Sociolinguistics

York St Jc
Fount?

Linguistics: The Essential Readings

This series consists of comprehensive collections of classic and contemporary reprinted articles in a wide range of fields within linguistics. The primary works presented in each book are complemented by outstanding editorial material by key figures in the field. Each volume stands as an excellent resource on its own, as well as an ideal companion to an introductory text.

1   *Phonological Theory: The Essential Readings*, edited by John A. Goldsmith
2   *Formal Semantics: The Essential Readings*, edited by Paul Portner and
                                                                      Barbara H. Partee
3   *Sociolinguistics: The Essential Readings*, edited by Christina Bratt Paulston and
                                                                      G. Richard Tucker

Sociolinguistics

The Essential Readings

Edited by

Christina Bratt Paulston
and
G. Richard Tucker

Blackwell
Publishing

350 Main Street, Malden, MA 02148-5018, USA
108 Cowley Road, Oxford OX4 1JF, UK
550 Swanston Street, Carlton South, Melbourne, Victoria 3053, Australia
Kurfürstendamm 57, 10707 Berlin, Germany

First published 2003 by Blackwell Publishing Ltd

Library of Congress Cataloging-in-Publication Data

Sociolinguistics : the essential readings / edited by Christina Bratt Paulston and G. Richard Tucker.
p.   cm. – (Linguistics ; 3)
Includes bibliographical references and index.
ISBN 0-631-22716-4 (alk. paper) – ISBN 0-631-22717-2 (pbk. : alk. paper)
1. Sociolinguistics.   I. Paulston, Christina Bratt, 1932–   II. Tucker, G. Richard.
III. Linguistics (Malden, Mass.) ; 3.

P40 .S5659 2003
306.44 – dc21

2002026251

A catalogue record for this title is available from the British Library.

Set in 10.5 on 12.5pt Ehrhardt
by SNP Best-set Typesetter Ltd., Hong Kong
Printed and bound in the United Kingdom
by MPG Books Ltd, Bodmin, Cornwall

For further information on
Blackwell Publishing, visit our website:
http://www.blackwellpublishing.com

Contents

Notes on Authors   ix
Preface   xiv
Acknowledgments   xvi

Part I: History of Sociolinguistics
Introduction   1

1 A Brief History of American Sociolinguistics 1949–1989   4
    Roger W. Shuy

2 Reflections on the Origins of Sociolinguistics in Europe   17
    Louis-Jean Calvet

Discussion Questions   25

Part II: Ethnography of Speaking
Introduction   27

3 Models of the Interaction of Language and Social Life   30
    Dell Hymes

4 Lands I Came to Sing: Negotiating Identities and Places in the
    Tuscan "*Contrasto*"   48
    Valentina Pagliai

Discussion Questions   69

Part III: Pragmatics
Introduction   71

5 Narrative Analysis: Oral Versions of Personal Experience   74
    William Labov and Joshua Waletzky

6 "Narrative Analysis" Thirty Years Later   105
    Emanuel A. Schegloff

7 Narrative Structure: Some Contrasts Between Maori and Pakeha
    Story-telling   114
    Janet Holmes

8   Contextualization Conventions   139
     John J. Gumperz

9   The Pronouns of Power and Solidarity   156
     Roger Brown and Albert Gilman

10   Complimenting: A Positive Politeness Strategy   177
     Janet Holmes

Discussion Questions   196

Part IV: Language and Gender
Introduction   199

11   Selections from *Language and Woman's Place*   203
     Robin Lakoff

12   The Relativity of Linguistic Strategies: Rethinking Power and Solidarity
     in Gender Dominance   208
     Deborah Tannen

Discussion Questions   229

Part V: Language and Variation
Introduction   231

13   Some Sociolinguistic Principles   234
     William Labov

14   On the Construction of Vernacular Dialect Norms   251
     Walt Wolfram

15   The Linguistic Individual in an American Public-Opinion Survey   272
     Barbara Johnstone

Discussion Questions   286

Part VI: Pidgins and Creoles
Introduction   287

16   Trade Jargons and Creole Dialects as Marginal Languages   290
     John E. Reinecke

Discussion Questions   299

Part VII: Individual Bilingualism
Introduction   301

17   A Social Psychology of Bilingualism   305
     Wallace E. Lambert

18   BICS and CALP: Origins and Rationale for the Distinction   322
     Jim Cummins

19   Linguistic Diversity, Schooling, and Social Class: Rethinking Our
     Conception of Language Proficiency in Language Minority Education   329
     Jeff MacSwan and Kellie Rolstad

Discussion Questions   341

Part VIII: Diglossia
Introduction   343

20   Diglossia   345
     Charles Ferguson

21   Bilingualism With and Without Diglossia; Diglossia With and Without
     Bilingualism   359
     Joshua A. Fishman

22   Toward the Systematic Study of Diglossia   367
     Alan Hudson

Discussion Questions   377

Part IX: Group Multilingualism
Introduction   379

23   Empirical Explorations of Two Popular Assumptions: Inter-Polity
     Perspective on the Relationships between Linguistic Heterogeneity,
     Civil Strife, and Per Capita Gross National Product   382
     Joshua A. Fishman

24   Linguistic Minorities and Language Policies   394
     Christina Bratt Paulston

Discussion Questions   407

Part X: Language Policy and Planning
Introduction   409

25   Dialect, Language, Nation   411
     Einar Haugen

26   Language Planning Goals: A Classification   423
     Moshe Nahir

27   Literacy and Language Planning   449
     Nancy H. Hornberger

Discussion Questions   460

Part XI: Multilingualism, Policies, and Education
Introduction   461

28   A Global Perspective on Bilingualism and Bilingual Education   464
     G. Richard Tucker

29   Language Policies and Language Rights   472
     Christina Bratt Paulston

Discussion Questions   483

Index   484

Notes on Authors

Roger Brown was Professor of Social Psychology at Harvard University from 1952 until his retirement in 1995 (with a brief interim appointment at MIT). He was the author of numerous seminal papers and books related to language acquisition including "How shall a thing be called?," *A first language: The early stages* (1973), and *Social Psychology* (1986). Brown died in 1997.

Louis-Jean Calvet was Professor of Linguistics at the Sorbonne (Paris) from 1970 to 1999 and is now professor at the University of Provence (Aix-en-Provence). His work mainly concerns multilingualism in Africa, Asia, and Latin America, and language planning and policies.

Jim Cummins teaches in the Department of Curriculum, Teaching and Learning of the Ontario Institute for Studies in Education of the University of Toronto. His research has focused on the nature of language proficiency and second language acquisition with particular emphasis on the social and educational barriers that limit academic success for culturally diverse students. Among his publications are *Language, Power and Pedagogy: Bilingual Children in the Crossfire* (2000) and *Negotiating Identities: Education for Empowerment in a Diverse Society* (2nd edition, 2001).

Charles Ferguson was Professor of Linguistics at Stanford for many years until his retirement in the early 1990s. Previously, he had served as founding director of the Center for Applied Linguistics in Washington, DC for eight years before returning to academia. His research interests included child language, especially the acquisition of phonology; sociolinguistics, particularly language planning and register variation; and linguistic studies of Arabic and Bengali. Ferguson died in 1998.

Joshua Fishman is Distinguished University Professor of Social Sciences, Emeritus, at Yeshiva University, New York, with which he has been affiliated since 1960. He is currently also a visiting professor at Stanford University, New York University and the Graduate Center of the City University of New York. His major interests are in language and ethnicity, language planning, and reversing language shift.

Albert Gilman (PhD, University of Michigan) was Professor of English at Boston University for 36 years. He specialized in modern drama as well as the works of Shakespeare. Gilman died in 1989.

John Gumperz is Professor Emeritus of Anthropology at the University of California, Berkeley. He has done linguistic anthropological fieldwork in India, Britain, Norway, Germany, and the urban United States on linguistic representations of social boundaries, communicative practice in polyglossic situations, and theories of discourse interpretation. He is currently working on a follow-up to Gumperz and Hymes's *Directions in Sociolinguistics* (Blackwell, 1971), which will apply ethnography of communication perspectives to today's communicative issues.

Einar Haugen received his PhD in 1931 with a dissertation on Aasen's New Norwegian. He served as Professor of Scandinavian Languages at the University of Wisconsin from 1931 to 1964. In 1964 he became Victor S. Thomas Professor of Scandinavian and Linguistics at Harvard University where he remained until his retirement. He was president of the Linguistic Society of America in 1950. Haugen died in 1994.

Janet Holmes is Professor of Linguistics at Victoria University of Wellington, where she teaches a variety of sociolinguistics courses. She is director of the Wellington Corpus of Spoken New Zealand English and of the Wellington Language in the Workplace Project. She has published on a wide range of topics including New Zealand English, language and gender, sexist language, pragmatic particles, compliments and apologies, and most recently on workplace discourse. Her publications include *An Introduction to Sociolinguistics* (1992), *Women, Men and Politeness* (1995), and an edited collection, *Gendered Speech in Social Context* (2000).

Nancy Hornberger is Professor of Education and Director of Educational Linguistics at the University of Pennsylvania Graduate School of Education, where she also convenes the annual Ethnography in Education Research Forum. She specializes in sociolinguistics and linguistic anthropology, language planning and policy, bilingualism and biliteracy, and educational policy and practice for indigenous and immigrant language minorities in the United States and internationally. She teaches, lectures, and consults internationally on these topics and serves on numerous international journal and book series editorial boards.

Alan Hudson has been a faculty member in the Department of Linguistics at the University of New Mexico since 1974, and was chair of the department from 1982 to 1990. He received his undergraduate degree in Celtic languages at University College, Dublin and his PhD in Language and Behavior from Yeshiva University, New York. His main research interests have been diglossia and the maintenance of Spanish in the southwestern United States.

Dell Hymes has taught at Harvard, Berkeley, Pennsylvania, and the University of Virginia, where he is now retired as Commonwealth Professor of Anthropology and of English. He has been president of the Linguistic Society of America, the American Anthropological Association and the American Association for Applied Linguistics. He founded the journal *Language in Society* and was its editor for 22 years.

Barbara Johnstone (PhD, University of Michigan) is Professor of Rhetoric and Linguistics at Carnegie Mellon University. She is the author of *Stories, Community, and Place: Narratives from Middle America* (1990), *The Linguistic Individual* (1996), and two textbooks, *Qualitative Methods in Sociolinguistics* (2001), and *Discourse Analysis* (Blackwell, 2002). Her recurrent interests have to do with how the individual and the social are related and the ways people evoke and shape places in discourse.

William Labov (PhD, Columbia, 1964) is Professor of Linguistics and Director of the Linguistics Laboratory at the University of Pennsylvania. His major studies include *The Social Stratification of English in New York City* (1966), *Sociolinguistic Patterns* (1972), *Language in the Inner City* (1972), and *Principles of Linguistic Change* (1994, 2000). He is the director of the Atlas of North American English and the Urban Minorities Reading Project and co-editor of *Language Variation and Change*. He also served as president of the Linguistic Society of America (1979), and is a member of the National Academy of Science. Home page: http://www.ling.upenn.edu/~labov.

Robin Lakoff is Professor of Linguistics at the University of California, Berkeley. She is the author of numerous books including *Language and Woman's Place* (1975), *Talking Power: The Politics of Language* (1991), and *The Language War* (2000). She has also published about eighty scholarly papers, reviews, and articles in newspapers and magazines on topics including the semantics of modality, the relationship between *some* and *any*, language and law, language and gender, language in psychotherapy, advertising language, narrative in group and individual identity formation, and the analysis of political rhetoric.

Wallace Lambert came to McGill University in 1954 from Chapel Hill and is currently Professor Emeritus at McGill. He has been a visiting professor at various universities around the world and is now working with the Cambridge Massachusetts Board of Education on a long-range investigation of foreign-language immersion programs and "two-way" immersion programs, oriented more by an English-Plus than by an English-Only ideology.

Jeff MacSwan is Assistant Professor of Language and Literacy in the Division of Curriculum and Instruction at Arizona State University. He has served as Associate Editor of the *Bilingual Research Journal*, and has published several articles and book chapters on bilingualism and the education of language minority students. He is the author of *A Minimalist Approach to Intrasentential Code Switching* (1999).

Moshe Nahir (PhD, University of Pittsburgh) is Professor of Linguistics in the Department of Linguistics at the University of Manitoba, Canada. He also served as head of its Department of Near Eastern and Judaic Studies (1979–90) and as director of its Language Center (1995–2001). His major research focuses on language planning, language planning in the revival of Hebrew, and recently also on language planning in Catalan. His research interests also cover attitudes to language planning, language normativism, and second language acquisition.

Valentina Pagliai (PhD, University of California, Los Angeles, 2000) is an Assistant Professor of Linguistic Anthropology at Oberlin College, Ohio. Her research focuses on verbal art and performance, aesthetic systems, ethnic and gender identities, language ideologies, and nationalism. She has conducted fieldwork in Italy and with Italian-Americans in the United States. Her most recent article is "Poetic dialogues: Performance and the construction of politics in the Tuscan Contrasto," *Ethnology*, 2002.

Christina Bratt Paulston is Professor Emerita of Linguistics at the University of Pittsburgh. She served as chair of the department from 1974 to 1989 and as director of the English Language Institute from 1969 to 1998. Her numerous publications include *Memories and Reflections: The Early Days of Sociolinguistics* (1997, edited with G. Richard Tucker), *Linguistic Minorities of Central and Eastern Europe* (1998, edited with Don Peckham), and *Sociolinguistic Perspectives on Bilingual Education* (1992).

John E. Reinecke had a varied career in public school and university teaching and working with organized labor. His MA thesis, "Language and Dialect in Hawaii" from the University of Hawaii in 1935, was published in 1969. His PhD dissertation, from the Department of Race Relations of Yale University, was the massive "Marginal Languages: A Sociological Survey of the Creole Languages and Trade Jargons" which was written in 1937 and laid the foundation for much subsequent work on these once maligned languages. It forms the basis for the article included here. Reinecke died in 1982.

Kellie Rolstad is Assistant Professor of Language and Literacy in the Division of Curriculum and Instruction at Arizona State University. She has published articles and chapters on language diversity, bilingual education, two-way immersion, and language shift in indigenous communities of Mexico. Examples of her work appear in the *Bilingual Review*, the *NABE News*, the *Bilingual Research Journal*, and *Teachers College Record*.

Emanuel Schegloff is Professor of Sociology with a joint appointment in applied linguistics at the University of California, Los Angeles and was co-founder of the Center for Language, Interaction, and Culture there. Educated at Harvard and the University of California, Berkeley, he has taught at Columbia University as well as UCLA. His research interests center on the naturalistic study of talk and other conduct in interaction and what we can learn about human beings and the organization of social life and experience from it.

Roger Shuy is Distinguished Research Professor of Linguistics, Emeritus, at Georgetown University, where he founded the sociolinguistics program in 1970 and headed it for many years. He has researched and published on language variation, medical discourse, literacy, classroom language and, for the past 25 years, on the intersection of language and law. His most recent books include *Language Crimes* (1993), *The Language of Confession, Interrogation and Deception* (1998), *Bureaucratic Language* (1998), *A Few Months to Live* (2000), and *Linguistic Battles in Trademark Disputes* (2002).

Deborah Tannen is a University Professor and Professor of Linguistics at Georgetown University. She has published eighteen books and nearly one hundred articles on such topics as cross-cultural communication, modern Greek discourse, the poetics of everyday conversation workplace interaction, and family interaction. Among her books are *Gender and Discourse* (1994), *You Just Don't Understand: Women and Men in Conversation* (1990), and *Talking from 9 to 5: Women and Men at Work* (1994). Her book *The Argument Culture* (1998) received the Common Ground Book Award; her most recent book, *I Only Say This Because I Love You* (2001), received the Books for a Better Life Award.

G. Richard Tucker was Professor of Psychology at McGill University (1969–78) and President of the Center for Applied Linguistics (1978–91) before assuming his present position as Professor of Applied Linguistics and Head of the Department of Modern Languages at Carnegie Mellon University. His major research focuses on diverse aspects of second language learning and teaching in North America, the Middle East and North Africa, and Southeast Asia.

Joshua Waletzky was a student at Horace Mann High School at the time he collaborated with William Labov on the article included. He is currently a filmmaker and musician in New York City.

Walt Wolfram is William C. Friday Professor at North Carolina State University where he directs the North Carolina Language and Life Project. He has also directed the Research Program at the Center for Applied Linguistics and taught at the University of the District of Columbia in Washington, DC. His primary interest is in vernacular dialects of English in the US and around the world.

Preface

This reader is designed to provide the student of sociolinguistics with introductory readings that range over a wide variety of topics. As you will discover from the first two chapters, sociolinguistics as an academic field of study is about fifty years old, and many of the early seminal articles were published in edited collections which are now out of print or in fairly obscure journals which are difficult to find – even in well-stocked major research-university libraries.

Introductory texts typically paraphrase, in a second-hand account, earlier seminal work; but our students throughout the years have insisted that they want to read these classic articles for themselves, not just someone else's synopsis of Hymes or Labov, to use but two examples, and so you will find the first reading for most topics to be an original article which carved out a new area of study (Brown and Gilman, for example), defined and delimited new concepts (Hymes on communicative competence), or organized concepts and suggested a new way to study them (Labov; Gumperz).

But, of course, in such a new and dynamic field, an enormous amount of progress has taken place, so we have also included up-to-date articles representative of work currently done in the various topics. Sometimes these articles elaborate on the initial work (Fishman), sometimes they disagree (MacSwan and Rolstad); but they all, in one way or another, have their intellectual roots in the initial work. Therefore the articles under each topic heading are probably best read in the order they are presented as they represent *cumulative* intellectual work. The topics, on the other hand, can be juggled to fit individual curricula or tastes. They are loosely ordered to represent work in sociolinguistics and then in the sociology of language.

The reader is intended, for course work, to be used with a general introductory text, of which there are many, inter alia Holmes 1992, Mesthrie et al. 2000, Romaine 2000, and Wardhaugh 2002. The basic idea is that students can use the present text to augment the material presented in the introductory text with a reading of selected original and follow-up works. The various topic readings are then best assigned to accompany the topics of the general introduction text.

The reader can of course also be read for its own sake, as a basic introduction to sociolinguistics for the individual reader. The editorial introductions to each section with their many references are designed to give such a reader general guidance to each new topic, an overview from which to pick and choose from the Further Reading.

We wish to acknowledge the contributions and assistance of a number of individuals whose help was invaluable to us as we conceptualized and then implemented this project. In particular, we wish to thank our colleagues Louis-Jean Calvet, Jim Cummins, Joshua Fishman, Alan Hudson, Dell Hymes, Barbara Johnstone, Bill Labov, Jeff MacSwan, Kellie Rolstad, and Walt Wolfram. Each of them helped us by providing important advice at a critical juncture during the project or by composing new or significantly revised material specifically for this reader.

We also wish to thank University of Pittsburgh doctoral student Stephanie Maietta-Pircio who provided the initial formulation of the Discussion Questions, Glynis Baguley, desk editor, whose attention to detail notably strengthened the manuscript, as well as Tami Kaplan and Sarah Coleman, both from Blackwells, who were responsive to any and all of our queries and a pleasure to work with.

References

Holmes, Janet. 1992. *An Introduction to Sociolinguistics*. London and New York: Longman.

Mesthrie, Rajend, Joan Swann, Andrea Deumert, and William Leap. 2000. *Introducing Sociolinguistics*. Philadelphia: John Benjamins.

Romaine, Suzanne. 2000. *Language in Society: An Introduction to Sociolinguistics*. Oxford: Oxford University Press.

Wardhaugh, Ronald. 2002. *An Introduction to Sociolinguistics*. Oxford: Blackwell.

Acknowledgments

The editors and publisher gratefully acknowledge the following for permission to reproduce copyright material:

1. Roger W. Shuy, "A Brief History of American Sociolinguistics 1949–1989," pp. 184–202, 206–7 from *Historiographia Linguistica* 23:1–2 (1990). © John Benjamins Publishing Co., Amsterdam. Reprinted by permission of the publisher;
2. Louis-Jean Calvet, "Reflections on the Origins of Sociolinguistics in Europe," translated from the French by Christina Bratt Paulston;
3. Dell Hymes, pp. 38–43, 52–65 excerpted from "Models of the Interaction of Language and Social Life: Ethnographic Description and Explanation" in John J. Gumperz and Dell Hymes (eds.), *Directions in Sociolinguistics: The Ethnography of Communication* (Oxford: Blackwell, 1986). Copyright © Dell Hymes. Reprinted with the kind permission of the author;
4. Valentina Pagliai, "Lands I Came to Sing: Negotiating Identities and Places in the Tuscan *Contrasto*," pp. 125–46 from *Pragmatics* 10:1 (2000), published by International Pragmatics Association (IPrA), Belgium. Reprinted by permission of the publishers;
5. William Labov and Joshua Waletzky, "Narrative Analysis: Oral Versions of Personal Experience," pp. 12–44 in June Helm (ed.), *Essays on the Verbal and Visual Arts: Proceedings of the 1966 Annual Spring Meeting of the American Ethnological Society* (Seattle: University of Washington Press, 1967). Not for sale or further reproduction. Reprinted by permission of American Anthropological Association;
6. Emanuel A. Schegloff, "'Narrative Analysis' Thirty Years Later," pp. 97–106 from *The Journal of Narrative and Life History* 7:1–4. Copyright © 1997, Lawrence Erlbaum Associates, Inc. Reprinted by permission of Lawrence Erlbaum Associates, Inc.;
7. Janet Holmes, "Narrative Structure: Some Contrasts between Maori and Pakeha Story-telling," pp. 25–57 from *Multilingua* 17:1 (1998). Reprinted by permission of Mouton de Gruyter;
8. John J. Gumperz, "Contextualization Conventions," pp. 130–52 from *Discourse Strategies* (Cambridge: Cambridge University Press, 1982). Reprinted by permission of the publisher;
9. Roger Brown and Albert Gilman, "The Pronouns of Power and Solidarity," pp. 253–76 from T. A. Sebeok (ed.), *Style in Language* (Cambridge, MA: MIT Press, 1960). Reprinted by permission of MIT Press, USA;

10. Janet Holmes, "Complimenting – A Positive Politeness Strategy," pp. 100–20 from Jennifer Coates (ed.), *Language and Gender: A Reader* (Oxford: Blackwell, 1998). Reprinted by permission of the publishers;

11. Robin Lakoff, pp. 4–5, 28–33, 35 from *Language and Woman's Place* (Harper & Row, 1975). Copyright © 1975 by Robin Lakoff. Reprinted by permission of HarperCollins Publishers Inc.;

12. Deborah Tannen, pp. 20–52 from *Gender and Discourse* (New York: Oxford University Press, Inc., 1994). Copyright © 1994 by Deborah Tannen. Used by permission of Oxford University Press, Inc.;

13. William Labov, "Some Sociolinguistic Principles," pp. 19–38 from *The Study of Nonstandard English* (Champaign, Ill.: National Council of Teachers of English, by special arrangement with the Center for Applied Linguistics, 1969). Reprinted by permission of the author and the Center for Applied Linguistics;

14. Walt Wolfram, "On Constructing Vernacular Dialect Norms," from John P. Boyle and Arika Okrent (eds.), *CLS 36: The 36th Meeting of the Chicago Linguistic Society, 2000* (Chicago: Chicago Linguistic Society, 2000). Reprinted by permission of the Chicago Linguistic Society;

15. Barbara Johnstone, "The Linguistic Individual in an American Public-opinion Survey," shortened for this volume by Barbara Johnstone from "Individual Style in an American Public-opinion Survey: Personal Performance and the Ideology of Referentiality"; originally published in *Language in Society* 20 (1991), pp. 557–76. Reprinted by permission of the publishers, Cambridge University Press;

16. John E. Reinecke, "Race, Cultural Groups: Trade Jargons and Creole Dialects as Marginal Languages," pp. 107–18 from *Social Forces* 17 (1938). Reprinted with permission;

17. Wallace E. Lambert, "A Social Psychology of Bilingualism," pp. 91–109 from *The Journal of Social Issues* 23:2 (1967). Reprinted by permission of Blackwell Publishers Ltd;

18. Jim Cummins, "BICS and CALP: Origins and Rationale for the Distinction." Written especially for this collection;

19. Jeff MacSwan and Kellie Rolstad, "Linguistic Diversity, Schooling, and Social Class: Rethinking our Conception of Language Proficiency in Language Minority Education." Written especially for this collection;

20. Charles Ferguson, "Diglossia," pp. 325–40 from *Word* 15 (1959). International Linguistic Association, New York;

21. Joshua A. Fishman, "Bilingualism With and Without Diglossia; Diglossia With and Without Bilingualism," pp. 29–38 from *The Journal of Social Issues* 23:2 (1967). Reprinted by permission of Blackwell Publishers Ltd;

22. Alan Hudson, shortened by the author from "Toward the Systematic Study of Diglossia," pp. 1–22 from *Southwest Journal of Linguistics* 10:1 (1991);

23. Joshua A. Fishman, "Empirical Explorations of Two Popular Assumptions: Inter-Polity Perspective on the Relationships between Linguistic Heterogeneity, Civil Strife, and Per Capita Gross National Product," pp. 209–25 in Gary Imhoff (ed.), *Learning in Two Languages: From Conflict to Consensus in the Reorganization of Schools*. New Brunswick: Transaction Publishers, 1990. Reprinted by permission of Transaction Publishers;

24.   Christina Bratt Paulston, pp. 55–64, 70–9 from "Linguistic Minorities and Language Policies – Four Case Studies" in Willen Fase, Koen Jaspaert, and Sjaak Kroon (eds.), *Maintenance and Loss of Minority Languages.* Amsterdam/Philadelphia: John Benjamins Publishing Co., 1992. Reprinted by permission of the publisher.
25.   Einar Haugen, "Dialect, Language, Nation," pp. 922–35 from *American Anthropologist* 68:4 (1966). Reprinted by permission of Camilla Haugen Cai and the American Anthropological Association;
26.   Moshe Nahir, "Language Planning Goals: A Classification," pp. 294–327 from *Language Problems and Language Planning* 8:3 (1984). Reprinted by permission of John Benjamins Publishing Co., Amsterdam;
27.   Nancy H. Hornberger, "Literacy and Language Planning," pp. 75–86 from *Language and Education* 8:1–2 (1994). Copyright © 1994 N. H. Hornberger. Reprinted by permission of Multilingual Matters Limited and the author;
28.   G. Richard Tucker, "A Global Perspective on Bilingualism and Bilingual Education" from Georgetown University Round Table on Languages and Linguistics (eds. James E. Alatis and Ai-Hui Tan), *Language in our Time: Bilingual Education and Official English, Ebonics and Standard English, Immigration and the Unz Initiative.* Washington, DC: Georgetown University Press, 2001. Reprinted by permission of the author and Georgetown University Press;
29.   Christina Bratt Paulston, "Language Policies and Language Rights," pp. 73–85 from *Annual Review Anthropology* 26 (1997). Copyright © 1997 by Annual Reviews Inc. Reprinted by permission of Annual Reviews Inc., www.annualreviews.org.

The publisher apologizes for any errors or omissions in the above list and would be grateful to be notified of any corrections that should be incorporated in future reprints or editions of this book.

Part I

History of Sociolinguistics

Introduction

Sociolinguistics as an academic field of study, as a discipline if you like, only developed within the last fifty years, in the latter part of the last century. Certainly, an interest in the social aspects of language, in the intersection of language and society, has been with us probably as long as mankind has had language, but its organized formal study can be dated to quite recently; 1964 is a good year to remember as you can find out when you read Roger Shuy's chapter. The word *sociolinguistics* was apparently coined already in 1939 in the title of an article by Thomas C. Hodson, "Sociolinguistics in India" in *Man in India*; it was first used in linguistics by Eugene Nida in the second edition of his *Morphology* (1949: 152), but one often sees the term attributed to Haver Currie (1952), who himself claimed to have invented it.

When sociolinguistics became popularized as a field of study in the late 1960s, there were two labels – sociolinguistics and sociology of language – for the same phenomenon, the study of the intersection and interaction of language and society, and these two terms were used interchangeably. Eventually a difference came to be made, and as an oversimplification one might say that while sociolinguistics is mainly concerned with an increased and wider description of language (and undertaken primarily by linguists and anthropologists), sociology of language is concerned with explanation and prediction of language phenomena in society at the group level (and done mainly by social scientists as well as by a few linguists). But in the beginning, no difference was intended, as no difference is intended in the essays by Shuy and Calvet.

Sociolinguistics turned out to be a very lively and popular field of study, and today many of its subfields can claim to be fields in their own right, with academic courses, textbooks, journals, and conferences; they include pragmatics, language and gender studies, pidgin and creole studies, language planning and policy studies, and education of linguistic minorities studies. The two articles here by Roger Shuy and Louis-Jean Calvet do not attempt an analysis of the history of thought of sociolinguistics; rather they describe and document the genesis, the origin, of sociolinguistics. There is to date no history of the entire field of sociolinguistics; it has after all only been around for about fifty years.

Tucker (1997) summarizes five cross-cutting themes that he found salient, based on 23 autobiographical sketches by the major founding members of sociolinguistics. First, these recollections describe an interdisciplinary field whose beginning can be pinpointed with reasonable accuracy (the major fields contributing to sociolinguistics were linguistics, anthropology, sociology, and social psychology, with an occasional political scientist). Second, the field appears to have emerged partially in response to a number of well-articulated and compelling social issues. Many of the autobiographies comment that the coalition of members from various disciplines was the natural outcome of the movement for social justice (cf. the US Civil Rights Act of 1964, later a precedent for the Bilingual Education Act of 1968) and for educational reform; an interest in confronting racial segregation, poverty, and the intractability of social structures. There was also a growing awareness that many recently independent ex-colonial governments were making policy decisions involving language, often without an adequate research or knowledge base. This post-colonial sensibility also informs Calvet's essay. As a partial consequence, many of the early US activities were problem- rather than theory-driven. In contrast, Calvet discusses how many of the early European sociolinguists were influenced by classical Marxist theory, still common today in the Latin American literature, while critical theory, a variation of Marxism, with its focus on the twinned concepts of power and conflict has become common today in all the anglophone literature.

Third, Tucker continues, all the evidence points to a small number of key individuals whose work in leadership, publications, and conferences, was essential to nurturing the young field. Fourth, not surprisingly, he finds a difference in worldview, models, questions, and problems between participants from the center and those from the periphery. Fifth and finally, theoretically uninteresting perhaps but still very important: "The early initiatives prospered at least in part because of continuing 'patronage' from a small number of organizations and associations, and because of the availability of ample funding from private as well as public sources for initiatives such as conferences, surveys, the establishment of graduate programs, and publications" (Tucker, 1997: 318).

This part on the genesis of sociolinguistics is meant to set the stage for the readings which follow. Most parts have an early "classic" essay from the time of the early development of the field followed by more recent work which builds on, develops or criticizes the early work. It may be, though, that students new to sociolinguistics will find a better understanding if they read this part last.

References

Currie, Haver. 1952. "A projection of socio-linguistics: the relationship of speech to social status," *Southern Speech Journal*, 18: 28–37.
Hodson, Thomas C. 1939. "Sociolinguistics in India," *Man in India*, XIX: 94.
Nida, Eugene A. 1949. *Morphology; The Descriptive Analysis of Words.* Ann Arbor: University of Michigan Press.
Tucker, G. Richard. 1997. "Epilogue" in C. B. Paulston and G. R. Tucker (eds.), *The Early Days of Sociolinguistics: Memories and Reflections.* Dallas, TX: Summer Institute of Linguistics, pp. 317–24.

Further Reading

Ammon, Ulrich, Norman Dittmar and Klaus J. Mattheier (eds.). 1987. "History of sociolinguistics as a discipline," *Sociolinguistics: An International Handbook of the Science of Language and Society*, 4: 379–469. Berlin: de Gruyter.

Ervin-Tripp, Susan. 1974. "Two decades of council activity in the rapprochement of linguistics and social science." Social Science Research Council. *Items*, 28 (1): 1–4.

Koerner, Konrad. 1991. "Towards a history of modern sociolinguistics," *American Speech* 66 (1): 57–70.

Le Page, Robert B. 1997. "The evolution of a social theory of language," in Florian Coulmas (ed.), *The Handbook of Sociolinguistics*, pp. 15–32. Oxford: Blackwell.

Murray, Stephen O. 1994. *Theory Groups and the Study of Language in North America: A Social History*. Amsterdam: Benjamins.

Shuy, Roger. 1990. "A brief history of American sociolinguistics," *Historiographia Linguistica* 17 (1/2): 183–209. The original and unabbreviated version.

1

A Brief History of American Sociolinguistics 1949–1989

Roger W. Shuy

[. . .]

1 Linguistic Ancestry

It is appropriate for modern-day linguists to regularly reexamine the works of leaders of our field upon whose shoulders we continue to stand (despite our apparent need to claim originality for our own recent breakthroughs and revolutions). Koerner (1988) traces much of our current sociolinguistic thought through Saussure by way of William Dwight Whitney (1827–1894), citing the following crucial passage:

> Speech is not a personal possession but a social: it belongs, not to the individual, but to the member of society. No item of existing language is the work of an individual; for what we may severally choose to say is not language until it be accepted and employed by our fellows. The whole development of speech, though initiated by the acts of individuals, is wrought out by the community. (Whitney 1867:404)

Koerner goes on to show that there is an intellectual passing along of this concept from Whitney to Saussure to Meillet to Martinet to Weinreich to Labov. There is much to be said for the validity of Koerner's suggestion. On the other hand, it must also be noted that there is seldom a simple strand of development of a truth or a concept. The great psychologist, Carl Gustav Jung, spoke of the development of a collective unconscious, an almost simultaneous awareness of something in many disparate settings at the same period of time. A perusal of the works of the giants of linguistics in the past century reveals a similar awareness. Bloomfield, for example, devoted an entire chapter to Speech Communities (Bloomfield 1933:42–56). Much of the more modern work in social dialect, gender differences and age-grading, for example, can be linked to Bloomfield's earlier observations. There are those, including Paul Kiparsky, who claim that Labov's variable rule actually can be traced back to Pāṇini (Kiparsky 1979). But, as Koerner points out, most texts and collections on sociolinguistics skip over historical antecedents, noting only such generalities as "sociolinguistics has been established as a distinct discipline for some years" (Pride & Holmes 1972:7).

Labov, as one might expect, does *not* overlook the thinking of those who preceded modern times, devoting several pages to the topic, "Some Earlier Studies of Language in Its Social Context" (Labov 1966). He cites the lecture notes of Antoine Meillet in 1905 in which Meillet expressed unwillingness to accept the historical laws discovered in the 19th century and observed that there must be variables as yet undiscovered, continual, even rapid, variation:

> . . . but from the fact that language is a social institution, it follows that linguistics is a social science, and the only variable to which we can turn to account for linguistic change is social change, of which linguistic variations are only consequences. We must determine which social structure corresponds to a given linguistic structure and how, in a general manner, changes in social structure are translated into changes in linguistic structure. (Labov, p.15)

Meillet's words seem strangely modern, yet neither he nor his colleagues and students seem to have followed up on the idea that social and linguistic phenomena were interrelated. The reason for this is obvious when we examine the theoretical development of the period in which he worked. In the 19th century, language change, etymology and language origins dominated the thinking of linguists. By the 20th century the major interest became the structure of language. The idea of cultural relativity emerged strongly in the work of anthropologists, turning away from what Edward Sapir referred to as "the evolutionary prejudice" of previous concerns about language (Sapir 1921). This relativism in the view of language and culture was accompanied in linguistics proper by a turn toward structuralism, led by Saussure and others. As Labov points out, little was accomplished until the field had developed a more explicit theory of phonological structure, the development of tape recorders, spectrograms, sampling procedures and, even more recently, computers, that were equipped to process large quantities of data (Labov 1966). However right Meillet was in his assessment, the technological and social contexts were simply not yet appropriate for the development of his ideas.

Meanwhile, as structuralism developed with Bloomfield, Sapir, Bloch, Hockett, Pike and others, the focus of linguistics turned inward to the basic outline of languages in general rather than upon variation within those languages. There was nothing essentially wrong with such a direction, for linguistics probably needed to develop in this manner.

2   Anthropological Ancestry

There are some who say that sociolinguistics is actually a modern version of what used to be called anthropological linguistics. There is something to be said in favor of such a position since, in a broad sense at least, sociolinguists extend the description and analysis of language to include aspects of the culture in which it is used. In that sense, sociolinguistics constitutes something of a return to anthropology, in which many believe it had its origins. The classic four-pronged definition of anthropology – cultural anthropology, physical anthropology, archeology and linguistics – however, focuses on the larger analysis of human behavior, its patterns and principles while modern sociolinguistics examines in depth more minute aspects of language in social context.

An early indication of the future development of sociolinguistics can be seen in *Horizons of Anthropology* edited by Sol Tax in 1964, in which Hymes noted that the salient trait of linguistics in the first half of the 20th century, from the viewpoint of anthropology, "has been its quest for autonomy". He predicted, however, that in the second half of this century "the salient trait will be the quest for integration, and the noted accomplishments will concern the engaging of linguistic structures in social contexts – in short, in the analysis of function" (Hymes 1964b:92).

American anthropology has always recognized language as a branch of its domain, probably because of the importance it has placed on American Indian studies. In the 19th century, the association of linguistics and anthropology was called by many names, such as 'ethnological philology' and 'linguistic ethnology'. In the 20th century this intersection of interests became known as 'ethnolinguistics', 'metalinguistics' and 'anthropological linguistics'. In the sixties, Hymes proposed the term 'linguistic anthropology', defining it broadly as the study of language in an anthropological context. Hymes noted that fields like anthropology and linguistics overlap in practice, but do not coincide. Anthropology uses linguistics to shed light on its proper task, coordinating knowledge about language from the viewpoint of humanity. The proper task of linguistics, on the other hand, is to coordinate knowledge about language from the viewpoint of culture.

Courses called "Language and Culture" had been offered, for example, as early as 1955 at Harvard (by Hymes in the Department of Social Relations), at the University of California at Berkeley and at the University of Pennsylvania. Hymes reports that such courses became increasingly sociolinguistic over time but that they depended increasingly upon prerequisite courses in descriptive linguistics. This was important, as Hymes notes, because:

> One wanted an introduction to linguistic description that recognized the need to specify social position and context for the data; and that recognized in phonetics the manifestation of a plurality of functions (identificational, expressive, directive, metalinguistic), as well as the processes of change. In fact to consider descriptive linguistics from a social point of view is to reconsider it, and to begin to envisage a somewhat distinctive content and mode of presentation. (Hymes 1966)

In this same report, Hymes goes on to point out that the more traditional minimal training of social scientists in only descriptive linguistics, though essential, was not sufficient for the kinds of research they were increasingly attempting to carry out. Social scientists need to know how to control linguistic forms, to be sure, but also how to control social valuations of language varieties, of their use with regard to persons, channels, topics and settings. In effect, the social scientist needs to apply the results of a sociolinguistic description.

[. . .]

3   Sociological Ancestry

The anthropological origins of sociolinguistics were not the only progenitor. As early as April of 1966, sociologists had organized a session on sociolinguistics as part of the

Ohio Valley Sociological Society's annual meeting. Hymes reports that one of the most prominent questions asked at that meeting was "Where can a sociologist go to study sociolinguistics?" (1966). To address this question more deeply, a follow-up meeting was held in Los Angeles three months later. To emphasize the fact that disciplinary developments do not require the trappings of an academic society annual meeting, this meeting was held in the home of William Bright. A number of scholars who would become the leaders in this emerging field happened to be in Los Angeles that summer and were invited, including Charles A. Ferguson, Joshua A. Fishman, Harold Garfinkel, Erving Goffman, John Gumperz, Dell Hymes, William Labov, Harvey Sacks, Edgar Polomé, Leonard Savitz and Emanuel Schegloff. The sociologists present shared their experiences in teaching sociolinguistics at their universities. Savitz stressed the need for training in linguistics for sociologists. Fishman supported this notion and added that sociologists were interested in linguistic variables but not necessarily in linguistics while linguists seemed interested in broad contextualization but not necessarily in sociology. It might be noted that this distinction of concerns appears to be current to this day (Hymes 1966).

In sociology, comparative studies programs began to develop in the early sixties, and many sociology students were sent to foreign countries. They were made aware of the need for language competence but not the need for linguistics. That is, these students wanted to learn the language of the people they were studying but they apparently did not see language as a source of sociological data.

Most of the early courses in sociolinguistics taught by sociologists were called 'Sociology of Language'. Joshua Fishman first taught a course by that name in 1960, at the University of Pennsylvania. Subsequently he continued to teach that course at Yeshiva, primarily to psychology majors. Fishman's approach reflected his own special interests in this area: language maintenance, language displacement and the social context of language planning.

In 1965 Joyce O. Hertzler's book, *The Sociology of Language*, was published. A sociologist himself, Hertzler noted:

> Among the social scientists, the chief contributors to language study have been anthropologists and psychologists. The anthropologists have been concerned with language as a cardinal aspect of culture, language origins and development, the analysis of primitive languages and the reciprocal relationships of these languages with primitive mental and social life. [. . .] The general, social educational and abnormal psychologists have been concerned with the stages of speech development in human beings, especially the speech development of children, the relationships of speech and abnormal psychological states, the strategic significance of language in personality development and in the socialization of the individual, and its relationship to the processes of thought. (Hertzler 1965:4–5)

[. . .]

Other sociologists interested in language were also pursuing their own special research concerns in the sixties. Although there was no course called the sociology of language at UCLA at that time, Harold Garfinkel reported that this subject entered into all of his teaching. In the same department, Harvey Sacks was teaching the analysis of conversation to sociology and anthropology majors. It appears that individual sociologists pursued their own language topics in sociology departments but without labels that might identify them as linguistic. Erving Goffman's research interest, for example, in the sixties, was in lying in public and on small social behaviors in public order. He saw linguistics as essential to the description of the structure and organization of small pieces of behavior. Most linguistically oriented sociologists, however, were at odds with the larger departmental requirements. If a sociology major were to invest the time and effort to become well enough grounded in linguistics to replicate the work of a Goffman, a Garfinkel or a Sacks, they ran the serious risk of sacrificing other aspects of sociological knowledge required by that field. Naturally, the same thing could be said of anthropologists and, conversely, of linguists.

4 The Cross-Disciplinary Dilemma

In order for the field of sociolinguistics to fully benefit from the combined disciplines upon which it was based, something had to give in the traditional academic structure. The ethnographic insights of anthropologists, the social theory and methods of sociology and the basic information of linguistics had to be merged more comfortably. To this point, they obviously were not. Anthropology students were getting a taste of linguistics, but not enough to do the type of work visualized by Hymes. Sociology departments were even less willing to stretch their traditional curricula to accommodate enough linguistics to further the seminal work of Sacks, Garfinkel, Fishman, and Goffman.

At the same time, there seems to have been considerably less concern on the part of linguists concerning the need for their students to be trained in anthropology and sociology. By 1966 Ferguson had taught a course called Sociolinguistics at two LSA Institutes and at Georgetown University. His students had a background in linguistics but not in sociology. Likewise Edgar Polomé reports that by then he had taught a course called sociolinguistics at the University of Texas, but almost exclusively to linguists. Labov argued that the sheer amount of linguistic training needed to bring about a change in the character of basic linguistic research and theory was so great that he preferred to train only those committed to linguistics. This thought was supported by Gumperz who also argued for a serious commitment to sociolinguistic analysis, not just an interest in it. Thus the mid sixties revealed great ferment and coming together of social scientists to try to determine how to cooperate across traditional disciplinary lines. There was both agreement and disagreement.

The agreement centered on the growing need for a kind of cross-cultural research that cut across disciplinary territories. Some saw the world as becoming reintegrated as one society, growing smaller in a sense, while at the same time there was a reestablishment of the plurality of societies and languages within societies. Both trends required a shift in focus and theory by sociologists, anthropologists and linguists.

In American society, it was the time of increased problems with racial segregation, poverty education and social structures. The problems were clear enough and these three disciplines had some of the tools needed to address them, but not apart from each other. But these fields faced the traditional problems that academics always face. Social scientists did not want to give up anything to get linguistics. Nor did linguists want to give up anything to get social science. Each wanted to keep its own field, goals and theory-building foremost while enjoying the most minimal fruits of the other.

We have already noted some of the origins of sociolinguistic thought in the giants of linguistics who preceded us, Saussure, Meillet and Bloomfield in particular. In England, the Firthian heritage of linguistics created a strong tradition for a sociolinguistic perspective, most recently in the work of Michael Halliday. In fact in 1966, Basil Bernstein wrote a memorandum called "Culture and Linguistics" which encouraged the development of the field of sociolinguistics in England. One of the recommendations of Hymes to the Social Science Research Council (1966) was to develop a handful of training centers or 'laboratories' for training in aspects of sociolinguistics, including London, New York, and Washington, D.C. One can assume that Hymes recommended London largely because the theoretical tradition of linguistics was oriented to a more functional rather than formal approach.

American linguistics in the mid sixties had clearly taken a more formalist bent. The period of structuralist, descriptive grammars, in particular, was now waning. Since much of what the modern sociolinguists such as Hymes, Gumperz, Labov and Ferguson had envisaged depended first on rich description, the advent of a modern sociolinguistics seemed out of time with the rapidly developing dominant linguistic theory. A major thread of continuity for a sociolinguistic tradition was found, however, in regional dialectology, in which language variability had been celebrated for many years.

5 Linguistic Geography

Linguistic geography, at least in Western countries, is said to have its origins in late 19th century Germany, when Georg Wenker mailed out forty sentences to thousands of village schoolmasters. These sentences contained words which were known to vary locally in pronunciation. With whatever semi-phonetic skills they could muster, these schoolmasters dutifully responded, creating a data base which still exists in Marburg and is now being computerized. The point here, however, is that the focus of Wenker's effort was on the rich *variation* that characterizes the German language.

[. . .]

In 1896, a French Atlas was devised and directed by Jules Gilliéron, who determined that it would be possible to achieve more consistent and accurate representations of the actual speech of informants if a single field worker with good phonetics skills would interview subjects and transcribe their speech phonetically. So he sent Edmond Edmont out on his bicycle to various French communities. In a period of four years, Edmont completed the 200-item questionnaire with 700 informants and the *Atlas Linguistique de la France* was published between 1902 and 1910.

[. . .]

The American atlas project, under the initial direction of Hans Kurath, began in 1931. The original idea was to produce a dialect dictionary. Concerned scholars, including George Kittredge and James Russell Lowell, gathered in Cambridge, Massachusetts, in 1889 and formed the American Dialect Society. After thirty years, although the society had not come close to publishing a dialect dictionary, it had collected over 26,000 interesting dialect words and phrases in its publication, *Dialect Notes*.[1] By 1929 the interests of many American dialectologists had turned away from a dialect dictionary to that of a linguistic atlas. With the assistance of the American Council of Learned Societies, a plan for such an atlas was published and Kurath was appointed its director. The plan was to produce a set of 'work sheets' containing over seven hundred items arranged roughly according to topics. This unique approach formulated the informants' answers but did not specify the questions, leaving that to the ingenuity of the fieldworker.

[. . .]

Linguistic Atlas research in the United States continues on a somewhat regular but slow pace today, aided by computerization of data and by the hard work of a few talented scholars. Many scholars question the value of the methods by which the data were elicited, the accuracy of pre-tape-recorded phonetic transcriptions, the biases of sampling, the focus only on lexicon and pronunciation, the omission of analytical procedures such as discourse analysis and pragmatic meaning, that developed after the atlas procedure was unchangeably determined.

[. . .]

In linguistic geography, there were many early features of modern sociolinguistics. The American Atlas traditionally attempted to get informants of three general social classes in more urban communities, but it was Raven I. McDavid who made the clearest connection between social factors and pronunciation variables. In his classic article, "Postvocalic /-r/ in South Carolina: A Social Analysis" (1948), he noted that in communities where postvocalic /r/ occurs with constriction, three variables decrease it: the more urban, younger, better educated speakers use less constriction. Such sensitivity to social influences of variation were not common, however, until the sixties, when language variation studies in America entered a kind of renaissance.

5.1 Developments

As new interest in minorities developed, the country, under President Kennedy's leadership, began viewing its citizens in a new way. Those who are products of later societies might not realize the tremendous impact such ideas had on linguistics at that time. As it often happens, a specific set of events framed the staging ground for a number of changes within our field, some related but others more serendipitous. One of these events was the annual Linguistic Institute at Indiana University in 1964. The major proponents of structuralism and generative grammar were matched against each other in a series of week-long lectures, first by Chomsky, then by Pike. It was an unusually well-attended institute that summer and, along with the Linguistic Society of America summer meeting, it provided one of the most exciting programs in the history of the field. One reason that the Institute was so well attended has already been mentioned – the arm-to-arm combat for theoretical leadership in the field. But there were other reasons as well.

In May of 1964, a month or so before the LSA Institute, the UCLA Center for Research in Language and Linguistics sponsored a conference on 'Sociolinguistics' at Lake Arrowhead, California. The edited papers of this conference appeared under the title, *Sociolinguistics* (Bright 1966). To give an idea of the recency of the term 'sociolinguistics', it should be noted that the 1961 Third Edition of Webster's New

International Dictionary does not list this word at all, although the term had appeared as early as 1952 in an article by Haver C. Currie in the *Southern Speech Journal*. At the time of the Lake Arrowhead conference, a number of scholars had been investigating the relationship between language and society, including Henry M. Hoenigswald, John Gumperz, Einar Haugen, Raven I. McDavid, Jr., Dell Hymes, John Fischer, William Samarin, Paul Friedrich, and Charles Ferguson. One bright new star on the horizon, a student of Uriel Weinreich at Columbia, named William Labov, was also invited to Lake Arrowhead to describe his dissertation research on New York City speech. This cadre of participants represented a number of quite different research traditions – linguistic geography, language contact, historical changes, ethnography, and language planning. Out of this conference-induced blending of traditions it was only natural to find terms into which each research tradition might fit. 'Language and Society' and 'Sociolinguistics' were the most logical choices and it was determined that two courses by these names should be offered at the 1964 LSA Institute.

John Gumperz had been carrying out earlier research in India and Norway on the differences in language used among people of various castes and social status. Those who had heard him talk about this in the past prevailed upon him to offer a summer institute course dealing with the broad issues involved in such variability. Gumperz had been trained in the linguistic geography tradition at Michigan but had found, in his recent work, new territories to study besides geographical variety. He taught the course called "Language and Society".

Charles Ferguson's research began with Bengali and Arabic studies, which led him to focus on different uses and/or varieties of those languages. By the fifties he had written about Arabic politeness and baby talk, for example. In the early sixties he, along with Gumperz, edited an issue of IJAL called "Linguistic Diversity in South Asia". He also wrote about diglossia as a language teaching problem. At the 1964 Institute he conducted a seminar in sociolinguistics. It is often the coming together of a nucleus of scholars with the same growing concerns that frees it and lets new ideas bloom. It is not my purpose to pinpoint the creation of modern sociolinguistics at the Lake Arrowhead conference or LSA Institute alone, but rather the combination of both in a continuous period from mid-May to mid-August of 1964. Just as linguistic geographers had broken from the view of language study which treated languages as homogenous and unified, so sociolinguists broke from structural linguists in their treatment of languages "as completely uniform, homogeneous or monolithic in their structure" (Bright 1966:11).

In addition to Gumperz' and Ferguson's courses in sociolinguistics, the 1964 LSA summer institute provided still another impetus for the development of language variation study. Alva L. Davis, a linguistic geographer then at Illinois Institute of Technology, along with Robert F. Hogan, of the National Council of Teachers of English, secured funding for a conference on Social Dialects and Language Learning, to be held in conjunction with this same LSA Summer Institute at Bloomington. Twenty-five participants, including linguists, educators, sociologists and psychologists, were invited. Gumperz, Labov, McDavid, and Ferguson represented continuity from the Lake Arrowhead group. All other linguists were from dialectology, language contact or multilingualism specialties. The publications of the papers at this meeting (Shuy 1965) focused on the equality of dialects, on the need for research on urban language,

on the adequacy of past approaches to dialectology research, on the pedagogical usefulness of deeper information about language variation, and on whether non-standard
varieties should be eliminated or added to by standard English.

Today, these topics seem rather common. But in the Summer of 1964 they were start-
lingly new issues. Several of the educators present argued, traditionally, for holding the
line against substandard English. The conference came to grips with terminological
issues such as 'substandard' vs. 'nonstandard' and 'culturally deprived' vs. 'culturally
different'. Haugen called into question the approach suggested by many: that we use
English as a Second Language methodology to teach English as a second dialect. He
pointed out that language learning and dialect learning are not the same things, despite
what seemed to be similarities.

With the Lake Arrowhead meeting, with the LSA Institute, with Gumperz' and
Ferguson's courses in sociolinguistics and with the conference on Social Dialects, the
Summer of 1964 was very important for the establishment of the field of sociolinguistics. What happened afterward proves this. Many of the participants in these meetings
began teaching courses called sociolinguistics at their home universities.

[. . .]

Concurrent with the growth of the sort of work carried out by Labov in New York
and others in Detroit and Washington DC in the sixties was the development of more
ethnographic research on language variation. Hymes, Gumperz and their colleagues
and students focused on language as a social fact and studied the interaction between
communication and culture. Perhaps out of dissatisfaction with the generativists' lim-
itation of 'competence' to grammatical knowledge, Hymes extended the notion to 'communicative competence', the most general term for the speaking and hearing capabilities
of a person (Hymes 1964a). Although Newmeyer asserts that Hymes intended 'communicative competence' to exclude grammatical competence (Newmeyer 1983), this
was not Hymes' intention at all. Hymes did not reject grammatical competence, rather,
he believed it to be a part of a larger competence that was worthy of study.

By the late 1960s, then, several strands of research approaches were fermenting and
coming together. The regional dialectology strand had been around for almost a century,
the language contact strand, evidenced by the work of Ferguson, Haugen, Weinreich,
Fishman, and others, had strongly made its presence known, and the ethnography of
communication strand had made a powerful impact in a relatively short time. All strands
were concerned with language in its social context and all were composed of scholars
who considered themselves to be doing linguistics. The term 'sociolinguistics', began
to crop up in university course catalogues, in journal articles and in book titles. With
this approaching harmony, however, were discordant tones brought about by the fact
that the practitioners of this work were found in separate academic disciplines, at least
as university structure defined them.

6   Changes from the Ancestral Heritage

It should be clear that modern linguistics was in severe labor pains in the mid-sixties,
ready and apparently eager to deliver its offspring, sociolinguistics. One might expect
this child to bear certain resemblances to both its parents, linguistics and social science.

One would even like to believe that the new child would bring these two parents closer together. In the period described in some detail earlier, from 1964 to 1966, the problems in doing this were recognized. What to name this new child was discussed by the leaders in this field (Hymes 1966). How to rear this child was discussed at virtually every meeting of such scholars (training at universities). Once this child was born it would need professional conferences, journals, meetings, institutes, texts, and training centers to help it grow to maturity.

Now, one quarter of a century after those mid-sixties planning meetings, early courses and collections of papers, it is time to take inventory of what actually happened. Did the disciplines of linguistics, sociology and anthropology ever accomplish the rapprochement that was so eagerly wished in the sixties? Did the young child get christened with an enduring name? Did the field of linguistics come to accept sociolinguistics as one of its own offspring? How is sociolinguistics doing in the fields of anthropology and sociology? Have specialized journals been created?

It is not accidental that many of the early sociolinguists looked to the analytical routines of sociology in addition to anthropology. Quantifiable approaches to socio-economic status were one such routine. Census data were also found useful, along with the more sophisticated sampling procedures and data gathering procedures of sociology.

7 Methodology

Sociolinguists charted their own course, however, even when borrowing from sociology and, for this reason, suffered criticism from that field. It became clear early on, for example, that language data are quite different from conventional sociological data. A sociologist could interview subjects concerning voting or purchasing patterns, daily activities, attitudes or values and still remain uncertain about the accuracy or truthfulness of their responses. It is relatively easy to stretch the truth about how many times one brushes one's teeth or exactly who one voted for but it is much more difficult for humans to consciously change or modify the consonants or vowels they use as they produce coherent ideas in their speech.[2] This relative stability of language used in natural contexts makes a small sample of language more useful to researchers than would be an equally small sample of the type of self-report data found in other social science research.

Sociolinguists also argue for parting company with the methods of determining socio-economic status that are common in sociology, while acknowledging that they benefited greatly from sociological procedures, particularly in the early days of sociolinguistic research. The first large sociolinguistic research projects (Labov 1965; Shuy, Wolfram & Riley 1968) essentially used language data to correlate with socio-economic status (SES) as defined by the Warner scale. As knowledge and theory grew, however, sociolinguists began to ask themselves: "Why should language be selected as the variable to correlate with SES? Why not let language *be* the SES?". If sociolinguists were true to their belief that language is the best available window to social structure and cognition, why use it to correlate with other, less adequate windows?

With the development of sociolinguistic quantitative analysis came more sophisticated statistical analyses. It has been said that there are two types of linguistic analysts:

those who search for universals (what languages have in common), and those who search for variability (how languages differ).

It became apparent that the search for language universals required less quantitative measures than the search for variability. To be sure, research in universals can use statistical analysis and it is also true that our long tradition of dialectology research had essentially avoided statistics. But as tightly focused research projects made use of multiple occurrences of language samples in different contexts, it became evident that a very important feature of language was that of frequency of occurrence, not just categorical presence or absence. [. . .]

In the 1960s, sociolinguistic quantification resulted in rather simple statistics, usually represented in percentages. There is nothing wrong with such statistics, of course, as long as the claims are clear and accurate. In fact, such statistical representation was a tremendous improvement over previous representations of all-or-none presence or absence of a feature. As linguists became acquainted with computers, however, larger and more sophisticated statistical routines became popular (Fasold 1984). From anthropology, some sociolinguists have borrowed the methodology of participant observation and ethnography. Although ethnographic approaches to language analysis existed for many years, it is noteworthy that the University of Pennsylvania is responsible for a burst of training and research in the sixties, one that produced a major impact on work in this area. Dell Hymes was largely responsible for this flurry of activity.

It should be stressed that even though sociolinguists reached out for ideas and approaches from sociology and anthropology, such ideas and approaches were not borrowed in their entirety or in their purest form. They were modified to the specific purposes of the newly perceived field. Both sociologists and anthropologists might complain, with justification perhaps, that these modifications dilute or distort the purposes of their own field. However true this may be, the criticism has less force when we recognize that sociolinguistics is *not* sociology and it is *not* anthropology, per se. There are those who agree, in fact, that neither is it linguistics per se, since sociolinguists go beyond the traditional limits of linguistic analysis, but this criticism is tempered by the fact that sociolinguists recognize this fact by calling the field sociolinguistics.

From the onset of the existence of a field of study called sociolinguistics, there has been debate about whether or not there should be something called sociolinguistics at all. Labov, regarded by most as one of the major forces in this field's birth, himself objected to the term as early as 1965. For Labov, there was no need for calling this field by a separate name. He preferred that the parent field, linguistics, adjust and accept social variability within its scope. In short, Labov didn't have any particular need for a concept or field like sociolinguistics. [. . .]

8 Names

In November of 1966, when Hymes submitted his report on Training in Sociolinguistics, no name for the field had been agreed upon. He reports that sociolinguistic subject matter was then being taught under the headings of 'linguistics', 'language and culture', 'sociology of language' and 'language behavior' as well as 'sociolinguistics'. Over twenty years later, the same labels appear, although, among linguists at least, 'sociolinguistics' has come to be the common term. Annual meetings of the Linguistic Society of America have had sessions labeled 'sociolinguistics' for over 15 years. In fact a recent brochure describing the entire field of linguistics, distributed by the LSA, describes sociolinguistics as one of the major components of our discipline. Today sociolinguistics may be defined differently by different scholars but there is general agreement that it includes topics such as language planning, language variability (social and regional dialects), registers, and pidgins and creoles. There is mixed agreement about whether sociolinguistics includes language change or whether the study of language change includes a subcategory of study which is sociolinguistic. Likewise, the more recent developments of discourse analysis, pragmatics and speech acts are by some scholars considered to be a part of sociolinguistics proper and by others to be separate areas of study in themselves. David Crystal, in *The Cambridge Encyclopedia of Language*, defines 'sociolinguistics' as "The study of the interaction between language and the structures and functioning of society" (p. 412). Absent from the above topics are fields of study such as 'the ethnography of communication' and 'language and culture', which are still generally believed to be the province of anthropology, and 'the sociology of language' and 'ethnomethodology', which are still generally believed to be the province of sociology. Few, if any, departments of linguistics offer all of the above-mentioned topics as specializations in which students can receive training.

[...]

Notes

This reading is much abbreviated from the full version in *Historiographia Linguistica* XVII (1/2): 183–209, 1990, to which the interested reader is referred.

1 The title of this journal was later changed to *Publications of the American Dialect Society* and remains the same today.
2 The same essential truthfulness or validity has been noted for morphological and syntactic features as well.

References

Bernstein, Basil B. 1966. "Culture and Linguistics". Memorandum.
Bloomfield, Leonard. 1933. *Language*. New York: Henry Holt & Co.
Bright, William, ed. 1966. *Sociolinguistics*. The Hague: Mouton.
Crystal, David, ed. 1987. *The Cambridge Encyclopedia of Language*. Cambridge: Cambridge Univ. Press.
Currie, Haver C. 1952. "A Projection of Sociolinguistics: The relationship of speech to social status". *Southern Speech Journal* 18.28–37.
Fasold, Ralph. 1984. *The Sociolinguistics of Society*. Oxford: Basil Blackwell.
Ferguson, Charles & John Gumperz. 1960. "Introduction". *Linguistic Diversity in South Asia*. (= *IJAL* 26:3.) Bloomington, Indiana.
Gilliéron, Jules & Edmond Edmont. 1902–1910. *Atlas linguistique de la France*. Paris: Champion.
Hertzler, Joyce O. 1965. *The Sociology of Language*. New York: Random House.

Hymes, Dell. 1964a. "Introduction: Toward ethnographies of communication". *The Ethnography of Communication* ed. by John J. Gumperz & D. H. Hymes (*American Anthropologist* 66, no.6, part 2), 1–34.

Hymes, Dell. 1964b. "A Perspective for Linguistic Anthropology". *Horizons of Anthropology* ed. by Sol Tax, 92–107. Chicago: Aldine.

Hymes, Dell. 1966. *Teaching and Training in Sociolinguistics*. Report to Social Science Research Council, 1 November, 1966.

Kiparsky, Paul. 1979. *Pāṇini as Variationist*. Cambridge, Mass.: MIT Press.

Koerner, Konrad. 1988. "Toward a History of Modern Sociolinguistics". Paper presented at the Fifteenth LACUS Forum. [A revised and extended version appeared in *American Speech* 66(1): 57–70.]

Labov, William. 1965. "Stages in the Acquisition of Standard English". *Social Dialects and Language Learning* ed. by Roger Shuy, 77–104. Champaign, Ill.: National Council of Teachers of English.

Labov, William. 1966. *The Social Stratification of English in New York City*. Washington, D.C.: Center for Applied Linguistics.

McDavid, Raven I., Jr. 1948. "Postvocalic /-r/ in South Carolina: A social analysis". *American Speech* 23.194–203.

Meillet, Antoine. 1921. *Linguistique historique et linguistique générale*. Paris: Société de Linguistique de Paris.

Newmeyer, Frederick J. 1983. *Grammatical Theory, Its Limits and Its Possibilities*. Chicago: University of Chicago Press.

Pride, John & Janet Holmes, eds. 1972. *Sociolinguistics*. Baltimore: Penguin.

Sapir, Edward. 1921. *Language: An introduction to the study of speech*. New York: Harcourt & Brace.

Shuy, Roger W., ed. 1965. *Social Dialects and Language Learning*. Champaign, Ill.: National Council of Teachers of English.

Shuy, Roger W. 1988. "The Social Context of the Study of the Social Context of Language Variation". *Synchronic and Diachronic Approaches to Linguistic Variation and Change* ed. by Thomas J. Walsh, 293–309. Washington, D.C.: Georgetown Univ. Press.

Shuy, Roger W., Walter A. Wolfram, & William K. Riley. 1968. *Field Techniques in an Urban Language Study*. Washington, D.C.: Center for Applied Linguistics.

Whitney, William Dwight. 1867. *Language and the Study of Language*. New York: Scribner, Armstrong and Co.

2

Reflections on the Origins of Sociolinguistics in Europe

Louis-Jean Calvet

At the beginning of the twentieth century, French linguistics experienced a strange debate in which the adversaries never really crossed swords. In 1906 Antoine Meillet, borrowing from the sociologist Emile Durkheim the notion of "social fact," forcefully stated his conception of language ("language is after all eminently a social fact. It fits exactly the definition which Durkheim proposed"[1]). The same year Ferdinand de Saussure was assigned a course in general linguistics at the University of Geneva. On November 12 of that year, some days before assuming his post, he wrote to Meillet essentially to discuss with him his own research on anagrams in Saturnian poetry, research on which he soon gave up and of which he does not breathe a word in his lectures. Meillet was not to know what Saussure was teaching; in 1913 in writing his obituary, he only refers to *Mémoire sur le système primitif des voyelles dans les langues indo-européennes*. It is not until 1916, after the posthumous publication of *Cours de linguistique générale*, that he discovers the propositions to which he strongly objected. Thus Saussure nowhere expressed his opinion about the theses of Meillet, whose name does not even appear in the index of the *Cours*, and Meillet was not able to criticize Saussure until after his death. Nevertheless, we have here the germ of a debate which is still going on between two conceptions of language and linguistics: on the one hand, Saussure's idea of language as an abstract structure, which one can study synchronically, without reference to change; on the other, Meillet's idea of language as a social fact, in constant evolution.

1 A First Birth of the Idea of Sociolinguistics: From Meillet to Sommerfelt

Some have seen in Meillet the origin of sociolinguistics, but things are a bit more complicated, and the first years of that century were witness to a number of interventions which all headed in the same direction but did not seem to know about each other. The publication of the volumes of the *Linguistic Atlas of France* by Gilliéron and Edmont stretches from 1902 to 1914. During this period, Meillet, who was working with Durkheim's journal *L'Année sociologique*, set forth his conception of language as social fact, and Raoul Guerin de la Grasserie, in an article published in 1909, launched the idea of a "sociology of language."[2] Gilliéron's atlas makes visible "linguistic variation by projecting it on a map"; Meillet insists on the social character of language, la Grasserie suggests the examination of "the reciprocal actions and reactions between society and language," but there is no convergence of these different approaches, like a chemical reaction which didn't take. This is to say that a large part of the questions we discuss today were already posited but without order, without relation to each other. Furthermore, Meillet, who had a central university position and enjoyed great prestige, never elaborated on a linguistic theory based on the conception of language as social fact, which remained with him only as a pious wish. He never, never even used any expression like "linguistic sociology," "sociological linguistics," "sociology of language" or "sociolinguistics," and his major articles were published under the title *Historical Linguistics and General Linguistics*. In particular, even though he could take into account the social and historical character of language when he studied the lexicon (for example in his articles on the names of man, or those of oil and wine) or the development of languages (for example the history of Latin), this was much more difficult for him in the area of syntax or phonology.

In the 1930s, according to Polomé, Professor Grégoire, "the pioneer in this field" (Polomé 1997: 213), gave a course at the University of Brussels devoted to the "sociology of language." But one has to wait until 1938 for the Norwegian linguist Alf Sommerfelt to attempt the first sociolinguistic description of a language.[3] The first sentence of his book is clear: "this book is an attempt at a sociological linguistics", and he writes later: "As language is a social fact comparable to religion, morals or rules of law, it is obvious that one should study it in the same way as the latter, which is to say that one should use the same general methods of sociology which one combines with the specific methods of linguistics" (Sommerfelt 1938: 6). He does cite Meillet to whose memory the work is dedicated, but mainly he draws on Durkheim, Mauss, Malinowski, Lévy-Bruhl, Radcliffe-Brown, that is, the major sociologists and anthropologists of his time. Sommerfelt also worked on Aranta, an Australian aboriginal language whose culture has played an important role in social anthropology, for matters which deal with totemism (cf. Durkheim, *Formes élémentaires de la vie religieuse, le système totémique en Australie*, 1912) as well as with comparison of religious and matrimonial systems, in sections and subsections. This tribe forms a typical example, used time and again by anthropologists and sociologists (up to Claude Lévi-Strauss in *Les Structures élémentaires de la parenté* and *La Pensée sauvage*), and it is thus not by accident that Sommerfelt is interested in Aranta. His approach became integrated into the humanities movement of his time, which was much influenced by evolutionism, and his knowledge and understanding make his arguments move persuasive than Meillet's. He is furthermore even more "radical" than Meillet and suggests studying "in the light of the social organization" systems of reference and categories of grammar (Sommerfelt 1938: 13) "to determine whether there exists a correlation between the phonological character of archaic languages and the sound systems of these languages and the structure of the societies which speak them," a program that Meillet never formulated in these terms. And that guides his approach: "in order to determine the relationship which exists between language and society, it stands to reason that one should begin with the languages which belong to the most archaic societies which are known" (Sommerfelt 1938: 14).

When one rereads him today, Sommerfelt's work is not very convincing in its results, but it is his system, a maximalist program, which is noteworthy, attempting to put sociolinguistics at the center of linguistics, a program which has hardly been followed until very recently. Immediately following World War II, there were a number of publications which took up the theme of a relationship between language and society: in 1946, the Italian Bruno Migliorini dedicated a chapter of a book on linguistics to "*la lingua e la società*",[4] and the Swede Torgny Segerstedt put in the title of one of his books the phrase "sociology of language",[5] the Briton M. M. Lewis published in 1947 a work with an enticing title,[6] but none of this challenged theoretically the weight of Saussurian structuralism, which became established. It is the same with the works of Basil Bernstein (Bernstein 1975) who has furthermore recently emphasized that in his opinion "if socio and linguistics are to illuminate language as a truly social construct, then there must be mutually translatable principles of description which enable the dynamics of the social to enter these translatable principles" (Bernstein 1997: 48).

2   A Second Birth of the Idea of Sociolinguistics: In the USSR

If we have here, by evidence, a first birthplace of the appearance in Europe of the relationships between language and society, there is another, very different and geographically far away, which played a not negligible role: it concerns the USSR, Marxism and "Marrism." Nicholas Marr had worked out a theory according to which all the languages in the world had the same origin, four syllables or "elements" (sal, ber, yon, rosh) whose combination would have given the different words of the different languages. Language, considered as superstructure, reflected for him dialectically the confrontation of classes, and so the forms of speech of similar social classes in different countries are closer to each other than the forms of speech of different social classes in the same country. It followed from this, in the same way as socialism was the future of the world, that this world would have in the future one single uniform language (which incidentally explains why the USSR had for a long time supported an Esperanto movement: Esperanto could have been an early manifestation of this proletarian world language).

For a long time the Soviet regime considered Marr's (he died in 1934) new theory of language and his school as official opinion. Some, like Valentin Volochinov, paid with their lives for having a different opinion. In his work, *Le Marxisme et la philosophie du langage*, published in 1929 (Volochinov 1977 in French translation), Volochinov insisted on the fact that the structure of speech is a social structure, that language is a continuous generative process, tied to the relationship among the speakers, and above all that language considered as a stable system of invariant forms is an abstraction without ties to a concrete reality. Volochinov disappeared in the Stalin camps, and his book was not translated until much later into English (1973) and then into French, but Stalin himself intervened in the debate in 1950, by the expedient of an interview in *Pravda* in which he undertook to "de-Marr" Soviet linguistics.[7] Language is not a superstructure, he said; it does not have the nature of social class (the Russian language, for example, did not change after the Revolution) and even if it is a social fact, it is above all "an instrument with whose aid human beings communicate," a tool.

This intervention, which formed an unexpected guarantee for linguistic structuralism (André Martinet, for example, defined language as "an instrument of communication"), even if it certainly did not reinstate Volochinov, it did however bring a certain freedom to communist linguists, anxious to align themselves with the political and theoretical positions of the USSR and who until now had not dared attack Marr's opinions head-on. Thus Marcel Cohen could write in 1956 that Marr "had tried to impose a pseudo-Marxist linguistics, in spite of the resistance of some Soviet linguists," and that Stalin refuted "the Marr doctrine with some correct interpretations of dialectical materialism and in so doing settled several important points of Marxist sociology" as applied to language (Cohen 1956: 26). He does not say a word about the fate of these linguists, but his work *Matériaux pour une sociologie du language* was to play a not negligible role. However, it was not a question of a structured, theoretical work which suggested a new conception of language and linguistics. But Cohen, a Marxist and communist, besides having worked with Meillet, was concerned with the relationship between language and society, and he attempted to add, in the margin of the structural conception of language, some varied sociological viewpoints. This book thus comes across as a series of illustrated notations in an extensive bibliography on themes as varied as language and social groups, language of cities and of the countryside, "distinguished" language and "common" language, the spread of the language of conquerors, language contact, etc. As Andrée Tabouret-Keller writes, it was "an attempt at mapping the terrain, stating the questions, and organizing the field of desirable investigations" (Tabouret-Keller 1997: 226). In fact, Cohen's work is characterized by two traits. On the one hand, he shows the way, indicating that it would be interesting to explore this or that theme, to work in this or that direction, every time giving numerous bibliographic citations, but he does not make any methodological suggestions. On the other hand, all his suggestions point in the same direction: study language use. This is to say that one looks in vain in Cohen's work for a new theory which could form a counterweight to structuralism, and that his insistence on the social usage of language supported structuralism: there was linguistics, the central science, and other peripheral approaches, sociolinguistics, ethnolinguistics, psycholinguistics . . .

But it remains true nevertheless that this was an important moment in the European history of sociolinguistics which does not seem well known to North American linguists. If, for example, we go back to Koerner's chart (Koerner 1991), intended as a summary of the history of sociolinguistics, we see that the central column, in which some of the European scholars I have cited appear, is somewhat simplified:

Sources of sociolinguistics according to Koerner (1991)

Dialectology	Historical linguistics	Bi- and multilingual studies
Wrede (1902)	Meillet (1905)	M. Weinreich (1931)
Gauchat (1905)	Vendryes (1921)	U. Weinreich (1951)
Jaberg (1908)	Sommerfelt (1932)	Haugen (1953)
Hermann (1929)		Ferguson (1959)
McDavid (1946–, 1948)	Martinet (1946 {1939})	Friedrich (1961)
	Weinreich (1953)	
	Labov (1963)	

Missing from this chart is not only Marcel Cohen but also any reference to Soviet linguistics and Stalin's intervention. Now, even if one can historically understand that the communist or Marxist quality of these linguists has "scared off" certain American writers, the fact remains that it is difficult to understand what happened in Europe without analyzing the 1950 debate in *Pravda* and its fallout. In the Marr/Stalin debate (which like the Saussure/Meillet debate took place in the absence of one of the protagonists) we find, in fact, the contradiction between a linguistics which attempts to read the traces of a social division in language (even if, with Marr, this attempt leads to a caricature) and, on the other hand, a linguistics which sees language as an instrument of "neutral" communication. The first, whatever you think about it, is not a stranger to the idea of "sociolinguistics"; the second is much closer to formal linguistics, which makes a "social" approach to the facts of language difficult. Some have seen a contradiction in Stalin: in the case of the Lyssenko affair, he came down, in the field of genetics, in favor of two sciences (a proletarian science and a bourgeois science); in the case of the "Marr affair," he settled, in the field of linguistics, against a proletarian science, for a single science. In fact, the debate is without doubt about something else; Stalin's position was tied more to political problems (the development of agriculture in the Lyssenko case, the national language in the Marr case) than to theoretical.[8] But the fact remains that his intervention, and the reading several European linguists[9] gave to it, helped push linguistics toward formalism, helped distance it from a sociolinguistic problematics.

3   What Concrete Work Followed?

The emergence of what was later to be called sociolinguistics is thus tied in Europe to the coming together of different factors, among them the theoretical tradition and the political environment which I have just discussed, but also actual circumstances of time and place. I will briefly call to mind three trends, which are not the only trends but without doubt the most important: 1) dialectology, 2) regional languages, and 3) the linguistic situation of the colonized countries.

The tradition in dialectology has prepared the ground for numerous works and for several dozens of linguistic atlases of different regions of France and of overseas *départements*. Even if these publications are directly concerned with variation, in particular geographical variation, they remain relatively distant from the major debates I have discussed here: dialectology is part of the origins of sociolinguistics but has stayed aloof, seemingly little concerned with the theoretical implications of its development. Besides, the new dialectology had, for research-methodological reasons, avoided the cities. When one looks, for example, at the six-hundred-point survey of Gilliéron and Edmont, one cannot find a single large city. This rural or semi-rural survey methodology was then replicated in Italy, Spain, Romania, etc., with always the same principle, which is perfectly understandable: in order to describe the "purest" dialectal forms, one could not survey in towns where one finds an intermingling of languages. Perhaps as a reaction against this rural aspect of dialectology, sociolinguistics today often studies urban landscapes (in Germany, Dittmar and Schlobinski 1988; in Spain, Villena Ponsoda 1994; in France, Calvet 1994) which yet again forced sociolinguistics to leave to linguistics proper the problems of language description and rather to focus on the usage and contact of languages. It is only quite recently that people have begun to do work on the effects of function on form, in particular on the urban process of creolization or on rural languages (see for example Thiam 1990, and Calvet and Moussirou-Mouyama 2000). I said that some Europeans who attempted to analyze language from a social viewpoint adhered to the Marxist tradition (Marcel Cohen, Jean Baptiste Marcellesi, in France; F. Rossi-Landi in Italy, etc.). Now, this reference implied a sociology aimed more at the class struggle and the balance of power than at just the distribution of income or the level of education. This school of thought was applied to the analysis of situations with minority languages (in Catalonia, Occitania, creole-speaking islands) as well as to a criticism of concepts which had come from the USA, like diglossia revisited from the viewpoint of a power struggle between dominant and dominated languages. And that which some have called "native" linguistics places practice (especially political practice) at the center of theoretical reflections. The study of regional language situations in France (Alsatian, Breton, Occitan, etc.) or in Spain (Catalan, Basque, Galician) has also nourished theoretical concern (see for example Aracil 1982).

In the same way, the existence of prior colonial empires for certain European countries (France, the United Kingdom, the Netherlands, Portugal) led linguists from these countries either to describe multilingual situations, language contact and creolization (Whiteley 1969, Houis 1971, Hill and Polomé 1980, Polomé 1984, 1985, etc.) or to analyze linguistic practice and epilinguistic discourse associated with colonialism (Calvet 1974, Phillipson 1992). In the same way that Guerin de la Grasserie and Sommerfelt looked for their corpus in the margins of society, one in slang, the other in an "archaic" society, European sociolinguistics has similarly positioned itself in the margin of linguistics, interested in language usage rather than in language itself. The present situation, and not only the European, is hardly different. In spite of Labov's frequently reiterated assertion according to which sociolinguistics is linguistics, and that the term sociolinguistics "implies that there can be a successful linguistic theory or practice which is not social" (Labov 1997: 147), European sociolinguistics has not illustrated this principle either methodologically or theoretically. In this, in spite of its particular mode of emergence, it is today no different from that on other continents.

Notes

1   "Comment les mots changent de sens," *L'année sociologique*, 1905–6.
2   "De la sociologie linguistique," 1909, *Sonderabdruck aus der Monatsschrift für Sociologie*, 1, Leipzig: Fritz Eckart Verlag.
3   Alf Sommerfelt, 1938. *La Langue et la société: caractères sociaux d'une langue de type archaïque*. Oslo: Aschehoug.
4   B. Migliorini. 1946. *Linguistica*. Florence.
5   In German translation, 1947. *Die Macht des Wortes: eine Sprachsoziologie*. Zurich. American edition, New York: Arno Press, 1975.
6   Morris Michael Lewis. 1947. *Language and Society*. London. American edition, New York: Social Sciences Publishers, 1948.
7   In fact, between May 9 and August 2, *Pravda* published numerous contributions on this theme, one for Marr, the other against. On June 20 and on July 4, Stalin intervened directly, and

afterwards everybody, including those who had until then defended Marr, stressed the theoretical importance of Stalin's text.

8 Stalin was not a linguist so it is remarkable that he would write letters to the editor about linguistics. In fact he probably didn't; although not officially acknowledged, it is considered by specialists that in all likelihood his writings on matters linguistic were ghost-written by the prominent Georgian linguist Arnold(i) Chikobava (with thanks to Professor Alice C. Harris). For the reader who would like to pursue the Marr controversy, see *The Soviet Linguistic Controversy*, translated from the Soviet press by John V. Murra, Robert M. Hankin, and Fred Holling (New York: King's Crown Press, 1951). (Translator's remarks.)

9 Marcel Cohen pays homage to this intervention in an article with the non-ambiguous title of "A lesson of Marxism for linguistics" (Cohen, 1950).

References

Aracil, Lluis. 1982. *Conflicte linguistic i normalitzacio lingüística a l'Europa nova*, Barcelona: Edicions de la Magrana.

Bernstein, Basil. 1975. *Langage et classes sociales*, Paris: Minuit.

Bernstein, Basil. 1997. "Sociolinguistics: A Personal View," in C. Paulston and R. Tucker (eds.), *The Early Days of Sociolinguistics*, Dallas, TX: SIL.

Calvet, Louis-Jean. 1974. *Linguistique et colonialisme, petit traité de glottophagie*. Paris: Payot.

Calvet, Louis-Jean. 1994. *La Voix de la ville, introduction à la sociolinguistique urbaine*, Paris: Payot.

Calvet, Louis-Jean and Auguste Moussirou-Mouyama (eds.). 2000. *Le plurilinguisme urbain*, Paris: Didier.

Cohen, Marcel. 1950. "Une leçon de marxisme à propos de linguistique," *La Pensée*, no. 34, November–December.

Cohen, Marcel. 1956. *Matériaux pour une sociologie du langage*, Paris: Armand Colin.

Dittmar, Norbert and Peter Schlobinski (eds.). 1988. *The Sociolinguistics of Urban Vernaculars*, Berlin, New York: de Gruyter.

Durkheim, Emile. 1915. *The Elementary Forms of Religious Life*. London: Allen & Unwin. English translation.

Ferguson, Charles. 1959. "Diglossia," *Word*, 15.

Gilliéron, Jules and Edmont, E. 1920. *Atlas linguistique de la France*. Paris: E. Champion.

Guerin de la Grasserie, Raoul. 1909. "De la sociologie linguistique," *Sonderabdruck aus der Monatsschrift für Sociologie*, 1, Leipzig: Fritz Eckart Verlag.

Hill, Peter C. and Polomé, Edgar. 1980. *Language in Tanzania*, IAI of London and Oxford University Press.

Houis, Maurice. 1971. *Anthropologie linguistique de l'Afrique noire*, Paris: PUF.

Koerner, Konrad. 1991. "Toward a History of Modern Sociolinguistics," *American Speech*, 6 (1).

Labov, William. 1997. "Sociolinguistic Patterns," in C. Paulston and R. Tucker (eds.), *The Early Days of Sociolinguistics*, Dallas, TX: SIL.

Lévi-Strauss, Claude. 1966. *The Savage Mind*. Chicago: University of Chicago Press. English translation.

Lévi-Strauss, Claude. 1969. *The Elementary Structures of Kinship*. Boston: Beacon Press. English translation.

Lewis, Morris Michael 1947. *Language in society*. London, New York: Social Sciences Publishers, 1948.

McDavid, Raven I., 1948. "Postvocalic /-v/ in South Carolina: A social analysis," American Speech, 23.

Marr, Nikolai. 1976. *Iazyk i sovremennost* (On language). Letchworth, Herts.: Prideaux Press.

Meillet, Antoine, 1905–6. "Comment les mots changent de sens," in *L'Année sociologique*, Paris.

Meillet, Antoine. 1913–14. "Ferdinand de Saussure." *Annuaire de l'école pratique des hautes études*, Paris.

Meillet, Antoine. 1916. "Compte rendu du Cours de linguistique générale de Ferdinand de Saussure," *Bulletin de la société linguistique de Paris*.

Migliorini, Bruno. 1946. *Linguistica*, Florence.

Phillipson, Robert, 1992. *Linguistic Imperialism*, Oxford: Oxford University Press.

Polomé, Edgar, 1984. "Standardization of Swahili," in C. Hagège and I. Fodor (eds.), *Language Reform, History and Future*, Hamburg: Buske.

Polomé, Edgar, 1985. "A study on the creole Shaba Swahili," in J. Maw and D. Parkin (eds.), *Swahili Language in Society*, Vienna: Institut für Afrikanistik, University of Vienna.

Polomé, Edgar, 1997. "Notes on the Development of Sociolinguistics," in C. Paulston and R. Tucker (eds.), *The Early Days of Sociolinguistics*, Dallas, TX: SIL.

Segerstedt, Torgny. 1947. *Die Macht des Wortes, eine Sprachsoziologie*, Zurich: Pan Verlag. New York: Arno Press. 1975. Translated from the Swedish.

Sommerfelt, Alf. 1938. *La Langue et la société: caractères sociaux d'une langue de type archaïque*, Oslo: Aschehoug.

Tabouret-Keller, Andrée, 1997. "From Sociolinguistics to the Anthropology of Language," in C. Paulston and R. Tucker (eds.), *The Early Days of Sociolinguistics*, Dallas, TX: SIL.

Thiam, Ndiassé. 1990. "L'Évolution du wolof véhiculaire en milieu urbain sénégalais: le contexte dakarois," *Plurilinguismes* no. 2, Paris.

Villena Ponsoda, Juan Andrés. 1994. *La ciudad lingüística, fundamentos criticos de la sociolingüística urbana*, Granada: University of Granada.

Volochinov, V. N. 1973. *Marxism and the Philosophy of Language*. Cambridge, MA: Harvard University Press. English translation.

Volochinov, V. N. 1977. *Le Marxisme et la philosophie du language*, French translation, Paris: Minuit.

Whiteley, Wilfred. 1969. *Swahili: The Rise of a National Language*, London: Methuen.

(translated from the French by Christina Bratt Paulston)

Discussion Questions

1. Some say that sociolinguistics was born out of the overlap of anthropology with structural linguistics, while others view the origins of the field as mostly from sociology. In fact, both anthropology and sociology played a part in the development of sociolinguistics. Discuss the contribution each has made to the development of sociolinguistics as a field in its own right.

2. Discuss why and how sociolinguists' focus on *language variation* was a departure from the generativists' analysis of language.

3. Sociolinguistics is quite broad in the range of inquiry that can be included in its scope. Shuy states: "There is mixed agreement about whether sociolinguistics includes language change or whether the study of language change includes a sub-category of study which is sociolinguistics" (p. 15). List three arguments that could be made *for* and *against* the inclusion of language change under the umbrella of sociolinguistics. Do you agree or disagree with the description of studies of pragmatics as sociolinguistic? Why?

4. Calvet quotes Stalin as stating that language is "'an instrument with whose aid human beings communicate,' a tool" (p. 19). How did Stalin's playing down the existence of social variation (vis-à-vis the inquiry early European sociolinguists were exploring at that time) serve his [Stalin's] political agenda?

5. Calvet states: "we find, in fact, the contradiction between a linguistics which attempts to read the traces of a social division in language . . . and on the other hand, a linguistics which sees language as an instrument of 'neutral' communication" (p. 21). Give three examples of how language can exemplify social division. Discuss whether language could ever be "an instrument of neutral communication".

Part II

Ethnography of Speaking

Introduction

Some scholars have claimed that sociolinguistics was designed as a countermovement to Noam Chomsky and his transformational generative grammar (TGG). Not so, as a perusal of the previous section makes clear. They were simply two schools of thought which appeared around the same time, with one notable exception.

That exception is the anthropological linguist Dell Hymes's concept of "communicative competence" intended as a counterconcept to Chomsky's "linguistic competence." By linguistic competence, an important building block then of TGG, Chomsky meant the ideal hearer–speaker's intuitive knowledge of all and only the grammatical sentences of English. What came out of the mouth was "linguistic performance," merely degenerate data of no interest. In defense of Chomsky, one should point out that he considered linguistics a cognitive science and asked different questions than did the sociolinguists.

But Hymes was not amused. Were a man to stand on a street corner and utter all and only the grammatical sentences of English, he would likely be institutionalized, he declared. In other words, knowledge of a language is infinitely more than some specified grammar rules. You have to know whom you can speak to, when you can speak, how you choose what terms. In other words, you have to know how it is appropriate to speak all the grammatical sentences, and appropriateness is as important as grammaticality. Clearly Hymes includes linguistic competence within the knowledge of communicative competence but he leaves that to others to work out. Gumperz explains: "Whereas linguistic competence covers the speaker's ability to produce grammatically correct sentences, communicative competence describes his ability to select, from the totality of grammatically correct expressions available to him, forms which appropriately reflect the social norms governing behavior in specific encounters" (1972: 205).

What Hymes is concerned with in the article here is developing a descriptive theory and working out the components of communicative competence which need to be identified, examined and analyzed within the framework of the ethnography of speaking (variously referred to as ways of speaking, ethnography of communication, ethnography of speech). The ethnography of speaking approach to the study of language was worked out in California in the early 1960s by junior faculty (you rarely get change from the top, be it societal change, language change or new schools of thought) who included the anthropological linguist John Gumperz, psycholinguist Susan Ervin-Tripp, sociologist Erving Goffman, philosopher John Searle and many others (Murray 1994). But the core was anthropological linguists and their concern was to describe (for which they needed models and theories) the sociolinguistic resources of a community, that is, the grammar but also the complex of linguistic potentials for social use and social meaning; how these resources figured in discourse and social interaction; and how they fitted into the larger society (Scherzer 1992). Hymes's title says it in a nutshell: "Models for the interaction of language and social life."

A "model" or a "theoretical framework" is in effect a mini-theory, a part of a larger theory. It is built of key concepts that are made to fit together into a coherent whole. The meaning of "concept" is notoriously difficult to define, and it is easier to understand if one looks instead at the function of concept, what concepts are supposed to do. Concepts are the organizational labels for data and the ideas that connect the data; they function much like pigeonholes in which you sort the data. The way you connect the pigeonholes builds your model; models pinpoint what to collect for description, how to analyze the data, and maybe even how to explain it.

In the last scene from G. B. Shaw's play *Pygmalion* (most people know it better as the musical "My Fair Lady"), Professor Higgins says rather surlily, "Fetch me my slippers, Eliza"; not even a please. How are we to understand that this is really a proposal of marriage? Professor Higgins was in fact patterned after Henry Sweet, Oxford phonetician and a notorious misogynist, and Shaw had no intention of marrying him off to Eliza – his play was social commentary, not romance. But early audiences rebelled; they wanted a happy ending and Shaw gave in and complied, if minimally. But this is a literary explanation; it explains why Shaw wrote as he did but not why we understand it. Enter Hymes; he gives us the concepts of speech situation, speech events and speech acts; which is to say context and how to do things with words, followed by a list of components of speech, each of which needs close attention.

We learn that speech act intention does not necessarily match surface form: "How charming you look," said to a disheveled wife at the end of a rough day is not much of a compliment and, taken as intended, ironic. Key (see chapter 3, p. 43) almost always overrides surface form. In the example from Shaw, the speech situation had been one of a formal ball with chaperones and the like social conventions; now the speech event is one of only two participants, marked for intimacy, and presumably Professor Higgins speaks his famous lines, not as an order but with sweet fondness: key overrides form and the meaning of order, Eliza may stay, which in Victorian England could only mean marriage, in turn relating the discourse to the larger society. And so we get the meaning, and hopefully Eliza does too.

But people do misunderstand the meaning, the intention of speech acts, and several schools of research studies, besides pragmatics per se, have resulted from this ethnographic approach to communication. John Gumperz (1982) explores the development of an interpretive sociolinguistics approach, the Scollons wrote about *Intercultural Communication* (1995) and such miscommunication, and Deborah Tannen in *You Just Don't Understand* (1990) applied the same approach to gender studies.

Hymes is not always easy to understand, and you may want to take a look at Saville-Troike's *The Ethnography of Communication: An Introduction*, which is based on Hymes's work and gives many additional examples and explanations.

We asked Dell Hymes to suggest some recent writings which exemplified his work. From his suggestions we chose Valentina Pagliai's "Lands I came to sing"; it gives us a glimpse of the land where Dante once sang but of which we have very little insight in the anglophone sociolinguistic literature. Enjoy!

References

Gumperz, John J. 1982. *Discourse Strategies*. Cambridge: Cambridge University Press.

Murray, Stephen O. 1994. *Theory Groups and the Study of Language in North America: A Social History*. Amsterdam: Benjamins.

Saville-Troike, Muriel. 1982. *The Ethnography of Communication: An Introduction*. Baltimore: University Park Press.

Scherzer, Joel. 1992. "The ethnography of speaking," (I: 419–20) in Wm. Bright (ed.), *International Encyclopedia of Linguistics*. Oxford: Oxford University Press.

Scollon, Ron and Suzanne Wong Scollon. 1995. *Intercultural Communication: A Discourse Approach*. Oxford: Blackwell.

Tannen, Deborah, 1990. *You Just Don't Understand: Women and Men in Conversation*. New York: Morrow.

Further Reading

Bauman, Richard and Joel Scherzer (eds.). 1974. *Explorations in the Ethnography of Speaking*. Cambridge: Cambridge University Press.

Carbaugh, Donal. 1990. *Cultural Communication and Intercultural Contact*. Hillsdale, NJ: Lawrence Erlbaum Associates.

Gumperz, John J. and Dell Hymes (eds.). 1972. *Directions in Sociolinguistics: The Ethnography of Communication*. New York: Holt, Rinehart and Winston.

Gumperz, John J. (ed.). 1982. *Language and Social Identity*. Cambridge: Cambridge University Press.

Heath, Shirley Brice. 1983. *Ways With Words: Language, Life, and Work in Communities and Classrooms*. Cambridge: Cambridge University Press.

Hymes, Dell. 1974. *Foundations in Sociolinguistics: An Ethnographic Approach*. Philadelphia: University of Pennsylvania Press.

Philips, Susan U. 1983. *The Invisible Culture: Communication in Classroom and Community on the Warm Springs Indian Reservation*. New York: Longman.

Schieffelin, Bambi B. and Elinor Ochs (eds.). 1986. *Language Socialization Across Cultures*. Cambridge: Cambridge University Press.

3

Models of the Interaction of Language and Social Life[1]

Dell Hymes

Diversity of speech has been singled out as the hallmark of sociolinguistics. Of this two things should be said. Underlying the diversity of speech within communities and in the conduct of individuals are systematic relations, relations that, just as social and grammatical structure, can be the object of qualitative inquiry. A long-standing failure to recognize and act on this fact puts many now in the position of wishing to apply a basic science that does not yet exist.

Diversity of speech presents itself as a problem in many sectors of life – education, national development, transcultural communication. When those concerned with such problems seek scientific cooperation, they must often be disappointed. There is as yet no body of systematic knowledge and theory. There is not even agreement on a mode of description of language in interaction with social life, one which, being explicit and of standard form, could facilitate development of knowledge and theory through studies that are full and comparable. There is not even agreement on the desirability or necessity of such a mode of description.

Bilingual or bidialectal phenomena have been the main focus of the interest that has been shown. Yet bilingualism is not in itself an adequate basis for a model or theory of the interaction of language and social life. From the standpoint of such a model or theory, bilingualism is neither a unitary phenomenon nor autonomous. The fact that two languages are present in a community or are part of a person's communicative competence is compatible with a variety of underlying functional (social) relationships. Conversely, distinct languages need not be present for the underlying relationships to find expression.

Bilingualism par excellence (e.g., French and English in Canada, Welsh and English in North Wales, Russian and French among prerevolutionary Russian nobility) is a salient, special case of the general phenomenon of linguistic repertoire. No normal person, and no normal community, is limited to a single way of speaking, to an unchanging monotony that would preclude indication of respect, insolence, mock seriousness, humor, role distance, and intimacy by switching from one mode of speech to another.

Given the universality of linguistic repertoires, and of switching among the ways of speaking they comprise, it is not necessary that the ways be distinct languages. Relationships of social intimacy or of social distance may be signaled by switching between distinct languages (Spanish: Guarani in Paraguay (Rubin 1962, 1968)), between varieties of a single language (standard German: dialect), or between pronouns within a single variety (German *Du:Sie*). Segregation of religious activity may be marked linguistically by a variety whose general unintelligibility depends on being of foreign provenance (e.g., Latin, Arabic in many communities), on being a derived variety of the common language (Zuni (Newman 1964)), or on being a manifestation not identifiable at all (some glossolalia). Conversely, shift between varieties may mark a shift between distinct spheres of activity (e.g., standard Norwegian: Hemnes dialect (see Blom and Gumperz 1972), or the formal status of talk within a single integral activity (e.g., Siane in New Guinea (Salisbury 1962)), Latin in a contemporary Cambridge University degree ceremony (e.g., *Cambridge University Reporter* 1969).

A general theory of the interaction of language and social life must encompass the multiple relations between linguistic means and social meaning. The relations within a particular community or personal repertoire are an empirical problem, calling for a mode of description that is jointly ethnographic and linguistic.

If the community's own theory of linguistic repertoire and speech is considered (as it must be in any serious ethnographic account), matters become all the more complex and interesting. Some peoples, such as the Wishram Chinook of the Columbia River in what is now the state of Washington, or the Ashanti of Nigeria, have considered infants' vocalizations to manifest a special language (on the Wishram, see Hymes 1966a; on the Ashanti, Hogan 1967). For the Wishram, this language was interpretable only by men having certain guardian spirits. In such cases, the native language is in native theory a second language to everyone. Again, one community may strain to maintain mutual intelligibility with a second in the face of great differentiation of dialect, while another may declare intelligibility impossible, although the objective linguistic differences are minor. Cases indistinguishable by linguistic criteria may thus be now monolingual, now bilingual, depending on local social relationships and attitudes (discussed more fully in Hymes 1968).

While it is common in a bilingual situation to look for specialization in the function, elaboration, and valuation of a language, such specialization is but an instance of a universal phenomenon, one that must be studied in situations dominantly monolingual as well. Language as such is not everywhere equivalent in role and value; speech may have different scope and functional load in the communicative economies of different societies. In our society sung and spoken communication intersect in song; pure speaking and instrumental music are separate kinds of communication. Among the Flathead Indians of Montana, speech and songs without text are separate, while songs with text, and instrumental music as an aspect of songs with text, form the intersection. Among the Maori of New Zealand instrumental music is a part of song, and both are ultimately conceived as speech. (It is interesting to note that among both the Flathead and Maori it is supernatural context that draws speech and music together, and makes of both (and of animal sounds as well among the Flathead) forms of linguistic communication.)[2] With regard to speaking itself, while Malinowski has made us familiar with the importance of phatic communication, talk for the sake of something being said, the ethnographic record suggests that it is far from universally an important or even accepted motive (see Sapir 1949b:16, 11). The Paliyans of south India "communicate very little at all times and become almost silent by the age of 40. Verbal, communicative persons are regarded as abnormal and often as offensive" (Gardner 1966: 398). The distribution of required and preferred silence, indeed, perhaps most immediately reveals in outline form a community's structure of speaking (see Samarin 1965; Basso 1970).

Finally, the role of language in thought and culture (Whorf's query) obviously cannot be assessed for bilinguals until the role of each of their languages is assessed; but the same is true for monolinguals since in different societies language enters differentially into educational experience, transmission of beliefs, knowledge, values, practices, and conduct (see Hymes 1966a). Such differences may obtain even between different groups within a single society with a single language.

What is needed, then, is a general theory and body of knowledge within which diversity of speech, repertoires, ways of speaking, and choosing among them find a natural place. Such a theory and body of knowledge are only now being built in a sustained way. Social scientists asking relevant functional questions have usually not had the training and insight to deal adequately with the linguistic face of the problem. Linguistics, the discipline central to the study of speech, has been occupied almost wholly with developing analysis of the structure of language as a referential code, neglecting social meaning, diversity, and use. There have been notable exceptions (as in the work of Firth, Jakobson, and Sapir), but the main course of linguistic work has been from the then newly captured sector of phonology (before World War II) through morphology and syntax. Now that the inner logic of linguistics itself brings it to deal with semantics and speech acts, and now that the social sciences generally in the United States are engaged in the sort of cross-cultural and educational research that makes language differences of concern, there has emerged something tantamount to a movement to redress the situation. The movement is commonly called *sociolinguistics*, especially when seen as relating language to sociological categories, or as mediating between linguistics and social science as a whole.

It is not necessary to think of sociolinguistics as a novel discipline. If linguistics comes to accept fully the sociocultural dimensions, social science the linguistic dimensions, of their subject matters and theoretical bases, sociolinguistic will simply identify a mode of research in adjacent sectors of each. As disciplines, one will speak simply of linguistics, anthropology, and the like (see Hymes 1964, 1966b, 1970). But, as just implied, the linguistics, anthropology, etc., of which one speaks will have changed. In order to develop models, or theories, of the interaction of language and social life, there must be adequate descriptions of that interaction, and such descriptions call for an approach that partly links, but partly cuts across, partly builds between the ordinary practices of the disciplines. This is what makes sociolinguistics exciting and necessary. It does not accept, but it is a critique of the present partitioning of the subject of man among the sciences of man. Its goal is to explain the meaning of language in human life, and not in the abstract, not in the superficial phrases one may encounter in essays and textbooks, but in the concrete, in actual human lives. To do that it must develop adequate modes of description and classification, to answer new questions and give familiar questions a novel focus.

1 The Case for Description and Taxonomy

For some of the most brilliant students of language in its social setting, the proper strategy is to select problems that contribute directly to current linguistic and social theory. A primary concern is relevant to particular problems already perceived as such in the existing disciplines, although the modes of work of those disciplines must often be transformed for the problems to find solutions. Field studies in societies exotic to the investigator, where strong control over data and hypothesis testing cannot easily be maintained, are not much valued. A concern to secure reports from such societies is thought pointless since it suggests a prospect of endless descriptions which, whatever their quantity and quality, would not as such contribute to theoretical discovery.

My own view is different. I accept an intellectual tradition, adumbrated in antiquity, and articulated in the course of the Enlightenment, which holds that mankind cannot be understood apart from the evolution and maintenance of its ethnographic diversity. A satisfactory understanding of the nature and unity of men must encompass and organize, not abstract from, the diversity. In this tradition, a theory, whatever its logic and insight, is inadequate if divorced from, if unilluminating as to, the ways of life of mankind as a whole. The concern is consonant with that of Kroeber, reflecting upon Darwin:

> anthropologists . . . do not yet clearly recognize the fundamental value of the humble but indispensable task of classifying – that is, structuring, our body of knowledge, as biologists did begin to recognize it two hundred years ago. (1960: 14)

Even the ethnographies that we have, though almost never focused on speaking, show us that communities differ significantly in ways of speaking, in patterns of repertoire and switching, in the roles and meanings of speech. They indicate differences with regard to beliefs, values, reference groups, norms, and the like, as these enter into the ongoing system of language use and its acquisition by children. Individual accounts that individually pass without notice, as familiar possibilities, leap out when juxtaposed, as contrasts that require explanation. The Gbeya around the town of Bossangoa in the western Central African Republic, for example, are extremely democratic, and relatively unconcerned with speech. There is no one considered verbally excellent even with regard to traditional folklore. Moreover,

> Gbeya parents and other adults focus little attention on the speech of children. No serious attempt is made to improve their language. In fact, a child only uncommonly takes part in a dyadic speech event with an adult. . . . Among the Gbeya "children are seen and not heard." Finally, there appears to be very little interest in reporting *how* a person speaks. . . . (Samarin 1969)

The Anang (Nigeria) received their name from neighboring Ibo, the term meaning "ability to speak wittily yet meaningfully upon any occasion."

> The Anang take great pride in their eloquence, and youth are trained from early childhood to develop verbal skills. This proverb riddle [not quoted here, but see discussion] instructs young people to assume adult duties and responsibilities as early as possible, even if doing so is difficult and unpleasant at times. As the vine must struggle to escape growing into the pit [the riddle], so must the child strive to overcome his shyness and insecurity and learn to speak publicly [the proverbial answer], as well as perform other adult roles. (Messenger 1960: 229)

Or, to consider the word and the sword, among the Araucanians of Chile the head of a band was its best orator, and his power depended upon his ability to sway others through oratory. Among the Abipon of Argentina no desired role or status depended upon skill in speaking; chiefs and members of the one prestigious men's group were selected solely on the basis of success in battle. The Iroquois value eloquence in chiefs and orators as much as bravery in war; the two are usually mentioned together and with equal status. A chief could rise equally quickly by either.

Since there is no systematic understanding of the ways in which communities differ in these respects, and of the deeper relationships such differences may disclose, we have it to create. We need taxonomies of speaking, and descriptions adequate to support and test them.

Such description and taxonomy will share in the work of providing an adequate classification of languages. If the task of language classification is taken to be to place languages in terms of their common features and differences, and if we consider the task from the standpoint of similarities, then four classifications are required. Languages are classified according to features descended from a common ancestor (genetic classification), features diffused within a common area (areal classification), features manifesting a common structure or structures, irrespective of origin or area (typological classification), and features of common use or social role (as koine, standard language, pidgin, etc.) (functional classification) (see Hymes 1968; Greenberg 1968: 133–135). The processes underlying the classifications (various kinds of retention, divergence, convergence) all can be viewed in terms of the adaption of languages to social contexts, but the forms of classification in which the dependence on social processes can be most readily excluded (genetic, typological) are the forms that have been most developed. Sociolinguistic research reinforces the intermittent interest that areal classification has received, and can properly claim the most neglected sector, functional classification, the interaction between social role and features of languages, for its own. The natural unit for sociolinguistic taxonomy (and description), however, is not the language but the speech community.

Of course, sociolinguistic taxonomy is not an end in itself, any more than is language classification. A taxonomy is not in itself a theory or explanation, though it may conceal or suggest one. There will indeed be a variety of taxonomies, answering to a variety of significant dimensions, as well as taxonomies of whole communities, societies, and social fields. (For a step in the latter direction, see Ferguson 1966.) The work of taxonomy is a necessary part of progress toward models (structural and generative) of sociolinguistic description, formulation of universal sets of features and relations, and explanatory theories. (I shall say something about each of these later.) Just the demonstration that the phenomena of speaking are subject to comparative study may help end the obscuring of actual problems by descant on the function of language in general. Those who do so should be received as if they were continuing to discuss physics in terms of the Ionian controversies as to the primordial element.[3]

2   Toward a Descriptive Theory

The primary concern now must be with descriptive analyses from a variety of communities. Only in relation to actual analysis will it be possible to conduct arguments analogous to those now possible in the study of grammar as to the adequacy, necessity, generality, etc., of concepts and terms. Yet some initial heuristic schema are needed if the descriptive task is to proceed. What is presented here is quite preliminary – if English and its grammarians permitted, one might call it "toward toward a theory." Some of it may survive the empirical and analytical work of the decade ahead.

Only a specific, explicit mode of description can guarantee the maintenance and success of the current interest in sociolinguistics. Such interest is prompted more by practical and theoretical needs, perhaps, than by accomplishment. It was the development of a specific mode of description that ensured the success of linguistics as an autonomous discipline in the United States in the twentieth century, and the lack of it (for motif and tale types are a form of indexing, distributional inference a procedure common to the human sciences) that led to the until recently peripheral status of folklore, although both had started from a similar base, the converging interest of anthropologists, and English scholars, in language and in verbal tradition.

The goal of sociolinguistic description can be put in terms of the disciplines whose interests converge in sociolinguistics. Whatever his questions about language, it is clear to a linguist that there is an enterprise, description of languages, which is central and known. Whatever his questions about society and culture, it is clear to a sociologist or an anthropologist that there is a form of inquiry (survey or ethnography) on which the answers depend. In both cases, one understands what it means to describe a language, the social relations, or culture of a community. We need to be able to say the same thing about the sociolinguistic system of a community.

Such a goal is of concern to practical work as well as to scientific theory. In a study of bilingual education, e.g., certain components of speaking will be taken into account, and the choice will presuppose a model, implicit if not explicit, of the interaction of language with social life. The significance attached to what is found will depend on understanding what is possible, what universal, what rare, what linked, in comparative perspective. What survey researchers need to know linguistically about a community, in selecting a language variety, and in conducting interviews, is in effect an application of the community's sociolinguistic description (see Hymes 1969). In turn, practical work, if undertaken with its relevance to theory in mind, can make a contribution, for it must deal directly with the interaction of language and social life, and so provides a testing ground and source of new insight.

Sociolinguistic systems may be treated at the level of national states, and indeed, of an emerging world society. My concern here is with the level of individual communities and groups. The interaction of language with social life is viewed as first of all a matter of human action, based on a knowledge, sometimes conscious, often unconscious, that enables persons to use language. Speech events and larger systems indeed have properties not reducible to those of the speaking competence of persons. Such competence, however, underlies communicative conduct, not only within communities but also in encounters between them. The speaking competence of persons may be seen as entering into a series of systems of encounter at levels of different scope.

An adequate descriptive theory would provide for the analysis of individual communities by specifying technical concepts required for such analysis, and by characterizing the forms that analysis should take. Those forms would, as much as possible, be formal, i.e., explicit, general (in the sense of observing general constraints and conventions as to content, order, interrelationship, etc.), economical, and congruent with linguistic modes of statement. Only a good deal of empirical work and experimentation will show what forms of description are required, and of those, which preferable. As with grammar, approximation to a theory for the explicit, standard analysis of individual systems will also be an approximation to part of a theory of explanation.

Among the notions with which such a theory must deal are those of speech community, speech situation, speech event, speech act, fluent speaker, components of speech events, functions of speech. etc.

2.1   Social units

One must first consider the social unit of analysis. For this I adopt the common expression *speech community*.

2.1.1   Speech community

Speech is here taken as a surrogate for all forms of language, including writing, song and speech-derived whistling, drumming, horn calling, and the like. Speech community is a necessary, primary term in that it postulates the basis of description as a social, rather than a linguistic, entity. One starts with a social group and considers all the linguistic varieties present in it, rather than starting with any one variety.

Bloomfield (1933) and some others have in the past reduced the notion of speech community to the notion of language (or linguistic variety). Those speaking the same language (or same first language, or standard language) were defined as members of the same speech community. This confusion still persists, associated with a quantitative measure of frequency of interaction as a way of describing (in principle) internal variation and change, as speculatively postulated by Bloomfield. The present approach requires a definition that is qualitative and expressed in terms of *norms for the use* of language. It is clear from the work of Gumperz, Labov, Barth, and others that not frequency of interaction but rather definition of situations in which interaction occurs is decisive, particularly identification (or lack of it) with others. (Sociolinguistics here makes contact with the shift in rhetorical theory from expression and persuasion to identification as key concept (see Burke 1950: 19–37, 55–59).)

Tentatively, a *speech community* is defined as a community sharing rules for the conduct and interpretation of speech, and rules for the interpretation of at least one linguistic variety. Both conditions are necessary.

The sharing of grammatical (variety) rules is not sufficient. There may be persons whose English I can grammatically identify but whose messages escape me. I may be ignorant of what counts as a coherent sequence, request, statement requiring an answer, requisite or forbidden topic, marking of emphasis or irony, normal duration of silence, normal level of voice, etc., and have no metacommunitative means or opportunity for discovering such things. The difference between knowledge of a variety and knowledge of speaking does not usually become apparent within a single community, where the two are normally acquired together. Communities indeed often mingle what a linguist would distinguish as grammatically and as socially or culturally acceptable. Among the Cochiti of New Mexico J. R. Fox was unable to elicit the first person singular possessive form of "wings," on the grounds that the speaker, not being a bird, could not say "my wings" – only to become the only person in Cochiti able to say it on the grounds that "your name is Robin."

The nonidentity of the two kinds of rules (or norms) is more likely to be noticed when a shared variety is a second language for one or both parties. Sentences that translate each other grammatically may be mistakenly taken as having the same functions in speech, just as words that translate each other may be taken as having the same semantic function. There may be substratum influence, or interference (Weinreich 1953) in the one as in the other. The Czech linguist J. Neustupny has coined the term *Sprechbund* "speech area" (parallel to *Sprachbund* "language area") for the phenomenon of speaking rules being shared among contiguous languages. Thus, Czechoslovakia, Hungary, Austria, and southern Germany may be found to share norms as to greetings, acceptable topics, what is said next in a conversation, etc.

Sharing of speaking rules is not sufficient. A Czech who knows no German may belong to the same *Sprechbund*, but not the same speech community, as an Austrian.

The *language field* and *speech field* (akin to the notion of social field) can be defined as the total range of communities within which a person's knowledge of varieties and speaking rules potentially enables him to move communicatively. Within the speech field must be distinguished the *speech network*, the specific linkages of persons through shared varieties and speaking rules across communities. Thus in northern Queensland, Australia, different speakers of the same language (e.g., Yir Yoront) may have quite different networks along geographically different circuits, based on clan membership, and involving different repertoires of multilingualism. In Vitiaz Strait, New Guinea, the Bilibili islanders (a group of about 200–250 traders and potmakers in Astrolabe Bay) have collectively a knowledge of the languages of all the communities with which they have had economic relations, a few men knowing the language of each particular community in which they have had trading partners.

In sum, one's speech community may be, effectively, a single locality or portion of it; one's language field will be delimited by one's repertoire of varieties; one's speech field by one's repertoire of patterns of speaking. One's speech network is the effective union of these last two.

Part of the work of definition obviously is done here by the notion of community, whose difficulties are bypassed, as are the difficulties of defining boundaries between varieties and between patterns of speaking. Native conceptions of boundaries are but one factor in defining them, essential but sometimes partly misleading (a point stressed by Gumperz on the basis of his work in central India). Self-conceptions, values, role structures, contiguity, purposes of interaction, political history, all may be factors. Clearly, the same degree of linguistic difference may be associated with a boundary in one case and not in another, depending on social factors. The essential thing is that the object of description be an integral social unit. Probably, it will prove most useful to reserve the notion of speech community for the local unit most specifically characterized for a person by common locality and primary interaction (Gumperz 1962: 30–32). Here I have drawn distinctions of scale and of kind of linkage within what Gumperz has termed the *linguistic community* (any distinguishable intercommunicating group). Descriptions will make it possible to develop a useful typology and to discover the causes and consequences of the various types.

2.1.2   Speech situation

Within a community one readily detects many situations associated with (or marked by the absence of) speech. Such contexts of situation will often be naturally described as ceremonies, fights, hunts, meals, lovemaking, and the like. It would not be profitable to convert such situations en masse into parts of a sociolinguistic description by the simple expedient of relabeling them in terms of speech. (Notice that the distinctions made with regard to speech community are not identical with the concepts of a general communicative approach, which must note the differential range of communication by speech, film, art object, music.) Such situations may enter as contexts into the statement of rules of speaking as aspects of setting (or of genre). In contrast to speech events, they are not in themselves governed by such rules, or one set of such rules throughout. A hunt, e.g., may comprise both verbal and nonverbal events, and the verbal events may be of more than one type.

In a sociolinguistic description, then, it is necessary to deal with activities which are in some recognizable way bounded or integral. From the standpoint of general social description they may be registered as ceremonies, fishing trips, and the like; from particular standpoints they may be regarded as political, esthetic, etc., situations, which serve as contexts for the manifestation of political, esthetic, etc., activity. From the sociolinguistic standpoint they may be regarded as speech situations.

2.1.3   Speech event

The term *speech event* will be restricted to activities, or aspects of activities, that are directly governed by rules or norms for the use of speech. An event may consist of a single speech act, but will often comprise several. Just as an occurrence of a noun may at the same time be the whole of a noun phrase and the whole of a sentence (e.g., "Fire!"), so a speech act may be the whole of a speech event, and of a speech situation (say, a rite consisting of a single prayer, itself a single invocation). More often, however, one will find a difference in magnitude: a party (speech situation), a conversation during the party (speech event), a joke within the conversation (speech act). It is of speech events and speech acts that one writes formal rules for their occurrence and characteristics. Notice that the same type of speech act may recur in different types of speech event, and the same type of speech event in different contexts of situation. Thus, a joke (speech act) may be embedded in a private conversation, a lecture, a formal introduction. A private conversation may occur in the context of a party, a memorial service, a pause in changing sides in a tennis match.

2.1.4   Speech act

The *speech act* is the minimal term of the set just discussed, as the remarks on speech events have indicated. It represents a level distinct from the sentence, and not identifiable with any single portion of other levels of grammar, nor with segments of any particular size defined in terms of other levels of grammar. That an utterance has the status of a command may depend upon a conventional formula ("I hereby order you to leave this building"), intonation ("Go!" vs. "Go?"), position in a conversational exchange ["Hello" as initiating greeting or as response (perhaps used when answering the telephone)], or the social relationship obtaining between the two parties (as when an utterance that is in the form of a polite question is in effect a command when made by a superior to a subordinate). The level of speech acts mediates immediately between the usual levels of grammar and the rest of a speech event or situation in that it implicates both linguistic form and social norms.

To some extent speech acts may be analyzable by extensions of syntactic and semantic structure. It seems certain, however, that much, if not most, of the knowledge that speakers share as to the status of utterances as acts is immediate and abstract, depending upon an autonomous system of signals from both the various levels of grammar and social settings. To attempt to depict speech acts entirely by postulating an additional segment of underlying grammatical structure (e.g., "I hereby X you to . . .") is cumbersome and counterintuitive. (Consider the case in which "Do you think I might have that last bit of tea?" is to be taken as a command.)

An autonomous level of speech acts is in fact implicated by that logic of linguistic levels according to which the ambiguity of "the shooting of the blacks was terrible" and the commonality of "topping Erv is almost impossible" and "it's almost impossible to top Erv" together requires a further level of structure at which the former has two different structures, the latter one. The relation between sentence forms and their status as speech acts is of the same kind. A sentence interrogative in form may be now a request, now a command, now a statement; a request may be manifested by a sentence that is now interrogative, now declarative, now imperative in form.

Discourse may be viewed in terms of acts both syntagmatically and paradigmatically; i.e., both as a sequence of speech acts and in terms of classes of speech acts among which choice has been made at given points.

2.1.5   *Speech styles*

Style has often been approached as a matter of statistical frequency of elements already given in linguistic description, or as deviation from some norm given by such description. Statistics and deviations matter, but do not suffice. Styles also depend upon qualitative judgments of appropriateness, and must often be described in terms of selections that apply globally to a discourse, as in the case of honorific usage in Japanese (McCawley 1968: 136), i.e., there are consistent patternings of speaking that cut across the components of grammar (phonology, syntax, semantics), or that operate within one independently of the selectional restrictions normally described for it. Whorf adumbrated as much in his conception of "fashions of speaking"; Joos has made and illustrated the point with regard to English; Pike (1967) has considered a wide variety of contextual styles as conditions on the manifestation of phonological and morphological units. Besides the existence of qualitatively defined styles, there are two other points essential to sociolinguistic description. One is that speech styles involve elements and relations that conventionally serve "expressive" or, better, stylistic, as well as referential function (e.g., the contrast in force of aspiration that conventionally signals emphasis in English). The second point is that speech styles are to be considered not only in terms of cooccurrence within each but also in terms of contrastive choice among them. Like speech acts, they have both syntagmatic and paradigmatic dimensions. (Ervin-Tripp treats rules of cooccurrence and of alternation in detail in Ervin-Tripp 1972.) The coherence, or cohesion, of discourse depends upon the syntagmatic relation of speech acts, and speech styles, as well as of semantic and syntactic features.

2.1.6 Ways of speaking

Ways of speaking is used as the most general, indeed, as a primitive, term. The point of it is the regulative idea that the communicative behavior within a community is analyzable in terms of determinate ways of speaking, that the communicative competence of persons comprises in part a knowledge of determinate ways of speaking. Little more can be said until a certain number of ethnographic descriptions of communities in terms of ways of speaking are available. It is likely that communities differ widely in the features in terms of which their ways of speaking are primarily organized.

2.1.7 Components of speech

A descriptive theory requires some schema of the components of speech acts. At present such a schema can be only an etic, heuristic input to descriptions. Later it may assume the status of a theory of universal features and dimensions.

Long traditional in our culture is the threefold division between speaker, hearer, and something spoken about. It has been elaborated in information theory, linguistics, semiotics, literary criticism, and sociology in various ways. In the hands of some investigators various of these models have proven productive, but their productivity has depended upon not taking them literally, let alone using them precisely. All such schemes, e.g., appear to agree either in taking the standpoint of an individual speaker or in postulating a dyad, speaker–hearer (or source–destination, sender–receiver, addressor–addressee). Even if such a scheme is intended to be a model, for descriptive work it cannot be. Some rules of speaking require specification of *three* participants (addressor, addressee, hearer (audience); source, spokesman, addressees; etc.); some of but *one*, indifferent as to role in the speech event; some of *two*, but of speaker and audience (e.g., a child); and so on. In short, serious ethnographic work shows that there is one general, or universal, dimension to be postulated, that of *participant*. The common dyadic model of speaker–hearer specifies sometimes too many, sometimes too few, sometimes the wrong participants. Further ethnographic work will enable us to state the range of actual types of participant relations and to see in differential occurrence something to be explained.

Ethnographic material so far investigated indicates that some sixteen or seventeen components have sometimes to be distinguished. No rule has been found that requires specification of all simultaneously. There are always redundancies, and sometimes a rule requires explicit mention of a relation between only two, message form and some other. (It is a general principle that all rules involve message form, if not by affecting its shape, then by governing its interpretation.) Since each of the components may sometimes be a factor, however, each has to be recognized in the general grid.

Psycholinguistic work has indicated that human memory works best with classifications of the magnitude of seven, plus or minus two (Miller 1956). To make the set of components mnemonically convenient, at least in English, the letters of the term SPEAKING can be used. The components can be grouped together in relation to the eight letters without great difficulty. Clearly, the use of SPEAKING as a mnemonic code word has nothing to do with the form of an eventual model and theory.

1. *Message form.* The form of the message is fundamental, as has just been indicated. The most common, and most serious, defect in most reports of speaking prob-

ably is that the message form, and, hence, the rules governing it, cannot be recaptured. A concern for the details of actual form strikes some as picayune, as removed from humanistic or scientific importance. Such a view betrays an impatience that is a disservice to both humanistic and scientific purposes. It is precisely the failure to unite form and content in the scope of a single focus of study that has retarded understanding of the human ability to speak, and that vitiates many attempts to analyze the significance of behavior. Content categories, interpretive categories, alone do not suffice. It is a truism, but one frequently ignored in research, that *how* something is said is part of *what* is said. Nor can one prescribe in advance the gross size of the signal that will be crucial to content and skill. The more a way of speaking has become shared and meaningful within a group, the more likely that crucial cues will be efficient, i.e., slight in scale. If one balks at such detail, perhaps because it requires technical skills in linguistics, musicology, or the like that are hard to command, one should face the fact that the human meaning of one's object of study, and the scientific claims of one's field of inquiry, are not being taken seriously.

Especially when competence, the ability of persons, is of concern, one must recognize that shared ways of speaking acquire a partial autonomy, developing in part in terms of an inner logic of their means of expression. The means of expression condition and sometimes control content. For members of the community, then, "freedom is the recognition of necessity"; mastery of the way of speaking is prerequisite to personal expression. Serious concern for both scientific analysis and human meaning requires one to go beyond content to the explicit statement of rules and features of form.

While such an approach may seem to apply first of all to genres conventionally recognized as esthetic, it also applies to conversation in daily life. Only painstaking analysis of message form – how things are said – of a sort that indeed parallels and can learn from the intensity of literary criticism can disclose the depth and adequacy of the elliptical art that is talk.

2. *Message content.* One context for distinguishing message form from message content would be: "He prayed, saying '. . .'" (quoting message form) vs. "He prayed that he would get well" (reporting content only).

Content enters analysis first of all perhaps as a question of *topic*, and of change of topic. Members of a group know what is being talked about, and when what is talked about has changed, and manage maintenance, and change, of topic. These abilities are parts of their communicative competence of particular importance to study of the coherence of discourse.

Message form and message content are central to the speech act and the focus of its "syntactic structure"; they are also tightly interdependent. Thus they can be dubbed jointly as components of "act sequence" (mnemonically, A).

3. *Setting.* Setting refers to the time and place of a speech act and, in general, to the physical circumstances.

4. *Scene.* Scene, which is distinct from setting, designates the "psychological setting," or the cultural definition of an occasion as a certain type of scene. Within a play on the same stage with the same stage set the dramatic time may shift: "ten years later." In daily life the same persons in the same setting may redefine their interaction as a changed type of scene, say, from formal to informal, serious to festive, or the like.

(For an example of the importance of types of scene to analysis of speech genres, see Frake's contrast of the Subanun and Yakan in Frake 1972.) Speech acts frequently are used to define scenes, and also frequently judged as appropriate or inappropriate in relation to scenes. Settings and scenes themselves, of course, may be judged as appropriate and inappropriate, happy or unhappy, in relation to each other, from the level of complaint about the weather to that of dramatic irony.

Setting and scene may be linked as components of act situation (mnemonically, S). Since scene implies always an analysis of cultural definitions, setting probably is to be preferred as the informal, unmarked term for the two.

5.   *Speaker*, or *sender*.
6.   *Addressor*.
7.   *Hearer*, or *receiver*, or *audience*.
8.   *Addressee*.

These four components were discussed in introducing the subject of components of speech. Here are a few illustrations. Among the Abipon of Argentina -*in* is added to the end of each word if any participant (whatever his role) is a member of the Hocheri (warrior class). Among the Wishram Chinook, formal scenes are defined by the relationship between a source (e.g., a chief, or sponsor of a ceremony), a spokesman who repeats the source's words, and others who constitute an audience or public. The source whose words are repeated sometimes is not present; the addressees sometimes are spirits of the surrounding environment. In the presence of a child, adults in Germany often use the term of address which would be appropriate for the child. Sometimes rules for participants are internal to a genre and independent of the participants in the embedding event. Thus male and female actors in Yana myths use the appropriate men's and women's forms of speech, respectively, irrespective of the sex of the narrator. Use of men's speech itself is required when both addressor and addressee are both adult and male, "women's" speech otherwise. Groups differ in their definitions of the participants in speech events in revealing ways, particularly in defining absence (e.g., children, maids) and presence (e.g., supernaturals) of participation. Much of religious conduct can be interpreted as part of a native theory of communication. The various components may be grouped together as participants (mnemonically, P).

9.   *Purposes – outcomes*. Conventionally recognized and expected outcomes often enter into the definition of speech events, as among the Waiwai of Venezuela, where the central speech event of the society, the *oho-chant*, has several varieties, according to whether the purpose to be accomplished is a marriage contract, a trade, a communal work task, an invitation to a feast, or a composing of social peace after a death. The rules for participants and settings vary accordingly (Fock 1965). A taxonomy of speech events among the Yakan of the Philippines (analyzed in Frake 1972) is differentiated into levels according jointly to topic (any topic, an issue, a disagreement, a dispute) and outcome (no particular outcome, a decision, a settlement, a legal ruling).

10.   *Purposes – goals*. The purpose of an event from a community standpoint, of course, need not be identical to the purposes of those engaged in it. Presumably, both sides to a Yakan litigation wish to win. In a negotiation the purpose of some may be to obtain a favorable settlement, of others simply that there be a settlement. Among the Waiwai the prospective father-in-law and son-in-law have opposing goals in arriving at a marriage contract. The strategies of participants are an essential determinant of the

form of speech events, indeed, to their being performed at all (see Blom and Gumperz 1972).

With respect both to outcomes and goals, the conventionally expected or ascribed must be distinguished from the purely situational or personal, and from the latent and unintended. The interactions of a particular speech event may determine its particular quality and whether or not the expected outcome is reached. The actual motives, or some portion of them, of participants may be quite varied. In the first instance, descriptions of speech events seek to describe customary or culturally appropriate behavior. Such description is essential and prerequisite to understanding events in all their individual richness; but the two kinds of account should not be confused (see Sapir 1949a: 534, 543).

Many approaches to communication and the analysis of speech have not provided a place for either kind of purpose, perhaps because of a conscious or unconsciously lingering behaviorism. (Kenneth Burke's (1945) approach is a notable exception.) Yet communication itself must be differentiated from interaction as a whole in terms of purposiveness. The two aspects of purpose can be grouped together by exploiting an English homonymy, *ends* in view (goals) and *ends* as outcomes (mnemonically, E).

11.   *Key*. Key is introduced to provide for the tone, manner, or spirit in which an act is done. It corresponds roughly to modality among grammatical categories. Acts otherwise the same as regards setting, participants, message form, and the like may differ in key, as, e.g., between *mock: serious* or *perfunctory: painstaking*.

Key is often conventionally ascribed to an instance of some other component as its attribute; seriousness, for example, may be the expected concomitant of a scene, participant, act, code, or genre (say, a church, a judge, a vow, use of Latin, obsequies). Yet there is always the possibility that there is a conventionally understood way of substituting an alternative key. (This possibility corresponds to the general possibility of choosing one speech style or register as against another.) In this respect, ritual remains always informative. Knowing what should happen next, one still can attend to the way in which it happens. (Consider, for example, critics reviewing performances of the classical repertoire for the piano.)

The significance of key is underlined by the fact that, when it is in conflict with the overt content of an act, it often overrides the latter (as in sarcasm). The signaling of key may be nonverbal, as with a wink, gesture, posture, style of dress, musical accompaniment, but it also commonly involves conventional units of speech too often disregarded in ordinary linguistic analysis, such as English aspiration and vowel length to signal emphasis. Such features are often termed *expressive*, but are better dubbed *stylistic* since they need not at all depend on the mood of their user. Revill (1966: 251) reports, for instance, that "some forms have been found which *cannot* [emphasis mine] be described as reflecting feelings on the part of the speaker, but they will be used in certain social situations" (for emphasis, clarity, politeness).

12.   *Channels*. By choice of channel is understood choice of oral, written, telegraphic, semaphore, or other medium of transmission of speech. With regard to channels, one must further distinguish modes of use. The oral channel, e.g., may be used to sing, hum, whistle, or chant features of speech as well as to speak them. Two important goals of description are accounts of the interdependence of channels in interaction and the relative hierarchy among them.

13.   *Forms of speech*. A major theoretical and empirical problem is to distinguish the verbal resources of a community. Obviously, it is superficial, indeed misleading, to speak of the language of a community (Ferguson and Gumperz 1960). Even where there is but a single "language" present in a community (no cases are known in the contemporary world), that language will be organized into various forms of speech. Three criteria seem to require recognition at the present time: the historical provenience of the language resources; presence or absence of mutual intelligibility; and specialization in use. The criteria often do not coincide. *Language* and *dialect* are suggested for the first; *codes* for the second; and *varieties* and *registers* for the third. One speaks normally of the English language, and of dialects of English, wherever forms of speech are found whose content is historically derived from the line of linguistic tradition we call "English." The different dialects are not always mutually intelligible (see Yorkshire and Indian English), and their social functions vary considerably around the world, from childhood vernacular to bureaucratic lingua franca. "Code" suggests decoding and the question of intelligibility. Unintelligibility may result when speech is in a language historically unrelated to one's own, but also from use of a simple transformation of one's own speech, e.g., Pig Latin, or "op" talk. In short, some forms of speech derive from others by addition, deletion, substitution, and permutation in various combinations. Finally, forms of speech are commonly specialized to uses of various sorts. *Register* has become familiar in English linguistic usage for reference to specific situations; varieties, or "functional varieties," has been used in American linguistics in relation to broad domains (e.g., vernacular vs. standard).

For sociolinguistics, *varieties* has priority as a standpoint from which to view the forms of speech of a community. The criteria of provenience and intelligibility have to do with sources and characteristics of the criterion of use with the functional organization, of the forms of speech. Channels and forms of speech can be joined together as means or agencies of speaking and labeled, partly for the sake of the code word, partly with an eye on the use of the term *instrumental* in grammar, as *instrumentalities* (mnemonically, I).

14.   *Norms of interaction*. All rules governing speaking, of course, have a normative character. What is intended here are the specific behaviors and proprieties that attach to speaking – that one must not interrupt, for example, or that one may freely do so; that normal voice should not be used except when scheduled in a church service (whisper otherwise); that turns in speaking are to be allocated in a certain way. Norms of interaction obviously implicate analysis of social structure, and social relationships generally, in a community. An illustration follows:

> The next morning during tea with Jikjitsu, a college professor who rents rooms in one of the Sodo buildings came in and talked of koans. "When you understand Zen, you know that the tree is really *there*." – The only time anyone said anything of Zen philosophy or experience the whole week. Zenbos never discuss koans or sanzen experience with each other. (Snyder 1969: 52)

15.   *Norms of interpretation*. An account of norms of interaction may still leave open the interpretation to be placed upon them, especially when members of different communities are in communication. Thus it is clear that Arabic and American students differ on a series of interactional norms: Arabs confront each other more directly (face

to face) when conversing, sit closer to each other, are more likely to touch each other, look each other more squarely in the eye, and converse more loudly (Watson and Graves 1966: 976–977). The investigators who report these findings themselves leave open the meanings of these norms to the participants (p. 984).

The problem of norms of interpretation is familiar from the assessment of communications from other governments and national leaders. One often looks for friendliness in lessened degree of overt hostility. Relations between groups within a country are often affected by misunderstandings on this score. For white middle-class Americans, for example, normal hesitation behavior involves "fillers" at the point of hesitation ("uh," etc.). For many blacks, a normal pattern is to recycle to the beginning of the utterance (perhaps more than once). This black norm may be interpreted by whites not as a different norm but as a defect. (I owe this example to David Dalby.)

Norms of interpretation implicate the belief system of a community. The classic precedent in the ethnographic analysis of a language is Malinowski's (1935) treatment of Trobriand magical formulas and ritual under the heading of *dogmatic context*. (Malinowski's other rubrics are roughly related to these presented here in the following way: His *sociological context* and *ritual context* subsume information as to setting, participants, ends in view and outcome, norms of interaction, and higher level aspects of genre; *structure* reports salient patterning of the verbal form of the act or event; *mode of recitation* reports salient characteristics of the vocal aspect of channel use and message form.)

The processes of interpretation discussed by Garfinkel (1972), including "ad hocing" generally, would belong in this category. These two kinds of norms may be grouped together (mnemonically, N).

16.   *Genres.* By genres are meant categories such as poem, myth, tale, proverb, riddle, curse, prayer, oration, lecture, commercial, form letter, editorial, etc. From one standpoint the analysis of speech into acts is an analysis of speech into instances of genres. The notion of genre implies the possibility of identifying formal characteristics traditionally recognized. It is heuristically important to proceed as though all speech has formal characteristics of some sort as manifestation of genres; and it may well be true (on genres, see Ben-Amos 1969). The common notion of "casual" or unmarked speech, however, points up the fact that there is a great range among genres in the number of and explicitness of formal markers. At least there is a great range in the ease with which such markers have been identified. It remains that "unmarked" casual speech can be recognized as such in a context where it is not expected or where it is being exploited for particular effect. Its lesser visibility may be a function of our own orientations and use of it; its profile may be as sharp as any other, once we succeed in seeing it as strange.

Genres often coincide with speech events, but must be treated as analytically independent of them. They may occur in (or as) different events. The sermon as a genre is typically identical with a certain place in a church service, but its properties may be invoked, for serious or humorous effect, in other situations. Often enough a genre recurs in several events, such as a genre of chanting employed by women in Bihar state in India; it is the prescribed form for a related set of acts, recurring in weddings, family visits, and complaints to one's husband (K. M. Tiwary, personal communication). A great deal of empirical work will be needed to clarify the interrelations of genres, events, acts, and other components (mnemonically, G).

As has been shown, the sixteen components can be grouped together under the letters of the code word SPEAKING: settings, participants, ends, act sequences, keys, instrumentalities, norms, genres. That the code word is not wholly ethnocentric appears from the possibility of relabeling and regrouping the necessary components in terms of the French PARLANT: *participants*, *actes*, *raison* (*résultat*), *locale*, *agents* (instrumentalities), *normes*, *ton* (key), *types* (genres).

Notes

1 This chapter is excerpted from a longer article in John J. Gumperz and Dell Hymes (eds.), *Directions in Sociolinguistics: The Ethnography of Communication* (Oxford: Blackwell, 1986).
2 These examples draw on a study by Judith Temkin Irvine (1968).
3 For recent examples of uncritical praise and intransigent indictment of language, see J. O. Hertzler 1965 and Brice Parain 1969. On "high and low evaluations of language" as an integral part of the history of philosophy and human culture, see Urban 1939: 12, 23–32.

References

Basso, Keith, 1970, "To give up on words: Silence in the Western Apache Culture." *Southwestern Journal of Anthropology*, 26 (3): 213–30.
Ben-Amos, Dan, 1969, "Analytical categories and ethnic genres." *Genre*, 2: 275–301.
Blom, Jan-Petter and John J. Gumperz, 1972, "Social meaning in linguistic structures: Code-switching in Norway." In John J. Gumperz and Dell Hymes (eds.), pp. 407–34.
Bloomfield, Leonard, 1933, *Language*. New York: Holt, Rinehart and Winston.
Burke, Kenneth, 1945, *A Grammar of Motives*. Englewood Cliffs, New Jersey: Prentice-Hall. (Republished by University of California Press, Berkeley, 1969.)
Burke, Kenneth, 1950, *A Rhetoric of Motives*. Englewood Cliffs, New Jersey: Prentice-Hall. (Republished by University of California Press, Berkeley, 1969.)
Cambridge University Reporter, January 15, 1969, p. 890.
Ervin-Tripp, Susan, 1972, "On sociolinguistic rules: alternation and co-occurrence." In John J. Gumperz and Dell Hymes (eds.), pp. 213–50.
Ferguson, Charles A., 1966, "National sociolinguistic profile formulas." In William Bright (ed.), *Sociolinguistics*, pp. 309–314. The Hague: Mouton.
Ferguson, Charles A. and Gumperz, John J., 1960, "Linguistic diversity in South Asia: Studies in regional, and functional variation." [RCAFL-P 13; *International Journal of American Linguistics*, 26 (3), pt. III].
Fock, Niels, 1965, "Cultural aspects of the 'oho' institution among the Waiwai." *Proceedings of the International Congress of Americanists*, pp. 136–40.
Frake, Charles O., 1972, "Struck by speech: The Yakan concept of litigation." In John J. Gumperz and Dell Hymes (eds.), pp. 106–29.
Gardner, Peter M., 1966, "Symmetric respect and memorate knowledge: The structure and ecology of individualistic culture." *Southwestern Journal of Anthropology*, 22: 389–415.
Garfinkel, Harold, 1972, "Remarks on ethnomethodology." In John J. Gumperz and Dell Hymes (eds.), pp. 301–24.
Greenberg, J. H., 1968, *Anthropological Linguistics: An Introduction*. New York: Random House.
Gumperz, John J., 1962, "Types of linguistic communities." *Anthropological Linguistics*, 4, 1: 28–40.

Gumperz, John J. and Dell Hymes, 1972, *Directions in Sociolinguistics: The Ethnography of Communication*. New York: Holt, Rinehart and Winston. Reprinted 1986, Oxford: Blackwell.

Hertzler, Joyce O. 1965, *Sociology of Language*. New York: Random House.

Hogan, Sister Helen Marie, 1967, *An Ethnography of Communication among the Ashanti*. MA dissertation, Department of Anthropology, University of Pennsylvania, Philadelphia.

Hymes, Dell, 1964, "Directions in (ethno-)linguistic theory." In Romney and D'Andrade (eds.), *Transcultural Studies in Cognition. American Anthropologist*, 66, 3, pt. II: 6–56.

Hymes, Dell (ed.), 1964, "Modes of address" (Reference Note). *Language in Culture and Society*, pp. 225–7. New York: Harper & Row.

Hymes, Dell, 1966a, "Two types of linguistic relativity." In W. Bright (ed.), *Sociolinguistics*, pp. 114–65. The Hague: Mouton.

Hymes, Dell, 1966b, "On 'anthropological linguistics' and Congeners." *American Anthropologist*, 68: 143–53.

Hymes, Dell, 1968, "Linguistics – the field." *International Encyclopedia of Social Sciences*, 9: 351–71.

Hymes, Dell, 1970, "Linguistic theory and the functions of speech." *Proceedings of International Days of Sociolinguistics*. Rome: Istituto Luigi Sturzo.

Kroeber, Alfred L., 1960, "Evolution, history and culture." In S. Tax (ed.), *Evolution after Darwin*, pp. 1–16. Chicago: University of Chicago Press.

Malinowski, Bronislaw, 1935, *Coral Gardens and their Magic*, vol II. London: Allen and Unwin.

McCawley, James, 1968, "The role of semantics in grammar." In Bach and Harms (eds.), *Universals in Linguistic Theory*, pp. 125–70. New York: Holt, Rinehart and Winston.

Messenger, John C. Jr., 1960, "Anang proverb riddles." *Journal of American Folklore*, 73: 225–35.

Miller, G. A., 1956, "The magical number seven, plus or minus two: Some limits on our capacity for processing information." *The Psychological Review*, 63: 81–97.

Newman, Stanley S., 1964, "Vocabulary levels: Zuni sacred and slang usage." In Hymes (ed.), *Language in Culture and Society*. New York: Harper and Row.

Parain, Brice, 1969, *Petite metaphysique de la parole*. Paris: Gallimard.

Pike, Kenneth L., 1967, *Language in Relation to the Unified Theory of the Structure of Human Behavior*. (2nd rev. ed.). The Hague: Mouton.

Revill, P. M., 1966, "Preliminary report on paralinguistics in Mbembe (Eastern Nigeria)." *Tagmemic and Matrix Linguistics Applied to Selected African Languages*. By K. L. Pike, 245–54, appendix VIII. Final Report, contract no. OE-5-14-065. Washington, DC, US Department of Health, Education and Welfare, Office of Education, Bureau of Research.

Rubin, Joan, 1962, "Bilingualism in Paraguay." *Anthropological Linguistics*, 4 (1): 52–8.

Rubin, Joan, 1968, *National Bilingualism in Paraguay*. The Hague: Mouton.

Salisbury, R. F., 1962, "Notes on bilingualism and linguistic change in New Guinea." *Anthropological Linguistics*, 4 (7): 1–13.

Samarin, William, 1965, "The language of silence." *Practical Anthropology*, 12: 115–19.

Samarin, William, 1969, "The art of Gbeya insults." *International Journal of American Linguistics*, 35: 323–9.

Sapir, Edward, 1949a, "Language." In D. G. Mandelbaum (ed.), *Selected Writings of Edward Sapir*, pp. 7–32. Berkeley: University of California Pres.

Sapir, Edward, 1949b, "Speech as a personality trait." In D. G. Mandelbaum (ed.), *Selected Writings of Edward Sapir*, pp. 533–43. Berkeley: University of California Press.

Snyder, Gary, 1969, *Earth Household: Technical Notes and Queries to Fellow Dharma Revolutionaries*. New York: New Directions.

Urban, Wilbur M. 1939, *Language and Reality*. New York: Macmillan.

Watson, O. Michael and Graves, T. D., 1966, "Quantitative research in proxemic behavior." *American Anthropologist*, 68: 971–85.

Weinreich, Uriel, 1953, *Languages in Contact*. Linguistic Circle of New York.

4

Lands I Came to Sing: Negotiating Identities and Places in the Tuscan "*Contrasto*"

Valentina Pagliai

1 Introduction[1]

This paper explores the representation and negotiation of ethnic identity and place in verbal art performances, through the analysis of the *Contrasto* (pl. *Contrasti*), a Tuscan[2] Italian genre of sung improvised poetry. I show that these Tuscan poets use performance to create images of the self and the other. Language is used to give shape to images of identity. Bauman defines performance as "a mode of communication, a way of speaking, the essence of which resides in the assumption of responsibility to an audience for a display of communicative skill" (1986: 3; see also Hymes 1981: 132). This display can lead to an enhancement of experience. Further, Bauman considers events themselves to be "abstractions from narratives" (1986: 5). Performance becomes a way of creating, not just representing, the past and social reality itself.

This conceptualization of performance leads to further implications. The idea of responsibility gives back to art its agency in society. Therefore, we can look at a particular form of verbal art, like poetry, as a form of social action. This is fundamental to an understanding of how the construction of identity, and the construction of images of ethnicity, happens in poetry. Bourdieu (1977, 1990) has already shown how reality is constructed in everyday practices. Following, I show how particular realities are emergent in (Tuscan) performance, and connected to places and placenames. The poetical *Contrasto* is improvised; it is made and unmade in the moment of performance, and only in the performance it acquires its social relevance. In the same fashion, there is a continuous making and unmaking of images in performances. These images are concretized and reflected in the innumerable repetition of their representation in everyday use of language in Tuscany, thus becoming continuously performed.

While working on the *Contrasti*, I started to realize that the definitions of ethnic identity found in anthropological theory were insufficient and unsatisfactory for looking at how Tuscans think about and construct their identities. The word "ethnic" also seemed inadequate. It became more obvious instead, that places, named places, were relevant.

The word *identity* is ambiguous. On one side, it refers to the person's perception of him or her self. On the other side, it refers to a process of external labeling, such as in the connected process of identification, or attribution of an I.D., of a particular place in a group and in a society. In this second sense, it becomes possible to talk about policies of identification, or categorization, of inclusion and exclusion, of establishment of borders and border-crossing.[3] "Classic" definitions of ethnicity see ethnic groups as stable and self-perpetuating social units to which the individual belongs by birth or primary socialization, and which can be defined through sets of *traits*.[4] This model, as Kroskrity has noted, tends to "reify" the concept of ethnicity (1993: 191) ignoring the space of free decisionality that identity offers to the person, and possibly offering a supposedly objective base to racist and discriminatory claims.

In this fixed definition, ethnicity is defined through boundaries. For example, Barth proposed considering ethnic groups as "categories of ascription and identification by the actors themselves" (Barth 1969: 10). Those categories that a group regards as important (*diacritica of ethnicity*) will enter the definition of the boundaries. According to Barth, once the boundaries are established, movements of people through them and relative converging of cultural content between the groups will not diminish for the people involved the feeling of belonging to different communities. Peterson Royce, aware of the presence of a duality in the concept of ethnic identity, proposed the concept of *double boundary*: "The boundary maintained from within, and the boundary imposed from outside" (1982: 29). 'Objective definitions' of ethnicity correspond to ascription of traits from outside; 'subjective definitions' refer to the internal, individual awareness of belonging to a group.

The risk here is to forget that the focus on boundaries is in itself an ideological choice, influenced by Western worldviews and historical events that stressed the importance of national borders, of contours, limits, and forms. The ideological attention on boundary maintenance defines people as people only as long as they remain inside an established boundary, and negates the humanity of those who refuse the boundary, those who trespass them. Cohen (1978) notices that every attempt to define an ethnic group by creating a boundary is artificial, and cannot account for the many *situational* transformations of ethnic identity and/or ethnic groups. The idea of situational ethnicity (Cohen 1978: 389) implies that it is constructed in interaction. The person will enact and communicate the particular ethnic identity of the ethnic group that is taken as referential in a given moment/context.

Theories of identity and ethnicity are not free from power relationships. The preference given to one model rather than another has political and social resonance. In Italy today, "traits" definitions are used by separatist movements, or associated with discriminatory statements against Southern Italians or recent immigrant groups.[5] They imply a desire to fix both the self and the "other" in a stable and stabilizing identity. For these reasons, I believe it is important to reaffirm the constructedness, the multiplicity, and the instability of social and ethnic identities. Only in this way, we can recover the *centrifugal* potential of identity and the space of free decisionality that it offers to the person as an agent.

Kroskrity has proposed to study "a given social identity in its interrelationships to other available social identities" (1993: 209). The sum of the available identities would then constitute a "repertoire" (1993) from which the person can choose. In this model, the individual is seen as an agent strategically using particular identities and actively redefining them and the roles associated with them. This model is in agreement with the studies done by Kroskrity himself on the Arizona Tewa ethnic identity (1993), and with

Zentella's ethnography on the New York Puertoricans (1990, 1997). Similar findings can be seen in the work of Duranti, Ochs and Ta'ase with the Samoan Americans in Los Angeles (1995). Similarly, I have discussed elsewhere the presence of a repertoire of identities in my work with the Italian American community in Los Angeles (Pagliai, 1995, 1996a, 1996b). See also Anzaldua's writings on Chicano and Mexican American identities (1987). In all these cases, people can shift among different ethnic identifications. Since natural belonging to a group is no longer a necessary nor sufficient condition to present the self through it, how the presentation of self is achieved and why becomes the new question.[6] As I show below, in the *Contrasti* a repertoire of identities becomes evident in the way the artists choose to represent themselves across contexts.

As identities become contested and are negotiated in performance, so are places. In traditional scholarship on ethnicity a "place" is inhabited by a specific ethnic group (maybe a nation, a region, or more often a ghetto), fixed in the same way in which ethnic groups are seen as fixed and defined. However, the recognition of a repertoire of identities goes against the view of identity[7] as stable/stabilizing. Instead, identities emerge only in the context in which they are performed.[8] Places are constituted through negotiations and re-negotiations (see Blu 1996: 198–99). Identities are connected to places, but places can shift. If not like the Wamirans stones, which move around at night (Kahn 1996: 181), they can shift in poetry, through the way the poets call on each of them.

Performance creates places, and places are continuously performed. In every word, in every encounter, we perform being Tuscan,[9] and we perform our belonging to places that are at the same time the depository of us being Tuscan. As the poets tell their stories, they contextualize them by recalling names of villages, cities, or particular features of the landscape. The answer of recognition by the audience defines a shared memory and knowledge. As Frake writes: "The use of placenames implicates much more than their denotation. In their phonological forms and their semantic suggestiveness, names often become remarkable – worthy of a story – in their own right" (1996: 238). Or, expressed in a parallel way by Vizenor, talking about Native American names and nicknames: "Native American Indian identities are created in stories, and names are essential to a distinctive personal nature" (1994: 56). Thus, acts of identity are also acts of naming, or renaming, where memory has been canceled.

Talking about placenames, Basso writes: "Because of their inseparable connection to specific localities, placenames may be used to summon forth an enormous range of mental and emotional associations – associations of time and space, of history and events, of persons and social activities, of oneself and stages in one's life" (1988: 103). To give a name is to reconstruct the reality of an object into a dimension of belonging. Vizenor again writes (1994: 104):

> Nicknames are personal stories that would, to be sure, trace the individual in tribal families and communities rather than cause separations by personal recognition. Even so, nicknames and stories change, a condition that liberates personal identities from the melancholy of permanence.

Thus a metonymic chain connects names to stories, stories to memories, memories to places, and places to identities. Though, as Vizenor also warns us, stories change, and so do identities.

2 The Tuscan Context

The area where my research focused is the northeastern part of Tuscany and includes the provinces of Florence, Prato and Pistoia. Historically Florence has been the main cultural and political center of Tuscany. Prato was constituted as a province only in the 80s. Before the territory was part of the provinces of Florence and Pistoia. Both Prato and Pistoia were traditionally subject to the political control of Florence. Tuscany as a region has been characterized historically by periods of very high political fragmentation and internal divisions.

Provincial identities today in Tuscany are very strong. People tend to identify with the main town, the provincial capital, but also with their village and town and the particular area or valley, etc. These identifications may also create antagonisms. In general, Tuscan towns have been traditionally antagonistic to each other. This antagonism is usually dated back, by the people themselves, to the medieval ages, the time when Tuscany was divided into city-states.[10]

The term used to describe this situation, in Italy, is *campanilismo*. This term, which has no translation in English (the Webster suggests 'parochialism' but this, I believe, is incorrect), is semantically very similar to the term *nazionalismo*, 'nationalism,' to which indeed it is compared in conversations in Italy. Nationalism implies an allegiance to a nation, and a series of associated feelings of pride, of belonging, of common history, etc. – but nationalism is also associated with national expansion, encroachments, colonialism, war and domination. The first series of meanings can also describe the term *campanilismo*, with one difference: The focus is not on the nation, but on the city, the town, and the village. In fact the term etymologically derives from the word *campanile*, 'bell tower' (we could think of a translation as 'bell-tower-ism'), and makes a clear reference to what could be considered an ubiquitous landmark in Italy: The tower of the main church of the city, town or village.

In Tuscany *campanilismo* takes up also, in part, the second series of meanings of the word "nationalism": The memory of the city-state of medieval times, when "*non c'era* posto *indoe un facessen guerra*" ('there was no *place* that wasn't at war' – verse from a traditional sung poem in octets, "*Pia dei Tolomei*"). Notice the word *posto*, namely 'place,' in this verse. Antagonisms among villages and towns today have lost any violent side, although many elders in Tuscany still remember that rivalries leading to violence were still a common happening at the beginning of the century. The poet Realdo Tonti, for example, recalls that:

Campanilismo is like this. In the past, among towns and towns, I don't know; here, when I was a boy, if a young man would pass the limit to go to San Niccoló, if he would pass a certain limit he would find himself hit with stones. You know, the ignorance. Maybe he was in love with a girl of that town, and then it was even worse. The evening when he would go in that town, they would do him the worst tricks. It is the same with *campanilismo*. It was like this in the towns. To you it may sound something difficult to believe. . . . You are young. . . . Yes, at the beginning of this century, but even until the war. Even until the 1930, 1935. . . . There was *campanilismo* between San Pietro and San Niccoló, San Michele. That was better, because there was the soccer team, you understand; here there was the music band. The music band of San Niccoló was better than the one of San

> Pietro, and so on. It was like this. Then there were *Contrasti*. . . . Better, the Poeti a Braccio would win their bread with it.[11]

This phenomenon is in some way similar to what Blu describes for the towns in Carolina (1996).

The antagonism is today only expressed in jokes and blasons, rarely offensive. Blasons are particular forms of stereotyping in which the stereotype is known and accepted by both the in-group and the out-group, and which are defined through oppositions. Thus an identification as *pianigiano*, 'plains person,' will recall the relevant opposition, namely *montanino* or 'mountain person.' Blasons are very common in Tuscany and practically every town and village has its own, as shown by the studies of scholars like De Simonis (1984/85), Pecori (1975) and Cortellazzo (1984). De Simonis, regarding the Tuscans, talks about a "precise consciousness of the diversity of the other" (1984/85: 8–9), even among small villages very near to each other.[12]

Talking about "ethnic identity" is not a common Tuscan experience. I doubt that most people would even understand what the terms mean. As Tamanoi writes of Japanese rural women: "Perhaps they had many identities or none at all; 'identity' is just not the way they talk about their living histories" (1998: 207–8). Conversations about places, instead, are continuous. The names, the roads to get there, the way people talk "there" and "here," together with innumerable acts of placing people, making sense of their actions, reckoning their *razza* ('race,' but in the Tuscan meaning of 'family ancestry'). "*Che* razza *di gente enno là a X?*" ('What *kind* of people are those in X?') they will ask me when I come back from the United States. As I shrug my shoulders in the impossibility of an answer, they will answer with the proverb: "*Tutto il mondo è paese*" ('the entire world is a town,' or 'the entire world is made out of towns').

In the performance of the *Contrasto*, the articulation of "repertoires" of ethnic identities depends on several factors, including the context, the audience, the negotiated meaning of the event, and the individuality of the artists. All of these factors, in turn, come to be reshaped by the performance itself. As Bauman has shown,

> Performance, like any other form of communication, carries the potential to rearrange the structure of social relations within the performance event and perhaps beyond it. The structure of social roles, relations, and interactions; the oral literary text and its meaning; and the structure of the event itself are all emergent in performance. (1986: 4)

In the *Contrasto*, identity itself can be seen as emerging in performance. The analysis of this genre, thus, underlines the active role of the individual in choosing and enacting a "repertoire" of identities.

3   Structure of the *Contrasto*

The *Contrasto* takes its name, 'contrast,' from the fact that two different figures, ideas, or things are depicted in it. Each is in turn defended and attacked, in an attempt to demonstrate the general inferiority of the one and superiority of the other. Thus, the *Contrasto* is a dialogue with the tendency to become a "duel." Following Del Giudice's definition, the *Contrasti* are "poetic 'contests', traditionally improvised, between two specific and stated adversaries . . . Although they are often musically lively and border on dance tune, *Contrasti* are also dramatic and heated debates" (Del Giudice 1995). The performances are public, usually done during local events, including feasts organized by the various district units of the parties, or by the parishes. The topics treated in a *Contrasto* vary and are potentially limitless. *Contrasti* between various Tuscan cities are common, as well as those involving political figures, gender distinctions and social roles.[13]

The *Contrasti* are performed by artists called *Poeti Bernescanti*,[14] or simply *poeti*, 'poets.' The structure is quite complex. The *Contrasti* are formed by a series of chained octets, where the first six verses have an alternated rhyme (example 1, lines 1–6), while the last two have a "coupled" rhyme (example 1, lines 7–8). Each of the verses in the octet must be formed by 11 syllables[15] (example 1, line 1). The poets use different varieties of the Tuscan dialect and code-switch among them. The "poetic language" also allows a high degree of semantic and grammatical creativity.[16]

(1)
1-A   C'è/ le/ bel/lez/ze/ ve/di/ le/ più/ ra/*re*
     There are the beauties, you see, the most rare
2-B   o quella l' è la tera degli am*ori*
     oh, that is the land of loves
3-A   doe si coltivano cose-e molto r*are*
     where the rarest things are cultivated
4-B   o specialmente delle rose e fi*ori*
     and especially roses and flowers
5-A   o lì non avrai delusioni am*are*
     oh there you will not have bitter delusions
6-B   o dove che si incontrano gli am*ori*
     where loves are encountered
7-C   invece te che abiti a Scand*icci*
     instead you, living in Scandicci
8-C   e tu ti trovi sempre ne past*icci*.
     you always find yourself in a mess.

4   Tuscan Identities as Connected to Place: Places Named

In the *Contrasto*, the contestation of each other's presentation and claim of identity passes through the metonymic association of the person (self and other) with places. These places can be named, hinted at, evoked through metaphors, and they are actively constructed and deconstructed. The act of naming, then, in verbal art performance, becomes fundamental and can furnish a key to understand a Tuscan vision of things. The Tuscan repertoire of identities could be articulated in a series of places, to which the person can claim or be claimed as belonging. Belonging itself, in turn, is articulated in terms of "knowing" or "being known," naming or being named. Names then become part of the way the claiming gets done.

At the beginning of a performance, the poets usually sing a series of "opening octets" in which they introduce themselves and greet the public. While they introduce themselves, the poets situate (identify) themselves each time in relation to the audience, the setting, and the other poet(s) present. This is the first of a series of layers of identity that they portray and of which they are invested during the *Contrasti* (often indissolubly mixed as well with their own identities as artists and as persons). The identity chosen can be portrayed through many means (for example by using particular varieties of the Tuscan dialect). Here, I focus on the conscious verbal self-identification in the opening octets. It is here, in fact, that we can see the connection between place-names and identity. The poets rarely present themselves as "being Tuscan" in their songs. Identity instead is connected to towns, villages, valleys and mountains, monuments and historical events and legends.

The poets whose performances I will discuss here are Altamante Logli and Realdo Tonti. Both of them are renowned and expert poets. Altamante lives in Scandicci, in the province of Florence. Realdo, a middle-aged man, lives in Agliana, in the province of Pistoia. Realdo is all in his name (lit. 'king Aldo'), regal. He could have been a king of ancient times, a tall and big man, with a powerful voice. He is also a kind person, down to earth and ready to accord you a benevolent smile. I was captured very soon by his continuous effort at introspection, his frequent bending on himself, and the incredible depth of his mind. Altamante is a seventy-eight year old man with the energy of a child, and of a child at times the temper. A short man with small penetrating eyes and a smile that makes you wonder if he is really fooling you about something. He is a little man, with a heart big like the world, that I could not avoid to love at first sight. Good natured and mellow, he becomes a true tiger on the stage, a poet with a fast and aggressive tongue that can give quite a bit of trouble to any adversary.

Schema #1   Altamante's repertoire of identities

Repertoire of identities	Place where he has invoked them	Setting
Apennine Mountains, Mountains, Cantagallo (town, province of Pistoia, Apennine mountains), Migliana	Migliana (town, province of Prato, on the Apennine mountains)	Local feast
Florence (city)	1) Papone (village, southern part of the province of Pistoia) 2) Lido di Pandoiano (village, province of Livorno)	1) Festival of Liberation 2) Local traditional feast
Scandicci (town, province of Florence), Tuscan	Florence	Festival of the ARCI
Political identities: Communist	Papone	Festival of Liberation

As shown in Schema #1, Altamante identified himself, in different performances, alternatively as Florentine, from Migliana, from Scandicci, from Cantagallo, from the Apennines, etc. (see also map 1). Only once he identified himself as Tuscan, during a performance in Florence, notably at an event organized by a national association, the ARCI (Italian Recreational and Cultural Association). He would otherwise refer to the particular Tuscan sub-groups or sub-cultures.[17]

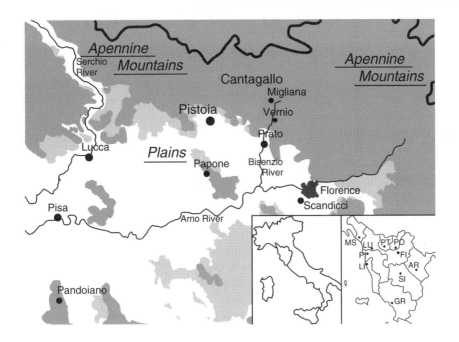

Naming indexes local knowledge. It affirms the presence of a relationship. The poets call in places as witnesses of their ability to belong to those places/identities. If they can name places, they can say that they are part of them, that they have that identity.[18] The identity declared by the other poet is also relevant. Usually poets tend to propose different identifications from each other. Thus, when singing with Realdo, Altamante would rather not declare himself from Pistoia. This seems to set the base for subsequent oppositional role-taking.

The connection that the Tuscan poets build with their audience through their performance is fundamental. It is important to understand the audience as co-performers. Artists and audience influence each other, and both a reflective and reflexive relationship is established among them. The audience usually requests the particular topic of the *Contrasto*. They may furnish various kinds of feedback, including evaluations, interpretations (see also Fretz 1987: 306–307), laughing and applause. They can even address the poets in rhyme.[19] The fact that the poets often insist on participation, on the possibility for everyone to "take the microphone," on the "we are here for you, to do what you ask us to do," is enlightening.

The performance is created in the interaction between speaker and listeners, and through this interaction, a certain social reality is upheld or criticized; a certain representation of identity can be legitimated or delegitimated. According to Heritage (1984), an objective reality exists so far as people agree on it. It is the ability of the poets in performance to obtain the agreement of the audience on the identities that they portray themselves or about themselves, that makes the poets part of their public. The identification can be contested, as I will show later. The point is that it is in the moment that the people accept the poets as part of them that the poets become able to express the audience's voice. The people recognize the poets and thus recognize the poets' ability to express Tuscan voices. They recognize the poets by accepting the performance and by co-constructing it. As Georges writes: "Everything human beings say and do when they assume the contrastive, but complementary, communicative roles of narrator and listener is an integral part of the event generated by their interacting; and this includes what they say or do in terms of such identities as those rooted in their sex, age, religious affiliation, ethnicity, occupations, etc." (1981: 251). Thus, the Tuscan ethnic identities and the communities to which they refer are *imagined* in the dialogue between the poets and their public.

The poet portrays the identity that allows him to feel closer to the audience. For example, in Migliana (see schema #1) Altamante creates an association through a series of towns in the Apennine Mountains. When this is not possible using an ethnic category, he uses class identities, professional identities, or others. For example in Papone, a small village in the southern part of the province of Pistoia, the setting being a festival organized by the Party of Communist Refoundation, he prefers to identify himself through a political identity, as Communist (see schema #1). This declaration of affiliation to the audience is revealing. These artists are not "heroic" figures. They escape from the hegemonic definition of the artist as hero; they share the same life, problems, unsettling questions, common sense, or limits of their audience. They do not stand out against the background of their communities, but find in their communities their strength and their voices. The relationship of the Tuscan poets with their audiences situates them close to the heart of the social network.

5   Place and Identity as Performed

In performance, the poets contest places and their definitions. Places are constructed and reconstructed in the *Contrasto* (see Blu 1996: 199). Metaphors of places overlap through the octets like realities overlap over the landscape (Blu 1996). Places (towns) become contested sources of identification, discursively constructed, thus pointing at contestable, unstable and contested identities.

I now turn to the analysis of a short excerpt from a *Contrasto*, done toward the end of the performance in Papone[20] (8th of August 1997). The context was a Festival of Liberation, taking place in the large courtyards of the local *Casa del Popolo* ('house of the people'). At the northern side of the building, there was a large paved space where, on other evenings, dances would be held. On one side stood a small stage erected for the occasion, and paraded with red Communist flags. This stage was used for musical groups, theater, political speakers, or other performances. At the other side of the paved dance ground, under the trees or along the side of the building, were the lines of the chairs where the audience sat. From the bar inside the building, voices and noises of dishes being washed created a droning accompaniment to the poets' singing.

The performance had started quite late, around 10 pm. In part for this reason, the audience was smaller than usual. The *Contrasto* I am analyzing was the last done, toward 11:30pm, when there was even less audience left (about 45–50 people). Because of it, the poets were getting ready to quit their rather short performance (usually performances run more than two hours). The remaining audience had been instead requesting to hear something more. The *Contrasto* started as a "closing octet" (the octet used to close a performance), then developed into a *Contrasto* of "plains vs. mountains" and then "city vs. countryside." The poets' indecision may explain why they start the closing octets, but then they end up doing another *Contrasto*.

In this *Contrasto* (spanning over 21 octets), the poets switch and shift among several Tuscan identities, and contest the other's identity as well as those attributed to the self by the other person. Altamante had started his closing octet, evoking his travel back to Scandicci (see map 1), where he lives. Realdo also evokes the travel back to the plains (where Pistoia is located). At this point, Altamante produces a third octet attacking Pistoia (octet #3):

(Octet #3) ALTAMANTE[21]

1 *Torna a s- Pistoia lá in quell'accquazione*
   Go back to Pistoia, there, in that stormy downpour
2   Realdo: ⟨*He! Ho! Ora comincia (vai)!*⟩[22]
           He! Ho! Now you start (go on)!
3 *torna lá nel mezzo ai* ⟨*gineprai*⟩[23]
   go back there, in the middle of those tangles of troubles
4 *io ritorno alla mia abitazione*
   I go back to my abode
5 ⟨*che a Pistoia un ci*⟩ *tornerei mai*
   since I would never go back to Pistoia
      AUD?: (   )
6 *c'é la paura po' dell'infezione*
   there is also the fear of the infection
7 *e poi ci sono tanti paretai*
   and then there are so many tangles of walls
8 *ci son delle giornate tant' amare*
   there are some days so bitter
9 *a forza sí di mosche e di zanzare.*
   by force, indeed, of flies and of mosquitoes
10   AUD: ((laughing))
11   AUD?: [(*e infatti*) *ce l'ho*
         (and in fact) I have them[24]
12   AUD?: [Ha! Ha! Ha ha ha ha!

Notice that Altamante uses characteristics of the environment, its rainy and humid weather, and recalls the fact that in the past the area had malaria (line 6: The infection). Belonging to Pistoia, thus, is metonymically connected to sickness. The verses evoke ugly weather, unhealthy waters, and a general sense of a place where you cannot avoid feeling uncomfortable: The tangles of bushes become tangles of walls: Ravines and an inhospitable place. A place where people live in fear, where the days are bitter in the continuous siege of the mosquitoes (themselves carriers of malaria) and the flies.

The harshness of Altamante's attack is proportional to the authenticity of the portrait. Talking about Kaluli songs, Feld writes: "Its evocative power depends not on the quantity of detail of places named, but on their connectedness, on the extent to which they map a place narrative that emotionally resonates with personal, biographical, and historical self-consciousness" (1996: 125). Notice, for example, the comment from a person in the audience (line 11), confirming the presence of flies and mosquitoes. The plains used to be a swamp. They were slowly drained over almost two thousand years by the peasants. Pistoia's original hamlet was built on the swamp itself, like a pile-dwelling. The name, Pistoia, comes from the Latin "pistores," people stamping their feet, making the land solid with that movement. It evokes to me the image of an unstable soil, continuously on the verge of sinking back in the swamp from which it was stolen. Altamante's derision of such an effort creates a powerful attack, and evokes powerful memories. Realdo defends Pistoia and attacks Scandicci in turn. In doing so, he creates another powerful image of Pistoia:

(#4) REALDO

1 *C'è le bellezze vedi le più rare*
     There are the beauties, you see, the most rare
2 *o quella l' è la tera degli amori*
     o, that is the land of loves
3 *doe si coltivano cose-e molto rare*
     where the rarest things are cultivated
4 *o specialmente delle rose e fiori*
     and especially roses and flowers
5 *o lì non avrai delusioni amare*
     o there you will not have bitter delusions
6 *o dove che si incontrano gli amori*
     where loves are encountered
7 *invece te che abiti a Scandicci*
     instead you, living in Scandicci
8 *e tu ti trovi sempre ne pasticci.*
     you always find yourself in a mess.
9   AUD: [((scattered applause))
10   AUD: [((laughing)
11   AUD?: (..........)

Realdo cancels the image of a painful past with that of a prosperous present. After the Second World War, there were many changes in the cultivation of the Pistoiese plains. The end of the sharecropping economy was associated with the development of nurseries. The humid climate makes the plains an ideal place for the production of flowers and ornamental plants. In Realdo's verses, these flowers that cover the land become a symbol of love. Suddenly, Pistoia is a sunny colorful heaven. As Blu writes: "How the land is to be construed, interpreted, and used is very much a matter of negotiation and often contestation" (1996: 198).

The land as constructed resonates and indexes realities of economic change and exploitation. The layers of human activity over the soil of the plains: The slow draining of the swamps, the cultivation, and then the recent changes that brought the construction of the nurseries that today bless Pistoia with flowers, money and cancer

(from the chemical pesticides used). Old illnesses and new ones: In the performance, the history of our Tuscan land passes in front of us audience. Each verse is a
memory.

Scandicci, in turn, is an industrial town that boomed after the Second World War
from a small agricultural center; today it is fused with Florence and constitutes one of
its suburban areas. Although Realdo does not describe Scandicci, the single mention at
the end of the description of Pistoia already hints at the juxtaposition between the
beauty of Pistoia and the ugliness of Scandicci. The juxtaposition is all in one word,
the "instead" that opens the two final verses. But Altamante, instead of picking up the
challenge of defending Scandicci, proposes for himself a new identity as "mountain
person" (*Montanino*), an inhabitant of the Apennine mountains:

(#5) ALTAMANTE

1 *Ma -o son- ((coughing)) son venuto da le castagne e ricci*
  But I came from the chestnuts and the husks[25]
2 *dove nasce i Bbisenzio sopra l'Appennino*
  where the Bisenzio River[26] is born over the Appenine
3   AUD: ((laughing))
4 *l'acqua colava giù da que' renicci*
  the water was dripping down from those sliding sand deposits
5 *e ti bagnó i' ssolo poverino*
  and soaked your soil poor one[27]
6 *voglio vedere ome ti tu spicci*
  I want to see how you can unstick yourself
7 *son nato fra la ch- fra i ccastagno e i'biancospino*
  I was born between the chestnut tree and the hawthorn
8 *a Pistoia tu fa' di' mmormorio*
  in Pistoia you make murmurs/grumble
9 *tu bevi l'acqua dove piscio io*
  you drink the water where I piss
10   AUD: ((laughing))
11   AUD: ((scattered applause))

This switch leads the confrontation from one between Pistoia and Scandicci, to one
between the Mountains and the Plains. Here, naming is substituted by metaphors,
which in turn presuppose common knowledge, or common memories. To the cultivated
flowers of the plains, Altamante juxtaposes the wild flowers and trees of the mountains.
The pure, running water of the Bisenzio River, decaying in its downward movement,
becomes the polluted, motionless waters of the plains. Notice how the effectiveness of
the poetry lies in great part in the ability to isolate the core elements of each construction of place, and attack those elements.

In the following octets (#6 through #13, not presented here), Realdo attacks the
Mountain people in turn, identifying Altamante with the town of Cantagallo (see map
#1). Altamante then attacks Pistoia. Later (octets #14 through #21) Realdo shifts the
theme by associating Pistoia with Florence, thereby contrasting the city with the coun-

tryside, and ends up claiming a Florentine identity. Thus in the end the poets switch their initial identifications around. The switch does not happen without opposition from Altamante. This can be seen better by looking at three octets (#14, #15, and #18) where Realdo starts (#14) and then completes (#18) the switch:

(#14) REALDO

1 ⟨*Si vede l'ignorante [come è scortese*⟩
   it can be seen how the ignorant is impolite
2   AUD: [((laughing))
3   Altamante: [*ndiamo si va via (......). Ora un vó via più*
                        come on, let's go away (......). Now I won't go away anymore
4 *tu l'ha messa la firma di mmontanaro*
   you put your signature as hillbilly
5 ⟨*guardatevi intorno*⟩ *nel nostro paese*
   look around in our country
6 *ndove gli è un'arte di ppiù raro*
   where there is an art of the most rare
7 *voglio di' di Firenze, i ppistoiese*
   I mean to say about Florence, the area of Pistoia
8   Altamante: (che c'entra) Firenze (......)
                       (what does) Florence (have to do with it) (......)
9 *e ora tu lo ngolli [boccone*[28] *amaro*
   and now you will swallow a bitter pill
10   Altamante: [(*parlá di Firenze*) (......)
                       (to talk about Florence) (......)
11 *dimmi te i piazza di ddomo e i Bbargello*
   tell me, the plaza of the cathedral and the Bargello[29]
12 *un tu gl' ha visti ncima a Diavello*
   you did not see them on top of Diavello[30]
13   AUD: ((laughing))
14   AUD?: (bravo)
15   AUD: ((scattered applauses))

Realdo starts by labeling Altamante as an ignorant hillbilly. This is the first part of what is going to be shown soon as a dichotomy between the uncivilized country-folk versus the civilized urbanite. In fact, immediately after, Realdo addresses the public asking them to look around themselves, to notice the artistic heritage of the region. Notice that he uses the pronoun "ours" together with the term paese, namely 'country' or 'town,' thus theorizing a unit that includes him (as Pistoiese) as well as the audience (Papone is situated between the provinces of Pistoia and Florence) in this address. Then in the fourth verse he makes explicit reference to Florence and Pistoia. By mentioning Florence, he is presenting the second term of the dichotomy: The urban space. The closure is highly humorous: The beauty of art, symbolized by the cathedral and the museum of Bargello, cannot be found on top of a mountain. The answer of the audience is one of roaring laughing and approval ("Bravo" in line 14).

Notice that Altamante, at the mentioning of Florence, starts objecting (lines 8 and 10). As an experienced poet, I think he already knows what is coming. Claiming Florence is to claim a powerful ally, especially when the association is done through art. More than a Tuscan capital, Florence is often felt by Tuscans as a world capital of art. As such, it is the homeplace of all poetry. To claim Florence is to empower one's poetical ability. Altamante at this point is left with the alternative of attacking Florence, or refusing Realdo's claim to a Florentine identification. He chooses the second possibility:

(#15) ALTAMANTE

1   AUD: [((still laughing after previous octet))
2 *[Ma sentite i cche dice sto zimbello*[31]
   But listen what he is saying this laughing stock
3   AUD: ((laughing))
4 ⟨*vo mettere*⟩ *Pistoia con Fiorenza*
   he wants to compare Pistoia with Florence
5 *io dio gli è malato ni ccervello*
   I say that he is sick in the brain
6 *oppure gli ha poca* ⟨*intelligenza*⟩
   or he has little intelligence
7   AUD: ((laughing))
8 *io parlavo d'i mmonte morto bello*
   I was talking of the mountain very beautiful
9 *indoe gli è nato la mia residenza*
   where it was born my residence
10 *se porto un pistoiese in piazza Signoria*
    if I bring a Pistoiese in the Signoria Plaza[32]
11 *l'acchiappahani se lo porta via.*
    the dog-catcher would carry him away.
12   AUD?: [Nooo! ((laughing))
13   AUD: [((lots of laughing))
14   AUD: ((applause))
15   AUD?: (tu sta' in filo) (gli attacca) Pistoia, è?
           (you are in trouble) (he is attacking) Pistoia, right?

Altamante bases his attack on the presupposed impossibility/absurdity to make a comparison between Pistoia and Florence. He thus reinterprets Realdo's attempt to build an association as an attempt to make a confrontation. Then, he re-establishes his own claim to talk of the beauty of the mountain: Since he was born there he can claim residence – thus he can speak for it. In turn, the claim of a Pistoiese to talk for Florence is derided: Like a dog in the central plaza of Florence, less than human, carried away like a madman. Altamante thus contests Realdo's right to "name" Florence, to call the city as witness to his argument. The negotiation of identity happens on multiple levels: The construction of the image, and the claim of belonging. Altamante also escalates the violence of his attack, to which the audience answers in various ways. They laugh and applaud (lines 3, 4, 6, 7, 13), but they also express recognition of the strength of the attack (line 12), or seem to comment on Realdo's position (line 15). In the next two octets (#16 and #17, not presented here), Realdo reaffirms his allegiance to the plains, and Altamante again contests the possibility of an association with Florence. Then, in the third octet, Realdo brings about his strongest argument:

(#18) REALDO

```
1        AUD?: Ovvia!
2                That's it!
3 Ecco tu l'ha scoperte [                         ] ⟨le tue carte⟩
    There! You have discovered your cards/hand
4            Altamante: [ndiamo si va via per Dio]
                    let's go away, by God!
5 se se' nato laggiú sull'Appennino
    if you were born far there on the Apennine
6 io nacqui lo sai da un'antra parte
    I was born you know in another place
7 vicino a i ssolo quello fiorentino
    near to the soil, the Florentine one
8 e gli è lì che gli è nata tutta l'arte
    and it is there that all art is born
9 ma te non lo sapevi [          ] pove[rino
    but you did not know it, poor one
10       Altamante: [(c'era Cino)]      [Cino (......)
                    (there was Cino³³) Cino (......)
11 finché un venivi ni ssolo di Pistoia [e Ferenza
    before you came in the soil of Pistoia and Florence
12       AUD?:                    [(......)
13 anlon- ancor nun lla sapei la differenza.
    you did not know the difference yet.
```

Here Realdo first recalls the attention to Altamante's previous affirmation to be born on the mountain (the Apennine, line 5). Then he affirms to be born near Florence (line 7). Notice that Realdo does not really inform us as to what he means by "near." Thus he is able to turn the table around against Altamante: As Altamante had claimed the ability to speak for the mountain since he was born there, so Realdo was born "near" Florence. There was born all art: Indirectly this means that since Altamante was born elsewhere, he cannot be a very good artist. Excluding Altamante from Florence is to disempower his poetic ability.

This is a very dangerous attack against a poet, one that threatens to enrage, and thus reveal, the person behind the personage.³⁴ Perhaps for this reason, the next phrases are full of ambiguity: Altamante did not know – but what? That Realdo was from Florence, or that all art is born there? The next verse also has a double meaning: It may make an indirect reference to the fact that Altamante moved to Scandicci later in life; alternatively it refers to the fact that to learn about art (to understand the difference) he had to come to the cities. The last verse may mean that only by coming to the cities he would understand the difference between Pistoia and Florence, but also the difference between art and non-art. Notice how during this octet, differently from the previous ones, the audience does not laugh at all, thus showing their perception of Realdo's dangerous attack.

Contesting the name taking of the poet is contesting his ability to identify with a community. Accepting the name taking is to accept his belonging. The poets continuously rename themselves, and call the audience to witness their ability to rename themselves as part of those places. They call on places as witnesses of their ability to recall stories, memories, to belong to those places, to claim those identities.

The artist, in this process of identification, can become, be seen and speak as a series of cultural personae, each in turn representing a particular version of the world. These personifications are not just constructed in performance but co-constructed in the dialogue between the artists and with the audience. The audience relinquishes or bestows on the artists the power to speak for them, about them, and especially *from* them (as part of them). This co-construction is the base for the establishment of a reflexive relationship between artists and audience. A reflexive relationship in which portrayals of the essence of particular social identities are offered (presented) and at the same time attacked, praised, derided, offended, deconstructed, reorganized and *imagined*. The audience, through their co-performance, can accept, refuse, negotiate those images. Bauman affirms that "Performance is formally reflexive – signification about signification. . . . Performance may be seen as broadly metacultural, a cultural means of objectifying and laying open to scrutiny culture itself, for culture is a system of systems of signification" (1992: 47). Each poet disturbs the constructed objectivity of the portrayal of identity proposed by the other. The *Contrasti* are powerful, also because one poet is always going to shake the reality that the other poet is constructing.

As people share the same places, they can have different definitions of them. Each of these definitions implies a reality, so that realities are overlapping. Tuscan places are created historically; they are sediments in these definitions of places. There are layers to Tuscan places. The poets actively deploy each of these layers in their presentation of different definitions of the same places. Not every Tuscan shares the same definitions of the places they live in. It is this non-sharing that the performances underline. They lay bare the contradictions, but they do so with a smile. They challenge the ability of Tuscans to say "this is our place," and they invite the audience to join them on a more complex level of thinking.

Having shown the importance of "place" in the definition of identity, I stated that places are also "performed," or emergent in performance. As Casey notices, "places not only *are*, they *happen*" (1996: 27, italics in the original). As the landscape is constituted in speech acts, the connection between the landscape and peoples is also constituted (see Basso 1996: 54). "Thus represented and enacted", writes Basso, "places and their meaning are continuously woven into the fabric of social life" (1996: 57). This also implies that performance allows play with each other's reality, a game that can be highly destructive, as the duel of the *Contrasto* can be destructive. Poets offend and humiliate each other as well as their audiences. The freedom of rethinking our selves is not (and maybe cannot be) free from a bit of prickly pain, that at times may make us grind our teeth in the middle of a laugh. Then, would the absence of that sting make us happier, or just more bored and dull people?

6   Conclusions

The *Contrasti*'s complex structure has, ingrained in itself, the elements that make it so important in showing contested identities. Its bipolar organization allows and requires that two opposite voices (or two opposite discourses) may be heard, and both in turn be attacked. Thus, ethnic identity in the *Contrasti* is always shifting, bipolar or multipolar, dual or multiple, and defined in opposition to others. The *Contrasti* mine at its root the sense of the absoluteness of a particular identity, showing to the public how it lies in the eye of the beholder. Identity is revealed as constructed, multiple, unstable.

As recent waves of immigration are changing the ethnic makeup of the Italian nation, many Italians have started to interrogate themselves on their cultural and ethnic identities. The arrival of immigrants is often seen as the moment of starting, the cause of the overlapping of different realities on the landscape. I have tried to show that the overlapping has always been present. It is part of the way people construct their vision of things, not just a phenomenon of modernity or postmodernity. It is not something due to supposed anomic conditions of present times. The contradictions do not take place on a substratum that once was uncontradictory (the pristine unity of one people). Recognizing the necessity of the overlapping of realities, then, can be a first step toward creating new memories together, landmarks that bear our joint names. An old view is still lurking in the background, one that would like to see a happy state in the absence of diasporas and displacements. However, displacement can be a powerful strategy, and the contestation of place can be done with a smile. The Tuscan poets continuously deplace, replace and emplace themselves. By doing this they augment their power. Deplacing and re-emplacing are strategies that create the universality of a certain discourse; they are strategies of power and empowerment.

While waging their ethnic wars with words, Realdo, Altamante and the other poets offer to their public the possibility to see the relativity of ethnic divisions. What is important is that we, the public, can laugh together about them, and as we listen to the praises and the offenses, we reflect on the various sides of our selves. Tuscan people need their poets today more than ever, as shown by the renewed interest in this ancient genre. They ask the poets to discuss new topics that witness to the need of making sense, of finding a place for other cultures in the constellation of relevant Tuscan identities. Once each portrayal has been in turn constructed and deconstructed, what the public is left with is, in Realdo's closing verses (Octet #20), the final refusal of the individual to be bounded by birth or other "IDs":

> *fin da i' momento che siamo nelle fasce*
> since the moment we are swaddled
> *l'artista un si sa mai ndove nasce*
> no one knows where the artist is born

Notes

1   My analysis is based on my fieldwork in Tuscany between 1994 and 1998, where I spent a total of more than two years. My ethnographic method privileged participant observation, and I followed the artists in their performances, videotaping them. I also conducted interviews with them afterwards. The research itself was made possible by two grants I received from the Department of Anthropology, University of California Los Angeles.

2   Tuscany is a region in central Italy, with about 3.5 million people. It is closed to the north and east by the Apennine Mountains, and by the Tirreno Sea to the west, while a series of hillsides and plains connects it to the Lazio region to the south. Tuscany today is an economically prosperous and highly industrialized region. Culturally speaking, Tuscany is a transition area in which we find elements of Northern, Middle-European cultures and Southern, Mediterranean cultures. The Tuscan language includes many varieties (Giacomelli 1984/85). The language spoken in Pistoia, is the 'Pistoiese, Occidental, Tuscan' language. The language spoken in Florence, to the south-east of Pistoia, is the 'Fiorentino Tuscan.'

3   In this sense Visweswaran (1995) writes that: "Identities, no matter how strategically deployed, are not always chosen, but are in fact constituted by relations of power always historically determined" (1995: 8).

4   An example of such lists comes from the Random House College Dictionary: "*Ethnic Group*: A group of People of the same race or nationality who share a common and distinctive culture."

5   I cannot overstress the way in which "traits" definitions of Ethnicity are used as a base for ethnic hate crimes and discriminatory behaviors, such as the Holocaust and other attempted genocides. They can be seen at work today in the war between Serbs and Albanians.

6   This has also been seen as a problem in Rampton's recent study of language crossing (1998). Though Rampton's distinction between "interactive", "reactive" and "deracinated" ethnicity (with the connected idea of a "true" belonging versus "commodified" belonging) presupposes again the existence of an ethnic group outside or before people's creation of an identification to one (before its creation in everyday practices or shared participation into it). This is like presupposing a reality outside of its social construction. Here, Rampton does not seem to have done any theoretical progress and be still abiding to some kind of "trait/fixed" definition of ethnic group.

7   Here, I focus more on the "subjective" side of identity, although by no means I intend to negate the importance of looking at the "boundary imposed from the outside" (Peterson Royce 1982: 29).

8   This emergence, in turn, implies the contextual creation of a shared knowledge regarding the identity itself (its characteristics, boundaries, etc. including possible beliefs in fixed traits).

9   I include myself here, as I was born and grew up in Tuscany, in Pistoia.

10   Although the antagonism could possibly date back further to the Etruscan time. In fact, it is now known that the Etruscans were also organized in city-states.

11   Excerpts from an interview conducted in Realdo Tonti's home, in Agliana, on June 18, 1997.

12   Important oppositional identities in the area under study are the ones between the city and the countryside. For example, Florence versus the rest of its province, the plains versus the mountain, and the juxtaposition between Pistoia and Prato. These are also reflected in several *Contrasti*.

13   Examples of topics are: "Husband and Wife," "Hunter and Jackrabbit," "Blonde and Brunette," "Science and Nature," "Water and Wine," "Peasant and Landowner," etc. The topics are supposed to be sung by two poets. When three poets are present, themes can be proposed that require the expression of three different points of view and thus three participants.

14   Literally 'poets in Berni's style,' after F. Berni, a Tuscan writer of the 16th century who is supposed to have first used this kind of poetry in its modern form. The poets are also called *poeti a braccio*, 'poets at arms.' The meaning and origins of this second name are obscure.

15   I believe that the number of syllables in each verse depends on the way it is performed. The melody, for example, allows a multiplication of the syllables through pausing, division of the diphthongs, elision, or melodic prolongation of vowels.

16   The language of the *Contrasti* disparages and ignores the common rules governing grammar and phrase formation in Italian. The prominence given to the sound, to the internal organization of the genre itself against the external organization/constraints of grammar, is striking. Even the semantic use is particular. The poet can create new words whose semanticity is null and at the same time reconstructed by the listeners, often through assonance of meaning. Word use follows the needs of musicality as well, even the music is more important than the semantic meaning.

17   Of course, this might have been different if he had found himself outside of Tuscany (he performed many times in Lazio and once in Emilia) or outside of Italy (he performed in Switzerland), but I lack data for those occasions. Insight can be used, anyway, by comparing him to another poet, Mariani, from Lazio, whose performance was recorded in Tuscany. Mariani actually never presented a Lazio identity, but rather his sub-cultural group in Lazio. He also declared himself akin to the Tuscan people.

18   This idea I share with Sepa Sete, since it was formed through a dialogue with her.

19   The audience is not homogeneous, but there are various kinds of audiences, and each of them can have a different role in respect to the performance (Goodwin 1986). Moreover the people in the audience have an influence on each other's peformance as audience (Goodwin 1986). The audience can also be divided into "supporters" and "antagonists" in respect to the performance.

20   Papone is a village near the town of Lamporecchio, in the province of Pistoia, but very close to the border with the Florence province, and separated from Pistoia by a chain of Hills, the San Baronto. It is also high country, over the hills themselves.

21   The following transcription conventions apply:
(words in parenthesis) = words are in parenthesis when their transcription is unsure.
(......) = words I cannot hear and transcribe.
((double parenthesis)) = indicate production of specified sound by the speaker or audience, including applause and laughing.
[   ] or [= square brackets indicate overlapping between two different speakers.
⟨   ⟩ = laughter from the audience overlapping the speaker's words or singing.
AUD = audience
AUD? = unknown person in the audience
Notice that I transcribe sentences spoken by other than the singer by indenting them and indicating the name of the speaker, followed by a colon. These sentences are also numbered, although they are not part of the octet.

22   Note the audience's laughing answer to Altamante's first verse. It underlines the passage from the closing octets to a new *Contrasto*, at the same time recognizing and encouraging it.

23   Literally, *gineprai* means 'bushes of juniper,' but it is generally used in its idiomatic sense of 'troubles from which it is difficult to extricate oneself.'

24   Referring to the presence of flies and mosquitoes, very common in summer.

25   The chestnut trees that cover the Apennine Mountains are an important symbol for the people living in them. They also furnish an important staple food. The chestnuts are gathered and cooked in various ways or ground to make flour, from which a sweet bread is made.

26   See map 4.1.

27   The swampy plains receive their waters from the Apennine Mountains.

28   *Boccone* literally means 'mouthful of food' or 'bite of food.'

29   The museum of Bargello, one of the most important in Florence.

30   This reference to Diavello is only partially clear to me. It seems that he is referring to a mountaintop with that name. Unfortunately, I do not know its exact location.

31   *Zimbello* literally a 'decoy,' often a bird or in the shape of a bird.

32   Florence's central plaza, where are the Museum of *Palazzo Vecchio* 'Old Palace,' the connected Uffizi Museum, the Loggia of Orcagna, and the Marzocco Fountain.

33 Probably referring to the medieval poet Cino Da Pistoia, who lived in the 13th century; Cino was part of the *Stil Novo,* 'New Style,' and friend of Dante Alighieri. Here Altamante seems to be suggesting to Realdo a possible ending of the verse, and a possible defense of Pistoia.

34 As you may notice, the offenses leveled at each other are quite heavy. However, while the offense exchanged offends the personage, the poet remains untouched and calmly smiling. For example, in line #2 of octet #3, Realdo greets the beginning of Altamante's attack with a "go on." He will wait and give the other time to finish, and then he will take his turn at offending. What is at stake is not actually losing face for having been offended, but losing face for not having been able to answer to the offense appropriately and destructively while following all the dictates of the genre. The public itself is very sensitive to the way emotions are displayed by the poets. They will laugh a lot at the offense they give to each other, commenting on the ability to effectively counter each of them. However, the public will stop laughing if they perceive that the rage is true.

References

Anzaldua, Gloria (1987) *Borderlands/La frontera: The new mestiza.* San Francisco: Aunt Lute.

Barth, Fredrik (1969) *Ethnic groups and boundaries. The social organization of culture difference.* Boston: Little, Brown & Co.

Basso, Keith H. (1988) Speaking with names: Language and landscape among the Western Apache. *Cultural Anthropology* 3: 99–130.

Basso, Keith H. (1996) Wisdom sits in places: Notes on Western Apache landscape. In S. Feld & K. H. Basso (eds.), *Senses of place.* Santa Fe: School of American Research Press.

Bauman, Richard (1986) *Story, performance and event: Contextual studies of oral narrative.* Cambridge: Cambridge University Press.

Bauman, Richard (1992) *Folklore, cultural performances, and popular entertainments.* New York and Oxford: Oxford Unviersity Press.

Bourdieu, Pierre (1977) *Outline of a theory of practice.* Translated by Richard Nice. Cambridge: Cambridge University Press.

Bourdieu, Pierre (1990) *The logic of practice.* Translated by Richard Nice. Stanford: Stanford Unviersity Press.

Blu, Karen I. (1996) "Where do you stay at?": Homeplace and community among the Lumbee. In S. Feld & K. H. Basso (eds.), *Senses of place.* Santa Fe: School of American Research Press.

Casey, Edward S. (1996) How to get from space to place in a fairly short stretch of time: Phenomenological prolegomena. In S. Feld & K.H. Basso (eds.), *Senses of place.* Santa Fe: School of American Research Press.

Cohen, Ronald (1978) Ethnicity: Problem and focus in anthropology. *Annual Review of Anthropology* 7: 379–403.

Cortellazzo, Mario (1984) *Curiosità linguistica nella cultura popolare.* Lecce: Milella.

De Simonis, Paolo (1984/85) 'Noi' e 'loro'. Note su identità e confini linguistici e culturali in Toscana. *Quaderni Dell'Atlante Lessicale Toscano,* 2/3 – 1984/85. Florence: L. S. Olschki Editore.

Del Giudice, Luisa (1995) *Italian traditional songs.* Los Angeles: Istituto Italiano di Cultura.

Duranti, A., E. Ochs, and E. K. Ta'ase (1995) Change and tradition in literacy instruction in a Samoan American community. *Educational Foundations,* 9.4: 57–74.

Feld, Steven (1996) Waterfalls of song: An acustemology of place resounding in Bosavi, Papua New Guinea. In S. Feld & K. H. Basso (eds.), *Senses of place.* Santa Fe: School of American Research Press.

Frake, Charles O. (1996) Pleasant places, past times, and shared identity in rural East Anglia. In S. Feld & K. H. Basso (eds.), *Senses of place.* Santa Fe: School of American Research Press.

Fretz, L. Rachel (1987) In performance: Narrating skills and listener responses. Unpublished Ph.D. Dissertation.

Georges, Robert A. (1981) Do narrators really digress? A reconsideration of "audience asides" in narrating. *Western Folklore* 15.3: 245–252.

Giacomelli, Gabriella (1984/85) Parole *toscane*. *Quaderni Dell'Atlante Lessicale Toscano* 2/3 – 1984/85. Florence: L. S. Olschki Editore.

Goodwin, Charles (1986) Audience diversity, participation and interpretation. *Text* 6.3: 283–316.

Heritage, John (1984) *Garfinkel and Ethnomethodology*. Cambridge: Polity Press.

Hymes, Dell (1981) *"In vain I tried to tell you": Essays in Native American Ethnopoetics*. Philadelphia: Pennsylvania University Press.

Kahn, Miriam (1996) Your place and mine: Sharing emotional landscapes in Wamira, Papua New Guinea. In S. Feld & K. H. Basso (eds.), *Senses of place*. Santa Fe: School of American Research Press.

Kroskrity, Paul V. (1993) *Language, history, and identity: Ethnolinguistic studies of the Arizona Tewa*. Tucson: University of Arizona Press.

Pagliai, Valentina (1995) The Italian Americans in Los Angeles: Representations of identity and community. Unpublished Master Thesis, Department of Anthropology, University of California Los Angeles.

Pagliai, Valentina (1996a) Code-switching and the communicative construction of the Italian American identity. Unpublished paper.

Pagliai, Valentina (1996b) Narrando l'identità etnica: Gli Italoamericani a Los Angeles. *Etnosistemi*, Anno IV, N(4 – Gennaio: 61–82.

Pecori, Giulio (1975) *Blasoni popolari toscani e modi proverbiali*. Florence: Libreria Editrice Fiorentina.

Rampton, Ben (1998) Language crossing and the redefiniton of "minority." *Working Papers in Applied Linguistics*, 5/December: 15–30.

Royce, Anya Peterson (1982) *Ethnic identity. Strategies of diversity*. Bloomington: Indiana Univeristy Press.

Tamanoi, Mariko Asano (1998) *Under the shadow of nationalism: Politics and poetics of rural Japanese women*. Honolulu: University of Hawaii Press.

Visweswaran, Kamala (1994) *Fictions of feminist ethnography*. Minneapolis & London: University of Minnesota Press.

Vizenor, Gerald R. (1994) *Manifest manners: Postindian warriors of survivance*. Hanover: Wesleyan University Press.

Zentella, Ana C. (1990) Returned migration, language and identity: Puerto Rican bilinguals in dos worlds/two mundos. *International Journal of the Sociology of Language*, Special Issue, 84.

Zentella, Ana C. (1997) *Growing up bilingual*. Oxford: Blackwell Publishers.

Discussion Questions

1. Considering Hymes's definition of speech community, discuss what would be your personal speech community. Who would you include? Do you have more than one?
2. Discuss whether Hymes's definition of speech community would need to be altered to include the most modern means of communication, e.g. email, internet chat rooms. Why or why not?
3. In most cases, would the following be speech acts, speech events or speech situations?

   an apology

   a wedding reception

   the introduction of a conference speaker

   a monologue in a play

   intermediate Spanish class

   a child's little white lie to mother
4. In chapter 1 Shuy refers to Newmeyer's assertion that Hymes "intended 'communicative competence' to exclude grammatical competence" (p. 12). Why would there be some confusion about the inclusion of grammatical competence in Hymes's concept of communicative competence? What arguments for and against the inclusion of grammatical competence in communicative competence can be made?
5. In part I both Calvet and Shuy discuss the presence of two camps in linguistics: one which looks at languages as static, but with universal tendencies, and the other which focuses on variation and/or continual change. As Shuy states, "there are two types of linguistic analysts: those who search for universals (what languages have in common), and those who search for variability (how languages differ)" (pp. 13–14). Discuss how Hymes in chapter 3 reconciles these seemingly dichotomous approaches.
6. Discuss how Hymes's criticism of the notion that a participant is always part of a dyad (chapter 3, p. 37) applies to the *Contrasti* described by Pagliai. What are the components of speech in the *Constrasti*? Who are the participants?
7. Pagliai discusses the importance of place and place names in creating identity in Tuscany. How does place play a role in the creation of identity in your own community? Considering the homogeneous nature of Italy and the heterogeneous nature of countries such as Australia, Canada, Great Britain, and the United States of America, what factors might contribute to the conception of identity in these more heterogenous societies that might not play a role in Italy?
8. Discuss how Pagliai's discussion of place and identity might relate to Hymes's concept of speech community.
9. Observe a public event in your society that might be analyzed to see how the entertainers/performers interact with the audience. Write a brief description of this interaction and describe its role in the culture.

Part III

Pragmatics

Introduction

Pragmatics is not one coherent field of study; it is a topic in the philosophy of language which deals with implicatures and presuppositions: "it involves the context-dependent aspects of meaning, which are systematically abstracted away from in the pure semantics of logical form" (Horn 1992: 260). Pragmatics is studied in stylistics and psycholinguistics as well as in sociolinguistics, and the result is a set of conflicting definitions, diversity of subject-matter, and a range of methodologies. At present pragmatics is in the process of developing into a field in its own right, with its own courses, journals, and conferences. The broadest perspective sees "pragmatics as the study of the principles and practice underlying all interactive linguistic performance – this including all aspects of language usage, understanding, and appropriateness" (Crystal 1987: 120).

Formal linguistics typically deals with the analysis of language at the sentence level. Narrative and discourse analysis, also called text linguistics, examines the coherence and structure of language in extended text, spoken and written. Sociolinguistics studies the social meaning of communicative choices among available alternatives, and Hymes's essay outlined a range of possible considerations in observing such choices. In telling stories, narrators also "need to make certain choices – about the inclusion of certain episodes, the description of peoples and events, and in many communities the use of one (or more) language varieties rather than others, as well as choices between different linguistic forms and structures" (Swann 2000: 191). Narratives are always representations, constructed to make a point, and the choices the narrator makes allow him a certain "presentation of self" (Goffman 1959) as well as a judgment of the actors and events of the constructed text.

William Labov (1966) in the fieldwork for his enormously influential dissertation also collected stories, partially to distract the informants' attention from the language elicited, on exciting topics like being in danger of death or in a fight. He then analyzed characteristics of these narratives, and the article presented here by Labov and Waletzky, "Narrative analysis: oral versions of personal experience," became the seminal article of an entire school of work. Emanuel Schegloff, a sociologist and an important contributor to the development of this school, reflects on the work of the last thirty years, while Janet Holmes demonstrates that narrative structure is not a universal (as was thought in the early days) but is culture–sensitive and differs from community to community.

Conversational analysis as developed by John J. Gumperz (1982a, b) was grounded in the basic assumption of anthropology that language and ways of speaking are socially and culturally relative; there are no universal ways of saying no, of asking for a drink, or of apologizing. All discourse is culture–specific. Gumperz very early on attempted to develop what he called "interpretive sociolinguistic approaches to the analysis of real time processes in face to face encounters. . . . an individual's choice of speech style has symbolic value and interpretive consequences that cannot be explained simply by correlating the incidence of linguistic variants with independently determined social and contextual categories" (1982a: vii). Interpretive, or what later became called interactional, sociolinguistics is here contrasted by Gumperz to the correlational approach of Labovian variationist sociolinguistics (not to Labov's narrative analysis approach). See part V.

Gumperz's concern was not only theoretical; many of his studies on conversations across cultural boundaries documented misunderstandings caused by marginal features of language of which the speakers were unaware – intercultural miscommunication. These differential features of language Gumperz calls "contextualization cues: aspects of language and behavior (verbal and nonverbal signs) that relate what is said to contextual presuppositions, that is background knowledge that allows situated inferences about what one's interlocutor intends to convey" (Schiffrin 1996: 313). Gumperz's "Contextualization conventions" is from the body of work which seeks to develop this framework.

Other areas of interactional sociolinguistics built on philosophers' work on speech acts (Austin 1965; Searle 1969), on doing things with words. Another very productive topic has drawn on Brown and Gilman's inspirational work on address forms, which was one of the very earliest descriptions of language to explicitly introduce the notion of 'power' as an explanatory concept. The original Brown and Gilman article is presented here; a more recent work by the New Zealander Janet Holmes on the speech act of complimenting reveals a shift away from focus on form to an analysis of the functions of compliments – and how men and women differ in giving them.

References

Austin, J. L. 1965. *How to Do Things With Words*. Oxford: Oxford University Press.
Crystal, David. 1987. *The Cambridge Encyclopedia of Language*. Cambridge: Cambridge University Press.
Goffman, Erving. 1959. *The Presentation of Self in Everyday Life*. New York: Anchor Books.
Gumperz, John J. 1982a. *Discourse Strategies*. Cambridge: Cambridge University Press.
Gumperz, John J. 1982b. *Language and Social Identity*. Cambridge: Cambridge University Press.
Horn, Laurence R. 1992. "Pragmatics, implicatures, and presupposition," in William Bright (ed.), *International Encyclopedia of Linguistics*, pp. 260–6. Oxford: Oxford University Press.
Labov, William. 1966. *The Social Stratification of English in New York City*. Washington, DC: Center for Applied Linguistics.
Schiffrin, Deborah. 1996. "Interactional sociolinguistics," in Sandra Lee McKay and Nancy H. Hornberger (eds.), *Sociolinguistics and Language Teaching*, pp. 307–28.

Searle, John R. 1969. *Speech Acts: An Essay in the Philosophy of Language*. Cambridge: Cambridge University Press.

Swann, Joan. 2000. "Language in Interaction," in Rajend Mesthrie, Joan Swann, Andrea Deumert and William L. Leap, *Introducing Sociolinguistics*. Amsterdam: Benjamins.

Further Reading

Brown, Penelope and Stephen Levinson. 1987. *Politeness: Some Universals in Language Use*. Cambridge: Cambridge University Press.

Christie, Christine. 2000. *Gender and Language: Towards a Feminist Pragmatics*. Edinburgh: Edinburgh University Press.

Eckert, Penelope. 2000. *Linguistic Variation as Social Practice*. Oxford: Blackwell.

Kasper, Gabriele and Shoshana Blum-Kulka (eds.) 1993. *Interlanguage Pragmatics*. Oxford: Oxford University Press.

Mey, Jacob L. 1993. *Pragmatics: An Introduction*. Oxford: Blackwell.

Philips, Susan. 1983. *The Invisible Culture: Communication in Classrooms and Communities on the Warm Springs Indian Reservation*. New York: Longman.

Rose, Kenneth R. and Gabriele Kasper. 2001. *Pragmatics in Language Teaching*. Cambridge: Cambridge University Press.

Schiffrin, Deborah. 1994. *Approaches to Discourse*. Oxford: Blackwell.

5

Narrative Analysis: Oral Versions of Personal Experience

William Labov and Joshua Waletzky

Most attempts to analyze narrative have taken as their subject matter the more complex products of long-standing literary or oral traditions. Myths, folk tales, legends, histories, epics, toasts, and sagas seem to be the results of the combination and evolution of simpler elements; they contain many cycles and recycles of basic narrative structures; in many cases, the evolution of a particular narrative has removed it so far from its originating function that it is difficult to say what its present function is.

In our opinion, it will not be possible to make very much progress in the analysis and understanding of these complex narratives until the simplest and most fundamental narrative structures are analyzed in direct connection with their originating functions. We suggest that such fundamental structures are to be found in oral versions of personal experiences: not the products of expert storytellers that have been retold many times, but the original production of a representative sample of the population. By examining the actual narratives of large numbers of unsophisticated speakers, it will be possible to relate the formal properties of narrative to their functions. By studying the development of narrative technique from children to adults, and the range of narrative techniques from lower-class to middle-class speakers, it will be possible to isolate the elements of narrative.

In this article, we will present an analytical framework for the analysis of oral versions of personal experience in English. We will first introduce definitions of the basic units of narrative and then outline the normal structure of the narrative as a whole. Finally, we present some general propositions about the relation of formal properties to narrative functions, based on our examination of a moderate body of data.

The analysis will be *formal*, based upon recurrent patterns characteristic of narrative from the clause level to the complete simple narrative. We will rely upon the basic techniques of linguistic analysis, isolating the invariant structural units, which are represented by a variety of superficial forms. From this analysis it is possible to derive a considerable amount of information on the syntax and semantics of English below the sentence level, but this direction of research will not be exploited here. We will be concerned primarily with the characteristics of narrative itself.

The analysis is *functional*: Narrative will be considered as one verbal technique for recapitulating experience – in particular, a technique of constructing narrative units that match the *temporal sequence* of that experience. Furthermore, we find that narrative that serves this function alone is abnormal: it may be considered empty or pointless narrative. Normally, narrative serves an additional function of personal interest, determined by a stimulus in the social context in which the narrative occurs. We therefore distinguish two functions of narrative: (a) *referential* and (b) *evaluative*.

In most previous studies of folk narrative, the basic unit for analysis has been a substantial piece of thematic material, defined at various levels of abstraction by the type of action referred to. Thus the work of Propp (1958) was devoted to the formal structure of such large semantic units. The present study assumes as a basic task the analysis of narratives that might appear as fundamental, unanalyzable units in Propp's scheme. We will be concerned with the smallest unit of linguistic expression that defines the functions of narrative – primarily the clause, although we will refer to cases where phrases and words are relevant to evaluative function. Colby's work (1966) took as data the frequencies of individual words according to a semantic subcategorization; a linguistic approach is quite opposite in direction, focusing upon the syntagmatic structure of words and phrases operating in clauses and higher levels of organization. Schatzman and Strauss (1955) studied class differences in narrative technique by informal means; it is hoped that the methods developed in the present discussion will permit a more reliable and objective approach to studies of this type.

We will be dealing with tape-recorded narratives taken from two distinct social contexts. One is a face-to-face interview where the narrator is speaking only to the interviewer, a person not a member of a narrator's primary group. In the second situation, the narrator is recorded in interaction with his primary group, he is speaking in part to the members of his group, and in part to an outsider on the margins of the group, who provides only a part of the stimulus for the narrative.

The following pages provide 14 examples of the data on hand, drawn from about 600 interviews gathered in the course of four linguistic studies.[1] The narrators include speakers from Black and White communities, rural and urban areas, and they range in age from 10 to 72 years old. In one respect the range is limited: There are no highly educated speakers represented here; in fact, none of the narrators finished high school.

The ultimate aims of our work require close correlations of the narrator's social characteristics with the structure of their narratives, since we are concerned with problems of effective communication and class and ethnic differences in verbal behavior.[2] In this article, however, we are concerned with the narratives themselves, and so these fourteen examples appear as anonymous narrations, arranged in descending order of the speakers' ages.

Narrative 1
(Were you ever in a situation where you thought you were in serious danger of getting killed?) I talked a man out of – Old Doc Simon I talked him out of pulling the trigger. (What happened?)

Well, in the business I was associated at that time, the Doc was an old man . . . He had killed one man, or – had done time. But he had a – young wife, and those days I dressed well. And seemingly she was trying to make me.

I never noticed it. Fact is, I didn't like her very well, because she had – she was a nice looking girl until you saw her feet. She had big feet. Jesus, God, she had big feet!

Then she left a note one day she was going to commit suicide because he was always raising hell about me. He came to my hotel. Nice big blue 44, too.

I talked him out of it; and says, "Well, we'll go look for her, and if we can't find her, well you can – go ahead, pull the trigger if you want to." I was maneuvering.

So he took me up on it. And we went to where they found her handkerchief – the edge of a creek – and we followed down a little more, and we couldn't find anything. And got back – it was a tent show – she was laying on a cot with an ice bag on her head. She hadn't committed suicide.

But – however – that settled it for the day. But that night the manager, Floyd Adams, said, "You better pack up and get out because that son of a bitch never forgives anything once he gets it in his head."

And I did. I packed up and got out. That was two.

That was two.

After I came out from New York . . .

NARRATIVE 2

I had dogs that could do everything but talk. And by gorry, sir, I never licked 'em.

(When you have small kids, they're always asking for one more thing, like a drink of water, to keep from going to bed at night. I wonder if you had that problem, and what you did about it?) Yeah, but – a lot of the children I've seen, that their excuse they've got to go to the bathroom, and they don't have to go at all. (How do you cope with it. You can't – you never know . . .) No. I don't remember how we coped with it. I never believed a whole lot in licking. I was never – with my children, and I never – when it was with my animals, dogs; I never licked a dog, I never had to. A dog knew what I meant; when I hollered at a dog, he knew the – what I meant. I could – I had dogs that could do everything but talk. And by gorry, sir, I never licked 'em.

I never come nearer bootin' a dog in my life. I had a dog – he was a wonderful retriever, but as I say he could do everything but talk. I could waif him that way, I could waif him on, I could waif him anywhere. If I shot a crippled duck he went out after it; he didn't see it in the water, he'd always turn around look at me, and I'd waif him over there, if the duck was there, or if it was on the other side of where we're on, I could waif him straight ahead, and he'd turn and he'd go. If he didn't see me, he'd turn around, he'd look at me, and I'd keep a-awaifin' him on. And he'd finally catch sight of him, and the minute he did, you know, he would bee-line and get that duck.

I was gunnin' one night with that dog – we had to use live decoys in those days – a fellow named Jack Bumpus was with me; I was over at a place called Deep Bottom, darker than pitch. And – uh – heard a quackin' off shore. And, I said to Jack, "Keep quiet. There's one comin' in." And – uh – finally Jack said to me, "I think I see 'im." I said, "Give 'im a gun. Give 'im a gun. Try it."

So he shot, and this duck went for the shore with his wings a-goin' like that for the shore. Went up on the shore. Well this dog never lost a crippled duck on shore, he'd take a track just the same as a hound would take a rabbit track. And I sent him over. I said, "Go ahead."

So he went over there. And – gone a while and come back and he didn't have the duck. And that was unusual – I said, "You git back there and get that duck!" And he went back there; and he stayed a little while longer, longer than he did the first time, and he come back and he didn't have that duck.

And I never come nearer shootin' a dog. By gorry. I come pretty near. "*You git back there and get that duck!*" And that dog went back there, and he didn't come back. And he didn't come back. By gorry, we went over there – I walked over there, and here he was; one of my tame ducks that I had tethered out there had got the strap off her leg, and had gone out there, and when this fellow shot, he hadn't hit the duck. The duck came to the shore, he hadn't hit the duck; but the duck was scared and come for the shore. My dog was over there, and he had his paw right on top of that duck, holdin' him down just as tight as could be, and – by gorry, boy, I patted that dog, I'll tell you if I ever walloped that dog I'd have felt some bad. He knew more 'n I did: the dog knew more than I did. He knew that was that tame duck: he wasn't gonna pick him up in his mouth and bring him, you know. He was just holdin' him right down on the ground.

NARRATIVE 3

(Were you ever in a situation where you were in serious danger of being killed?) My brother put a knife in my head. (How'd that happen?) Like kids, you get into a fight and I twisted his arm up behind him.

This was just a few days after my father had died, and we were sitting shive. And the reason the fight started . . . He sort of ran out of the yard – this was out on Coney Island – and he started talk about it. And my mother had just sat down to have a cup of coffee. And I told him to cut it out.

Course kids, you know – he don't hafta listen to me. So that's when I grabbed him by the arm, and twisted it up behind him. When I let go his arm, there was a knife on the table, he just picked it up and he let me have it. And I started bleed like a pig.

And, naturally, first thing was – run to the doctor. And the doctor just says, "Just about this much more," he says, "and you'd a been dead."

NARRATIVE 4

. . . They didn't believe in calling the law or anything like that. They just took things in their own hands. (Did you ever see any shooting of that sort?) Oh, yes. I can remember real well. I w's just a girl. 'Fact, stayed with me quite a while.

Well, there's a fellow, his name was Martin Cassidy 'n' Bill Hatfield. Mr. Cassidy's mother gave him some money an' tell him to go get a bushel of peaches. An' he went down to Martin's house. An' Martin had some moonshine there.

Back down there, they make their own liquor, you know. So – we call it moonshine. Today, they call it white lightnin'; but at that time we call it moonshine.

An' I remember real well what happened. Bunch of us kids was out there playin'; an' no one meanin' any harm about it. But anyway, Mrs. Hatfield come down an' took away her money from Mr. Hatfield, you know, for the peaches, cause she know what he was gonna buy drinks with it. 'Nd Mr. Cassidy was laying out there in the yard.

And Mr. Cassidy just looked up, and he said to Bill, just – just jokin', just in a kiddin' way, he said "Uh huh," he says, "that's – another dollar bill you won't get to spend for drinks, hunh?"

'Nd Bill said, "I'll fix you, ya so-and-so."

So he walked in Martin Cassidy's *house*, his own house, came out with a double-bitted axe, hit him down 'crost the head once, turned over and hit him again, then throwed the axe down and run through the woods.

Just over two dollars that he was sent for peaches with.

NARRATIVE 5

(Were you ever in a situation where you were in serious danger of being killed?) Yes. (What happened?) I don't really like to talk about it. (Well, tell me as much about it as you can?)

Well, this person had a little too much to drink, and he attacked me, and a friend came in, and she stopped it.

NARRATIVE 6

(Were you ever in a situation where you were in serious danger of being killed?)

Yeah, I was in the Boy Scouts at the time. And we was doing the 50-yard dash, racing, but we was at the pier, marked off, and so we was doing the 50-yard dash. There was about eight or nine of us, you know, going down, coming back.

And going down the *third* time, I caught cramps and I started yelling "Help!", but the fellows didn't believe me, you know. They thought I was just trying to catch up, because I was going on or slowing down. So all of them kept going. They leave me.

And so I started going down. Scoutmaster was up there. He was watching me. But he didn't pay me no attention either. And for no reason at all there was another guy, who had just walked up that minute . . . He just jumped over and grabbed me.

NARRATIVE 7

(And what about the street fight?) Then – ah – well, street fight, the most important, lemme see. (You know, the one that you remember the most.) Well, I had quite a lot. Well, one, I think, was with a girl [laughter]. Like, I was a kid, you know.

And she was the baddest girl – *the baddest girl in the neighborhood.* If you didn't bring her candy – to school, she'd punch you in the mouth. And you had to kiss her when she['d] tell you. This girl was only about twelve years old, man, but she was a killer. She didn't take no junk. She whupped all her brothers.

And I came to school one day, and I didn't have no money; my ma wouldn't give me no money. And I played hookies one day. First time I played hookies, man, put sump'n on me, so I said, you know, I'm not gonna play hookies no more, 'cause I don't want to get a whuppin'.

So I go to school, and this girl says, "Where's the candy?" I said, "I don't have it." She says, powwww!! So I says to myself, "Well, there's gonna be times my mother won't give me money because a poor family, and I can't take this all – and and, you know – every time she don't give me any money. So I say, well, I just gotta fight the girl. She gonna hafta whup me. I hope she [don't] whup me."

And I hit the girl: powwww!!

NARRATIVE 8

(Were you ever in a situation where you were in serious danger of being killed?) I'm gonna die? When I was drownin', I didn't know – like, I was turnin' tumblesauts. But that was the only time.

I – I was in a fight downtown once. Like – I went down to a party, and – this – this guy was a soldier – and this guy was a soldier, and he comes on, "gimme a cigarette."

I said, "I don't have any cigarette."

"Well, lemme search you."

I said, "You're not gonna search me."

"Well – I'm a soldier, and I know judo."

I said, "Well, I don't – I don't care if you're a *cop* and you know karate, you're not gonna search me."

And he hit me, man, like I hit him. And like, I – I got next to the guy. He didn't get a chance to use nothing, and I put sump'm on him.

I had – had a couple of guys with me. So we walked around the corner, – after, you know, I knocked him down a couple of times. I said "Well, you know, we'll soon get it."

I walk around the corner about twenty guys come after us, down by the projects. And we're runnin' – and, like – I couldn't run as fast as the other guys. And they was catchin' up to me. And I crossed the street, and I tripped, man. And, like, when I tripped, they kicked me and they was on me and I said, "Like this is it, man"; I pulled a knife.

But – a guy I know from the projects came over and gave me a hand.

And that – that was it, you know. That was it.

NARRATIVE 9

(Did you ever have a feeling, or a premonition, that something was gonna happen, and it did?) Yes, I did. (Tell me about it.)

I was goin' with a girl, one time; we were layin' on a bed – we weren't doin anything, we were talkin' – and, I don't know, I looked into her face, and I saw, like, horns coming out of her head. You know. You know – like – I said, "You look like the devil!"

She said, "What do you mean, I look like the devil?"

"Don't kid around," I said, "I'm not kiddin'. I saw horns comin' out of your head."

And the girl got very angry and walked out. But, we got together, and we went together for about four months.

And, like, this girl tried to put me in a couple of tricks. Like she tried to get some boys to hurt me. You know. And she was a devil.

So, now, anything I see I believe it's going to happen.

NARRATIVE 10

(Did you ever see anybody get beat up real bad?)

I know a boy name Harry. Another boy threw a bottle at him right in the head, and he had to get seven stitches.

NARRATIVE 11

(What was the last cartoon you saw on television?) I don't know, I was watching the Sandy Becker show. (What was the story about?) About this pig. (What happened?)

See he – they threw him out, you know. So he wanted to get back in, 'cause, you know, it was sn– raining hard. So he got on this boat and tried to – go somewhere else. And the boat went over. And he tried to swim.

So this other man was fishing in the rain. So he seen the pig, and went over there and, and picked the pig up and put it in the boat and brought it back to shore, so he would land there.

And that was that.

NARRATIVE 12

(What was the most important fight you remember?)

When I was in fourth grade – no – it was third grade – there was this boy, he stole my glove.

He took my glove, and say that his father found it downtown on the ground. I told him that he – it's impossible for him to find downtown, 'cause all those people were walking by, and just his father is the only one that find it? So he get all upset.

Then I fought him. I knocked him all in the street. So he say he give. And I kept on hitting him. Then he start crying and run home to his father.

And his father told him, he ain't find no glove.

NARRATIVE 13

. . . See, Napoleon he took the ring and put it on the maiden. It was a statue of the maiden. Then he put it on her finger where the ring's supposed to be, and then he put it on the 45° angle. And then he looked in, and then he saw the place where the project was made at. And everything wh – the doctor who made it was dead.

So he came. He took him and the boy – the boy asked could he see it, and when the boy started to see it, he had this thing on – this patch or something – on his back. The Japanese leader could trace him by that patch because, you know, by radar.

And then – he started – so he took the patch off the boy and put it on the dog. And he took a stick and threw it in the water and the dog ran after it. And the radar – it went in the water with the dog.

And then – Napoleon and the dog started running – I mean, Napoleon and the boy started running, and they started running to the place where the project was made. And they started running to the place. And then, when they got there, they found that all of it was dried up and everything.

So when they started to leave out, he had a Japanese man first tell him to surrender. And before he told him to surrender, the dog – the dog came in there. The dog had found them. And the Japanese man came and told 'em to surrender.

See, they was inside the cave and the Japanese man was outside. And he told them to surrender. And he didn't surrender. He first – he told them that he made a trap. Then he said, "You can come in and make sure the project is all washed up," 'cause it was no more there. And they came.

When he sent one of his men to India . . .

NARRATIVE 14

(Did Calvin do something that was really wild?) Yeah. We made Calvin hit – I say, "Calv –"

See, we – it was on a Sunday, and we didn't have nothin' to do after I – after we came from church. Then we ain't had nothin' to do.

So I say, "Calvin, let's go get out – put our dirty clothes on so we can play in the dirt."

And so Calvin say, "Let's have a rock – a rock war." And I say, "All right."

So Calvin had a rock and we, you know – here go a wall and a faraway go a wall. Calvin threw a rock. I was lookin' and – uh – and Calvin threw a rock. It oh – it almost hit me.

So I looked down to get another rock.

Say "Sssh!" an' it pass me.

I say, "Calvin, I'm bust your head for that."

Calvin stuck his head out. I th'ew the rock, and the rock went up, I mean it went up, came down, and say [slap], and smacked him in the head and his head busted.

These fourteen examples cover a wide variety of types, from extremely short to relatively long, from highly organized structures to simple serial types. In addition to the narrative themselves, enough preliminary quotation is given so that one can obtain some idea of the stimulus to which the narratives respond – a matter quite relevant to the functional analysis of narrative.

Some difficult questions arise as we examine these narratives:

1. Though each is presented as a single narrative, how in fact do we know whether one or more narratives are contained in a given example? Is narrative structure well enough defined that we can answer this question? For instance, is Narrative 5 a narrative or a fragment of a narrative? Is Narrative 13 a fragment of a narrative or three separate narratives?

2. The structural framework of the narrative cannot be studied profitably without saying something about the sequence of events to which it refers. The fundamental

question of narrative analysis appears to be this: How can we relate the sequence of clauses in the narrative to the sequence of events inferred from the narrative?

We will attempt to answer these questions in the following discussion.

1 The Basic Framework of Narrative

1.1 Temporal sequence

We have defined narrative informally as one method of recapitulating past experience by matching a verbal sequence of clauses to the sequence of events that actually occurred. For example, in Narrative 5 we have four independent clauses that refer to four successive events or situations:

(5)
 a   Well, this person had a little too much to drink
 b   and he attacked me
 c   and the friend came in
 d   and she stopped it.

The temporal sequence of narrative is an important defining property that proceeds from its referential function. Narrative is not the only method for referring to a sequence of events; all recapitulation of experience is not narrative. For example, the events of Narrative 5 might have been presented in the following way:

(5′)
 c   A friend of mine came in
 d   just in time to stop
 a   this person who had a little too much to drink
 b   from attacking me.

This form of presenting events depends on syntactic embedding. However, not all alternatives to narrative require this type of subordination. The following series of four independent clauses presents the same material in reverse order:

(5″)
 d   A friend of mine stopped the attack.
 c   She had just come in.
 b   This person was attacking me.
 a   He had had a little too much to drink.

Despite the fact that these two formulations are perfectly logical, orderly, and acceptable ways of representing a sequence of events, they are not narratives as we are about to define the concept. The basic narrative units that we wish to isolate are defined by the fact that they recapitulate experience in the same order as the original events.

However, inspection of the other examples shows that the relationships between clauses and events are not simple. For instance, in Narrative 3:

(3)
d   and we were sitting shive.
e   And the reason the fight started . . .
f   He sort of ran out in the yard –
g   this was out on Coney Island –
h   and he started talk about it;
i   and my mother had just sat down to have a cup of coffee
j   and I told him to cut it out.

The sequence of clauses d through j does not match the sequence of events and situations inferred from the narrative. The situation described in g ("This was out on Coney Island") certainly did not follow f ("He sort of ran out of the yard"); the event of i ("and my mother had just sat down to have a cup of coffee") did not follow h ("and he started talk about it") – rather, it preceded it; the referent of clause e is not temporally ordered with relation to any of the events ("and the reason the fight started"). The clauses that do refer to events clearly in the sequence are:

(3′)
f   He sort of ran out in the yard
h   and he started talk about it
j   and I told him to cut it out.

So far, we have discussed clauses in general as narrative units. But it can quickly be seen that only independent clauses are relevant to temporal sequence. Subordinate clauses (like the embedded clauses seen in formulation 5′) may be placed anywhere in the narrative sequence without disturbing the temporal order of the semantic interpretation, as in the next example taken from Narrative 1:

(1)
k   Then she left a note one day
l   she was going to commit suicide
m   because he was always raising hell about me.

Here clause l ("she was going to commit suicide") is the familiar construction of indirect discourse in which we refer to the fact that a person in the past referred to an event that would occur sometime in the future. Clause m, on the other hand, refers to events prior to clause k. One can quote any number of examples to show that any subordinate clause is removed from the temporal sequence of narrative, even if it retains its own temporal reference.

These considerations illustrate the motivation for the definitions of the narrative clause to be developed later in this article. These elements will be characterized by *temporal sequence*: Their order cannot be changed without changing the inferred sequence of events in the original semantic interpretation.

1.2   Displacement sets

The following operations provide a formal basis for establishing temporal sequence among the independent clauses of a narrative. Each clause is assigned a sequential symbol (using lowercase letters), as in the next example from Narrative 8:

(8)

w   and they was catchin' up to me
x   and I crossed the street
y   and I tripped, man.

Each clause is then tested for the potential range of displacement by examining the semantic interpretation that results when the clause in question is moved to all possible positions in the remaining sequence. For example, we find that x can be placed before w without changing the original semantic interpretation, since we can infer that the process of catching up extended throughout the sequence:

(8′)

x   and I crossed the street
w   and they was catchin' up to me
y   and I tripped, man.

But x cannot be placed after y without changing the original interpretation, as in:

(8″)

w   and they was catchin' up to me
y   and I tripped, man
x   and I crossed the street.

The result of these operations is indicated in the following system of subscripts. For the clause c, the symbol $_a c_p$ indicates that c can be placed before any and all of the preceding a clauses and after any of the following p clauses without changing the temporal sequence of the original semantic interpretation.

The set consisting of the clauses before which c can be placed, c itself, and the clauses after which c can be placed, is the *displacement set* of c, symbolized DS(c).

Thus, for the partial sequence of w, x, and y discussed previously, we have

(8‴)

$_0 w_2$ and they was catchin' up to me $DS(w) = \{w, x, y\}$
$_1 x_0$ and I crossed the street $DS(x) = \{w, x\}$
$_0 y_0$ and I tripped, man. $DS(y) = \{y\}$

1.3   Narrative clauses and free clauses

Two extreme types of displacement ranges that result from this operation are

$_0 c_0$ and $_{x-1} c_{n-x}$

in which n is the total number of clauses in a sequence. The $_0c_0$ clause, with a displacement set of $\{c\}$, is locked in position in the sequence; it evidently functions as a *narrative clause* of the simplest kind, maintaining the strict temporal sequence that is the defining characteristic of narrative. The $_{x-1}c_{n-x}$ clause, on the other hand, has a displacement set equal to the entire narrative and can range freely through the narrative sequence. This type may be termed a *free clause*.

1.4   Coordinate clauses

Although the free clause has no fixed relation to the temporal sequence, and the simple $_0c_0$ narrative clause is strictly ordered by temporal sequence, there are other types of clauses that have more complex relations to narrative sequence. We frequently find sequences of the type $_0c_1$ $_1d_0$, as in this extract from Narrative 14:

(14)

$_0s_0$ [and the rock] came down

$_0t_1$ and smacked him in the head

$_1u_0$ and say (slap!)

Clauses t and u might just as well have been reversed:

(14′)

$_0s_0$ [and the rock] came down

$_0u_1$ and say (slap!)

$_1t_0$ and smacked him on the head

Both t and u have identical displacement sets, $DS(t) = \{t, u\}$, $DS(u) = \{t, u\}$, and they may be freely interchanged without any change in temporal sequence. Clauses with identical displacement sets may be termed *coordinate clauses*. (All free clauses are coordinate in this sense, since they all have the same displacement sets, but it is the coordinate nature of certain narrative clauses that is our primary concern.)

   One can, of course, have three or more coordinate clauses in a single sequence, as in the following extract from Narrative 1:

(1)

$_0l_0$ He came to my hotel. Nice big blue 44 too.

$_0m_3$ I talked him out of it,

$_1n_2$ and says, "Well, we'll go look for her,

$_2o_1$ and if we can't find her, well you can – go ahead, pull the trigger if you want to."

$_3p_0$ I was maneuvering.

$_0q_0$ So he took me up on it.

Here clauses m, n, o, and p are coordinate, with identical displacement sets (m, n, o, p), because they could occur in any of the six possible permutations without altering the temporal sequence of the original semantic interpretation. But none of these could be placed before l ("He came to my hotel") or after q ("So he took me up on it").

1.5 Restricted clauses

The narrative clauses that we have considered are of two general forms, $_0c_0$ and $_0c_1$ $_1d_0$, and appear to have one feature in common. Their displacement sets range from a left zero subscript to a right zero subscript, with no zeros in between. We also find in narratives a third type of clause that does not range freely over the entire narrative, yet has a wider range than the narrative clause. This type of clause has a displacement set that may range across several left or right zero subscripts. Such clauses, which are neither free nor temporally ordered in the strict sense, may be termed *restricted clauses*.

It may be now helpful to consider a narrative as a whole to illustrate the nature of free clauses, coordinate clauses, and restricted clauses and to show how the displacement sets of such clauses are determined. Narrative 6 may be analyzed as follows:

(6)

$_0a_{18}$	yeh I was in the boy scouts at the time	DS {a–s}
$_1b_{17}$	and we was doing the 50-yard dash	"
$_2c_{16}$	racing	"
$_3d_{15}$	but we was at the pier, marked off	"
$_4e_{14}$	and so we was doing the 50-yard dash	"
$_5f_{13}$	there was about eight or ten of us, you know, going down, coming back	"
$_6g_0$	and, going down the *third* time, I caught cramps	{a–g}
$_0h_0$	and I started yelling "Help!"	{h}
$_0i_1$	but the fellows didn't believe me, you know,	{i–j}
$_1j_0$	they thought I was just trying to catch up because I was going on or slowing down	{i–j}
$_0k_1$	so all of them kept going	{k–l}
$_1l_0$	they leave me	{k–l}
$_0m_3$	and so I started going down	{m–p}
$_{13}n_5$	Scoutmaster was up there	{a–s}
$_6o_3$	he was watching me	{i–r}
$_7p_2$	but he didn't pay me no attention either	{i–r}
$_0q_0$	and for no reason at all there was another guy, who had just walked up that minute . . .	{q}
$_0r_0$	he just jumped over	{r}
$_0s_0$	and grabbed me	{s}

Narrative 6 begins with six free clauses, all of which can range over the entire narrative; for each of these, the sum of the subscripts is 18. The third clause, *racing*, is in apposition with *doing* in the second clause, and is treated as derived from *we was racing*. It must be analyzed separately, because it is possible that such an appositive could be temporally ordered in respect to other clauses.[3] The situation and action described in these six clauses prevails throughout the entire narrative: that is, the *8 or 9 of us* continue racing even when the narrator himself is in trouble.

The first narrative clause is g, with a displacement set of {a, b, c, d, e, f, g}, ranging from the left zero of a to its own right zero. Clauses i and j are coordinate clauses of the type just discussed, and so are k and l.

Clause m is a narrative clause with a displacement set ranging over the three following clauses. These following clauses are not in strict narrative sequence; the first one, n, is a free clause ("Scoutmaster was up there"). It should be understood that the test for displacement range must include a procedure for adjusting anaphoric reference. "Scoutmaster was up there" would be a strange utterance in initial position, but if we supply the referent of "there – at the pier," we have "Scoutmaster was up at the pier," which could stand in initial position without changing the temporal sequence of the original semantic interpretation. The reverse situation would apply if a specific free clause in initial position, with several proper names, was displaced to a point later in the narrative: pronoun substitution would be made.

The second clause, o, ("He was watching me") is a restricted clause, with DS(o) = {i–r} extending before n. It could have been placed at any point after h ("I started yelling 'Help!'"), that is, after the action that called the scoutmaster's attention to the narrator and logically motivated his action. It is worth following the logic of this argument in detail, because it is typical of the method for establishing the displacement sets of restricted clauses.

While it is true that the scoutmaster's job was to watch everyone, we interpret the statement o ("He was watching me") to mean that there was a significant change at one point, from watching everyone to watching the narrator in particular. This interpretation hinges on the word "either" – this word coordinates the negation of "He didn't pay me no attention" with some previous negative statement; the first preceding negative clause is i ("the fellows didn't believe me."). Therefore, we can conclude that both of these statements refer to events that responded to clause h ("and I started yelling 'Help!'"). Therefore, the displacement sets of o and p cannot include h without a change in the temporal sequence of the original semantic interpretation.

On the other hand, clause o could range towards the end, at any point up to clause s. If clause o appeared after s, then the same temporal inference that we now draw – that the scoutmaster began watching after the cry for help – would be altered. It would be the grabbing of the narrator by the "other guy" that would mark the beginning of the scoutmaster's watching.

The same argument holds for clause p, which is a restricted clause with the same range as o.

The rest of the narrative consists of simple $_0c_0$ narrative units. Clause q ("for no reason at all there was another guy") has the temporal status of a punctual act, appearance: the viewpoint is clearly that of the narrator.

Figure 1 is a graphic display of these statements about the displacement sets of the clauses concerned. Each clause is represented by a mark opposite the alphabetic symbol, and the vertical line running through this mark represents the displacement set. We will return to this diagram later in discussing the normal structure of narrative as a whole.

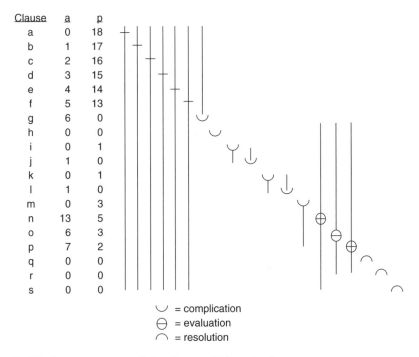

Clause	a	p
a	0	18
b	1	17
c	2	16
d	3	15
e	4	14
f	5	13
g	6	0
h	0	0
i	0	1
j	1	0
k	0	1
l	1	0
m	0	3
n	13	5
o	6	3
p	7	2
q	0	0
r	0	0
s	0	0

⌣ = complication
⊖ = evaluation
⌢ = resolution

Figure 1   Displacement ranges of the clauses of Narrative 6

1.6   Temporal juncture

If narrative clauses succeed each other in uninterrupted sequence, the zero subscripts alone would show the temporal segmentation of the narrative. But because any number of free or restricted units can intervene between two narrative clauses, we must define temporal relations between any two clauses in the narrative, not necessarily contiguous. We wish to define formally the condition under which any two clauses are ordered with respect to each other and cannot be interchanged without change in the temporal sequence of the original semantic interpretation. Such a condition is met when the displacement range of a given clause does not extend past the actual location of some following clause, and conversely, the displacement range of this following clause does not extend past the actual location of the given preceding clause. More concisely, their displacement sets do not include each other. Two such clauses are temporally ordered with respect to each other. Their displacement sets may in fact overlap, but the displacement set of c will not include d, and that of d will not include c if c and d are temporally ordered.

Two clauses that are temporally ordered with respect to each other are said to be separated by *temporal juncture*. This juncture has no relation to any free or restricted clauses that may fall in between the temporally ordered clauses. In Narrative 6, given in full previously, we find temporal junctures between g and h, h and i, j and k, l and m, m and q, q and r, r and s. Since i and j, k and l are coordinate, we can best represent these junctures by the following diagram:

g   I caught cramps
h   and I started yelling
ij   the fellows didn't believe; they thought I was
kl   all of them kept going; they leave me
m   I started going down
q   there was another guy
r   he just jumped over
s   and grabbed me.

1.7   Definition of the narrative clause

We can now proceed to define the basic unit of narrative, the narrative clause, in terms of temporal juncture and displacement sets. It is characteristic of a narrative clause that it cannot be displaced across a temporal juncture without a change in the temporal sequence of the original semantic interpretation. Therefore if the displacement set of a given clause does not contain two clauses that are temporally ordered with respect to each other, then that clause is a *narrative clause*. More simply, we can say that a narrative clause has an *unordered displacement set*. If the displacement set is ordered – that is, if some members are temporally ordered with respect to each other – then the given clause is a restricted clause or a free clause. If such an ordered set is equal to the narrative as a whole, the clause is a *free clause*; if not, a *restricted clause*.

We can restate these definitions formally in the following manner. A narrative N may be represented as a set of n clauses

$$c^1, c^2 \ldots c^i \ldots c^n$$

in which $0 \leq I \leq n$. Then

1. $c^i \in DS(c^j)$ if $c^i \ldots c^j$ and $c^j \ldots c^i$ yield the same temporal sequence in semantic interpretation [or if $c^i = c^j$]
2.   If $c^i \in DS(c^k)$ and $c^j \in DS(c^k)$
     and $c^i \notin DS(c^i)$ and $c^j \notin DS(c^i)$
     a.   and $DS(c^k) = N$, then c^k is a free clause.
     b.   and $DS(c^k) < N$, then c^k is a restricted clause.
3.   If condition 2 does not hold, c^k is a narrative clause.

1.8   Definition of a narrative

We can now define quite simply those sequences of clauses that we will consider as narratives. Any sequence of clauses that contains at least one temporal juncture is a narrative. Thus

(10)
$_0a_2$ I know a boy name Harry.
$_1b_0$ Another boy threw a bottle at him right in the head,
$_0c_0$ and he had to get seven stitches.

is a narrative, because a temporal juncture is found between b and c. A statement such as "I shot and killed him" would be a narrative, because it contains a temporal juncture, but not "I laughed and laughed at him." There are many ambiguous cases that allow two distinct interpretations: "I punched him in the head, the mouth and the chest" is normally a list, which does not imply that he was punched first in the head, then in the mouth, and then in the chest. But the temporal interpretation is possible, and it is more likely in "I beat him up and stomped on him."

The upper bound of narrative is not set by this approach, and the question of deciding between one narrative or two must be left to the section that deals with the overall structure of narrative.

1.9   Narrative heads

The finite verb of a narrative clause, which carries the tense marker of the clause, is the *narrative head* of that clause. Heads of coordinate clauses are coordinate heads.

(2)
$_0u_0$ And – gone a while
$_0v_0$ and come back
$_0w_1$ and he didn't have the duck.
$_0x_{31}$ And that was unusual –
$_1y_0$ I said, "You git back there
$_0z_0$ and get that duck."[4]
$_0aa_0$ And he went back there;

Here, the narrative heads are *gone, come, did-, was, said, said*, and *went*. The types of grammatical forms and categories that can function as grammatical heads are extremely limited. The principal forms are simple past and simple present. As a rule, no modals appear; abstractly considered, it is possible that *could* could function as a narrative head, though no examples have been found in our materials to date. The progressive (past and possibly present) does appear occasionally as a narrative unit:

(1)
$_0u_1$ and got back
$_{21}v_9$ it was a tent show
$_1w_1$ she was laying on a cot with an ice bag on her head.
$_{12}x_7$ She hadn't committed suicide.
$_1y_0$ But – however – that settled it for the day.

In this example, "was laying" is in temporal order; it can be displayed before the free unit v and after the restricted unit x, but not before u or after y without changing the temporal sequence of the semantic interpretation. There is considerable semantic and syntactic interest in the questions raised by this use of the past progressive,[5] and many other such issues are raised by the data of narrative analysis; however, this article is confined to the description of the basic units and framework of narrative, and such questions are not pursued here.

In general, the present perfect does not appear in narrative.[6] The past perfect, as noted before, does not function as a narrative head. However, if the clause with the past perfect refers to an event developed in the narrative, rather than to some event preceding the entire narrative, it can function as a restrictive clause. This is the case in Clause x in Narrative 1. Although x would have been true in initial position, it would not have referred to the particular suicide threatened in Clause k. In its present position, x asserts that the threat of k was not consummated at some time prior to the moment in which x is stated – necessarily before the next preceding narrative unit. Therefore, x can be placed before the disclosure of w, at any point after k. It can also occur at any point after the disclosure w with no change in temporal sequence.

A series of past perfect narrative heads can be used to describe a set of events in temporal sequence, placing the entire set at some point prior to the preceding narrative unit.

(2)

$_0$nn$_0$	I walked over there
$_0$oo$_{18}$	And here he was;
$_{42}$pp$_{17}$	one of my tame ducks that I had tethered out there had got the strap off her leg,
$_{43}$qq$_{16}$	and had gone out there,
$_{30}$rr$_{15}$	and when this fellow shot he hadn't hit the duck

It is true that the three clauses pp, qq, and rr are here in temporal sequence. But no permutation of their order will produce a different temporal sequence in semantic interpretation:

$_0$oo$_{18}$	and here he was
$_{28}$rr$_{17}$	and when this fellow shot he hadn't hit the duck
$_{43}$qq$_{16}$	one of my tame ducks that I had tethered out there had gone out there
$_{44}$pp$_{15}$	She had got the strap off her leg.[7]

As indicated by the subscripts, pp and qq are free clauses, and rr is restricted – it cannot precede the shot itself, but can follow at any later point.

1.10   Related narrative sequences

The definitions we have given for narrative units are deliberately applied to the linear sequence presented by the narrator. This linear sequence may be considered the *surface structure* of the narrative; there are often many narratives with rather different surface structures, but with equivalent semantic interpretations. In the same way, there are many sentences with different surface structures that correspond to the same underlying string of formatives in the original phrase structure of a grammar:

a   The rock say "shhh!"
b   "shhh!" is what the rock say
c   What the rock say is "shhh!"
d   It's a fact that the rock say "shhh!"
e   The rock's saying "shhh!"

In previous discussions, we showed that for each series of events described in a narrative, there are other equivalent means of verbal statement besides narrative. There are also equivalent narratives with the same semantic (temporal) interpretation. It is useful to relate all of these to a single underlying form, just as sentences b through e are related to the simplest form, a. To do this, we must consider the fundamental semantic relation in narrative.

The semantic interpretation of a narrative, as we have defined it, depends on the expectation that the events described did, in fact, occur in the same order as they were told in. Thus the sequence

$_0a_0$ he attacked me
$_0b_0$ the friend came in

with temporal juncture between a and b, is equivalent in its semantic interpretation to

$_0a_0$ he attacked me
       then
$_0b_0$ the friend came in

That is, the temporal juncture is semantically equivalent to the temporal conjunction *then*.

Of course, the a-then-b relation is not the only one at work in narrative. If it were, we would have only a succession of narrative clauses. One also finds implied relations between clauses such as a-and at the same time-b, or a-and now that I think back on it-b. But among these temporal relations, the a-then-b is in some sense the most essential characteristic of narrative. Some narratives (see Narrative 5) may use it exclusively, and every narrative must, by definition, use it at least once.

Though some of these relations are marked explicitly, the majority of them are implied by certain lexical and grammatical features. Moreover, these implicit markers are, in a given situation, often ambiguous: They may stand for more than one relation. Consider the following sequence from Narrative 4:

$_1b_2$ Martin Cassidy's mother give him some money
$_2c_0$ an' tell him to go get a bushel of peaches
$_0d_0$ an' he went down to Martin's house

Though both c and d are connected to the preceding clause by *and*, and though d is clearly ordered with respect to b, b and c are not clearly ordered. The lexical meanings of *give* and *tell* imply a possible simultaneity between b and c. If we substitute for *tell* a verb whose lexical meaning (virtually) denies the possibility or simultaneity with *give*, then b and c are unambiguously ordered:

$_0b_0$ Martin Cassidy's mother give him some money
$_0c'_0$ an' bring up a bushel of peaches from the cellar

One more important point can be drawn from this example. The two possible relations between b and c as they stand are b-then-c and b-and at the same time-c, not c-then-

b. This again suggests that the x-then-y relation is the fundamental one in narrative, which is then added to or modified by marked lexical or grammatical forms.

1.11   Isolating primary sequences

If we give primacy in narrative to the a-then-b relation, we may wish to select the narrative sequence with the most explicit statement of this relation as the basic underlying form and derive other equivalent narratives from it. Such a basic form we term the *primary sequence*. As we will see, the derivation of other forms from the primary sequence has an important interpretation in the functional organization of the narrative structure as a whole. The procedure for isolating primary sequence can be set out as four steps, and illustrated by the following operations on Narrative 6, previously analyzed in Figure 1:

1. A displacement range is assigned to each clause of the narrative.

    $_0a_{18}$ $_1b_{17}$ $_2c_{16}$ $_3d_{15}$ $_4e_{14}$ $_5f_{13}$ $_6g_0$ $_0h_0$ $_0i_1$ $_1j_0$ $_0k_1$ $_1l_0$ $_0m_3$ $_{13}n_5$ $_6o_3$ $_7p_2$ $_0q_0$ $_0r_0$ $_0s_0$

2. Free clauses are moved to the beginning of the narrative.

    $_0a_{18}$ $_1b_{17}$ $_2c_{16}$ $_3d_{15}$ $_4e_{14}$ $_5f_{13}$ $_6n_{12}$ $_7g_0$ $_0h_0$ $_0i_1$ $_1j_0$ $_0k_1$ $_1l_0$ $_0m_2$ $_5o_3$ $_6p_2$ $_0q_0$ $_0r_0$ $_0s_0$

3. Restricted clauses are moved to a point as early as possible in the narrative without changing the temporal sequence of the original semantic interpretation.

    $_0a_{18}$ $_1b_{17}$ $_2c_{16}$ $_3d_{15}$ $_4e_{14}$ $_5f_{13}$ $_6n_{12}$ $_7g_0$ $_0h_0$ $_0o_8$ $_1p_7$ $_2i_1$ $_3j_0$ $_0k_1$ $_1l_0$ $_0m_0$ $_0q_0$ $_0r_0$ $_0s_0$

4. Coordinate clauses are coalesced to single units.

    $_0a\!-\!n_9$ $_1g_0$ $_0h_0$ $_0o\!-\!p_5$ $_1i\!-\!j_0$ $_0k\!-\!l_0$ $_0m_0$ $_0q_0$ $_0r_0$ $_0s_0$

The string of 10 symbols given here represents the primary sequence of the narrative, in which the a-then-b relation is developed most explicitly. The operation of moving free clauses and restricted clauses as far to the left as possible is a method of minimizing the total amount of delay in the statement of any given event or condition. We can, in fact, define both of these as a specific operation: the minimizing of left subscripts.

Formally, we consider a narrative $c^1, c^2 \ldots c^i \ldots c^n$ with left displacement ranges a^1, $a^2 \ldots a^i \ldots a^n$, in which $0 \leq i \leq n$. A *left displacement function* $y(N_i)$ is defined for each permutation $N_1, N_2 \ldots N_m$ of the clauses $c^2, c^2 \ldots c^n$ that preserves the temporal sequence of the original semantic interpretation:

$$y(N_i) = \sum_{i=1}^{n} a^i$$

When $y(N_i)$ is minimal, any sequence c^i, c^i in which $DS(c^i) = DS(c^j)$ is rewritten as c^k and displacement ranges reassigned. The resulting string is the *primary sequence* of the series $N_1, N_2 \ldots N_m$.

We now proceed to show why in most narratives the linear ordering of clauses departs significantly from the order of the primary sequence. For this purpose, we will have to outline the overall structure of narratives as governed by narrative functions.

2 Overall Structure of Narratives

2.1 Orientation

Figure 1 shows a group of six free clauses occurring together at the beginning of Narrative 6. This is characteristic of most narratives to a greater or lesser degree. Of the 14 examples given in the beginning of this article, 11 have such groups of free clauses. When we examine these groups of free clauses in relation to referential function, we find that they serve to orient the listener in respect to person, place, time, and behavioral situation. We will therefore refer to this structure feature as an *orientation section*: formally, the group of free clauses that precede the first narrative clause. Not all narratives have orientation sections, and not all orientation sections perform these four functions. Furthermore, some free clauses with these functions occur in other positions. Finally, we find that the orientation function is often performed by phrases or lexical items contained in narrative clauses. Despite these limitations, the overall view of narrative shows that the orientation section is a structural feature of a narrative structure. When orientation sections are displaced, we frequently find that this displacement performs another function, evaluation, to be discussed later. Furthermore, we find that orientation sections are typically lacking in narratives of children and less verbal adults whose narratives fail in other ways to carry out referential functions, for example, to preserve temporal sequence. This is the case with Narrative 13, the narrative of vicarious experience from a television show, *The Man From UNCLE*. An interesting example is Narrative 5, where the suppression of full narrative structure is plainly motivated by the explicit reluctance of the narrator to identify persons and places. Here, as in many of the critical issues discussed below, it is essential to preserve the context of the narrative. Because such originating context is often missing and cannot be reconstructed in traditional folk tales, it is more difficult to relate analysis to the originating functions.

2.2 Complication

The main body of narrative clauses usually comprises a series of events that may be termed the complication or complicating action. In Figure 1, the complicating action section of Narrative 6 runs from clause g to m.

In many cases, a long string of events may actually consist of several cycles of simple narrative, with many complication sections. This is the case with Narrative 2, the product of a practiced storyteller who is widely known in his community (Martha's Vineyard) as an expert in this traditional art.[8] The subdivisions of Narrative 2 are plainly marked by structural features to be discussed later, but in Narrative 13, this task is much more difficult and must depend upon informal semantic criteria.

The complication is regularly terminated by a result, as in the simple Narrative 5: clause d – or perhaps c and d – is the result that ends the complicating action of a and b, as shown in Figure 2.

To isolate the result in Narrative 5, we are forced to use semantic criteria that are often difficult to apply and seldom consistent. Without further functional analysis, it will usually be hard to tell when a narrative is actually over – when the result begins and when it has been given in full.

Figure 2   Overall structure of Narrative 5

2.3   Evaluation

Before proceeding to discuss the result of narratives, we would like to suggest that a narrative that contains only an orientation, complicating action, and result is not a complete narrative. It may carry out the referential function perfectly, and yet seem difficult to understand. Such a narrative lacks significance: it has no point. This is the case with Narratives 11 and 13. Narrative 11 is difficult to follow, although the complicating action and the result seem to be clearly stated.

(11)

$_0a_0$	See he – they threw him out, you know.
$_0b_0$	So he wanted to get back in, 'cause, you know, it was sn– raining hard.
$_0c_0$	So he got on this boat
$_0d_0$	and he tried to – go somewhere else.
$_0e_0$	And the boat went over.
$_0f_1$	And he tried to swim.
$_6g_6$	And this other man was fishing in the rain.
$_1h_0$	So he seen the pig
$_0i_0$	and he want over there
$_0j_0$	and picked the pig up
$_0k_0$	and put it in the boat
$_0l_0$	and brought it back to the shore, so he would land there.
$_0m_0$	And that was that.

There are 13 independent clauses, and 12 of them are narrative clauses. A diagram of displacement ranges for this narrative offers little justification for any internal segmentation (see Figure 3).

Narrative 13 is actually a very detailed statement of a sequence of events and their results – a series of at least three narrative cycles. Yet, the overall effect of Narrative 13 is confusion and pointlessness. This is true for the whole narrative, which is actually 10 times as long as the extract.

Both Narratives 11 and 13 are examples of narratives of vicarious experience, not, as in the other cases, of personal experience. They are lacking the evaluation section that is typical of narratives of personal experience. When we compare Narrative 13 with Narrative 14, a narrative of personal experience, we can appreciate the great difference between unevaluated and evaluated narration.

Clause	a	p
a	0	0
b	0	0
c	0	0
d	0	0
e	0	0
f	0	1
g	6	6
h	1	0
i	0	0
j	0	0
k	0	0
l	0	0
m	0	0

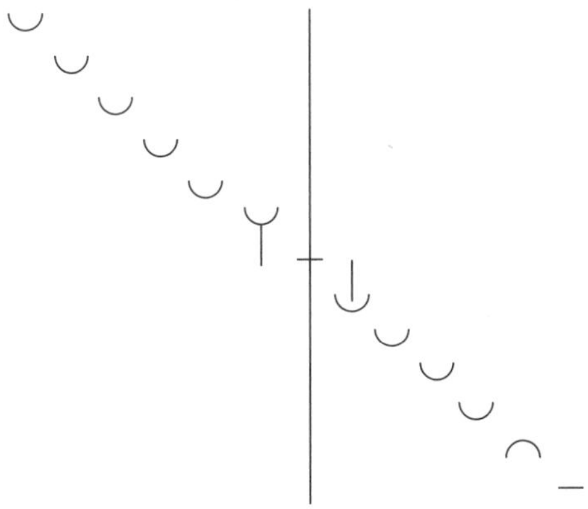

Figure 3   Overall structure of Narrative 11

Narratives are usually told in answer to some stimulus from outside and to establish some point of personal interest. For example, among the narratives given here we find many examples of narratives dealing with the danger of death. When the subject is asked if he were ever in serious danger of being killed, and he says "Yes," then he is asked: "What happened?". He finds himself in a position in which he must demonstrate to the listener that he really was in danger. The more vivid and real the danger appears, the more effective the narrative. If the narrative is weak and uninteresting, he will have made a false claim. (See Narratives 1, 3, 6, and 8.)

Beyond such immediate stimulus, we find that such narratives are so designed as to emphasize the strange and unusual character of the situation – there is an appeal to the element of mystery in most of the narratives. (See Narratives 2, 3, and especially 9). Then, too, many narratives are designed to place the narrator in the most favorable possible light: a function which we may call self-aggrandizement. (See Narratives 7, 8, and especially 12.)

The functions of narrative have an effect on the narrative structure. A simple sequence of complication and result does not indicate to the listener the relative importance of these events or help him distinguish complication from *resolution*. We also find that in narratives without a point it is difficult to distinguish the complicating action from the result.

Therefore, it is necessary for the narrator to delineate the structure of the narrative by emphasizing the point where the complication has reached a maximum: the break between the complication and the result. Most narratives contain an evaluation section that carries out this function.

Many evaluation sections are defined formally. Multicoordinate clauses or groups of free or restricted clauses are frequently located at the break between the complicating action and the resolution of these complications. This is the case in Figure 1, for the clauses n, o, and p. As the narrator is going down, in the water, the moment of crisis is suspended by three clauses that do not occur in this position by any necessity of temporal sequence. They are restricted clauses that could have occurred much earlier in the narrative – in fact, before the first temporal juncture. After these three clauses, the narrative moves swiftly to a conclusion.

In many narratives, the evaluation section is fused with the result: that is, a single narrative clause both emphasizes the importance of the result and states it. This is the case with Narratives 3 and 12. In Narrative 3, the doctor's statement: "you'd a been dead" tells us simultaneously that the narrator was close to death and that he survived. The evaluation is here shown as related directly to the originating function – to demonstrate that the narrator was indeed close to death.

In the case of Narrative 1, we find more than one evaluation section. Narrative 1 begins with a long orientation section of 10 clauses.

(1)

$_0a_{30}$ Well, in the business I was associated at that time, the Doc was an old man . . .

$_1b_{29}$ He had killed one man,

$_2c_{28}$ or – had done time.

$_3d_{27}$ But he had a young wife

$_4e_{26}$ and those days I dressed well.

$_5f_{25}$ And seemingly, she was trying to make me.

$_6g_{24}$ I never noticed it.

$_7h_{23}$ Fact is, I didn't like her very well, because she had – she was a nice looking girl until you saw her feet.

$_8i_{22}$ She had big feet.

$_9j_{21}$ Jesus, God, she had big feet!

$_{10}k_0$ Then she left a note one day she was going to commit suicide because he was always raising hell about me.

$_0l_0$ He came to my hotel. Nice big blue 44 too.[9]

$_0m_3$ I talked him out of it,

$_1n_2$ and says, "Well, we'll go look for her,

$_2o_1$ and if we can't find her, well, you can – go ahead, pull the trigger if you want to."

$_3p_0$ I was maneuvering.

$_0q_0$ So he took me up on it.

$_0r_0$ And we went to where they found her handkerchief – the edge of a creek –

$_0s_0$ And we followed down a little more,

$_0t_0$ And we couldn't find anything.

$_0u_1$ And got back –

$_{21}v_9$ it was a tent show –

$_1w_1$ she was laying on a cot with an ice bag on her head.

$_{12}x_7$ She hadn't committed suicide.

$_1y_0$ But – however – that settled it for the day.

$_0z_0$ But that night the manager, Floyd Adams, said, "You better pack up

$_0aa_0$ and get out, because that son of a bitch never forgives anything once he gets it in his head."

$_0bb_1$ And I did.

$_1cc_0$ I packed up

$_0dd_0$ and got out.

$_0ee_0$ That was two.

The first narrative unit is k ("Then she left a note one day . . ."), followed by l ("He came to my hotel") and m ("I talked him out of it"). We then have two clauses coordinated with m – clauses n ("And says") and o ("I was maneuvering."). These multicoordinate clauses suspend the action at a critical moment – when the danger of death is greatest, and they contain an explicit statement of the attitude of the narrator. His coolness in a moment of crisis emphasizes the danger and reflects well on himself.

Five narrative clauses follow this suspension, resolving the crisis introduced by l and m. A second evaluation section occurs at a subsidiary point when the situation is further resolved – the fate of the lady in question is determined, and simultaneously the immediate threat to the narrator. The action is suspended at this point by the use of a free clause that might have occurred in the orientation section, v ("it was a tent show"), and a direct comment, x, that might have been inferred from w. The resolution is stated with some finality in y ("that settled it"). Finally, there is an added explicit evaluation of a third party that confirms the implications of the previous evaluation section, followed by a conclusion. The overall diagram shows how evaluation sections outline the structure of the narrative.

It should be apparent here that the evaluation sections are responsible for those deviations from the order of the primary sequence of the narrative that complicate the a-then-b relation of narrative. The functions of the evaluation section must be added to the primary narrative function in order to understand how the primary sequence is transformed into the more complex structure that we see here. All of the evaluation sections shown here are related to the originating function of the narrative. From a structural point of view, the first section is the major break in the complicating action.[10]

Not all evaluation sections have the structural feature of suspending the complicating action, as shown in Figure 4. In many cases, the evaluation may be present as lexical or phrasal modification of a narrative clause, or it may be itself a narrative clause or coincide with the last narrative clause. For this reason, the fundamental definition of evaluation must be semantic, although its implications are structural.

The *evaluation* of a narrative is defined by us as that part of the narrative that reveals the attitude of the narrator towards the narrative by emphasizing the relative importance of some narrative units as compared to others. This may be done by a variety of means:

Semantically defined evaluation:

1. direct statement: "I said to myself: this is it."
2. lexical intensifiers: "He was beat up real, real bad."
   "I whupped that dude half to death."

Formally defined:

3. suspension of the action:
   a. through coordinate clauses and restricted clauses: See Figure 1
   b. repetition (subtype of the above): See Narrative 2, at the moment of crisis when the dog is gone for the 3rd time: "And he didn't come back. And he didn't come back."

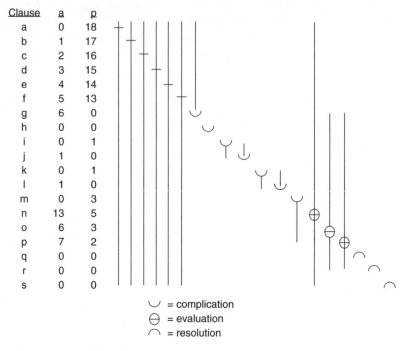

Clause	a	p
a	0	18
b	1	17
c	2	16
d	3	15
e	4	14
f	5	13
g	6	0
h	0	0
i	0	1
j	1	0
k	0	1
l	1	0
m	0	3
n	13	5
o	6	3
p	7	2
q	0	0
r	0	0
s	0	0

⌣ = complication
⊖ = evaluation
⌢ = resolution

Figure 4   Overall structure of Narrative 1

Culturally defined:

4.   symbolic action: "They put an egg on his door."
     "I crossed myself."
     "You could hear the rosaries clicking."
5.   judgment of a third person: here the entire narrative is reported to a person not
     present at the narrative.

Narrative 12 is a heavily evaluated narrative that shows three of these characteristic
forms of evaluation. It is typical of many fight narratives in its two-part structure. The
first subcycle deals with the events leading up to the fight, and its conclusion is the
beginning of the second subcycle, the fight itself. In this case, the evaluation of the first
section is a statement of the narrator:

$_0$d$_0$ I told him that – it's impossible for him to find downtown, cause all those people
        were walking by, and just his father is the only one that find it?

Although the very length of this closely reasoned argument serves to suspend the action,
the structural criteria we have been using show it as a single narrative clause. We identify this clause as an evaluation on semantic grounds: It is an explicit statement by the
narrator of his attitude towards the situation.

   The conclusion of Narrative 12 is also an evaluative statement that coincides with
the last narrative unit: The statement of a third person after the entire sequence of
events is reported to him.

$_0j_0$ Then he start crying
$_0k_0$ and run home to his father.
$_0l_0$ And his father told him, he ain't find no glove

In addition, we have the evaluation of the act of clause i

$_0h_0$ So he say he give
$_0i_0$ And I kept on hitting him.

It is normal not to hit someone after he says "I give." This incident evaluates the narrative by indicating that the anger of the narrator was so great – due to excessive and unreasonable provocation – that he was carried away to the extent of violating this norm. The other boy had placed himself outside of normal sanctions by his behavior.

All of these forms of evaluation serve the function of self-aggrandizement, showing the narrator in a favorable position as compared to the other boy. It is evident that there are a great variety of evaluation types, more or less deeply embedded in the narrative. But this variety should not obscure the fact that unevaluated narratives are exceptional as representations of personal experience, and unevaluated narratives lack structural definition.

An important characteristic of narratives is the degree of embedding of the evaluation in the narrative framework. There is a wide range, from the most highly internalized type – a symbolic action or the evaluation of a third person – to the most external – a direct statement of the narrator to the listener about his feelings at the time. In the examples given previously, we find internalized evaluation in Narrative 1, in the dramatic statements of narrator and manager; and in Narrative 3, in the statement of the doctor ("just about this much more," he says, "and you'd a been dead."). The last narrative, Narrative 14, has a dramatic statement of the narrator ("I say, 'Calvin, I'm bust your head for dat.'").

Sometimes the evaluation occurs in a statement of the narrator to himself, less well integrated into the narrative, as in Narrative 7: "So I says to myself, 'Well, there's gonna be times . . .'".

The other end of the scale is shown by a comment at the end of the narrative directed towards the listener, as in Narrative 13: "Just over two dollars that he was sent for peaches with." Still more direct is Narrative 2: "I'll tell you if I had ever walloped that dog I'd have felt some bad."

We might construct a scale of degrees of embedding of evaluation, following examples of the following sort:

Internal 1. And when we got down there, her brother turned to me and whispered, "I think she's dead, John!"
2. And when we got down there, I said to myself, "My God, she's dead!"
3. And when we got down there, I thought, "She's dead."
4. And when we got down there, I thought she was dead.
5. Later, the doctors told us she was close to death.
6. I think she must have been close to death.
External 7. You know, in cases like this, it's clear that she was likely as not dead.

2.4   Resolution

With this definition of evaluation, we can now return to the problem of defining the result of a narrative. The problem is now quite simple. We can establish the break between the complicating and resolving action by locating the placement of the evaluation. Thus, the *resolution* of the narrative is that portion of the narrative sequence that follows the evaluation. If the evaluation is the last element, then the resolution section coincides with the evaluation. In the examples given previously, the complicating clauses are symbolized $\cup$ and the resolving clauses $\cap$.

2.5   Coda

Many narratives end with a resolution section, but others have an additional element that we may call the *coda*.

The actual sequence of events described in the narrative does not, as a rule, extend up to the present. The coda is a functional device for returning the verbal perspective to the present moment. This is accomplished by a variety of means, so that the codas cannot be identified by such simple tag lines as "And they lived happily ever after."

a.   One device used in a coda is *deixis*. This is the linguistic category that points to a referent instead of naming it explicitly: In this case, it has the effect of standing at the present moment of time and pointing to the end of the narrative, identifying it as a remote point in the past.

(1)
$_0aa_0$ I packed up
$_0bb_0$ and got out.
$_0cc_0$ That was two.

(7)
$_0bb_0$ That was one of the most important.

(8)
$_0gg_1$ And that – that was it, you know.
$_1hh_0$ That was it.

(11)
$_0m_0$ And that was that.

This use of the obviate deictic category – *that, there, those* – contrasts sharply with the use of the proximate in the body of the narrative – *this, here, these*. For example, we have the following proximate evaluation in Narrative 8:

(8)
$_0bb_0$ and they was on me and
$_0cc_0$ and I said "Like this is it, man."
$_0dd_0$ I pulled a knife

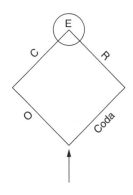

Figure 5   The normal form of narrative

b.   Another device used in codas is an incident in which one of the actors can be followed up to the present moment in actions that may not be totally relevant to the
narrative sequence:

And you know that man who picked me out of the water?
he's a detective in Union City,
and I see him every now and again.

c.   The effect of the narrative on the narrator may be extended to the present moment:

I was given the rest of the day off,
and ever since then I haven't seen the guy, 'cause I quit.
I quit, you know.
No more problems.

It is interesting to note that all codas are separated from the resolution by temporal
juncture. At the same time, it seems that some semantic criterion is necessary to identify codas: The fact that they are frequently not descriptions of events, or of events
necessary to answer the question: "What happened?"

The overall structure of the narratives that we have examined is not uniform; there
are considerable differences in the degree of complexity, in the number of structural
elements present, and how various functions are carried out. However, a composite view
of narrative performance leads us to posit a *normal form* for oral versions of personal
experience; the degree to which any one narrative approximates this normal form is a
significant fact about that narrative – perhaps more significant than any other in terms
of fulfilling the originating function of the narrative.

The normal form is quite distinct from the primary sequence of the narrative. As
noted above, the need for an evaluation section motivates the transformation of the
primary sequence into the more characteristic normal form that appears in the linear
sequence presented by the narrator.

One can represent the normal form of narrative using the diagram in Figure 5. Here
the originating function of the narrative is applied at the base of the diamond; we

proceed up and to the left with the orientation section, then up to the apex with the complication. Frequently, but not always, the evaluation suspends the action at this apex, as represented by the circle. The resolution proceeds downward and to the right, and the coda is represented by the line that returns to the situation (point in time) at which the narrative was first elicited. The simplest possible narrative would consist of the single line of the complication, without a clear resolution; frequently we find minimal narratives that have both complication and resolution ("He hit me hard and I hit him back"). As we proceed to more complex narratives, told by speakers with greater overall verbal ability, we find a higher percentage of narratives that duplicate the exact form of this diagram. Perhaps the most frequent variant is the case in which the evaluation ends the resolution: jokes, ghost stories, and surprise endings take this form, as the story is reshaped by many retellings.

3 Conclusion

This view of narrative structure helps us to answer the two questions raised at the beginning of this discussion. First, we have related the sequence of narrative elements to the inferred sequence of events in the experience that is being recapitulated, through the definitions of narrative units, restricted clause, free clause, and narrative clause. Secondly, we have outlined the principal elements of simple narratives that perform both referential and evaluative functions. We have shown that the evaluative function requires the transformation of the primary sequence, based on the a-then-b relation, into the more complex normal form of the narrative as presented by the narrator.

With this framework, we are beginning to analyze relative effectiveness and completeness of narrative structure among various subgroups of our population, and, furthermore, to analyze the more complex types of narration developed by skilled storytellers and preserved by oral tradition. It is clear that these conclusions are restricted to the speech communities that we have examined. This view of narrative structure will achieve greater significance when materials from radically different cultures are studied in the same way.

Notes

The work described in this article was supported in part by the U.S. Office of Education in connection with Cooperative Research Branch Project No. 3288, "A Study of Non-Standard English of Negro and Puerto Rican Speakers in New York City," under the overall program of Project Literacy.

1 The materials include: 70 interviews with speakers from various occupations, ethnic membership, and ages on Martha's Vineyard, Massachusetts; 230 interviews with speakers representing a stratified random sample of the Lower East Side of New York City; 250 interviews of children and adults from our current research in Central Harlem; and 50 interviews from exploratory work in Cleveland, Boston, Philadelphia, Chicago, Phoenix, and Beaufort County, South Carolina. The basic interview techniques are described in Labov (1964, 1966) and Labov, Cohen, and Robins (n.d.).
2 In our current research in Central Harlem, we are concerned with the functional conflicts between standard English and the nonstandard English of Black and Puerto Rican children.

Many of these children show great verbal ability in many areas, including the construction of narratives, but cannot read at all. One purpose of this work on narrative analysis is to show how children use language to carry out the functions that are important in their system of values.

3   As in, "We were running, walking, and then creeping down the road." We might better say that an apparent appositive turns out to be a coordinated clause. Coordinate verbs are always analyzed separately if they are independent, and in most cases in which they are subordinated to verbs of saying and telling. See narrative 2, which follows: "I said, 'You git back there/ and get that duck.'" If the narrator had cited himself as saying, "You get that duck and get back there," he would have been reversing the inferred sequence of events – in this case, two utterances. The same argument holds for the example in Narrative l (cited previously), clauses n and o. On the other hand, if someone says: "You try and get it," we cannot understand these as two independent verbs, but rather the use of "and" is equivalent to an infinitive embedding, the same as "You try to get it."

4   As noted previously, the subordination of "get back there" and "get that duck" to "I said" is not the type of subordination that removes clauses from temporal sequence. We can consider this coordination: "I said, 'you git back there,' and I said, 'You get that duck.'"

5   If "was laying" is accepted as a narrative clause, it cannot have the basic grammatical meaning of "simultaneous" as stated by Diver (1963). It would rather differ from the simple past *lay* by the feature "extended." The meaning of "simultaneous" can be supported by arguing that these clauses are equivalent to "When we got back, she was laying . . ." In other cases, Diver pointed out, the use of the past progressive may force a metaphorical interpretation "the action was so swift that it was as if it was simultaneous with the preceding," as in " I was on the masthead; the ship gave a lurch; I was falling through the air; I hit the water." These and other interpretations can be subjected to an increasing number of empirical tests through the analysis of narratives such as the ones given here.

6   Diver (1963) showed this form in his narrative axis with the meaning of "present, before," and gives a constructed example: "All day the sun has warmed the Spanish steps. . . ." One can find such examples in literary works that use historical present sequences freely, perhaps, but they have not occurred in the material we have examined to date.

7   Here the usual adjustments in anaphoric reference have been made. It may be noted that this series of past perfect clauses is one answer to a difficult problem produced by a narrative of this type. The result would lose its surprising effect if these clauses were placed in narrative sequence with regular preterit verbs. By placing the three clauses well out of temporal sequence, it is more difficult for the listener to follow the explanation and surprise is achieved at the risk of a certain awkwardness and confusion. Again, we find that even partial success signals the fact that the narrator of Narrative 2 is a practiced storyteller and has probably told this story many times. We do not take narratives of this type as primary data.

8   As noted previously, Narrative 2 has many formal features that set it aside from the others and identify it as the product of a practiced storyteller. One can point to the embedding of an essentially anonymous "other" in the complicating action, frequent if traditional metaphor, the triple subcycle typical of developed folk tales, strategic repetition, and also the determination shown by the narrator in introducing the story. The preliminary material illustrates how a narrator of this sort will get the topic of his favorite stories into the conversation despite the fact that the original stimulus was only marginally relevant. The transition of the interview theme was accomplished solely by the subject, and the actual stimulus for the narrative was his own.

Despite the fact that features appear in this narrative that are distinct from the simpler examples, a formal analysis of Narrative 2 is possible only after consideration of the simpler narratives or, at least, a formal analysis based on such functional considerations as we have introduced.

9   The phrase "Nice big blue 44 too" might as well be considered a narrative clause, derived from "He had a nice big blue 44 too." However, the status of *had* as the head of a narrative clause is still at issue, and it would be tendentious to use a deleted form as evidence. We have therefore been treating this phrase as subordinated to "He came to my hotel," equivalent to "with a nice big blue 44 too."

10   The three evaluation sections of Narrative 1 raise the possibility that we can analyze this narrative as consisting of three distinct subcycles: that it is a complex narrative consisting of three structural units. This article is limited to the consideration of simple narratives, and this possibility must be postponed to a later study of subcycles and complex narratives.

References

Colby, B. (1966). Cultural patterns in narrative. *Science, 151*, 793–798.

Diver, W. (1963). The chronological system of the English verb. *Word, 19*, 141–148.

Labov, W. (1964). Phonological correlates of social stratification. *American Anthropologist, 66*(6, Pt. 2), 164–176.

Labov, W. (1966). *The social stratification of English in New York City*. Washington, DC: Center for Applied Linguistics.

Labov, W., Cohen, P., & Robins, C. (n.d.). *Final report on Project 3091*. Washington, DC: U.S. Office of Education, Cooperative Research Branch.

Labov, W., & Waletzky, J. (1967). Narrative analysis: Oral versions of personal experience. In J. Helm (Ed.), *Essays on the verbal and visual arts: Proceedings of the 1996 Annual Spring Meeting of the American Ethnological Society* (pp. 12–44). Seattle: University of Washington Press.

Propp, V. (1958). *Morphology of the folk tale* (Publication 10). Bloomington, IN: Research Center in Anthropology, Folklore and Linguistics.

Schatzman, L., & Strauss, A. (1955). Social class and modes of communication. *American Journal of Sociology, 60*, 329–338.

6

"Narrative Analysis" Thirty Years Later
Emanuel A. Schegloff

For the most part, people tell stories to do something – to complain, to boast, to inform, to alert, to tease, to explain or excuse or justify, or to provide for an interactional environment in whose course or context or interstices such actions and interactional inflections can be accomplished (M. H. Goodwin, 1989, 1990). Recipients are oriented not only to the story as a discursive unit, but to what is being done by it, with it, through it; for the story and any aspect of its telling, they can attend the "why that now" question (Schegloff & Sacks, 1973). It should not be surprising that the projects that are being implemented in the telling of a story inform the design and constructional features of the story, as well as the details of the telling (Sacks, 1978). They inform as well the moment-to-moment manner of the story's uptake by its recipients (C. Goodwin, 1984; C. Goodwin & M. H. Goodwin, 1987), and that uptake in turn is taken up by the teller (if indeed there is a single teller; cf. Duranti & Brenneis, 1986; C. Goodwin, 1986; Lerner, 1992; Mandelbaum, 1993) and feeds back to affect the next increment of telling.

Design and constructional features of stories are shaped as well by an orientation to who the recipient(s) is, to how many of them there are, and who they are to one another and to the teller and what they can (or should) be supposed to know (C. Goodwin, 1981, 1986). Such quotidian storytellings arise in, or are prompted by, the ongoing course of an interactional occasion or the trajectory of a conversation or are made to interrupt it (Jefferson, 1978; Sacks, 1974, 1992). On the story's completion the interaction and its participants have been brought to some further state of talk and interaction, transformed or not – talk and interaction whose further trajectory will in some fashion be related to that story's telling (Jefferson, 1978; Sacks, 1974, 1992; Schegloff, 1992). Ordinary storytelling, in sum, is (choose your term) a coconstruction, an interactional achievement, a joint production, a collaboration, and so forth.

Although the 1967 Labov and Waletzky paper, "Narrative Analysis: Oral Versions of Personal Experience" (chapter 5; henceforth L&W), was important in attracting attention to the interest of ordinary persons' stories of personal experience,[1] it obscured part of what is involved in their very constitution by setting their formative examination in the context of the sociolinguistic interview, an interactional and situational context masked by the term "oral versions [of personal experience]." This formulation of their subject elevated the issue of "oral vs. written" into central prominence and glossed the telling differences (if I may put it that way) between contrasting auspices of speaking and organizations of talking in the interview on the one hand and less academically occasioned settings of storytelling on the other. Although we are celebrating

the positive consequences of their paper on its 30th anniversary, it is worth detailing
its unintended, less beneficial consequences in the hope of redirecting subsequent work
toward a differently targeted and more compelling grasp of vernacular storytelling.

This tack may strike readers as tangential to the occasion, and in a sense it is. It starts
not from an interest in *narrative* as a field for whose development L&W is central, but
from a more general interest in quotidian talk-in-interaction – a domain into which
most occurrences of "oral versions of personal experience" are likely to fall. Taking
narrative as the focus, one opts for a discursive unit, genre, and activity across contexts
of realization, pushing to the background the consequences of those contexts – however
conceived – for the actual constitution of stories. Taking "talk-in-interaction" as the
relevant domain, an analyst is constrained to take into account the different settings of
"orality" (henceforth "talking") – in which different speech-exchange systems with different turn-taking practices differentially shape stories and the practices of storytelling,
not to mention the different practical activities in whose course, and on whose behalf,
storytelling may be undertaken. An analyst is so constrained because the participants
embody these differences in their conduct.[2]

Taking the practices of conversation as a baseline for talk-in-interaction, what can
be said about the sociolinguistic interview as a setting in which to describe an object
generically formulated as "oral versions of personal experience" or narrative?

For one thing, the context of the sociolinguistic elicitation plays havoc with the
motive force of the telling – the action and interactional precipitant of the telling –
by making the elicitation question itself the invariant occasion for telling the story.[3]
Though the authors would surely now disavow or reject it, this seems to have em-
bodied something of an ideal of a "null context" in which one might get at the pure
shape of storytelling itself, freed of the diverse situated motives and contingencies of
actual tellings. It would not be the first time in the western intellectual and scientific
tradition, or even in the context of contemporary linguistics, in which an ideal form is
extracted from transient "distortions" of its idiosyncratic situated occasions, however
ironic such an effort appears in the midst of otherwise sustained and innovative preoccupation with linguistic variation. However, the variationism of sociolinguistics has
been couched more in terms of groups and sociodemographic categories than in terms
of situations and interactional contexts (Goffman, 1964).[4]

Actually, the image at work here appears to take the story or narrative as already
formed, as waiting to be delivered, to fit in or be trimmed to fit the context into which
it is to be inserted. In this regard it resembles common conceptions of speech acts,
whose constitutive conditions and properties are autonomous, which have their origins
in the psychology of the individual (whether in intentions or experiences and memories) and which are then stitched into the occasions on which they are enacted. One
does not find here the sense of an ongoing interaction in which consequential next
moments of the participants' lives are being lived together (in contrast to the content
of the stories being elicited, in which that property is valued) with the stories being
touched off or mobilized by those moments, with the telling constituted to serve the
exigencies of those moments and being shaped thereby.

This image of narrative was (and is) both reflected in, and fostered by, the data with
which L&W worked, at least as displayed in the 1967 paper. Although it was an important step to present the data, to devote a whole separate section of the paper to the

"texts," when we look at "the data" today, a number of striking observations present themselves:

1. They report nothing (no talk or other conduct) by the recipient(s) in the course of the telling.
2. They report nothing (no talk or other conduct) by the recipient(s) at the end, on the completion of the story.
3. They report no silences "in the course" of the story to indicate where else (earlier) the story might have been (designed to be) possibly complete, without fruition.
4. They report no hesitations, hitches, or other deviations from smooth delivery in the course of the telling, nor any problems in its uptake during the course of the telling.

In short, there is nothing interactional in the data at all other than the eliciting question, which takes on a role much like that of an experimental stimulus to occasion the production of the already formed story waiting to be told.

Of course, L&W could not do everything, could not take everything into account, could not anticipate developments that were still embryonic at the time of the 1967 paper. Still, it is striking to what degree features of the 1967 paper have remained characteristic of treatments of narrative. This analytic tack has remained acceptable, and indeed celebrated, because it has fit so well with the academic tradition of ex cathedra decisions on analytic focus. I speak here of the academy, not of L&W.

Academics – whether literary, linguistic, psychological, and so forth – have wished to focus on narrative per se, so that is what they studied or how they formulated what they studied. A focus on the structure of narrative as an autonomous discursive form was consistent with the structuralism that dominated academic culture in the 1960s from the anthropology of Lévi-Strauss to the then-recent turn of literary studies, and which allowed an extension of themes familiar from literary studies to the study of the vernacular. They have collectively disattended the fact that, unlike the narratives examined in literary studies that are ordinarily singly authored (however sensitive to social and cultural context), in the natural social world narrative – in the form of the telling of stories in ordinary talk-in-interaction – is an organic part of its interactional environment. If it is disengaged from its environment, much is lost that is constitutive of its occurrence there. Even many of those otherwise committed to "coconstruction" as a theme of social, cultural, and linguistic practice might be drawn to disengage stories from the detailed interactional context of their telling by this effort to focus on narrative structure per se or by the uses to which it may be put. Thereby, the "product-narrative," or an idealized version of narrative structure, logic, rhetoric, and so forth, has been disengaged from its context of production and reception and has become reinforced as a rich discursive resource, deployable for a wide variety of other interpretive undertakings, unconstrained by the symbiotic relation otherwise obtaining between a story and the occasion of its telling. But back to L&W.

L&W took the key problems of securing oral narratives of personal experience for analysis to be those of authenticity and spontaneity – how to get their tellers to transcend Labov's version of the observer's paradox (Labov, 1970, p. 47), the formality and hypercorrection of speech that set in with overt observation by outsiders, a problem which Labov had already encountered and described in other work. Part of the solution was to elicit stories so exciting and engaging to tell that the tellers would lose themselves in the very drama of the telling (hence stories about "a time you were almost killed," etc.). At the same time, avoiding "contamination" by the observer led to an enforced reserve in the uptake of stories by the elicitor that could not but problematize the trajectory of the telling and the shape of the resultant story – especially in the case of a dramatic or "exciting" story. In this respect, in treating the recipient as basically extraneous (and hence a source of "bias"), in treating the narrative as "belonging to" the basic unit of western culture – the individual doing the telling (the talking head) – the opportunity was missed to re-situate the narrative in social context, to see that the recipient(s) is an irremediable component of a story's telling. Even if recipients stay blank (and perhaps especially then), their presence and conduct enters into the story's telling. Nor are the consequences of having proceeded in this way trivial or incidental. They go to the heart of the matter – the characterization of the anatomy of ordinary storytelling. For example, the presence of a summary theme or evaluation in L&W's account may well reflect the formative effect of the elicitation session and the eliciting inquiry as the occasion for telling. When stories come up "naturally," such summings-up by teller are often not present (they may rather be articulated by recipients as part of a receipt sequence), and if they are present, it can testify to "trouble" in the uptake of the story (Jefferson, 1978, pp. 228–237).

Or consider the possible effects of the decision to solicit "stories of almost being killed" for their capacity to secure involved and spontaneous telling. This seems to be predicated on the view that "type of story" or "topic of story" is nonconsequential for its anatomy or structure and that only spontaneity is specially associated with it. This may well be so, but there is some past experience with this issue and some evidence that what stories are about (given their recipients, etc.) may be nonarbitrarily related to the trajectory of telling.

Jefferson (1980, 1988), for example, observed that she was initially reluctant to get involved in a proposed study of "talk about troubles," suspecting that it was a structurally nonconsequential matter, focused on a topic designed to be of interest for analytically extraneous reasons. Once engaged with the data, however, she found that "troubles-telling" mobilized distinctive interactional stances from both teller and recipients, engendered distinctive trajectories of telling and uptake (Jefferson & Lee, 1981), and so forth. Similarly, Schegloff (1976/1984) found that "opposition-type stories in which teller was one of the protagonists" served to pose issues of alignment for recipients which could in turn have consequences for how the telling was brought to a close.

However "obvious" in retrospect, neither of these distinctive features, nor that these were relevant ways of "typologizing" stories, was accessible in advance. Whatever the virtues of stories about having almost been killed, when disengaged from the details of the context of their telling and in particular from their uptake-in-their-course by their recipients, we cannot know what distinctive features of structure or interactional enactment they occasion.[5]

To sum up, there have been some developments over these 30 years in our understanding of talk-in-interaction and conversation in particular, and they suggest some directions of inquiry that merit more serious attention by those interested in narrative as a dressed-up version of storytelling. For example:

Consider the differences between storytellings by reference to their conditions of launching – between those which themselves launch a sequence and those which are "responsive," that is, between storytellings that have to "make their own way" and those that are responsive to inquiry, to invitation, to solicitation, or can be introduced under that guise. Here we are noting not only the special character of stories "in second position" in the sense of being produced in answer to a question as compared to ones that launch a spate of talk, but that there can be striking differences between stories that have been *sol*icited (and further between those already-known stories that are solicited and those not previously known) and those that are *el*icited, in which a question gets a story without having specifically asked for one (as in the excerpt reproduced in Footnote 2).

Consider the differences between stories analyzably used to do something and those apparently told "for their own sake."

Consider the relation between a story proper and the practices of storytelling, and the storytelling sequence, by which it is constructed and conveyed.

Consider the fact that one consequence of a storytelling can be the touching off of another storytelling (Sacks, 1992, Vol. 1, pp. 764–772; Vol. 2, pp. 3–17, 249–268). Subsequent stories are mobilized in recipients' memory by a story's telling just because they can serve as displays of understanding of, and alignment (or misalignment) with, prior stories. Such a consequence is both background and prospect for storytelling in conversation. A "subsequent story" is designed for the place in a course of tellings that it is to occupy. Consider, then, the differences in storytellings by reference to their place in such a sequence of tellings. This is especially relevant for stories of personal experience, and much is lost by not incorporating it, for example, in collecting stories of the Holocaust. However, this is a consequence of severing narratives from their origins as stories told in real-life interaction.

Whatever findings may emerge from such inquiries, given that story recipients may contest the initial premises of the telling (C. Goodwin, 1986, pp. 298–301; Sacks, 1974, pp. 340–344), that the telling can be substantially shaped by such contestation (C. Goodwin, 1986, 301–302), or by other "interpolations" by recipients (Lerner, 1992; Mandelbaum, 1993), and that whether, where, and how the story and storytelling end can be contingent on the occurrence and form of recipient uptake (Jefferson, 1978, pp. 228–237; Schegloff, 1992, pp. 203–214), one might entertain the possibility that the constitutive practices of storytelling incorporate recipients and that storytelling abstracted from its interactional setting, occasioning, and uptake is an academically hybridized form. A search for the vernacular or quotidian counterpart to literary narrative could benefit from a redirection from this path.

A body of conversation-analytic work over the last several decades has found that the organization and practices of talk-in-interaction in specialized (often work) settings is generally best described as a modification or transformation of the organization of talk in ordinary conversation (Drew & Heritage, 1992a, 1992b; Heritage, 1984; Heritage & Greatbatch, 1991). For example, the practices and organization of talk in classrooms, courts, news interviews, therapy sessions, and so forth all stand in systematic, describable relations to the organization and practices of ordinary conversation.[6] "Elicitation sessions" appear to be a specialized setting and speech exchange system (Sacks, Schegloff, & Jefferson, 1974) as well. They ought to be understood by reference to ordinary interaction, as should the activities (like storytelling) that occur in them – and not the other way around.

Just because L&W was an early entry, very likely the first, in the effort to describe "ordinary" narrative does not mean that other story types, otherwise contexted and occasioned, should be described by comparison to their account. Although stories like those described by L&W surely get told, in ordinary conversation they take work to achieve, work that may vary from occasion to occasion, yielding stories that vary from occasion to occasion, or ones whose invariance took doing. We do not get to see any of that in L&W or to suspect it.

I have focused attention on the half of the cup that is empty, not the half that is full. L&W sought to bring attention from the stories that preoccupied students of high literature to those of ordinary folks. They sought to bridge the chasm between formalism and functionalism by taking on both jobs. This is the full half. They isolated the ordinary folks in the artificial environment of the academic elicitation and thereby suppressed the possibility of observing the very functions they hoped to link to their formal account. This is the empty half. There is, then, ample work remaining to be done.

Notes

This article was prepared in response to an invitation to contribute to a special issue of the *Journal of Narrative and Life History*, assessing and reflecting on the article, "Narrative Analysis: Oral Versions of Personal Experience" by William Labov and Joshua Waletzky, 30 years after its publication. My thanks to Steven Clayman, Charles and Marjorie Goodwin, and John Heritage for reacting to earlier versions of this contribution.

1   It may be worth recalling "the times" in which L&W was produced by reference to other work and workers active in related areas, in order to complement the line drawn from L&W to this issue of *Journal of Life History and Narrative*. Recall, then, that the special issue of the *American Anthropologist* on "The Ethnography of Communication," edited by John Gumperz and Dell Hymes, appeared in 1964. Goffman's influential "The Neglected Situation" appeared in that special issue, as did Labov's "Phonological Correlates of Social Stratification," in which the basic interview techniques used by L&W are described (L&W, 1967, fn. 5). Garfinkel's *Studies in Ethnomethodology* appeared in 1967. The first of Sacks' *Lectures on Conversation* (1992) were delivered in 1964 and mimeographed transcripts began circulating informally shortly thereafter. The lectures for Spring 1966 began with several lectures on storytelling (later published as "On the Analyzability of Stories by Children," Sacks, 1972), including observations on the mapping of sentence order to event order (Sacks, 1992 Vol. 1, pp. 236–266; cf. the notes for an earlier version of these lectures in Fall 1965, Vol 1, 223–231). Schegloff's "Sequencing in Conversational Openings" appeared in the *American Anthropologist* in 1968. There was an informal meeting during the 1966 Linguistic Institute at UCLA at which many of these people – Garfinkel, Gumperz, Labov, Sacks, Schegloff – and others – Aaron Cicourel and Michael Moerman come to mind – met, some for the first time. For example, though Bill Labov and I had then been colleagues at Columbia for a year, we met for the first time at that UCLA encounter; it was also the first meeting of Labov and Sacks, as I recall. A few days later, there was an informal meeting at Bill Bright's house involving a partially overlapping set of people – including Goffman, for example, but not Garfinkel or Sacks – to discuss the teaching of sociolinguistics. In short, the mid-60s was a time when a range of related ways of addressing a related range of subject matters at the intersection of language, interaction, discourse, practical action and inference, and the like was being explored.

2   "Personal experience" in this way emerges as a "type" of the larger class "narrative," a taxonomy
fitted to academic and investigatory preoccupations – such as the task of collecting examples of
narrative by soliciting their telling and needing to specify "what kind of story" is wanted. This,
however, is an unusual way for the matter to come up in ordinary interaction. Rather than starting with "narrative" and choosing some "type," participants are likely to have something to tell,
with design considerations bearing on whether to tell it minimally in a single-unit utterance, as a
story, and so forth, and, if as a story, what design features for story construction to adopt. For
example, in the brief excerpt that follows, Hyla and Nancy are two college students with tickets
to the theater that evening to see The Dark at the Top of the Stairs. In this telephone conversation several hours before they are to meet, Nancy asks Hyla how she came to get the tickets.

Hyla, 5:06–17
```
 1                            (0.8)
 2   Hyla:    [·hhhhhh]
 3   Nancy:          [How did]ju hear about it from the pape[r?
 4   Hyla:                                                  [·hhhhh I sa:w-
 5                            (0.4)
 6   Hyla:    A'right when was: it,
 7                            (0.3)
 8   Hyla:    The week before my birthda:[y,]
 9   Nancy:                              [Ye] a[:h,
10   Hyla:                                     [I wz looking in the Calendar
11            section en there was u:n, (·) on a:d yihknow a liddle:: u-
12            thi:ng, ·hh[hh
13   Nancy:              [Uh hu:h,=
```

Here the question asked at Line 3 is ostensibly to be answered with a simple response: "I
saw . . ." ("ostensibly" because this may be belied by the audibly deep in-breath which precedes
it ("·hhhhh") and which may project a rather longer telling in the works). That initial response-
in-progress is abandoned shortly after onset, and a storytelling format begins to be deployed,
the story going on for a good two pages of single-spaced transcript. This is one type of instance
of having something to tell and choosing among alternative formats of telling, in contrast with
starting with a story-to-be-told and choosing among types of story.

3   If the inquiry for a story was designed to implement some other action or interactional tack, or
was so understood by its recipients, L&W do not tell us. The same goes for the telling that ensued,
though we might suppose the common "motive" of "helping science" to have been mobilized (cf.
Orne, 1959, 1962; Rosenthal, 1966).

4   The problem is not the aim of arriving at some underlying practices or structures of narrative,
only the effort to do so by stripping away naturally occurring circumstantial detail by intervening
in the data collection (thereby distorting the data), rather than by arriving at it by analysis of
naturally occurring "specimens."

5   Here again there are analytic particulars, not hypothetical speculations, to be considered. For
example, in the stretch of talk taken up in C. Goodwin, 1986, and Schegloff, 1987, 1992, the telling
of a story is prompted for its dramatic, exciting character to escape the displayed boring character of the talk otherwise going on. However, the telling is no sooner launched than the auspices
of its telling, the premise of its dramatic character, are challenged, and turn out to compromise
the course of the telling. Where "excitement" is offered as relief from ennui, it may be taken as a
complaint about the current active speakers and prompt responses which impact the teller quite
differently from the "exciting" stories elicited in the L&W. These too might have been compro-
mised (or differently told) had others, familiar with the tale and the events it reported, been present
to the telling. However, the elicitation setting provides a more antiseptic and hothouse environment, and in this respect at least, an unnatural one.

6   This goes specifically to the practices of storytelling in such settings as well. For example, with respect to talk in therapy sessions, Sacks (1992, vol. 1, pp. 767–768) called attention to Fromm-Reichmann's observation that a key problem in the training of therapists and in the practice of therapy is listening to the stories of others without having those stories mobilize in the therapist subsequent stories ("second stories") of their own experience. Her remarks exemplify the notion of specialized settings as transformations of ordinary conversational practice – therapists-in-training have to neutralize or suppress practices of story reception in ordinary conversation in favor of ones fitted to the technical tasks of therapeutic interaction. For another setting, see also Pomerantz (1987).

References

Drew, P., & Heritage, J. (1992a). Analyzing talk at work: An introduction. In P. Drew & J. Heritage (Eds.), *Talk at work* (pp. 3–65). Cambridge, England: Cambridge University Press.

Drew, P., & Heritage, J. (Ed.). (1992b). *Talk at work.* Cambridge, England: Cambridge University Press.

Duranti, A., & Brenneis, D. (Eds.). (1986). The audience as co-author. *Text, 6,* 239–347.

Garfinkel, H. (1967). *Studies in ethnomethodology.* Englewood Cliffs, NJ: Prentice-Hall.

Goffman, E. (1964). The neglected situation. *American Anthropologist, 66*(6, Part II), 133–136.

Goodwin, C. (1981). *Conversational organization: Interaction between speakers and hearers.* New York: Academic.

Goodwin, C. (1984). Notes on story structure and the organization of participation. In M. Atkinson & J. Heritage (Eds.), *Structures of social action* (pp. 225–246). Cambridge, England: Cambridge University Press.

Goodwin, C. (1986). Audience diversity, participation and interpretation. *Text, 6*(3), 283–316.

Goodwin, C., & Goodwin, M. H. (1987). Concurrent operations on talk: Notes on the interactive organization of assessments. *IPrA Papers in Pragmatics, 1*(1), 1–52.

Goodwin, M. H. (1989). Tactical uses of stories: Participation frameworks within girls' and boys' disputes. *Discourse Processes, 13,* 33–71.

Goodwin, M. H. (1990). *He-said-she-said: Talk as social organization among black children.* Bloomington: Indiana University Press.

Gumperz, J. J., & Hymes, D. (Eds.). (1964). The ethnography of communication [Special issue]. *American Anthropologist, 66*(6, Part II).

Heritage, J. (1984). *Garfinkel and ethnomethodology.* Cambridge, England: Polity.

Heritage, J., & Greatbatch, D. (1991). On the institutional character of institutional talk: The case of news interviews. In D. Boden & D. H. Zimmerman (Eds.), *Talk and social structure* (pp. 93–137). Cambridge. England: Polity.

Jefferson, G. (1978). Sequential aspects of storytelling in conversation. In J. Schenkein (Ed.), *Studies in the organization of conversational interaction* (pp. 219–248). New York: Academic.

Jefferson, G. (1980). *End of grant report on conversations in which "troubles" or "anxieties" are expressed* (Rep. No. HR 4805/2). London: Social Science Research Council.

Jefferson, G. (1988). On the sequential organization of troubles – Talk in ordinary conversation. *Social Problems. 35,* 418–441.

Jefferson, G., & Lee, J. L. (1981). The rejection of advice: Managing the problematic convergence of a "troubles-telling" and a "service encounter." *Journal of Pragmatics, 5,* 399–422.

Labov, W. (1964). Phonological correlates of social stratification. *American Anthropologist, 66*(6, Part II).

Labov, W. (1970). The study of language in its social context. *Studium Generale, 23,* 30–87.

Labov, W., & Waletzky, J. (chapter 5 of this book). (Original work published 1967).

Lerner, G. (1992). Assisted storytelling: Deploying shared knowledge as a practical matter. *Qualitative Sociology, 15,* 247–271.

Mandelbaum, J. (1993). Assigning responsibility in conversational storytelling: The interactional construction of reality. *Text*, *13*, 247–266.

Orne, M. T. (1959). The nature of hypnosis: Artifact and essence. *Journal of Abnormal and Social Psychology*, *58*, 277–299.

Orne, M. T. (1962). On the social psychology of the psychological experiment: With particular reference to demand characteristics and their implications. *American Psychologist*, *17*, 776–783.

Pomerantz, A. (1987). Descriptions in legal settings. In G. Button & J. R. E. Lee (Eds.), *Talk and social organisation* (pp. 226–243). Clevedon, England: Multilingual Matters.

Rosenthal, R. (1966). *Experimenter effects in behavioral research*. New York: Appleton-Century-Crofts.

Sacks, H. (1972). On the analyzability of stories by children. In J. J. Gumperz & D. Hymes (Eds.), *Directions in sociolinguistics: The ethnography of communication* (pp. 325–345). New York: Holt, Rinehart & Winston.

Sacks, H. (1974). An analysis of the course of a joke's telling in conversation. In R. Bauman & J. Sherzer (Eds.), *Explorations in the ethnography of speaking* (pp. 337–353). Cambridge, England: Cambridge University Press.

Sacks, H. (1978). Some technical considerations of a dirty joke. In J. Schenkein (Ed.), *Studies in the organization of conversational interaction* (pp. 249–69). New York: Academic.

Sacks, H. (1992). *Lectures on conversation* (Vols. 1 & 2). Oxford, England: Blackwell.

Sacks, H., Schegloff, E. A., & Jefferson, G. (1974). A simplest systematics for the organization of turn-taking for conversation. *Language*, *50*, 696–735.

Schegloff, E. A. (1968). Sequencing in conversational openings. *American Anthropologist*, *70*, 1075–1095.

Schegloff, E. A. (1984). On some questions and ambiguities in conversation. In J. M. Atkinson & J. Heritage (Eds.), *Structures of social action: Studies in conversation analysis* (pp. 28–52). Cambridge, England: Cambridge University Press. (Reprinted from Pragmatics Microfiche, 22, D8-G1, 1976, Department of Linguistics, Cambridge University).

Schegloff, E. A. (1987). Analyzing single episodes of interaction: An exercise in conversation analysis. *Social Psychology Quarterly*, *50*, 101–114.

Schegloff, E. A. (1992). In another context. In A. Duranti & C. Goodwin (Eds.), *Rethinking context: Language as an interactive phenomenon* (pp. 193–227). Cambridge, England: Cambridge University Press.

Schegloff, E. A., & Sacks, H. (1973). Opening up closings. *Semiotica*, *8*, 289–327.

7

Narrative Structure: Some Contrasts Between Maori and Pakeha Story-telling

Janet Holmes

1 Introduction

(1) Middle-aged educated non-Maori woman describing her experience at a meeting:

> he was trying to explain how Maori people see these things you know and he he started to tell a story + I suppose to make his- + to illustrate the point I don't know + but anyway I just couldn't follow it II couldn't see what he was GETTING at I mean I simply got lost ++ I could understand the words but somehow I missed the point (Transcription conventions are provided at the end of the paper.)

Stories are remarkably flexible discourse units which can serve a range of purposes. They can be used to instruct, to entertain, to illustrate arguments, to establish connections, to mark social boundaries, and for many other functions. They occur in all kinds of contexts from the most formal social occasion to the most casual conversation. This paper explores some of the features of narratives told by New Zealanders in relaxed conversation. In particular, it focuses on differences in structural characteristics of the stories told by Maori New Zealanders compared to Pakeha New Zealanders, and explores some of the implications of these differences.

The paper begins with a brief description of differences between New Zealand Maori and Pakeha culture to provide a context for the subsequent analysis. This is followed by an outline of the analytical framework used to compare Maori and Pakeha narrative. Structural differences are then examined from two main perspectives: firstly in terms of the way the narrative is presented and secondly in terms of the listener's response to the narrative. In the final section the implications of the patterns are explored with some discussion of the cross-cultural issues they raise.

1.1 Maori and Pakeha culture

Maori are the indigenous people of New Zealand currently constituting about 13 percent of the population. 'Pakeha' is a Maori term widely used to refer to those New Zealanders of European (mainly British) origin who colonised New Zealand in the nineteenth century, and who now make up the majority of the population.[1] English is the dominant language in New Zealand in most domains for both Maori and Pakeha people, and the Maori language is in very real danger of disappearing; the contexts in which

Maori is heard have rapidly contracted over the past fifty years (Benton 1991). Recent estimates suggest that, despite efforts to revive it, the number of really fluent adult speakers of Maori has dropped to as low as 22000 (National Maori Language Survey 1995), or about 5 percent of the Maori population, with perhaps 10–20 percent moderately fluent speakers. Though Maori and Pakeha interact freely, there are many aspects of Maori and Pakeha culture which differ, some of them very subtle (see Metge 1995). Pakeha culture, a culture derived from Europe, and from Britain in particular, is the dominant culture (King 1985, 1991). Hence much descriptive research has been undertaken from a predominantly Pakeha perspective without this being explicitly acknowledged. Maori culture is much less prominent, and it is neither understood nor appreciated by the majority of Pakeha New Zealanders. It is Maori who are of necessity bicultural; most Pakehas 'are far from knowledgeable about any culture but their own' (Metge 1976: 322).

Metge and Kinloch (1978) discuss a variety of differences in Maori and Pakeha ways of communicating, pointing out that unrecognised differences are often the source of misunderstandings and of people 'talking past each other' (1978: 8–9). Maori people, for instance, emphasise non-verbal signals more and verbalisation less than Pakeha; indeed many Pakeha tend to define communication in terms of verbal expression. As a result, Pakeha often consider Maori unresponsive and difficult to talk to, while to Maori, Pakeha often miss the intended message because 'they are listening with their ears instead of their eyes' (1978: 10).

Moreover, in Maori culture silence in face-to-face interaction is not negatively evaluated as it tends to be in most Western cultures (Metge and Kinloch 1978). Silence is not seen as impolite, a failure to signal positive politeness, but rather functions for Maori in many contexts as a negative politeness device, in that it avoids imposing on others. On the other hand, silence in conjunction with non-verbal signals may be used to signal positive politeness. For example, a Maori might walk into a pub and greet acquaintances simply by making eye contact and giving a brief head nod, where a Pakeha would feel constrained to enter into a verbal routine of greeting (Stubbe 1998). Of course, depending on the context, silence can be seen as positive or negative in any culture (Tannen 1985: 98). This point is nicely illustrated by the observation that in formal public contexts, Maori will often interject verbally with *ae* or *kia ora*[2] to acknowledge or signal their approval of what the speaker is saying during their address, whereas Pakeha in the same context generally listen in silence punctuated by head nods, or at most, laughter. This example illustrates the principle of cultural relativity: the same interactional goals may be achieved by different means by members of different groups. The analysis in this paper explores a number of areas where there appear to be differences in Maori and Pakeha ways of telling stories, and discusses the potential for miscommunication arising from these differences. I have discussed my analysis with a number of Maori women and men, but it is unavoidably an analysis undertaken from a female Pakeha perspective.

1.2   A brief description of the data

The stories analysed below occurred spontaneously in the course of 30 excerpts from conversations between friends which were collected for the one million word Wellington

Corpus of Spoken New Zealand English (WCSNZE). Each conversation was a relaxed chat between two friends of the same age, gender, social class and ethnicity: i.e., 60 contributors in all. 24 of the conversationalists were people who self-identified as Maori and 36 were Pakeha; half were women and half men. Most of the conversations were collected in the home of one of the participants; in a few cases recordings were made at work in a coffee or lunch break. In all cases, only the participants were present and they recorded themselves. This conversational data base yielded 96 narratives.

Both Maori and Pakeha used stories in their everyday conversations with friends in this sample of conversational New Zealand English. While the Maori told more stories than the Pakeha, the difference was not great: the Maori people produced 45 stories in the 12 conversational excerpts analysed compared to 51 stories in the 18 Pakeha excerpts. Given the problems of deciding where to draw boundaries between stories, the greatly differing lengths of stories, and the fact that the excerpts in the WCSNZE were generally taken from longer conversations, no particular weight should be put on this difference. Moreover, not all conversations are equally conducive to story-telling. Conversational topics and 'moods' differ greatly, though in fact all but two of the recorded conversations included at least one story. In both the story-less interactions the conversations developed into task-oriented discussions of the merits and demerits of a proposed course of action – one concerning plans to buy a piece of land, the other about plans to build a ramp. The remaining conversations include a range from one to nine stories. There are examples of very short and very long stories in both the Maori and the Pakeha conversations. Indeed, in relation to story length, age was a more relevant factor than gender: older contributors tended to produce longer stories than younger ones. The next section outlines the framework used to compare structural features of Maori and Pakeha narratives.

2   Analysing Narrative

2.1   Defining a narrative

So far I have been assuming that we all know what counts as a story or a narrative, but the use of spontaneously occurring rather than elicited stories highlights the fact that this is not always self-evident. There is an extensive literature analysing narratives, and definitions range from very simple to very sophisticated. Jennifer Coates (1996: 72), for example, provides a definition which fits the preconceptions of most lay people about what constitutes a story:

> By *story*, I mean both autobiographical accounts of things that have happened to us, and anecdotes about other people and events. To count as a story, these accounts must be structured in a particular way, which in our culture basically entails having a beginning, a middle and an end.

Like many others, Coates then proceeds to use the analytical framework provided by William Labov. Labov's definition is more formal. A narrative is 'one method of recapitulating past experience by matching a verbal sequence of clauses to the sequence of events which (it is inferred) actually occurred' (Labov and Waletzky (chapter 5), p. 81; Labov 1972: 359–60).

In other words, a narrative uses a sequence of temporally ordered clauses to recapitulate past experience. As Linde (1993: 67–8) notes, this definition was developed to account for oral narratives of personal experience, and on the basis of extensive application by researchers has proved the most useful for studying 'naturally occurring oral data'. I will use it in this paper.

2.2   Labov's analytical framework

The structural framework introduced by Labov (1972) contains six components: abstract, orientation, complicating action, evaluation, resolution, coda. These can be briefly described as follows:

Abstract: What is the story about?
The abstract serves as a preface indicating what the story will be about. It may summarise and establish the point of the story.

Orientation: Who, where, when and why?
The orientation sets the scene, providing information on the characters, the time, the place and the circumstances of the story.

(Complicating) Action: What happened?
This provides the bones of the narrative and takes the form of simple-past tense main clauses which typically follow chronological order in personal experience narratives.

Evaluation: Why is this story worth telling?
This conveys the point of the story and answers the question 'so what?'

Resolution: how did it all end?

Coda: That's it.
The coda provides a wrap-up or summary and returns the conversation to present time.

Of these six components, the complicating action is technically the only essential component – what Toolan (1988: 153) calls the 'obligatory nucleus'. Hence, minimally, the structure of a story may involve just two narrative clauses, as illustrated in example (2).[3]

(2)   I went down the shops yesterday
      but I forgot my purse

As it stands, this is an example of what Labov calls an 'unevaluated' narrative. However, there is little doubt that most people would consider (2) a rather inadequate story. In white western culture the layperson's notion of a story is generally much closer to what Labov describes as an 'evaluated' story which 'makes a point', i.e., includes the evaluation component. A third clause, as illustrated in example (3), produces an 'evaluated' story.

(3)   I went down the shops yesterday
      but I forgot my purse
      so the whole expedition was a complete waste of time

As Labov notes:

> Pointless stories are met (in English) with the withering rejoinder, 'So what?' Every good narrator is continually warding off this question. (1972: 366)

The evaluation contained in the third clause, constitutes a response to this question.

Labov's definition of a narrative has been widely adopted (e.g., Polanyi 1989; A. Bell 1991; Johnstone 1993; Linde 1993; Rymes 1995; Coates 1996), and most subsequent researchers have assumed that evaluation is an integral and essential component of a narrative. Charlotte Linde (1993: 71) claims, for instance, that narratives 'crucially contain evaluations', and describes the evaluation as 'socially the most important part of the narrative' (1993: 72). However, it is clear that the issue of what counts as a story differs between social and cultural groups (cf. Heath 1983; Polanyi 1989; M. Goodwin 1991). Goodwin notes, for example, that the 'instigating' stories told by working class young black girls do not fit Labov's definition. She describes them as emerging from the social action in which talk is naturally embedded, and comments that stories might better be described as 'cultural objects designed to operate in ongoing social projects' (1991: 275–6). Goodwin focusses here on the function of the narratives for the group she was working with. Similarly Heath (1983) points to the great contrast in the definition of a story between the small-town black and white working class communities she worked with; for the white community the black community's stories 'would be lies' while for the black community, the white community's stories 'would not even count as stories' (1983: 189). Some of the differences between Maori and Pakeha story-telling which will be discussed below relate to the issue of what counts as a story. The most obvious area of contrast between Pakeha and Maori stories, for example, is the range of variation in the expression of the evaluation, and, in particular, the inexplicitness, from a Pakeha perspective, of the evaluative component in a number of Maori stories.

The evaluation is undoubtedly the most linguistically heterogeneous element of a narrative. Labov (1972) distinguishes between evaluation which is expressed outside the narrative clause(s), and evaluation which is narrative-clause-internal. The third clause of example (3), 'so the whole expedition was a complete waste of time', exemplifies a narrative-clause-external evaluation; the function of the clause is to express the evaluation. Clause-internal evaluation, is categorised by Labov into different sub-types (such as 'intensifiers' and 'comparators') which convey the narrator's attitude to the events described. In example (4) the second clause contains a narrative-clause-internal evaluation in the form of the phrase 'like a fool'.

(4)   I went down the shops yesterday
      but like a fool I forgot my purse
      so the whole expedition was a complete waste of time

Others have also noted the range of linguistic means by which the evaluation may be conveyed. Linde (1993: 72) illustrates evaluation conveyed through adverbials, repeated structures, and the contrast between direct and indirect speech. Listening to the stories in my corpus, it is clear that evaluation may also be conveyed prosodically and paralinguistically; and observation suggests that evaluation may also be expressed non-verbally, through gesture or facial expression, for instance (cf. Wolfson 1982; Linde 1993: 72).

3   Structural Features of Maori and Pakeha Narrative

3.1   The narrator's role

Many of the stories told both by Maori and Pakeha in the sample conform to Labov's suggested structure in broad outline, though few explicitly express each of the six components, and there is some variation in almost every example. Here is a very brief example from a young Pakeha woman.[4,5]

(5)   ANN: mm + I went for my driving test last week   *Abstract/Orientation*
      BEV: oh did you
      ANN: yeah
      BEV: how did that go
      ANN: oh I was good   *Action/Evaluation*
             apart from I forgot to um [laughs] stop at the red light
               Action/Evaluation
             and so I went straight through it   *Action/Evaluation*
      BEV: really
      ANN: so I have to resit it   *Resolution*
             but I'll get it next time   *Coda*

As is often the case, the evaluation extends throughout the action, since the statement 'I was good' (which implies she drove well) is said ironically, and influences the interpretation of the following two clauses. In other words, the evaluative component is expressed mainly through an ironic tone of voice.

Example (6) is a story told by a young Maori woman which illustrates the six components in Labov's analytical framework.

(6)   MAY: talking about set-ups   *Abstract*
             oh I'm getting sick of it man   *Evaluation*
             um Sam said to me after land today   *Action/Orientation*
             oh so Rachel who're you going to the ball with   *Action*
             and I said um why [laughs]   *Action*
             she said because I've got someone for you to go with   *Action*
             I said I'm going with Jonathan Davis [laughs]   *Action*
             she said oh I've got this really gorgeous nephew
             and I want him to meet you [laughs]   *Resolution*
      LYN: [laughs]
      MAY: I said well bring him along anyway [laughs]   *Coda*

Overall, there were many similarities in the structure of the stories told by members of each ethnic group. There were also, however, a number of interesting differences. I turn now to consideration of two particular areas where Maori patterns of telling a story sometimes differed from Pakeha:

(i)   A tendency to omit or truncate story components:
        A number of the Maori stories have no explicit resolution or coda and as a result, from a Pakeha perspective, the story seems to have been left unfinished.[6]
(ii) The reduction of lexicalised structural support for complicating action:
        There are elements of the complicating action, in particular when reported speech is involved, which are often assumed or left implicit by Maori narrators, or which are conveyed prosodically rather than lexically. Again, these stories sometimes appear incomplete or reduced from a Pakeha perspective.

3.1.1   Reduced narrative structure

It should first be recognised that many of the stories told by the Maori participants are structurally complete in terms of Labov's framework, though this is sometimes achieved very economically. In fact, stories told by both Maori and Pakeha often end with a clause which serves the dual function of resolution and evaluation.

(7)   i.   Story of an experience in a recording studio told by young Pakeha man:
              that was a really weird experience
        ii.   Story about wisdom teeth operation told by young Pakeha woman:
              but it's all been fine
        iii. Story about escapade in a video parlour told by young Maori man:
              oh what eggs man
        iv. Story of a confrontation with a student told by young Maori woman:
              I wanted him to know that I could see where he was doing right and that you know I'm not too big to say you're doing a good job

These final clauses serve to bring the account of the action to a close, though their main function is clearly evaluative; and they illustrate lexically explicit evaluations.

Stories told by Pakeha, however, very often end with an overt resolution clause too. (8) is a particularly clear example where Tom makes the point of his story quite explicit.

(8)   Story of how he 'drove' his video told by middle-aged Pakeha man:
        but the whole point about this is I solved the technology problem

These final resolution clauses are often introduced by the discourse particle 'so':

(9)   i.   Story of failing driving test told by young Pakeha woman:
              so I have to resit it
        ii.   Story of visit to father told by middle-aged Pakeha woman:
              so Annie stayed there and made him some lunch
              and then we went back afterwards
        iii. Story of why he hadn't been in his office all day told by middle-aged Pakeha man:
              so you see this is why I haven't been in my office

iv.   Story of a series of phone calls which disrupted his evening told by young
      Pakeha man:
      she rang back and said how good it was   *Action/Evaluation*
      so that was four phone calls   *Resolution*
v.   Story told by young Pakeha woman about a dessert with sherry added at
      one end of the dish:
      so I had a second helping at the other end

In some of the Maori stories, however, the evaluation is much less lexically explicit,
and the resolution and coda may be omitted entirely. The listener is left to draw their
own conclusion, or, perhaps more accurately from the Maori participants' viewpoint,
the narrator considers the point of the story requires no elaboration.[7] When this
happens and there is no explicit evaluation, resolution clause or coda, the effect from a
Pakeha point of view is that the story seems incomplete.

Example (10), which was narrated by an older Maori woman, illustrates a story where
the resolution and evaluation are nowhere expressed by the narrator in explicit lexicalised form.

(10) NINA: yep see I used to smoke f-first thing in the morning   *Orientation*
      HANA: yeah
      NINA: and one famous morning I nearly set fire to my bedding
                  Orientation/Abstract
      HANA: [laughs] I know it's not funny but [laughs]
      NINA: I reached over and grabbed a fag and lit up   *Action*
      HANA: mm
      NINA: ++ and um + then I (used) to smoke all the time at work and now I don't
                  care now
      HANA: mm

The last two clauses are prosodically marked as not part of the narrative. They are separated by pauses and distinct intonation contours from the previous clauses. They are
descriptive clauses containing information on habitual behaviour rather than relating to
a particular experience as a story does. They are included to make it clear that Nina's
story finishes at the line marked 'Action'. This might be regarded as a very embryonic
story, but it progresses beyond an abstract to a clause that is clearly classifiable as constituting complicating action. The narrator provides no explicit evaluation, resolution
or coda. However, the point of the story, as well as its resolution, are apparently adequately indicated as far as the listener, Hana, is concerned. Hana herself provides a
potential evaluation by indicating that she finds the story amusing, but the narrator
nowhere indicates the 'point' of the story explicitly. It appears that, in context, the
implicit signal provided in the abstract is perfectly adequate from the point of view of
both conversationalists. So, although this story seems incomplete from a Pakeha perspective, the Maori narrator assumes the point does not need to be made lexically
explicit in a resolution clause; the discourse context provided is sufficient.

Another example involves a much longer story, but once again it appears to finish
very abruptly from a Pakeha perspective. Kay recounts at great length, and with con-

siderable descriptive detail, the story of how her son, Sam, wooed his wife, Lynnette. Kay tells, for example, how she advised Sam on effective courtship strategies. Kay's story ends with an account of how Sam would turn up at Lynnette's workplace in his navy officer's uniform (with a digression about how smart he looked in it) and

(11)   with a bunch of flowers
        and take [laughs] Lynnette out to lunch
        she goes it was [drawls] lovely
        I said that's the way to do it [laughs]
        and he said and I listened to you Mum [laughs]
        yeah which is good

This last section is clearly a closing evaluation but there is no explicit statement spelling out the resolution: e.g., 'and so he won her' or 'and so that's how they got together'. The story grew out of a discussion of Lynnette's vow that she would never marry a navy man because her two sisters had done so, and she knew the costs. In this context, and especially given its length and the level of detail with which the complicating action is elaborated, a Pakeha listener expects an ending conveying the message 'so in fact Lynnette came to marry a navy man after all/despite her vow'. But the narrator assumes this point is quite clear on the basis of the earlier contextualisation of the story, and indeed, it is a comment from her addressee, Hine, 'and then she ended up marrying a navy man', which encourages her to elaborate and develop the story at such length. The narrator clearly assumes the point does not need to be made lexically explicit in a resolution clause; the discourse context already provided is sufficient.

This tendency to leave the story 'unfinished' or open-ended is typical of Maori narratives, myths or 'life stories' told in Maori contexts. One never finishes a story because the narrative continues and is continually up-dated. On the next appropriate occasion, speakers may pick up and continue the ongoing narrative. It seems possible that the tendency to avoid closing off a story in English reflects this practice in Maori cultural contexts.

The tendency in Maori stories to leave meanings implicit is apparent not only in the narratives, but also in other aspects of the conversation between the Maori participants. From a Pakeha point of view, ideas are often introduced and left undeveloped, in an embryonic state. Points are sometimes sketched in outline and left to sit, briefly mentioned, gently tossed into the conversation, and left there – presumably for the other person to consider and pick up if they are interested. Discussing these features with Pakeha teachers of Maori language, it became clear that these are features which characterise interactions among Maori in the Maori language. One teacher, who is married to a fluent Maori speaker and who mixes often in Maori contexts, commented that one needed to be a very active listener when communicating in Maori; the speaker leaves a great deal unstated and expects the listener to work hard to decode meaning. The implications of such interactional strategies for cross-cultural communication in a range of contexts are well worth further consideration.

3.1.2   Reduced lexical scaffolding in 'action' component

A second feature which characterises some of the Maori stories involves the degree to which the complicating action is lexically elaborated. There are a number of stories where rather than components of the larger narrative structure being omitted, assumed or implied, components within the complicating action are implied rather than stated. This is especially apparent in sections involving reported speech where the listener is expected to infer who is speaking.

(12)   REWI: well it's like I tried learning off the old um my grandmother
                   and she was saying like
                   I thought how how much do you
                   how do you leave it in
                   how long do you leave it in the fridge for
                   oh till you knead (need?) it
         PETER: yeah [laughs] [laughs]
         REWI: (I said how long's that)
                   I don't know
                   how long are you going to knead it
         PETER: (yeah)
         REWI: next I said well who knows
         PETER: yeah
         REWI: is it two weeks can you leave it
                   oh I suppose so
         PETER: [laughs]
         REWI: couldn't get any answers out of her like
         PETER: [laughs] yeah
         REWI: you know how do you make it-
                   she goes oh well you get a bit of flour
                   you put it in you put a bit of
                   you put a bit of sugar in
                   and then you put a bit of water in
                   how much?
                   oh as much as you need
         PETER: [laughs] yeah [laughs]
         REWI: sorry Nana I sort of
                   I don't understand those /sort of instructions\
         PETER: /yeah\
                   Mum got hoohaa [cross] with me
                   cause she said I was too impatient

A similar story told by a Pakeha would typically be provided with more overt lexicalised scaffolding in the form of signals of speakerhood, such as 'she said' and 'I said' throughout.[8] In example (12) the listener is expected to follow the story with very few explicit lexical signals; some of the (from a Pakeha perspective) 'missing' information is conveyed by the intonation and prosody, but there remains a considerable amount of work to be done by the listener to follow who is saying what. Yet Peter gives no indication that he has any trouble following the story. Indeed he follows it with a story of his own which makes a related point about Maori ways of doing things.

There are a number of examples of older Maori speakers using this strategy of presenting direct reported speech without indicating explicitly who produced the quoted utterance. Example (13) begins with conventional (by Pakeha standards) lexical scaffolding but then abandons it. The only remaining signal of speaker change is the discourse marker *well* which introduces the reported speech (Schiffrin 1987).

(13)   LEN: he's he said to me the other day
              dad I've been in this city for eighteen years
              he says I'm sick of everything
              I want-
              I said oh well what do you want to do
       JO: yeah I know how he feels
       LEN: what do you want to do I said
              well I want to go to australia
              well how're you gonna get there
              how you go- you gonna fly there
       JO: yeah

The effect of withdrawing the lexical framing is to emphasise and give impact and immediacy to the quoted words, and this can be used to convey evaluative affect (cf. Toolan 1988: 121). This strategy is used not only in stories but also in the analysis of issues, when different people's viewpoints are cited. For example, in example (14), discussing why a colleague, Hera, would not accept the name suggested for a teaching unit, Te Moana suddenly switches to direct speech with no overt linguistic signal that she is hypothesising about what Hera might say. She uses direct reported speech as a device for conveying Hera's position sympathetically.

(14)   ANA: anyway she started to come round towards the towards the end of the year
              but I think it was just a
              I think it was a um um [tut] a confidence thing
              you know she's just a bit
       TM: or on-
              I was also thinking that maybe it was more because um
              I didn't choose the name
              it's not necessarily my choice

Though it is clear what is intended, a Pakeha person might well have inserted a phrase such as 'she might think/say/take the position' before 'I didn't choose the name'. Here the hesitation *um* serves to introduce the reported speech which is signalled prosodically by a shift in pitch, rather than lexically.

By contrast, the following example, taken from a conversation between two young Pakeha men, illustrates extensive explicit lexical attributions of speakerhood, using forms of the verbs *say* and *go*.

(15)   CON: she says oh you're not going to work on the night fills
              (and) I go oh no
              Wally just only said he'd give me three hours a week
              and she goes yeah I know
              which means what Wally was telling me about the ten hours
              was all bullshit

'cause she goes yeah I know I've had the productivity through and
        everything . . .
    and then I rung up Wally on Tuesday
    and says oh is that okay you know the dates I put down there and every
        thing for leaving
    and he said oh what's this I see on my desk what's this
    and I go well I'm leaving you know
BEN: yeah
CON: he said WHY [laughs]
    I said well you can only offer me three hours a week it's hardly worth my while
BEN: yep
CON: and he goes um what did he say
    he goes I could've given you anywhere up to ten
BEN: [laughs]
CON: and I go oh

The features I have described – the omission of an explicit resolution clause
and the reduction of lexical scaffolding for reported speech in the complicating
action – are more frequent in the Maori than the Pakeha stories, but it is certainly
not the case that they characterise only Maori stories or all Maori stories. As mentioned above, there are many stories told by Maori contributors in which an explicit evaluation clearly also serves as a resolution, and many which provide overt lexical
scaffolding for dialogue. Example (16), for instance, is a brief story told by a young
female Maori teacher of adults to a fellow teacher. Its main point is to convey the narrator's attitude to the request made of her by an older male student, and this is made
very clear indeed; moreover, the reported dialogue is quite explicitly attributed to
specific speakers.

(16)   PANE: old um John Smithson came up to me today   *Abstract/Orientation*
            and said oh do I pay my thirty dollars to you   *Action*
            and I said [tut] well have you been receiving letters
            to say that you owe them thirty dollars   *Action*
            and he goes oh yeah   *Action/Evaluation*
            and I went well THAT'S who you pay it to   *Resolution/Evaluation*
    KATH: [laughs] [laughs] smarmy   *Evaluation*
    PANE: [laughs] that's eXACtly how I said it too   *Evaluation*
            I said it to him like that   *Evaluation*
            oh it was so funny   *Evaluation*

Pane constructs the student as a bothersome and rather stupid man who can't read
or accurately interpret simple communications. The evaluation is quite explicit in her
tone of voice as well as the content and syntax which involves Pane, a young woman,
speaking to an older Pakeha man as if he were a small child or intellectually limited in
some way. Kath responds 'smarmy', lexicalising the negative attitude conveyed by
Pane's tone and syntax. The implicit evaluation expressed by the tone of voice and
prosody of the clause identified as the resolution is externalised and emphasised in the

subsequent overtly evaluative clauses. So this story conveys Pane's attitude to an older Pakeha male student, and the final evaluative clause spells out the point of the story. And this example also clearly illustrates the use of explicit verb forms (*say* and *go*) to report utterances attributed to the different speakers.

3.1.3   Interpreting the point

As indicated in the previous section, as a Pakeha woman listening to these Maori conversations on tape, I often felt that stories seemed unfinished and incomplete. This was partly due to the fact that the Pakeha stories conformed to a structure which I could recognise and which felt very familiar: they always had a beginning, a middle and an end which I could identify. In particular, I had little difficulty in recognising their point; I had confidence that I knew at least the overt reason why the narrator had told the story, and why they considered it worth telling. But this was not always true for the Maori stories, particularly those told by the older Maori contributors. I was often left wondering what exactly the story had been about, and unclear as to why it had been told. The point was sometimes embedded deep within the story, implicit rather than overt, expressed prosodically, paralinguistically or non–verbally, rather than lexically, and in some cases, heavily dependent on the social and discourse context for its significance.

The following example may help in suggesting the importance of knowing a great deal of background cultural and sometimes historical context in interpreting stories. [. . .]

[The] story relates the death of an old man in a house where the narrator and his addressee (who is his brother) were staying as young boys. The story is . . . redolent with cultural significance, and the two conversationalists allude to one aspect of this quite explicitly in the coda. The story ends as follows:

(18)   LEN: yeah they had him in a sheet yeah on the
       Jo: on on (. . .)
      LEN: verandah
      Jo: well yeah yeah and they bought him bought him inside after a while at night
      LEN: (was) yeah yeah
      Jo: they bought him in (late at night)
      LEN: yeah + on the front of the house there
          out on the porch there
      Jo: yeah I could you know I I
          from that from that day to this day I could feel something about that old fella
      LEN: yeah
      Jo: you know the- the- there was something that he we never we never ever got
          but knew was there eh

The story is clearly highly significant for the narrator; the old man had made a deep impression on him. The final two clauses simply hint at this, and are opaque to those who had not shared the experience, and even more opaque to those unfamiliar with the significance for the young Maori boys of the death of a highly respected elder in a Maori household.

Overall, then, the Pakeha narrators tend to spell out the significance of their stories more explicitly than do the Maori. They tend to indicate the end of a story quite explicitly, generally with a clause expressing a resolution, often introduced by 'so'. And components of the story such as the evaluation, resolution and coda, as well as elements of the complicating action tend to be signalled and expressed lexically more extensively than in some Maori stories.

The features I have identified as characteristic of some Maori stories occur most often in contexts where the conversationalists are well-versed in Maori culture. They also typify contexts where the conversationalists know each other well; indeed in some cases the two participants were related. Hence, the implicit meanings conveyed by narrators may reflect the closeness of the relationship between the conversationalists. However, this was not always the case and, in particular, there was a contrast between the younger and the older Maori women where the relationships between the conversationalists were very comparable. While the older Maori women's stories were often characterised by truncated structures of various kinds, suggesting they expected their listeners to follow without needing to spell everything out, the stories of the young Maori women were least characterised by the features I have described in this section. (See, for instance, examples (6) and (16) above where speaker attributions are explicitly made throughout.) I will return to this point in the conclusion.

3.2 The listener's role in narrative

Jennifer Coates (1996) notes that within the women's conversations she analysed, the structure of stories is unusual. Stories are much more of a solo performance than other parts of the conversations where a genuinely collaborative floor generally develops, which she describes as 'polyphonic talk', analogous to a musical 'jam session' (Coates 1996: 133). While it is true that during the telling of a story the floor is generally dominated by one speaker, it is also true that the listener's role may be a relatively active one. Spontaneous conversational stories can often be analysed as joint productions or interactive achievements, involving both the narrator and the addressee to differing extents. Indeed, there is a good deal of research on American and white Western narrative illustrating the ways in which the audience contributes to the creation of a story (e.g., Wolfson 1976; Duranti 1986; C. Goodwin 1986; S. E. Bell 1988; Riessman 1993; Corston 1993; Rymes 1995). In Polynesian contexts, Watson (1975) describes an overlapping style used by Hawaiian children in narration, and Besnier (1990) found that Nukulaelae gossip on Tuvalu was characterised in part by the use of contrapuntal co-constructed narratives. Moerman (1988: 23) similarly notes the phenomenon of 'talking as a team' in Thai conversations.

In the New Zealand data there was a great deal of variation in the extent to which the 'audience' contributed to a story. At one end of the scale the co-conversationalist's role was expressed by minimal verbal indications of interest and attention, while at the other there were a few stories which were much more jointly constructed. These could be described as collaborative, interactive or 'dialogic' in structure (Cheepen 1988).[9] Hence, in analysing this aspect of the New Zealand data, it was useful to consider two distinct continuums, the first relating to the role of narrator, the second to the role of addressee or listener. Figure 1 focuses on the narrator role.

Solo construction .... Joint construction

Figure 1   Narrator role

Supportive ....Unsupportive

Figure 2   Listener role

At one extreme a narration may be completely solo, quintessential 'one-at-a-time' talk (Coates 1989), as when a story is read aloud. At the other, a story may be co-constructed from contributions by two or more subjects. In theory, the way in which these contributions are integrated is another area of potential variation: they could, for example, be sequential, as in games where each contributor must pick up the story from where the previous person stops, or, at the other extreme, contributions may be simultaneous, with co-construction an on-going dynamic process (e.g., Sheldon 1996).

Turning to the role of the listener(s) or audience, one continuum on which this role can be evaluated is the degree of support that the addressee gives to the narrator in telling the story. Figure 2 represents this continuum.

The two continuums are obviously closely related in that one extreme type of supportive behaviour might be to share the narrator's role. But, while this may accurately describe verbal interaction in some social and cultural contexts, it is not always the case, and at the conceptual level it is useful to distinguish the two roles. There are certainly some social contexts where the most supportive audience behaviour involves allowing the narrator uncontested access to the floor, and there are also contexts where a completely silent response can be totally supportive, indicating appreciation, respect or understanding (Holmes and Stubbe 1997; Stubbe 1998). In more formal contexts, for instance, silence is interpreted positively, speakers are allowed to continue uninterrupted until they have finished, and there is no expectation of immediate verbal feedback. In the pub, on the other hand, a familiar story may well attract a range of different supportive contributions from the audience in the course of its narration.

The New Zealand corpus illustrated a range of points on both the narrator and the listener continuums. Each of the conversations involved only two contributors, and the most common pattern was for stories to clearly 'belong to' one or other speaker. On the other hand, there were examples of jointly constructed stories. These were typically reminiscences of shared experiences or re-livings of past shared adventures. In this data, these tended to occur more often in the Maori conversations, but they were so few in number that no great significance can be attached to this.

From the point of view of ethnic contrast, the listener's role was the area of most interest. Though there was much in common in the way listeners from both ethnic groups in the New Zealand corpus responded to narratives, there were also two areas where interesting differences were apparent: firstly, the amount of feedback given by Maori and Pakeha listeners differed; and secondly, there was a contrast in the type of feedback they provided.

3.2.1   Amount of feedback

There has been considerable research establishing that different cultural groups vary widely in the amount of verbal feedback they consider appropriate or polite in interaction. Polanyi (1989: 48), for example, describes how white middle class Americans listening to a story are expected to respond: 'there is a strong expectation that they will show their appreciation . . . while the story is being told using nods, minimal responses, laughter, and comments to express interest, sympathy, or surprise'. Japanese listeners are expected to be even more responsive. White (1989) demonstrated that the Japanese he recorded had a higher overall baseline for verbal backchannelling than Americans from mid-western USA: the Japanese used approximately three times as many minimal responses as the Americans. White relates this finding to the Japanese cultural value of omoiyari (literally 'being kind, generous to others') which places great emphasis on the creation and maintenance of harmonious interaction. At the other end of the scale, Lehtonen and Sajavaara (1985: 195) report that the use of vocalisations and verbal backchannels is less frequent in Finnish than in many Central European languages or in British or American English, and that interruptions are generally unacceptable. Listener feedback occurs primarily via non-verbal signals, making the typical Finn a silent listener.

An analysis of the verbal feedback provided by a sample of Maori and Pakeha listeners from this New Zealand corpus made it clear that different norms prevail between these groups too (Stubbe 1998). There was a striking and statistically significant difference in the overall rates of verbal feedback, with the Maori conversationalists producing, on average, approximately a third less verbal feedback than the Pakeha. By comparison with Pakeha, Maori conversationalists seem to have a lower baseline for providing verbal feedback.

This finding is consistent with the ethnographic observations of Metge and Kinloch (1978), mentioned above (as well as the patterns discussed in the previous section), that verbalisation is of relatively greater importance to Pakeha than it is to Maori. The lower Maori level of verbal feedback should not be interpreted to mean that the Maori speakers were less involved than the Pakeha speakers in the collaborative production of narrative. It is important to bear in mind that an attentive silence is an important way of signalling listener interest in many contexts. And, in fact, much of the time Maori listeners demonstrated their attention and involvement in the ongoing discourse by means of verbal feedback in similar ways to the Pakeha speakers. Moreover, anecdotal evidence and observation suggest that there is a correspondingly greater use of a range of non-verbal feedback strategies by Maori listeners, but this is an area where further investigation is clearly needed.

3.2.2   Type of feedback

In recent work, researchers have begun to pay attention not only to the amount of verbal feedback given by different social groups but also to its function and placement in interaction. Moreover, the set of forms that has been examined has been extended to include a more open-ended set of short utterances, often together with vocalisations such as laughter (e.g., Stenstrom 1994; Reid 1995). And, as mentioned above, there has been considerable, mainly American, research, on the ways in which and the extent to which the 'audience' typically contributes to the construction of a narrative.

In this area too, appropriate listener behaviour varies cross-culturally. Cooperative overlapping, for instance, is often used to signal active listening and conversational involvement, but the form, placement and interpretation of such overlaps differ between cultures and speech communities, and even between sub-groups of the same speech community (e.g., Scollon 1985).

Analysing the conversations in this New Zealand sample, Maria Stubbe (1998) distinguished supportive from neutral minimal responses, as well as more extended overtly supportive feedback, such as cooperative overlaps, from neutral verbal feedback. Though there were no overall significant differences in the numbers of these produced by Maori vs Pakeha listeners, detailed qualitative analysis suggested that the listener's responses were sensitive to a range of factors such as the nature of the relationship between the conversationalists, and the type of talk in which they are engaged. Ethnic variation in listener responses according to the type of talk is the focus of the analysis in the next section.

3.2.3   *Questioning the narrator*

Focusing specifically on narrative, one area where the Maori and Pakeha listeners in this corpus clearly differed was in the extent to which the Pakeha listeners actively asked questions of the story tellers. It was quite common for Pakeha listeners to contribute to the story by asking questions which encouraged the narrator to proceed with the story, to elaborate on particular aspects (especially the orientation), or to develop it further. By contrast, there were very few examples of this kind of interactive behaviour among the Maori contributers. Maori listeners tended to listen silently, or to provide instances of minimal feedback or short supportive comments. They rarely actively inserted a question into the course of the narrative.

Looking in more detail at the questions asked by those listening to a narrative, it was clear that questions functioned differently at different points in the narrative. Firstly, a question or encouraging comment could serve to elicit a narrative. At the simplest level, a question such as 'so what have you been up to recently?' might well elicit a story. In many cases, speakers would mention topics which held the potential for elaboration. Permission to tell a story might then be overtly negotiated, as illustrated in the following example from the brief narrative quoted in full as example (5) above.

(19)   ANN: mm + I went for my driving test last week *Abstract*
       BEV: oh did you?
       ANN: yeah
       BEV: how did that go?

Ann's abstract serves as a signal that she has a story to tell, but she waits till Bev's prompt *how did that go?* before telling more.

Example (20) provides another example where the listener's comment 'licenses' the story. The topic of how he came to resign from his job is first briefly mentioned by Sam's co-conversationalist. At a later point in the conversation Sam says:

(20)   SAM: so er you've handed in your resignation

Sam is clearly inviting a fuller account of the resignation; the particle 'so' signals that this information has already been provided. There are a number of examples of such 'licensing' questions which invite or give permission for the story to be told.

(21) Story about cooking Maori bread is produced in response to the question:
      can you do that can you cook them?

(22) Mark's question licenses a story about cooking a huge variety of sausages:
      BRIAN: I've done all the butcher's sausages now
      MARK: you've done all the butcher's sausages?

Licensing comments in Maori conversations are often quite laconic:

(23) Hine's response licenses a story explaining why the child's grandmother is not proficient in Maori:
      KAY: she can beat her nanny and auntie to speak Maori
      HINE: yeah?

Whether the story emerges as a response to a question or licensing comment, or is volunteered, does not differ markedly between the ethnic groups. Both Maori and Pakeha use questions which lead to the telling of a story, and there are no noticeable ethnic differences in this respect.

   Where ethnic difference become apparent is when questions occur during the course of the narration. As Coates (1996: 95–96) comments, narratives are unusual because they are much more solo performances than is typical of conversational interaction. However, in a number of the Pakeha stories particular components – especially elements of the orientation and evaluation – are elicited by the co-conversationalist's questions. (The relevant questions are italicised.)

(24) VERA: OH and um did I tell you Jude's got married?
      MEG: JUDE
      VERA: yeah
      MEG: *when did that happen?*

(25) ANN: I gave blood today
      BEV: *did you whereabouts?*

(26) JOE: we played- [laughs] played the top team
      MICK: *who- who are they?*

(27) TOM: and I picked up the video thingy you know the
      GARY: *is this the G code?*

In each case, the questions encourage the narrator to supply further details. Questions such as these during the course of a narrative are much rarer in the Maori interactions.

Though such questions can disrupt the flow of the story (see Holmes 1997), there is evidence that they are often perceived as supportive by Pakeha narrators, serving as evidence of the listener's attention and interest.[10] So during a long story told by a Pakeha woman, Helen, to her friend, Joan, about how she looks after her elderly father, Joan asks a question which is clearly welcomed by Helen as an opportunity to elaborate on her daughter Annie's relationship with Helen's father, Jason (Annie's grandfather).

(28)   HEL: so we went in and visited him
and I said Annie'll stay with you and make you some lunch
and she gets on quite–
and she chats away with Jason and they have quite a nice–
JOAN: *she's very good with adults isn't she?*
HEL: yes she is she's–
well she's good with him too
I don't know they sort of get along nicely
and um better than the other two do really you know

Joan's question functions as a positive politeness strategy indicating an interest in Annie, Helen's daughter, with a positive comment which Helen clearly appreciates.

Finally, when a narrator appears to have finished a story, Pakeha listeners often ask questions which extend the story or develop it into a discussion. I will give just two examples. At the end of a story about having her wisdom teeth out, Maria's listener asks a question which sets off another story.

(29)   PAT: *how much did it cost to get your teeth out?*

In example (30) Mona is recounting a long story about how a hair-dressing salon made a mess of colouring her hair. The questions asked by her conversational partner, Carol, are similarly facilitative; and, as Mona appears to be winding up the story, Carol encourages her to elaborate with some interpretive comment.

(30)   MONA: so I'm going to phone the salon tomorrow and speak to the owner if she's there
CAROL: yeah
MONA: and um just ask her to do something about it
CAROL: *gosh that's pretty poor isn't it*
MONA: well I don't have his home phone number or I'd phone him at home
CAROL: yeah [tut] *oh so they're trying to avoid you?*

By asking questions in this way, listeners are expressing positive politeness. Indicating interest in another's topic is clearly a way of signalling positive affect, and suggesting that both listener and speaker share similar attitudes and values. And asking questions which elicit further information about the topic is one linguistic strategy for indicating interest in it.

Maori listeners by contrast generally do not ask such questions. Often they simply do not provide any overt comment at the end of a story, apart from general minimal feedback. When they do, it is often just a brief evaluative comment indicating understanding.

(31)   Following a story about a woman who resisted smoking at an emotionally demand-
        ing event when all around her were smoking:

yes that's hard

Sometimes the Maori listener responds with a sympathetic mirroring story, as indicated at the end of example (12) above:

(32)   REWI: sorry Nana I sort of
                I don't understand those /sort of instructions\
        PETER: /yeah\
                Mum got hoohaa [cross] with me
                cause she said I was too impatient

Peter goes on to tell a story which makes a similar point. Sometimes a story was picked
up and extended or commented on much later in the conversation, where, from the perspective of a Pakeha listener, it did not obviously seem to 'fit' (another example perhaps of
the pervasiveness of implicit contextualisation in Maori exchanges).[11] Overall, however,
there seems to be an assumption by Maori conversationalists that the listener is providing
an adequate response by simply attending to the story. Being polite in Maori interaction,
it seems, does not involve initiating further talk or asking questions to extend a person's
narrative. Indeed such behaviour may be perceived and experienced as overly intrusive.

To summarise, there are many respects in which Maori and Pakeha responded similarly to the stories of their conversational partners. However, there were also examples
where contrasting responses were evident, and it seems possible that these reflect different attitudes to the listener's role in conversation, a point which is discussed further
below. Maori listeners tended to listen relatively silently compared to Pakeha. They provided less overt verbal feedback of any kind in conversation than Pakeha. Pakeha listeners, by contrast, not only supplied ongoing explicit verbal feedback, but also often
asked questions to elicit more information in the course of a narrative, and at the end
of a narrative. These intra-textual and post-narrative questions occurred much more
often in the Pakeha than in the Maori conversations.

It seems very likely that Maori listeners use non-verbal strategies as well as minimal
responses for signalling attention and interest and doing the ongoing work of being a
good co-conversationalist. This is certainly consistent with observation of Maori interaction in more public settings. More systematic analysis of Maori non-verbal behaviour
in private informal settings using well-trained participant observers or video equipment
is an obvious area for further research.

4   Conclusion

Maori people are necessarily bicultural. There is no such requirement for Pakeha in
New Zealand whose language and culture dominate almost every social domain. As a

result Maori patterns of interaction in English are indistinguishable from those of Pakeha in many respects. This encourages the assumption that there are no cultural differences in this area. In fact, however, differences do exist, as illustrated in this paper, though they are not widespread, and they may be most frequent in private social contexts between Maori people.

In both cultures it is assumed that one does not need to spell out the obvious. Indeed, to do so in intimate contexts can be insulting. In both cultures solidarity licenses assumptions about shared values, cultural knowledge and attitudes. However, the precise areas and ways in which these assumptions become relevant, and the interactive strategies through which they are realised sometimes differ.

The areas of difference identified in this paper suggest that Maori people feel that explicitness is unnecessary more often than Pakeha. The stories told by Maori were sometimes considerably less lexically explicit than the Pakeha. Using Labov's framework, the evaluation component was often conveyed through tone of voice, prosody or paralinguistic strategies; the resolution and coda were sometimes omitted. The Maori narrators assumed more often than the Pakeha that these elements were self-evident. Similarly, there were examples where reported speech was not attributed explicitly to specific characters in a story; the lexical scaffolding typical of reported speech in narrative was omitted. As listeners, Maori conversationalists were also less verbally explicit than Pakeha. Firstly, they used less overt verbal feedback than Pakeha listeners. Secondly, where Pakeha listeners often asked questions in the course of a narrative to elicit further detail, Maori listeners rarely did so.

These differences suggest that behaving as a polite conversationalist may involve different responses from Maori and Pakeha. Pakeha tend to make things clear, spelling out the point of a story for maximum impact. Listening to the stories in the sample, it seems that narrators used this strategy in order to make their stories more entertaining, more of a performance for their listener's benefit. In some of the Maori stories, by contrast, the denouement is low key, underplayed and inexplicit. The narrator seems to assume that the point is self-evident, a climactic ending unnecessary. The emphasis is on the intimacy of the relationship between the two conversationalists – things do not need spelling out.

As listeners, there was a consistent tendency for the Maori informants to produce verbal feedback at a markedly lower overall frequency than the Pakeha informants, suggesting that the two groups operate according to different baseline levels when providing this type of feedback. In conversational contexts, Maori listeners sometimes indicate attention and interest by keeping silent, rather than providing verbal feedback and asking questions as Pakeha do. Silent attentive behaviour is a strategy for signalling interest in both cultures, but it is less common in one-to-one interaction among Pakeha.

Hence, while both groups have experience of the behaviour patterns I have described, the contexts in which they use them and the extent to which they use them seems to differ. Pakeha tend to use active positively polite behaviour, asserting interest and indicating shared attitudes more overtly. Maori tend to use negatively polite strategies more often than Pakeha in these contexts, avoiding verbal intrusion on the speaker's floor. If these patterns occur in cross-cultural interaction, there is a possibility of misinterpretation. And because it is Maori who are bicultural, it is Pakeha who are most likely to misunderstand.

[. . .]

Finally, it is worth noting that the patterns identified in this analysis may raise problems not only for inter-cultural communication but also in the area of education. Many children find it difficult to meet the demand for explicitness which characterises western education. In written work, in particular, young writers are often admonished for making assumptions about the reader's level of familiarity with the subject, and standard exam advice exhorts students to make their knowledge explicit and avoid being too cryptic. In this context a tendency to assume knowledge and avoid spelling out matters which seem self-evident may be a disadvantage. Similarly, relatively silent listening may be misunderstood as inattentiveness in contexts where higher levels of verbal feedback are the majority group norm.

This analysis has focused on areas of difference between Maori and Pakeha telling stories in informal conversational contexts. Many of the patterns I have identified are by no means widespread or typical. They are of interest, however, because it seems possible that they are indicative of patterns which may be misinterpreted or cause inter-ethnic communication problems when they do occur.[12] The analysis has explored areas where Pakeha tend to be more explicit than Maori, but it is important to note the cultural relativity of all such behaviour. In other contexts, it is Pakeha who are less explicit and Maori who make issues clear. Pakeha tend to 'skip the formalities' of formal welcomes, for instance, thus giving offence to Polynesian people for whom greeting rituals are crucial symbols in the process of extablishing contact between people (Metge and Kinloch 1978: 15; Metge 1995). On the other hand, Pakeha often react negatively to the repetition, paraphrase and other rhetorical features of formal Maori oratory, perceiving these discourse patterns as over-elaborated and redundant. Because we internalise the norms of our own culture, we may be insensitive to the arbitrariness of particular patterns. Such norms operate largely below the level of conscious awareness, and so the possibility of different meanings often goes unrecognised. In the area of discourse, this can lead to misinterpretation of the speaker's intentions. And in New Zealand, because the conventions of the dominant social or cultural group, the Pakeha, are widely regarded as the norm, it is Maori who are typically required to adapt or to suffer the negative consequences of any resulting miscommunication. This paper is intended to assist in identifying at least some of these areas of potential miscommunication.

Transcription conventions

YES	Capitals indicate emphatic stress
[laughs]	Paralinguistic features in square brackets
[drawls]	
+	Pause of up to one second
++	Two second pause
(4)	Indicates length of longer pauses in seconds
..../......\...	Simultaneous speech
..../.......\...	
(hello)	Transcriber's best guess at an unclear utterance
?	Rising or question intonation
-	Incomplete or cut-off utterance

Notes

I would like to express my appreciation to Maria Stubbe, Chris Lane and Harima Fraser who read drafts of this paper and provided valuable comments which have greatly improved it. I have also discussed the material with a number of the Maori narrators who prefer not to be identified by name but for whose insights and assistance I here record a great debt of gratitude. The paper has also benefited from the comments of two anonymous referees. The research was made possible by a grant from the New Zealand Foundation for Research, Science and Technology.

1   As a shorthand device and for convenience, I use the terms 'Maori' and 'Pakeha' as if they designated clear-cut groups. Recent social constructionist approaches emphasise the relativist status of ethnic (and gender) identities, and define the categories of Maori and Pakeha ethnicity as having emerged *as such* as a result of colonisation and its aftermath (King 1985, 1991; Ritchie 1992; Walker 1989).

2   *Ae* is the Maori word for 'yes', while in this context the greeting *kia ora* similarly signals affirmation of what the speaker has just said.

3   In presenting narrative excerpts I have adopted the widely accepted convention of dividing the transcript into lines corresponding to narrative clauses which makes it easier for readers to follow the analysis.

4   In order to keep this paper to a reasonable length I have selected brief examples wherever possible.

5   All names have been changed to protect identities. I have done some minor editing for ease of reading: e.g., each clause is generally given a separate line and overlapping speech is not indicated where it is not relevant to the point being made.

6   Compare Scollon and Scollon's comments (1981: 33, 119–120) on the relative inexplicitness of Athabaskan Indian narratives from an American Anglo viewpoint. Though the historical and political context is very different, their discussion suggests possible reasons for this feature.

7   Compare Scollon and Scollon's comments on Athabaskan stories. When told to an Athabaskan audience 'the best telling of a story is the briefest', they do not need 'to be expanded with explanations or motivations. These are understood' (1981: 119).

8   My earliest research on discourse analysis (Holmes 1970) explored the many functions of such reported speech forms (e.g., providing planning time, emphasis etc.) in a sample of British working class oral narratives.

9   'This dialogic form of story telling means that the distinction between "storyteller" and "audience" becomes blurred, because what is happening in such a situation is that the speakers are collaborating in a story-telling' (Cheepen 1988: 54).

10   There are interesting gender differences in how facilitatively such questions appear to function in the context of a narrative. This issue is explored in Holmes (1997).

11   I owe this point to Maria Stubbe.

12   The fact that there are examples of these features in this sample of material which was recorded for the WCSNZE suggests that they may be more frequent in more relaxed social contexts where people know each other well. If they are carried over into cross-cultural contexts, there is clearly potential for misunderstanding.

References

Bell, Allan. 1991. *The Language of News Media*. Oxford: Blackwell.

Bell, Susan E. 1988. Becoming a political woman: The reconstruction and interpretation of experience through stories. In Todd, Alexandra D. and Sue Fisher (eds.), *Gender and Discourse: The Power of Talk*. Norwood, NJ: Ablex, 97–123.

Benton, Richard A. 1991. The Maori language: dying or reviving. East–West Centre Association Working Paper No. 28. Honolulu: East-West Centre Association.

Besnier, Niko. 1990. Conflict management, gossip, and affective meaning on Nukulaelae. In Watson-Gegeo, Karen Ann and Geoffrey M. White (eds.), *Disentangling. Conflict discourse in Pacific Societies*. Stanford: Stanford University Press, 290–334.

Cheepen, Christine. 1988. *The Predictability of Informal Conversation*. London: Pinter.

Coates, Jennifer. 1989. Gossip revisited: language in all-female groups. In Coates, Jennifer and Deborah Cameron (eds.), *Women in their Speech Communities*. London: Longman, 94–121.

Coates, Jennifer. 1996. *Women Talk*. Oxford: Blackwell.

Corston, Simon. 1993. On the interactive nature of spontaneous narrative. *Te Reo* 36, 69–97.

Duranti, Alessandro. 1986. The audience as co-author. *Text* 6–3, 239–247.

Goodwin, Charles. 1986. Audience diversity, participation and interpretation. *Text* 6–3, 283–316.

Goodwin, Marjorie Harness. 1991. Retellings, pretellings and hypothetical stories. *Research on Language and Social Interaction* 24, 263–276.

Heath, Shirley Brice. 1983. *Ways with Words: Life and Work in Communities and Classrooms*. Cambridge: Cambridge University Press.

Holmes, Janet. 1970. The Language of Spoken Monologue. M. Phil thesis. University of Leeds.

Holmes, Janet. 1997. Story-telling in New Zealand women's and men's talk. In Wodak, Ruth (ed.), *Gender and Discourse*. London: Sage.

Holmes, Janet and Maria Stubbe. 1997. Good listeners: gender differences in New Zealand conversation. *Women and Language* xx: 2, 7–14.

Johnstone, Barbara. 1993. Community and contest: midwestern men and women creating their worlds in conversational story-telling. In Tannen, Deborah (ed.), *Gender and Conversational Interaction*. Oxford: Oxford University Press, 62–80.

King, Michael. 1985. *Being Pakeha*. Auckland, London: Hodder and Stoughton.

King, Michael (ed.) 1991. *Pakeha: the Quest for Identity in New Zealand*. Auckland, Harmondsworth: Penguin.

Labov, William. 1972. The transformation of experience in narrative syntax. *Language in the Inner City: Studies in the Black English Vernacular*. Philadelphia: University of Pennsylvania. 354–396.

Labov, William and Joseph Waletzky. 1967. Narrative analysis: oral versions of personal experience. In Helm, June (ed.), *Essays on the Verbal and Visual Arts*. Seattle: University of Washington Press, 12–44. (Chapter 5 of this volume.)

Lehtonen, Jaako and Kari Sajavaara. 1985. The silent Finn. In Tannen, Deborah and Muriel Saville-Troike (eds.), *Perspectives on Silence*. Norwood, NJ: Ablex, 193–201.

Linde, Charlotte. 1993. *Life Stories: The Creation of Coherence*. Oxford: Oxford University Press.

Metge, Joan. 1976. *The Maoris of New Zealand*. London: Routledge and Kegan Paul.

Metge, Joan. 1995. *New Growth from Old: The Whaanau in the Modern World*. Wellington: Victoria University Press.

Metge, Joan and Patricia Kinloch. 1978. *Talking Past Each Other: Problems of Cross-cultural Communication*. Wellington: Victoria University Press/Price Milburn.

Moerman, Michael. 1988. *Talking Culture. Ethnography and Conversation Analysis*. Philadelphia: University of Pennsylvania Press.

National Maori Language Survey. Provisional Findings. 1995. Wellington: Maori Language Commission.

Polanyi, Livia. 1989. *Telling the American Story: A Structural and Cultural Analysis of Conversational Storytelling*. Cambridge, MA: MIT Press.

Reid, Julie. 1995. A study of gender differences in minimal responses. *Journal of Pragmatics* 24, 489–512.

Riessman, Catherine Kohler. 1993. *Narrative Analysis*. London: Sage.

Ritchie, James. 1992. *Becoming Bicultural*. Wellington: Huia Publishers and Daphne Brasell Associates.

Rymes, Betsy. 1995. The construction of moral agency in the narratives of high-school drop-outs. *Discourse and Society* 6–3, 495–516.

Schiffrin, Deborah. 1987. *Discourse Markers*. Cambridge: Cambridge University Press.

Scollon, Ron. 1985. The machine stops: silence in the metaphor of malfunction. In Tannen, Deborah and Muriel Saville-Troike (eds.), *Perspectives on Silence*. Norwood, NJ: Ablex, 21–30.

Scollon, Ron and Suzanne B. Scollon. 1981. *Narrative, Literacy and Face in Interethnic Communication*. Norwood, NJ: Ablex.

Sheldon, Amy. 1996. Sharing the same world, telling different stories: gender differences in co-constructed narratives. In Slobin, D., J. Gerhardt, J. Guo and A. Kyratzis (eds.), *Social Interaction, Social Context and Language: Festschrift presented to Susan Ervin-Tripp*. Hillsdale, NJ: Lawrence Erlbaum Associates, 803–829.

Stenstrom, Anna-Brita. 1994. *An Introduction to Spoken Interaction*. London: Longman.

Stubbe, Maria. 1998. Are you listening? Cultural influences on the use of verbal feedback in conversation. *Journal of Pragmatics* 29, 257–289.

Tannen, Deborah. 1985. Silence: anything but. In Tannen, Deborah and Muriel Saville-Troike (eds.), *Perspectives on Silence*. Norwood, NJ: Ablex, 93–112.

Toolan, Michael J. 1988. *Narrative: A Critical Linguistic Introduction*. London: Routledge.

Walker, Ranginui. 1989. Maori identity. In Novitz, David and Bill Willmott (eds.), *Culture and Identity in New Zealand*. Wellington: Government Printing Books, 35–52.

Watson, Karen Ann. 1975. Transferable communicative routines: strategies and group identity in two speech events. *Language in Society* 2, 53–72.

White, Sheida. 1989. Backchannels across cultures: a study of Americans and Japanese. *Language in Society* 18, 59–76.

Wolfson, Nessa. 1976. Speech events and natural speech: some implications for sociolinguistic methodology. *Language in Society* 5, 189–209.

Wolfson, Nessa. 1982. *The Conversational Historical Present in American English Narrative*. New York: Foris.

8

Contextualization Conventions

John J. Gumperz

[I] have argued (Gumperz 1982) that linguistic diversity is more than a fact of behavior. Linguistic diversity serves as a communicative resource in everyday life in that conversationalists rely on their knowledge and their stereotypes about variant ways of speaking to categorize events, infer intent and derive expectations about what is likely to ensue. All this information is crucial to the maintenance of conversational involvement and to the success of persuasive strategies. By posing the issue in this way, one can avoid the dilemma inherent in traditional approaches to sociolinguistics, where social phenomena are seen as generalizations about groups previously isolated by non-linguistic criteria such as residence, class, occupation, ethnicity and the like, and are then used to explain individual behavior. We hope to be able to find a way of dealing with what are ordinarily called sociolinguistic phenomena which builds on empirical evidence of conversational coöperation and does not rely on a priori identification of social categories, by extending the traditional linguistic methods of in-depth and recursive hypothesis testing with key informants to the analysis of the interactive processes by which participants negotiate interpretations.

Initially we approach the problem of the symbolic significance of linguistic variables by discovering how they contribute to the interpretation of what is being done in the communicative exchange. The hypothesis is that any utterance can be understood in numerous ways, and that people make decisions about how to interpret a given utterance based on their definition of what is happening at the time of interaction. In other words, they define the interaction in terms of a frame or schema which is identifiable and familiar (Goffman 1974). I will refer to the basic socially significant unit of interaction in terms of which meaning is assessed as the *activity type* or *activity* (Levinson 1978). The term is used to emphasize that, although we are dealing with a structured ordering of message elements that represents the speakers' expectations about what will happen next, yet it is not a static structure, but rather it reflects a dynamic process which develops and changes as the participants interact. Moreover, its basis in meaning reflects something being *done*, some purpose or goal being pursued, much as Bartlett (1932), who originated the concept of 'schema' as an organizing principle in interpreting events, stated that he preferred the term 'active developing patterns.' Thus the activity type does not determine meaning but simply constrains interpretations by channelling inferences so as to *foreground* or make relevant certain aspects of background knowledge and to underplay others.

1   Contextualization Cues

A basic assumption is that this channelling of interpretation is effected by conversational implicatures based on conventionalized co-occurrence expectations between content and surface style. That is, constellations of surface features of message form are the means by which speakers signal and listeners interpret what the activity is, how semantic content is to be understood and *how* each sentence relates to what precedes or follows. These features are referred to as *contextualization cues*. For the most part they are habitually used and perceived but rarely consciously noted and almost never talked about directly. Therefore they must be studied in process and in context rather than in the abstract.

Roughly speaking, a contextualization cue is any feature of linguistic form that contributes to the signalling of contextual presuppositions. Such cues may have a number of such linguistic realizations depending on the historically given linguistic repertoire of the participants. The code, dialect and style switching processes, some of the prosodic phenomena we have discussed as well as choice among lexical and syntactic options, formulaic expressions, conversational openings, closings and sequencing strategies can all have similar contextualizing functions. Although such cues carry information, meanings are conveyed as part of the interactive process. Unlike words that can be discussed out of context, the meanings of contextualization cues are implicit. They are not usually talked about out of context. Their signalling value depends on the participants' tacit awareness of their meaningfulness. When all participants understand and notice the relevant cues, interpretive processes are then taken for granted and tend to go unnoticed. However, when a listener does not react to a cue or is unaware of its function, interpretations may differ and misunderstanding may occur. It is important to note that when this happens and when a difference in interpretation is brought to a participant's attention, it tends to be seen in attitudinal terms. A speaker is said to be unfriendly, impertinent, rude, uncooperative, or to fail to understand. Interactants do not ordinarily notice that the listener may have failed to perceive a shift in rhythm or a change in pronunciation. Miscommunication of this type, in other words, is regarded as a social faux pas and leads to misjudgements of the speaker's intent; it is not likely to be identified as a mere linguistic error.

The cues involved here are basically gradual or scalar; they do not take the form of discrete qualitative contrasts. What is involved is a departure from normal in one or another direction. But while the signalling potential of semantic directionality is, in large part, universal, the situated interpretation of the meaning of any one such shift in context is always a matter of social convention. Conversationalists, for example, have conventional expectations about what count as normal and what count as marked kinds of rhythm, loudness, intonation and speech style. By signalling a speech activity, a speaker also signals the social presuppositions in terms of which a message is to be interpreted. Notions of normality differ within what, on other grounds, counts as a single speech community. When this is the case, and especially when participants think they understand each others' words, miscommunication resulting in mutual frustration can occur.

The conversational analyses described in this chapter extend the methodological principle of comparing ungrammatical and grammatical sentences, by which linguists derive generalizations about grammatical rules, to the analysis of contextualization phenomena that underlie the situated judgements conversationalists make of each other. Naturally occurring instances of miscommunication are compared with functionally similar passages of successful communication in the same encounter or findings from other situations to derive generalizations about subculturally and situationally specific aspects of inferential processes.

The following example illustrates the type of miscommunication phenomena we look for and shows how we begin to isolate possible linguistic sources of misunderstanding. The incident is taken from an oral report by a graduate student in educational psychology who served as an interviewer in a survey.

(1)   The graduate student has been sent to interview a black housewife in a low income, inner city neighborhood. The contact has been made over the phone by someone in the office. The student arrives, rings the bell, and is met by the husband, who opens the door, smiles, and steps towards him:

> HUSBAND: So y're gonna check out ma ol lady, hah?
> INTERVIEWER: Ah, no. I only came to get some information. They called from the office.

(Husband, dropping his smile, disappears without a word and calls his wife.)

The student reports that the interview that followed was stiff and quite unsatisfactory. Being black himself, he knew that he had 'blown it' by failing to recognize the significance of the husband's speech style in this particular case. The style is that of a formulaic opening gambit used to 'check out' strangers, to see whether or not they can come up with the appropriate formulaic reply. Intent on following the instructions he had received in his methodological training and doing well in what he saw as a formal interview, the interviewer failed to notice the husband's stylistic cues. Reflecting on the incident, he himself states that, in order to show that he was on the husband's wave-length, he should have replied with a typically black response like "Yea, I'ma git some info" (I'm going to get some information) to prove his familiarity with and his ability to understand local verbal etiquette and values. Instead, his Standard English reply was taken by the husband as an indication that the interviewer was not one of them and, perhaps, not to be trusted.

The opener "So y're gonna check out ma ol lady" is [a] formulaic phrase identifiable through co-occurrent selections of phonological, prosodic, morphological and lexical options. Linguists have come to recognize that, as Fillmore (1976) puts it, "an enormous amount of natural language is formulaic, automatic and rehearsed, rather than propositional, creative or freely generated." But it must be emphasized that although such formulas have some of the characteristics of common idioms like *kick the bucket* and *spill the beans*, their meaning cannot be adequately described by lexical glosses. They occur as part of routinized interactive exchanges, such as Goffman describes as "replies and responses" (1981). Their use signals both expectations about what is to be accomplished and about the form that replies must take. They are similar in function to code switching strategies. Like the latter they are learned by interacting with others in institutionally defined networks of relationships. Where these relationships are ethnically specific they are often regarded as markers of ethnic background. But, as our example shows, their use in actual encounters is ultimately determined by activity specific presuppositions so that failure to react is not in itself a clear sign of ethnic identity. Basically, these formulaic phrases reflect indirect conversational strategies that make conditions favorable to establishing personal contact and negotiating shared interpretations.

Because of the indirect ways in which they function, and the variety of surface forms they can take, empirical analysis of contextualization strategies presents a major problem. New kinds of discovery methods are needed to identify differences in the perception of cues. The procedures we have begun to work out rely either on verbatim description of remembered happenings or on passages isolated from tape recorded or videotaped naturalistic encounters by methods patterned on those described in Erickson & Schultz (1982). The passages in question may vary in length, but a basic requirement is that they constitute self-contained episodes, for which we have either internal or ethnographic evidence of what the goals are in terms of which participants evaluate component utterances. These passages are then transcribed literally bringing in as much phonetic, prosodic and interactional detail as necessary, described in terms of the surface content and ethnographic background necessary to understand what is going on and, finally, analyzed interpretively both in terms of what is intended and what is perceived.

In what follows we present additional examples illustrating interpretive differences. These will be analyzed and elicitation strategies will be discussed that are capable of making explicit the unverbalized perceptions and presuppositions that underlie interpretation.

(2)   A husband sitting in his living room is addressing his wife. The husband is of middle class American background, the wife is British.
They have been married and living in the United States for a number of years:

HUSBAND: Do you know where today's paper is?
WIFE: *I'll* get it for you.
HUSBAND: That's O.K. Just tell me where it is.
           I'll get it.
WIFE: No, I'LL get it.

The husband is using a question which literally interpreted inquires after the location of the paper. The wife does not reply directly but offers to get the paper. Her "I'll" is accented and this could be interpreted as 'I will if you don't.' The husband counter-suggests that he had intended to ask for information, not to make a request. He also stresses "I'll." The wife then reiterates her statement, to emphasize that she intends to get it. The "I'll" is now highly stressed to suggest increasing annoyance.

(3)   A mother is talking to her eleven year old son who is about to go out in the rain:

MOTHER: Where are your boots?
SON: In the closet.
MOTHER: I want you to put them on *right* now.

The mother asks a question which literally interpreted concerns the location of the son's boots. When he responds with a statement about their location, the mother retorts with a direct request. Her stress on "right now" suggests that she is annoyed at her son for not responding to her initial question as a request in the first place.

It would seem at first glance that what is at issue here is listeners' failure to respond appropriately to an indirect speech act (Searle 1975). But directness is often itself a matter of socio-cultural convention. Few Americans would claim for example that "Have you got the time?" is not a direct request. Although it would be premature to make definitive claims on the basis of these two examples, interpretive differences of this type have been found to be patterned in accordance with differences in gender and ethnic origin.

(4)   Telephone conversation between a college instructor and a student. The individuals know each other well since the student, who is black, had previously worked as an office helper in the white instructor's office for several years. The telephone rings:

INSTRUCTOR:	Hello.
STUDENT:	How's the family?
	(pause)
INSTRUCTOR:	Fine.
STUDENT:	I'll get back to you next month about that thing.
INSTRUCTOR:	That's O.K. I can wait.
STUDENT:	I'm finished with that paper. It's being typed.
INSTRUCTOR:	Come to the office and we'll talk about it.

The student answers the instructor's hello with what sounds like a polite inquiry about the instructor's family. The fact that he fails to identify himself can perhaps be explained by assuming that he would be recognized by his voice. But he also fails to give the customary greeting. More than the normal interval elapses before the instructor responds with a hesitant "Fine." He seems unsure as to what is wanted. The instructor has less difficulty with the student's next statement which makes indirect reference to the fact that the student has borrowed some money which he was promising to return soon. The topic then shifts to a paper which has not yet been turned in. When the instructor later refused to give the student a grade without seeing the finished paper, the student seemed annoyed. He claimed that the telephone call had led him to hope he would be given special consideration.

(5)   Conversation in the office between a black undergraduate employed as a research assistant, who is busy writing at his desk, and a faculty member, his supervisor, who is passing by at some distance. The two are on first name terms:

STUDENT:	John, help me with this. I'm putting it all down.
SUPERVISOR:	What is it?
STUDENT:	I'm almost done. I just need to fix it up a little.
SUPERVISOR:	What do you want me to do?
STUDENT:	I'm writing down everything just the way you said.
SUPERVISOR:	I don't have the time right now.

The student opens with what sounds like a request for help. But the supervisor's request for more information is answered with further factual statements about what the student is doing. The second, more insistent question also fails to elicit an adequate reply. It seems as if the student, having asked for help, then refuses to say what he wants done.

Passages such as the above were played to sets of listeners including some who did and others who did not share participants' backgrounds. Each incident was first heard in its entirety and then repeated more slowly with frequent pauses. Initial questions tended to yield very general replies about what was ultimately intended, what listeners thought, how they felt, how well they did, and what they did wrong. Subsequent questioning attempted to induce respondents to relate their judgements more closely to what they actually heard. The aim here is to test the analyst's hypotheses about more immediate communicative goals, illocutionary force of particular utterances, and about the way listeners interpret speakers' moves. We therefore focus on particular exchanges such as question–answer pairs rather than on single utterances or on an entire passage. Respondents' answers are followed up with elicitation techniques patterned on those developed by linguistic anthropologists (Frake 1969) to recover native speakers' perceptual and inferential processes. For example, if a respondent states that the speaker, A, is making a request, we may then ask a series of questions such as the following: (a) What is it about the way A speaks that makes you think . . . ?; (b) Can you repeat it just about the way he said it?; (c) What is another way of saying it?; (d) Is it possible that he merely wanted to ask a question?; (e) How would he have said it if he . . . ?; (f) How did the answerer interpret what A said?; (g) How can you tell that the answerer interpreted it that way? These elicitation procedures yield hypotheses about the actual cues processed and the paradigmatic range of alternatives in terms of which evaluations are made. The analyst can then use this to reanalyze the passage at hand, deal with additional data and develop more specific elicitation procedures for particular types of situations. The main goal of all these procedures is to relate interpretations to identifiable features of message form, to identify chains of inferences, not to judge the absolute truth value of particular assessments.

Examination of our examples in these terms reveals significant differences in interpretation. Some judges identify the first utterance in (2) as a factual question, others as a request, others again suggest that it is ambiguous. The mother's remark in (3) is seen by some as an order to put on boots; others feel it could be a request for information. In (5) a number of judges note the student's failure to state clearly what he is doing and what he wants the supervisor to help him with. These same judges also note the student's failure to say hello in the telephone conversation of (4) and suggest that this omission seems rude. Others, however, instead of mentioning the student's vagueness in (5) claim that the supervisor's insistence on asking what is wanted is out of place. A common comment was: "Why didn't the supervisor say that he doesn't have any time in the first place?"

At first glance, these evaluations seem to reflect individual interpretations of what are essentially inherent ambiguities or differences in degree. Although some trends begin to emerge, it would be premature to claim that they relate to cultural background. But when we examine choice of alternative expressions and sequencing strategies, more systematic relationships begin to emerge.

Judges who identify the husband's opener in (2) as a request also state that the wife's annoyance is justified since, if he did not want her to get the paper, he would not have used that expression. They argue he would have said something like "I wonder where the paper is." These same judges also claim that the child's answer to the mother's order in (3) is impertinent, and that this justified the mother's annoyance. They say that to justify himself the child should have answered indirectness with indirectness and replied with something like "Why, is it raining?" Thus there seems to be an empirically recoverable implicational ordering to evaluations such that assessment at the speech act level of illocutionary force forms the basis for more specific interpretations.

Everyone listening to (2) and (3) recognized the opening utterances as meaningful strategies. The situation is different however with (4). Here judges point to the caller's failure (a) to identify himself and (b) to open with a greeting, such as "Hi." They argue that the participants know each other and can be presumed to recognize each other's voices, and that self-identification is not necessary, but the lack of a greeting evokes different responses. Some judges merely see it as a failure to say something that should have been said, an inappropriate strategy that seems odd, or perhaps rude. Others, however, recognize it as part of a meaningful gambit, an indirect way of suggesting that the speaker wants something. When pressed further they illustrate their comments with anecdotes from their own experience, listing other expressions that exemplify similar verbal strategies. These same judges point to the speaker's failure to state what he wants in (5) as a similar instance of indirectness. The strategy underlying both examples seems to be something like this: Do not verbalize explicitly what the conversation is about, rely on the listener's ability to use his background knowledge. If he is a friend, he will guess what is wanted and will cooperate, so that if he enters into this type of interaction and responds at all he can be presumed to understand.

The failure to say something that is normally expected is thus interpreted in attitudinal terms by some listeners, while others see it as having identifiable signalling value. For the latter group it counts as a contextualization strategy which is meaningful in the same sense that the idiomatic opener in example (1) [is] meaningful. Since the signalling mechanisms involved are covert, highly context bound and learned only through intensive formal contact under conditions allowing maximum feedback, such as we find in home and peer settings, they tend to reflect commonality of family or ethnic background. Therefore, whenever one set of listeners (a) identifies such features as conventionalized and (b) agrees on their interpretation and on appropriate sequencing strategies, while another group does not see such cues as meaningful, we have fairly good evidence that the interpretive differences also reflect significant variations in sociocultural background. In fact judges who see meaningful indirectness in (4) and (5) are either black or familiar with black rhetoric. We might therefore tentatively identify the features in question as reflecting black style. The evidence for differences in cultural background is somewhat weaker in the case of examples (2) and (3), but it is of interest that the mother and wife are English and that other English judges tend to favor the request interpretation, while Americans tend toward the question interpretation.

More data are needed, based on larger and more varied records of interaction. It should be pointed out, however, that by relating perception and interpretation of contextualization cues to cultural background, we are not attempting to predict usage or to relate the incidence of linguistic variables to other characteristics. Our procedures serve to identify strategies of interpretation that are potentially available to speakers of certain backgrounds and to alert people to the ways in which discourse level signs can affect interpretation of seemingly unambiguous messages.

Once such strategies are identified, it becomes possible to test our understanding of their meaning and distribution by constructing more systematic tests to be used with larger samples of judges. These tests take the form of alternate paraphrases of similar socially realistic episodes, built on naturally occurring examples which are recorded by good mimics who are familiar with the relevant strategies. These can be submitted to ethnically and occupationally stratified samples, and results are subject to statistical analysis of the usual kind.

The following key sentence, extracted from a test that we are constructing to deal with communication problems of students from India who are used to Indian styles of English, may serve as an example:

(6)   A: You may run all the way to the post office, but I'm sure it will be closed by the time you get there,
   Question: Which of the following two statements is closest to what the speaker really meant?
      a.   It doesn't matter whether or not I give you permission to go to the post office. Even if I do and if you run, you won't make it before closing time.
      b.   It is possible that you could run to the post office, but it will be closed by the time you get there.

The linguistic issue here hinges on the meaning of the modal "may." Speakers of American English use *may* to mean either 'permission' or 'possibility.' Speakers of Indian English in India use it only to indicate permission. Our results with this type of question show that recently arrived speakers of Indian English unanimously choose interpretation (a); speakers of American English choose interpretation (b). Indian students who have lived in the United States for some time will be aware of interpretation (b) if they have lived in typically American settings and have formed close friendships with Americans. Those who have lived there surrounded by other Indian friends are less likely to be aware of interpretation (b). Understanding of communicative strategies is, thus, less a matter of length of residence than of communicative experience.

2   The Perceptual Bases of Contextualization Cues

Apart from the formulaic expressions, code switching phenomena and prosodic signs discussed so far, there are other less readily noticed phonetic and rhythmic signs that enter into the contextualization process. Their nature and cultural functioning is best discussed in relation to recent work in the micro-analysis of nonverbal signs. Students of non-verbal communication, among whom Hall (1959, 1966) is perhaps the most widely known, have long argued that what is involved in cross-cultural understanding is much more than value difference or racial or ethnic stereotyping. A large proportion of misunderstandings are traceable to variant perceptions and interpretations of seemingly trivial facial and gestural signs.

Systematic analysis of these signs was pioneered by Birdwhistell (1970), who along with his collaborators developed techniques of frame by frame analysis of filmed natural interaction sequences. He demonstrated that in the act of talking, eyes, face, limbs and torso all emit automatically produced signs which tend to go unnoticed yet neverthe-less convey information. These nonverbal signs are language like in the sense that they are learned through interaction, culturally specific and analyzable in terms of underly-ing processes. They are coordinated with verbal signs both at the micro-level of sylla-bles (Condon & Ogston 1967, Byers 1976) and at the level of clauses and longer discourse segments. Ekman's (1979) studies provide basic information on the physio-logical bases of facial movements and also show how these can be read to provide infor-mation about speakers' emotional states. Scheflen (1972) has made a detailed study of body postures employed by patients and analysts in psychiatric interviews. He shows how these serve to frame the interaction and simultaneously reflect and signal the tran-sition from one stage of an encounter to another. We can thus talk of human commu-nication as channelled and constrained by a multilevel system of learned, automatically produced and closely coordinated verbal and nonverbal signals.

The most significant insights into how such signs affect verbal exchanges come from studies in speaker–listener coordination (Kendon, Harris & Key 1975). When the rela-tionship of speakership moves to listeners' responses was measured, it was found that these tend to be synchronized in such a way that moves and responses follow each other at regular rhythmic intervals. The timing of responses, moreover, is much faster than one would expect if unpredictable stimuli were responded to (Kempton 1981). This suggests that conversational synchrony requires some degree of predictability and rou-tinization, such as is most commonly acquired by shared culture and similarity of inter-active experience.

Of key importance for work in modern urban societies is Erickson's recent work on interethnic counselling sessions (Erickson & Schultz 1982). Erickson filmed and tape recorded a series of student–counselor advising sessions in which ethnic backgrounds of both counselors and students varied. Interaction in such sessions is usually seen as expressively neutral or instrumental, directed toward the goal of helping the student in planning course work or discovering academic strengths and weaknesses. Counselors can hardly be said to be prejudiced, as defined by the usual attitude measures. Yet Erick-son's highly detailed and subtle indices showed significant, if complex, relationships between the amount of useful information that the student obtained and the ethnicity of participants.

The interviews were analyzed on three levels or channels of communication: (a) non-verbal signals, such as gaze direction, proxemic distance, kinesic rhythm or timing of body motion and gestures; (b) paralinguistic signals – voice, pitch and rhythm; (c) semantic content of messages. A series of indices were constructed which served to isolate instances of interactional asymmetry or 'uncomfortable moments' in the inter-view. Identification of such passages was found to be highly reliable when checked both across coders and against the evaluations of original participants who were shown the films.

The results reveal a direct relationship between these indices of asynchrony and the amount of usable information that the student derived from the interview. The lower the asynchrony was, the greater was the amount of practical information obtained. Asynchrony, in turn, was related to (a) similarity of ethnic background of participants and (b) the ability to find some common base of experience on which to build the interaction.

What seems to happen is that, at the beginning of each conversation, there is an introductory phase when interpersonal relationships are negotiated and participants probe for common experiences or some evidence of shared perspective. If this maneuver is successful, the subsequent interaction is more likely to take the form of an interrelated series of moves in which speakers cooperate to produce a well-coordinated sequence of exchanges. The ability to establish a common rhythm is a function, among other factors, of similarity in ethnic background. Thus, in spite of the socially neutral nature of the interviews, it seems that Poles, for example, communicate most comfortably, easily and efficiently with other Poles, less easily with Italians, even less easily with Jews, and least easily with Puerto Ricans and blacks. It is important to note that, while participants can learn to identify moments of uncomfortableness when viewing their own tapes, their interpretations of what happened and why often differ greatly. Furthermore, black counselors seem somewhat less affected by ethnically different students than their white counterparts. Perhaps the communication difficulties they experience in their own everyday lives make them more tolerant of differences in communication styles.

Work on conversational synchrony highlights the role that automatic reactions to nonverbal cues, revealed only through microanalysis, play in creating the conditions under which successful communication can take place. Moreover, if it can be shown that smooth, synchronous exchanges favor the establishment of shared interpretive frames, then measures of speaker–listener response rhythms can provide a basis for indices of communicative effectiveness that are independent of lexical content.

What is it about languages that mediates the relationship between information transfer and synchrony? Contextualization processes, in as much as they give rise to predictions about the course of an interaction, must certainly play an important role. We have talked (in Gumperz 1982) about the role that prosodic mechanisms such as tone grouping, accent placement and tune play in segmenting the stream of talk, signalling thematic connections and providing information about activities. When basic tone grouping and accentuation conventions differ, predictability in conversation suffers, although sentences in isolation may be easily comprehensible. Our discussion of formulaic expressions and code switching phenomena (ibid.) has also stressed the role they play in indicating discourse expectations. In situations of linguistic diversity, formulaicness as well as code alternation are frequently marked by co-occurrent selections of phonetic variables and prosodic and grammatical options. This means that experience in making the proper discriminations in the first place plays an important role in conversational synchrony.

Black English illustrates this point. Ethnographers of communication like Mitchell-Kernan (1971) point to the many subtle communicative functions dialect variants have in creating an atmosphere of warmth and responsiveness in group settings. Kochman (1973) has provided a series of highly interesting examples illustrating the role that features such as rhythmicity and sound symbolism, among others, play in black groups. Piestrup (1973) builds on this ethnographic work in examining the effect of dialect usage on children's reading achievement in Standard English. The findings, based on tape recordings of more than twenty classroom sessions, show that previous research that saw a direct connection between phonological deviance and performance is in need of modification. There is a third factor, 'teaching style,' which mediates the relationship. With teachers whose teaching is responsive to student cues, who are tolerant of different communication styles and who succeed in setting up what Piestrup refers to as rhythmic teacher–student exchanges, dialect speakers do as well or better than others in achieving control of expository English prose. With unresponsive teachers, these dialect differences have a negative effect.

Clearly, shared history and communicative experience are important factors in facilitating conversational cooperation. The following examples will show how instances of miscommunication and asynchrony can be identified in order to resolve situations where cooperation in conversation breaks down. In each case we will seek to identify the cues that are operating and determine their sources within the linguistic system so as to form hypotheses about what they reflect about participants' social background.

(7)   *Who's the artist?*

When a house painter arrived at the home of a middle class couple in California, he was taken around the house to survey the job he was about to perform. When he entered a spacious living room area with numerous framed original paintings on the walls, he asked in a friendly way, "Who's the *ar*tist?" The wife, who was British, replied, "The painter's not too well known. He's a modern London painter named —." The house painter hesitated and then, looking puzzled, said, "I was wondering if someone in the family was an artist."

The exchange is part of a casual encounter between strangers who were aware of the dissimilarity in backgrounds because of the differences in their accents. Yet they were not prepared for the interpretive problems they encountered.

"Who's the *ar*tist?" is a formulaic comment that fits a paradigm often uttered by Americans being escorted around a house. That is, one might just as well say, "Who's the *cook*?" on seeing an array of kitchen utensils on a pegboard, or "Who's the *gar*dener?" on looking out the window and seeing rows of seed packages on sticks in the tilled earth. Such formulas are often a conventionalized way of fulfilling the expectation that a complimentary comment be made upon seeing someone's house for the first time. The compliment in the formulaic paradigm generally initiates a routine in which the addressee indirectly acknowledges the indirect compliment by saying, for example, "It's just a hobby," or "I'm just a fan," or by making some other self-deprecatory remark, in response to which the compliment is reasserted: "But they're really very good." The British wife in the above example was not familiar with this paradigm and its attendant routine, and therefore took the house painter's question to reflect an objective interest in the paintings. The questioner's puzzled look after her response was an indication that his question had not been understood as intended.

As sociolinguists, we need to know how the formulaic nature of utterances is signalled. In the example given here, there are both extra-linguistic and linguistic cues. The extralinguistic signals lie in the setting and the participants' knowledge of what preceded the interaction. There are at least three linguistic signals: first, the semantic content; second, the syntactic paradigm; and third, the contextualization cues such as prosody (e.g. the stress and high pitch on the first syllable of "*ar*tist," and its marked high falling intonation). The contextualization cues here alert the listener to the possibility of a formulaic interpretation, even if the specific utterance has never been heard before. Formulaic use of language is always a problem for non–native speakers. It is perhaps even more of a danger, however, between people who ostensibly speak the same language but come from different social or regional backgrounds. Since they assume that they understand each other, they are less likely to question interpretations.

(8)   *The fingers of the hand*
     This exchange is [an] extract from [a] graduate student discussion. Five graduate students of various backgrounds were video–taped discussing a first–year graduate course. A difference of opinion had developed concerning the need for the course to integrate various approaches to anthropology. One of the two male students in the group argued that, given the complexity of research in the field, such integration was no longer possible. Three women students, on the other hand, maintained that the connection still existed and therefore should be brought out. One of these women attempted to summarize their line of argument. Notice when she was interrupted by her friend:

> A: It's like all parts of the hand. The fingers operate independently, but they have the same
> B: [What I would like to say is . . .

The videotape clearly shows that A was disconcerted by B's interruption. She turned suddenly to B and uttered an expression of frustration.

When the participants in this discussion viewed the tape, B insisted that she had agreed fully with what A had said, but she had thought A was finished, and therefore had taken a turn to talk. A asserted that she had been interrupted just when she had been about to make her point based on the simile she had introduced. It may be relevant to note at this point that A is black, from an inner-city neighborhood in northern California, and the extended simile she was using is recognized by those familiar with black rhetoric as fitting a formulaic paradigm for summing up an argument or commenting on what someone has said.

Elsewhere in the same discussion, A made another statement which fits a formulaic paradigm: "You hear one thing, you read another." One indication of the formulaic nature of this expression lies in the fact that in in-group conversation frequently only the first part of such a sequence is uttered, i.e. one would say, "You hear one thing," or "It's like all parts of the hand," and stop at that, relying on the hearer's cultural knowledge to supply the rest and give the appropriate response. Our examples, however, arose in a mixed group session, and we see that A intended to complete the simile. Her intonation rose on "independently," signalling that she was going to continue, and presumably a native speaker of American English would have known from this signal that she was not relinquishing the floor. Although B has spoken English most of her life, she is from India, and her Indian English has some of the prosodic and paralinguistic features described in Gumperz 1982, chapter 5.

Throughout the entire discussion B had tended to team up with the other two female discussants, supporting their position vis à vis the two males and there is no indication that she has changed her mind in this case. Yet B interrupted much more than the other participants, despite her subsequent assertion that she did not intend to do so; moreover, she was frequently interrupted by others, who also later asserted that they had thought she was finished with what she wanted to say. Thus, it can be seen that cross-cultural differences, which consist of more generalized discrepancies in use of prosody and paralinguistic cues, can lead to the disruption of conversational rhythm and thematic progression.

(9) *I don't wanna read*

In a taped elementary school classroom session, the teacher told a student to read. The student responded, "I don't wanna read." The teacher got annoyed and said, "All right, then, sit down."

When this interchange was played to others, some said that the child was being un-cooperative. Others said the child meant, "Push me a little and I'll read. I can do it, but I need to know that you really want me to." This latter group interpreted the child's statement, "I don't wanna read," as indirect. While whites opted for the 'refusal' inter-pretation of the present example, black informants generally favored the 'encourage me' interpretation. Those who chose the second interpretation agree that it is the child's rising intonation at the end of his sentence that led to their conclusion, and many of them furthermore volunteered the information that if the child had intended to refuse, he would have stressed "want." The two possible intonation contours, then, seem to form a contrast set for blacks.

The same pattern can be seen in other interchanges in which rising intonation is used in this way by speakers who employ this system. For example, note the following classroom interchange.

(10) *I don't know*

T: James, what does this word say?
J: I don't know.
T: Well, if you don't want to try someone else will. Freddy?
F: Is that a *p* or a *b*?
T: (encouragingly) It's a *p*.
F: Pen.

James (J) spoke with rising intonation and therefore, in his system at least, implied, 'I need some encouragement.' The teacher missed this and thought James was refusing to try. Freddy's (F's) question in effect had the same 'meaning' (communicative func-tion) as James' statement 'I need some encouragement.' However, Freddy communi-cated his hesitancy in a way the teacher expected, so she furnished that encouragement, and Freddy proceeded. Witnessing this interchange, James then 'saw' that the teacher was willing to encourage Freddy but not him. He therefore concluded that she was 'picking on him' or 'prejudiced against him.'

(11) *A bridge*

Our last example is taken from the same discussion among graduate students as was (8). At this point, the main topic has been the failure of the course program to show the relationship between linguistic anthropology and social anthropology:

> A: But if you took a core that was designed by the linguistics department and one by the socio-cultural, and both of them had Boas there would be some connection. Then why is it important in both areas? What's the difference? And I
>
> B: Do you think it's because people in socio-cultural sort of monopolize the field?
>
> C: Wait a minute wait a minute!
>
> A: You pick up what you need, you don't pick up the whole package. You pick out what *you* need. You don't need the whole box.
>
> D: Both of them are justified. Anthropologists have their own emphasis, linguists have their own emphasis and . . . but ah there is no connection. What we need is a bridge ah . . .
>
> C: Maybe the problem is that there is no faculty person that really has that oversight.

D finished a sentence and has followed it by "ah . . . ," and C took a turn to speak. Speakers of American English do not see C's contribution as an interruption. D, however, seemed annoyed at this point, and when viewing the tape afterward, he commented that he had been interrupted and prevented from making his point. Up until the time that C broke in, D had simply been repeating what had been previously said in order to set the stage for his contribution. D, who is Indian, further stated that this happened to him continually with Americans. Later on in the discussion he did succeed in making his point, which was that, to be successful, the course should be built on a common intellectual foundation. He made it, however, only when an outsider intervened and asked each participant to state his/her own opinion in turn.

An examination of D's use of prosody shows significant differences from American conventions in the way he signalled relationships between clauses in longer stretches of discourse, reflecting features of Indian English prosody. . . . His second and third statements were intended to contrast with each other; he was saying that anthropologists and linguists have different emphases. Since he used the same syntax and lexicon in both statements, the Americans would not hear these as contrasting unless he differentiated them through prosody (e.g. contrastive stress on "their"). D, however, seemed to be using the same stress pattern on both sentences. The Americans, using their own system, perceived this as simply 'listing.' D's next two statements were: "but there is no connection. What we need is a bridge." Here he puts what sounds to Americans like emphatic stress on "connection," "we," and "bridge." Americans are therefore likely to assume, as C did, that these two statements represent D's main point.

Our studies of Indian in-group conversation reveal at least two characteristics of Indian rhetorical strategy which operate differently from American English: (a) in making an argument, Indian speakers take great care to formulate the background for what they are going to say; and (b) they use increased stress to mark this background information, then shift to low pitch and amplitude on their own contributions.

Using this strategy, D in our example instinctively expected to be listened to attentively because he had thus set the stage for his contribution. On the contrary, he was interrupted, since his American interlocutors didn't share his system of signalling and therefore did not expect anything important to follow. The tragic outcome of such signalling differences lies in the judgements made by participants and observers about the intellectual quality of conversational contributions. As it stands, D's contribution sounds unoriginal, repetitive and not logically connected. In reality he never got to make his point at all.

Independent ethnographic evidence from work in urban school settings highlights the importance of some of the interpretive issues illustrated here. Note that the "help me" of example (5), the "I don't wanna read" of (9) and the "I don't know" of (10) have similar formulaic interpretations which are specific to black cultural traditions. They all tend to be understood as requests for cooperation which may be motivated by no more than a desire for company, or friendly support. The formulaicness of such utterances is marked syntactically by phrases like "I don't," "I can't," followed by a predicate and prosodically by a characteristic intonation contour. This contour accents the predicate and thus serves to identify the formula. Other American listeners, however, who are not attuned to these cues tend to rely on their own system to interpret these phrases as confessions of inability to perform the task at hand or expressions of helplessness and indirect requests for assistance.

In the initial months of a one year study of classroom communication, a research assistant trained in linguistics and discourse analysis worked as a teacher's aide and participant observer in a first grade classroom. As a regular part of their daily school routine, children were given paper and crayons, asked to draw anything they liked and then show it to the teacher. The white children took their materials and sat down quietly by themselves and soon produced pictures. Many of the black children, on the other hand, took much longer over the task and regularly called for help using phrases like "Help me Sarah, I can't do this." The differences between the two groups seemed so pronounced that the assistant at first interpreted the black children's behavior as one more confirmation of social scientists' findings that black children do not have the home experience to prepare them for school. But informal visits to homes showed that this clearly was not the case. Moreover, the children in the class had all had preschool experiences where work with paper and crayon was done.

Experience with exchanges like those in the examples given above led us to look for cues suggesting formulaic interpretations. Thereafter a pattern emerged, and what seemed like lack of experience came to be identified for what it is, a difference in verbal strategy. In saying "I can't do this" children like those in examples (9) and (10) simply seemed to be asking for encouragement or company. Such differences, if they remain undetected, may have serious consequences for how children's performance is evaluated.

3   Conclusion

Miscommunication caused by contextualization conventions reflects phenomena that are typically sociolinguistic, in the sense that their interpretive weight is much greater than their linguistic import as measured by the usual techniques of contrastive grammar. Whenever they occur, they have the effect of retrospectively changing the character of what has gone before and of reshaping the entire course of an interaction. A mistake in one such feature would lead the listener to think, "I thought we were on the same wavelength, but we are obviously not." Discrepant practices may persist despite years of intergroup contact. Often, speakers may be aware of vague difficulties in communication or of their inability to involve others in serious talk, yet rarely do they see, nor does conventional grammatical analysis suggest, that such difficulties may have linguistic causes.

While all the processes we have described trigger different inferential chains, the grammatical and semantic nature of the cues involved, and particularly the level of discourse at which they operate, differ. This has important consequences both for conversationalists engaged in an encounter and for analysts seeking to derive generalizations concerning the historical origin of interpretive traditions.

In the case of Americans interacting with Indian English speakers differences affect interpretation on several levels of generality. This includes the level of rhetorical principles governing such matters as how to respond to a preceding speaker's move, how to elaborate a point and in what order to present information. It also includes more local conventions that determine how the stream of talk is divided into information units, how accentuation works to identify focused items, distinguish given from new information and main points from qualifying structures. All these are matters that are basic, affecting the ability to establish conversational synchrony, to effect smooth turn taking and to cooperate in working out common themes. The formulaic usages and directness conventions in the other passages, by contrast, are considerably less basic.

Example (2) illustrated this point. In each utterance of the exchange that follows the husband's opener which is misinterpreted, "I'll" is accented to convey different connotations which are clearly understood by both participants. This indicates that the tone grouping and accent placement principles which affect conversational synchrony are shared, and that the misunderstanding is due primarily to lexicon and to conventions for inferring nonverbalized information. If the husband had spoken a style of Indian English which employs the prosodic conventions illustrated in Gumperz 1982, chapter 5, the likelihood that the two could have maintained such an exchange would have been very low. The Black English speech formulas in examples (4), (5), (8) and (9) are marked prosodically, but this is a matter of stylized tunes which affects only isolated utterances. Note that in example (4) it is the fact that the professor and the student did sustain a cooperative exchange after the opening sequence that led the student to misread the professor's intent. Similarly, a native American who differed from the black speaker in (8), and consequently failed to understand that a simile was intended, might nevertheless have realized that rising intonation indicated the speaker was not ready to relinquish her turn.

There is reason to believe that the differences between Western – i.e. native British and American – and Indian English are matters of basic cultural norms and of the interaction of prosody and syntax reflecting long established, historical traditions that arose in distinct culture areas, and are maintained through networks of interpersonal relationships. Individuals reared in these traditions often learn the clause level grammar of another language, but in using it they rely on their own native discourse conventions. These conventions . . . are subconscious and for the most part tend to remain unverbalized. They are learned only through prolonged and intensive face to face contact. Yet the very linguistic features that cause the comprehension problem also make it difficult to enter into the type of contact and elicit the type of feedback that is necessary to overcome them. In this way casual intergroup contacts may reinforce distance and maintain separateness unless stronger outside forces intervene to create the conditions that make intensive interaction possible.

References

Bartlett, F. C. 1932. *Remembering*. Oxford: Oxford University Press.

Birdwhistell, R. L. 1970. *Kinesics and Context*. Philadelphia: University of Pennsylvania Press.

Byers, P. 1976. Biological rhythms as informational channels in communicative behavior. In *Perspectives in Ethology*, vol. 2, ed. P. G. Bateson & P. H. Klopfer. New York: Plenum Press.

Condon, J. C. & Ogston, D. 1967. Speed and body motion. In *Perception of Language*, ed. P. Kjeldergaard. Columbus, Ohio: Charles Merrill.

Ekman, P. 1979. About brows, emotional and conversational signals. In *Human Ethology*, ed. M. von Cranach, K. Foppa, W. Lepenies & D. Ploog. Cambridge: Cambridge University Press.

Erickson, F. & Schultz, J. J. (eds.) 1982. *The Counselor as Gatekeeper: Social and Cultural Organization of Communication in Counselling Interviews*. New York: Academic Press.

Fillmore, C. 1976. The need for a frame semantics in linguistics. In *Statistical Methods in Linguistics*. Stockholm: Skriptor.

Frake, C. 1969. The ethnographic study of cognitive systems. In *Cognitive Anthropology*, ed. S. A. Tyler. New York: Holt, Rinehart & Winston.

Goffman, E. 1974. *Frame Analysis*. New York: Harper & Row.

Goffman, E. 1981. *Forms of Talk*. Philadelphia: University of Pennsylvania Press.

Gumperz, J. J. 1982. Discourse Strategies. Cambridge: Cambridge University Press.

Hall, E. T. 1959. *The Silent Language*. New York: Doubleday.

Hall, E. T. 1966. *The Hidden Dimension*. New York: Doubleday.

Kempton, W. 1981. The rhythmic basis of interactional micro-synchrony. In *Aspects of Non-Verbal Communication*, ed. W. von Raffler-Engel & B. Hoffer. San Antonio, Texas: Trinity University Press.

Kendon, A., Harris, R. M. & Key, M. R. (eds.) 1975. *Organization of Behavior in Face-to-Face Interaction*. The Hague: Mouton.

Kochman, T. 1973. *Rappin' and Stylin' Out: Communication in Urban Black America*. Urbana-Champaign: University of Illinois Press.

Levinson, S. C. 1978. *Activity Types and Language*. Pragmatics Microfiche 3: 3-3 D1-G5.

Mitchell-Kernan, C. 1971. *Language Behavior in a Black Urban Community*. Language Behavior Research Laboratory, University of California, Berkeley, Monograph no. 2.

Piestrup, A. M. 1973. *Black Dialect Interference and Accommodation of Reading Instruction in the First Grade*. Language Behavior Research Laboratory, University of California, Berkeley, Monograph no. 4.

Scheflen, A. E. 1972. *Body Language and the Social Order*. Englewood Cliffs, New Jersey: Prentice-Hall.

Searle, J. R. 1975. Indirect Speech Acts. In *Syntax and Semantics*, vol. 3, ed. P. Cole & J. Morgan. New York: Academic Press.

9

The Pronouns of Power and Solidarity

Roger Brown and Albert Gilman

Most of us in speaking and writing English use only one pronoun of address; we say 'you' to many persons and 'you' to one person. The pronoun 'thou' is reserved, nowadays, to prayer and naïve poetry, but in the past it was the form of familiar address to a single person. At that time 'you' was the singular of reverence and of polite distance and, also, the invariable plural. In French, German, Italian, Spanish and the other languages most nearly related to English there are still active two singular pronouns of address. The interesting thing about such pronouns is their close association with two dimensions fundamental to the analysis of all social life – the dimensions of power and solidarity. Semantic and stylistic analysis of these forms takes us well into psychology and sociology as well as into linguistics and the study of literature.

This paper is divided into five major sections. The first three of these are concerned with the semantics of the pronouns of address. By semantics we mean covariation between the pronoun used and the objective relationship existing between speaker and addressee. The first section offers a general description of the semantic evolution of the pronouns of address in certain European languages. The second section describes semantic differences existing today among the pronouns of French, German and Italian. The third section proposes a connection between social structure, group ideology, and the semantics of the pronoun. The final two sections of the paper are concerned with expressive style by which we mean covariation between the pronoun used and characteristics of the person speaking. The first of these sections shows that a man's consistent pronoun style gives away his class status and his political views. The last section describes the ways in which a man may vary his pronoun style from time to time so as to express transient moods and attitudes. In this section it is also proposed that the major expressive meanings are derived from the major semantic rules.

In each section the evidence most important to the thesis of that section is described in detail. However, the various generalizations we shall offer have developed as an interdependent set from continuing study of our whole assemblage of facts, and so it may be well to indicate here the sort of motley assemblage this is. Among secondary sources the general language histories (Baugh, 1935; Brunot, 1937; Diez, 1876; Grimm, 1898; Jespersen, 1905; Meyer-Lübke, 1900) have been of little use because their central concern is always phonetic rather than semantic change. However, there are a small number of monographs and doctoral dissertations describing the detailed pronoun semantics for one or another language – sometimes throughout its history (Gedike, 1794; Grand, 1930; Johnston, 1904; Schliebitz, 1886), sometimes for only a century or so (Kennedy, 1915; Stidston, 1917), and sometimes for the works of a particular author (Byrne, 1936; Fay, 1920). As primary evidence for the usage of the past we have drawn on plays, on legal proceedings (Jardine, 1832–5), and on letters (Devereux, 1853; Harrison, 1935). We have also learned about contemporary usage from literature but, more importantly, from long conversations with native speakers of French, Italian, German and Spanish both here and in Europe. Our best information about the pronouns of today comes from a questionnaire concerning usage which is described in the second section of this paper. The questionnaire has thus far been answered by the following numbers of students from abroad who were visiting in Boston in 1957–8: 50 Frenchmen, 20 Germans, 11 Italians and two informants, each, from Spain, Argentina, Chile, Denmark, Norway, Sweden, Israel, South Africa, India, Switzerland, Holland, Austria and Yugoslavia.

We have far more information concerning English, French, Italian, Spanish and German than for any other languages. Informants and documents concerning the other Indo-European languages are not easily accessible to us. What we have to say is then largely founded on information about these five closely related languages. These first conclusions will eventually be tested by us against other Indo-European languages and, in a more generalized form, against unrelated languages.

The European development of two singular pronouns of address begins with the Latin *tu* and *vos*. In Italian they became *tu* and *voi* (with *Lei* eventually largely displacing *voi*); in French *tu* and *vous*; in Spanish *tu* and *vos* (later *usted*). In German the distinction began with *du* and *Ihr* but *Ihr* gave way to *er* and later to *Sie*. English speakers first used 'thou' and 'ye' and later replaced 'ye' with 'you'. As a convenience we propose to use the symbols *T* and *V* (from the Latin *tu* and *vos*) as generic designators for a familiar and a polite pronoun in any language.

1   The General Semantic Evolution of T and V

In the Latin of antiquity there was only *tu* in the singular. The plural *vos* as a form of address to one person was first directed to the emperor and there are several theories (Byrne, 1936; Châtelain, 1880) about how this may have come about. The use of the plural to the emperor began in the fourth century. By that time there were actually two emperors; the ruler of the eastern empire had his seat in Constantinople and the ruler of the west sat in Rome. Because of Diocletian's reforms the imperial office, although vested in two men, was administratively unified. Words addressed to one man were, by implication, addressed to both. The choice of *vos* as a form of address may have been in response to this implicit plurality. An emperor is also plural in another sense; he is the summation of his people and can speak as their representative. Royal persons sometimes say 'we' where an ordinary man would say 'I'. The Roman emperor sometimes spoke of himself as *nos*, and the reverential *vos* is the simple reciprocal of this.

The usage need not have been mediated by a prosaic association with actual plurality, for plurality is a very old and ubiquitous metaphor for power. Consider only the several senses of such English words as 'great' and 'grand'. The reverential *vos* could have been directly inspired by the power of an emperor.

Eventually the Latin plural was extended from the emperor to other power figures. However, this semantic pattern was not unequivocally established for many centuries. There was much inexplicable fluctuation between T and V in Old French, Spanish, Italian and Portuguese (Schliebitz, 1886), and in Middle English (Kennedy, 1915; Stidston, 1917). In verse, at least, the choice seems often to have depended on assonance, rhyme, or syllable count. However, some time between the twelfth and fourteenth centuries (Gedike, 1794; Grand, 1930; Kennedy, 1915; Schliebitz, 1886), varying with the language, a set of norms crystallized which we call the nonreciprocal power semantic.

1.1   The power semantic

One person may be said to have power over another in the degree that he is able to control the behavior of the other. Power is a relationship between at least two persons, and it is nonreciprocal in the sense that both cannot have power in the same area of behavior. The power semantic is similarly nonreciprocal; the superior says T and receives V.

There are many bases of power – physical strength, wealth, age, sex, institutionalized role in the church, the state, the army or within the family. The character of the power semantic can be made clear with a set of examples from various languages. In his letters, Pope Gregory I (590–604) used T to his subordinates in the ecclesiastical hierarchy and they invariably said V to him (Muller, 1914). In medieval Europe, generally, the nobility said T to the common people and received V; the master of a household said T to his slave, his servant, his squire, and received V. Within the family, of whatever social level, parents gave T to children and were given V. In Italy in the fifteenth century penitents said V to the priest and were told T (Grand, 1930). In Froissart (late fourteenth century) God says T to His angels and they say V; all celestial beings say T to man and receive V. In French of the twelfth and thirteenth century man says T to the animals (Schliebitz, 1886). In fifteenth century Italian literature Christians say T to Turks and Jews and receive V (Grand, 1930). In the plays of Corneille and Racine (Schliebitz, 1886) and Shakespeare (Byrne, 1936), the noble principals say T to their subordinates and are given V in return.

The V of reverence entered European speech as a form of address to the principal power in the state and eventually generalized to the powers within that microcosm of the state – the nuclear family. In the history of language, then, parents are emperor figures. It is interesting to note in passing that Freud reversed this terminology and spoke of kings, as well as generals, employers and priests, as father figures. The propriety of Freud's designation for his psychological purposes derives from the fact that an individual learning a European language reverses the historical order of semantic generalization. The individual's first experience of subordination to power and of the reverential V comes in his relation to his parents. In later years similar asymmetrical power relations and similar norms of address develop between employer and employee, soldier and officer, subject and monarch. We can see how it might happen, as Freud believed, that the later social relationships would remind the individual of the familial prototype and would revive emotions and responses from childhood. In a man's personal history recipients of the nonreciprocal V are parent figures.

Since the nonreciprocal power semantic only prescribes usage between superior and inferior, it calls for a social structure in which there are unique power ranks for every individual. Medieval European societies were not so finely structured as that, and so the power semantic was never the only rule for the use of T and V. There were also norms of address for persons of roughly equivalent power, that is, for members of a common class. Between equals, pronominal address was reciprocal; an individual gave and received the same form. During the medieval period, and for varying times beyond, equals of the upper classes exchanged the mutual V and equals of the lower classes exchanged T.

The difference in class practice derives from the fact that the reverential V was always introduced into a society at the top. In the Roman Empire only the highest ranking persons had any occasion to address the emperor, and so at first only they made use of V in the singular. In its later history in other parts of Europe the reverential V was usually adopted by one court in imitation of another. The practice slowly disseminated downward in a society. In this way the use of V in the singular incidentally came to connote a speaker of high status. In later centuries Europeans became very conscious of the extensive use of V as a mark of elegance. In the drama of seventeenth century France the nobility and bourgeoisie almost always address one another as V. This is true even of husband and wife, of lovers, and of parent and child if the child is adult. Mme de Sévigné in her correspondence never uses T, not even to her daughter the Comtesse de Grignan (Schliebitz, 1886). Servants and peasantry, however, regularly used T among themselves.

For many centuries French, English, Italian, Spanish, and German pronoun usage followed the rule of nonreciprocal $T–V$ between persons of unequal power and the rule of mutual V or T (according to social-class membership) between persons of roughly equivalent power. There was at first no rule differentiating address among equals but, very gradually, a distinction developed which is sometimes called the T of intimacy and the V of formality. We name this second dimension *solidarity*, and here is our guess as to how it developed.

1.2   The solidarity semantic

The original singular pronoun was T. The use of V in the singular developed as a form of address to a person of superior power. There are many personal attributes that convey power. The recipient of V may differ from the recipient of T in strength, age, wealth, birth, sex or profession. As two people move apart on these power-laden dimensions, one of them begins to say V. In general terms, the V form is linked with differences between persons. Not all differences between persons imply a difference of power. Men are born in different cities, belong to different families of the same status, may attend different but equally prominent schools, may practice different but equally respected professions. A rule for making distinctive use of T and V among equals can be formulated by generalizing the power semantic. Differences of power cause V to emerge in one direction of address; differences not concerned with power cause V to emerge in both directions.

The relations called *older than, parent of, employer of, richer than, stronger than*, and *nobler than* are all asymmetrical. If A is older than B, B is not older than A. The relation called 'more powerful than', which is abstracted from these more specific relations, is also conceived to be asymmetrical. The pronoun usage expressing this power relation is also asymmetrical or nonreciprocal, with the greater receiving V and the lesser T. Now we are concerned with a new set of relations which are symmetrical; for example, *attended the same school* or *have the same parents* or *practice the same profession*. If A has the same parents as B, B has the same parents as A. Solidarity is the name we give to the general relationship and solidarity is symmetrical. The corresponding norms of address are symmetrical or reciprocal with V becoming more probable as solidarity declines. The solidary T reaches a peak of probability in address between twin brothers or in a man's soliloquizing address to himself.

Not every personal attribute counts in determining whether two people are solidary enough to use the mutual T. Eye color does not ordinarily matter nor does shoe size. The similarities that matter seem to be those that make for like-mindedness or similar behavior dispositions. These will ordinarily be such things as political membership, family, religion, profession, sex, and birthplace. However, extreme distinctive values on almost any dimension may become significant. Height ought to make for solidarity among giants and midgets. The T of solidarity can be produced by frequency of contact as well as by objective similarities. However, frequent contact does not necessarily lead to the mutual T. It depends on whether contact results in the discovery or creation of the like-mindedness that seems to be the core of the solidarity semantic.

Solidarity comes into the European pronouns as a means of differentiating address among power equals. It introduces a second dimension into the semantic system on the level of power equivalents. So long as solidarity was confined to this level, the two-dimensional system was in equilibrium (see Figure 1a), and it seems to have remained here for a considerable time in all our languages. It is from the long reign of the two-dimensional semantic that T derives its common definition as the pronoun of either condescension or intimacy and V its definition as the pronoun of reverence or formality. These definitions are still current but usage has, in fact, gone somewhat beyond them.

The dimension of solidarity is potentially applicable to all persons addressed. Power superiors may be solidary (parents, elder siblings) or not solidary (officials whom one seldom sees). Power inferiors, similarly, may be as solidary as the old family retainer and as remote as the waiter in a strange restaurant. Extension of the solidarity dimension along the dotted lines of Figure 1b creates six categories of persons defined by their relations to a speaker. Rules of address are in conflict for persons in the upper left and lower right categories. For the upper left, power indicates V and solidarity T. For the lower right, power indicates T and solidarity V.

The abstract conflict described in Figure 1b is particularized in Figure 2a with a sample of the social dyads in which the conflict would be felt. In each case usage in one direction is unequivocal but, in the other direction, the two semantic forces are opposed. The first three dyads in Figure 2a involve conflict in address to inferiors who are not solidary (the lower right category of Figure 1b), and the second three dyads involve conflict in address to superiors who are solidary (the upper left category in Figure 1b).

Well into the nineteenth century the power semantic prevailed and waiters, common soldiers and employees were called T while parents, masters and elder brothers were called V. However, all our evidence consistently indicates that in the past century the

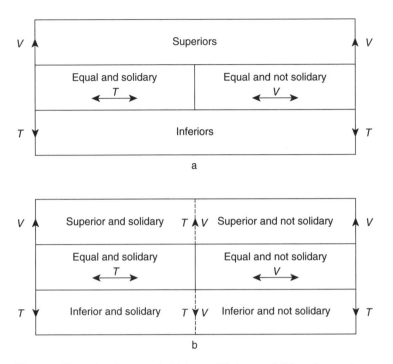

Figure 1   The two-dimensional semantic (a) in equilibrium and (b) under tension

solidarity semantic has gained supremacy. Dyads of the type shown in Figure 2a now reciprocate the pronoun of solidarity or the pronoun of nonsolidarity. The conflicted address has been resolved so as to match the unequivocal address. The abstract result is a simple one-dimensional system with the reciprocal *T* for the solidary and the reciprocal *V* for the nonsolidary.

It is the present practice to reinterpret power-laden attributes so as to turn them into symmetrical solidarity attributes. Relationships like *older than, father of, nobler than*, and *richer than* are now reinterpreted for purposes of *T* and *V* as relations of *the same age as, the same family as, the same kind of ancestry as*, and *the same income as*. In the degree that these relationships hold, the probability of a mutual *T* increases and, in the degree that they do not hold, the probability of a mutual *V* increases.

There is an interesting residual of the power relation in the contemporary notion that the right to initiate the reciprocal *T* belongs to the member of the dyad having the better power-based claim to say *T* without reciprocation. The suggestion that solidarity be recognized comes more gracefully from the elder than from the younger, from the richer than from the poorer, from the employer than from the employee, from the noble than from the commoner, from the female than from the male.

In support of our claim that solidarity has largely won out over power we can offer a few quotations from language scholars. Littré (1882), writing of French usage, says: 'Notre courtoisie est même si grande, que nous ne dédaignons pas de donner du vous et du monsieur à l'homme de la condition la plus vile.' Grand (1930) wrote of the Italian *V*: 'On commence aussi à le donner aux personnes de service, à qui on disait tu

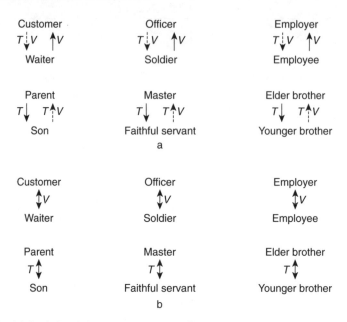

Figure 2   Social dyads involving (a) semantic conflict and (b) their resolution

autrefois.' We have found no authority who describes the general character of these many specific changes of usage: a shift from power to solidarity as the governing semantic principle.

The best evidence that the change has occurred is in our interviews and notes on contemporary literature and films and, most importantly, the questionnaire results. The six social dyads of Figure 2 were all represented in the questionnaire. In the past these would have been answered in accordance with asymmetrical power. Across all six of these dyads the French results yield only 11 per cent nonreciprocal power answers, the German 12 per cent, the Italian 27 per cent. In all other cases the usage is reciprocal, as indicated in Figure 2b. In all three of the languages, address between master and servant retains the greatest power loading. Some of the changes toward solidarity are very recent. Only since the Second World War, for instance, has the French Army adopted a regulation requiring officers to say V to enlisted men.

Finally, it is our opinion that a still newer direction of semantic shift can be discerned in the whole collection of languages studied. Once solidarity has been established as the single dimension distinguishing T from V the province of T proceeds to expand. The direction of change is increased in the number of relations defined as solidary enough to merit a mutual T and, in particular, to regard any sort of camaraderie resulting from a common task or a common fate as grounds for T. We have a favorite example of this new trend given us independently by several French informants. It seems that mountaineers above a certain critical altitude shift to the mutual T. We like to think that this is the point where their lives hang by a single thread. In general, the mutual T is advancing among fellow students, fellow workers, members of the same political group, persons who share a hobby or take a trip together. We believe this is the direction of current change because it summarizes what our informants tell us about the pronoun usage of the 'young people' as opposed to that of older people.

2   Contemporary Differences among French, Italian and German

While *T* and *V* have passed through the same general semantic sequence in these three languages, there are today some differences of detailed usage which were revealed by the questionnaire data. Conversations with native speakers guided us in the writing of questionnaire items, but the conversations themselves did not teach us the characteristic semantic features of the three languages; these did not emerge until we made statistical comparison of answers to the standard items of the questionnaire.

The questionnaire is in English. It opens with a paragraph informing the subject that the items below all have reference to the use of the singular pronouns of address in his native language. There are 28 items in the full questionnaire, and they all have the form of the following example from the questionnaire for French students:

1.(a) Which pronoun would you use in speaking to your mother?
        T (definitely) ——
        T (probably) ——
Possibly *T*, possibly *V* ——
        V (probably) ——
        V (definitely) ——
1.(b) Which would she use in speaking to you?
        T (definitely) ——
        T (probably) ——
Possibly *T*, possibly *V* ——
        V (probably) ——
        V (definitely) ——

The questionnaire asks about usage between the subject and his mother, his father, his grandfather, his wife, a younger brother who is a child, a married elder brother, that brother's wife, a remote male cousin, and an elderly female servant whom he has known from childhood. It asks about usage between the subject and fellow students at the university at home, usage to a student from home visiting in America, and usage to someone with whom the subject had been at school some years previously. It asks about usage to a waiter in a restaurant, between clerks in an office, fellow soldiers in the army, between boss and employee, army private and general. In addition, there are some rather elaborate items which ask the subject to imagine himself in some carefully detailed social situation and then to say what pronoun he would use.

The most accessible informants were students from abroad resident in Boston in the fall of 1957. Listings of such students were obtained from Harvard, Boston University, MIT, and the Office of the French Consul in New England. Although we have data from a small sample of female respondents, the present analysis is limited to the males. All the men in the sample have been in the United States for one year or less; they come from cities of over 300,000 inhabitants, and these cities are well scattered across the country in question. In addition, all members of the sample are from upper-middle-class, professional families. This homogeneity of class membership was enforced by the factors determining selection of students who go abroad. The occasional informant from a working-class family is deliberately excluded from these comparisons. The class from which we draw shows less regional variation in speech than does the working class and, especially, farmers. At the present time we have complete responses from 50 Frenchmen, 20 Germans and 11 Italians; many of these men also sent us letters describing their understanding of the pronouns and offering numerous valuable anecdotes of usage. The varying numbers of subjects belonging to the three nationalities result from the unequal representation of these nationalities among Boston students rather than from national characterological differences in willingness to answer a questionnaire. Almost every person on our lists agreed to serve as an informant.

In analyzing the results we assigned the numbers 0–4 to the five response alternatives to each question, beginning with 'Definitely V' as 0. A rough test was made of the significance of the differences among the three languages on each question. We dichotomized the replies to each question into: (a) all replies of either 'Definitely T' or 'Probably T'; (b) all replies of 'Definitely V' or 'Probably V' or 'Possibly V, possibly T'. Using the chi-squared test with Yates's correction for small frequencies we determined, for each comparison, the probability of obtaining by chance a difference as large or larger than that actually obtained. Even with such small samples, there were quite a few differences significantly unlikely to occur by chance ($P = .05$ or less). Germans were more prone than the French to say T to their grandfathers, to an elder brother's wife, and to an old family servant. The French were more prone than the Germans to say T to a male fellow student, to a student from home visiting in America, to a fellow clerk in an office, and to someone known previously as a fellow student. Italians were more prone than the French to say T to a female fellow student and also to an attractive girl to whom they had recently been introduced. Italians were more prone than the Germans to say T to the persons just described and, in addition, to a male fellow student and to a student from home visiting in America. On no question did either the French or the Germans show a significantly greater tendency to say T than did the Italians.

The many particular differences among the three languages are susceptible of a general characterization. Let us first contrast German and French. The German T is more reliably applied within the family than is the French T; in addition to the significantly higher T scores for grandfather and elder brother's wife there are smaller differences showing a higher score for the German T on father, mother, wife, married elder brother, and remote male cousin. The French T is not automatically applied to remote relatives, but it is more likely than the German pronoun to be used to express the camaraderie of fellow students, fellow clerks, fellow countrymen abroad, and fellow soldiers. In general it may be said that the solidarity coded by the German T is an ascribed solidarity of family relationships. The French T, in greater degree, codes an acquired solidarity, not founded on family relationship but developing out of some sort of shared fate. As for the Italian T, it very nearly equals the German in family solidarity and it surpasses the French in camaraderie. The camaraderie of the Italian male, incidentally, is extended to the Italian female; unlike the French or German student the Italian says T to the co-ed almost as readily as to the male fellow student.

There is a very abstract semantic rule governing T and V which is the same for French, German, and Italian and for many other languages we have studied. The rule is that usage is reciprocal, T becoming increasingly probable and V less probable as the number of solidarity-producing attributes shared by two people increases. The respect in which French, German, and Italian differ from one another is in the relative weight given to various attributes of persons which can serve to generate solidarity. For German, ascribed family membership is the important attribute; French and Italian give more weight to acquired characteristics.

3 Semantics, Social Structure and Ideology

A historical study of the pronouns of address reveals a set of semantic and social psychological correspondence. The nonreciprocal power semantic is associated with a relatively static society in which power is distributed by birthright and is not subject to much redistribution. The power semantic was closely tied with the feudal and manorial systems. In Italy the reverential pronoun *Lei* which has largely displaced the older *voi* was originally an abbreviation for *la vostra Signoria* 'your lordship' and in Spanish *vuestra Merced* 'your grace' became the reverential *usted*. The static social structure was accompanied by the Church's teaching that each man had his properly appointed place and ought not to wish to rise above it. The reciprocal solidarity semantic has grown with social mobility and an equalitarian ideology. The towns and cities have led the way in the semantic change as they led the way in opening society to vertical movement. In addition to these rough historical correspondences we have made a collection of lesser items of evidence favoring the thesis.

In France the nonreciprocal power semantic was dominant until the Revolution when the Committee for the Public Safety condemned the use of V as a feudal remnant and ordered a universal reciprocal T. On 31 October, 1793, Malbec made a Parliamentary speech against V: 'Nous distinguons trois personnes pour le singulier et trois pour le pluriel, et, au mépris de cette règle, l'esprit de fanatisme, d'orgueil et de féodalité, nous a fait contracter l'habitude de nous servir de la seconde personne du pluriel lorsque nous parlons à un seul' (quoted in Brunot, 1927). For a time revolutionary 'fraternité' transformed all address into the mutual *Citoyen* and the mutual *tu*. Robespierre even addressed the president of the Assembly as *tu*. In later years solidarity declined and the differences of power which always exist everywhere were expressed once more.

It must be asked why the equalitarian ideal was expressed in a universal T rather than a universal V or, as a third alternative, why there was not a shift of semantic from power to solidarity with both pronouns being retained. The answer lies with the ancient upper-class preference for the use of V. There was animus against the pronoun itself. The pronoun of the 'sans-culottes' was T (Gedike, 1794), and so this had to be the pronoun of the Revolution.

Although the power semantic has largely gone out of pronoun use in France today native speakers are nevertheless aware of it. In part they are aware of it because it prevails in so much of the greatest French literature. Awareness of power as a potential factor in pronoun usage was revealed by our respondents' special attitude toward the saying of T to a waiter. Most of them felt that this would be shockingly bad taste in a way that other norm violations would not be, apparently because there is a kind of seignorial right to say T to a waiter, an actual power asymmetry, which the modern man's ideology requires him to deny. In French Africa, on the other hand, it is considered proper to recognize a caste difference between the African and the European, and the nonreciprocal address is used to express it. The European says T and requires V from the African. This is a galling custom to the African, and in 1957 Robert Lacoste, the French Minister residing in Algeria, urged his countrymen to eschew the practice.

In England, before the Norman Conquest, 'ye' was the second person plural and 'thou' the singular, 'You' was originally the accusative of 'ye', but in time it also became the nominative plural and ultimately ousted 'thou' as the usual singular. The first uses of 'ye' as a reverential singular occur in the thirteenth century (Kennedy, 1915), and seem to have been copied from the French nobility. The semantic progression corresponds roughly to the general stages described in the first section of this paper, except that the English seem always to have moved more freely from one form to another than did the continental Europeans (Jespersen, 1905).

In the seventeenth century 'thou' and 'you' became explicitly involved in social controversy. The Religious Society of Friends (or Quakers) was founded in the middle of this century by George Fox. One of the practices setting off this rebellious group from the larger society was the use of Plain Speech, and this entailed saying 'thou' to everyone. George Fox explained the practice in these words:

> 'Moreover, when the Lord sent me forth into the world, He forbade me to put off my hat to any, high or low; and I was required to Thee and Thou all men and women, without any respect to rich or poor, great or small.' (quoted in Estrich and Sperber, 1946)

Fox wrote a fascinating pamphlet (Fox, 1660), arguing that T to one and V to many is the natural and logical form of address in all languages. Among others he cites Latin, Hebrew, Greek, Arabick, Syriack, Aethiopic, Egyptian, French, and Italian. Fox suggests that the Pope, in his vanity, introduced the corrupt and illogical practice of saying V to one person. Farnsworth, another early Friend, wrote a somewhat similar pamphlet (Farnsworth, 1655), in which he argued that the Scriptures show that God and Adam and God and Moses were not too proud to say and receive the singular T.

For the new convert to the Society of Friends the universal T was an especially difficult commandment. Thomas Ellwood has described (1714) the trouble that developed between himself and his father:

> But whenever I had occasion to speak to my Father, though I had no Hat now to offend him; yet my language did as much: for I durst not say YOU to him, but THOU or THEE, as the Occasion required, and then would he be sure to fall on me with his Fists.

The Friends' reasons for using the mutual T were much the same as those of the French revolutionaries, but the Friends were always a minority and the larger society was antagonized by their violations of decorum.

Some Friends use 'thee' today; the nominative 'thou' has been dropped and 'thee' is used as both the nominative and (as formerly) the accusative. Interestingly many Friends also use 'you'. 'Thee' is likely to be reserved for Friends among themselves and 'you' said to outsiders. This seems to be a survival of the solidarity semantic. In English at large, of course, 'thou' is no longer used. The explanation of its disappearance is by no means certain; however, the forces at work seem to have included a popular reaction against the radicalism of Quakers and Levelers and also a general trend in English toward simplified verbal inflection.

In the world today there are numerous examples of the association proposed between ideology and pronoun semantics. In Yugoslavia, our informants tell us, there was, for a short time following the establishment of Communism, a universal mutual *T* of solidarity. Today revolutionary *esprit* has declined and *V* has returned for much the same set of circumstances as in Italy, France, or Spain. There is also some power asymmetry in Yugoslavia's 'Socialist manners'. A soldier says *V* and *Comrade General*, but the general addresses the soldier with *T* and surname.

It is interesting in our materials to contrast usage in the Afrikaans language of South Africa and in the Gujerati and Hindi languages of India with the rest of the collection. On the questionnaire, Afrikaans speakers made eight nonreciprocal power distinctions; especially notable are distinctions within the family and the distinctions between customer and waiter and between boss and clerk, since these are almost never power-coded in French, Italian, German, etc., although they once were. The Afrikaans pattern generally preserves the asymmetry of the dyads described in Figure 2, and that suggests a more static society and a less developed equalitarian ethic. The forms of address used between Afrikaans-speaking whites and the groups of 'coloreds' and 'blacks' are especially interesting. The Afrikaner uses *T*, but the two lower castes use neither *T* nor *V*. The intermediate caste of 'coloreds' says *Meneer* to the white and the 'blacks' say *Baas*. It is as if these social distances transcend anything that can be found within the white group and so require their peculiar linguistic expressions.

The Gujerati and Hindi languages of India have about the same pronoun semantic, and it is heavily loaded with power. These languages have all the asymmetrical usage of Afrikaans and, in addition, use the nonreciprocal *T* and *V* between elder brother and younger brother and between husband and wife. This truly feudal pronominal pattern is consistent with the static Indian society. However, that society is now changing rapidly and, consistent with that change, the norms of pronoun usage are also changing. The progressive young Indian exchanges the mutual *T* with his wife.

In our account of the general semantic evolution of the pronouns, we have identified a stage in which the solidarity rule was limited to address between persons of equal power. This seemed to yield a two-dimensional system in equilibrium (see Figure 1a), and we have wondered why address did not permanently stabilize there. It is possible, of course, that human cognition favors the binary choice without contingencies and so found its way to the suppression of one dimension. However, this theory does not account for the fact that it was the rule of solidarity that triumphed. We believe, therefore, that the development of open societies with an equalitarian ideology acted against the nonreciprocal power semantic and in favor of solidarity. It is our suggestion that the larger social changes created a distaste for the face-to-face expression of differential power.

What of the many actions other than nonreciprocal *T* and *V* which express power asymmetry? A vassal not only says *V* but also bows, lifts his cap, touches his forelock, keeps silent, leaps to obey. There are a large number of expressions of subordination which are patterned isomorphically with T and V. Nor are the pronouns the only forms of nonreciprocal address. There are, in addition, proper names and titles, and many of these operate today on a nonreciprocal power pattern in America and in Europe, in open and equalitarian societies.

In the American family there are no discriminating pronouns, but there are non-reciprocal norms of address. A father says 'Jim' to his son but, unless he is extraordinarily 'advanced', he does not anticipate being called 'Jack' in reply. In the American South there are no pronouns to mark the caste separation of Negro and white, but there are nonreciprocal norms of address. The white man is accustomed to call the Negro by his first name, but he expects to be called 'Mr Legree'. In America and in Europe there are forms of nonreciprocal address for all the dyads of asymmetrical power; customer and waiter, teacher and student, father and son, employer and employee.

Differences of power exist in a democracy as in all societies. What is the difference between expressing power asymmetry in pronouns and expressing it by choice of title and proper name? It seems to be primarily a question of the degree of linguistic compulsion. In face-to-face address we can usually avoid the use of any name or title but not so easily the use of a pronoun. Even if the pronoun can be avoided, it will be implicit in the inflection of the verb. 'Dîtes quelque chose' clearly says *vous* to the Frenchman, A norm for the pronominal and verbal expression of power compels a continuing coding of power, whereas a norm for titles and names permits power to go uncoded in most discourse. Is there any reason why the pronominal coding should be more congenial to a static society than to an open society?

We have noticed that mode of address intrudes into consciousness as a problem at times of status change. Award of the doctoral degree, for instance, transforms a student into a colleague and, among American academics, the familiar first name is normal. The fledgling academic may find it difficult to call his former teachers by their first names. Although these teachers may be young and affable, they have had a very real power over him for several years and it will feel presumptuous to deny this all at once with a new mode of address. However, the 'tyranny of democratic manners' (Cronin, 1958) does not allow him to continue comfortably with the polite 'Professor X'. He would not like to be thought unduly conscious of status, unprepared for faculty rank, a born lickspittle. Happily, English allows him a respite. He can avoid any term of address, staying with the uncommitted 'you', until he and his addressees have got used to the new state of things. This linguistic *rite de passage* has, for English speakers, a waiting room in which to screw up courage.

In a fluid society crises of address will occur more frequently than in a static society, and so the pronominal coding of power differences is more likely to be felt as onerous. Coding by title and name would be more tolerable because less compulsory. Where status is fixed by birth and does not change each man has enduring rights and obligations of address.

A strong equalitarian ideology of the sort dominant in America works to suppress every conventional expression of power asymmetry. If the worker becomes conscious of his unreciprocated polite address to the boss, he may feel that his human dignity requires him to change. However, we do not feel the full power of the ideology until we are in a situation that gives us some claim to receive deferential address. The American professor often feels foolish being given his title, he almost certainly will not claim it as a prerogative; he may take pride in being on a first-name basis with his students. Very 'palsy' parents may invite their children to call them by first name. The very President of the Republic invites us all to call him 'Ike'. Nevertheless, the differences of power are real and are experienced. Cronin has suggested in an amusing piece (Cronin, 1958) that subordination is expressed by Americans in a subtle, and generally unwitting, body language. 'The repertoire includes the boyish grin, the deprecatory cough, the unfinished sentence, the appreciative giggle, the drooping shoulders, the head-scratch and the bottom-waggle.'

4 Group Style with the Pronouns of Address

The identification of style is relative to the identification of some constancy. When we have marked out the essentials of some action – it might be walking or speaking a language or driving a car – we can identify the residual variation as stylistic. Different styles are different ways of 'doing the same thing', and so their identification waits on some designation of the range of performances to be regarded as 'the same thing'.

Linguistic science finds enough that is constant in English and French and Latin to put all these and many more into one family – the Indo-European. It is possible with reference to this constancy to think of Italian and Spanish and English and the others as so many styles of Indo-European. They all have, for instance, two singular pronouns of address, but each language has an individual phonetic and semantic style in pronoun usage. We are ignoring phonetic style (through the use of the generic T and V), but in the second section of the paper we have described differences in the semantic styles of French, German and Italian.

Linguistic styles are potentially expressive when there is covariation between characteristics of language performance and characteristics of the performers. When styles are 'interpreted', language behavior is functionally expressive. On that abstract level where the constancy is Indo-European and the styles are French, German, English and Italian, interpretations of style must be statements about communities of speakers, statements of national character, social structure, or group ideology. In the last section we have hazarded a few propositions on this level.

It is usual, in discussion of linguistic style, to set constancy at the level of a language like French or English rather than at the level of a language family. In the languages we have studied there are variations in pronoun style that are associated with the social status of the speaker. We have seen that the use of V because of its entry at the top of a society and its diffusion downward was always interpreted as a mark of good breeding. It is interesting to find an organization of French journeymen in the generation after the Revolution adopting a set of rules of propriety cautioning members against going without tie or shoes at home on Sunday and also against the use of the mutual T among themselves (Perdiguier, 1914). Our informants assure us that V and T still function as indications of class membership. The Yugoslavians have a saying that a peasant would say T to a king. By contrast, a French nobleman who turned up in our net told us that he had said T to no one in the world except the old woman who was his nurse in childhood. He is prevented by the dominant democratic ideology from saying T to subordinates and by his own royalist ideology from saying it to equals.

In literature, pronoun style has often been used to expose the pretensions of social climbers and the would-be elegant. Persons aping the manners of the class above them usually do not get the imitation exactly right. They are likely to notice some point of difference between their own class and the next higher and then extend the difference too widely, as in the use of the 'elegant' broad [a] in 'can' and 'bad'. Molière gives us his 'précieuses ridicules' saying V to servants whom a refined person would call T. In Ben Jonson's *Everyman in his Humour* and *Epicoene* such true gallants as Wellbred and Knowell usually say 'you' to one another but they make frequent expressive shifts between this form and 'thou', whereas such fops as John Daw and Amorous-La-Foole make unvarying use of 'you'.

Our sample of visiting French students was roughly homogeneous in social status as judged by the single criterion of paternal occupation. Therefore, we could not make any systematic study of differences in class style, but we thought it possible that, even within this select group, there might be interpretable differences of style. It was our guess that the tendency to make wide or narrow use of the solidary T would be related to general radicalism or conservatism of ideology. As a measure of this latter dimension we used Eysenck's Social Attitude Inventory (1957). This is a collection of statements to be accepted or rejected concerning a variety of matters – religion, economics, racial relations, sexual behavior, etc. Eysenck has validated the scale in England and in France on Socialist, Communist, Fascist, Conservative and Liberal party members. In general, to be radical on this scale is to favor change and to be conservative is to wish to maintain the status quo or turn back to some earlier condition. We undertook to relate scores on this inventory to an index of pronoun style.

As yet we have reported no evidence demonstrating that there exists such a thing as a personal style in pronoun usage in the sense of a tendency to make wide or narrow use of T. It may be that each item in the questionnaire, each sort of person addressed, is an independent personal norm not predictable from any other. A child learns what to say to each kind of person. What he learns in each case depends on the groups in which he has membership. Perhaps his usage is a bundle of unrelated habits.

Guttman (Stouffer, Guttman, *et al.*, 1950) has developed the technique of Scalogram Analysis for determining whether or not a collection of statements taps a common dimension. A perfect Guttman scale can be made of the statements: (a) I am at least 5′ tall; (b) I am at least 5′ 4″ tall; (c) I am at least 5′ 7″ tall; (d) I am at least 6′ 1″ tall; (e) I am at least 6′ 2″ tall. Endorsement of a more extreme statement will always be associated with endorsement of all less extreme statements. A person can be assigned a single score – a, b, c, d, or e – which represents the most extreme statement he has endorsed, and from this single score all his individual answers can be reproduced. If he scores c he has also endorsed a and b but not d or e. The general criterion for scalability is the reproducibility of individual responses from a single score, and this depends on the items being interrelated so that endorsement of one is reliably associated with endorsement or rejection of the others.

The Guttman method was developed during World War II for the measurement of social attitudes, and it has been widely used. Perfect reproducibility is not likely to be found for all the statements which an investigator guesses to be concerned with some single attitude. The usual thing is to accept a set of statements as scalable when they are 90 per cent reproducible and also satisfy certain other requirements; for example, there must be some statements that are not given a very one-sided response but are accepted and rejected with nearly equal frequency.

The responses to the pronoun questionnaire are not varying degrees of agreement (as in an attitude questionnaire) but are rather varying probabilities of saying T or V. There seems to be no reason why these bipolar responses cannot be treated like yes or no responses on an attitude scale. The difference is that the scale, if there is one, will be the semantic dimension governing the pronouns, and the scale score of each respondent will represent his personal semantic style.

It is customary to have 100 subjects for a Scalogram Analysis, but we could find only 50 French students. We tested all 28 items for scalability and found that a subset of them made a fairly good scale. It was necessary to combine response categories so as to dichotomize them in order to obtain an average reproducibility of 85 per cent. This coefficient was computed for the five intermediate items having the more-balanced marginal frequencies. A large number of items fell at or very near the two extremes. The solidarity or T-most end of the scale could be defined by father, mother, elder brother, young boys, wife or lover quite as well as by younger brother. The remote or V-most end could be defined by 'waiter' or 'top boss' as well as by 'army general'. The intervening positions, from the T-end to the V-end are: the elderly female servant known since childhood, grandfather, a male fellow student, a female fellow student and an elder brother's wife.

For each item on the scale a T answer scores one point and a V answer no points. The individual total scores range from 1 to 7, which means the scale can differentiate only seven semantic styles. We divided the subjects into the resultant seven stylistically homogeneous groups and, for each group, determined the average scores on radicalism–conservatism. There was a set of almost perfectly consistent differences,

In Table 1 appear the mean radicalism scores for each pronoun style. The individual radicalism scores range between 2 and 13; the higher the score the more radical the person's ideology. The very striking result is that the group radicalism scores duplicate the order of the group pronoun scores with only a single reversal. The rank-difference correlation between the two sets of scores is .96, and even with only seven paired scores this is a very significant relationship.

There is enough consistency of address to justify speaking of a personal-pronoun style which involves a more or less wide use of the solidary T. Even among students of the same socioeconomic level there are differences of style, and these are potentially expressive of radicalism and conservatism in ideology. A Frenchman could, with some confidence, infer that a male university student who regularly said T to female fellow students would favor the nationalization of industry, free love, trial marriage, the abolition of capital punishment, and the weakening of nationalistic and religious loyalties.

What shall we make of the association between a wide use of T and a cluster of radical sentiments? There may be no 'sense' to it at all, that is, no logical connection between the linguistic practice and the attitudes, but simply a general tendency to go along with the newest thing. We know that left-wing attitudes are more likely to be found in the laboring class than in the professional classes. Perhaps those offspring of the professional class who sympathize with proletariat politics also, incidentally, pick up the working man's wide use of T without feeling that there is anything in the linguistic practice that is congruent with the ideology.

Table 1   Scores on the pronoun scale in relation to scores on the radicalism scale

Group pronoun score	Group mean radicalism score
1	5·50
2	6·66
3	6·82
4	7·83
5	6·83
6	8·83
7	9·75

On the other hand perhaps there is something appropriate in the association. The ideology is consistent in its disapproval of barriers between people: race, religion, nationality, property, marriage, even criminality. All these barriers have the effect of separating the solidary, the 'in-group', from the nonsolidary, the 'out-group'. The radical says the criminal is not far enough 'out' to be killed; he should be re-educated. He says that a nationality ought not to be so solidary that it prevents world organization from succeeding. Private property ought to be abolished, industry should be nationalized. There are to be no more out-groups and in-groups but rather one group, undifferentiated by nationality, religion, or pronoun of address. The fact that the pronoun which is being extended to all men alike is *T*, the mark of solidarity, the pronoun of the nuclear family, expresses the radical's intention to extend his sense of brotherhood. But we notice that the universal application of the pronoun eliminates the discrimination that gave it a meaning and that gives particular point to an old problem. Can the solidarity of the family be extended so widely? Is there enough libido to stretch so far? Will there perhaps be a thin solidarity the same everywhere but nowhere so strong as in the past?

5   The Pronouns of Address as Expressions of Transient Attitudes

Behavior norms are practices consistent within a group. So long as the choice of a pronoun is recognized as normal for a group, its interpretation is simply the membership of the speaker in that group. However, the implications of group membership are often very important; social class, for instance, suggests a kind of family life, a level of education, a set of political views and much besides. These facts about a person belong to his character. They are enduring features which help to determine actions over many years. Consistent personal style in the use of the pronouns of address does not reveal enough to establish the speaker's unique character, but it can help to place him in one or another large category.

Sometimes the choice of a pronoun clearly violates a group norm and perhaps also the customary practice of the speaker. Then the meaning of the act will be sought in some attitude or emotion of the speaker. It is as if the interpreter reasoned that variations of address between the same two persons must be caused by variations in their attitudes toward one another. If two men of seventeenth century France properly exchange the *V* of upper-class equals and one of them gives the other *T*, he suggests that the other is his inferior since it is to his inferiors that a man says *T*. The general meaning of an unexpected pronoun choice is simply that the speaker, for the moment, views his relationship as one that calls for the pronoun used. This kind of variation in language behavior expresses a contemporaneous feeling or attitude. These variations are not consistent personal styles but departures from one's own custom and the customs of a group in response to a mood.

As there have been two great semantic dimensions governing *T* and *V*, so there have also been two principal kinds of expressive meaning. Breaking the norms of power generally has the meaning that a speaker regards an addressee as his inferior, superior, or equal, although by usual criteria, and according to the speaker's own customary usage, the addressee is not what the pronoun implies. Breaking the norms of solidarity generally means that the speaker temporarily thinks of the other as an outsider or as an intimate; it means that sympathy is extended or withdrawn.

The oldest uses of *T* and *V* to express attitudes seem everywhere to have been the *T* of contempt or anger and the *V* of admiration or respect. In his study of the French pronouns Schliebitz (1886) found the first examples of these expressive uses in literature of the twelfth and thirteenth centuries, which is about the time that the power semantic crystallized in France, and Grand (1930) has found the same thing for Italian. In saying *T*, where *V* is usual, the speaker treats the addressee like a servant or a child, and assumes the right to berate him. The most common use of the expressive *V*, in the early materials, is that of the master who is exceptionally pleased with the work of a servant and elevates him pronominally to match this esteem.

Racine, in his dramas, used the pronouns with perfect semantic consistency. His major figures exchange the *V* of upper-class equals. Lovers, brother and sister, husband and wife – none of them says *T* if he is of high rank, but each person of high rank has a subordinate confidante to whom he says *T* and from whom he receives *V*. It is a perfect nonreciprocal power semantic. This courtly pattern is broken only for the greatest scenes in each play. Racine reserved the expressive pronoun as some composers save the cymbals. In both *Andromaque* and *Phèdre* there are only two expressive departures from the norm, and they mark climaxes of feeling.

Jespersen (1905) believed that English 'thou' and 'ye' (or 'you') were more often shifted to express mood and tone than were the pronouns of the continental languages, and our comparisons strongly support this opinion. The 'thou' of contempt was so very familiar that a verbal form was created to name this expressive use. Shakespeare gives it to Sir Toby Belch (*Twelfth Night*) in the lines urging Andrew Aguecheek to send a challenge to the disguised Viola: 'Taunt him with the license of ink, if thou thou'st him some thrice, it shall not be amiss.' In life the verb turned up in Sir Edward Coke's attack on Raleigh at the latter's trial in 1603 (Jardine, 1832–5): 'All that he did, was at thy instigation, thou viper; for I thou thee, thou traitor.'

The *T* of contempt and anger is usually introduced between persons who normally exchange *V* but it can, of course, also be used by a subordinate to a superior. As the social distance is greater, the overthrow of the norm is more shocking and generally represents a greater extremity of passion. Sejanus, in Ben Jonson's play of that name, feels extreme contempt for the emperor Tiberius but wisely gives him the reverential *V* to his face. However, soliloquizing after the emperor has exited, Sejanus begins: 'Dull, heavy Caesar! Wouldst thou tell me . . .' In Jonson's *Volpone* Mosca invariably says 'you' to his master until the final scene when, as the two villains are about to be carted away, Mosca turns on Volpone with 'Bane to thy wolfish nature.'

Expressive effects of much greater subtlety than those we have described are common in Elizabethan and Jacobean drama. The exact interpretation of the speaker's attitude depends not only on the pronoun norm he upsets but also on his attendant words and actions and the total setting. Still simple enough to be unequivocal is the ironic or mocking 'you' said by Tamburlaine to the captive Turkish emperor Bajazeth. This exchange occurs in Act IV of Marlowe's play:

> TAMBURLAINE: Here Turk, wilt thou have a clean trencher?
> BAJAZETH: Ay, tyrant, and more meat.
> TAMBURLAINE: Soft, Sir, you must be dietee; too much eating will make you surfeit.

'Thou' is to be expected from captor to captive and the norm is upset when Tamburlaine says 'you'. He cannot intend to express admiration or respect since he keeps the Turk captive and starves him. His intention is to mock the captive king with respectful address, implying a power that the king has lost.

The momentary shift of pronoun directly expresses a momentary shift of mood, but that interpretation does not exhaust its meaning. The fact that a man has a particular momentary attitude or emotion may imply a great deal about his characteristic disposition, his readiness for one kind of feeling rather than another. Not every attorney general, for instance, would have used the abusive 'thou' to Raleigh. The fact that Edward Coke did so suggests an arrogant and choleric temperament and, in fact, many made this assessment of him (Jardine, 1832–5). When Volpone spoke to Celia, a lady of Venice, he ought to have said 'you' but he began at once with 'thee'. This violation of decorum, together with the fact that he leaps from his sick bed to attempt rape of the lady, helps to establish Volpone's monstrous character. His abnormal form of address is consistent with the unnatural images in his speech. In any given situation we know the sort of people who would break the norms of address and the sort who would not. From the fact that a man does break the norms we infer his immediate feelings and, in addition, attribute to him the general character of people who would have such feelings and would give them that kind of expression.

With the establishment of the solidarity semantic a new set of expressive meanings became possible – feelings of sympathy and estrangement. In Shakespeare's plays there are expressive meanings that derive from the solidarity semantic as well as many dependent on power usage and many that rely on both connotations. The play *Two Gentlemen of Verona* is concerned with the Renaissance ideal of friendship and provides especially clear expressions of solidarity. Proteus and Valentine, the two Gentlemen, initially exchange 'thou', but when they touch on the subject of love, on which they disagree, their address changes to the 'you' of estrangement. Molière (Fay, 1920) has shown us that a man may even put himself at a distance as does George Dandin in the soliloquy beginning: 'George Dandin! George Dandin! Vous avez fait une sottise . . .'

In both French and English drama of the past, *T* and *V* were marvelously sensitive to feelings of approach and withdrawal. In terms of Freud's striking amoeba metaphor the pronouns signal the extension or retraction of libidinal pseudopodia. However, in French, German and Italian today this use seems to be very uncommon. Our informants told us that the *T*, once extended, is almost never taken back for the reason that it would mean the complete withdrawal of esteem. The only modern expressive shift we have found is a rather chilling one. Silverberg (1940) reports that in Germany in 1940 a prostitute and her client said *du* when they met and while they were together but when the libidinal tie (in the narrow sense) had been dissolved they resumed the mutual distant *Sie*.

We have suggested that the modern direction of change in pronoun usage expresses a will to extend the solidary ethic to everyone. The apparent decline of expressive shifts between *T* and *V* is more difficult to interpret. Perhaps it is because Europeans have seen that excluded persons or races or groups can become the target of extreme aggression from groups that are benevolent within themselves. Perhaps Europeans would like to convince themselves that the solidary ethic once extended will not be withdrawn, that there is security in the mutual *T*.

Note

Our study was financed by a Grant-in-Aid-of-Research made by the Ford Foundation to Brown, and the authors gratefully acknowledge this assistance.

References

Baugh, A. C. (1935), *A History of the English Language*, New York.
Brunot, F. (1927), *La pensée et la langue*, Paris.
Brunot, F. (1937), *Histoire de la langue française*, Paris.
Byrne, Sister St G. (1936), 'Shakespeare's use of the pronoun of address', dissertation, Catholic University of America, Washington.
Châtelain, É. (1880), 'Du pluriel de respect en Latin', *Revue de philologie*, vol. 4, pp. 129–39.
Cronin, M. (1958), 'The tyranny of democratic manners', *New Republic*, vol. 137, pp. 12–14.
Devereux, W. B. (1853), *Lives and Letters of the Devereux, Earls of Essex, in the Reigns of Elizabeth, James I and Charles I, 1540–1646*, London.
Diez, F. (1876), *Grammaire des langues romanes*, Paris.
Ellwood, T. (1714), *The History of the Life of Thomas Ellwood*, London.
Estrich, R. M., and Sperber, H. (1946), *Three Keys to Language*, New York.
Eysenck, H. J. (1957), *Sense and Nonsense in Psychology*, Penguin.
Farnsworth, R. (1655), *The Pure Language of the Spirit of Truth . . . or 'Thee' and 'Thou' in its Place. . . .*, London.
Fay, P. B. (1920), 'The use of "tu" and "vous" in Molière', *University of California Publications in Modern Philology*, vol. 8, pp. 227–86.
Fox, G. (1660), *A Battle-Doore for Teachers and Professors to Learn Plural and Singular*, London.
Gedike, F. (1974), *Über Du und Sie in der deutschen Sprache*, Berlin.
Grand, C. (1930), '*Tu, voi, lei*': *étude des pronoms allocutoires italiens*, Ingebohl.
Grimm, J. (1898), *Deutsche Grammatik*, vol. 4, Gütersloh.

Harrison, G. B. (ed.) (1935), *The Letters of Queen Elizabeth*, London.

Jardine, D. (1832–5), *Criminal Trials*, vols. 1–2, London.

Jespersen, O. (1905), *Growth and Structure of the English Language*, Leipzig.

Johnston, O. M. (1904), 'The use of "ella," "lei" and "la" as polite forms of address in Italian', *Modern Philology*, vol. 1, pp. 469–75.

Kennedy, A. G. (1915), *The Pronoun of Address in English Literature of the Thirteenth Century*, Stanford University Press.

Littré, É. (1882), *Dictionnaire de la langue française*, vol. 4, Paris.

Meyer-Lübke, W. (1900), *Grammaire des langues romanes*, vol. 3, Paris.

Muller, H. F. (1914), 'The uses of the plural of reverence in the letters of Pope Gregory I', *Romanic Review*, vol. 5, pp. 68–89.

Perdiguier, A. (1914), *Mémoires d'un compagnon*, Moulins.

Schliebitz, V. (1886), *Die Person der Anrede in der französischen Sprache*, Breslau.

Silverberg, W. V. (1940), 'On the psychological significance of "Du" and "Sie"', *Psychoanalytic Quarterly*, vol. 9, pp. 509–25.

Stidston, R. O. (1917), *The Use of Ye in the Function of Thou: A Study of Grammar and Social Intercourse in Fourteenth-Century England*, Stanford University Press.

Stouffer, S. A., Guttman, L., *et al.* (1950), *Measurement and Prediction*, Princeton University Press.

10

Complimenting: A Positive Politeness Strategy

Janet Holmes

1 Paying Compliments

Example 1
Two colleagues meeting in Pat's office to discuss a report.

> CHRIS: Hi Pat. Sorry I'm late. The boss wanted to set up a time for a meeting just as
> I was leaving.
> PAT: That's OK Chris. You're looking good. Is that a new suit?
> CHRIS: Mm. It's nice isn't it. I got it in Auckland last month. Have you had a break since
> I last saw you?
> PAT: No, work work work I'm afraid. Never mind. Have you got a copy of the report with
> you?

Positive politeness can be expressed in many ways but paying a compliment is one of the most obvious. A favourable comment on the addressee's appearance, as illustrated in example 1, is a very common way of paying a compliment as we shall see. Compliments are prime examples of speech acts which notice and attend to the hearer's 'interests, wants, needs, goods', the first positive politeness strategy identified and discussed by Brown and Levinson (1987: 102).

1.1   What is a compliment?

But what is a compliment? There are a number of positively polite speech acts in the exchange between Pat and Chris – greetings, friendly address terms, expressions of concern and compliments. I would want to count *you're looking good* and *is that a new suit* as examples of compliments. The first is a direct compliment, while the fact that the second counts as a compliment is inferable from the discourse context and the fact that things which are new are generally highly valued in western society (see Manes 1983). When collecting and analysing examples of a particular speech act, it is important to have a clear definition in order to decide what counts and what does not. This is how I have defined a compliment:

> A compliment is a speech act which explicitly or implicitly attributes credit to some-
> one other than the speaker, usually the person addressed, for some 'good' (possession,

characteristic, skill, etc.) which is positively valued by the speaker and the hearer. (Holmes 1986: 485)

As the utterance *is that a new suit* illustrates, a compliment may be indirect, requiring some inferencing based on a knowledge of the cultural values of the community. There are other ways in which a compliment may be indirect too. Compliments usually focus on something directly attributable to the person addressed (e.g. an article of clothing), but examples 2 and 3 demonstrate that this is not always the case.

Examples 2 and 3

(2)   *Rhonda is visiting an old schoolfriend, Carol, and comments on one of Carol's children.*

RHONDA: What a polite child!
CAROL: Thank you. We do our best.

(3)   *Ray is the conductor of the choir.*

MATT: The choir was wonderful. You must be really pleased.
RAY: Yes, they were good weren't they.

The complimenters' utterances in these examples may look superficially like rather general positive evaluations, but their function as compliments which indirectly attribute credit to the addressee for good parenting in (2), and good conducting in (3), is unambiguous in context.

1.2   Why give a compliment?

Compliments are usually intended to make others feel good (see Wierzbicka 1987: 201), The primary function of a compliment is most obviously affective and social, rather than referential or informative. They are generally described as positively affective speech acts serving to increase or consolidate the solidarity between the speaker and addressee (see Wolfson 1981, 1983; Holmes 1986; Herbert 1989; Lewandowska-Tomaszczyk 1989). Compliments are social lubricants which 'create or maintain rapport' (Wolfson 1983: 86), as illustrated in all the examples above, as well as in example 4.

Example 4

Two women, good friends, meeting in the lift at their workplace.

SAL: Hi how are you? You're looking just terrific.
MEG: Thanks. I'm pretty good. How are things with you? That's a snazzy scarf you're wearing.

Compliments are clearly positive politeness devices which express goodwill and solidarity between the speaker and the addressee. But they may serve other functions too. Do compliments have any element of referential meaning, for instance? While the primary function of compliments is most obviously affective, they also convey some information in the form of the particular 'good' the speaker selects for comment. They provide a positive critical evaluation of a selected aspect of the addressee's behaviour or appearance, or whatever, which in some contexts may carry some communicative weight. Johnson and Roen (1992), for instance, argue that the compliments they analysed in written peer reviews simultaneously conveyed both affective (or inter-personal) meaning and referential (or ideational) meaning in that a particular aspect of the review was chosen for positive attention. It is possible that some compliments are intended and perceived as conveying a stronger referential message than others. Very clearly, the relationship between the complimenter and recipient is crucial in accurately interpreting the potential functions of a compliment.

In some contexts, compliments may function as praise and encouragement. In an analysis of over a thousand American compliments, Herbert (1990: 221) suggests some compliments serve as expressions of praise and admiration rather than offers of solidarity. This seems likely to reflect the relationship between the participants. Praise is often directed downwards from superordinate to subordinate. So the teacher's compliment about a student's work in example 5 would generally be regarded as praise.

Example 5

TEACHER: This is excellent Jeannie. You've really done a nice job.

Tannen seems to be referring to this function of compliments when she identifies compliments as potentially patronising.

> Giving praise . . . is . . . inherently asymmetrical. It . . . frames the speaker as one-up, in a position to judge someone else's performance. (Tannen 1990: 69)

It is possible, then, that in some relationships compliments will be unwelcome because they are experienced as ways in which the speaker is asserting superiority. Com-pliments directed upwards from subordinate to superordinates, on the other hand, are often labelled 'flattery'. In analysing differences in the way women and men use and interpret compliments, it will clearly be important to consider compliments between status unequals, exploring the possible alternative interpretations which they may be given.

Compliments may have a darker side then. For some recipients, in some contexts, an apparent compliment may be experienced negatively, or as face-threatening. They may be patronising or offensively flattering. They may also, of course, be sarcastic. When the content of a compliment is perceived as too distant from reality, it will be heard as a sarcastic or ironic put-down. I was in no doubt of the sarcastic intent of my brother's comment 'You play so well' as I was plonking away at the piano, hitting far more wrong than right notes. Focusing on a different perspective, Brown and Levinson suggest (1987: 66) that a compliment can be regarded as a face-threatening act to the extent that it implies the complimenter envies the addressee in some way, or would like something belonging to the addressee. This is perhaps clearest in cultures where an expression of admiration for an object imposes an obligation on the addressee to offer it to the complimenter, as in example 6.

Example 6
Pakeha woman to Samoan friend whom she is visiting.

> SUE: What an unusual necklace. It's beautiful.
> ETI: Please take it.

In this particular instance, Sue was very embarrassed at being offered as a gift the object she had admired. But Eti's response was perfectly predictable by anyone familiar with Samoan cultural norms with respect to complimenting behaviour. In other cultures and social groups too, compliments may be considered somewhat face-threatening in that they imply at least an element of envy and desire to have what the addressee possesses, whether an object or a desirable trait or skill (see Brown and Levinson 1987: 247). And in 'debt-sensitive cultures' (1987: 247), the recipient of a compliment may be regarded as incurring a heavy debt. In such cultures, then, the function of a compliment cannot be regarded as simply and unarguably positively polite.

Even if intended as an expression of solidarity, a compliment might be experienced as face-threatening if it is interpreted as assuming unwarranted intimacy. Lewandowska-Tomaszczyk (1989: 75) comments that in her Polish and British compliment data, compliments between people who did not know each other well caused embarrassment. Compliments presuppose a certain familiarity with the addressee, she suggests. This is likely to be true of certain types of compliments in many cultures. Compliments on very personal topics, for instance, are appropriate only from intimates, as in example 7.

Example 7
Young woman to her mother who is in hospital after a bad car accident.
Oh mum you've got your false teeth – they look great

The mother had been waiting for some time to be fitted with false teeth to replace those knocked out or broken in the car accident. There are not many situations in which such a compliment could be paid without causing embarrassment.

At the darkest end of the spectrum are utterances which have been called 'stranger compliments' or 'street remarks' (Kissling and Kramarae 1991; Kissling 1991).

Example 8
Man on building site to young woman passing by.
Wow what legs. What are you doing with them tonight sweetie?

These serve a very different interpersonal function from compliments between friends and acquaintances. Though some women interpret them positively as expressions of appreciation, others regard them as examples of verbal harassment. It seems likely that both the speaker's intentions and the hearer's interpretations of these speech acts are extremely variable, and require detailed analysis in context. Though I have mentioned them here for completeness, the discussion below is not based on data which included 'stranger compliments'.

Different analysts have thus identified a number of different functions of compliments in different contexts:

1   to express solidarity;
2   to express positive evaluation, admiration, appreciation or praise;
3   to express envy or desire for hearer's possessions;
4   as verbal harassment.

These functions are not necessarily mutually exclusive, but the relationship between the participants is crucial in interpreting the primary function of a particular compliment: analysis in context is essential. Distributional data can also be suggestive, however, as we shall see in the next section which describes the way compliments are used between New Zealand women and men, and discusses what this suggests about their function as politeness devices.

2   Who Pays Most Compliments?

Shall I compare thee to a summer's day?
The following analysis of the distribution of compliments between New Zealand women and men is based on a corpus of 484 naturally occurring compliments and compliment responses. The data was collected using an ethnographic approach (Holmes 1986), a method which derives from anthropology, and which has been advocated by Hymes over many years (1962, 1972, 1974), and very successfully adopted by researchers such as Nessa Wolfson (e.g. 1983, 1988). This approach combines some of the advantages of qualitative research with the generalisability gained from quantitative analysis. Compliments and their responses are noted down, together with relevant features of the participants, their relationship, and the context in which the compliment occurred. Using a number of people as data collectors, it was possible to gather a large number of compliments from a wide variety of contexts. Most, however, were produced by adult Pakeha New Zealanders, and it is therefore the compliment norms of this group which are being described.

The New Zealand compliments collected in this way revealed a very clear pattern. Women gave and received significantly more compliments than men did, as figure 1 illustrates.

Women gave 68 per cent of all the compliments recorded and received 74 per cent of them. By contrast, compliments between males were relatively rare (only 9 per cent), and, even taking account of females' compliments to males, men received overall considerably fewer compliments than women (only 26 per cent). On this evidence, complimenting appears to be a speech behaviour occurring much more frequently in interactions involving women than men.[1]

Other researchers report similar patterns. Compliments are used more frequently by women than by men, and women are complimented more often than men in two different American studies (Wolfson 1983; Herbert 1990), and in research on compliments between Polish speakers (Lewandowska-Tomaszczyk 1989). This same pattern also turned up in a rather different context – that of written peer reviews (Johnson and Roen 1992). In this more information-orientated context which involved writing rather than speech, one would not have predicted gender contrasts. But even in writing women tended to use more compliments (or 'positive evaluative terms' to quote Johnson and

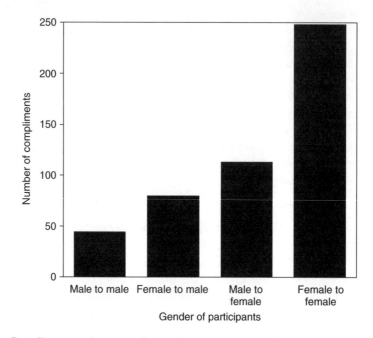

Figure 1   Compliments and gender of participants

Roen's precise measure) than men, though the differences were not quite statistically significant (Johnson and Roen 1992: 38).

These differences in the distribution of compliments between women and men have led to the suggestion that women and men may perceive the function of compliments differently. Women may regard compliments as primarily positively affective speech acts, for instance, expressing solidarity and positive politeness, while men may give greater weight to their referential meaning, as evaluative judgements, or to the potentially negative face-threatening features discussed above.

Herbert (1990), for instance, draws a parallel between the lower frequency of compliments given by South Africans compared to Americans, and the lower frequency of compliments between men compared to women. Where compliments are frequent, he suggests, they are more likely to be functioning as solidarity tokens; where they are less frequent they are more likely to be referentially orientated or what he calls 'genuine expressions of admiration' (1990: 221). In support of this, he points to the fact that in his data the responses elicited by the rarer male–male compliments were more likely to be acceptances, reflecting the recipients' recognition of their evaluative function.

Example 9
Mick and Brent are neighbours. They meet at Brent's gate as he arrives home.

MICK:	New car?
BRENT:	Yeah.
MICK:	Looks as if it will move.
BRENT:	Yeah it goes well I must say.

Female compliments, however, were more likely to elicit alternative responses, such as shifting or reducing the force of the compliment.

Example 10
Friends arriving at youth club.

> HELEN: What a neat outfit!
> GERRY: It's actually quite old.

Responses which shift or reduce the compliment's force reflect the function of such compliments as tokens of solidarity, he suggests, since they indicate the recipient's desire to restore the social balance between speakers. There were no such gender differences in compliment responses in the New Zealand corpus, so this explanation cannot account for the less frequent use of compliments by New Zealand men.

It is possible, however, that men may more readily perceive compliments as face-threatening acts than women do. They may feel embarrassed or obligated by these unsolicited tokens of solidarity. The male threshold for what counts as an appropriate relationship to warrant mutual complimenting may differ from the female. Wolfson's 'bulge' theory (Wolfson 1988) suggested that certain linguistic behaviours, such as compliments, occurred more frequently between friends than between strangers or intimates. The bulge represented the higher frequency of such polite speech acts to friends and acquaintances. But the 'bulge' or the range of relationships within which compliments are acceptable politeness tokens may be much narrower for men than women. Female and male norms may differ. While one cannot be sure of the reasons for the imbalance in the distribution of compliments in women's and men's speech, it is widely agreed that women appear to use compliments mainly as a means of expressing rapport, while they do not appear to function so unambiguously for men.

This interpretation would be consistent with research which suggested that women's linguistic behaviour can often be broadly characterised as facilitative, affiliative, and cooperative, rather than competitive or control-orientated. In much of the research comparing patterns of male and female interaction, women's contributions have been described as 'other-orientated'. If women regard compliments as a means of expressing rapport and solidarity, the finding that they give more compliments than men is consistent with this orientation. Conversely, if men regard compliments as face-threatening or controlling devices, at least in some contexts, this could account for the male patterns observed.

In studies of compliments elsewhere, women also received more compliments than men (Wolfson 1984; Holmes 1988; Herbert 1990; Johnson and Roen 1992). Compliments between women are most frequent in all the studies, but it is noteworthy that men compliment women more often than they compliment other men. One explanation for this might be that women's positive attitude to compliments is recognised by both women and men in these speech communities. Perhaps people pay more compliments to women because they know women value them.

Alternatively, one might focus on why people do not compliment men as often as they do women. It appears to be much more acceptable and socially appropriate to compliment a woman than a man. One possible explanation based on an analysis of the power relations in society points to women's subordinate social position. Because compliments express social approval one might expect more of them to be addressed 'downwards' as socialising devices, or directed to the socially insecure to build their confidence. Nessa Wolfson (1984: 243) takes this view:

> women because of their role in the social order, are seen as appropriate recipients of all manner of social judgements in the form of compliments . . . the way a woman is spoken to is, no matter what her status, a subtle and powerful way of perpetuating her subordinate role in society.

In other words, she suggests, compliments addressed to women have the same function as praise given to children, that is they serve as encouragement to continue with the approved behaviour. They could be regarded as patronising socialisation devices. Interestingly, even in classrooms it seems that females receive more praise or positive evaluations than males (e.g. de Bie 1987). It is possible that one of the reasons people do not compliment males so often as females is an awareness of men's ambivalence about compliments and of the possibility that men may regard some compliments as face-threatening acts, as embarrassing and discomfiting, or experience them as patronising strategies which put the speaker 'one-up'. If this is the case, then it is not surprising that the fewest compliments occur between men.

The way compliments are distributed suggests, then, that women and men may use and interpret them differently. While women appear to use them as positive politeness devices, and generally perceive them as ways of establishing and maintaining relationships, men may view them much more ambiguously as potentially face-threatening acts, or as having a more referential evaluative message which can serve a socialising function. In the next section an examination of the syntactic patterns of compliments will throw a little further light on these speculations.

3   How Do Women and Men Pay Compliments?

Examples 11–15
(11)   You're looking nice today.
(12)   What great kids!
(13)   That's a beautiful skirt.
(14)   I really love those curtains.
(15)   Good goal.

Compliments are remarkably formulaic speech acts. Most draw on a very small number of lexical items and a very narrow range of syntactic patterns. Five or six adjectives, such as *good*, *nice*, *great*, *beautiful*, and *pretty* occurred in about two-thirds of the New Zealand compliments analysed. Wolfson noted the same pattern in her American corpus of nearly 700 compliments (1984: 236). And syntactic patterns prove similarly unoriginal. One of just four different syntactic patterns occurred in 78 per cent of all the compliments in the New Zealand corpus (Holmes 1986). Similarly, three alternative syntactic patterns accounted for 85 per cent of the compliments in the American

Table 1 Syntactic patterns of compliments and speaker gender

Syntactic formula*	Female %	Male %
1 NP BE (LOOKING) (INT) ADJ e.g. *That coat is really great*	42.1	40.0
2 I (INT) LIKE NP e.g. I *simply love that skirt*	17.8	13.1
3 PRO BE (a) (INT) ADJ NP e.g. *That's a very nice coat*	11.4	15.6
4 What (a) (ADJ) NP! e.g. *What lovely children!*	7.8	1.3
5 (INT) ADJ NP e.g. *Really cool ear-rings*	5.1	11.8
6 Isn't NP ADJ! e.g. *Isn't this food wonderful!*	1.5	0.6
Subtotals	85.7	82.4
7 All other syntactic formulae	14.3	17.6
Totals	100.0	100.0

Note: *Following Manes and Wolfson (1981) copula BE represents any copula verb; LIKE represents any verb of liking: e.g. *love, enjoy, admire*; ADJ represents any semantically positive adjective; and INT represents any boosting intensifier: e.g. *really, very*.

corpus (Manes and Wolfson 1981). Compliments may be polite but they are rarely creative speech acts.

Nor are there many gender differences in this aspect of politeness behaviour. Most of the syntactic patterns and lexical items occurring in compliments seem to be fairly equally used by women and men, as table 1 demonstrates.

There are, however, two patterns which differ between women and men in an interesting way in the New Zealand corpus. Women used the rhetorical pattern *What (a) (ADJ) NP!* (e.g. *What lovely children!*) significantly more often than men. Men, by contrast, used the minimal pattern *(INT) ADJ (NP)* (e.g. *Great shoes*) significantly more often than women. The former is a syntactically marked formula, involving exclamatory word order and intonation; the latter, by contrast, reduces the syntactic pattern to its minimum elements. In other words, a rhetorical pattern such as *What a splendid hat!* can be regarded as emphatic and as increasing the force of the speech act. (D'Amico-Reisner (1983: 111–12) makes the same point about rhetorical questions as expressions of disapproval.) Using a rhetorical pattern for a compliment stresses its addressee- or interaction-orientated characteristics.

But the minimal pattern represented by *nice bike*, which was used more by men, tends to reduce the force of the compliment; it could be regarded as attenuating or hedging the compliment's impact. Interestingly, too, there were no examples of the more rhetorical pattern (*what lovely children!*) in the male–male interactions observed.

So there seems good reason to associate this pattern with female complimenting behaviour.

Examples 16–18

(16)   I love those socks. Where did you get them?

(17)   I like those glasses.

(18)   *Referring to a paper written by the addressee.*
       I really liked the ending. It was very convincing.

Studies of compliments by other researchers provide support for this suggestion that women's compliments tend to be expressed with linguistically stronger forms than men's. Having analysed over one thousand American compliments, Herbert (1990: 206) reported that only women used the stronger form *I love X* (compared to *I like X*), and they used it most often to other women. In written peer reviews, Johnson and Roen (1992) noted that women used significantly more intensifiers (such as *really, very, particularly*) than men did, and, as in Herbert's data, they intensified their compliments most when writing to other women.

These observations provide further support for the point that it is important in analysing hedging and boosting behaviour to examine the particular types of speech acts which are being boosted, and, in particular, to note whether the speech act is intended and perceived as affectively positive or negative. It is possible to strengthen or alternatively to reduce the force of a positively affective speech act such as a compliment in a variety of ways. By their selections among a narrow range of syntactic formulae and lexical items, men more often choose to attenuate the force of their compliments, while women tend to increase their compliments' force. This supports the suggestion that women expect addressees to interpret compliments as expressions of solidarity rather than as face-threatening speech acts. By contrast, men's tendency to attenuate compliments supports the proposal that men perhaps perceive compliments as less unambiguously positive in effect. In other words, the differences which have been noted in the distribution of syntactic and lexical patterns between women and men is consistent with the view that women tend to regard compliments as primarily positively affective acts while men may feel more ambivalent about using them.

Examples 19 and 20

(19)   You're looking stunning.

(20)   I especially liked the way you used lots of examples.

In general, it is also true that women use more personalised compliment forms than men, while men prefer impersonal forms. There is some evidence for this in the New Zealand data, as table 1 illustrates, but it is even more apparent in Herbert's (1990) American corpus, and Johnson and Roen's (1992) written peer reviews. Well over half (60 per cent) of the compliments offered by men in Herbert's corpus were impersonal forms, for example, compared to only a fifth of those used by women. By contrast women used many more forms with a personal focus (Herbert includes both *you* and *I* as personalised forms). Almost 83 per cent of female–female interactions used personalised forms compared to only 32 per cent of male–male compliments (Herbert 1990:

205). The peer reviews analysed by Johnson and Roen revealed a similar pattern. The women used more personal involvement strategies, especially to other women (1992: 44).

This evidence echoes the patterns noted in research on verbal interaction, which suggested that women tend to prefer personalised and expressive forms as opposed to impersonalised forms (see Kalcik 1975; Swacker 1979; Aries 1982), and supports a view of women's style as more interpersonal, affective and interaction-orientated compared to the impersonal, instrumental and content-orientated style more typical of male inter-action (e.g. Piliavin and Martin 1978; Baird and Bradley 1979; Preisler 1986; Aries 1976, 1987; Schick Case 1988; Tannen 1990). So, where the linguistic features of women's compliments differ from men's, the differences tend to support the proposition that women regard compliments as other-orientated positive politeness strategies which they assume will be welcome to addressees, whereas for men, and especially between men, their function may not be so clear-cut.

4   What Do Women and Men Compliment Each Other About?

Examples 21–24
(21)   *Appearance compliment.*
         I like your outfit Beth. I think I could wear that.
(22)   *Ability/performance compliment.*
         Wow you played well today Davy.
(23)   *Possessions compliment.*
         Is that your flash red sports car?
(24)   *Personality/friendliness.*
         I'm very lucky to have such a good friend.

Women and men tend to give compliments about different things. To be heard as a compliment an utterance must refer to something which is positively valued by the participants and attributed to the addressee. This would seem to permit an infinite range of possible topics for compliments, but in fact the vast majority of compliments refer to just a few broad topics: appearance, ability or performance, possessions, and some aspect of personality or friendliness (Manes 1983; Holmes 1986). In fact, compliments on some aspect of the addressee's appearance or ability accounted for 81 per cent of the New Zealand data.

Within these general patterns, there is a clearly observable tendency for women to be complimented on their appearance more often than men. Over half (57 per cent) of all the compliments women received in the New Zealand data related to aspects of their appearance. And women give compliments on appearance more than men do, so that 61 per cent of all the compliments between women related to appearance compared to only 36 per cent of the compliments between males, as figure 2 demonstrates. Men, by contrast, appear to prefer to compliment other men, but not women, on possessions.

Provided it is not sarcastic, a compliment on someone's appearance such as *you're looking wonderful* is difficult to interpret as anything other than a positively polite utterance. An appearance compliment is clearly an expression of solidarity, a positively

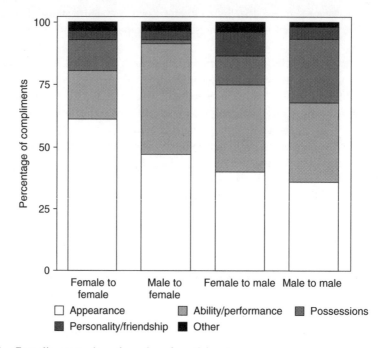

Figure 2   Compliment topic and gender of participants

affective speech act. The predominance of this type of compliment in women's inter-actions is consistent with the view that women use compliments primarily for their pos-itively polite function. Compliments on possessions, on the other hand, are much more vulnerable to interpretation as face-threatening acts since, as illustrated in example 6 above, there is the possibility that the complimenter will be heard as expressing desire for or envy of the object referred to. To this extent, men's greater use of these com-pliments reinforces the suggestion that they are more likely to perceive and experience compliments as potential face-threatening acts. In other words, if possession-orientated compliments are experienced as more face-threatening than others – which seems fea-sible since they focus on things which are in theory transferable from complimenter to recipient – then men certainly use more potentially face-threatening compliments than women.

Compliments on appearance seem to cause some men embarrassment.

Example 25
Middle-aged male to elderly male at a concert.

> MALE 1:   I haven't seen you since the Festival.
> MALE 2:   We haven't been here much since the Festival.
> MALE 1:   You've got a new tie in the meantime.
> MALE 2:   It's a very old one actually.
> MALE 1:   It's quite splendid anyway.
> MALE 2:   (*Looks extremely embarrassed.*) No no. What have you been up to anyway?

The recipient's response to the first somewhat indirect compliment is a disclaimer, while his response to the second overt compliment is acute embarrassment followed by a rejection. Wolfson comments (1983: 93) that appearance compliments are remarkably rare between American males. It seems that in America compliments on appearance may be experienced by males as very big face-threatening acts. And while New Zealand men do give and receive compliments on their appearance, there are a number of examples where compliments on their appearance clearly caused surprise.

Example 26
Two colleagues meet at coffee machine at work.

> BILL: You're looking very smart today.
> TOM: (*Looking very embarrassed.*) I'm meeting Mary and her mother for lunch.

Appearance compliments are clearly not the common currency of politeness between men that they are between women.

A number of men have commented that at least one of the reasons for the scarcity of appearance compliments between men is fear of the possible imputation of homosexuality.

> To compliment another man on his hair, his clothes, or his body is an *extremely* face threatening thing to do, both for speaker and hearer. It has to be very carefully done in order not to send the wrong signals. (Britain, personal communication)

In support of this David Britain provided the following example.

Example 27
Male flatmate, Alex, to Dave, referring to the latter's new haircut.
Jesus Christ tell me who did that and I'll go and beat him up for you!
Laughter. Then
No it's OK.
Finally, a week later.
That's a good haircut.

In this case, it took a week for Alex to get round to saying he liked Dave's haircut, that is to pay a clearly identifiable compliment on his appearance to another male.

Figure 2 also shows that nearly half (44 per cent of all) the compliments given by males to females were compliments on abilities, skills or performance. Women do not compliment men or other women so often on this topic. This raises the question of whether a compliment can act as a power play. As mentioned above, praise is often directed downwards. A compliment could be experienced as patronising if the recipient felt it was given as encouragement rather than as a token of solidarity. Compliments on skills and abilities are particularly vulnerable to being interpreted in this way.

Example 28
Husband to wife about her painting of a wall.
You've made a pretty good job of that.

One has the feeling that the husband is a little surprised his wife has done so well and is patting her on the head approvingly. The tendency for men to compliment women on their skills and abilities may reflect women's subordinate social status in the society as a whole, as well as, perhaps, a male tendency to perceive compliments as means of conveying referential or evaluative, as well as affective, messages. The next section will illustrate that the way compliments are used to those of different status provides further support for such an interpretation.

5   Can a Compliment Be a Power Play?

People pay most compliments to their equals. As Wolfson puts it, 'the overwhelming majority of all compliments are given to people of the same age and status as the speaker' (1983: 91). New Zealanders' compliments followed this pattern (see also Knapp et al. 1984; Herbert 1990). Almost 80 per cent of the corpus consisted of compliments between status equals. Compliments typically occur in informal interactions between friends.

The distribution of the small proportion of compliments that occurred between people of different status is interesting, however, because it throws further light on the question of the functions of compliments for women and men.

If it is true, as Wolfson suggests, that the fact that women receive more compliments than men reflects their subordinate status in the society as a whole, then one would also expect more compliments to subordinates than to superiors, regardless of gender. Wolfson's American data evidently confirmed this expectation. She comments that 'the great majority of compliments which occur in interaction between status unequals are given by the person in the higher position' (1983: 91).

Example 29
Manager to her secretary.
You are such a treasure Carol. What would I do without you!

Another American study, which was based on self-report data rather than observation, reports the same pattern (Knapp et al. 1984). Most compliments occurred between status equals, but when there was a status imbalance, higher status participants complimented more often than lower status ones. In other words, people seem generally less willing to compliment someone of higher rather than lower status. Neither of these studies examined the interaction of gender and status, however.

In the New Zealand data, as mentioned, the great majority of compliments occurred between status equals. There were no significant differences in the numbers addressed to those of higher rather than lower status. But, interestingly, it was found that higher status females were twice as likely to receive compliments as higher status men.

Example 30
Secretary to boss.
That's a lovely dress.

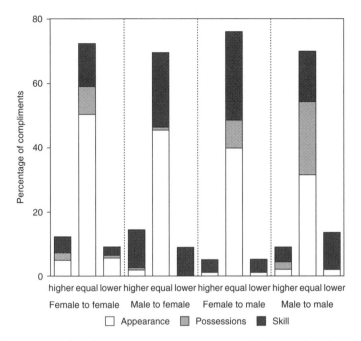

Figure 3   Compliments by relative status and gender of participants and topic

If high status generally reduces the likelihood that one will receive compliments, then this data indicates it reduces it less with women than with men. This is true whether the complimenter is male or female, as can be seen in figure 3. In fact, despite the general pattern that women pay more compliments than men, males are even more likely to compliment women of higher status than women are.

Example 31

Male caretaker to woman executive as she leaves work.
You're a hard working woman Mrs Thomas. I hope they pay you well.

This is further support for the view that it is more acceptable to compliment high status women than high status men.

Perhaps higher status women are perceived as more receptive to compliments (especially from men) than their male counterparts, because in the society as a whole women are generally regarded as socially subordinate, and less powerful and influential than men. This may legitimate behaviour that might otherwise be considered presumptuous. Tannen's (1990: 69) suggestion that giving praise 'frames the speaker as one-up' is again relevant here. Higher status males may be perceived as high risk addressees by both genders. But female gender apparently overrides high status in determining how risky a compliment is perceived as being. Alternatively, perhaps women are seen as more approachable because they value solidarity more highly than status, and tend to reduce rather than emphasise status differences (Troemel–Ploetz 1992).

This interpretation of the patterns is consistent with the suggestion that men are more likely to experience a compliment as a face-threatening act whereas women are more likely to perceive compliments as positively affective speech acts, regardless of relative status. If true, this would be likely to encourage complimenters to address compliments upwards to women, and discourage compliments to higher status men where the risk of offence would be too great. Note the male's discouraging reaction in the following example.

Example 32
Young woman to Minister's personal secretary at a reception.

WOMAN: What an interesting job you have. You must be very bright.
MAN: I just do my job.

The young woman was lively and friendly. The tone of the man's reply made it clear he thought her presumptuous. Complimenting a higher status male is obviously a risky business. There is further support for this interpretation when we look at differences in the way women and men use compliments on appearance, in particular. As figures 2 and 3 illustrate, appearance was the most common topic of compliments in this corpus, as in others. Figure 3 shows that appearance was also by far the most frequent topic of compliments between equals (30–50 per cent of all compliments). But status differences reduced the likelihood of appearance compliments quite dramatically, especially in cross-sex relationships. Fewer than 2 per cent of the compliments analysed were appearance compliments between cross-sex pairs of different status – a clear indication of the link between appearance compliments and solidarity-based relationships.

On the other hand, appearance compliments are the most obvious examples of compliments which are likely to be interpreted or experienced differently by women and men, as discussed above, and illustrated in the following example.

Example 33
Office receptionist to high status male whom she knew only slightly.

RECEPTIONIST: That's a nice suit.
MALE: Mr Avery's expecting me I think.

The man ignores the compliment completely. The receptionist was almost certainly being positively polite and intended her compliment as a solidarity signal. But an appearance compliment is vulnerable to being interpreted as presumptuous when addressed by a subordinate to a superior of either gender. If men also tend to regard compliments as potential face-threatening acts and find compliments on their appearance particularly discomfiting, the negative effect will be even greater.

The patterns revealed by the distribution of compliments in this corpus suggest, then, that women and men may use and interpret compliments differently. While women seem to use compliments to establish, maintain and strengthen relationships, they are much less clearly positive politeness devices for men, where they need to be used with care – especially to other men – since they can be face-threatening. The fact that men pay more compliments to women than they do to men may indicate that men are aware of the value of compliments in women's eyes – a solidarity-based explanation. Alternatively, this pattern may reflect the fact that men perceive compliments as appropriate encouragement or evaluative feedback to subordinates. In other words, male compliments to women may reflect the different social power positions of women and men.

[. . .]

6   Conclusion

In concluding this paper it is worth emphasising the range of functions any utterance may perform. The detailed analysis of compliments illustrated well that the 'same' utterance may simultaneously convey a range of meanings. The 'same' utterance may also be used and interpreted differently by different social groups, including women and men. Just as a gift expresses solidarity and appreciation in some cultures, but is a form of one-upping a rival in others (Tannen 1990: 295–6), so at least some compliments may be accepted as tokens of solidarity by women but experienced as an embarrassment by men. The same is likely to be true of other potential positive politeness devices. They are likely to be used and interpreted very differently in different contexts and cultures.

On the basis of a number of different aspects of the distribution of compliments in the New Zealand corpus, I have suggested that women tend to perceive and use compliments as positively affective speech acts and expressions of solidarity, whereas the responses of men may be more ambivalent. It seems possible that in some situations, at least, and with some types of compliment in particular, men may be more likely to interpret compliments as face-threatening acts. The pattern I have suggested provides an intriguing mirror-image of Kuiper's (1991) analysis of the way insults which would certainly be experienced as face-threatening acts by women, appear to perform a solidarity-maintaining function for at least some men. Kuiper describes the verbal interaction of members of a rugby team in the locker room before a match. The team members insult and abuse each other, using terms of address such as 'wanker', 'fuck-face' and the more overtly sexist 'fucking old woman', and 'girl's blouse'. For this group 'sexual humiliation is used as a means of creating group solidarity through the loss of face the individuals who belong to the group suffer' (1991: 200). (See also Labov 1972 on ritual insults among Black gang members and Dundes et al. 1972 on Turkish boys' verbal duelling.) Insults function for these men as expressions of solidarity, whereas the data in this chapter has suggested women prefer compliments for this function.

It also seems possible that the way men use compliments to women, in particular, may reflect the subordinate status of women in the society generally. Like endearments, compliments gain their force from the context of the relationship in which they are used. When used non-reciprocally by superiors to subordinates, these may underline patterns of societal power which place women in a clearly subordinate position to men. When used between equals and friends, on the other hand, and especially female equals and friends, a compliment could be considered a quintessential example of a positive politeness strategy.

Note

1   As noted in Holmes (1988), the predominance of females among the data collectors was a potential source of bias. The figures nevertheless suggest that even with equal numbers of female and
male data collectors, compliments between females will be more frequent than compliments
between males, though the imbalance would not be so dramatic.

References

Aries, E. J. (1976) 'Interaction patterns and themes of male, female and mixed groups'. *Small Group
Behaviour*, 7, 1, 7–18.
Aries, E. J. (1982) 'Verbal and non-verbal behaviour in single-sex and mixed-sex groups: are tradi-
tional sex roles changing?' *Psychological Reports*, 51, 127–34.
Aries, E. J. (1987) 'Gender and communication', pp. 149–76 in P. Shaver and C. Hendrick (eds) *Sex
and Gender*. Newbury Park, CA: Sage.
Baird, J. E. and Bradley, P. H. (1979) 'Styles of management and communication: a comparative study
of men and women'. *Communication Monographs*, 46, 101–11.
Brown, P. and Levinson, S. (1987) *Politeness: Some Universals in Language Use*. Cambridge:
Cambridge University Press.
D'Amico-Reisner, L. (1983) 'An analysis of the surface structure of disapproval exchanges', pp.
103–15 in N. Wolfson and E. Judd (cds) *Sociolinguistics and Language Acquisition*. Rowley, MA:
Newbury House.
De Bie, M. L. W. (1987) 'Classroom interaction: survival of the fittest', pp. 76–88 in D. Brouwer and
D. de Haan (eds) *Women's Language, Socialisation and Self-Image*. Dordrecht: Foris.
Dundes, A., Leach, J. W. and Özkök, B. (1972) 'The strategy of Turkish boys' verbal dueling rhymes',
pp. 130–60 in J. J. Gumperz and D. Hymes (eds) *Directions in Sociolinguistics*. New York: Holt,
Rinehart & Winston.
Herbert, R. K. (1989) 'The ethnography of English compliments and compliment responses: a con-
trastive sketch', pp. 3–35 in W. Olesky (ed.) *Contrastive Pragmatics*. Amsterdam: John Benjamins.
Herbert, R. K. (1990) 'Sex-based differences in compliment behaviour'. *Language in Society*. 19,
201–24.
Holmes, J. (1986) 'Compliments and compliment responses in New Zealand English'. *Anthropologi-
cal Linguistics*, 28, 4, 485–508.
Holmes, J. (1988) 'Paying compliments: a sex-preferred positive politeness strategy'. *Journal of
Pragmatics*, 12, 3, 445–65.
Hymes, D. (1962) 'The ethnography of speaking', pp. 15–53 in T. Gladwin and W. Sturtevant (eds)
Anthropology and Human Behaviour. Washington, DC: Anthropological Society of Washington.
Hymes, D. (1972) 'On communicative competence', pp. 269–93 in J. B. Pride and J. Holmes (eds)
Sociolinguistics. Harmondsworth: Penguin.
Hymes, D. (1974) 'Ways of speaking', pp. 433–51 in R. Bauman and J. Sherzer (eds) *Explorations in
the Ethnography of Speaking*. Cambridge: Cambridge University Press.
Johnson, D. M. and Roen, D. H. (1992) 'Complimenting and involvement in peer reviews: gender
variation'. *Language in Society*, 21, 1, 27–57.
Kalcik, S. (1975) '". . . like Ann's gynaecologist or the time I was almost raped" – personal narratives
in women's rap groups'. *Journal of American Folklore*, 88, 3–11.
Kissling, E. A. (1991) 'Street harassment: the language of sexual terrorism'. *Discourse and Society*, 2,
4, 451–60.
Kissling, E. A. and Kramarae, C. (1991) '"Stranger compliments": the interpretation of street
remarks'. *Women's Studies in Communication*, Spring, 77–95.

Knapp, M. L., Hopper, R. and Bell, R. (1984) 'Compliments: a descriptive taxonomy'. *Journal of Communications*, 34, 4 12–31.

Kuiper, K. (1991) 'Sporting formulae in New Zealand English: two models of male solidarity', pp. 200–9 in J. Cheshire (ed.) *English Around the World: Sociolinguistic Perspectives*. Cambridge: Cambridge University Press.

Labov, W. (1972) 'Rules for ritual insults', pp. 265–314 in T. Kochman (ed.) *Rappin' and Stylin' Out*. Chicago: University of Illinois Press.

Leech, G. N. (1983) *Principles of Pragmatics*. London: Longman.

Lewandowska-Tomaszczyk, B. (1989) 'Praising and complimenting', pp. 73–100 in W. Olesky (ed.) *Contrastive Pragmatics*. Amsterdam: John Benjamins.

Manes, J. (1983) 'Compliments: a mirror of cultural values', pp. 96–102 in N. Wolfson and E. Judd (eds) *Sociolinguistics and Language Acquisition*. Rowley, MA: Newbury House.

Manes, J. and Wolfson, N. (1981) 'The compliment formula', pp. 115–32 in F. Coulmas (ed.) *Conversational Routine*. The Hague: Mouton.

Piliavin, J. A. and Martin, R. R. (1978) 'The effects of the sex composition of groups on style of social interaction'. *Sex Roles*, 4, 281–96.

Preisler, B. (1986) *Linguistic Sex Roles in Conversation*. Berlin: Mouton de Gruyter.

Schick Case, S. (1988) 'Cultural differences, not deficiencies: an analysis of managerial women's language', pp. 41–63 in S. Rose and L. Larwood (eds) *Women's Careers: Pathways and Pitfalls*. New York: Praeger.

Swacker, M. (1979) 'Women's verbal behaviour at learned and professional conferences', pp. 155–60 in B. Dubois and I. Crouch (eds) *The Sociology of the Languages of American Women*. San Antonio, TX: Trinity University.

Tannen, D. (1990) *You Just Don't Understand: Women and Men in Conversation*. New York: William Morrow.

Troemel-Ploetz, S. (1992) 'The construction of conversational equality by women', pp. 581–9 in K. Hall, M. Bucholtz and B. Moonwomon (eds) *Locating Power. Proceedings of the Second Berkeley Women and Language Conference* (4 and 5 April 1992), vol 2. Berkeley, CA: Berkeley Women and Language Group, University of California.

Wierzbicka, A. (1987) *English Speech Acts Verbs: A Semantic Dictionary*. New York: Academic Press.

Wolfson, N. (1981) 'Compliments in cross-cultural perspective'. *TESOL Quarterly*, 15, 2, 117–24.

Wolfson, N. (1983) 'An empirically based analysis of complimenting in American English', pp. 82–95 in N. Wolfson and E. Judd (eds) *Sociolinguistics and Language Acquisition*. Rowley, MA: Newbury House.

Wolfson, N. (1984) '"Pretty is as pretty does": a speech act view of sex roles'. *Applied Linguistics*, 5, 3, 236–44.

Wolfson, N. (1988) 'The bulge: a theory of speech behaviour and social distance', pp. 21–38 in J. Fine (ed.) *Second Language Discourse: A Textbook of Current Research*. Norwood, NJ: Ablex.

Discussion Questions

1. Tape-record a personal narrative told by someone you know. Discuss the follow-ing elements of the narrative (as defined by Labov and Waletzky):
   a) What prompt or stimulus did you use to elicit the narrative?
   b) Describe the function(s) of the narrative.
   c) Make a transcript of the text comprising at least two temporal sequences in the narrative. Describe whether the speaker's clauses follow the temporal sequence of events.
   d) Is there an evaluation of the narrative by the speaker? Does the speaker express an attitude toward the narrative in any way?
   e) Describe the coda of the narrative.

2. Listen again to the recording you made for question 1 and discuss the following. Use examples to illustrate your points.
   a) What interactions did you have with the speaker during the narrative? Did you interrupt? . . . ask for clarification? . . . give encouragement? . . . other?
   b) How did your interactions with the speaker affect the telling of the story? For example, did they seem to encourage or discourage a particular topic or focus?
   c) Describe your relationship to the speaker. Do you believe that your relation-ship somehow influenced the narrative?
   d) If the speaker paused or in some way used silence, describe how that affected the narrative.

3. Compare your analyses in questions 1 and 2.
   a) Is the analysis in question 1 incomplete without the information in question 2?
   b) Consider Schegloff's criticisms of Labov and Waletzky. What is the effect of not including information about the social interaction in the data?

4. Gumperz discusses the use of directness/indirectness and how it might be mis-interpreted. Try to make three different requests of a colleague or friend in which you vary your level of directness. Report back on how your interlocutor responds. Was there any miscommunication? When you were most direct, was the request considered rude? Does the cultural or social background of the other parties influ-ence their reactions?

5. Gumperz discusses the expectation that people will understand and react appro-priately to various contextualization conventions.
   a) Observe conversations or classroom interactions in your daily life. List at least four contextualization conventions you notice and the response that they (are likely to) elicit.
   b) Interview a speaker of another language. Does that language use the same conventions?
   Compare your findings with those of your classmates. Do you notice any differ-ences that may be attributable to social or cultural backgrounds?

6. In some of your daily interactions with friends or family, ignore or misinterpret two or three contextualization conventions. Describe the situation, the convention, how you broke the convention and the reactions, if any, of your interlocutors.

7. (a)   Modern English does not have a T/V distinction, but we still have ways to demonstrate respect (or, in Brown and Gilman's words, we have "the power semantic") in conversations. Discuss examples of how English speakers show respect in their speech to, for example, an older stranger, a boss, a professor, their boyfriend or girlfriend's parents, or other person of higher status.

    (b)   Along the same lines, in English, we do not have a grammatical structure to show solidarity, but we can. Observe ways in which you show (or don't show) solidarity by how you typically address the following people:

    your mother or father
    your siblings
    co-workers or classmates
    good friends
    your doctor.

8. Consider the "social dyads involving semantic conflict and their resolution" in chapter 9, p. 162, figure 2. What might happen if the person in the subordinate position initiated the use of the T form? Consider the use of first names with English speakers. Who decides when and with whom it is appropriate to use first names?

9. Give a compliment to:

    a close friend or family member
    a stranger
    a co-worker or classmate
    a complete stranger.

    Make note of what the compliments were and whether the person you gave it to was male or female. Then answer the following questions based on the information in chapter 10:

    How did the recipient react?
    Which syntactic formula did your compliments use?
    What topic did you compliment them about (e.g. appearance, possessions)?
    Was the person of higher, equal or lower status than you?

10. As a class, calculate the gender patterns of the compliments you gave in exercise 9: Who gave compliments to whom (male to male, female to male, etc.)? What syntactic structures were used by whom? What topics were complimented on by whom and to whom?

11. In chapter 10, the dark side of compliments is discussed. Have you ever observed a compliment that is being used in a negative way or to gain power? Give some examples for discussion with the class.

12. Another speech act which can be used to gain solidarity or to show concern is the apology. Discuss the various types and uses of apologies that you observe. Do gender, status or age differences change the type or syntax of apologies?

Part IV

Language and Gender

Introduction

The subfield of sociolinguistics known as Language and Gender (L&G) Studies is best thought of as having begun as part of the much larger Women's movement, a social movement fought against the ever present inequality between the sexes. As Ruth Bleier wrote: "Not the least important aim, as in the rest of feminist scholarship and practices, is to win the struggle for the minds of those women, perhaps the majority, who are constrained or oppressed by internalized scientific judgments about our presumed biological limitations. For then, together we can change science and society" (1991: 1).

As early as 1949, Simone de Beauvoir wrote in *The Second Sex* "one is not born but rather becomes a woman," a foreshadowing of the role of culture in the very conceptualization of sex. Today feminists, male and female, make a distinction between sex and gender; sex is based on biology with criteria of genitalia and reproductive organs while gender is a social construct(ion), influenced by sociohistorical criteria and cultural conditioning. It is easily seen then that gender will vary from culture to culture, from community to community, and that universal statements and generalizations become useless and easily misleading. There is probably no area within sociolinguistics where postmodern ideas have had more influence. Here is a fairly typical postmodern statement on gender by historian Gail Bederman: "gender . . . is a historical, ideological process. Through that process, individuals are positioned and position themselves as men or women. Thus I don't see manhood as either an intrinsic essence or a collection of traits, attributes, or sex roles. Manhood . . . is a continual, dynamic process" (1995: 7); a definition quite similar to sociolinguists Freeman and McElhinney's "concept of gender as a cultural construct, a structure of relationships that is often reproduced, sometimes challenged, and potentially transformed in everyday linguistic practices" (1996: 221).

"The year 1973 was historic for language and gender research," writes Alice Freed (1995: 4); Robin Lakoff, a feminist who happened to be a linguist, published "Language and woman's place," the first article in a major journal devoted entirely to a discussion of women and language. Lakoff's claims, an articulation of what has been called the deficit theory, pointed out weaknesses in women's language like the use of rising question intonation in statements to express uncertainty, use of more tag questions, trivial topics, empty adjectives, etc. (Freeman and McElhinney (1996: 232) have a complete list of Lakoff's claims with a listing of later empirical research testing these claims.)

Lakoff was trained in formal linguistics (early transformational–generative grammar) and she used the tools of her trade for research, introspection and native speaker intuition. The amazing thing is that although most of her claims were later found not to be valid empirically, she still inspired decades of research on the interaction of language and gender. Clearly she had struck a nerve, and that nerve still reverberates in L&G studies.

The rest of the twentieth century saw the development of two "competing" perspectives, the so-called "dominance" framework and the "difference" framework. Many of the early L&G studies followed Labov and Trudgill in a variationist, quantitative approach to empirical research. (For a critique of this research, see Cameron 1992.) Their finding, replicated in other studies, that women, especially lower-middle-class women, tended to use more prestige forms or high-status forms was explained by women being more socially insecure and more status-conscious. But, as Joan Swann and many others have pointed out, such studies only represent statistical tendencies; correlational data do not imply causality, and "social class" as a variable was poorly conceptualized and operationalized. "Trudgill's claim about women's 'status-consciousness' has been the subject of some criticism and would not now be generally accepted, mainly because of the absence of convincing independent evidence that women actually are more status-conscious than men" (Swann 2000: 223). In other words, the L&G studies had proliferated with many and at times conflicting findings, and this situation led to a search for a theoretical framework that could be used to interpret the data (Freed 1995: 3).

The dominance perspective held that institutionalized male dominance was an important factor underlying male/female differences and language feature variation needed to be understood in such a larger sociopolitical context (Thorne and Henley 1975; Uchida 1992). The difference perspective borrowed from John Gumperz's work (1982) on intercultural comparisons and from the ethnography of speaking models and held that boys and girls were socialized into different subcultures and exhibited different communicative styles which frequently led to miscommunication. *You Just Don't Understand: Women and Men in Conversation* (1990), Deborah Tannen's controversial popularization of this approach, led to international recognition and discussion of this topic. Her scholarly work exemplifies an academic approach to a difference perspective. Uchida, in the widely cited "When 'difference' is 'dominance': a critique of the 'anti-power based' cultural approach to sex differences," writes "the dichotomization of 'power' and 'culture' as two separate, independent concepts is inappropriate, because social interaction always occurs in the context of a patriarchal society. As a direction for future research, I propose that the relationship between gender and language should be approached from the viewpoint that we are doing gender in interaction" (1992: 547). Tannen, in "The relativity of linguistic strategies: rethinking power and solidarity in gender dominance," continues this discussion.

Scholars writing in the 1990s did increasingly become dissatisfied with the conceptualization of gender, and one might in passing point out that for all the discussion of the distinction between sex and gender, in all the quantitative research studies gender had still been operationalized in terms of dichotomous sex. Gender now was taken to include, besides masculine and feminine, gay, lesbian, transsexual, eunuch, that is, whatever variation of gender an interactive and ethnographic approach to research turned up (Greenman 2001; Leap 1996; Livia and Hall 1997).

The work of the linguistic anthropologists especially has emphasized women's and men's lifestyles and interaction patterns (Burton, Dyson and Ardener 1994). Both Susan Gal's and Penelope Eckert's dissertations document and explain women's lifestyle choices as a powerful force in situations of language shift, deliberate and purposeful choices which make women look very different from the twits of much variationist research. Anthropological linguists also helped clarify the need to focus on language use and function rather than on form; there is not a one-to-one relationship between form and function, and a tag question can express several functions (Holmes 1995); or indeed, as Cameron et al. (1988) point out, utterances are often multifunctional: they carry out more than one function simultaneously. Swann comments that their "argument is in line with recent 'postmodernist' models of language, which tend to see the functions or meanings of any utterance as highly fluid and context-dependent. Meanings are not simply 'in the language', but are negotiated between speakers. . . . If the meanings of tag questions and overlapping speech are inherently uncertain and context-dependent, so too are the meanings of particular accent or dialect features. Charting the distribution of linguistic features . . . may conceal . . . what they mean in specific contexts." (2000: 239).

With the recent concern for the fluidity of gender and doing gender, and of language, there is also a realization that there is considerable group fluidity within the groups of men and women; that there is considerable variation between men and variation between women, which condition remains unexplored. As Wallace Lambert once said, there is always more intragroup variation than intergroup variation, and until now this has not been emphasized in the L&G studies. The next decade promises to be very exciting in this line of research with new conceptualizations and new questions.

References

Beauvoir, Simone de. 1949. *Le Deuxième Sexe.* Paris: Gallimard. Translated as *The Second Sex.* 1961. New York: Bantam Books.

Bederman, Gail. 1995. *Manliness and Civilization.* Chicago: University of Chicago Press.

Bleier, Ruth (ed.). 1991. *Feminist Approaches to Science.* Oxford: Pergamon Press.

Burton, Pauline, Ketaki Kushari Dyson, and Shirley Ardener. 1994. *Bilingual Women: Anthropological Approaches to Second-Language Use.* Oxford: Berg.

Cameron, Deborah. 1992. *Feminism and Linguistic Theory.* Basingstoke: Macmillan.

Cameron, Deborah, F. McAlinden and K. O'Leary. 1988. "Lakoff in context: the social and linguistic functions of tag questions," in Jennifer Coates and Deborah Cameron (eds.), *Women in Their Speech Communities*, pp. 74–93. London: Longman.

Eckert, Penelope. 1980. "Diglossia: separate and unequal," *Linguistics*, 18: 1053–64.

Freed, Alice F. 1995. "Language and Gender," *Annual Review of Applied Linguistics*, 15: 3–22.

Freeman, Rebecca and Bonnie McElhinny. 1996. "Language and Gender," in S. L. McKay and Nancy H. Hornberger (eds.), *Sociolinguistics and Language Teaching.* Cambridge: Cambridge University Press.

Gal, Susan. 1979. *Language Shift: Social Determinants of Linguistic Change in Bilingual Austria.* New York: Academic Press.

Gumperz, John J. (ed.). 1982. *Language and Social Identity.* Cambridge: Cambridge University Press.

Holmes, Janet. 1995. *Women, Men and Politeness.* Harlow, Essex: Longman.

Lakoff, Robin. 1973. "Language and woman's place," *Language in Society*, 2: 45–80. Reprinted and expanded, 1975. *Language and Woman's Place*. New York: Harper and Row.

Leap, William L. 1996. *Word's Out: Gay Men's English*. Minneapolis: University of Minnesota Press.

Livia, Anna and Kira Hall (eds.). 1997. *Queerly Phrased*. Oxford: Oxford University Press.

Swann, Joan. 2000. "Gender and language use," in Rajend Mesthrie, Joan Swann, Andrea Deumert and William Leap. *Introducing Sociolinguistics*. Amsterdam: Benjamins.

Tannen, Deborah. 1990. *You Just Don't Understand: Women and Men in Conversation*. New York: Morrow.

Thorne, Barrie and Nancy Henley (eds.). 1975. *Language and Sex: Difference and Dominance*. Rowley, MA: Newbury House.

Uchida, Aki. 1992. "When 'difference' is 'dominance': A critique of the 'anti-power based' cultural approach to sex difference," *Language in Society*, 21: 547–68.

Greenman, Gregory, II. 2001. *Studies on Gay and Lesbian Language: A Partial Bibliography*. www.msu.edu/~greenm14/outil/gaybib.html.

Further Reading

Coates, Jennifer (ed.). 1998. *Language and Gender: A Reader*. Oxford: Blackwell.

Johnson, Sally and Ulrike Hanna Meinhof (eds.). 1997. *Language and Masculinity*. Oxford: Blackwell.

Romaine, Suzanne. 1999. *Communicating Gender*. Mahwah, NJ: Erlbaum.

11

Selections from *Language and Woman's Place*

Robin Lakoff

[...]

This book (Lakoff 1975), then, is an attempt to provide diagnostic evidence from language use for one type of inequity that has been claimed to exist in our society: that between the roles of men and women. I will attempt to discover what language use can tell us about the nature and extent of any inequity; and finally to ask whether anything can be done, from the linguistic end of the problem: does one correct a social inequity by changing linguistic disparities? We will find, I think, that women experience linguistic discrimination in two ways: in the way they are taught to use language, and in the way general language use treats them. Both tend, as we shall see, to relegate women to certain subservient functions: that of sex object, or servant; and therefore certain lexical items mean one thing applied to men, another to women, a difference that cannot be predicted except with reference to the different roles the sexes play in society.

The data on which I am basing my claims have been gathered mainly by introspection: I have examined my own speech and that of my acquaintances, and have used my own intuitions in analyzing it. I have also made use of the media: in some ways, the speech heard, for example, in commercials or situation comedies on television mirrors the speech of the television-watching community: if it did not (not necessarily as an exact replica, but perhaps as a reflection of how the audience sees itself or wishes it were), it would not succeed. The sociologist, anthropologist or ethnomethodologist familiar with what seem to him more error-proof data-gathering techniques, such as the recording of random conversation, may object that these introspective methods may produce dubious results. But first, it should be noted that *any* procedure is at some point introspective: the gatherer must analyze his data, after all. Then, one necessarily selects a subgroup of the population to work with: is the educated, white, middle-class group that the writer of the book identifies with less worthy of study than any other? And finally, there is the purely pragmatic issue: random conversation must go on for quite some time, and the recorder must be exceedingly lucky anyway, in order to produce evidence of any particular hypothesis, for example, that there is sexism in language, that there is not sexism in language. If we are to have a good sample of data to analyze, this will have to be elicited artificially from someone; I submit I am as good an artificial source of data as anyone.

These defenses are not meant to suggest that either the methodology or the results are final, or perfect. I mean to suggest one possible approach to the problem, one set of facts. I do feel that the majority of the claims I make will hold for the majority of speakers of English; that, in fact, much may, *mutatis mutandis*, be universal. But grant-ing that this study does in itself represent the speech of only a small subpart of the community, it is still of use in indicating directions for further research in this area: in providing a basis for comparison, a taking-off point for further studies, a means of dis-covering what is universal in the data and what is not, and why. That is to say, I present what follows less as the final word on the subject of sexism in language – anything but that! – than as a goad to further research.

[. . .]

Sociologically it is probably fairly obvious that a woman in most subcultures in our society achieves status only through her father's, husband's, or lover's position. What is remarkable is that these facts show up linguistically in nonobvious ways.

Suppose we take a pair of words which, in terms of the possible relationships in an earlier society, were simple male–female equivalents, analogous to bull: cow. Suppose we find that, for independent reasons, society has changed in such a way that the primary meanings now are irrelevant. Yet the words have not been discarded, but have acquired new meanings, metaphorically related to their original senses. But suppose these new metaphorical uses are no longer parallel to each other. By seeing where the parallelism breaks down, we can intuit something about the different roles played by men and women in this culture. One good example of such a divergence through time is found in the pair *master* and *mistress*. Once used with reference to one person's power over another, these words became unusable in their original sense as the master–servant relationship became nonexistent. But the words are still common as used in sentences (18) and (19):

(18) (*a*) He is a master of the intricacies of academic politics.
      (*b*) *She is a mistress . . .

(19) (*a*) *Harry declined to be my master, and so returned to his wife.
      (*b*) Rhonda declined to be my mistress, and so returned to her husband.

Unless used with reference to animals or slaves, *master* now generally refers to a man who has acquired consummate ability in some field, normally nonsexual. But its femi-nine counterpart cannot be used in this way. It is practically restricted to its sexual sense of "paramour." We start out with two terms, both roughly paraphrasable as "one who has power over another." But the masculine form, once one person is no longer able to have absolute power over another, becomes usable metaphorically in the sense of "have power over *something*." The feminine counterpart also acquired a metaphorical inter-pretation, but the metaphor here is sexual: one's mistress "has power over" one in a sexual sense. And this expression is probably chivalrous, rather than descriptive of the real-world relationship between lovers. In terms of choice, of economic control, and so forth, it is generally the man who holds the power in such a relationship; to call a woman one's "mistress" is the equivalent of saying "please" in prefacing a request to a subor-dinate. Both are done for politeness and are done purely because both participants in the relationship, in both cases, know that the supposed inferiority of the mistress's lover and of the user of "please" is only a sham. Interesting too in this regard is the fact that "master" requires as its object only the name of some activity, something inanimate and abstract. But "mistress" requires a masculine noun in the possessive to precede it. One cannot say:

(20)   *Rhonda is a mistress.

One must be *someone's* mistress.

And obviously too, it is one thing to be an *old master*, like Hans Holbein, and another to be an *old mistress*: the latter, again, requires a masculine possessive form preceding it, indicating who has done the discarding. *Old* in the first instance refers to absolute age: the artist's lifetime versus the time of writing. But *old* in the second really means "discarded," "old" with respect to someone else.

[. . .]

So here we see several important points concerning the relationship between men and women illustrated: first, that men are defined in terms of what they do in the world, women in terms of the men with whom they are associated; and second, that the notion of "power" for a man is different from that of "power" for a woman: it is acquired and manifested in different ways. One might say then that these words have retained their principal meanings through time; what has changed is the kinds of interpersonal relationships to which they refer.

As a second example, the examples in (21) should be completely parallel semantically:

(21)   *(a)*   He's a professional.
         (b)   She's a professional.

Hearing and knowing no more about the subjects of the discourse than this, what would one assume about them in each case? Certainly in *(a)* the normal conclusion the casual eavesdropper would come to was that "he" was a doctor or a lawyer or a member of one of the other professions. But it is much less likely that one would draw a similar conclusion in *(b)*. Rather, the first assumption most speakers of English seem to make is that "she" is a prostitute, literally or figuratively speaking. Again, a man is defined in the serious world by what he does, a woman by her sexuality, that is, in terms of one particular aspect of her relationship to men.

[. . .]

The sexual definition of women, however, is but one facet of a much larger problem. In every aspect of life, a woman is identified in terms of the men she relates to. The opposite is not usually true of men: they act in the world as autonomous individuals, but women are only "John's wife," or "Harry's girl friend." Thus, meeting a woman at a party, a quite normal opening conversational gambit might be: "What does your husband do?" One very seldom hears, in a similar situation, a question addressed to a man: "What does your wife do?" The question would, to a majority of men, seem tautological: "She's my wife – that's what she does." This is true even in cases in which a woman is being discussed in a context utterly unrelated to her relationships with men, when she has attained sufficient stature to be considered for high public office. In fact, in a recent discussion of possible Supreme Court nominees, one woman was mentioned prominently. In discussing her general qualifications for the office, and her background, the *New York Times* saw fit to remark on her "bathing-beauty figure." Note that this is not only a judgment on a physical attribute totally removed from her qualifications for the Supreme Court, but that it is couched in terms of how a man would react to her figure. Some days later, President Nixon announced the nominations to his Price Board, among them one woman. In the thumbnail sketches the *Times* gave of each nominee, it was mentioned that the woman's husband was a professor of English. In the case of none of the other nominees was the existence of a spouse even hinted at, and much less was there any clue about the spouse's occupation. So here, although the existence of a husband was as irrelevant for this woman appointee as the existence of a wife was for any of the male appointees, the husband was mentioned, since a woman cannot be placed in her position in society by the readers of the *Times* unless they know her marital status. The same is not at all true of men. Similarly in the 1971 mayoral campaign in San Francisco, the sole woman candidate was repeatedly referred to as *Mrs. Feinstein*, never *Feinstein*, when her opponents were regularly referred to by first and last names or last names alone: *Joseph Alioto*, or *Alioto*, not *Mr. Alioto*. Again, the woman had to be identified by her relationship to a man, although this should bear no relevance to her qualifications for public office.

[. . .]

Also relevant here are the connotations (as opposed to the denotative meanings) of the words *spinster* and *bachelor*. Denotatively, these are, again, parallel to "cow" versus "bull": one is masculine, the other feminine, and both mean "one who is not married." But there the resemblance ends. *Bachelor* is at least a neutral term, often used as a compliment. *Spinster* normally seems to be used pejoratively, with connotations of prissiness, fussiness, and so on. Some of the differences between the two words are brought into focus in the following examples:

(22)   *(a)*   Mary hopes to meet an eligible bachelor.
       (b)   *Fred hopes to meet an eligible spinster.

It is the concept of an *eligible spinster* that is anomalous. If someone is a spinster, by implication she is not eligible (to marry); she has had her chance, and been passed by. Hence, a girl of twenty cannot be properly called a spinster: she still has a chance to be married. (Of course, *spinster* may be used metaphorically in this situation, as described below.) But a man may be considered a bachelor as soon as he reaches marriageable age: to be a bachelor implies that one has the choice of marrying or not, and this is what makes the idea of a bachelor existence attractive, in the popular literature. He has been pursued and has successfully eluded his pursuers. But a spinster is one who has not been pursued, or at least not seriously. She is old unwanted goods.

[. . .]

What all these facts suggest is merely this, again: that men are assumed to be able to choose whether on not they will marry, and that therefore their not being married in no way precludes their enjoying sexual activity; but if a woman is not married, it is assumed to be because no one found her desirable. Hence if a woman is not married by the usual age, she is assumed to be sexually undesirable, prissy, and frigid.

The reason for this distinction seems to be found in the point made earlier: that women are given their identities in our society by virtue of their relationship with men, not vice versa.

[. . .]

Reference

Lakoff, Robin. 1975. *Language and Woman's Place.* New York: Harper and Row.

12

The Relativity of Linguistic Strategies: Rethinking Power and Solidarity in Gender Dominance

Deborah Tannen

1 Introduction

In analyzing discourse, many researchers operate on the unstated assumption that all speakers proceed along similar lines of interpretation, so a particular example of discourse can be taken to represent how discourse works for all speakers. For some aspects of discourse, this is undoubtedly true. Yet a large body of sociolinguistic literature makes clear that, for many aspects of discourse, this is so only to the extent that cultural background is shared. To the extent that cultural backgrounds differ, lines of interpretation and habitual use of many linguistic strategies are likely to diverge. One thinks immediately and minimally of the work of Gumperz (1982), Erickson and Shultz (1982), Scollon and Scollon (1981), and Philips (1983). My own research shows that cultural difference is not limited to the gross and apparent levels of country of origin and native language, but also exists at the subcultural levels of ethnic heritage, class, geographic region, age, and gender. My earlier work (Tannen 1984, 1986) focuses on ethnic and regional style; my most recent work (Tannen 1990) focuses on gender-related stylistic variation. I draw on this work here to demonstrate that specific linguistic strategies have widely divergent potential meanings.[1]

This insight is particularly significant for research on language and gender, much of which has sought to describe the linguistic means by which men dominate women in interaction. That men dominate women is not in question; what I am problematizing is the source and workings of domination and other interpersonal intentions and effects. I will show that one cannot locate the source of domination, or of any interpersonal intention or effect, in linguistic strategies such as interruption, volubility, silence, and topic raising, as has been claimed. Similarly, one cannot locate the source of women's powerlessness in such linguistic strategies as indirectness, taciturnity, silence, and tag questions, as has also been claimed. The reason one cannot do this is that the same linguistic means can be used for different, even opposite, purposes and can have different, even opposite, effects in different contexts. Thus, a strategy that seems, or is, intended to dominate may in another context or in the mouth of another speaker be intended or used to establish connection. Similarly, a strategy that seems, or is, intended to create connection can in another context or in the mouth of another speaker be intended or used to establish dominance.

Put another way, the "true" intention or motive of any utterance cannot be determined from examination of linguistic form alone. For one thing, intentions and effects are not identical. For another, as the sociolinguistic literature has dramatized repeatedly (see especially McDermott and Tylbor 1983; Schegloff 1982, 1988; Erickson 1986; Duranti and Brenneis 1986), human interaction is a "joint production": everything that occurs results from the interaction of all participants. The source of the ambiguity and polysemy of linguistic strategies that I will explore here is the paradoxical relationship between the dynamics of power and solidarity.

2   Overview of the Chapter

In this chapter I first briefly explain the theoretical paradigm of power and solidarity. Then I show that linguistic strategies are potentially ambiguous (they could "mean" either power or solidarity) and polysemous (they could "mean" both). Third, I reexamine and expand the power and solidarity framework in light of cross-cultural research. Finally, I demonstrate the relativity of five linguistic strategies: indirectness, interruption, silence versus volubility, topic raising, and adversativeness (that is, verbal conflict).

3   Theoretical Background

3.1   Power and solidarity

Since Brown and Gilman's (1960) introduction of the concept and subsequent elaborations of it, especially those of Friedrich (1972) and Brown and Levinson ([1978]1987), the dynamics of power and solidarity have been fundamental to sociolinguistic theory. (Fasold (1990) provides an overview.) Brown and Gilman based their framework on analysis of the use of pronouns in European languages which have two forms of the second person pronoun, such as the French *tu* and *vous*. In English the closest parallel is to be found in forms of address: first name versus title–last name. In Brown and Gilman's system, power is associated with nonreciprocal use of pronouns; in English the parallel would be a situation in which one speaker addresses the other by first name but is addressed by title–last name (for example, doctor and patient, teacher and student, boss and secretary, building resident and elevator operator). Solidarity is associated with reciprocal pronoun use or symmetrical forms of address: both speakers address each other by *tu* or by *vous* (in English, by title–last name or by first name). Power governs asymmetrical relationships where one is subordinate to another; solidarity governs symmetrical relationships characterized by social equality and similarity.

In my previous work exploring the relationship between power and solidarity as it emerges in conversational discourse (Tannen 1984, 1986), I note that power and solidarity are in paradoxical relation to each other. That is, although power and solidarity, closeness and distance, seem at first to be opposites, each also entails the other. Any show of solidarity necessarily entails power, in that the requirement of similarity and closeness limits freedom and independence. At the same time, any show of power entails solidarity by involving participants in relation to each other. This creates a closeness that can be contrasted with the distance of individuals who have no relation to each other at all.

In Brown and Gilman's paradigm, the key to power is asymmetry, but it is often thought to be formality. This is seen in the following anecdote. I once entitled a lecture "The Paradox of Power and Solidarity." The respondent to my talk appeared wearing a three-piece suit and a knapsack on his back. The audience was amused by the association of the suit with power, the knapsack with solidarity. There was something immediately recognizable in this semiotic. Indeed, a professor wearing a knapsack might well mark solidarity with students at, for example, a protest demonstration. And wearing a three-piece suit to the demonstration might mark power by differentiating the wearer from the demonstrators, perhaps even reminding them of his dominant position in the institutional hierarchy. But wearing a three-piece suit to the board meeting of a corporation would mark solidarity with other board members, whereas wearing a knapsack in that setting would connote not solidarity but disrespect, a move in the power dynamic.

3.2   The ambiguity of linguistic strategies

As the preceding example shows, the same symbol – a three-piece suit – can signal either power or solidarity, depending on, at least, the setting (for example, a board meeting or student demonstration), the habitual dress style of the individual, and the comparison of his clothing with that worn by others in the interaction. (I say "his" intentionally; the range of meanings would be quite different if a man's three-piece suit were worn by a woman.) This provides an analogue to the ambiguity of linguistic strategies, which are signals in the semiotic system of language. As I have demonstrated at length in previous books (see especially Tannen 1984, 1986, 1990), all linguistic strategies are potentially ambiguous. The power–solidarity dynamic is one fundamental source of ambiguity. What appear as attempts to dominate a conversation (an exercise of power) may actually be intended to establish rapport (an exercise of solidarity). This occurs because (as I have worded it elsewhere) power and solidarity are bought with the same currency: The same linguistic means can be used to create either or both.

This ambiguity can be seen in the following fleeting conversation. Two women were walking together from one building to another in order to attend a meeting. They were joined by a man they both knew who had just exited a third building on his way to the same meeting. One of the women greeted the man and remarked, "Where's your coat?" The man responded, "Thanks, Mom." His response framed the woman's remark as a gambit in a power exchange: a mother tells a child to put on his coat. Yet the woman might have intended the remark as showing friendly concern rather than parental caretaking. Was it power (condescending, on the model of parent to child) or solidarity (friendly, on the model of intimate peers)? Though the man's uptake is clear, the woman's intention in making the remark is not.

Another example comes from a letter written to me by a reader of *You Just Don't Understand: Women and Men in Conversation*. A woman was at home when her partner arrived and announced that his archrival had invited him to contribute a chapter to a book. The woman remarked cheerfully how nice it was that the rival was initiating a rapprochement by including her partner in his book. He told her she had got it wrong: because the rival would be the editor and he merely a contributor, the rival was actually trying to solidify his dominance. She interpreted the invitation in terms of solidarity. He interpreted it as an expression of power. Which was right? I don't know. The invitation was ambiguous; it could have "meant" either. I suspect it had elements of both. In other words, it was polysemous.

3.3   The polysemy of power and solidarity

If ambiguity denotes meaning one thing *or* another, polysemy denotes meaning one thing *and* another – that is, having multiple meanings simultaneously. The question "Where's your coat?" shows friendly concern *and* suggests a parent–child constellation. The invitation to contribute a chapter to a book brings editor and contributor closer *and* suggests a hierarchical relationship.

One more example will illustrate the polysemy of strategies signaling power and solidarity. If you have a friend who repeatedly picks up the check when you dine together, is she being generous and sharing her wealth, or is she trying to flaunt her money and remind you that she has more of it than you? Although the intention may be to make you feel good by her generosity, her repeated generosity may nonetheless make you feel bad by reminding you that she has more money. Thus, both of you are caught in the web of the ambiguity of power and solidarity. It is impossible to determine which was her real motive, and whether it justifies your response. On the other hand, even if you believe her motive was purely generous, you may nonetheless feel denigrated by her generosity because the fact that she has this generous impulse is evidence that she has more money than you, and her expressing the impulse reminds you of it. In other words, both interpretations exist at once: solidarity (she is paying to be nice) and power (her being nice in this way reminds you that she is richer). In this sense, the strategy is not just ambiguous with regard to power and solidarity but polysemous. This polysemy explains another observation that initially surprised me: Paules (1991) reports that waitresses in the restaurant where she did ethnographic field work were offended not only by tips that were too small, but also by tips that were too large. The customers' inordinate beneficence implies that the amount of money left is insignificant to the tipper but significant to the waitress.

Brown and Gilman are explicit in their assumption that power is associated with asymmetrical relationships in which the power is held by the person in the one-up position. This is stated in their definition:

> One person may be said to have power over another to the degree that he is able to control the behavior of the other. Power is a relationship between at least two persons, and it is nonreciprocal in the sense that both cannot have power in the same area of behavior. (chapter 9, p. 158)

I have called attention, however, to the extent to which solidarity in itself can be a form of control. For example, a young woman complained about friends who "don't let you be different." If the friend says she has a particular problem and the woman says, "I don't have that problem," her friend is hurt and accuses her of putting her down, of acting superior. The assumption of similarity requires the friend to have a matching problem.[2]

Furthermore, although Brown and Gilman acknowledge that "power superiors may be solidary (parents, elder siblings)" and "power inferiors, similarly, may be as solidary as the old family retainer" (p. 160), most Americans are inclined to assume that solidarity implies closeness, whereas power implies distance.[3] Thus Americans regard the sibling relationship as the ultimate in solidarity: "sister" or "brother" are often used metaphorically to indicate closeness and equality.[4] In contrast, it is often assumed that hierarchy precludes closeness: employers and employees cannot "really" be friends. But being linked in a hierarchy necessarily brings individuals closer. This is an assumption underlying Watanabe's (1993) observation, in comparing American and Japanese group discussions, that whereas the Americans in her study saw themselves as individuals participating in a joint activity, the Japanese saw themselves as members of a group united by hierarchy. When reading Watanabe, I was caught up short by the term "united." My inclination had been to assume that hierarchy is distancing, not uniting.

The anthropological literature includes numerous discussions of cultural contexts in which hierarchical relationships are seen as close and mutually, not unilaterally, empowering. For example, Beeman (1986) describes an Iranian interactional pattern he dubs "getting the lower hand." Taking the lower-status position enables an Iranian to invoke a protector schema by which the higher-status person is obligated to do things for him or her. Similarly, Yamada (1992) describes the Japanese relationship of *amae*, typified by the parent–child or employer–employee constellation. It binds two individuals in a hierarchical interdependence by which both have power in the form of obligations as well as rights vis-à-vis the other. Finally, Wolfowitz (1991) explains that respect/deference is experienced by Suriname Javanese not as subservience but as an assertion of claims.

The Suriname Javanese example is particularly intriguing because it calls into question the association of asymmetry with power and distance. The style Wolfowitz calls respect politeness is characterized by both social closeness and negative politeness.[5] It is hierarchical insofar as it is directional and unequal; however, the criterion for directionality is not status but age. The prototypical relationship characterized by respect politeness is grandchild–grandparent: a relationship that is both highly unequal and very close. Moreover, according to Wolfowitz, the Javanese assume that familial relations are inherently hierarchical, including age-graded siblings. Equality, in contrast, is associated with formal relationships that are also marked by social distance.

We can display these dynamics in the following way. The model that reflects American assumptions conceptualizes power and solidarity as opposite ends of a single continuum simultaneously representing symmetry/asymmetry, hierarchy/equality, and distance/closeness (See figure 1.) In contrast, the cross-cultural perspective suggests a multidimensional grid of at least (and, potentially and probably, more) intersecting continua. The closeness/distance dimension can be placed on one axis and the hierarchy/equality one on another. (See figure 2.) Indeed, the intersection of these dimensions – that is, the co-incidence of hierarchy and closeness – may account, at least in part, for what I am calling the ambiguity and polysemy of power and solidarity.

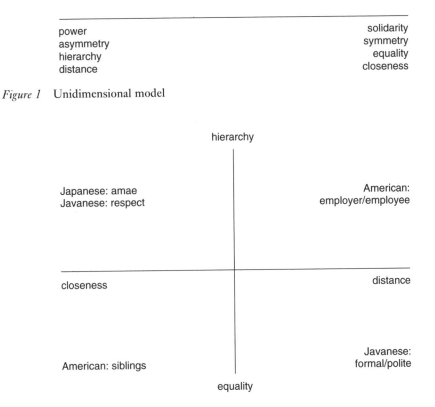

power   solidarity
asymmetry   symmetry
hierarchy   equality
distance   closeness

Figure 1   Unidimensional model

hierarchy

Japanese: amae   American:
Javanese: respect   employer/employee

closeness   distance

American: siblings   Javanese:
                                                               formal/polite

equality

Figure 2   Multidimensional model

3.4   Similarity/difference

There is one more aspect of the dynamics of power and solidarity that bears
discussion before I demonstrate the relativity of linguistic strategies. That is the
similarity/difference continuum and its relation to the other dynamics discussed.

For Brown and Gilman, solidarity implies sameness, in contrast to power, about
which they observe, "In general terms, the *V* form is linked with differences between
persons" (p. 159). This is explicit in their definition of "the solidarity semantic":

> Now we are concerned with a new set of relations which are symmetrical; for example,
> *attended the same school* or *have the same parents* or *practice the same profession*. If A has the
> same parents as B, B has the same parents as A. Solidarity is the name we give to the
> general relationship and solidarity is symmetrical. (p. 160; italics in original)

The similarity/difference continuum calls to mind what I have discussed elsewhere
(Tannen 1984, 1986) as the double bind of communication.[6] In some ways, we are all
the same. But in other ways we are all different. Communication is a double bind in the
sense that anything we say to honor our similarity violates our difference, and anything
we say to honor our difference violates our sameness. Thus a complaint can be lodged:
"Don't think I'm different." ("If you prick me, do I not bleed?" one might protest, like

Shylock.) But a complaint can also be lodged: "Don't think I'm the same." (Thus, women who have primary responsibility for the care of small children may be effectively excluded from activities and events at which day care is not provided.) Becker (1982:125) expresses this double bind as "a matter of continual self-correction between exuberance (that is, friendliness: you are like me) and deficiency (that is, respect: you are not me)." All these formulations elaborate on the tension between similarity and difference, or what Becker and Oka (1974) call "the cline of person," a semantic dimension they suggest may be the one most basic to language; that is, one deals with the world and the objects and people in it in terms of how close (and, I would add, similar) they are to oneself.

As a result of these dynamics, similarity is a threat to hierarchy. This is dramatized in Harold Pinter's play *Mountain Language*. Composed of four brief scenes, the play is set in a political prison in the capital city of an unnamed country that is under dictatorial siege. In the second scene, an old mountain woman is finally allowed to visit her son across a table as a guard stands over them. But whenever she tries to speak to her son, the guard silences her, telling the prisoner to tell his mother that it is forbidden to speak their mountain language in the capital. Then he continues: (Spaced dots indicate omitted text; unspaced dots are a form of punctuation included in the original text.)

GUARD

. . . And I'll tell you another thing. I've got a wife and three kids. And you're all a pile of shit.
Silence.

PRISONER

I've got a wife and three kids.

GUARD

You've what?
Silence.
You've got what?
Silence.
What did you say to me? You've got what?
Silence.
You've got *what?*
He picks up the telephone and dials one digit.
Sergeant? I'm in the Blue Room ... yes ... I thought I should report, Sergeant ... I think I've got a joker in here.

The Sergeant soon enters and asks, "What joker?" The stage darkens and the scene ends. The final scene opens on the same setting, with the prisoner bloody and shaking, his mother shocked into speechlessness.

The prisoner was beaten for saying, "I've got a wife and three kids." This quotidian statement, which would be unremarkable in casual conversation, was insubordinate in the hierarchical context of brutal oppression because the guard had just made the same statement. When the guard said, "I've got a wife and three kids. And you're a pile of shit," he was claiming, "I am different from you." One could further interpret his words to imply, "I'm human, and you're not. Therefore I have a right to dominate and abuse you." By repeating the guard's words verbatim, the prisoner was then saying, "I am the same as you."[7] By claiming *his* humanity and implicitly denying the guard's assertion that he is "a pile of shit," the prisoner challenged the guard's right to dominate him.[8] Similarity is antithetical to hierarchy.

The ambiguity of closeness, a spatial metaphor representing similarity or involvement, emerges in a nonverbal aspect of this scene. In the performance I saw, the guard moved steadily closer to the prisoner as he repeated the question "You've got what?" until he was bending over him, nose to nose. The guard's moving closer was a kinesic/proxemic analogue to the prisoner's statement, but with opposite effect: he was "closing in." The guard moved closer and brought his face into contact with the prisoner's not as a sign of affection (which such actions could signify in another context) but as a threat. Closeness, then, can mean aggression rather than affiliation in the context of a hierarchical rather than symmetrical relationship.

4   The Relativity of Linguistic Strategies

The potential ambiguity of linguistic strategies to mark both power and solidarity in face-to-face interaction has made mischief in language and gender research, wherein it is tempting to assume that whatever women do results from, or creates, their powerlessness and whatever men do results from, or creates, their dominance. But all the linguistic strategies that have been taken by analysts as evidence of subordination can in some circumstances be instruments of affiliation. For the remainder of this chapter I demonstrate the relativity of linguistic strategies by considering each of the following strategies in turn: indirectness, interruption, silence versus volubility, topic raising, and adversativeness or verbal conflict. All of these strategies have been "found" by researchers to express or create dominance or subordination. I will demonstrate that they are ambiguous or polysemous with regard to dominance/subordination (that is, power) or distance/closeness (that is, solidarity). Once again, I am not arguing that these strategies *cannot* be used to create dominance or powerlessness, much less that dominance and powerlessness do not exist. Rather, my purpose is to demonstrate that the "meaning" of any linguistic strategy can vary, depending at least on context, the conversational styles of participants, and the interaction of participants' styles and strategies. Therefore the operation of specific linguistic strategies must be studied more closely to understand how dominance and powerlessness are expressed and created in interaction.

4.1   Indirectness

Lakoff (1975) identifies two benefits of indirectness: defensiveness and rapport. Defensiveness refers to a speaker's preference not to go on record with an idea in order to be able to disclaim, rescind, or modify it if it does not meet with a positive response. The rapport benefit of indirectness results from the pleasant experience of getting one's way not because one demanded it (power) but because the other person wanted the same thing (solidarity). Many researchers have focused on the defensive or power benefit of indirectness and ignored the payoff in rapport or solidarity.

The claim by Conley, O'Barr, and Lind (1979) that women's language is really powerless language has been particularly influential. In this view, women's tendency to be indirect is taken as evidence that women don't feel entitled to make demands. Surely there are cases in which this is true. Yet it can also be demonstrated that those who feel entitled to make demands may prefer not to, seeking the payoff in rapport. Furthermore, the ability to get one's demands met without expressing them directly can be a sign of power rather than of the lack of it. An example I have used elsewhere (Tannen 1994, chapter 5) is the Greek father who answers, "If you want, you can go," to his daughter's inquiry about going to a party. Because of the lack of enthusiasm of his response, the Greek daughter understands that her father would prefer she not go and "chooses" not to go. (A "real" approval would have been "Yes, of course, you should go.") I argue that this father did not feel powerless to give his daughter orders. Rather, a communicative system was conventionalized by which he and she could both preserve the appearance, and possibly the belief, that she chose not to go rather than simply obeying his command.

Far from being powerless, this father felt so powerful that he did not need to give his daughter orders; he simply needed to let her know his preference, and she would accommodate to it. By this reasoning, indirectness is a prerogative of the powerful. By the same reasoning a master who says, "It's cold in here," may expect a servant to make a move to close a window, but a servant who says the same thing is not likely to see his employer rise to correct the situation and make him more comfortable. Indeed, a Frenchman who was raised in Brittany tells me that his family never gave bald commands to their servants but always communicated orders in indirect and highly polite form. This pattern renders less surprising the finding of Bellinger and Gleason (1982, reported in Gleason 1987) that fathers' speech to their young children had a higher incidence than mothers' of both direct imperatives (such as "Turn the bolt with the wrench") *and* implied indirect imperatives (for example, "The wheel is going to fall off").

The use of indirectness can hardly be understood without the cross-cultural perspective. Many Americans find it self-evident that directness is logical and aligned with power whereas indirectness is akin to dishonesty as well as subservience. But for speakers raised in most of the world's cultures, varieties of indirectness are the norm in communication. In Japanese interaction, for example, it is well known that saying "no" is considered too face-threatening to risk, so negative responses are phrased as positive ones: one never says "no," but listeners understand from the form of the "yes" whether it is truly a "yes" or a polite "no."

The American tendency to associate indirectness with female style is not culturally universal. The above description of typical Japanese style operates for men as well as women. My own research (Tannen 1981, 1984, 1986) suggests that Americans of some cultural and geographic backgrounds, female as well as male, are more likely than others to use relatively direct rather than indirect styles. In an early study (Tannen 1994, chapter 5) I compared Greeks and Americans with regard to their tendency to interpret a question as an indirect means of making a request. I found that whereas American women were more likely to take an indirect interpretation of a sample conversation, Greek men were as likely as Greek women, and more likely than American men *or women*, to take an indirect interpretation. Greek men, of course, are not less powerful vis-à-vis women than American men.

Perhaps most striking is the finding of Keenan (1974) that in a Malagasy-speaking village on the island of Madagascar, women are seen as direct and men as indirect. But this in no way implies that the women are more powerful than men in this society. Quite the contrary, Malagasy men are socially dominant, and their indirect style is more highly valued. Keenan found that women were widely believed to debase the language with their artless directness, whereas men's elaborate indirectness was widely admired.

Indirectness, then, is not in itself a strategy of subordination. Rather, it can be used either by the powerful or the powerless. The interpretation of a given utterance, and the likely response to it, depends on the setting, on individuals' status and their relationship to each other, and also on the linguistic conventions that are ritualized in the cultural context.

4.2   Interruption

That interruption is a sign of dominance has been as widespread an assumption in research as in conventional wisdom. One rarely encounters an article on gender and language that does not make this claim. Most frequently cited is West and Zimmerman's (1983) finding that men dominate women by interrupting them in conversation. Tellingly, however, Deborah James and Sandra Clarke (1993), reviewing research on gender and interruption, do not find a clear pattern of males interrupting females. Especially significant is their observation that studies comparing amount of interruption in all-female versus all-male conversations find more interruption, not less, in all-female groups. Though initially surprising, this finding reinforces the need to distinguish linguistic strategies by their interactional purpose. Does the overlap show support for the speaker, or does it contradict or change the topic? I explore this phenomenon in detail in Tannen (1994), chapter 2, but I will include a brief summary of the argument here.

The phenomenon commonly referred to as "interruption," but which is more accurately referred to as "overlap," is a paradigm case of the ambiguity of power and solidarity. This is clearly demonstrated with reference to a two-and-a-half-hour Thanksgiving dinner conversation that I analyzed at length (Tannen 1984). My analysis makes clear that some speakers consider talking along with another to be a show of enthusiastic participation in the conversation, of solidarity, creating connections; others, however, assume that only one voice should be heard at a time, so for them any overlap is an interruption, an attempt to wrest the floor, a power play. The result, in the conversation I analyzed, was that enthusiastic listeners who overlapped cooperatively, talking along to establish rapport, were perceived by overlap-resistant speakers as interrupting. This doubtless contributed to the impression reported by the overlap-resistant speakers that the cooperative overlappers had "dominated" the conversation. Indeed, the tape and transcript also give the impression that the cooperative overlappers had dominated, because the overlap-aversant participants tended to stop speaking as soon as another voice began.

It is worth emphasizing the role of symmetry, or balance, in determining whether an overlap becomes an interruption in the negative or power-laden sense. If one speaker repeatedly overlaps and another repeatedly gives way, the resulting communication is unbalanced, or asymmetrical, and the effect (though not necessarily the intent) is domination. But if both speakers avoid overlap, or if both speakers overlap each other and win out equally, there is symmetry and no domination, regardless of speakers' intentions. In an important sense, though – and this will be discussed in the last section under the rubric of adversativeness – the very engagement in a symmetrical struggle for the floor can be experienced as creating rapport, in the spirit of ritual opposition analogous to sports. Further, an imbalance can result from differences in the purpose for which overlap is used. If one speaker tends to talk along in order to show support, and the other chimes in to take the floor, the floor-taking overlapper will tend to dominate.

Thus, to understand whether an overlap is an interruption, one must consider the context (for example, cooperative overlapping is more likely to occur in casual conversation among friends than in a job interview), speakers' habitual styles (for example, overlaps are more likely not to be interruptions among those with a style I call "high involvement"), and the interaction of their styles (for example, an interruption is more likely to occur between speakers whose styles differ with regard to pausing and overlap). This is not to say that one cannot use interruption to dominate a conversation or a person, but only that it is not self-evident from the observation of overlap that an interruption has occurred, was intended, or was intended to dominate.

4.3   Silence versus volubility

The excerpt from Pinter's *Mountain Language* dramatizes the assumption that powerful people do the talking and powerless people are silenced. This is the trope that underlies the play's title and its central theme: By outlawing their language, the oppressors silence the mountain people, robbing them of their ability to speak and hence of their humanity. In the same spirit, many scholars (for example, Spender 1980) have claimed that men dominate women by silencing them. There are obviously circumstances in which this is accurate. Coates (1986) notes numerous proverbs that instruct women, like children, to be silent.

Silence alone, however, is not a self-evident sign of powerlessness, nor volubility a self-evident sign of domination. A theme running through Komarovsky's (1962) classic study of *Blue-Collar Marriage* is that many of the wives interviewed said they talked more than their husbands: "He's tongue-tied," one woman said (13); "My husband has a great habit of not talking," said another (162); "He doesn't say much but he means what he says and the children mind him," said a third (353). Yet there is no question but that these husbands are dominant in their marriages, as the last of these quotes indicates.

Indeed, taciturnity itself can be an instrument of power. This is precisely the claim of Sattel (1983), who argues that men use silence to exercise power over women. Sattel illustrates with a scene from Erica Jong's novel *Fear of Flying*, only a brief part of which is presented here. The first line of dialogue is spoken by Isadora, the second by her husband, Bennett. (Spaced dots indicate omitted text; unspaced dots are a form of punctuation included in the original text.)

"Why do you turn on me? What did I do?"
Silence.
"What did I do?"
He looks at her as if her not knowing were another injury.
"Look, let's just go to sleep now. Let's just forget it."
"Forget what?"
He says nothing.
. . .
"It was something in the movie, wasn't it?"
"What, in the movie?"
". . . It was the funeral scene. ... The little boy looking at his dead mother. Something got you there. That was when you got depressed."
Silence.
"Well, *wasn't* it?"
Silence.
"Oh come on, Bennett, you're making me *furious*. Please tell me. Please."

The painful scene continues in this vein until Bennett tries to leave the room and Isadora tries to detain him. The excerpt certainly seems to support Sattel's claim that Bennett's silence subjugates his wife, as the scene ends with her literally lowered to the floor, clinging to his pajama leg. But the reason his silence is an effective weapon is her insistence that he tell her what's wrong. If *she* receded into silence, leaving the room or refusing to talk to him, his silence would be disarmed. The devastation results not from his silence alone but from the interaction of his silence and her insistence on talking, in other words, the interaction of their differing styles.[9]

Researchers have counted numbers of words spoken or timed length of talk in order to demonstrate that men talk more than women and thereby dominate interactions. (See James and Drakich 1993 for a summary of research on amount of talk.) Undoubtedly there is truth to this observation in some settings. But the association of volubility with dominance does not hold for all settings and all cultures. Imagine, for example, an interrogation, in which the interrogator does little of the talking but holds all the power.

The relativity of the "meaning" of taciturnity and volubility is highlighted in Margaret Mead's (1977) discussion of "end linkage," a concept developed jointly by Mead, Gregory Bateson, and Geoffrey Gorer. The claim is that universal and biologically constructed relationships, such as parent–child, are linked to different behaviors in different cultures. One of their paradigm examples is the apportionment of spectatorship and exhibitionism. In middle-class American culture, children, who are obviously the weaker party in the constellation, are expected to exhibit while their more powerful parents are spectators. (Consider, for example, the American child who is prompted to demonstrate how well s/he can recite the alphabet for guests.) In contrast, in middle- and upper-class British culture, exhibition is associated with the parental role and spectatorship with children, who are expected to be seen and not heard.

Moreover, volubility and taciturnity, too, can result from style differences rather than speakers' intentions. As I (Tannen 1984, 1985) and others (Scollon and Scollon 1981,

Scollon 1985) have discussed, there are cultural and subcultural differences in the length of pauses expected between and within speaking turns. In my study of the dinner conversation, those who expected shorter pauses between conversational turns began to feel an uncomfortable silence ensuing while their longer-pausing friends were simply waiting for what they regarded as the "normal" end-of-turn pause. The result was that the shorter pausers ended up doing most of the talking, another sign interpreted by their interlocutors as dominating the conversation. But their intentions had been to fill in what to them were potentially uncomfortable silences, that is, to grease the conversational wheels and ensure the success of the conversation. In their view, the taciturn participants were uncooperative, failing to do their part to maintain the conversation.

Thus, silence and volubility cannot always be taken to "mean" power or powerlessness, domination or subjugation. Rather, both may imply either power or solidarity, depending on the dynamics discussed.

4.4   Topic raising

Shuy (1982) is typical in assuming that the speaker who raises the most topics is dominating a conversation. However, in a study I conducted (Tannen 1994, chapter 3) of videotaped conversations among friends of varying ages recorded by Dorval (1990), it emerged that the speaker who raised the most topics was not always dominant, as judged by other criteria (for example, who took the lead in addressing the investigator when he entered the room?). In a 20-minute conversation between a pair of sixth-grade girls who identified themselves as best friends, Shannon raised the topic of Julia's relationship with Mary by saying, "Too bad you and Mary are not good friends anymore." The conversation proceeded and continued to focus almost exclusively on Julia's troubled relationship with Mary.

Similarly, most of the conversation between two tenth-grade girls was about Nancy, but Sally raised the topic of Nancy's problems. In response to Nancy's question "Well, what do you want to talk about?" Sally said, "Your mama. Did you talk to your mama?" The ensuing conversation focuses on events involving Nancy's mother and boyfriend. Overall, Sally raised nine topics, Nancy seven. However, all but one of the topics Sally raised were questions focused on Nancy. If raising more topics is a sign of dominance, Sally controlled the conversation when she raised topics, although even this was subject to Nancy's collaboration by picking them up. It may or may not be the case that Sally controlled the conversation, but the nature of her dominance is surely other than what is normally assumed by that term if the topics she raised were all about Nancy.

Finally, the effect of raising topics may also be an effect of differences in pacing and pausing, as discussed above with regard to my study of dinner-table conversation. A speaker who thinks the other has no more to say on a given topic may try to contribute to the conversation by raising another topic. But a speaker who was intending to say more and was simply waiting for the appropriate turn-exchange pause will feel that the floor was taken away and the topic aggressively switched. Yet again, the impression of dominance might result from style differences.

4.5   Adversativeness: conflict and verbal aggression

Research on gender and language has consistently found male speakers to be competitive and more likely to engage in conflict (for example, by arguing, issuing commands, and taking opposing stands) and females to be cooperative and more likely to avoid conflict (for example, by agreeing, supporting, and making suggestions rather than commands). (Maltz and Borker (1982) summarize some of this research.) Ong (1981: 51) argues that "adversativeness" is universal, but "conspicuous or expressed adversativeness is a larger element in the lives of males than of females."

In my analysis of videotapes of male and female friends talking to each other (Tannen 1994, chapter 3), I have begun to investigate how male adversativeness and female cooperation are played out, complicated and contradicted in conversational discourse. In analyzing videotapes of friends talking, for example, I found a sixth-grade boy saying to his best friend,

Seems like, if there's a fight, me and you are automatically in it. And everyone else wants to go against you and everything. It's hard to agree without someone saying something to you.

In contrast, girls of the same age (and also of most other ages whose talk I examined) spent a great deal of time discussing the dangers of anger and contention. In affirming their own friendship, one girl told her friend,

Me and you never get in fights hardly,

and

I mean like if I try to talk to you, you'll say, 'Talk to me!' And if you try to talk to me, I'll talk to you.

These examples of gendered styles of interaction are illuminated by the insight that power and solidarity are mutually evocative. As seen in the statement of the sixth-grade boy, opposing other boys in teams entails affiliation within the team. The most dramatic instance of male affiliation resulting from conflict with others is bonding among soldiers, a phenomenon explored by Norman (1990).

By the same token, girls' efforts to support their friends necessarily entail exclusion of or opposition to other girls. This emerges in Hughes' (1988) study of girls playing a street game called four-square, in which four players occupy one square each and bounce a ball into each other's squares. The object of the game is to eliminate players by hitting the ball into their square in such a way that they fail to hit it back. But this effort to "get people out" is at odds with the social injunction under which the girls operate, to be "nice" and not "mean." Hughes found that the girls resolved the conflict, and formed "incipient teams" composed of friends, by claiming that their motivation in eliminating some players was to enable others (their friends) to enter the game, since eliminated players are replaced by awaiting players. In the girls' terms, "getting someone out" was "nice-mean," because it was reframed as "getting someone [a friend] in." This dynamic is also supported by my analysis of the sixth-grade girls' conversation: Most of their talk was devoted to allying themselves with each other in opposition to another girl who was not present. So their cooperation (solidarity) also entails opposition (power).

For boys power entails solidarity not only by opposition to another team, but by opposition to each other. In the videotapes of friends talking, I found that all the conversations between young boys (and none between young girls) had numerous examples of teasing and mock attack.[10] In examining preschool conversations transcribed and analyzed by Corsaro and Rizzo (1990: 34), I was amazed to discover that a fight could initiate rather than preclude friendship. In the following episode, a little boy intrudes on two others and an angry fight ensues. This is the way Corsaro and Rizzo present the dialogue:

Two boys (Richard and Denny) have been playing with a slinky on the stairway leading to the upstairs playhouse in the school. During their play two other boys (Joseph and Martin) enter and stand near the bottom of the stairs.

DENNY: Go!
(Martin now runs off, but Joseph remains and he eventually moves halfway up the stairs.)
JOSEPH: These are big shoes.
RICHARD: I'll punch him right in the eye.
JOSEPH: I'll punch you right in the nose.
DENNY: I'll punch him with my big fist.
JOSEPH: I'll-I-I-
RICHARD: And he'll be bumpety, bumpety and punched out all the way down the stairs.
JOSEPH: I-I-I'll- I could poke your eyes out with my gun. I have a gun.
DENNY: A gun! I'll-I-I- even if-
RICHARD: I have a gun too.
DENNY: And I have guns too and it's bigger than yours and it poo-poo down. That's poo-poo.
(All three boys laugh at Denny's reference to poo-poo.)
RICHARD: Now leave.
JOSEPH: Un-uh. I gonna tell you to put on- on the gun on your hair and the poop will come right out on his face.
DENNY: Well.
RICHARD: Slinky will snap right on your face too.
DENNY: And my gun will snap right-

Up until this point I had no difficulty interpreting the interaction: The boys were engaged in a fight occasioned by Joseph's intrusion into Richard and Denny's play. But what happened next surprised and, at first, perplexed me. Corsaro and Rizzo describe it this way:

At this point a girl (Debbie) enters, says she is Batgirl, and asks if they have seen Robin. Joseph says he is Robin, but she says she is looking for a different Robin and then runs off. After Debbie leaves, Denny and Richard move into the playhouse and Joseph follows. From this point to the end of the episode the three boys play together.

At first I was incredulous that so soon after their seemingly hostile encounter, the boys played amicably together. I finally came to the conclusion that for Joseph picking a fight was a way to enter into interaction with the other boys, and engaging him in the fight was Richard and Denny's way of accepting him into their interaction – at least after he acquitted himself satisfactorily in the fight. In this light, I could see that the reference to poo-poo, which occasioned general laughter, was the beginning of a reframing from fighting to playing.[11]

Folklore provides numerous stories in which fighting precipitates friendship among men. One such is attributed by Bly (1990: 243–44) to Joseph Campbell's account of the Sumerian epic, *Gilgamesh*. In Bly's rendition, Gilgamesh, a young king, wants to befriend a wild man named Enkidu. When Enkidu is told of Gilgamesh,

> his heart grew light. He yearned for a friend. "Very well!" he said. "And I shall challenge him."

Bly paraphrases the continuation: "Enkidu then travels to the city and meets Gilgamesh; the two wrestle, Enkidu wins, and the two become inseparable friends."[12]

A modern-day academic equivalent to the bonding that results from opposition is to be found in the situation of fruitful collaborations that began when an audience member publicly challenged a speaker after his talk. Finally, Penelope Eckert (personal communication) informs me that in her research on high school students (Eckert 1990) she was told by boys, but never by girls, that their close friendships began by fighting.

These examples call into question the correlation of aggression and power on one hand, and cooperation and solidarity on the other. Again the cross-cultural perspective provides an invaluable corrective to the temptation to align aggression with power as distinguished from solidarity. Many cultures of the world see arguing as a pleasurable sign of intimacy. Schiffrin (1984) shows that among lower-middle-class men *and women* of East European Jewish background, friendly argument is a means of being sociable. Frank (1988) shows a Jewish couple who tend to polarize and take argumentative positions, but they are not fighting; they are staging a kind of public sparring, where both fighters are on the same team. Byrnes (1986) claims that Germans find American students uninformed and uncommitted because they are reluctant to argue politics with new acquaintances. For their part, Americans find German students belligerent because they provoke arguments about American foreign policy with Americans they have just met.

Greek conversation provides an example of a cultural style that places more positive value, for both women and men, on dynamic opposition. Kakava (1989) replicates Schiffrin's findings by showing how a Greek family enjoy opposing each other in dinner conversation. In another study of modern Greek conversation, Tannen and Kakava (1992) find speakers routinely disagreeing when they actually agree, and using diminutive name forms and other terms of endearment – markers of closeness – precisely when they are opposing each other.[13] These patterns can be seen in the following excerpt from a conversation that took place in Greece between an older Greek woman and myself. The woman, whom I call Ms. Stella, has just told me that she complained to the police about a construction crew that illegally continued drilling and pounding through the siesta hours, disturbing her nap:

DEBORAH: Echete dikio.
STELLA: Ego <u>echo</u> dikio. Kopella mou, den xero an echo dikio i den echo dikio. Alla ego yperaspizomai ta symferonta mou kai ta dikaiomata mou.
DEBORAH: You're right.
STELLA: I <u>am</u> right. My dear girl, I don't know if I'm right or I'm not right. But I am watching out for my interests and my rights.

My response to Ms. Stella's complaint is to support her by agreeing. But she disagrees with my agreement by reframing my statement in her own terms rather than simply accepting it by stopping after "I *am* right." She also marks her divergence from my frame with the endearment "kopella mou" (literally, "my girl," but idiomatically closer to "my dear girl").

The following conversation is also taken from Tannen and Kakava (1992). It is, according to Kakava, typical of her family's sociable argument. The younger sister has said that she cannot understand why the attractive young woman who is the prime minister Papandreou's girlfriend would have an affair with such an old man. The older sister, Christina, argues that the woman may have felt that in having an affair with the prime minister she was doing something notable. Her sister replied,

Poly megalo timima re Christinaki na pliroseis pantos.
It's a very high price to pay, Chrissie, anyway.

I use the English diminutive form "Chrissie" to reflect the Greek diminutive ending -*aki*, but the particle *re* cannot really be translated; it is simply a marker of closeness that is typically used when disagreeing, as in the ubiquitously heard expression "Ochi, re" ("No, *re*").

5   Conclusion

The intersection of language and gender provides a rich site for analyzing how power and solidarity are created in discourse. But prior research in this area evidences the danger of linking linguistic forms with interactional intentions such as dominance. In trying to understand how speakers use language, we must consider the context (in every sense, including at least textual, relational, and institutional constraints), speakers' conversational styles, and, most crucially, the interaction of their styles with each other.

Attempts to understand what goes on between women and men in conversation are muddled by the ambiguity and polysemy of power and solidarity. The same linguistic means can accomplish either, and every utterance combines elements of both. Scholars, however, like individuals in interaction, are likely to see only one and not the other, like the picture that cannot be seen for what it is – simultaneously a chalice and two faces – but can only be seen alternately as one or the other. In attempting the impossible task of keeping both images in focus at once, we may at least succeed in switching from one to the other rapidly and regularly enough to deepen our understanding of the dynamics underlying interaction such as power and solidarity as well as gender and language use.

Notes

This chapter began as a paper entitled "Rethinking Power and Solidarity in Gender and Dominance," which was published in *Proceedings of the 16th Annual Meeting of the Berkeley Linguistics Society*, edited by Kira Hall, Jean-Pierre Koenig, Michael Meacham, Sondra Reinman, and Laurel A. Sutton, 519–29 (Berkeley: Linguistics Department, University of California, Berkeley, 1990). A significantly revised and expanded version appears in *Gender and Conversational Interaction*, a volume I edited, published by Oxford University Press in 1993. That rewriting was carried out while I was in residence at the Institute for Advanced Study in Princeton, New Jersey. Further revisions – improvements, I hope – which I made to the version that appears here (some in response to much-appreciated comments from Paul Friedrich) were carried out while I was a fellow at the Center for Advanced Study in the Behavioral Sciences in Palo Alto, California. I have lifted the summary of this chapter directly from the overview that appears in the 1993 publication.

1   I use the term "strategy" in its standard sociolinguistic sense, to refer simply to a way of speaking. No implication is intended of deliberate planning, as is the case in the common parlance use of such expressions as "military strategy." Neither, however, as Gumperz (1982) observes, are linguistic strategies "unconscious." Rather, they are best thought of as "automatic." That is, people speak in a particular way without "consciously" thinking it through, but are aware, if questioned, of how they spoke and what they were trying to accomplish by talking in that way. This is in contrast to the "unconscious" motives of Freudian theory about which an individual would be unaware if questioned. (For example, most men would vigorously deny that they want to kill their fathers and marry their mothers but a strict Freudian might claim that this wish is "unconscious.")

2   This example is taken from Tannen (1990).

3   I myself have made the observation that asymmetry is distancing whereas symmetry implies closeness, for example, with regard to the ritual of "troubles talk" and the way it often misfires between women and men (Tannen 1990). Many women talk about troubles as a way of feeling closer, but many men frequently interpret the description of troubles as a request for advice, which they kindly offer. I have observed that this not only cuts off the troubles talk, which was the real point of the discourse, but it also introduces asymmetry: If one person says she has a problem and another says she has the same problem, they are symmetrically arrayed and their similarity brings them closer. But if one person has a problem and the other has the solution, the one with the solution is one-up, and the asymmetry is distancing – just the opposite of what was sought by initiating the ritual.

4   This assumption is made explicit by Klagsbrun (1992), who, in a book about sibling relationships, writes, "Unlike the ties between parents and children, the connection among siblings is a horizontal one. That is, sibs exist on the same plane, as peers, more or less equals" (12). But Klagsbrun gives a pivotal example of how she was frustrated as a child (and continues to be hampered, as an adult) by always being bested by her *older* brother. It is clear from the example that she and her brother were not equals because of the difference in their ages – and, one might argue, their genders.

5   Negative politeness, as discussed by Brown and Levinson ([1978] 1987), entails honoring others' needs not to be imposed on.

6   Scollon (1982: 344–45) explains that all communication is a double bind because one must serve, with every utterance, the conflicting needs to be left alone (negative face) and to be accepted as a member of society (positive face). The term "double bind" traces to Bateson (1972).

7   I have demonstrated at length (Tannen 1987, 1989) that repeating another's words creates rapport on a metalevel: It is a ratification of the other's words, evidence of participation in the same universe of discourse.

8   Following the oral presentation of this paper at the Berkeley Linguistics Society in 1989, both Gary Holland and Michael Chandler pointed out that the prisoner may be heard as implying the second part of the guard's statement: "and you're a pile of shit."

9   This scene illustrates what Bateson (1972) calls "complementary schismogenesis": Each person's style drives the other into increasingly exaggerated forms of the opposing behavior. The more he refuses to tell her what's wrong, the more desperate she becomes to break through his silence. The more she pressures him to tell her, the more adamant he becomes about refusing to do so.

10   Some examples are given in Tannen (1990). Whereas the boys made such gestures as shooting each other with invisible guns, the girls made such gestures as reaching out and adjusting a friend's headband.

11   Elsewhere (Tannen 1990: 163–65) I discuss this example in more detail and note the contrast that the boys fight when they want to play, and the girl avoids disagreeing even when she in fact disagrees.

12   Another element of this epic, as Bly recounts it, is that Gilgamesh lures Enkidu away from the wild animals with which he had been happily living by sending a temple prostitute who throws off her clothes at the appropriate moment. She is simply the vehicle for the two men to get together. Much could be said about this aspect of the epic, but my purpose here is only to draw attention to the way the men use fighting as a means to friendship.

13   Sifianou (1992) independently observes the use of diminutives as solidarity markers in Greek conversation.

References

Bateson, Gregory. 1972. *Steps to an ecology of mind*. San Francisco: Chandler. Paperback: New York: Ballantine.

Becker, A. L. 1982. Beyond translation: Esthetics and language description. *Contemporary perceptions of language: Interdisciplinary dimensions*. Georgetown University Round Table on Languages and Linguistics 1982, ed. by Heidi Byrnes, 124–38. Washington, DC: Georgetown University Press.

Becker, A. L., and I Gusti Ngurah Oka. 1974. Person in Kawi: Exploration of an elementary semantic dimension. *Oceanic Linguistics* 13:229–55.

Beeman, William O. 1986. *Language, status, and power in Iran*. Bloomington: Indiana University Press.

Bellinger, David, and Jean Berko Gleason. 1982. Sex differences in parental directives to young children. *Sex Roles* 8:1123–39.

Bly, Robert. 1990. *Iron John: A book about men*. Reading, MA: Addison-Wesley.

Brown, Roger, and Albert Gilman. 1960. The pronouns of power and solidarity. *Style in language*, ed. by Thomas Sebeok, 253–76. Cambridge, MA: M.I.T. Press. (Chapter 9 in this volume.)

Brown, Penelope, and Stephen Levinson. [1978]1987. *Politeness: Some universals in language usage*. Cambridge: Cambridge University Press.

Byrnes, Heidi. 1986. Interactional style in German and American conversations. *Text* 6:2.189–206.

Campbell, Joseph. 1964. *The masks of god: Occidental mythology*. New York: Viking.

Coates, Jennifer. 1986. *Women, men and language*. London: Longman.

Conley, John M., William M. O'Barr, and E. Allen Lind. 1979. The power of language: Presentational style in the courtroom. *Duke Law Journal* 1978:1375–99.

Corsaro, William, and Thomas Rizzo. 1990. Disputes in the peer culture of American and Italian nursery school children. *Conflict talk*, ed. by Allen Grimshaw, 21–65. Cambridge: Cambridge University Press.

Dorval, Bruce (ed.). 1990. *Conversational coherence and its development*. Norwood, NJ: Ablex.

Duranti, Alessandro, and Donald Brenneis (eds.). 1986. The audience as co-author. Special issue of *Text* 6:3.239–47.

Erickson, Frederick. 1986. Listening and speaking. *Languages and linguistics: The interdependence of theory, data, and application*. Georgetown University Round Table on Languages and Linguistics 1985, ed. by Deborah Tannen, 294–319. Washington, DC: Georgetown University Press.

Erickson, Frederick, and Jeffrey Shultz. 1982. *The counselor as gatekeeper: Social interaction in interviews*. New York: Academic Press.

Fasold, Ralph W. 1990. *The sociolinguistics of language*. Oxford: Basil Blackwell.

Frank, Jane. 1988. Communicating "by pairs": Agreeing and disagreeing among married couples. Unpublished ms., Georgetown University.

Friedrich, Paul. 1972. Social context and semantic feature: The Russian pronominal usage. *Directions in sociolinguistics*, ed. by John J. Gumperz and Dell Hymes, 270–300. New York: Holt, Rinehart, and Winston. Reprinted: Oxford: Basil Blackwell.

Gleason, Jean Berko. 1987. Sex differences in parent–child interaction. *Language, gender, and sex in comparative perspective*, ed. by Susan U. Philips, Susan Steele, and Christine Tanz, 189–99. Cambridge: Cambridge University Press.

Gumperz, John J. 1982. *Discourse strategies*. Cambridge: Cambridge University Press.

Hughes, Linda A. 1988. "But that's not *really* mean": Competing in a cooperative mode. *Sex Roles* 19:11/12.669–687.

James, Deborah, and Sandra Clarke. 1993. Women, men and interruptions: A critical review. *Gender and conversational interaction*, ed. by Deborah Tannen, 231–80. New York and Oxford: Oxford University Press.

James, Deborah, and Janice Drakich. 1993. Understanding gender differences in amount of talk. *Gender and conversational interaction*, ed. by Deborah Tannen. 281–312. New York and Oxford: Oxford University Press.

Jong, Erica. 1973. *Fear of flying*. New York: Holt, Rinehart and Winston.

Kakava, Christina. 1989. Argumentative conversation in a Greek family. Paper presented at the Annual Meeting of the Linguistic Society of America, Washington, DC.

Keenan, Elinor. 1974. Norm-makers, norm-breakers: Uses of speech by men and women in a Malagasy community. *Explorations in the ethnography of speaking*, ed. by Richard Bauman and Joel Sherzer, 125–43. Cambridge: Cambridge University Press.

Klagsbrun, Francine. 1992. *Mixed feelings: Love, hate, rivalry, and reconciliation among brothers and sisters*. New York: Bantam.

Komarovsky, Mirra. 1962. *Blue-collar marriage*. New York: Vintage.

Lakoff, Robin. 1975. *Language and woman's place*. New York: Harper and Row.

Maltz, Daniel N., and Ruth A. Borker. 1982. A cultural approach to male–female miscommunication. *Language and social identity*, ed. by John J. Gumperz, 196–216. Cambridge: Cambridge University Press.

McDermott, R. P., and Henry Tylbor. 1983. On the necessity of collusion in conversation. *Text* 3:3.277–97.

Mead, Margaret. 1977. End linkage: A tool for cross-cultural analysis. *About Bateson*, ed. by John Brockman, 171–231. New York: Dutton.

Norman, Michael. 1990. *These good men: Friendships forged from war*. New York: Crown.

Ong, Walter J. 1981. *Fighting for life: Contest, sexuality, and consciousness*. Ithaca, NY: Cornell University Press; Amherst: University of Massachusetts Press.

Paules, Greta Foff. 1991. *Dishing it out: Power and resistance among waitresses in a New Jersey restaurant*. Philadelphia: Temple University Press.

Philips, Susan Urmston. 1983. *The invisible culture: Communication in classroom and community on the Warm Springs Indian reservation*. New York and London: Longman. Reprinted: Prospect Heights, IL: Waveland Press.

Pinter, Harold. 1988. *Mountain language*. New York: Grove Press.

Sattel, Jack W. 1983. Men, inexpressiveness, and power. *Language, gender and society*, ed. by Barrie Thorne, Cheris Kramarae, and Nancy Henley, 119–24. Rowley, MA: Newbury House.

Schegloff, Emanuel. 1982. Discourse as an interactional achievement: Some uses of 'uhuh' and other things that come between sentences. *Analyzing discourse: Text and talk*. Georgetown University Round Table on Languages and Linguistics 1981, ed. by Deborah Tannen, 71–93. Washington, DC: Georgetown University Press.

Schegloff, Emanuel. 1988. Discourse as an interactional achievement II: An exercise in conversation analysis. *Linguistics in context: Connecting observation and understanding*, ed. by Deborah Tannen, 135–58. Norwood, NJ: Ablex.

Schiffrin, Deborah. 1984. Jewish argument as sociability. *Language in Society* 13:3.311–35.

Scollon, Ron. 1985. The machine stops: Silence in the metaphor of malfunction. *Perspectives on silence*, ed. by Deborah Tannen and Muriel Saville-Troike, 21–30. Norwood, NJ: Ablex.

Scollon, Ron, and Suzanne B. K. Scollon, 1981. *Narrative, literacy and face in interethnic communication*. Norwood, NJ: Ablex.

Shuy, Roger W. 1982. Topic as the unit of analysis in a criminal law case. *Analyzing discourse: Text and talk*. Georgetown University Round Table on Languages and Linguistics 1981, ed. by Deborah Tannen, 113–26. Washington, DC: Georgetown University Press.

Sifianou, Maria. 1992. The use of diminutives in expressing politeness: Modern Greek versus English. *Journal of Pragmatics* 17:2.155–73.

Spender, Dale. 1980. *Man made language*. London: Routledge and Kegan Paul.

Tannen, Deborah. 1981. Indirectness in discourse: Ethnicity as conversational style. *Discourse Processes* 4:3.221–38.

Tannen, Deborah. 1984. *Conversational style: Analyzing talk among friends*. Norwood, NJ: Ablex.

Tannen, Deborah. 1985. Silence: Anything but. *Perspectives on silence*, ed. by Deborah Tannen and Muriel Saville-Troike, 93–111. Norwood, NJ: Ablex.

Tannen, Deborah. 1986. *That's not what I meant!: How conversational style makes or breaks your relations with others*. New York: William Morrow. Paperback: Ballantine.

Tannen, Deborah. 1987. Repetition in conversation: Toward a poetics of talk. *Language* 63:3.574–605.

Tannen, Deborah. 1989. *Talking voices: Repetition, dialogue and imagery in conversational discourse*. Cambridge: Cambridge University Press.

Tannen, Deborah. 1990. *You just don't understand: Women and men in conversation*. New York: William Morrow. Paperback: Ballantine.

Tannen, Deborah. 1994. *Gender and Discourse*. New York: Oxford University Press.

Tannen, Deborah, and Christina Kakava. 1992. Power and solidarity in Modern Greek conversation: Disagreeing to agree. *Journal of Modern Greek Studies* 10:12–29.

Watanabe, Suwako. 1993. Cultural differences in framing: American and Japanese group discussions, 176–208. *Framing in discourse*, ed. by Deborah Tannen. New York and Oxford: Oxford University Press.

Wolfowitz, Clare. 1991. *Language style and social space: Stylistic choice in Suriname Javanese*. Urbana and Chicago: University of Illinois Press.

West, Candace, and Don H. Zimmerman. 1983. Small insults: A study of interruptions in cross-sex conversations between unacquainted persons. *Language, gender and society*, ed. by Barrie Thorne, Cheris Kramarae, and Nancy Henley, 103–17. Rowley, MA: Newbury House.

Yamada, Haru. 1992. *American and Japanese business discourse: A comparison of interactional styles*. Norwood, NJ: Ablex.

Discussion Questions

1. Compare how two of the following sources use language to describe women and men. What differences do you notice? Why do you think these differences exist?
    Sports section of the newspaper
    Women's magazine
    Men's magazine
    Entertainment section of the newspaper
2. Lakoff discusses the differences in how parents treat little girls and boys and how the children are socialized differently. Observe how various parents interact with their small children. Do you notice any gender differences in how mothers and fathers treat boys and girls? Do you notice any differences in the parents' expectations for the behavior or speech of girls vs. boys?
3. Greetings often vary depending on our closeness or distance from the person we are greeting. Imagine you have just returned from a trip: how would you greet each of the following people?
    your mother
    your boss
    your sibling
    your best friend
    a co-worker or classmate.
    Why do the differences exist? Considering Tannen's discussion of power and solidarity, analyze your own strategies in the above greetings.
4. Compare your answers to question 3 with those of a classmate of the opposite sex. What differences do you notice in how you both greet people?
5. Tannen describes her analysis of the overlapping or interruptions in speech during a Thanksgiving dinner. Monitor the speech of your own family conversations, possibly at mealtimes. Who interrupts more and when? Are the interruptions supportive or are they viewed as dominating the conversation and taking the floor?
6. As Tannen points out, the use of silence and disagreement in conversation can be very different in different cultures. Responding or disagreeing may even be seen as "talking back." Interview someone who speaks another language to find out how they would react in the following situations. Do they believe there are any gender differences in how someone would react in their language to these situations?
    a) Your father wants you to come to the store with him, but you really wanted to go out with your friend.
    b) Your boss tells you to finish a job in a way that you think will waste your time.
    c) Your best friend has just gotten a haircut that you think looks terrible.
    Compare their reactions to your own. Discuss your findings with your classmates.

Part V

Language and Variation

Introduction

Sociolinguistics has deep roots in regional dialectology, or linguistic geography, the study of how the same language shows variation from region to region, as Calvet and Shuy both discuss in their chapters. We all know that an English lorry is the same as an American truck and that some people fry their eggs in a frying pan while others use a skillet. One is not better than another; they are just different. Words vary in pronunciation as well. In London *cot* and *caught* sound different, in Pittsburgh they are pronounced the same. When the radio announcer said "Would you like to hear some bar talk?" it sounded like a peculiar question, but he had just talked about interviewing a Russian conductor in New York so it was within the expectancies of Russian behavior; it turned out that the announcer was about to play some Bela Bartok. Such differences are at times mildly amusing but without the stigmatizing effects of social dialect differences. This is not to say that regional differences cannot at times acquire symbolic significance: the Old Testament has an early account (from warfare in days without uniforms) of testing group membership by the pronunciation of the word Shibboleth – if the answer was Sibboleth you belonged to the enemy and lost your life (Judges 12: 4–6).

Regional dialectology or dialect geography had long been part of the study of language change, of historical linguistics, and used many of its basic concepts, like family tree, phonemic split, comparative method of reconstruction, etc. (Wardhaugh, 1998: 131) as well as its research methodology. Old informants from rural and often isolated areas were sought out to respond to word list surveys, and no one really knew how representative and typical of the language variety their responses were. Cities were avoided for their linguistic heterogeneity, and variants were dismissed as occurring in free variation. These methodological weaknesses were recognized, and the Labovian school, variationist theory, quantitative sociolinguistics (there are many labels for the same body of work) set out to rectify these shortcomings.

Noam Chomsky's publications of *Syntactic Structures* (1957) and *Aspects of a Theory of Syntax* (1965) were held to bring about a revolution in linguistics, often cited as an exemplar of a classic paradigm shift (Kuhn 1970). While that revolution may now have come to an end (Searle 2002), the publication from that same time of William Labov's dissertation *The Social Stratification of English in New York City* still has a profound and lasting influence on the study of language. Labov's major point was to document structured heterogeneity, the notion that variability in language can be shown to be structured. Earlier linguists had believed that only uniform states could be structured and had dismissed language variation as random, in free variation. Labov and variationist linguists collected naturalistic speech from real speakers, tape-recorded and transcribed, and insisted on accounting for all the data – in stark contrast to Chomsky's native speaker intuition of all and only the grammatical sentences of English and the dismissal of linguistic performance as degenerate data. While some sociolinguists hold that Labovian variationist linguistics is the very heart of sociolinguistics, Labov himself considers it simply linguistics: "I have resisted the term sociolinguistics for many years, since it implies that there can be a successful linguistic theory or practice which is not social" (1972: xiii). Milroy and Milroy make the point that Labov is basically concerned with linguistic description and change; his major theoretical contributions may well have been to historical linguistics: "The key difference between the variationist paradigm and other empirical approaches [see parts II and III] is that the former is focused on understanding variation and change in the structural parts of *language* rather than the behavior of *speakers* or the nature of speaker interaction" (Milroy and Milroy, 1997: 48; see their excellent discussion on "Varieties and variation").

Labov's contributions are ubiquitous in anthologies and easily accessible; the selection here is a chapter from a hard-to-find, early work for the National Council of Teachers of English, where he spells out in plain language some of his working principles. Basically, variationist linguistics seeks to correlate a linguistic variable with externally preselected social variables, like age, gender, race or ethnicity, and social class and networks in order to identify and describe structured heterogeneity of language, usually within a monolingual speech community. Correlations do not indicate causality, and Labov has been much criticized for his interpretations of his data, especially of his famous cross-over line of lower-middle-class women, labeled hypercorrection, as indicative of women's higher linguistic insecurity, higher yearnings for upward social mobility, etc. (see Cameron 1990; Freeman and McElhinney 1996).

The other two chapters in this section also approach the topic of language and variation, if from two very different perspectives. Walt Wolfram asks the surprising question of how vernaculars, i.e. non-standardized dialects, become normed, how their speakers acquire a sense of *appropriate* language forms and usage. He answers this question through a comparative analysis of two speech communities, examining African-American Vernacular English and Lumbee Native American Indian English. Barbara Johnstone approaches language variation from the viewpoint of the "linguistic individual" (1996, 2000): "For a growing number of linguists, speakers and their utterances are replacing linguistic systems as the object of study. These linguists see language as residing in talk. Reluctant to abstract away from our actual experience of language – the experience of seeing people, not language, do things and possess linguistic attributes – they ask why actual, situated utterances take the shapes they do, aiming thereby to display the processes by which people create their own identities and communicate with others. In this view, the social is an artifact of the individual" (1996: 19).

References

Cameron, Deborah. 1990. "Demythologizing sociolinguistics: Why language does not reflect society," in John E. Joseph and Talbot J. Taylor (eds.), *Ideologies of Language*. London: Routledge.

Chomsky, Noam. 1957. *Syntactic Structures*. The Hague: Mouton.

Chomsky, Noam. 1965. *Aspects of the Theory of Syntax*. Cambridge, MA: MIT Press.

Freeman, Rebecca and Bonnie McElhinney. 1996. "Language and gender," in Sandra Lee McKay and Nancy H. Hornberger (eds.), *Sociolinguistics and Language Teaching*. Cambridge: Cambridge University Press.

Johnstone, Barbara. 1996. *The Linguistic Individual: Self-Expression in Language and Linguistics*. Oxford: Oxford University Press.

Johnstone, Barbara. 2000. "The individual voice in language," *Annual Review of Anthropology*, 29: 405–24.

Labov, William. 1972. *Sociolinguistic Patterns*. Philadelphia: University of Pennsylvania Press.

Kuhn, Thomas S. 1970. *The Structure of Scientific Revolutions*. Chicago: University of Chicago Press.

Milroy, James and Lesley Milroy. 1997. "Varieties and Variation," in Florian Coulmas (ed.), *Handbook of Sociolinguistics*. Oxford: Blackwell.

Searle, John R. 2002. "The end of the revolution," *The New York Review of Books*, XLIX: 3, 33–6.

Wardhaugh, Ronald. 1998. *An Introduction to Sociolinguistics*. Oxford: Blackwell.

Further Reading

Chambers, J. K. and Peter Trudgill. 1980. *Dialectology*. Cambridge: Cambridge University Press.

Cheshire, Jenny (ed.). 1991. *English Around the World: Sociolinguistic Perspectives*. Cambridge: Cambridge University Press.

Labov, William. 2001. *Principles of Linguistic Change: Social Factors*. Oxford: Blackwell. See the bibliography for further readings.

Milroy, James. 1990. *Linguistic Variation and Change*. Oxford: Blackwell.

Milroy, James. 1992. *Linguistic Variation and Change: On the Historical Sociolinguistics of English*. Oxford: Blackwell.

Milroy, James and Lesley Milroy. 1978. "Belfast: Change and variation in an urban vernacular," in Peter Trudgill (ed.), *Sociolinguistic Patterns in British English*. London: Arnold.

Rickford, John R. 1999. *African American Vernacular English*. Oxford: Blackwell.

Trudgill, Peter. 1974. *The Social Differentiation of English in Norwich*. Cambridge: Cambridge University Press.

Trudgill, Peter. 1986. *Dialects in Contact*. Oxford: Blackwell.

13

Some Sociolinguistic Principles

William Labov

Style shifting. One of the fundamental principles of sociolinguistic investigation might simply be stated as *There are no single-style speakers.* By this we mean that every speaker will show some variation in phonological and syntactic rules according to the immediate context in which he is speaking. We can demonstrate that such stylistic shifts are determined by (a) the relations of the speaker, addressee, and audience, and particularly the relations of power or solidarity among them; (b) the wider social context or "domain": school, job, home, neighborhood, church; (c) the topic. One must add of course that the stylistic range and competence of the speaker may vary greatly. Children may have a very narrow range in both the choices open to them and the social contexts they respond to. Old men often show a narrow range in that their motivation for style shifting disappears along with their concern for power relationships.

We apply the principle stated above in a very concrete way when carrying out research with face-to-face interviews. We do not judge the absolute stylistic level of the speaker by some absolute standard of "casualness." We know that, as long as we are asking questions and receiving answers, the speaker is using a relatively "careful" or "consultative" style, and that he possesses a more "casual" or intimate style with which he argues with his friends or quarrels with his family. There are techniques for obtaining casual speech in an interview situation, but the soundest approach is to observe the speaker interacting with the peers who control his speech in everyday life when the observer is not there.

Well-developed social variables show a systematic range of style shifting which is correlated to the amount of attention paid to speech. We can easily observe such style shifting in certain long-standing variables which are common to almost all dialects of English. The *th* of *thing* and *that* can appear as a smooth fricative "*th*" sound, the standard variant; as a "t"-like sound lightly or strongly articulated; as a combination of these two; or as a zero as in *Gimme 'at.* For most Americans, the proportions of these forms are nicely blended and graded for each stylistic level – at different absolute levels for different social groups and different regions. Similarly, the alternation of *-ing* and *-in'* in unstressed syllables is a systematic stylistic variable for most Americans – again at different levels for different classes and regions.

At one time, the dialect areas of the eastern United States were sharply divided into *r*-less and *r*-pronouncing areas, according to whether consonantal *r* is pronounced in words like *car* and *card.* But in the last two decades the *r*-pronunciation of "general American" has become accepted as the standard of broadcast networks and of careful middle class pronunciation almost everywhere. As a result, we find that the new "prestige" pronunciation of *r* in final and preconsonantal position has become a sociolinguistic variable in the older *r*-less areas. Almost all younger and middle-aged speakers will show some style shifting with *r*, so that in the more formal styles they will use more *r* and in casual speech practically none at all.

The grammatical variables that show style shifting are quite well known in general, though we usually lack the exact knowledge of where and when these features are used to signal change of style. Some are well-established stereotypes, like *ain't*. Although dictionaries may vary in the way they label *ain't*, most native speakers are quite clear in their sociolinguistic approach to this word – in their social *evaluation* of the form. To make the point clear, imagine a community in which *ain't* is the formal style and in which people correct *isn't* to *ain't* when they are careful. Such a community would be very odd indeed – obviously not a part of the same American speech community in which we all live.

The "double negative" or negative concord is an important stylistic marker; it allows nonstandard speakers to express negatives in a particularly emphatic fashion by reduplicating the negative forms (*Nobody don't know about that*) and at the same time register their adherence to the nonstandard form which is stylistically opposed to the standard (*Nobody knows anything about that*).

The passive has two forms in English, which are closely allied but perhaps not equivalent in meaning. If we ask "What happened to him?" the answer can be "He got run over" or "He was run over." The colloquial form is clearly the former; nonstandard dialects depend almost entirely upon this *got*-passive, to the exclusion of the *be*-passive. As a result, the *be*-passive has acquired a standard, rather careful flavor which it would not have if there were no opposing forms.

In all these examples, we can easily demonstrate the meaning of the stylistic alternation by observing the direction of correction in false starts. In almost every interview, one will find speakers making corrections like "Nobody told him noth– anything about it." No matter how rare or how common such corrections may be, we find that they uniformly run in the same direction, since the more formal style is associated with a mental set in which greater attention is paid to speech and the less formal style with a casual and spontaneous use of language in which the minimum attention is given to the speech process.

It should be clear that the various sociolinguistic variables found in American English are rarely confined to one or the other dialect but usually wander from one end of the stylistic range to the other. There are some which are never used in standard literary or formal English; but as a rule we find that dialects differ primarily in the way in which they use these variables – that is, in the distribution of frequencies along the stylistic range. It would follow that writing a different grammar for each dialect is a wasteful and unnatural procedure; rather, it seems likely that the various dialects of English can be organized within a single pandialectal grammar. However, there are cases in which dialects differ sharply and abruptly from each other and use forms which appear to be meaningless or contradictory to those from other communities; this is particularly common with nonstandard Negro English, as we shall see, and in a number of ways this dialect appears to be a different "system." It may be that single grammars can only be written for dialects whose speakers are actually in contact with each other – dialects which are mutually intelligible in the clearest sense. This problem has not been resolved, but in general we can say that few sociolinguistic variables are confined to single dialects.

So far we have been speaking of monolingual style shifting. On the face of it, the shift to another language in bilingual situations seems to be a radically different step. Bilingual speakers do not think of Spanish as another "style" of English. However, there is a functional relation between different languages and different styles which cannot be overlooked. Research in stable bilingual communities indicates that one natural unit of study may be the "linguistic repertoire" of each speaker rather than individual languages; such repertoires may include a wide range of styles in one language and a narrow range in another. The sum total of styles and languages occupies a given range of situations or contexts in which the person interacts with others – linguistic "domains" such as home, neighborhood, job, church, store, school, and newspaper. A monolingual individual uses and understands a wide range of styles which are specialized for various domains; bilingual individuals rarely use both languages over all domains but rather show a comparable specialization of languages and uneven distribution of styles within these languages. When we encounter an individual in one particular domain, at home or in school, we can often tell from the range of style shifting in what domain he uses that language. For example, a first-generation Spanish-English bilingual may use a fairly formal Spanish – learned at school – in interviews; he may use a very colloquial Spanish at home; but in English he may have only a nonstandard dialect which he learned on the streets. A second-generation Spanish speaker may reverse this pattern, with Spanish confined to a very informal pattern used at home.

1   The Social Stratification of Language

In 1948, John Kenyon introduced the distinction between *cultural levels* and *functional varieties* of English. He argued that we should recognize a colloquial standard and a formal nonstandard, as well as a formal standard and a colloquial nonstandard – in other words, that style and class stratification of language are actually independent. This would seem to be a common sense distinction, and it would obviously be useful and helpful if language were organized in this manner. Then, no matter how casually an educated person spoke, we would have no trouble in recognizing him as an educated person.

It is remarkable that this is not the case. In actual fact, the same variables which are used in style shifting also distinguish cultural or social levels of English. This is so for stable phonological variables such as *th-* and *-ing*; for such incoming prestige forms as *-r*; for the grammatical variables such as pronominal apposition, double negative, or even the use of *ain't*. If we plot the average values of these phonological variables for *both* style and social levels, we find such regular patterns as figures 1 and 2 for *th-* and *-ing*. The vertical axis is the proportion of the nonstandard variant used; the horizontal axis shows various styles, from casual speech to the reading of isolated words. Each point on this graph shows the average value of a group of speakers – a socioeconomic class in this case – in a particular style, and the lines connect all the values of (th) and (ing) for a given social group. Note that at each style there is social stratification: whether we are listening to casual speech or to reading, it is clear that the social background of

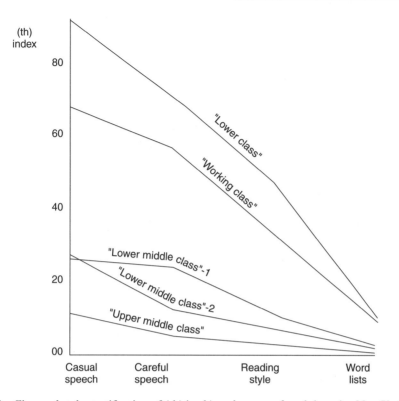

Figure 1 Class and style stratification of (th) in *thing, three,* etc., for adult native New York City speakers

the speaker is reflected in his use of these variables. But each group also shows regular style shifting in the same direction; although these social groups are very different in one sense, they are all very similar in another sense: they all *use* the variable in the same way. Members of a speech community are not aware of this fact; their experience is limited to (a) the whole range of speech styles used by their own family and friends, and (b) the speech of a wide range of social classes in one or two styles. Thus the teacher hears the differences between middle class and working class children in classroom recitation but does not follow his students home and hear them at their ease among their own friends. He does not realize how similar the students are to him – how they fit into the same sociolinguistic structure which governs his own behavior. Instead, teachers like most of us tend to perceive the speech of others categorically: John always says *dese* and *dose*, but Henry never does. Few teachers are able to perceive that they themselves use the same nonstandard forms in their most casual speech; as we will see, almost everyone hears himself as using the norm which guides his speech production in most formal styles. In a word, the differences between speakers are more obvious than their similarities.

Thus we see that the same linguistic features are used to register style shifting and social stratification – functional varieties *and* cultural levels. This situation is not unique to English. It is generally the case, even in the languages of Southeast Asia which have

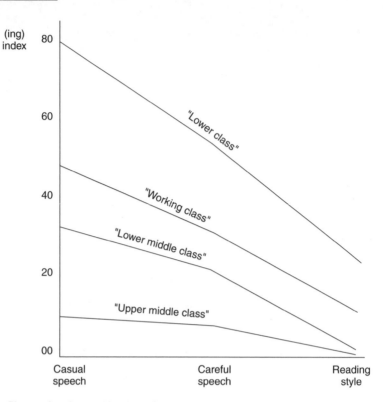

Figure 2 Class and style stratification of (ing) in *working, living*, etc., for white New York City adults

extremely complex systems for registering respect. True enough, there are general features of articulation and voice quality which tend to mark the educated speaker for us no matter what linguistic forms he uses, but such qualities are neither universal nor highly reliable. It may seem astonishing that sociolinguistic structure provides so much chance for confusion; given this interlocking of style and class markers, there is considerable opportunity for misjudging the background or attitude of strangers. Yet it is also logical that languages should develop in this fashion, for each group models its formal style on the speech behavior of those groups one or two steps above it in the social scale. The secretary patterns her formal speech on that of her boss, but the working man in the shop seldom hears the language of front-office people directly; his chief model for formal communication seems to be the speech of office clerks and secretaries. Unless the language shows extraordinarily strong prohibitions against "mixing levels," we will then see such regular patterns of shifting as in figures 1 and 2. Discrete stylistic levels or codes do exist in some societies, and even in our own – the archaic English of the King James Bible, for example, has a fairly well-established set of co-occurrence rules which are used productively in sermons but not elsewhere in standard English. Such a co-occurrence rule governs the agreement of the second singular *thou* with the verb form *hast*: one cannot switch from *you have* to *you hast* or *thou have*; instead both changes must be made together. One can also argue that lexical choices are determined by similar strict co-occurrence rules, that it is equally a violation to say *Thou hast been swell to me, Lord*. But this violation breaks a different kind of rule (termed a "Type II" rule below); such violations *do* occur, and they can be interpreted.

So far, we have been considering stable sociolinguistic situations. Wherever the language is in the process of change, there is a tendency for the new forms to be adopted first by one social group and only gradually spread to others. The social value attributed to these forms is derived from the values associated with the groups which introduced them. Thus hip slang such as *dig* and *boss* introduced from the Negro ghettos has one type of prestige and is used most frequently in the most casual speech. Spelling pronunciations such as *often* with a *t* or *calm* with an *l* are introduced by lower middle class speakers and gradually spread to higher and lower social groups. As these linguistic changes mature, the new feature normally becomes subject to an overt social stigma, and the variable develops a characteristic pattern of style shifting, with the pattern displayed in figures 1 and 2. When the change goes to completion, the possibility of choice disappears, and with it the social value associated with the item. Today, the spelling pronunciation of *recognize* with a *g* is standard, and it has lost the over-careful, insecure character it must have had when it was first introduced. But incoming pronunciations such as *"perculator"* or *"esculator"* now stand at the other end of the spectrum. At any one time, social groups will differ in their attitude towards particular linguistic variables in process of change. For some, there is no problem in *It's I* vs. *It's me*; *Whom do you want?* vs. *Who do you want?*; or *He does it as he should* vs. *He does it like he should*. For others, these are matters of paralyzing concern. The norms for pronouncing *vase* and *aunt* are now shifting, so that many people are baffled and embarrassed when they encounter these words in a text to be read aloud. Faced with two conflicting norms, speakers often find a meaningful use for both. As one woman said in an interview, "These little ones are my *vayses* [rhyming with mazes]; but these big ones are my *vahses* [rhyming with Roz's]."

The sharpness of the social stratification of language seems to vary with the degree of social mobility which exists in society as a whole. In London and its environs, we find that the use of initial *f-* for standard voiceless *th-* is a uniform characteristic of working class speech, but it is not heard in the standard speech of adults. Moreover, in their most careful, "posh" pronunciation, many working class speakers say *fings, free* and *frow* for *things, three* and *throw*. In the United States, we do not find such sharp stratification among white working class speakers: stops are common enough in *tings, tree*, and *trow*. But, as figures 1 and 2 show, even the lowest ranking social group has no difficulty in saying *things, three* and *throw* when reading word lists. We do find sharp social stratification between white and Negro speakers in the United States, where a pattern of caste rather than class differentiation has prevailed for a few centuries. We then can observe such differentiation between ethnic groups as the nonstandard Negro English difficulty with *-sps, -sts, -sks* clusters. Many Negro speakers literally cannot say *wasps, lists* or *desks*: these plurals are normally *wasses, lisses* and *desses*, forms which are quite unknown in the surrounding white community.

The ethnic stratification of society is thus reflected in linguistic patterns – sometimes partly independent of socioeconomic factors, sometimes closely interlocked with them. In New York City, the Jewish and Italian populations differ from each other in subtle ways as they both follow the general evolution of the vernacular. The Italians are far more forward in their raising of the vowel of *bad* to equal that of *beard*; the Jews, on the other hand, are somewhat more advanced in their tendency to raise the vowel of *law* to that of *lure*. In Phoenix, Arizona, the ongoing linguistic change which merges *cot* and *caught*, *Don* and *dawn*, is much more characteristic of the Anglo population than of the Negroes and Mexicans: the latter groups normally preserve this distinction between short *o* and long open *o*. In most urban ghetto areas, we find that the southern characteristic of merging *i* and *e* before nasals has become generalized among the Negro population, so that Negroes of all geographic backgrounds neither make nor hear the difference between *pin* and *pen*, *Jim* and *gem*, while the surrounding white population still preserves the distinction. This is one of many examples of a feature of a southern regional dialect transported to an urban setting to become an ethnic and class marker.

When the ethnic group still preserves a foreign language for at least one social domain, we find clear traces of it in their English. Some foreign accents have high prestige in the United States – French is the most outstanding example – but usually not if there is a large immigrant group which speaks this language. Even where bilingual speakers use a fairly native English, they are limited in their stylistic range. Thus many who have learned English as a second language in their late teens will show an excellent, even native, careful style but no casual or intimate style at all.

Breaks in social communication between groups in society are reflected in the failure of certain linguistic items to cross the barrier between the groups. While certain kinds of slang pass freely and continuously from the Negro community into the white community, other grammatical and lexical items remain fixed, and we can witness *pluralistic ignorance* where neither perceives the actual situation: one group knows nothing about the form at all, and the other assumes that its use is quite general. Negro speakers have traditionally used *mother wit* as the equivalent of *common sense*, but no white speakers know this term except as an archaic and literary form. The Negro vernacular uses dummy *it* for *there*, saying *it's a difference*; *it's no one there*; *it's a policeman at the door*; but despite their long contact with Negro speakers in person and in dialect literature, the neighboring white speakers know nothing of this pattern.

The regular pattern of figures 1 and 2 is that of a stable sociolinguistic marker. When the marker is in the process of change, we see patterns more like that of figure 3, which shows the incoming prestige marker of *r*-pronunciation. The steepness of the lines is not the same for all groups: in particular, we observe that the lower middle class shows the sharpest shift towards *r*-pronunciation in formal styles, going even beyond the highest social group in this respect. This "hypercorrect" behavior, or "going one better," is quite characteristic of second-ranking groups in many communities. We find similar behavior in the *r*-pronunciation of such distant areas as Hillsboro, North Carolina, as well as New York City, and in overcorrect grammatical behavior as well as in pronunciation. The sharpness of such style shifting is a direct reflection of the degree of linguistic insecurity felt by a particular group: that is, the tendency to shift away from the natural pattern of casual speech is proportionate to the recognition of an external standard of correctness. We can measure the strength of such feelings by various tests which reflect the extent to which people will say "*That* is the correct way to say it, but *this* is the way *I* say it." Since American school teachers have traditionally been drawn from the lower middle class, the strong tendency towards hypercorrect behavior

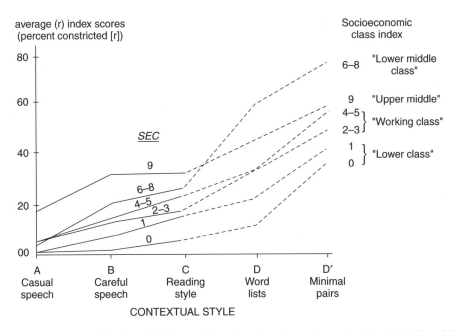

average (r) index scores
(percent constricted [r])

Socioeconomic
class index

Figure 3 Class stratification of (r) in *guard*, *car*, *beer*, *beard*, etc., for native New York City adults

which we see here must be reckoned with in designing any educational program. Along with linguistic insecurity and extreme range of style shifting, one encounters an extreme intolerance towards other dialects. For decades, educational leaders have asked teachers to regard the child's nonstandard language as "another" way of speaking, to recognize it as simply "different" from school language rather than condemning it as sloppy or illogical. But many teachers find it difficult to adopt this attitude, since they recognize in the child's language (perhaps unconsciously) the very pattern which they so sharply correct in themselves. It is extraordinary to witness how violently some people will express themselves on such apparently trivial points as the height of the vowel in *bad*. It is not uncommon for people to stigmatize a certain pronunciation by saying, "I would never hire a person who talked like *that*!" Such extreme reactions are quite common in our schools, and all teachers should be on the watch for them to the extent that they interfere with the process of education itself.

2 Types of Linguistic Rules

In the last few pages, we have been concerned with a kind of linguistic behavior which has seldom been studied in the past: variable rules. There is no fixed instruction in English as to how we must pronounce the *th* of *then* in any given case; instead, there are several choices. But these choices are not in free variation. There is an important variable rule which tells us that those who pronounce *then* with a *d*- sound with a certain frequency are to be stigmatized as "uneducated" or "lower class." Anyone who does not know this rule is not a very good speaker of English. Rules of this sort – which we will designate Type III – are quite common in English. Despite the fact that they cannot be violated with any given pronunciation of a word, they are an important part of our linguistic competence.

The kinds of rules which are generally taught in school are a different sort. They state "Do not do this at all!" For example, "Don't say *ain't*!" But there is an added provision, usually unstated: "unless you want to fail" or "unless you want to be known as stupid or uneducated." These rules are cast in categorical form, but they are what we might call *semi-categorical*: they are written in the full knowledge that people do indeed make violations, and that one can interpret such violations. There is a ready-made label or interpretation which goes with the breaking of the rules. This labeling is not, of course, a simple matter, because some utterances of *ain't* are taken as jokes, others as slips, and still others as evidence of habitual violations. But in the school situation, each utterance of *ain't* is marked as a violation and reprimanded as such. We may call such rules Type II rules. When Type II rules are overtly violated, the violation is rare enough to be worth reporting: such violations are thus *reportable*, and an appropriate response to the report is "He did?" "He did say that?" If a school teacher were to use *ain't* in the middle of a grammar class, it would indeed make a story worth telling. It is common to find Type II rules at the beginning or at the end of a linguistic change in progress, where the form is rare enough to be noticed whenever it occurs. The broad *a* pronunciation of *aunt* and *bath* is almost extinct as a prestige form among white speakers in the middle Atlantic states. "Bahth" and "ahnt" survive as rare examples of adherence to an older prestige pattern and are frequently stigmatized as false attempts to impress the listener. They survive in another way which is characteristic of Type II rules: "I'm going to the bahthroom," originally taken as a humorous play on the notion of falsely impressing someone, now is becoming fossilized into a common and almost unconscious form of ritualized humor.

Most linguistic rules are of an altogether different character. They are automatic, deep-seated patterns of behavior which are not consciously recognized and are never violated. Rules for contraction of *is* form one such set of automatic rules among countless others, which we may call Type I. No one is taught in school the very complex conditions under which one can, if desired, contract *is* to *'s*: that one can do so in *He's here*, but not **Here he's*; in *He's ready*, but not **What he's is smart*. Such automatic rules exist in all forms of social behavior, but they are extremely hard to detect simply because they are never violated and one never thinks about them at all. For example, in asking someone for directions, one thinks about who to ask, and what polite forms to use, but never about whether one should introduce oneself. "Hello, I'm Bill Labov, where's Grand Central Station?" is a violation which never occurs. If one artificially constructs such a violation, people are simply confused; they cannot interpret it, and the most appropriate response is "Wha'?" Linguists have been discovering and formulating such Type I rules for many centuries, and most of our studies are concerned with them. They form the very backbone of linguistic structure; without them we would find it very difficult to speak at all. If English teachers indeed had the job of "teaching the child the Type I rules of English," it would be incredibly more difficult than the job which they actually do face, which is to instruct children in a small number of Type II rules and some basic vocabulary for talking about language. We can summarize this discussion of rule typology by the following chart:

Rule type	How often rule operates	Violations	Response to violations	Example
I	100%	None in natural speech	Wha'?	Rules for when one can contract *is*: "He is" vs. *"He's."
II	95–99%	Rare and reportable	He did?	"Why you ain't never giving me no A's?"
III	5–95%	None by definition and unreportable	So what?	"He sure got an A" vs. "He surely got an A."

3 Linguistic Norms

We have seen that sociolinguistic behavior shows social differentiation. Such behavior reflects a set of norms, beliefs, or subjective attitudes towards particular features and language in general. The regular stratification of behavior shown above has a subjective counterpart: uniform linguistic norms, in which all speakers of the community agree in their evaluation of the feature in question. In our society, these values are middle class norms, since the middle class is the dominant group in school, business, and mass communications. Certain linguistic forms, like the fricative *th* in *then*, the *-ing* in *working*, the *-ly* in *surely*, are considered more suitable for people holding certain kinds of jobs. One can set up a scale of jobs requiring more or less excellent speech which will obtain very general agreement, such as television announcer, school teacher, office manager, salesman, post office clerk, foreman, factory worker. The converse values are equally uniform: that nonstandard language like the *d-* in *den* (*then*), the *-in'* in *workin'* or the *never* in *Nobody never knows* are characteristic of "tough" guys who not only like to fight but come out on top. Those familiar with street culture know that there is in fact little correlation between toughness and the use of nonstandard language, but the stereotype seems to be well established. The fact that both values – job suitability and toughness – are clearest in the reports of middle class speakers suggests to us that both sets are in fact taught in school. If the teacher does in fact identify nonstandard language with the tougher elements in school, it seems inevitable that he will convey this notion to the students in the class and so gradually reinforce the values already present in the mass media.

The stability and uniformity of social values in respect to language are quite extraordinary. Social revolutions, such as those which have taken place in Eastern European countries, characteristically fail to overturn the sociolinguistic norms of the society; on the contrary, prohibitions against using vernacular forms in writing may grow even stricter. We can judge from impressionistic reports that this seems to be the case in the Soviet Union as well as Czechoslovakia. In our own society, we find that all social groups share the same set of norms in correct and public language. Radical and revolutionary figures do not use nonstandard grammar in public or in print; on the contrary, they endorse the rules of grammar as strictly as the conservative journals do. There has been a long tradition in the United States for politicians to appeal to the public with a sprinkling of the vernacular in their platform speeches. But such displays are confined rather strictly to certain set situations, and the same speakers insist on correct or even formal grammar in formal or solemn statements. The leaders of the black nationalist movement among the Negro people do not use nonstandard Negro English in their public speeches. Their grammar is essentially standard. Although there is a growing tendency to use fragments of vernacular language in public speeches, careful analysis shows that these are isolated elements; the basic grammar and phonology used is that of the middle class community, essentially that which is taught in school.

In highly stratified situations, where society is divided into two major groups, the values associated with the dominant group are assigned to the dominant language by all. Lambert and his colleagues at McGill University have shown how regular are such unconscious evaluations in the French-English situation of Quebec, in the Arabic-Hebrew confrontation in Israel, and in other areas as well. When English Canadians heard the same person speaking Canadian French, on the one hand, and English, on the other, they unhesitatingly judged him to be more intelligent, more dependable, kinder, more ambitious, better looking and taller – when he spoke English. Common sense would tell us that French-Canadians would react in the opposite manner, but in fact they do not. Their judgments reflect almost the same set of unconscious values as the English-Canadians show. This overwhelming negative evaluation of Canadian French is a property of the society as a whole. It is an omnipresent stigma which has a strong effect on what happens in school as well as in other social contexts.

Such a uniform set of norms defines a speech community. People in the United States do not share the Canadian reaction to Canadian French. They do share a number of uniform values about nonstandard dialects, but they also differ considerably in their reaction to particular features, depending upon the underlying vernacular of the region. The short *a* of *mad, bad, glad*, is a crucial matter in New York City – in fact, it is probably the one feature of pronunciation which working class speakers pay most attention to in careful speech. In Philadelphia, the vowels are more strikingly different from the formal standard, but people don't care very much about it. A far more crucial issue for Philadelphia is the vowel of *go* and *road*. The Philadelphia and Pittsburgh vernacular forms have a centralized beginning, very similar to that of some high prestige British dialects. As a result, the Philadelphia vernacular forms sound elegant and cultivated to New York speakers, and the New York vernacular forms, with a lower, unrounded beginning, sound elegant and impressive to the Philadelphians. Conversely, the Philadelphians and the New Yorkers both despise their own vernacular forms. In general, it is an important sociolinguistic principle that *those who use the highest degree of a stigmatized form in their own casual speech are quickest to stigmatize it in the speech of others*. This principle has important consequences for the classroom situation. The teacher from the same community has the advantage that he can realistically detect and correct the most important nonstandard features of his students; but he has the disadvantage that he will react to these features in an extreme, sometimes unrealistic fashion. This is most relevant to questions of pronunciation. Grammatical norms are fairly uniform throughout the United States, and our chief sources of regional variation have to do with the pronunciation of vowels.

4   Differences between the Sexes

In some societies there are striking differences between men's and women's speech, but in the United States we do not find widespread variation in the actual features of language used by the sexes. There are marginal examples: men are more apt to say "*Fill 'er up*" than women are; men use more obscene language than women do – in public. But the major differences between the sexes are in the important areas of *attitudes* towards language. The sociolinguistic behavior of women is quite different from that of men because they respond to the commonly held normative values in a different way. Such differences appear in our earliest studies of sociolinguistic variables. In Fischer's 1958 study of the use of *-ing* and *-in'* in a New England village, we find that both boys and girls use both variants. But among the girls, ten out of twelve used more *-ing* than *-in'*, while among the boys, only five out of twelve did. In general, women are more sensitive to overt social correction and use more prestige forms than men. But this difference is not independent of social class. It is moderately true for the highest status group in a speech community, but the effect is far more striking in the *second highest* status group. Here the difference may appear in an extreme form. Below a certain point on the social scale, the effect is often reversed. Among lower class women who live at home, on welfare or without a regular occupation, we can observe less awareness of sociolinguistic norms and less response to them.

   A typical pattern is that shown by men and women in their use of pronominal apposition – that is, *My brother he's pretty good*. In Roger Shuy's sociolinguistic study of Detroit (1967), we find the following indices for the use of this nonstandard feature by men and women:

STATUS GROUP:	I	II	III	IV
Men	5.0	19.3	23.1	25.0
Women	4.8	9.2	27.2	23.7

Fischer

Men and women are practically the same for the highest status group. In the lower groups III and IV there are small differences with no clear direction. But in the second highest group there is a very great difference between men and women: women use less than half as much pronominal apposition as men.

   When we examine the full spectrum of stylistic behavior for men and women, it appears that the crucial differences lie in the steeper slope of style shifting for women: in all but the lowest status group they may actually use more of a nonstandard form in their casual speech than men, but in formal styles they shift more rapidly and show an excess of hypercorrect behavior at that end of the scale. Furthermore, women respond in a much more extreme fashion to subjective reaction tests than men and are far more prone to stigmatize nonstandard usage. The overall picture of women's behavior fits in with the general sociolinguistic principle stated above – that those who use more nonstandard forms in their own casual speech will be most sensitive to those forms in the speech of others. The hypercorrect pattern of the second highest status group is accentuated in women. This is particularly important for the schools, since the majority of our teachers are women, and it is their reaction to nonstandard language with which we must be concerned in examining the educational applications of these findings.

5   Stages in the Acquisition of Standard English

In the sociolinguistic study of language learning, we can begin with the fundamental observation that *children do not speak like their parents*. This is indeed surprising, since we obviously learn to speak from our parents. If the child's parents speak English, and he grows up in the United States, he will certainly have English as his native language. Yet in almost every detail, his English will resemble that of his peers rather than that of his parents. We have as yet no thoroughgoing studies of the relation of parent, child, and peer group, yet all of the available evidence shows that this is the case. With a few exceptions, second-generation speakers in a given area will be as fully native as the third and fourth generations. As a rule, the child becomes a native speaker of a particular dialect between the ages of roughly four and thirteen. If the child moves into a new area at the age of ten or eleven, the chances are that he will never acquire the local dialect pattern as completely as those who were born and raised in that area.

In some towns of northeastern New Jersey, for example, we find that adults do not equate *spirit* and *spear it*, nor do they rhyme *nearer* and *mirror* – that is, they distinguish the vowels of *beat* and *bit* before intervocalic *r*. But the children in this area use the higher vowel of *beat* for both *nearer* and *mirror*, *mysterious* and *delirious*. In the middle class sections of the same region, most parents come from New York City and have an *r*-less vernacular, but almost all children are solidly *r*-pronouncing. Most parents are not aware of how systematically their children's speech differs from their own; if they do inquire, they will be surprised to find that there is no fixed relation between their own rules and those of their children. Instead, it is the local group of their children's peers which determines this generation's speech pattern. This is the case with rules of nonstandard urban dialects as well as the more neutral rules of regional dialects considered here.

The full force of peer group influence may not indeed appear in the speech of the six-year-old in the first grade. It is in the fourth and fifth grade, when the ten-year-old begins to come under the full influence of the preadolescent peer group, that we obtain the most consistent records of his dialect. It should also be pointed out that it is at this age that many school records show sharp downward trends, and this is not unconnected with the fact that peer groups present a more solid resistance to the schoolroom culture than any individual child can.

In the process of language learning, there are many sections of the vocabulary which are acquired quite late. It is possible that the underlying linguistic system used by a child will be different from that of adults if he has learned very little of the latinate vocabulary before the age of thirteen. Word alternations, such as microscope ~ microscopy, decide ~ decision, pérmit ~ permít, give the crucial evidence which supports and justifies the spelling system of English. We are badly lacking in any systematic studies of children's total vocabulary (active and passive) in the early grades; it is this vocabulary which provides the input to whatever linguistic insight the child has into English spelling, and this is the equipment which he brings to the task of learning to read.

At an even later stage the child acquires the sociolinguistic norms discussed in the preceding sections. Whereas the adult community shows almost complete agreement in responses to subjective reaction tests, adolescents are quite sketchy in their perceptions of these value systems. Children certainly know that there is a great difference between school language and home language, teacher language and their own language; but they know surprisingly little of the social significance of these differences. A conversation with a twelve-year-old may run like this:

"Have you ever heard anyone say *dese*, *dat*, and *dose*?"
"Yeh."
"What kind of person says that?"
"I don't know."

Anything that can be done within the educational process to accelerate the learning of these adult norms will certainly have an effect upon the desire to learn standard English.

If we map the acquisition of the adult sociolinguistic pattern in families with many children, we find that there is a steady upward movement with age. Families of all social levels follow the same general direction, in that older children show more style shifting and more sensitive subjective reactions than younger children. But there is regular class stratification in this area too. Middle class families start at a higher level and accelerate faster, so that middle class children may have a fully adult sociolinguistic system in their late teens. In college, these children will receive the most intensive training in the use of middle class formal language. On the other hand, working class families start at a lower level, and their children may not converge on the adult system until their thirties or forties. At this point, it is obviously too late for them to acquire productive control of prestige patterns: their performance will be erratic and unreliable, even though they are capable of judging the performance of others.

In general, we find that norms acquired later in life, especially after puberty, never achieve the automatic regularity of a Type I rule. A certain amount of audio-monitoring, or attention paid to speech, is necessary if any degree of consistency is to be achieved with such patterns. When the speaker is tired, or distracted, or unable to hear himself, this acquired or "superposed" pattern gives way in favor of the native vernacular acquired early in life. He may also stop monitoring his speech for the opposite reasons – when he is intensely excited, emotionally disturbed, or very much involved in the subject. It is an important sociolinguistic principle that *the most consistent and regular linguistic system of a speech community is that of the basic vernacular learned before puberty*. The overt social correction supplied in the schoolroom can never be as regular or far-reaching as the unconscious efforts of "change from below" within the system. It is almost a matter of accident which words rise to the level of social consciousness and become overt stereotypes to be corrected. The *o* of *coffee*, *chocolate* and *door* has moved to a very high *u*-like vowel in the vernacular of New York and Philadelphia, and it has finally become subject to the process of social correction. The *o* of *boy* and *Lloyd* is the same *o*, and it has moved to the same *u*-like vowel, but it is never corrected to a low vowel like the others.

Overt correction applied in the schoolroom is useful to the student in that it makes him aware of the distance between his speech and the standard language – in grammar and pronunciation. This correction cannot in itself teach him a new Type I rule; it most often gives him a variable Type III rule which he will use in formal situations. At best he may achieve a semi-categorical Type II control of this feature. There are many educated Negro speakers who were raised speaking nonstandard Negro English, which has no third-singular *s* and has obligatory negative concord as in *Nobody know nothin' about it*. In formal situations such speakers can supply all third-singular *s*'s and avoid negative concord. But this requires continual monitoring of their own speech. In relaxed and casual circumstances, the rules of their basic vernacular will reappear. It is certainly a good thing that this is the case, for a speaker who can no longer use the nonstandard vernacular of the neighborhood in which he was raised cannot return to that neighborhood as the same person.

We may consider the important question as to whether any speaker ever acquires complete control of both standard English and a nonstandard vernacular. So far, the answer to this question seems to be no. We have observed speakers who maintain perfect control of their original vernacular in casual speech and have variable control of standard rules in their casual speech. Educated black speakers will show, even in their casual speech, far more third-singular *s* than the vernacular; their negative concord will be quite variable; in a word, the Type I or Type II rules of the nonstandard dialect are now variable Type III rules for them. This does not stop them from communicating effectively with their old neighbors and friends. But it does mean that they are very poor informants on the fundamental rules of the vernacular. Teachers raised in ghetto areas cannot use themselves for reliable information on the original nonstandard rules. The knowledge of one system inevitably affects the other. The rules of standard English and its nonstandard relatives are so similar that they are bound to interact. Languages and dialects are not so carefully partitioned from each other in the speakers' heads that the right hand does not know what the left hand is doing.

6   Social Differences in Verbal Skills

There is ample evidence to show that social classes differ in their use of language in ways that go beyond the use of stigmatized nonstandard forms. A number of studies show that middle class speakers use longer sentences, more subordinate clauses, and more learned vocabulary; they take a less personal verbal viewpoint than working class speakers. Our own studies of narratives of personal experience show that middle class speakers interrupt their narratives much more often to give evaluative statements, often cast in an impersonal style. Middle class speakers seem to excel in taking the viewpoint of the "generalized other."

There is also ample evidence to show that middle class children do better on a wide range of school tasks, in reading and mathematics, in achievement tests and nonverbal intelligence tests. In a word, they perform much better in school and do better at acquiring a number of important skills which they will need in later life. Everyone would like to see working class youth, especially Negro and Puerto Rican youth in the American urban ghettos, do as well.

There is, however, no automatic connection between these two sets of findings. Seeing these two correlations, many educators have immediately concluded that a third correlation exists: that working class children must be taught middle class verbal habits and be made to abandon the rules of their own dialect. Such a conclusion is without warrant, for we do not know at present how much of the middle class verbal pattern is functional and contributes to educational success and how much is not and does not.

The British social psychologist Basil Bernstein (1966) has devoted his attention to class differences in the use of language. He distinguishes a "restricted code" and an "elaborated code" which govern the selection of linguistic forms and suggests that working class speakers are confined to the former while middle class speakers have both. The chief characteristics of the "restricted code" may be summed up best in Bernstein's own language: speech is "fast, fluent, with reduced articulatory clues"; meanings are "discontinuous, dislocated, condensed and local"; there is a "low level of vocabulary and syntactic selection"; and most importantly, "the unique meaning of the person would tend to be implicit" (p. 62).

Bernstein's description of the restricted code is a good picture of the casual speech which we rely upon for our view of the basic vernacular of a language, with both working class and middle class subjects. The overall characteristic which he focuses on is greater or lesser *explicitness* – and in the formulation used earlier, more or less attention paid to the monitoring of speech. This is the style which is commonly used among those who share a great deal of common experience. The most explicit formal style is used in addressing a public audience or in writing, where we presuppose the minimum amount of shared information and experience.

Clearly, then, the verbal skills which characterize middle class speakers are in the area which we have been calling "school language" in an informal sense, which speakers confined to a nonstandard dialect plainly do not control. There is no reason to presuppose a deep semantic or logical difference between nonstandard dialects and such an elaborated style. Some aspect of the formal speech of middle class speakers may very well have value for the acquisition of knowledge and verbal problem solving. But before we train working class speakers to copy middle class speech patterns wholesale, it is worth asking just which aspects of this style are functional for learning and which are matters of prestige and fashion. The question must be answered before we can design an effective teaching program, and unfortunately we have not yet begun to answer it.

Working class speakers also excel at a wide range of verbal skills, including many not controlled by middle class speakers. In the urban ghettos, we find a number of speech events which demand great ingenuity, originality, and practice, such as the system of ritual insults known variously as *sounding, signifying, the dozens*, etc.; the display of occult knowledge sometimes known as *rifting*; the delivery, with subtle changes, of a large repertoire of oral epic poems known as *toasts* or *jokes*; and many other forms of verbal expertise quite unknown to teachers and middle class society in general. Most of these skills cannot be transferred wholesale to the school situation. Until now there has been no way of connecting excellence in the verbal activity of the vernacular culture with excellence in the verbal skills needed in school. Yet it seems plain that our educational techniques should draw upon these nonstandard vernacular skills to the better advantage of all concerned.

References

Bernstein, Basil. 1966. "Elaborated and restricted codes," in J. J. Gumperz and Dell Hymes (eds.), *The Ethnography of Communication*. (Special issue of *American Anthropologist*, 66 (6), part 2: 55–69.)

Fischer, J. L. 1958. "Social influences on the choice of a linguistic variant," *Word*, 14: 47–56.

14

On the Construction of Vernacular Dialect Norms

Walt Wolfram

1 The Neglected Consideration of Vernacular Norms

All language communities engage in _language norming_, that is, the establishment of appropriate models of language behavior for members of the speech community. In this respect, socially subordinate, vernacular-speaking communities are no different from their socially dominant, "mainstream" counterparts. Although we have a substantial base of knowledge about the development and codification of standard English norms, little attention has been paid to the process of instantiating, transmitting, and regulating vernacular norms within indigenous speech communities. Sociolinguistic inquiry into the norming process for vernacular speech communities is generally minimized or ignored completely. In fact, most accounts of English vernacular dialects are content to describe dialect forms simply by comparing them with the codified standard norm, even when describing the patterns of vernacular varieties as linguistically independent rules or processes. Thus, classic descriptive accounts of varieties such as African American Vernacular English (Labov, Cohen, Robins, and Lewis 1968; Fasold and Wolfram 1970; Labov 1972) or Appalachian English (Wolfram and Christian 1976) emphasize how the structures in these dialects differ from their idealized standard English counterparts without considering how the vernacular norms are instantiated, maintained, and regulated within their respective speech communities.

This discussion aims to address the neglected dimension of vernacular dialect norming by examining the status of two contrasting dialect situations, the case of African American Vernacular English (AAVE) and the case of Lumbee Vernacular English. The situations considered here demonstrate how linguistic, sociohistorical, sociolinguistic, sociopsychological, and ideological issues are implicated in the construction of vernacular norms. Perhaps more importantly, these contrasting situations underscore the need to examine in more careful detail the process of vernacular dialect norming as a legitimate and essential focus of sociolinguistic inquiry.

2 Fundamental Issues in Vernacular Norming

At least four major issues need to be recognized in the construction of vernacular dialect norms: (1) _the actuation issue_, (2) _the embedding issue_, (3) _the diffusion issue_, and (4) _the_ *dynamic issue.*[1] The *actuation issue* refers to the process whereby vernacular dialect structures are initiated. What circumstances and forces internally and externally give rise to the emergence of vernacular dialect norms? Explanations for the linguistic initiation of vernacular dialect structures may include differential language change, language contact, and independent language development.

Differential language change refers to the fact that structural features shared at one point by the speakers of the language at large may be retained by some speech communities while other groups of speakers undergo change. For example, the use of *a*-prefixing in structures like *She was a-working* was once a general trait of earlier English both in the US (Wolfram 1980) and in England (Trudgill 1990) that has been selectively maintained in some peripheral dialect areas.

Structures associated with vernacular varieties may also be activated through the linguistic negotiation of language contact situations, as various types of accommodation strategies (Trudgill 1986, Winford forthcoming) are enacted, including direct and indirect language transfer. Some of the vernacular language norms of AAVE, for example, are attributable to the long-term substratal transfer effects of an earlier language contact situation in the African diaspora, just as dialect norms in other ethnic communities may reflect the lingering effects of their heritage languages.

At the same time, some structures that develop into vernacular norms are actuated by internally motivated language changes. These may involve parallel independent development in different varieties, or Sapir's (1921) "drift", due to the operation of general processes of analogy and the universal tendency to move toward unmarked forms. For example, a survey of various vernacular dialects of English (Wolfram and Fasold 1994; Wolfram and Schilling-Estes 1998) shows a uniform tendency to regularize once-irregular plurals (e.g. *two sheeps*), to regularize past tense forms (e.g. *They growed up*), to adopt negative concord (e.g. *They didn't do nothing*), to stop syllable-onset, interdental fricatives (e.g. [dɪs] 'this'), and so forth. As Chambers (1995: 242) points out, "certain variables appear to be primitives of vernacular dialects in that they recur ubiquitously all over the world." These developments result from natural processes that guide changes quite independently from diffusion or language contact.

The *embedding issue* concerns the process whereby linguistic features are incorporated into and are established as part of the vernacular norm, including the assignment of sociolinguistic significance. On one level, the establishment of vernacular variants appears to be a relatively straightforward case of co-variance, in which particular linguistic variants become established as vernacular norms by virtue of their association with socially subordinate groups. On another level, however, the instantiation is a complex, selective process. There are *social indicators* (no conscious recognition), *social markers* (conscious recognition without overt comment), and *stereotypes* (conscious recognition and the object of overt commentary) within vernacular dialect communities, just as there are in the socially favored dialects (Labov 1966). Furthermore, there is also interaction between the linguistic principles that drive language change and the social mechanisms that ascribe social meaning in the construction of vernacular norms.

The *diffusion issue* concerns the spread of vernacular norms, both within localized speech communities and across different vernacular-speaking communities. Given the demographic distribution of different social and ethnic groups in the US, differential patterns of settlement, migration, re-settlement are involved, as well as diverse models of intra- and inter-community interaction. Traditional models of dialect diffusion focus on the *contagious model*, in which the spread of features follows a straightforward wave-like time and distance relation; the *hierarchical model*, in which features spread from areas of denser population to areas of sparser population; or the *contrahierarchical model*, in which features spread from more sparsely populated areas to more densely populated ones (Bailey, Wikle, Tillery, and Sand 1991). As useful as these macro models are, we cannot simply assume that they will apply to the spread of change among vernacular social groups as they do to mainstream groups. It is also possible that these models may be insufficient to explain how change and subsequent vernacular normativization takes place on a community level. In fact, we will see that mechanistic models of diffusion do not adequately account for some of the supra-regional normative development in contemporary AAVE.

The *dynamic issue* relates to the fact that vernacular varieties, like all other language varieties, are constantly undergoing change. Accordingly, their language norms also shift. What kinds of structural features change and how do such changes affect the reconfiguration of vernacular norms? How have the norms of different vernaculars changed over time, and what social mechanisms are used to transmit and regulate these changing norms? With reference to norming, there appears to be an essential difference in the establishment of norms for an overtly sanctioned variety recognized as the standard and the establishment of non-mainstream vernacular norms. Usage books, orthoepical guides, internet grammar "hotlines", and other venues provide for the codification of standard English, and various language guardians, including language specialists, teachers, and parents and caretakers, serve as gatekeepers. There is, however, no comparable codification of vernacular norms, and the transmission of norms seems to take place on a more covert, informal level. At this point, we know little about the regulatory procedures and mechanisms used to instantiate vernacular dialect norms.

There may also be important differences in the rate of normative change for vernacular varieties vis-à-vis their standard counterparts. Codified norms of socially dominant varieties tend to be relatively conservative and resistant to ongoing change. But this is not necessarily the case for vernacular norms. According to Chambers (1995: 246), a standard norm is "more restricted or tightly constrained in its grammar and phonology" due to the social pressures to resist some natural linguistic changes. Standard varieties may resist the natural pull of some of these processes because socially sanctioned mainstream norms tend to emphasize permanency and conscious resistance to some natural linguistic changes. At the same time, however, some characteristic traits of vernacular English norms have existed for centuries, therefore showing a kind of permanency in their own right.

It should be obvious that not all of the issues raised here can be addressed in the following description. My goal is more modest; I hope simply to explore two quite different vernacular situations to demonstrate important differences in the establishment and recognition of vernacular norms. In the process I hope to show that the construction of vernacular norms involves a complex array of intersecting linguistic, social, and psychological factors, and that it is fully deserving of more careful sociolinguistic scrutiny.

3   The Case of AAVE: A Developing Supra-regional Norm

No dialect of English has received more attention over the past four decades than AAVE. Descriptive attention to AAVE in a wide range of regional settings during this period has led to the often noted observation that there is cross-regional uniformity in many AAVE structures. Despite vast geographical separation, disparate urban and rural African American communities reveal an amazing recurrence of a common set of dialect structures that unites AAVE as it is set apart from other vernacular varieties of English. Grammatical structures such as habitual *be* (e.g. *Sometimes my ears be itching*), copula/auxiliary absence (e.g. *He taking too much time*), inflectional *-s* absence (e.g. *She go home: The lady house nice; four cent*), and completive *done* (e.g. *They done finished*) have been documented wherever AAVE is spoken in the US, as have prevocalic syllable-coda consonant cluster reduction (e.g. *wes' area*), syllable-coda labialization (e.g. *mouf*), postvocalic *r* vocalization (*bea'*), and so forth. The inventory of typical AAVE features has been amply documented over the last three decades (e.g. Fasold and Wolfram 1970; Labov 1972; Baugh 1983; Rickford 1999) and will not be repeated here. Furthermore, hundreds of other descriptions of selected AAVE features in varied geographical settings in the US have replicated these results.

The supra-regional dimension of AAVE seems even more noteworthy in light of recent studies of the earlier history of AAVE. In the late 1960s and 70s, it was commonly assumed that AAVE developed from a widespread creole predecessor and that current AAVE was a vestige of the incomplete process of decreolization. Such a reconstruction might certainly account for the commonality of features in contemporary AAVE. However, the emergence of new corpora on the speech of earlier African Americans in the last two decades has seriously challenged the creolist hypothesis, leading to a "neo-Anglicist" position (Montgomery, Fuller, and DeMarse 1993; Mufwene 1996; Poplack 1999). Some recent studies of the history of AAVE (Poplack and Sankoff 1987; Poplack and Tagliamonte 1989, 1991; Poplack 1999) suggest that earlier AAVE was really no different from earlier cohort Anglo-American vernacular varieties. This historical reconstruction of AAVE would thus make the emergence of common-core structures in contemporary AAVE a rather remarkable development of the twentieth century.

3.1   The regional base of earlier AAVE

Over the past several years, the staff of the North Carolina Language and Life Project has been investigating a unique sociolinguistic situation that has significant implications for the examination of the contemporary development of AAVE. The bi-racial community of Hyde County, North Carolina, located along the eastern seaboard of North Carolina by the Pamlico Sound, was initially inhabited by Europeans in the first decade of the 1700s, making it one of the oldest Anglo-American settlement communities in North Carolina. Shortly thereafter, African Americans were brought to the area (Kay and Cary 1995). After an early period of growth in the 1700s, the region became quite isolated, and has remained relatively insular to this day. In fact, the first official census conducted in 1790 (4,120) and the most recent census in 1990 (5,411) show that

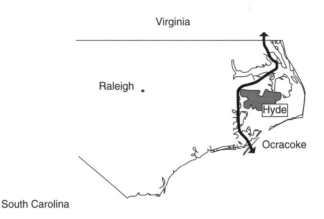

Virginia

Raleigh .

Hyde

Ocracoke

South Carolina

Figure 1   Hyde County and the boundaries of the Outer Banks dialect

Hyde County has gained less than 1,500 people over two centuries. African Americans have been between a quarter and a half of this population for almost three centuries now.

This remote coastal setting provides an ideal context for examining several critical issues regarding the historical development of African American speech and the establishment of AAVE norms. It offers a sociolinguistic context involving a long-term, relatively insular bi-racial situation featuring a distinctive Anglo-American variety; the Outer Banks dialect described in a number of recent publications (e.g. Wolfram and Schilling-Estes 1995, 1997; Wolfram, Hazen, and Schilling-Estes 1999) is found in the coastal mainland Hyde County region as well as on the Outer Banks. In fact, Ocracoke Island on the Outer Banks is a part of Hyde County. Figure 1 indicates the location of Hyde County and delineates the approximate isogloss for the traditional dialect encompassing the region.

An analysis of African American speakers and their cohort Anglo-American speakers of different generations from Hyde County offers insight into how African American speech has developed in relation to the local Anglo-American vernacular variety. Given the apparent time construct (Bailey, Wikle, Tillery, and Sand 1991), the data for the elderly speakers (born between 1898 and 1920) would most likely reflect the earlier speech of the County, whereas the younger speakers (1971–1985) would reflect the contemporary state of speech in Hyde County.

A representative set of diagnostic variables has now been scrutinized in considerable detail for different generations of African Americans and Anglo-Americans in Hyde County: the vowel system (Thomas forthcoming; Wolfram, Thomas, and Green 2000), phonotactic patterns such as syllable-coda consonant cluster reduction (Childs 2000), copula absence (Green 1998), past tense *be* leveling (Green 1998), and verbal *-s* marking (Wolfram, Thomas, and Green 2000). A summary of the results from these studies is given in table 1. The speech of elderly and younger Hyde County African Americans, elderly and younger Anglo-Americans, and contemporary urban AAVE in regions other than Hyde County (e.g. Fasold and Wolfram 1970; Labov 1972; Fasold 1972; Baugh 1983; and Rickford 1999) are included in the comparison. Shared, distinctive patterns

Table 1   Summary of Vernacular Dialect Alignment

Dialect Feature	Elderly Hyde Anglo–Amer.	Elderly Hyde African Amer.	Young Hyde Anglo–Amer.	Young Hyde African Amer.	Urban AAVE
Phonology					
Prevocalic CCR in *bes' egg*	–	+	–	+	+
Postvocalic –*r* in *year*	+	+	+	–	–
Backed /ay/ in *time*	+	+	+/–	–	–
Unglided /ay/ in *time*	–	–	+/–	–/+	+
Front-gliding /aw/ in *town*	+	+	–	–/+	–
Lowered /er/ in *bear*	+	+	–	–	–
Raised, unglided /▶/ in *caught*	+	+	–/+	–/+	–
Fronted /o/ in *coat*	+	+	+	+	–
Morphosyntax					
NP 3rd pl. subj. verbal –*s* e.g. *The dogs barks*	+	+	+/–	–	–
Pro 3rd pl. subj. verbal –*s* e.g. *They barks*	–	+	–	–	–
3rd sg. –*s* absence e.g. *The dog go*	–	+	–	+	+
Habitual *be* verb –*ing* e.g. *Sometimes the dog be barking*	–	–	–	+	+
Copula abs. e.g. *She nice*	–	+	–	+	+
Was regularization e.g. *The dogs was nice*	+	+	+	+	+
Weren't regularization e.g. *It weren't nice*	+	+	+/–	–	–

among the different groups are indicated by shading. The co-existence of patterns is indicated by +/− or −/+, with the dominant variant indicated first.

Table 1 shows that some earlier dialect features used by Hyde County African Americans paralleled the distinctive regional features used by their Anglo-American cohorts. The communities shared the distinctive Outer Banks vowel system and morphosyntactic features such as the leveling of past *be* based on polarity (i.e. *weren't* for negative constructions as in *I weren't there* and *was* for positive constructions as in *We was there*) and verbal -*s* marking with plural subjects (e.g. *The dogs barks*). At the same time, there is evidence for some long-standing, selective structural differences in the Anglo-American and African American varieties of Hyde County. The phonological process of syllable-coda consonant cluster reduction apparently operated differently for the two groups of speakers in the past, as it does in the present; both younger and older African American speakers have significant prevocalic cluster reduction whereas Anglo-

Americans do not. Furthermore, African American and Anglo-American communities have differed in their use of copula absence (e.g. *She nice*) and optional 3rd sg. verbal -*s* marking (e.g. *The dog bark*). The adoption of regional structures, however, was not always isomorphic, so that the African American version of verbal -*s* marking with 3rd pl. subjects is more general than that found among their Anglo-American cohorts. The Anglo-American version of verbal -*s* marking with third plural subjects restricts it to noun phrases (e.g. *The ducks likes food*) whereas the African American version general-izes the application to both noun phrases and pronouns (e.g. *The ducks likes food* and *They likes food*). And, of course, there are some apparent innovative features in AAVE that have been adopted by younger Hyde County African Americans, such as habitual *be* with verb -*ing*.

One of the important lessons to be taken from this examination concerns the selec-tion of structures for investigating earlier African American speech. An authentic picture of earlier African American speech can emerge only if a wide array of dialect structures is considered, including entire vowel systems and profiles of complete tense, aspect, and modal systems. Selective, single-structure studies may reveal significant insight into a particular linguistic process and/or a particular dimension of an ethno-linguistic boundary, but such studies may obscure or even distort our understanding of the overall relationship of African American speech to other varieties.

The data suggest that the English of African Americans at an earlier period in the history of Hyde County was considerably more regionalized than it is currently. Although there were some dialect differences, there was apparently much greater dialect congruity in the earlier speech of some African American and Anglo-American communities.

Finally, the comparison of dialect features of African Americans in Hyde County with some of the core structures of contemporary urban AAVE indicates change toward an external norm. A number of the dialect traits found in contemporary AAVE are absent in the speech of most elderly residents but present in the speech of younger speakers. For example, younger African American speakers have more extensive postvo-calic *r* vocalization and habitual *be* than the older generation. Not only do younger Hyde County African Americans lose some of the regionalisms used by previous generations but they adopt characteristic traits of AAVE that align them with the vernacular as it is used elsewhere. Evidence from ongoing change in Hyde County clearly supports the contention that African American speakers are diverging from their Anglo-American vernacular cohorts as local dialect features are being replaced by a more widespread, common-core set of AAVE features. In effect, the ethnic marking of speech in Hyde County seems to be superseding its regional locus.

To examine the subjective basis of our conclusion about the increasing ethnic role of AAVE, we constructed a speaker identification task with speech samples represent-ing several types of speakers.[2] We extracted passages of 20–30 seconds each from con-versational interviews with seven different speakers. The content of the passages consisted of human-interest stories that were neutral with respect to racial content, pre-cluding ethnic identification based on the content of the passage rather than the speech per se. The speakers included a middle-aged Anglo-American speaker from Hyde County, an elderly (born 1910) and a younger (born 1975) African American from Hyde County, an older African American speaker from the Piedmont area of North Carolina

Table 2   Results from ethnic identification task for representative African American and Anglo-American speech samples

Listener groups	Hyde Co. Anglo–Am.	Elderly Hyde Co. Af. Am.	Young Hyde Co. Af. Am.	Elderly Piedmont NC Af. Am.	Ex-slave Piedmont, Va
		Correct identification of ethnicity			
Total (N = 29)	100%	10.4%	89.7%	100%	69.6%
Anglo-American (N = 16)	100%	15.4%	84.6%	100%	76.9%
African American (N = 13)	100%	6.3%	93.8%	100%	62.5%

located near Raleigh, North Carolina, an ex-slave from Charlottesville, Virginia, who was born in 1848, and two other Anglo-American speakers from the coastal plains of North Carolina. For the purposes of this investigation, we concern ourselves only with the first five speakers.

We played the sample passages to groups of listeners in Raleigh, North Carolina, and asked them simply to identify the ethnicity of each speaker. Of the 29 listeners who participated in the task, 13 were African American.[3] The results of the ethnic identification task for the five speakers of relevance to this study are summarized in table 2. The significant differences in correct identification (chi square test of significance) are shaded.

Note the contrast between the correct identification of the elderly and young African American speakers from Hyde County. The elderly speaker is correctly identified as African American by only 10 percent of the listeners and the young speaker is correctly identified by 90 percent of the listeners, with no significant difference based on the ethnicity of the judge. The generational difference takes on more significance when we consider the background of the two speakers. Not only are both of the speakers lifetime residents of Hyde County, but they lived in the same home and are related; the elderly speaker is the great-grandfather of the young speaker. Yet the great-grandfather, whose speech reveals many of the regional dialect features found in the speech of cohort Anglo-Americans, is identified by both African American and Anglo-American listeners as "white" while his great-granddaughter, whose speech indicates many traits of contemporary AAVE, is identified as African American.

The generational split in ethnic identification within Hyde County should not be taken to mean that all earlier African American speakers were indistinguishable from their Anglo-American cohorts. The elderly African American speaker from the Piedmont area of North Carolina (taken from Hazen 2000) was, in fact, identified categorically as African American by listeners. Meanwhile, the correct ethnic identification of the ex-slave from Charlottesville, Virginia, was more inconsistent. The analysis of this ex-slave's vowel system by Thomas (forthcoming) shows traits characteristic of AAVE, but it also reveals the production of a traditional Virginia Piedmont production of the /au/ diphthong with a raised nucleus. It may be that this distinctly regional /au/ production moderates the ethnic classification of the speaker, since highly regionalized dialect traits tend to be associated with Anglo-American varieties.

Evidence from the speaker identification task and our detailed cross-generational linguistic analysis of dialect features in Hyde County, North Carolina, clearly support the contention that some earlier varieties of English spoken by African Americans were highly regionalized. However, younger speakers in these regions have not only lost regional vernacular features; as these features recede, they are replaced by structures representing the common core features of contemporary AAVE shared throughout the US, including linguistic developments of AAVE in the twentieth century (Bailey and Maynor 1987; Dayton 1996; Labov 1998).

3.2   Explaining the supra-regional norms of contemporary AAVE

How do we explain the development and maintenance of a supra-regional norm for AAVE? Several factors seem to converge in such an explanation. First, there is a historical, linguistic explanation. Although the speech of earlier African Americans showed considerable accommodation to regional variation in English, some distinctive, long-term ethnolinguistic structures apparently existed in earlier AAVE. For example, even in highly regionalized contexts where African Americans adopted many areal dialect features (Wolfram, Thomas, and Green 2000), structures such as prevocalic consonant cluster reduction (Childs 2000), copula absence (Green 1998; Winford 1998), and optional inflectional -s marking (Wolfram, Thomas, and Green 2000; Winford 1998) were present in the speech of African Americans. The most reasonable explanation for the existence of some of these structures is substrate influence from the earlier contact situation between speakers of African languages and speakers of English in the African diaspora.[4] Thus, a series of long-term, ethnolinguistically distinctive features provided an embryonic base for some of the structures characteristic of the past and contemporary vernacular. But that is obviously not the whole story. There is also evidence that some of the important features of the contemporary AAVE norm were creations of the twentieth century (Bailey and Maynor 1985, 1987; Dayton 1996; Labov 1998).

A partial explanation for the supra-regional status of AAVE may also be based in the expanded mobility and inter-regional, intra-ethnic contact situation characteristic of African Americans in the twentieth century (Johnson and Campbell 1981). African Americans in isolated rural regions of the South, including Hyde County, have much more expanded contact with other African Americans than they did a century ago. Whereas the elderly Hyde County African American used in our ethnic identification task did not leave the county until he was in his mid-30s, his great-granddaughter travels outside of the county on a regular basis and has traveled beyond the state on several occasions. Furthermore, residents who leave isolated, rural areas of the South often visit relatives and friends back home. In fact, various "homecoming" events and family reunions bring together those living within and outside of the Hyde County community on a semi-regular basis. This steady inter-regional contact seems much more typical of African American communities than it is of many Anglo-American communities.

Patterns of inter-regional contact and increased mobility thus may play a role in the transmission of a supra-regional vernacular norm.

At the same time, the continuing ex facto segregation of American society serves as a fertile environment for maintaining a distinct ethnic variety. Many Northern urban areas are, in fact, more densely populated by African Americans today than they were several decades ago (Graff et al. 1986), and the informal social networks of many urban African Americans remain quite segregated (Stack 1996).

Along with explanations based on population movement and segregation, however, is the role of cultural identity. Over the past half century, there has been a growing sense of ethnic identity associated with AAVE. This identity is supported through a variety of informal and formal social mechanisms that range from community-based social networks to stereotypical media projections of African American speech (Lippi-Green 1997). Part of the definition of African American speech is not simply the adoption of features associated with AAVE, but the avoidance of features that are associated with "white speech" (Ash and Myhill 1986; Graff et al. 1986), including regional dialect traits. Fordham and Ogbu (1986) suggest that the adoption of standard English is at the top of the list of behaviors listed as "acting white." So-called "oppositional identity", in which African Americans avoid conduct with strong associations of white behavior (Fordham and Ogbu 1986), may thus be an important part of the explanation for the rejection of regional dialect features that have strong white connotations.

During the twentieth century, AAVE has become much more of an urban than a rural phenomenon (Bailey and Maynor 1985, 1987). In this developing ethnolinguistic milieu, traditional rural dialects such as the Hyde County dialect would carry strong associations of white, rural speech. For example, younger African American subjects in our study describe the speech of older Hyde County African Americans as "sounding country" and sounding more white than the speech of younger African Americans. Younger speakers who identify strongly with African American culture contra "white culture" would therefore be inclined to change their speech toward the more generalized version of AAVE and away from the localized regional norm. An essential ingredient of the contemporary supra-regional norm for AAVE is thus the heightened symbolic role of language as an ethnic emblem of African American culture. Such an identity would accordingly enhance the role of a widespread supra-regional AAVE norm vis-à-vis accommodation to a regional dialect norm with strong connotations of white speech behavior.

4   The Case of Lumbee Vernacular English: A Localized Norm

Lumbee Vernacular English (LVE) presents a quite different case of vernacular dialect norming. The Lumbee Native American Indians of Robeson County, North Carolina, are the largest Native American group (47,000 in Robeson County) east of the Mississippi, yet they are virtually invisible on a national level. Their cultural status has been marginalized for well over a century, both in terms of the dominant Anglo-American culture and in terms of other Native American groups as well. They are federally recognized as a Native American Indian tribe but with no entitlements. An

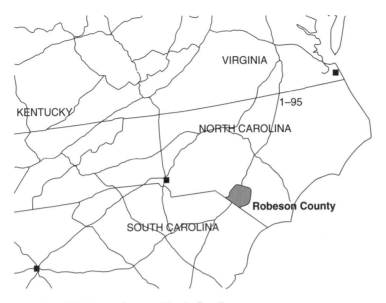

Figure 2   Location of Robeson County, North Carolina

important dimension of their marginalized status is their lack of a recoverable Native American language, as their ancestral language was lost early in their contact with Europeans. Their indeterminate status as a Native American group is summarized by Bordewich (1996: 62–63):

> The Lumbees' century-long quest for identity is a story as serpentine as the jungled Lumber River, whose swampy course shielded, and perhaps even created them and their ambiguous world. . . . There is, in fact, nothing at all about the Lumbees that fits conventional notions of what it means to be Native American. Yet for as long as any Lumbee can remember, they have possessed an unflagging conviction that they are simply and utterly Indian, a tenacious faith that is troubled only by the failure of most other Americans to recognize it.

The Lumbee are the dominant ethnic group in Robeson County (41 percent Lumbee vs. 34 percent white, 24 percent African American, and 1 percent other in the 1998 census estimate), and the proportion of Lumbee in relation to whites and African Americans has been increasing steadily.[5] The location of Robeson County is given in figure 2.

The English dialect spoken by many Lumbee is distinctive, and is often the topic of overt comment by those who have contact with them. In fact, the Congressional Act by the Congress of the United States recognizing their status includes a reference to speech:

> Whereas by reason of tribal legend, coupled with a distinctive appearance and *manner of speech* [emphasis mine] . . . shall, after ratification of this Act, be known and designated as Lumbee Indians of North Carolina.

(Act Relating to the Lumbee Indians of North Carolina, Congress of the United States. June 7, 1956)

Such a reference suggests that the dialect of English used by the Lumbee has had symbolic status as an identifying cultural trait for some time now.

4.1   The local base of Lumbee Vernacular English

Various studies by the North Carolina Language and Life Project staff over the past decade have examined a representative set of diagnostic variables in LVE, with particular focus on how these structures compare with cohort Anglo-American and African American vernacular dialect communities in Robeson County. Studies have focused on the vowel system (Schilling-Estes 1997; Thomas forthcoming), phonotactic patterns such as syllable–coda consonant cluster reduction (Torbert 2000), postvocalic r-lessness (Miller 1996; Schilling-Estes 1998), copula absence (Dannenberg 1999), past tense be leveling (Wolfram and Sellers 1999), finite be(s) (Dannenberg and Wolfram 1998), and perfective be (Wolfram 1996; Dannenberg 1999); a summary of these is provided in Wolfram and Dannenberg (1999). A comparative profile of selected grammatical variables based on these studies is given in table 3 and a summary of phonological variables is given in table 4. The tables compare LVE with the vernacular varieties spoken by their African American and Anglo-American cohorts in Robeson County. The regular incidence of a feature is indicated by ✓ and the limited occurrence of a feature is indicated by (✓).

Although the Lumbee share many vernacular dialect structures with their Robeson County Anglo-American and African American cohorts, they also have a few distinctive structures, such as past tense leveling based on polarity (e.g. *They was there, I weren't there*), perfective be (e.g. *I'm been there*), finite be(s) (e.g. *It bes that way*) and the backing and raising of the nucleus in /ai/.[6]

To examine the extent to which Lumbee speakers are identifiable to listeners, we designed a simple speaker identification task comparable to the one for AAVE discussed in the last section. Twelve passages of 20–30 seconds each were extracted from the natural conversational interviews conducted by the staff of the North Carolina Language and Life project, four from each of the three Robeson County ethnic groups. The samples, which were neutral with respect to ethnically identifiable content, included two men and two women from each ethnic group, one younger and one older speaker. The task was administered to two different groups of listeners, one to Lumbee Robeson County residents and one to listeners from Raleigh, North Carolina, located about 100 miles from Robeson County. The instructions given to listeners were simply to identify the speakers on the tape as white, Lumbee, or African American. Participants from the Raleigh area generally know who the Lumbee are but do not have substantive contact with them. The results of the task are given in table 5. Significant differences between the responses of the Raleigh listeners and the Robeson County listeners in the application of a chi square test of significance are shaded.

The results from the listening task indicate a dramatic difference in the ability of the two groups to correctly identify Lumbee speakers. The listeners from Raleigh were not able to identify the Lumbee speakers reliably, typically misidentifying them as white.

Table 3   Comparison of Anglo-American, Lumbee, and African American Vernacular grammatical structures in Robeson County, North Carolina

✓ = occurrence of structure; (✓) = restricted occurrence			
Grammatical structure	Anglo–Am.	Lumbee	Afr. Am.
finite *bes* e.g. *She bes there*	(✓)	✓	
Perfective *be* e.g. *I'm been there; They might be lost it*		✓	
weren't regularization e.g. *She weren't here*		✓	
was/is regularization e.g. *We was there*	✓	✓	✓
a–prefixing e.g. *He was a-fishin*	(✓)	✓	
copula absence e.g. *They nice, She nice*	(✓)	(✓)	✓
3rd sg. absence e.g. *She like_ cats*			✓
Plural noun phrase agreement e.g. *The dogs gets upset*	(✓)	✓	
plural absence with measurement nouns e.g. *twenty mile_*	✓	✓	✓

In contrast, the listeners from Robeson County identified Lumbee at significant levels of accuracy. While the two groups of listeners differed in their identification of Lumbee speakers, both groups reliably identified African Americans (over 90 percent) and Anglo-Americans, with no significant difference between the two groups of listeners. We thus conclude that insiders and outsiders differ only in their ability to correctly identify LVE speakers.[7]

4.2   Explaining the local basis of Lumbee Vernacular English

How do we explain the significant difference by community members and outsiders in their identification of Lumbee speakers? In part, the differential perceptual ability may be explained by appealing to their socialized dialect sensitivities. There are only a few diagnostic features that distinguish LVE from other dialects, but some of these are

Table 4 Comparison of Anglo-American, Lumbee, and African-American Vernacular phonological structures in Robeson County, North Carolina

Phonological structure	Anglo–Am.	Lumbee	Afr. Am.
[ay] backing, raising e.g. [tʌɪd] 'tide'		✓	
[ay] ungliding e.g. [tam] 'time'	✓	✓	✓
[h] retention in 'it', 'ain't' e.g. [hɪt] 'it'	(✓)	✓	(✓)
[æ] lowering preceding e.g. [ðar] 'there'	(✓)	✓	
[ayr]/[awr] reduction e.g. [tar] 'tire'	✓	✓	
intrusive r, unstressed final [o] e.g. [fɛlə] 'feller'	✓	✓	
unstressed initial [w] deletion [yʌŋ #ənz] 'young uns'	✓	✓	✓
[I]/[E] preceding [+nas] merger e.g. [pɪn] 'pin'/'pen'	✓	✓	✓
final θ labialization [bof] 'both'	✓	✓	✓
prevocalic cluster reduction [wɛs ɛn] 'wes' en'		(✓)	✓

Table 5 Results from speaker identification tasks of Robeson County Lumbee, Anglo-Americans and African Americans

Listener identification group	Lumbee	Anglo–American	African American
	Correct ethnic identification		
Raleigh, NC, non–Lumbee listeners (N = 38)	38.5%	80.4%	91.4%
Robeson County Lumbee listeners (N = 45)	82.8%	70.0%	91.1%
Chi square results	68.31 p >.001	4.66 p = n.s.	0.01 p = n.s.

recognized on a quite conscious level by the residents of Robeson County, even becoming stereotypical dialect traits associated with LVE. For example, forms such as finite *be(s)* and past *be* leveling to *weren't* are sometimes cited by community members as typical of and unique to the Lumbee dialect.

The Lumbee themselves also acknowledge language differences as a symbol of cultural distinctiveness, As noted earlier, their distinct "manner of speech" was even noted in the Congressional Act of 1956 as an identifying cultural trait. It is not uncommon to hear comments such as the following from the Lumbee:

> "That's [i.e. the dialect] how we recognize who we are, not only by looking at someone. We know just who we are by our language. You recognize someone is from Spain because they speak Spanish, or from France because they speak French, and that's how we recognize Lumbees. If we're anywhere in the country and hear ourselves speak, we know exactly who we are." (35-year-old Lumbee artist)

Although not all Lumbee make such a strong, overt connection between dialect and culture, there does seem to be a consensus among Lumbee that they can indeed be readily identified by their speech. In fact, in our ethnographic observations we have yet to find a Lumbee who did not think that Lumbee speech was distinctive.

Part of the strong sense of identity among the Lumbee may be related to the role that self-definition has played in their cultural identity. Outsiders have often expressed skepticism about the status of the Lumbee as "real Indians" due to their early departure from many conventional Native American customs and early loss of an ancestral language. Their response to this skepticism often has been to emphasize the role of self-definition in their identity. As one participant in our study put it:

> "We know who we are, we know, we have always known. Y'all are the ones who are always trying to identify something." (40+-year-old Lumbee male)

Such self-asserted identity clearly embraces dialect distinctiveness. Consequently, considerable cultural capital is vested in the distinctive vernacular dialect.

For most people outside of the immediate Robeson County area, ethnic identity is defined in terms of a bi-racial dimension. That is, listeners tend to react to speech solely in terms of a white–black ethnic dichotomy, following the primary black–white cultural relations that have historically defined the Mid-Atlantic and South region the past couple of centuries. Listeners may be attuned to regional dialect dimensions that differentiate the South from the North, the Outer Banks from the mainland, or the mountains from the plains and coast, but a bi-racial ideology still applies to ethnicity. In fact, Milroy (1999) has suggested that a bi-racial ideology takes precedence over class in the US, thereby distinguishing it from England, where class takes precedence over race.[8] In such a context, people outside of a localized context such as Robeson County would not be attuned to the essential tri-ethnic character of Robeson County. The ethnic composition of the County is, in fact, somewhat of an anomaly for the general region. In such a social milieu, there would be no socialized reason for extending ethnolinguistic distinctiveness beyond the basic black–white dimension that has dominated the South over the last couple of centuries. As noted, few people outside of North Carolina have even heard of the Lumbee and therefore have no basis for factoring them into an ethnolinguistic taxonomy. In this context, the Lumbee and their cohort Robeson County Anglo-American and African American communities are left with a highly localized construction of a vernacular norm.

5   Beyond Illustrative Cases in Explaining Vernacular Norms

Though our contrastive case studies reveal the construction of different vernacular norms, they are instructive in directing us to the kinds of factors that need to be included in any account of vernacular norming. First, there is a *linguistic dimension* to vernacular dialect norming. Although varieties such as AAVE and LVE certainly differentiate themselves dialectally, they share a pool of vernacular features that cannot be accounted for simply on the basis of diffusion or language contact. It is apparent that some vernacular forms arise through parallel, independent development, or "drift" due to the operation of general processes of analogy and a universal tendency to move toward unmarked forms. For example, a survey of various socially subordinate vernacular varieties in the US (Wolfram and Schilling-Estes 1998), England (Trudgill 1990) and around the world (Cheshire 1981) shows the uniform tendency to expand the regularization of once-irregular plurals (e.g. *two sheeps*), the regularization of past tense forms (e.g. *They growed up*), and the adoption of negative concord (e.g. *They didn't do nothing*), along with the stopping of syllable-onset, interdental fricatives (e.g. [dɪs] 'this'). These structures fit Chambers's (1995: 242) definition of "ubiquitous, primitive vernacular features." If, as Chambers (1995: 246) asserts, the prescriptive standard norm is "more restricted or tightly constrained in its grammar and phonology" than its vernacular counterparts, then vernacular norms would be under less social pressure to resist some of these natural linguistic changes. The unifying dimension of such common vernacular traits, referred to as the *principle of vernacular dialect congruity* (Wolfram forthcoming), seems to be the operation of natural linguistic processes in a social context more relaxed to the overt prescriptive norms that would otherwise impede naturally occurring changes.

There is also a *sociohistorical component* that has to be factored into the explanation of vernacular norms. Patterns of population settlement, migration, and diffusion are as vital for understanding the growth and maintenance of vernacular varieties as they are for socially sanctioned dialects. Thus, the migration of African Americans from the South in the early and mid-twentieth century (Johnson and Campbell 1981), as well as the maintenance of inter-regional connections and family ties, provides a communication network for the diffusion of vernacular norms from the South to the North and West. In more recent decades, the return of some African Americans to the South (Stack 1996) no doubt has also provided for the diffusion of vernacular norms from urban areas, the current focal area for AAVE, back to rural areas which were once the primary regions for earlier vernacular development. The ebb and flow of migration, along with the regular maintenance of inter-regional family ties has no doubt afforded a transmission route for contemporary supra-regional AAVE norms.

In contrast, the concentration of 90 percent of the Lumbee population within a single North Carolina county for an extended period of time is an important consideration in explaining the highly localized LVE norm. While there are small enclaves of transplanted Lumbee in cities such as Baltimore, Maryland, and Greensboro, North Carolina, who keep in regular contact with their relatives back home, their historical and current demographic profile is quite localized. Part of the reason that outside listeners could not identify Lumbee speakers in the identification task was no doubt related to the lack of firsthand experience with them and the general lack of Lumbee visibility beyond Southeastern North Carolina. Sociohistorical factors that include past and present settlement patterns, demographic distribution, population density, and patterns of migration are therefore essential to understanding the development and maintenance of vernacular norms.

There is also a *sociolinguistic component* to vernacular norming in the sense that vernacular structures are socially marked and instantiated within given speech communities. Communities may differ significantly in their social embedding of dialect structures, selectively focusing on some variants as dialect icons while ignoring others. Thus, Schilling-Estes and Wolfram (1999) show how two isolated island communities in the mid-Atlantic with similar dialect profiles, Smith Island in the Chesapeake Bay area and Ocracoke on the Outer Banks, differ significantly in their social marking of structures. For example, Smith Island, Maryland, has seized upon the front-gliding of the diphthong /aw/ ([æɪ]) as a symbolic marker of dialect identity while Ocracoke, North Carolina, has selected the backing and raising of /ay/ ([ʌ > ɪ]) as a dialect icon. Vernacular dialect norming therefore must take into account the process of social embedding as structures are selectively instantiated and differentially marked socially in particular vernacular dialect communities.

There is also a *sociopsychological component* in that individual and group identities are constructed and maintained through dialect variation. With respect to AAVE, for example, "oppositional identity" (Fordham and Ogbu 1986) may explain why younger African American speakers who have lived all of their lives in the isolated, distinctive dialect areas such as Hyde County are abandoning their regional dialect roots in favor of an external, supra-regional AAVE norm. Apart from the increased contact with outsiders and the expanded mobility of the younger generation, it must be recognized that present-day AAVE speakers want to sound neither "white" nor "country."

We also saw the role of identity as an essential part of Lumbee construction of a "linguistic other." The dialect norm of the Lumbee is centered in their self-proclaimed, unique identity that differentiates them from both African American and white varieties. Linguistic-cultural identity is obviously an essential ingredient of constructing a vernacular norm, whether covert or overt.

Finally, there is *an ideological dimension* to the construction of vernacular norms. Underlying assumptions and beliefs about ethnic group membership may influence the establishment of vernacular norms. Part of the reason that AAVE is so strongly defined along ethnic lines is no doubt the bi-racial ideology that has defined US society. Accordingly, the primacy of ethnolinguistic distinctiveness certainly has factored into the development of a supra-regional norm for AAVE as African Americans in Boston, Los Angeles, the rural South, and elsewhere in the US distinguish themselves from Anglo Americans in their speech.

In contrast, the Lumbee are neither white nor black in a bi-racial society. Correspondingly, their dialect is neither. By the same token, however, the Lumbee have had to distinguish themselves more from African Americans than from Anglo-Americans because they have historically been classified and subordinated along with African Americans. For example, in census classifications of race, they were designated as "free people of color" until the twentieth century and they were also subjected to Jim Crow laws along with African Americans. They have also had to contend with persistent claims that they are essentially African Americans who are trying to escape the social subordination of being black in US society. Their dialect therefore is more opposed to AAVE than it is to Anglo-American vernaculars. We thus see how racial ideology in the US enters into the construction of dialect differentiation and identity, both on a local and a non-local level.

Perhaps the most essential lesson in this discussion is that the construction of vernacular norms cannot be reduced to a single dimension or circumstance. As demonstrated in our illustrative cases, linguistic, demographic, sociohistorical, sociopsychological, and ideological factors all enter into the construction of vernacular norms. In various permutations, we would expect these factors to be involved in the construction of both vernacular and standard norms, although they might be instantiated and regulated in quite different ways.

Notes

Research reported here was funded by the National Science Foundation, BCS 99-10224 and SBR-96-16331, as well as the William C. Friday Endowment at North Carolina State University. Becky Childs assisted in the fieldwork and analysis of data, and Amy Gantt and Renee Hammonds assisted in the administration and analysis of speaker identification tasks. Dan Beckett offered helpful suggestions on a preliminary version of the paper.

1   Some of these issues obviously are connected to Weinreich, Labov, and Herzog's (1968) taxonomy of problems for an empirical theory of language change (viz., the *actuation, constraint, transition, embedding, and evaluation* problem). Our focus on the construction of vernacular norms leads us to emphasize a slightly different but complementary set of issues.
2   The listening task was constructed and administered by Amy Gantt.
3   The listeners were students enrolled for credit in courses at North Carolina State University who did not have a background in linguistics. The listening task was administered by Amy Gantt and Walt Wolfram in Raleigh, and by Renee Hammonds and Walt Wolfram in Robeson County. In Robeson County, the task was administered to a group of students at the University of North Carolina at Pembroke, a church youth group between 11 and 16 years of age, and a convenience sample of other selected individuals.
4   It should be noted that the appeal to the early contact situation as a basis for explaining some long-term substratal effects on AAVE does not imply the acceptance of the creolist hypothesis about its genesis.
5   Between 1990 and 1998, the Lumbee population growth has been 16 percent, African American growth 8 percent, and white population growth 5 percent.
6   Although it has sometimes been suggested (Craig 1991; Leap 1996) that there was a pan-Indian vernacular, the kinds of dialect features that set apart the Lumbee in Robeson County do not parallel the typical features set forth for this pan-Indian variety. Furthermore, the social circumstances that may have given rise to such a panlectal variety, such as the Indian Boarding Schools, did not pertain to the Lumbee situation. For the most part, the dialect features distinguishing the Lumbee here are thus quite localized.
7   Preliminary results from Robeson County Anglo-Americans and African Americans given the same speaker identification task suggest that they also identify Lumbee at high levels of accuracy but we do not yet have sufficient numbers of respondents in these categories to support this observation statistically.
8   Although I would agree with this assessment of the United States as it applies to the Mid-Atlantic region where this study takes place, I would be hesitant to apply this bi-racial ideology to the

United States without qualification. For example, in some parts of the Southwest where Native Americans and Mexican Americans are the primary ethnic groups along with Anglo–Americans, the racial ideology might be somewhat different than that for the East Coast of the US.

References

Ash, Sharon and Jon Myhill. 1986. Linguistic correlates of inter-ethnic contact. *Diversity and Diachrony*, ed. by David Sankoff, 33–44. Philadelphia/Amsterdam: John Benjamins.

Bailey, Guy and Natalie Maynor. 1985. The present tense of *be* in Southern Black folk speech. *American Speech* 60: 195–213.

Bailey, Guy and Natalie Maynor. 1987. Decreolization? *Language in Society* 16: 449–73.

Bailey, Guy, Thomas Wikle, Jan Tillery, and Lori Sand. 1991. The apparent time construct. *Language Variation and Change* 3: 241–64.

Baugh, John. 1983. *Black Street Speech: Its History, Structure, and Survival*. Austin: University of Texas Press.

Bordewich, Fergus M. 1996. *Killing the White Man's Indian: Reinventing Native Americans at the End of the Twentieth Century*. New York: Doubleday.

Chambers, J. K. 1995. *Sociolinguistic Theory*. Malden, MA Oxford: Basil Blackwell.

Cheshire, Jenny (ed.). 1981. *English around the World: Sociolinguistic Perspectives*. Cambridge: Cambridge University Press.

Childs, Becky. 2000. *A Hyde County Clusterfest: The Role of Consonant Cluster Reduction in a Historically Isolated African American Community*. MA thesis. Raleigh: North Carolina State University.

Craig, B. 1991. American Indian English. *English World-Wide* 12: 25–61.

Dannenberg, Clare. 1999. *Sociolinguistic Constructs of Ethnic Identity: The Syntactic Delineation of Lumbee English*. PhD dissertation. Chapel Hill: University of North Carolina at Chapel Hill.

Dannenberg, Clare and Walt Wolfram. 1998. Ethic identity and grammatical restructuring: *Be(s)* in Lumbee English. *American Speech* 73: 139–59.

Dayton, Elizabeth. 1996. *Grammatical Categories of the Verb in African-American Vernacular English*. Philadelphia: PhD dissertation. University of Pennsylvania.

Fasold, Ralph W. 1972. *Tense Marking in Black English: A Linguistic and Social Analysis*. Arlington: Center for Applied Linguistics.

Fasold, Ralph W. and Walt Wolfram. 1970. Some linguistic features of Negro dialect. *Teaching Standard English in the Inner City*, ed. by Ralph W. Fasold and Roger W. Shuy, 41–86. Washington, DC: Center for Applied Linguistics.

Fordham, Signithia and John Ogbu. 1986. Black students' school success: Coping with the burden of "acting white". *Urban Review* 18: 176–206.

Graff, David, William Labov, and Wendell A. Harris. 1986. Testing listeners' reactions to phonological markers of ethnic identity: A new method for sociolinguistic research. *Diversity and Diachrony*, ed. by David Sankoff, 45–58. Philadelphia/Amsterdam: John Benjamins.

Green, Elaine W. 1998. *A Marshland of Ethnolinguistic Boundaries: Conflicting Past and Present Tense be Paradigms in Coastal Carolina Speech*. MA thesis. Raleigh: North Carolina State University.

Hazen, Kirk. 1999. *Identity and Ethnicity in the Rural South: A Sociolinguistic view Through Past and Present Be*. Publications of the American Dialect Society No 82. Durham, NC: Duke University Press.

Johnson, Daniel M. and Rex R. Campbell. 1981. *Black Migration in America: A Social Demographic History*. Durham, NC: Duke University Press.

Kay, Marvin L. and Lorin Lee Cary. 1995. *Slavery in North Carolina, 1748–1775*. Chapel Hill/London: University of North Carolina Press.

Labov, William. 1966. *The Social Stratification of English in New York City*. Washington, DC: Center for Applied Linguistics.

Labov, William. 1969. Contraction, deletion and inherent variability of the English copula. *Language* 45: 715–62.

Labov, William. 1972. *Language in the Inner City: Studies in the Black English Vernacular*. Philadelphia: University of Pennsylvania Press.

Labov, William. 1998. Co-existent systems in African-American Vernacular English. *African-American English: Structure, History and Use*, ed. by Salikoko S. Mufwene, John R. Rickford, Guy Bailey, and John Baugh, 85–109. London/New York: Routledge.

Labov, William, Paul Cohen, Clarence Robins, and John Lewis. 1968. *A Study of the Non-Standard English of Negro and Puerto Rican Speakers in New York City*. United States Office of Education Final Report, Research Project 3288.

Leap, William. 1993. *American Indian English*. Salt Lake City: University of Utah.

Lippi-Green, Rosina. 1997. *Language Ideology and Discrimination in the United States*. London/New York: Routledge.

Miller, Jason P. 1996. *Mixed Sociolinguistic Alignment and Ethnic Identity: R-Lessness in a Native American Community*. MA thesis. Raleigh: North Carolina State University.

Milroy, Lesley. 1999. Standard English and language ideology in Britain and the United Sates. *Standard English: The Widening Debate*. ed. by Tony Bex and Richard Watts, 173–206. London/New York: Routledge.

Montgomery, Michael, Janet Fuller, and Sharon DeMarse. 1993. The black men has wives and sweet harts [and third person -s] jest like the white men: Evidence for verbal -s from written documents on nineteenth-century African American speech. *Language Variation and Change* 5: 335–57.

Mufwene, Salikoko S. 1996. The development of American Englishes: Some questions from a creole genesis perspective. *Focus on the USA*, ed. by Edgar W. Schneider 231–64. Philadelphia/Amsterdam: John Benjamins.

Poplack, Shana (ed.). 1999. *The English History of African American English*. Malden, MA/Oxford: Basil Blackwell.

Poplack, Shana and David Sankoff. 1987. The Philadelphia story in the Spanish Caribbean. *American Speech* 62: 291–314.

Poplack, Shana and Sali Tagliamonte. 1989. There's no tense like the present: Verbal -s inflection in Early Black English. *Language Variation and Change* 1: 47–84.

Poplack, Shana and Sali Tagliamonte. 1991. African American English in the diaspora: Evidence from old-line Nova Scotians. *Language Variation and Change* 3: 301–39.

Rickford, John R. 1999. *African American Vernacular English: Features, Evolution and Educational Implications*. Malden, MA/Oxford: Blackwell.

Sapir, Edward. 1921. *Language*. New York: Harcourt.

Schilling-Estes, Natalie. 1997. Intra-ethnic differentiation and cross-ethnic accommodation: /ay/ in Lumbee Native American Vernacular English. New Ways of Analyzing Variation 26. Quebec. October.

Schilling-Estes, Natalie. 1998. Situated ethnicities: Constructing and reconstructing identity in the sociolinguistic interview. Paper presented at New Ways of Analyzing Variation 27. Athens, GA. October.

Schilling-Estes, Natalie and Walt Wolfram. 1999. Alternative models of dialect death: Dissipation vs. concentration. *Language* 75: 486–521.

Stack, Carol. 1996. *Call to Home*. New York: HarperCollins.

Thomas, Erik R. forthcoming. *An Acoustic Analysis of Vowel Variation in New World English*, Publication of the American Dialect Society No. 85. Durham, NC: Duke University Press.

Torbert, Benjamin. 2000. *Consonant Cluster Reduction in North Carolina Native English Varieties*. MA thesis. Raleigh: North Carolina State University.

Trudgill, Peter. 1986. *Dialects in Contact*. Oxford: Basil Blackwell.

Trudgill, Peter. 1990. *The Dialects of England*. Oxford: Basil Blackwell.

Weinrich, Uriel, William Labov, and Marvin Herzog. 1968. Empirical foundations for a theory of language change. *Directions for Historical Linguistics*, ed. by Winford Lehman and Yalkiel Malkiel, 95–188. Austin, University of Texas Press.

Winford, Donald 1997. On the origins of African American Vernacular English – a creolist perspective, Part I: The sociohistorical background. *Diachronica* 14: 304–44.

Winford, Donald. 1998. On the origins of African American Vernacular English – a creolist perspective, Part II: The features. *Diachronica* 15: 99–154.

Winford, Donald. forthcoming. Creoles in the context of contact linguistics. *Pidgin and creole linguistics in the 21st century*, ed. by Glenn Gilbert. Amsterdam/Philadelphia: John Benjamins.

Wolfram, Walt. 1980. A-prefixing in Appalachian English. *Locating Language in Time and Space*, ed. by William Labov, 107–43. New York: Academic Press.

Wolfram, Walt. 1996. Delineation and description in dialectology: The case of perfective *I'm* in Lumbee English. *American Speech* 70: 5–26.

Wolfram, Walt. forthcoming. The sociolinguistic construction of remnant dialects. *Methods in Sociolinguistics*, ed. by Carmen Fought.

Wolfram, Walt, Becky Childs, and Benjamin Torbert. forthcoming. Tracing dialect history through consonant cluster reduction. *Southern Journal of Linguistics* 24.

Wolfram, Walt and Donna Christian. 1976. *Appalachian Speech*. Arlington, VA: Center for Applied Linguistics.

Wolfram, Walt and Chare Dannenberg. 1999. Dialect identity in a tri-ethnic context: The case of Lumbee American Indian English. *English World-Wide* 20: 79–116.

Wolfram, Walt and Ralph W. Fasold. 1974. *The Study of Social Dialects in American English*. Englewood Cliffs: Prentice-Hall.

Wolfram, Walt and Jason Sellers. 1999. Ethnolinguistic marking of past *be* in Lumbee Vernacular English. *Journal of English Linguistics* 27: 94–114.

Wolfram, Walt, Kirk Hazen, and Natalie Schilling-Estes. 1999. *Dialect Maintenance and Change on the Outer Banks*. Publications of the American Dialect Society 81. Tuscaloosa: University of Alabama Press.

Wolfram, Walt and Natalie Schilling-Estes. 1995. Moribund dialects and the endangerment canon: The case of the Ocracoke brogue. *Language* 71: 696–721.

Wolfram, Walt and Natalie Schilling-Estes. 1997. *Hoi Toide on the Outer Banks: The Story of the Ocracoke Brogue*. Chapel Hill: University of North Carolina Press.

Wolfram, Walt and Natalie Schilling-Estes. 1998. *American English: Dialects and Variation*. Malden, MA/Oxford: Basil Blackwell.

Wolfram, Walt, Erik Thomas, and Elaine W. Green. 2000. The regional context of Earlier African-American Speech: Reconstructing the development of African-American Vernacular English. *Language in Society* 28(3).

15

The Linguistic Individual in an American Public-Opinion Survey

Barbara Johnstone

More than perhaps any other, the telephone public-opinion survey is a speech event in which the display of an individual's linguistic voice is meant to be suppressed. It is a situation in which people are not only not evaluated on the basis of how well or clearly they express their individual identities, but in which variation from individual to individual is supposed to be avoided. The explicit goal of a public-opinion poll is the production of information, and this product is valued precisely to the extent that the interviews are not influenced by individual idiosyncrasy on the part of interviewers. If polls proceed the way they are intended to proceed, one might expect individual expression to be nonexistent. If it is not – if there is variation from interviewer to interviewer – then it is worth wondering why. If people perform linguistic tasks such as this, which they suppose "a machine could do" (and which machines sometimes do, in fact, do), in individually varied ways, it must be for the most pressing reasons.

I look in this paper at thirty-six telephone opinion-poll interviews conducted by twenty-four different interviewers, to see if there is individual variation, and if so where it occurs and what forms it takes. In these interviews, randomly selected respondents answer the same questions asked for the same purpose by a very homogeneous group of interviewers, all of whom use the same written questionnaire and have been trained to use it the same way. I find that there is individual variation throughout the poll interviews, even in the most completely scripted and least interactive portions. People appear to express their linguistic individuality not only when they are being judged on the basis of it, as in the composition of a poem or the performance of a story in conversation, but even when they are not required to, and in fact even when they are not supposed to. This suggests that we need ways of thinking about language and discourse in which variation from individual to individual is taken more seriously than it is in most current approaches.

1 How Telephone Surveys are Supposed to Work

The public-opinion poll interview is understood, by people who use its product, by its designers, by interviewers, and by many respondents, to be conversation at its most externally controlled and least self-expressive. Social facts about interlocutors such as age and occupation, which influence what speakers say and how they say it in other speech events, are supposed to be suppressed in telephone interviews. Such interviews are thus understood to be as anonymous as any sort of talk. They are also meant to be as referential as talk can get – interviewers are supposed to introduce the task, ask the questions, and respond to the answers exactly the same way other interviewers do and exactly the same way in each interview, and the only thing that counts for the statistics which result from the poll are the respondents' answers, coded by the interviewer on a copy of the questionnaire with a letter or a word or short phrase. If there is any speech task in which there should be no individual variation at all, one might expect it to be that of the poll interviewer.

Scholarship about interviewing has demonstrated that language does not act as a neutral code for the exchange of facts in this speech event, any more than it does in any other speech event. Interviewers inevitably affect the results of interviews (Hyman et al. 1954). Brenner (1981) found, for example, that almost 13% of all questions in face-to-face interviews were "significantly altered" by interviewers. In a study of how poll respondents' behavior varied depending on the sex of the interviewer, Johnstone, Ferrara, and Bean (1991) found that male respondents in interviews conducted by females, apparently often uncomfortable with the fact that the interviewer controls the flow of topics and turns in the interaction, sometimes attempted to break the interview frame by doing things like giving facetious or inappropriately formatted answers. Female respondents were more likely to be cooperative, treating the task as a test rather than a game. Theorists such as Cicourel (1964: 74–5) and Briggs (1986: 23–4) point out that the two goals of survey research – validity and reliability – are incompatible: a completely reliable interview would be completely standardized, so as to assure that the same results would occur another time, but a completely standardized interview is least likely to get at respondents' real feelings and opinions.

Nonetheless, directors of polls, interviewers, and consumers of survey information justify survey research in general, and interviewing in particular, with reference to the belief that discourse can be designed in such a way as to be impersonal, value-free, and purely referential. Practitioners like the director of the Texas Poll assume that variability, since it can lead to biased results, is error, and they train their staffs to stray from the written schedule as little as possible. Supervisors are supposed to check to see that interviewers stick to the script. Manuals for interviewers and textbooks about survey research reiterate that "differences among research interviewers must be minimized or eliminated" (Nathan 1986: 69; see also Stano and Reinsch 1982; Hoinville et al. 1978). Each instruction, question, transition, and acknowledgment is to be pre-planned word for word and delivered exactly as scripted. Interviewers are not supposed to rephrase or explain questions, provide clues about their own attitudes, talk about their own backgrounds, or provide any more than minimal acknowledgments of answers. The reputation of the polling agency, and hence its ability to attract clients, depends on assurance that interviews are always conducted the same way.

2   How Telephone Surveys Actually Work: Individual Variation Among Texas Poll Interviewers

To examine one aspect of how this speech event actually works, I looked at 36 interviews, taped and transcribed, from one run of the Texas Poll. The Texas Poll is conducted quarterly by the Public Policy Resources Laboratory at Texas A&M University. Respondents each quarter are approximately 1,000 residents of Texas. Most of the interviewers are college students, almost all are women, most are around 20 years old, and most are from middle- to upper-middle-class urban or suburban families from Texas. Like other such surveys, the Texas Poll is a standardized, scripted interview which includes both open-ended and multiple-choice questions. The questionnaire prescribes exact wording for the introductory portion of the interview and for each question, as well as for topic shifts between sets of questions ("On a different topic;" "On another subject;" "Now we want to ask some questions about . . ."). The subset I analyzed includes at least one from each of the 24 interviewers who conducted the survey on that occasion. (Three of these interviewers were male, 21 female; one was African-American and two were Hispanic.) In order to be able to examine the amount of variability in a single interviewer's performance of the task as well as variability among different interviewers, I also examined seven additional interviews by one of the female interviewers and five additional interviews by one of the male interviewers. In addition, since some of the interview tapes begin with repeated attempts to locate an appropriate respondent, I was able to examine multiple introductions by two other interviewers.

In what follows, I look at three elements of each interview: the interviewers' fully scripted introductions, interviewers' acknowledgments of respondents' answers (which are not scripted, but which are required, especially in telephone talk, so that respondents will know they have been heard), and interviewers' unelicited comments during or about responses, which are neither scripted nor required. For each of these three speech acts, I ask two questions. First, is there variation from speaker to speaker? The answer, in brief, is that in every case there is. Second, what are the continua along which interviewers' choices, in general, seem to vary? I will suggest two, one discourse-syntactic (more subordinative versus more coordinative ways of connecting clauses) and one interactional (how often and in what ways interviewers make reference to themselves and the people they are talking to).

2.1 Introductions

This bit of talk takes place at the very beginning of the interaction, immediately after someone at the number being called picks up the phone and says "Hello." The script printed on the schedule of questions is this:

> Hello, this is _____ calling for the Texas Poll, a statewide, nonpartisan public opinion poll. This month we are conducting a confidential survey of public opinion in Texas, and we'd really appreciate your help and cooperation.

There are five underlying clauses in this passage:

1. This is _____
2. [I am] calling for the Texas Poll
3. [The Texas Poll is] a statewide, nonpartisan public opinion poll
4. This month we are conducting a confidential survey of public opinion in Texas
5. we'd really appreciate your help and cooperation

Of the 21 occurrences of the complete introduction, only two are exactly the same as the script on the schedule. Only two others are identical to each other; both of these differ from the protocol in adding *I'm* before *calling* (thus making clause 2 finite), adding two *and*'s to the script, and substituting *with* for *for* in clause 2. Both interviewers choose to use their first and last names rather than first name only to fill in the blank in the first clause. (All interviewers have been given pseudonyms.)

Three of the 24 interviewers are making call-backs to respondents who were unavailable or unwilling to answer the survey on an earlier occasion. Interviewers begin these with part of the script, before shifting to an unscripted explanation of the function of the call:

Hello, this is Walt Field and I'm calling for the Texas Poll. And uh . . . I have uh, uh . . . a message to . . . We called a couple of days ago and that we should, we should try back today.
(Transcription conventions are provided at the end of the paper.)
Hi, my name is Jessica Whitman. ØI'm calling *with* the Texas Poll. [Respondent: Yeah.] I believe, uh, someone called for you yesterday.

Note that neither the first nor the second clauses in these two examples are identical. The dissimilarities are highlighted in the second example. Walt Field begins with "Hello," Jessica Whitman with "Hi." For Field's "this is" Whitman says "my name is." Both interviewers change the script's embedded "calling for the Texas Poll" to the independent clause "I'm calling;" Field connects the two clauses with *and*, and Whitman changes *for* to *with*.

Two introductions are quite deviant, involving the reordering and deletion of information in the script, as well as the addition of other information:

Hello, uh my name is Lianne and I'm calling for the Texas Poll. We're doing a statewide, nonpartisan public opinion poll, and it's a confidential survey of public opinion in Texas, sir.

Hello, my name is Elizabeth McMillan and I'm calling for Texas A&M University? for a Texas Poll that we're conducting? [Respondent: Uh-huh] and it's just a statewide, nonpartisan public opinion poll that we do three times a year. It's a confidential survey of public opinion in Texas? and we'd appreciate your help with it?

The remaining fifteen introductions differ from one another, and from the script, along two axes. The first has to do with how the five clauses in the script are connected. Any of the five clauses can be spoken as an independent clause; while in the script only three clauses are independent, in the interviews all five can be. With the exception of the first, each clause can be connected to the preceding clause with *and*. Thus the script, which includes several embedded clauses and only one *and*, can be spoken entirely in coordinate clauses connected with *and*:

Hello. My name is Mary Porter *and* I am calling from the Texas Poll *and* this is a statewide, nonpartisan public opinion poll *and* in this month we are conducting a confidential survey of public opinions in Texas *and* we would really appreciate your help and cooperation but first of all ma'am . . .

Five interviewers, on the other hand, connect clauses only once, in four cases between the third and fourth clauses ("*and* this month we are conducting . . .") and in one case between the second and third clauses ("*and* the Texas Poll is . . ."). In the middle of this range, two or three *and*'s may be employed, at the beginnings of any combination of clauses. The third clause, which appears in the script as the appositive noun phrase "a statewide, nonpartisan public opinion poll," is actually spoken that way by only six of the 24 interviewers. More often, it occurs as an independent clause. Seven options are employed:

It's a statewide . . .
It's just a statewide . . .
This is a statewide . . .
This is merely a statewide . . .
We're a statewide . . .
We're doing the statewide . . .
which is a statewide . . .

In summary, interviewers almost always speak a version of the introduction in which bits of information are less tightly packed into clauses and more explicitly linked than in the version on their script, but they do so in a wide variety of ways.

The other axis along which the introductions vary is what could be called "person-ability," or how often and in what way the introductions make reference to the people involved in the interaction. The script refers twice to *we* ("we are conducting;" "we'd really appreciate"), and the interviewer is required to refer to him or herself by name ("this is ____"). In all cases except two of the non-callback introductions, the two required *we*'s are included, and in every case at least one extra reference to "I" or "we" is added. Elaine Maldonado includes the two required *we*'s, as well as three extra first-person pronouns:

Hi, *my name* is Elaine and *I'm* calling for the Texas Poll. *We're* a statewide, nonpartisan public opinion poll. And this month *we are* conducting a confidential survey of public opinions in Texas. *We'd* really appreciate your help and cooperation. Do you have a few moments?

There is in addition another marker of personability in Elaine Maldonado's introduction: the appended question addressed to and about the respondent: "Do you have a few moments?" Other markers of personability are common as well. Ten of the interviewers use only their first names, but others choose to give both first and last names. This format suggests more clearly that they are real people than does the first-name-only format, which is used to identify the filler of the server role in many service encounters. Thirteen interviewers add *sir* or *ma'am*. Four exchange the script's *hello* for the more personable *hi*, though one makes a shift in the other direction with *good afternoon*.

If any part of the poll interviews could be expected to display little individual variation, it would be the introductions. This segment of the interview occurs before interviewer and respondent know anything about each other (except that the interviewer has heard the respondent's voice and may thereby have identified the subject's sex and ethnicity). The introduction is completely scripted on the questionnaire. Yet out of 24 cases the introduction occurs 22 different ways. The interviewers appear in almost all cases to be responding to the same troubles with the script: it is too writerly to be easily understandable, and too distancing to be effective in encouraging respondents to cooperate. But no two interviewers correct these problems the same way. The result is 24 different voices, doing 22 different things structurally.

2.2   Acknowledgment of answers

At the end of each answer and before making the transition to the next question, interviewers must indicate that the answer is satisfactory in format (i.e. codable on the interviewer's questionnaire) and complete, and that it has been heard. All 24 interviewers do this. Because the poll interviews take place over the phone, answer-acknowledgment needs to be done verbally (rather than, as often in face-to-face conversation, by eye movement or other gesture), and interviewers are instructed to provide it. This element of the interviewers' linguistic behavior is thus required, but, unlike the introduction, it is not scripted. I have examined the first five acknowledgments in each interview.

Interviewers almost invariably choose *okay* or some variant (*m'kay; 'kay*). This may have to do with the fact that Texas Poll trainers suggest this discourse marker to interviewers as appropriately neutral. But *okay* is rarely the whole of an answer acknowledgment. *Okay* may be spoken with question intonation. In addition to *okay*, an acknowledgment may repeat part or all of the answer, either before or after *okay*, in what Merritt (1977) refers to as a "playback:"

RESPONDENT: Well, right now, the economy right now.
INTERVIEWER: *The economy?* Okay.

An acknowledgment may also add a synonym to *okay*, such as *all right, right*, or *I see*, or *gotcha*:

RESPONDENT: Your education.
INTERVIEWER: Education. Okay, *gotcha*, education.

and/or announce that the interviewer needs time to encode the answer:

RESPONDENT: . . . I mean the work. Lot of people out of work.
INTERVIEWER: Okay, *let me get that down.*

Acknowledgments often include a transition to the next question. These include *and then, now, well now*, and *the next one is now.* Many interviewers, but not all, also use the scripted transitions on the questionnaire, which include *looking ahead, turning to x*, and *thinking about x.* Occasionally an interviewer will provide only a transition, without *okay*, or no acknowledgment at all. *Ma'am* can be part of the acknowledgment, as can a comment on the answer preceding *okay*:

You did? Okay, uhm, [next question]
Oh, is that right? Okay.

In a few cases, interviewers adopt riskier, ambiguous strategies for acknowledging answers, strategies which could appear evaluative:

That'll work.
Well that's, that's what we want Arturo.
That's great.

   Though individuals are not entirely consistent in the strategies they use for answer-acknowledgment, there is far less variation within interviews, and across interviews by the same interviewer, than across interviews by different interviewers. Some interviewers tend to repeat part of the answer; others do not. Some tend to repeat combinations like "okay, okay" or "okay, all right," whereas others do not. Some use *now* in making the transition to the next question while others do not.
   Though the range of variation is small, the choices individuals make for acknowledging answers tell their respondents something about them as individuals, and help shape the texture of the interview. If the interview were really the predictable, anonymous, referential sort of speech its users assume it is, then these small differences should not occur.

2.3   Unelicited comments on answers

I look next at an element of the interviewers' talk which is neither scripted nor required: interviewers' unelicited comments during or about respondents' answers. These are comments which are not responses to direct verbal prompts by the respondent such as "Could you repeat that?" or "How am I supposed to answer that?" To begin with a rather stunning example, during a respondent's anecdote in answering a question about whether abortion should be legal, one interviewer interjects:

That's, ah-hah, that's . that's really neat. That happened with a friend of mine too. So. that happened with a friend of mine's family too. They adopted a baby, a little girl.

This sort of commentary is not condoned by interviewer supervisors and directors of polling services, and interviewers can lose their jobs for it. Most unelicited commentary is not so extended: "I know what you mean," "goodness," "that's fine."
   Unelicited comments by interviewers appear to serve a number of functions, many of which have the effect of creating personality. Interviewers may reassure subjects that a "don't know" answer is acceptable. There is very little variation in how this is done:

Okay, that's fine.
That's okay.
Okay, that's fine.
Okay. That's fine. That's fine.
Okay sir, that's fine.

Interviewers sometimes comment on respondents' justifications of their answers:

> RESP: ((laugh)) I guess [the new President]'s done pretty good. He had a good
> party the other day.
>
> → INTERVIEWER: ((laugh)) That's a good start. 'Kay.

Or they may apologize for asking difficult questions:

I know you're going "Oh gosh."
I know it's kinda hard to think of 'em.

In these cases, comments always create personability by either mentioning or alluding directly to "I" and "you," and such apologetic comments are always style-shifted toward the informal from the formal prose of the questionnaire.

In addition, interviewers sometimes comment on respondents' answers:

> RESPONDENT: [justifies an answer about gun control]
>
> → INTERVIEWER: Right, I agree with you there.

> RESPONDENT: [responds to question about whether she has ever gone to a doctor to be checked for skin cancer by saying "No, but I worked for a dermatologist part time."]
>
> → INTERVIEWER: Hey . . . hey there you go, you don't . . . Hey, that's that's what you gotta do.

Interviewers may also use unelicited comments to instruct respondents about how to do the task at hand, after a hesitation,

> RESPONDENT: Um (.5) gosh ((laugh)) . um (.5)
>
> → INTERVIEWER: Just . j- . just how do you feel?

or when the respondent is answering too quickly,

> RESPONDENT: I think the most important issue is being certain that nuclear=
>
> → INTERVIEWER: =Wait. Being certain. I'm sorry, I'm writing this down word for word if you could be patient with me. Being certain that . . .

or when the answer is inappropriate to the question, as when one respondent answers a multiple choice question rating Texas as a place to live with "I like it just fine," when "fine" was not one of the choices that had been read to her:

Nkay. Most of our questions have a specific answer. You can just choose from the answers I read you.

Other functions interviewers' comments can serve include commentary on the poll's procedures or questions,

> RESPONDENT: Uh . . . well, that's kind of a loaded question. I'd say yeah, I'd say yes.
> → INTERVIEWER: Okay. . . . Yeah, now they're real simplified questions, I guess they have
> to be more or less.

or allusion to other respondents,

> RESPONDENT: [objects to the choices given in a fixed-alternative question]
> → INTERVIEWER: Okay. Well, talking to others I think we do need a . . . a middle category.

or commentary on their own performance:

Ah . . . I wasn't trying to insult your intelligence . . .

Okay. Okay. I'm still trying to figure out how to spell Wichita Falls. ((laughs)) I'm stupid.

In one interview, the respondent sounds congested and sneezes, and this provokes "Bless you. Did you sneeze?" and "Sounds like you're getting over a bad cold?" from the interviewer.

Variation in interviewers' unelicited comments, except in the case of reassurances, is enormous, both in structure and function. There are many ways to stray, slightly, from the task at hand, and many choices of words and syntax along each tangential path. What interviewers' unelicited comments have in common, though, is that they tend to create the sense that a real individual is speaking with another real individual.

3   Reasons for Individual Variation

Some of the deviation from the explicit and implicit script of the interview task has to do with enhancing its referential function. For example, interviewers make the introduction less subordinative in order to make it easier to understand by ear, and they reassure hesitant respondents and instruct confused ones in order to make the flow of answers continue. But most of the deviation from the scripted task has the effect of enhancing the individuality of the speaker. When interviewers deviate from the script they speak as themselves rather than as representatives of the Texas Poll. Interviewers express individual identities because talk will not continue unless they do. Seasoned poll interviewers are in fact perfectly aware of this and acknowledge that even though they know why they are supposed to stick to the script, interviewers who do stick to the script are less successful: potential respondents hang up the phone.

For Americans, unsolicited telephone calls from strangers are an infringement of privacy, a serious threat to a person's right to choose whom to interact with. Furthermore, the poll asks questions which may embarrass respondents, either by forcing them to admit ignorance or by requiring them to divulge private information (such as their income, age, and religion). Interviewers are required to violate strongly held beliefs about how people should treat one another. (For this reason, the job is perceived as very stressful, and the turnover rate is high.) In Brown and Levinson's (1987[1978]) terms, the interviewer's call is a "face threatening act," and such acts are rude unless they are mitigated by means of various "politeness strategies."

Many of the interviewers' deviations from the script can be seen as politeness strategies. For example, interviewers lessen the threat to respondents' face by allowing respondents to stray from the topic if it appears that respondents want to do so, by displaying personal interest in respondents' answers, and by identifying themselves with respondents. They reduce the imposition of requesting personal information by divulging information about themselves. They console respondents who are forced to admit ignorance. They act deferentially, in voices that sometimes sound tentative and hedged, showing respect with "sir" or "ma'am," apologizing for difficult questions, and thanking respondents. But while all interviewers are bound by the special requirements of this speech event for politeness, not all fulfill the obligation the same way. No two sound alike. Some are successful by being deferential and businesslike; others are equally successful with friendly, sympathetic, affiliative strategies. Some use a mixture. The need for politeness can help explain why interviewers deviate from the script, and why many of the deviations take the forms they do. But it does not explain why these extra expressions of politeness take so many different forms.

3.1   Individuation, culture, language ideology

Being polite means acting like a person and treating other people as people. People's ideas about what it means to be a person, though, are not everywhere the same. While it may be that some sort of conception of the self, as distinct from other selves and from non-human things, is universal (Hallowell 1955), specific ideologies about personhood vary from society to society and from era to era. In Bali, for example (Geertz 1984 [1974]), individuals are defined by titles and designations, as an actor is defined by a role; consistent performance of one's externally defined role is what matters. Idiosyncrasy is cause for shame, since when people let individuality show they fall out of character. The case has been made that this conception of person as social role was also characteristic of Classical Western society, until the Roman era, when "persona" as mask became "person" as individual legal entity (Mauss 1938).

The Texas Poll interviewers and respondents appear to share in a conception of person diametrically opposed to that of the Balinese. Being a person is being an individual, and self-expression is crucial for mental health and social acceptance. Americans' individualism has been remarked on for as long as Americans have been a nation, by outsiders such as De Tocqueville as well as by insiders such as Thoreau and Emerson. Sincerity is valued more than conformity, and even the most traditional forms of speech (such as wedding vows), which must elsewhere be repeated verbatim, are often seen as meaningless unless done differently by different people. "Playing a role" or speaking "lines" is dishonest, and not true to the self. What it means to be a "character" is not to play a preordained part, but rather the opposite: if someone is a "character" it is because she behaves differently than others and thus sets herself apart for special notice. It is insincere, rude, and, increasingly, illegal to treat a person as the filler of a role rather than as a distinct individual.

The required expression of individuality occurs in many modalities, among them language. To use language completely idiosyncratically would be to be incomprehensible, but the existence, in humans, of strategies for figuring out what someone might mean even if one has not heard it said that way before means that it is possible to do new things with language. And, crucially for our purposes here, it is more polite to express one's individuality than it is to be completely conventional, because being different means being engaged, paying attention to what one is doing, not "being a machine." This, then, is why politeness strategies in the survey interviews, though all chosen from a conventional set of possibilities, take the varied form they do rather than a more consistent form. Individual variation, in short, is polite, because poll interviewers are culturally required to act as individuals and treat others as individuals.

4 Discussion

The research I have reported on here raises issues for linguistic practice and linguistic theory. The first has to do with anonymous telephone public-opinion surveys. As mentioned above, previous research has shown that public-opinion polls are flawed by their nature. But public-opinion surveys continue to be widely used, and their results, in the United States, are enormously powerful.

The continued use of public-opinion surveys has in part to do with conscious decisions about the cost–benefit ratio of the procedure; people use it in spite of its shortcomings. But it also has to do with ideologies about language and language users. Language is understood by pollsters and poll-users as a code, a tool for exchanging objective information which, if used carefully, can be infallible. For survey work, this means that if the questions are worded correctly, and the interviewers trained well, facts can be elicited. Poll interviewers, on the other hand, need to express individuated personalities. By their design, polls require identical wordings, but if the interviewers in fact all talked the same way, refusing to depart from the script, they would be perceived as machine-like and unresponsive to the individuated personalities of their respondents, and the respondents might stop cooperating. The problem is thus more radical, and perhaps less easily soluble, than has been previously suggested.

Though poll interviewers express their individuality by means of linguistic choices drawn from relatively restricted conventional sets, the result of all their ways of deviating from the script is that each one has an individual style, an individual voice which can be tracked across interviews with very different respondents who are making very different interactional demands. Most theories of language, focused on what is theoretically "shared" among speakers and what is empirically observable across utterances, do not take this fact seriously, treating individual idiosyncrasy as deviance or ignoring it altogether (Johnstone 1996, 2000).

In one way of doing linguistics, however, deriving from the discourse-based philological tradition of close reading of texts, individual differences are treated as a "vantage point from which to consider questions of method and theory in the study of language in general" (Hymes 1979: 36). In this view, people create grammar by talking; the language, linguistic competence, or *langue* usually seen as prior to talk, performance, or *parole* is in fact a consequence of discourse. Hopper (1988), for example, speaks of "emergent grammar"; Tannen (1989) of a "poetics of talk" in which utterances are created out of snatches of remembered speech and of others' phrases; Becker (1984, 1988) of a "linguistics of particularity" in which "languaging" is the focus. Since the goal of linguists in this more humanistic paradigm is to work toward understanding language through coming to understand particular instances of language use, describing what makes a given text *different* from others – its individual, particular language – is as important as understanding what makes it *similar* to others. So, for example, Friedrich and Redfield (1979 [1978]: 435) suggest that "our models of language and of linguistics should include individual language and speech as significant variables," and Becker (1981: 5) points out that "the most difficult task for the philologist is to hear the individual voice." The Texas Poll suggests that individual voice is not only present, but crucial, in every speech event. It suggests a need for a linguistics of individuality based in the stylistics of the most mundane forms of everyday talk.

Transcription Conventions

. . .	short pause of up to half a second (number of dots corresponds roughly to the length of the pause
(.5)	longer pause of half a second or more, in seconds
:	following a vowel, indicates elongated vowel sound
((laugh))	extralinguistic sounds
=	links two conversational turns, where the second follows directly on the first without a pause
→	highlights key lines
Ø	highlights a missing item

Note

This is a shortened and somewhat updated version of Johnstone 1991. Dawn Washington provided invaluable help in analyzing the data; an Undergraduate Research Opportunity grant from the Department of English at Texas A&M University funded her work. I am also grateful to James Dyer of the Texas A&M Public Policy Resources Laboratory for allowing the January 1989 Texas Poll to be taped, and to Guy Bailey for taping it and making the tapes available to me, as well as to the student volunteers who transcribed some of the tapes I discuss. I received useful reactions to drafts of this paper from members of the Texas A&M Linguistics Colloquium and the Discourse Studies Group and from Dell Hymes, Jane Hill, Lesley Milroy, Carol Myers Scotton, Ellen Barton, and Neal Norrick. Christina Bratt Paulston made valuable suggestions about how to edit the paper for an introductory reader like this one.

References

Becker, A. L. 1981. "On Emerson on language." *Georgetown University Round Table on Languages and Linguistics 1981*, ed. by Deborah Tannen, 1–11. Washington, DC: Georgetown University Press.

Becker, A. L. 1984. "The linguistics of particularity: Interpreting superordination in a Javanese text." In Claudia Brugman and Monica Macaulay (eds) (with Amy Dahlstrom, Michele Emanatian, Birch Moonwomon, and Catherine O'Connor), *Proceedings of the Berkeley Linguistics Society, Tenth Annual Meeting*, 425–36. Berkeley, CA: Berkeley Linguistics Society.

Becker, A. L. 1988. "Language in particular: A lecture." In *Linguistics in Context: Connecting Observation and Understanding*, ed. by Deborah Tannen, 17–35. Norwood, NJ: Ablex.

Brenner, Michael. 1981. "Aspects of conversational structure in the research interview." In *Conversation and Discourse: Structure and Interpretation*, ed. by Paul Werth, 19–40. London: Croon Helm.

Briggs, Charles L. 1986. *Learning How to Ask: A Sociolinguistic Appraisal of the Role of the Interview in Social Science Research* (Studies in the Social and Cultural Foundations of Language 1). Cambridge: Cambridge University Press.

Brown, Penelope and Stephen C. Levinson. 1987. *Politeness: Some Universals in Language Usage*. Cambridge: Cambridge University Press. (First published 1978 in *Questions and Politeness*, ed. by Esther Goody.)

Cicourel, Aaron. 1964. *Method and Measurement in Sociology*. New York: The Free Press of Glencoe.

Friedrich, Paul and James Redfield. 1979. "Speech as a personality symbol: The case of Achilles." In *Language, Context, and the Imagination: Essays by Paul Friedrich*, selected and introduced by Anwar S. Dil, 402–40. Stanford, CA: Stanford University Press. (First published in *Language* 54(1978): 263–88.)

Geertz, Clifford. 1984. "From the native's point of view: On the nature of anthropological understanding." In *Culture Theory: Essays on Mind, Self, and Emotion*, ed. by Richard A. Shweder and Robert A. LeVine, 123–36. Cambridge: Cambridge University Press. (First published in *Bulletin of the American Academy of Arts and Sciences* 28 (1974), no. 1.)

Hallowell, A. I. 1955. "The self and its behavioral environment." In *Culture and Experience*, ed. by A. I. Hallowell, 75–110. Philadelphia: University of Pennsylvania Press.

Hoinville, Gerald, Roger Jowell and associates. 1978. *Survey Research Practice*. London: Heinemann Educational Books.

Hopper, Paul. 1988. Emergent grammar and the a priori grammar postulate. In *Linguistics in Context: Connecting Observation and Understanding*, ed. by Deborah Tannen, 117–34. Norwood, NJ: Ablex.

Hyman, H. et al. 1954. *Interviewing in Social Research*. Chicago: University of Chicago Press.

Hymes, Dell. 1979. "Sapir, competence, voices." In *Individual Differences in Language Ability and Language Behavior*, ed. by Charles J. Fillmore, Daniel Kempler, and William S.-Y. Wang, 33–45. New York: Academic Press.

Johnstone, Barbara. 1991. "Individual style in an American public-opinion survey: Personal performance and the ideology of referentiality." *Language in Society*, 20 (4), 557–76.

Johnstone, Barbara. 1996. *The Linguistic Individual: Self-expression in Language and Linguistics*. New York: Oxford University Press.

Johnstone, Barbara. 2000. "The individual voice in language." *Annual Review of Anthropology*, 29, 405–24.

Johnstone, Barbara, Kathleen Ferrara, and Judith. M. Bean. 1992. "Gender, politeness, and discourse management in same-sex and cross-sex opinion-poll interviews." *Journal of Pragmatics*, 18, 405–30.

Mauss, Marcel. 1938. "Une catégorie de l'esprit humain: La notion de personne, celle de 'moi'." *Journal of the Royal Anthropological Institute* 68. (Trans. by H. D. Wells, A category of the human mind: The notion of person; the notion of self, in Carrithers, Michael, Steven Collins, and Steven Lukes (eds), 1985. *The Category of the Person: Anthropology, Philosophy, History*, 1–25. Cambridge: Cambridge University Press.)

Merritt, Marilyn. 1977. "The playback: An instance of variation in discourse." In *Studies in Language Variation: Semantics, Syntax, Phonology, Pragmatics, Social Situations, Ethnographic Approaches* (Colloquium on New Ways of Analyzing Variation, 3, Georgetown University, 1974), ed. by Ralph W. Fasold and Roger W. Shuy, 198–208. Washington, DC: Georgetown University Press.

Nathan, Harriet. 1986. *Critical Choices in Interviews: Conduct, Use, and Research Role.* Berkeley: Institute of Governmental Studies, University of California, Berkeley.

Stano, Michael E. and N. L. Reinsch Jr. 1982. *Communication in Interviews.* Englewood Cliffs, NJ: Prentice-Hall.

Tannen, Deborah. 1989. *Talking Voices: Repetition, Dialogue, and Imagery in Conversational Discourse.* Cambridge: Cambridge University Press.

Discussion Questions

1. Observe and describe at least two speech situations which differ in their level of formality (for example, a politician's speech and a conversation between friends). Make note of any differences in language/linguistic style that you notice. Does pronunciation, vocabulary or grammar differ? How?

2. With a classmate, role-play discussing a test on which you did poorly with the following people:

   Your best friend
   Another classmate
   Your professor
   Your mother.

   What linguistic elements, if any, changed in your language? What does this say about how you switch linguistic style for different speech situations? Does the gender of your interlocutor have any impact on the language you use?

3. In primary or secondary school, were you explicitly taught that some linguistic forms were not proper or non-standard? List them and describe why they are considered non-standard. Are there times nonetheless when you would use them? What are examples of some of these times. Are there any groups of speakers that do use these forms? Who are they? What is the general perception of these groups?

4. Consider the forms you listed in answer to question 3. Which of Labov's types do they correspond to (pp. 241–3)?

5. Interview three people from different age groups. Ask their opinions about the use of the "nonstandard" forms you reported in answer to question 3. Do they all agree? Is there any evidence of language change, related to age, in their evaluations?

6. Conduct six telephone interviews (modeled after Johnstone's interviews) and test for the presence or absence of any of the forms you discussed in questions 3–5.

Part VI

Pidgins and Creoles

Introduction

The interest in and study of pidgins and creoles have been around a lot longer than sociolinguistics has. Hugo Schuchardt (1842–1927) was the first scholar of international standing to take the study of pidgins and creoles seriously at a time when scholars considered them unworthy of academic concern. As Bickerton notes, in Schuchardt's "essays, one can find virtually all the ideas of the 20th-century creole studies, in embryonic form" (1979: viii). Pidgins and creoles were not considered "proper" full-fledged languages; they were thought to have no grammar and structure, just individual aberrations by speakers with no prestige; much of the early data came from African (ex)-slave speakers in the Caribbean and the Americas.

Today this picture has changed. The field, in Rickford and McWhorter's (1997) words, has much "frictious energy," by which they mean that many scholars don't agree with the views of many other scholars, and these arguments are being debated in the journals, especially in *The Journal of Pidgin and Creole Studies*. Sociolinguists are interested in this field for a number of reasons. First, the sociohistorical settings are more than just background; they form a very part of these languages: "the processes of pidginization and creolization . . . seem to represent the extreme to which social factors can go in shaping the transmission and use of language" (Hymes 1971: 5). Second, pidgins and creoles are wonderful data sources for theory testing of models of sociolinguistic variation and change: "researchers interested in the study of sociolinguistic variation, multilingualism, and code-switching, are often attracted to pidgin and creole speaking communities, for the opportunities they offer to study these topics and related ones, such as the relation of language to social class, power, and identity" (Rickford and McWhorter 1997: 239). Third, because so many of the pidgins and creoles studied so far have been varieties based on European languages in ex-colonial settings, they tend(ed) to exemplify and epitomize situations of social injustice where language is used to index and legitimate social inequality: "Not the least of the crimes of colonialism has been to persuade the colonialized that they, or ways in which they differ, are inferior – to convince the stigmatized that the stigma is deserved," in Hymes's (1971: 3) felicitous phrase. This situation has attracted scholars (and funding) concerned with issues in language planning and policies, literacy and illiteracy, language attitudes, and standard and non-standard languages, in applying the knowledge base of sociolinguistics in pragmatic ways. And finally, pidgins and creoles are just plain fun to study; who wouldn't like a language which expressed the notion of "moustache" as "grass belong mouth" as in Tok Pisin (pidgin talk), a Melanesian English Pidgin from Papua New Guinea?

Pidgins are contact languages between speakers of different languages who want to communicate but do not share a common language, in situations of discovery, trade, conquest, slavery, migration, etc. Pidgins have no native speakers, and when the contact situation disappears, so does the pidgin; typically they are not stable languages. An exception was the famous Lingua Franca, Sabir, the language of trade and crusades in the Mediterranean from the Middle Ages until the twentieth century. Tok Pisin is another exception; in fact, a good creolist can find exceptions to most general statements about pidgins and creoles.

Pidgins are a mixture of their source languages, often with most of the vocabulary from one language and most of the grammar from another, simplified from both the original languages. Here is an example from Tok Pisin, translated by the Reverend Paul Freyberg, chief translator of the Nupela Testamen:

Tripella liklik pik i stop long bush. Ol i no gat haws, na i gat wanpela waildok tu.
Three little pigs lived in the forest. They had no house, and there was a wolf there too.

tripella = three fellow; pella, a classifier
liklik = little; reduplication
pik = pig; devoicing and zero plural morpheme
i = predicate marker
stop = live
long = belong; all purpose preposition
bush = (here) forest
ol = all; plural marker
wanpela = one
waildok = wild dog, wolf

Note that the vocabulary comes from English with a pronunciation influenced by the sound systems of the local languages while much of the grammar reflects the structure of the Eastern Oceanic languages; Tok Pisin is called an English-based pidgin. On Haiti, they speak a French-based creole:

Rive Jan rive Mari pati.
As soon as John arrived, Mary left

rive = arriver, in predicate doubling
pati = partir (Muysken and Veenstra, 1995: 158)

In "classical" creole theory, a creole is a pidgin which has acquired native speakers (from the offspring of the pidgin speakers). Today, there is considerable scholarly disagreements over the relationship of pidgins to creoles and their origin. But scholars do agree that as native tongues, creoles expand in grammar and lexicon to meet all the needs required of them; they become regular full-fledged languages. But, and it is an important but, since many creoles coexist with their lexicon-base as the standard, official language, like standard French on Haiti, standard English on Jamaica, the language attitudes towards the creole become complicated. Although the language of home and hearth, of intimacy and solidarity, the creole gets 'no respect'; it has low social status, is considered ignorant or slang, jive and the like, and often its very existence is denied by its own speakers. It makes for a problematic and difficult educational setting.

There is a considerable literature on pidgins and creoles, which discusses issues like creole–standard diglossia, creole continuum with its acrolect and basilect, decreolization and relexification, as well as many educational and language planning issues. The article we have chosen for inclusion here is often cited and rarely read; it is one of the earliest academic studies on the sociological aspects of creole languages and based on Reinecke's 1937 PhD thesis in sociology at Yale University. You take it from there yourself!

References

Bickerton, Derek. 1979. "Introduction," in T. L. Markey (ed.), *Hugo Schuchardt: The Ethnography of Variation. Selected Writings on Pidgins and Creoles*, pp. vii–xvii. Ann Arbor, MI: Karoma Press.

Freyberg, Paul. No date. "Three little Pigs" translated into pidgin and adapted to a Melanesian setting. Broadcast by Superintendent Mike Thomas in the ABC's daily learning pidgin series. Boroko, T.P.N.G.: Australian Broadcasting Commission.

Hymes, Dell (ed.). 1971. *Pidginization and Creolization of Languages*. Cambridge: Cambridge University Press.

Muysken, Pieter and Tonjes Veenstra. 1995. "Haitian," in J. Arends, P. Muysken and N. Smith (eds.), *Pidgins and Creoles: An Introduction*, pp. 153–64. Amsterdam: Benjamins.

Rickford, John R. and John McWhorter. 1997. "Language contact and language generation: Pidgins and creoles," in F. Coulmas (ed.), *The Handbook of Sociolinguistics*, pp. 238–56. Oxford: Blackwell.

Further Reading

Arends, Jacques, Pieter Muysken and Norval Smith. 1995. *Pidgins and Creoles: An Introduction*. Amsterdam: Benjamins.

Bickerton, Derek. 1990. *Language and Species*. Chicago: University of Chicago Press.

McWhorter, John H. 2000. *The Missing Spanish Creoles: Recovering the Birth of Plantation Contact Languages*. Berkeley: University of California Press.

Mühlhäusler, Peter. 1986. *Pidgin and Creole Linguistics*. Oxford: Blackwell.

Romaine, Suzanne. 1988. *Pidgin and Creole Languages*. London: Longman.

Romaine, Suzanne. 1992. *Language, Education and Development: Urban and Rural Tok Pisin in Papua New Guinea*. Oxford: Clarendon Press.

Singler, John Victor. 1996. "Theories of creole genesis, sociohistorical considerations, and the evaluation of evidence: The case of Haitian creole and the relexification hypothesis," *Journal of Pidgin and Creole Languages*, 11: 2, 185–230.

Thomason, Sarah G. (ed.). 1997. *Contact Languages: A Wider Perspective*. Amsterdam: Benjamins.

Valdman, Albert. 1977. Pidgin and Creole Linguistics. Bloomington: Indiana University Press.

16

Trade Jargons and Creole Dialects as Marginal Languages

John E. Reinecke

1

When men of different speech are thrown into contact and must reach an understanding, four courses are open to them. If their contact is brief and discontinuous and limited to very simple transactions, speech may be dispensed with. Dumb barter is a form of accommodation reported from many parts of the world. Nevertheless one may suspect that it does not always preclude bilingualism; it is probably more a mechanism of defence than an expedient of ignorance. In any case, it is of limited usefulness and little used.[1] Members of two linguistic groups may speak a third language which they have already learned in other contact, *i.e.*, a lingua franca. Members of one group may learn efficiently the language of a second group. In the long run one of these two accommodations usually prevails; and the social importance of effective bilingualism is hard to overestimate. But there is a fourth possible course, which in the initial stages of intergroup contact is of great importance, and which may leave a permanent mark upon linguistic and social history. Neither group may be in a position to learn the other's language or a common third tongue at all correctly, so that both will be content with an imperfect approximation to one of the languages: a debased or pidginized or jargonized form, (as Jespersen terms it) a minimum or makeshift language.

   [. . .]

2

[It is with this form of linguistic accommodation that we are concerned here]: the forms of language known, with various degrees of accuracy, as trade languages or jargons, creole languages, mixed languages, lingua francas, minimum or makeshift languages, substitute languages, pidgins.[2] None of these terms appears to be sufficiently exact and at the same time broad enough to be applied to all the languages under consideration. As a general appellation the present writer therefore proposes the term *marginal languages*, with the following definition: The marginal languages arise in areas of pronounced culture contacts, in situations where, broadly speaking, it is impossible or impracticable for the peoples concerned to learn each other's language well. Their structure, relative to that of the languages from which they have been derived rather recently, is greatly broken down and simplified. Largely because of this broken-down structure, but also because of the circumstances under which they are spoken, they are often held in contempt by a large section of their speakers, by speakers of the parent languages, or by both.

These jargonized languages are marginal in reference both to their parent languages and to the cultural environment in which their parent languages are spoken. By those who know the languages from which they are derived, they are usually despised as being beneath the level, not only of standard or common languages, but also of the various patois and class dialects – themselves often despised – which do at least share in the linguistic structure of the accepted standard dialects. The marginal languages are dismissed, not merely as "bad grammar" or "dialect," but as "lingoes," "hodge-podge," "*Kauderwelsch*," "no language." Often they are in fact so broken down and deviant from the parent dialects as to become new, unintelligible languages. Merely as aggregates of linguistic tools they are therefore regarded as marginal. Their speakers, too, being restricted by such divergent, and presumably imperfect, forms of language, are regarded as marginal to the main body of speakers of English, French, or whatever the parent language may be. Furthermore, the term "marginal" as developed by the Chicago school of sociologists bears the connotations of lack of full participation in a society – of standing on the border between two societies or two cultures. The languages to which the word marginal is here applied usually arise on very pronounced frontiers of culture; they are in fact a rather characteristic phenomenon of certain types of the frontier. [. . .]

To the general observer, the marginal languages have enough of a distinct character (chiefly because of their simplified, minimum-approaching rather than minimum, structure) to be treated together and for peculiar attitudes to develop regarding them. They constitute a distinct field for the study of what has been called, perhaps prematurely, *Sprachsoziologie*.

A number of tolerably good studies have been made of particular marginal dialects, but almost invariably from a strictly linguistic point of view. Historical data have been introduced usually only in order to illustrate points in the structure of the languages, and data of sociological significance is scattered and incidental at the best. Nevertheless, from these studies a reasonably accurate idea may be reached of the nature of the marginal languages, of the circumstances of their formation, and thus of the divisions into which they fall.

An inductive examination of the literature on more than forty of the languages defined as marginal shows that they are divisible into several classes on the double basis of the milieu in which they took shape and of their functions. While these classes are not sharply distinguished one from another, yet it is economical to discuss the marginal languages by categories. The present writer distinguishes three important general classes, which constitute probably the only groups of relatively permanent jargons: the trade jargons, the plantation creole dialects, and the settlers' creole dialects.

Previous discussions of the so-called creole *or* trade languages have mostly suffered in clarity because they have all been lumped together – a practice perfectly justified on linguistic grounds. A common-sense dichotomy into trade jargons *and* creole dialects was adumbrated by several writers and stated in passing by the great creolist Hugo Schuchardt;[3] but the first attempt at a formal classification of the marginal languages did not appear until 1933, in an article by Professor Ernst Schultze of Leipzig, the title of which may be translated as "Slaves' and Servants' Languages (So-called Trade Languages), an Essay in the Sociology of Language and Migration."[4] This, as the pioneer sociological essay in its field, deserves special attention, and is a provocative piece of work, though marred by confused reasoning and an insufficient acquaintance with the source materials.

[. . .]

Schultze is correct in his original distinction between the trade jargons and the slaves' and servants' languages, and at error in his over-emphasis upon the importance of domination in all situations where jargons are spoken. Schultze also overlooks what the present writer considers the main point of difference between the trade jargons and the creole dialects (of both classes), namely that the former remain supplementary languages whilst the latter become primary languages.

3

The trade jargons may be regarded as the least developed forms of marginal language that have attained considerable fixity. Originally they arise out of the casual intercourse of traders (generally seamen) with a fixed population, although later they may be extended to serve the intercourse between the native population and resident foreigners who for some reason do not learn the native language. In the beginning they are truly makeshift, and since they tend to be short-lived, disappearing as soon as one or the other party finds it expedient to learn a standard tongue to serve as a common medium, some of them retain much of their makeshift character till their end. They remain very fluid, full of circumlocutions owing to their small vocabulary, inadequate for any but the simpler transactions. [. . .]

It is worth pointing out that the master-and-dependent relationship emphasized by Schultze does not obtain very strongly in trade situations. Between trading peoples there must be a modicum of mutual respect and freedom of action. Consequently the foreign trader may sometimes adopt the indigenous language as the basis of a jargon. Nootka and Chinook are the foundation of the Chinook Jargon, though today its vocabulary is mostly English. The Eskimo trade jargon of Alaska, the pidgin Motu of Papua, and the "Kitchen Kafir" of Natal are other examples of the adoption of a native base; so is the Tupi Lingua Geral of parts of Brazil, though this is not strictly speaking a jargon. The Pidgin English of Canton, however, to some extent illustrates Schultze's thesis, though in a different sense than he believed; for the English were originally in a position of dependence and their jargon was deliberately fostered by the Chinese in order to hold them at arm's length.

If the advance of trade is marked by the creation of jargons, the consolidation of trade relations and the foreign conquest which so often follows trade are marked by the disappearance of jargons. Those current within the past century must be but a small proportion of the total spoken within historic times, or even since the beginning of Western expansion about 1500. Alongside the speakers of any jargon are usually some persons who, enjoying special advantages, have learned the language more adequately. In case the language is akin to the native tongues or is easy to acquire, the jargonized varieties may be of limited extent and quickly yield place to the standard speech. This appears, on the strength of the scanty evidence, to be the case with Hausa and Swahili among the African tribes. On the other hand, English, so foreign in sound and structure to the Sudanese-speaking people, remains predominantly a pidgin in West Africa. Among literate peoples, too, the advantages of a correct writing and speaking knowledge of a trade language are obvious. While the "Russenorsk" jargon that had been current in northern Norway for four or five generations was abruptly killed by the World War, it would soon have been extinguished in any case, because young Russians connected with commercial firms saw the need of learning good Norwegian. The Lingua Franca of the Mediterranean was quickly ended by steam navigation and the French conquest of North Africa.

Only in exceptional circumstances do trade jargons gain a long lease of life, and still more exceptionally do they become established as permanent lingua francas of a region. Cantonese-English owes its tenacity (*c.* 1715 to the present) to the peculiar restrictions placed upon foreign trade before 1842, which allowed the jargon of a small community to become standardized to the point where it was even studied from textbooks by Chinese tradesmen. But since the diffusion of true English among all classes of the Chinese ports, the Pidgin is clung to only by some die-hard foreigners accustomed to use it in talking down to their servants, and its use is resented even by houseboys. The Lingua Franca, the archetype of trade jargons, had an existence of perhaps eight centuries, but this was only because the name Lingua Franca was applied to several Romance jargons differing from time to time and from place to place. Naturally, the more polyglot an area, the better chance has a pidgin to spread and to remain in use for a long time. [. . .]

Very seldom does a trade language spontaneously become the mother tongue of a group. Perhaps the only example in the literature is that of the Chinook Jargon, which is said to have been for a time the sole language of a few children of French Canadian *voyageurs* and squaws in Oregon Territory.

Certain dialects which may be classed with the trade jargons arise, it must be admitted, from master-and-servant relationships; but, since the servant is to a large extent a free agent and is in communication with his own society while the master remains an alien in the land he rules, these dialects remain supplementary and tend to disappear without attaining a stable structure. [. . .]

4

As opposed to the trade jargons, the creole languages or jargons are now primary languages, and the result of very definite domination of one people by another. Since the term "creole languages" is popularly applied to any European (especially a Romance) tongue spoken overseas in a debased form, it is, therefore, used of two distinct classes of language, sociologically considered.

One of these, the one more akin to the trade jargons in its origin, the present writer has called "settlers' creole dialects." These languages arise in situations where a small group of foreigners settle as colonists or traders in the midst of a very much larger native population. Instead of becoming assimilated linguistically, they are able because of commercial, cultural, or military-political advantages to impose their language as a lingua franca of trade – usually in a simplified and corrupted form. At the same time they assimilate a part of the native population through intermarriage, domestic slavery, and conversion to their religion and customs. (These are the only marginal languages in the formation of which intermarriage plays a direct and important rôle). This mixed population, having apprehended the colonists' language imperfectly, reduces its flexion and introduces idioms and words from its own languages. Clearly defined local dialects take shape. With the decline of the parent language as a medium of trade and admin-istration, the creole dialects remain in use as the domestic language of the mixed-blood groups, who now adopt some other tongue as their lingua franca with the surrounding population. The chief present examples of this type of language are the Portuguese-speaking communities of southern Asia and formerly of West Africa, débris of the Portuguese trade empire of the sixteenth and seventeenth centuries. The descendants of the *Bounty* mutineers on Pitcairn Island, however, probably illustrate in miniature the same phenomenon.

[. . .]

5

Quite distinct in their nature are the plantation creole dialects. These languages are the result of a set of circumstances which, so far as the literature indicates, are peculiar to a particular stage in the colonial exploitation of the tropics by Europeans, involving the introduction of African slave labor (*c.* 1500–1875). The West Indies, Guiana, French Louisiana, the Portuguese islands off West Africa, and the Mascarenes are the chief seats of these dialects, though the Gullah-speaking Sea Islands of South Carolina are also included, and also perhaps at one time Bahia in Brazil. Sierra Leone and Fernando Po in West Africa, settled by liberated West Indian slaves, speak dialects derived partly from America, partly from the mistakes of assimilated African natives, which therefore are on the borderline between the two types of creole language.

The plantation creole tongues are true *Sklavensprachen*. Although they owe some-thing to the sailors' trade jargons, they began essentially as makeshift means of com-munication between masters and field hands. The slaves, of very diverse origin, either quickly forgot their native languages or found them of very limited usefulness. The first creole generation was usually monolingual in an imperfectly apprehended, flexionless or at least greatly simplified dialect of their masters' language.[5] As spoken by the raw slaves the dialect was a crude makeshift, by no means improved by the masters' efforts to talk down to their chattels. Newcomers, turned over to old hands for seasoning, learnt the jargon from them: "matty a larn matty," as an old African of Guiana phrased it. The creole Negroes, in somewhat closer touch with the whites, improved their speech, enriching their vocabulary until it was adequate for their rather simple culture, and in some cases building up a new conjugation by means of auxiliaries. A new dialect – in extreme cases, such as the Negro-"English" of Suriname, a new language – has emerged; this, if through some historic accident it can be removed from the influence of the parent language, follows the usual laws of linguistic development. But since the creole dialects are usually subject more or less to such influence, they tend even under conditions of slavery "to constant leveling-out and improvement in the direction" of the masters' tongue.[6] Indeed, unless the slave population was overwhelmingly in the majority and fairly stable of residence (conditions obtaining especially on the sugar cane-growing islands), only the initial makeshift jargon was spoken; or, if a creole dialect did form, it was soon ironed out and the Negroes came to speak practically the same dialect as the neighboring whites. This leveling-out occurred in most parts of the Southern States and Brazil, as well as in Cuba, Santo Domingo, and Puerto Rico. Especially in the Hispanic colonies, where manumission was common and the freedmen often were merged socially and racially with the whites, conditions were unfavorable to the consolidation of a creole dialect.

The whites, having to speak creole constantly in directing their establishments, and surrounded by creole-speaking nurses and playmates during early childhood, appear usually to have spoken creole more than their standard dialect, though in a somewhat refined form. Their attitudes toward the creole were ambivalent. On the one hand a greater social distance existed between master and black than between an educated person and a peasant in, say, a German patois-speaking district. So the whites, at least in some colonies – for there were differences from place to place and from time to time – despised creole as a low-caste dialect, the imperfect jargon of an inferior race. It was something that one spoke to slaves, horses, and dogs, but not to one's equals unless *en famille*. On the other hand they came to have a sentimental attachment to it as a softer, more expressive medium – at least for everyday and intimate affairs – than the European tongue. A century and a half ago a Swiss traveler in Haiti expressed his annoyance at the fond complacency with which the white creoles regarded their patois. He was sharply answered by a creole, who declared: "There are a thousand things one dares not say in French, a thousand voluptuous images which one can hardly render successfully, which the Creole expresses or renders with infinite grace."[7]

As long as class and caste lines nearly coincided, and all of African descent except a few mulattoes were debarred from participation in the European community, the creole language was accepted by the masses as their proper tongue. Indeed, many of the field hands must have been scarcely aware of the standard language. Then too, even after emancipation, the whites in many colonies resented as presumptuous the use of the standard dialect by a colored person. At the same time, the Negroes developed a feeling for their patois as deep if not as sophisticated as that of the whites. The creole had its own rules and nuances, of which they were aware; they ridiculed the raw Africans who spoke it brokenly, and they enjoyed manipulating it in song and proverb.[8]

With emancipation and the consequent increased participation of the Negroes in the whites' culture – incomplete though this still is – , the attitudes of both races toward the use of creole changed. In some colonies, the liberated slaves at once saw in the acquisition of their masters' tongue a considerable step toward bridging the gap between themselves and the whites. Two years after emancipation in British Guiana a planter observed:

> It is wonderful how fond they have become already of speaking like the buckras [whites], and how sharp they are in picking up phrases, although they do mispronounce the words very "ingeniously."[9]

In general, the attitude of the colored population has come to be much like that of European patois-speakers: the patois is sentimentally dear, it is one's true mother tongue; for an ordinary person to speak any other among his own group is snobbish; but to speak crude patois before or to an educated person is impolite and displays one's ignorance. Lafcadio Hearn used to hear the colored mothers of New Orleans admonish their children: "*Allons, Marie! Eugène! faut pas parler crèole devant monsieur; parlez Français, donc!*"[10] When an educated foreigner enters a Haitian shop, the gossip in creole ceases and everybody assumes his French, such as it may be. Conversely, an educated creole Negro is insulted if addressed in patois.[11]

The whites (and the educated mulattoes who pattern after them) have been slower to give up the traditional linguistic distinction between the classes. In some places they still insist that their inferiors speak creole to them. But the colonial governments, under pressure of European democratic and nationalistic ideology, have insisted that the masses be instructed in the standard tongue. Having accepted this policy, the educated classes in still other places express their superiority by disparaging the creole and regretting its persistency.

Under the double pressure of emulation of the whites and government educational policy, the speakers of the creole dialects tend to modify their speech slowly but steadily in the direction of the standard languages – or, in case the patois is not derived from the official tongue, to drop the former completely. Thus far, however, none of the plantation creole dialects has been assimilated in structure to a standard language, and only one – the Creole Dutch of the Virgin Islands – has gone out of use. This slowness of change is attributable in the first place to the inertia of the hopelessly poor, geographically and culturally isolated colored masses, whose assimilation of European culture is still in large part superficial. Next in importance is the maintenance or development of an attitude of pride in the creole as a regional idiom. This attitude is shared by both races, though among the whites it appears to take a rather condescending aspect. Writers both white and colored have produced literature in a refined creole, and a mulatto of Cayenne even achieved the *tour de force* of a sizable novel written entirely in Guyanais French.[12] Only in a few areas, however, is the creole dialect generally regarded as better than a mere patois; and here the reason for its superior status must be sought in a complex of local conditions. Wide difference between the official tongue and the folk language accounts in part for the strength of Taki-taki "English" and Papiamento Spanish in the Dutch colonies of Suriname and Curaçao respectively. Missionaries, beginning their work in these colonies under slavery, before the authorities would allow the blacks to be taught Dutch, reduced the patois to writing and created a considerable religious literature, thus giving the creole a dignity which it still enjoys. In Curaçao a widely read press, under ecclesiastical direction but increasingly secular in content, has kept the Papiamento vigorous in spite of its discontinuance as a medium of instruction; and the 80,000 inhabitants of all social classes, loyal Dutch subjects but conscious of at least a semi-national tradition, regard Papiamento as in a fashion a national tongue. Papiamento has for the time attained a prestige unequalled by any other creole tongue, but, spoken by so small a group and crowded by Dutch, English, and Spanish, its position is more precarious than that of the creole French of Haiti. All the two and a half million Haitians speak Créole, and most of them, being illiterate peasants, speak nothing else. Toward this dialect the handful of cultivated people display an equivocal attitude.

On the one hand they pride themselves on their mastery of Parisian French, their link with the culture of France and a protection against the assimilative power of the United States. On the other hand they are attached to their patois and realize that it is the true national tongue of a considerable nation. Some believe that only in the Créole will the Haitians attain literary autonomy. The problem of lifting the masses to a knowledge of literary French is almost insoluble; and a compromise has been attempted (at least to a slight extent) through the use of school texts written in parallel Créole and French. Thus under favorable circumstances the creole dialects may attain the respectability of the minor European languages formerly spoken only by peasants, such as Estonian or Lettish.[13]

6

The three major classes discussed above are the only forms of marginal language relatively stable enough to allow them to be described grammatically. Another form, the broken speech of free immigrants, is of great social significance and considerable literary importance (*cf.* the comic stage in particular, and such writings as *Hans Breitmann's Ballads*). But Italian-Spanish or Yiddish-English, for example, is not an entity with its own norms. It is an amorphous mass of what Schuchardt called "individual corruptions," attempts, varying widely in degree of success, to reach the norm of the native language. These attempts show a resemblance but have no common denominator. Under modern conditions of free immigration they cannot endure, for the second or third generation of immigrant stock is exposed to so many contacts with the native stock that it becomes completely assimilated linguistically.

A partial exception may be observed only in a few places where there is already a plantation creole or a trade jargon tradition to build upon. Thus in Hawaii, where a broken English containing many Hawaiian words had long been spoken between natives and foreign seamen, Asiatic and Portuguese coolies imported to work under partially servile conditions on the sugar cane plantations gave rise to a Pidgin English of a certain stability and consistency. This has been perpetuated for sixty years from one group of immigrants to another; but the immigrants' own children, educated in American schools, speak a dialectal but increasingly standardized English. The Hawaiian linguistic situation, therefore, falls part way between that of free immigration and that of the servile plantation colonies.[14]

Notes

1   See P. J. Hamilton Grierson, *The Silent Trade*, etc. (Edinburgh, 1903). The widespread gesture codes, such as the Sign Language of the Plains Indians, are a special form of lingua franca which may have had their origin within a single language group, and which in any case depend upon bilingualism for their spread. Drum languages and similar codes have in general nothing to do with inter-group communication.

2   These expressions are popular, except for minimum and makeshift languages, terms coined by Otto Jespersen (*Language*, p. 232), and substitute languages, a term coined by Ernst Schultze (in *Sociologus*, 9: 377–418).

3   Schuchardt (1842–1927) was in his time the foremost authority on the so-called creole languages. The reference is in *Zeitschrift f. romanische Philologie*, 33: 441 (1909).

4   "Sklaven- und Dienersprachen (sogen. Handelssprachen) Ein Beitrag zur Sprach- und Wanderungs-Soziologie," *Sociologus*, 9: 377–418 (Dec. 1933).

5   There were exceptions. In some colonies the major nationalities among the slaves were recruited for generations and had their slave "kings." In Brazil, for reasons not wholly clear, but which are probably connected with the early use of the Tupi Lingua Geral on the coast and the close trade connection with Guinea and Angola, no impressive Creole Portuguese dialect ever arose; but several African languages, notably Yoruba, have been maintained down to the present date. Both fetishistic and Muhammedan cults have used African tongues in their services. Some groups of independent runaway Africans, notably the Saramacca tribe in Suriname, have also retained many African expressions, particularly in their semi-esoteric religious songs.

6   Leonard Bloomfield, *Language*, p. 474.

7   L. E. Moreau de Saint-Méry, *Description . . . de l'isle Saint-Domingue* (1797), Vol. I, p. 65; see Girod-Chantrans, *Voyage d'un Suisse*, etc. (1785), pp. 189–191.

8   J. Vendryes wrote of the creole: "[The natives'] apprenticeship to this language was never completed. It was limited to its superficial characteristics, to expressions representing the ordinary objects and essential acts of life; the inner essence of the language, with its fine complexities, was never assimilated by the native." (Vendryes, *Language*, p. 295.) This is much exaggerated. A new set of complexities was evolved; the creole came to have its own "inner essence" and to be applicable to social and religious concepts of considerable subtlety.

9   "Barton Premium," *Eight Years in British Guiana* (1850), p. 66.

10   Lafcadio Hearn, *An American Miscellany*, Vol. II, p. 146 (reprinted from *Harper's Weekly*, 1885).

11   Such attitudes are, of course, possible only where interracial contact and education have been widespread. Among the tribal Bush Negroes and the isolated Haitian peasantry creole is accepted in a matter of fact way as the national tongue.

12   Alfred Parépou, *Atipa, roman guyanais* (1885).

13   Afrikaans, now a full-fledged language almost fanatically cultivated by a nationality fewer than the Haitians, but imperialists, was originally at least a semi-creole patois. With the Portuguese-Dutch-English of the Bush Negroes there is no question of prestige or linguistic competition; it is simply their tribal language. A correspondent in Sierra Leone, where a "Sierra Leonese" English strongly colored by the Sudanese tongues is spoken by the masses, indicates that in spite of the official attitude of contempt toward it among the educated Negroes, they cherish it as a mark of their Sierra Leonese seminationality, just as they cherish English *per se* as distinguishing them from the tribal Africans.

14   See articles by William C. Smith in *American Speech*, 8: 15–19, and John E. Reinecke and Aiko Tokimasa, *ibid.*, 9: 48–58, 122–131. For further references to the marginal languages, see Carlo Tagliavini, article "Creole, Lingue," in *Enciclopedia Italiana*, 11: 833–835; *Hugo Schuchardt-Brevier*, ed. by Leo Spitzer (Halle, 1928); L. Göbl-Gáldi, "Esquisse de la structure grammaticale des patois français-créoles," *Zeit. f. französische Sprache u. Literatur*, 58: 257–295.

Discussion Questions

1. Language change and adaptation are often viewed negatively. Interview someone from your grandparents' generation to find out his or her opinions about how your generation speaks. Give at least four examples of expressions or slang that you use with your friends and see if the representative of the older generation knows what they mean and if he or she thinks they are proper.

2. The term "jargon" is also used to describe the vocabulary of a particular field or profession. Look in a professional journal or publication and identify five words with special meaning in the context of that field. Use a dictionary or interview a professional in that field to find out the special meaning of the words.

3. Have you even been in a situation where you did not speak the language well enough to express yourself and yet needed to communicate? How did you communicate? Describe some of the communication strategies you used or would need to use in such a situation.

4. Reinecke repeatedly uses negative words and terms to describe the so-called marginal languages, for example "inadequate", non-standard, imperfect. Considering the strategies you described in question 3, discuss why this opinion of creoles has existed.

Part VII

Individual Bilingualism

Introduction

The number of bilingual or multilingual individuals in the world is greater than the number of monolingual individuals. And as we know, many more children throughout the world have been, and continue to be, educated via a second or a later-acquired language – at least for some portion of their formal education – than the number of children educated exclusively via a first language. In many parts of the world, bilingualism or multilingualism and innovative approaches to education which involve the use of two or more languages constitute the normal everyday experience (see, for example Dutcher 1994; World Bank 1995).

The tone for this section, and for the complexity and importance of the underlying issues, is perhaps best captured by alluding briefly to recent demographic changes and their potential implications for individuals seeking access to educational and occupational opportunities. The initial analyses of the year 2000 US census data indicate that the population grew more during the period 1990–2000 (from 249 million to approximately 281 million) than during any previous decade. Perhaps what was most surprising was that the minority population grew by 35% during this time while the non-Hispanic white population grew by only 3.4% (Business–Higher Education Forum, 2002, p. 23). In similar fashion, Extra and Vallen (1997) reported that approximately one-third of the population in urbanized western Europe under 35 years of age would have an immigrant background by the year 2000. All indicators point to the likelihood that the early years of the twenty-first century at least will be characterized by a growing interdependence among culturally and linguistically diverse groups of peoples for purposes of commerce, education, security, and tourism.

The three papers in this section have been purposely selected to provide readers with an introduction to, and comment on, a strand of work that has been enormously influential. In the first paper, Lambert presents an integrative review of his early research on the social influences on bilinguals' behaviors and on the social repercussions of bilingualism on these individuals – work that he conducted collaboratively with a rotating group of graduate students from approximately 1956–1966. It seems fair to conclude that the course of inquiry into the nature of the correlates and consequences of individual bilingualism was significantly altered following the pioneering contribution of Lambert and his students. Lambert raised a number of fundamental questions, such as "How does the way that a bilingual individual presents him- or herself in one or the other of his or her languages affect the way that he or she is perceived?" How, and in what ways, and to what ends does the bilingual individual consciously or unconsciously adopt different guises in varying social situations depending upon the ethnicity and the language proficiency of the interlocutors? How do an individual's knowledge about and feelings toward the group whose language is the object of study affect the course of study of that language? What types of social factors affect the allegiances that bilingual individuals develop and how do these allegiances change over time? Lambert appears to have had a remarkable penchant for turning common-sense observations regarding everyday life and behavior into research questions. And his research clearly foreshadowed the burgeoning of interest that we have seen in recent years in the so-called Heritage-language Learner (see, for example, Peyton, Ranard and McGinnis 2001). In later years, Lambert's interests focused even more sharply on understanding the educational, social, and personal consequences of the increasing heterogeneity of North American society (see for example Lambert and Taylor 1990; Lambert 1992; Taylor and Lambert 1996). As he and his colleagues pursued their later research in multicultural and multilingual communities such as Detroit, Michigan and Miami, Florida, Lambert continued to argue that ethnic minorities in North America can effectively and comfortably double their cultural identity, that "they can have two cultures and two languages for the price of one" (Lambert 1991).

Jim Cummins, too, focuses on the bilingual individual in chapter 18, in which he recounts the history and the evolution of the distinction that he drew between the development of basic interpersonal communicative skills (BICS) and cognitive academic language proficiency (CALP). A comprehensive overview of Cummins's writings on this and other topics is available in Baker and Hornberger (2001). This distinction, BICS vs. CALP, although provocative as Cummins and more particularly MacSwan and Rolstad both note, has had profound implications for the assessment and placement of so-called English language learners in North America (see, for example, Hamayan 1997; Cloud, Genesee and Hamayan 2000). Indeed, the issues about which Cummins and MacSwan and Rolstad write will likely come to assume greater and greater importance during the early part of the twenty-first century, particularly in the United States as the number and proportion of minority students in schools continues to increase with the expectation that they will become, in fact, the majority of all students by the year 2030. For example, between 1972 and 1999, the percentage of Hispanics in elementary and secondary schools in the United States increased from 6% to 16%. However, during this time fewer than two-thirds of the Hispanics graduated from secondary school (as opposed to approximately 90% of white and black students) and only 11% of Hispanic students entering college completed their bachelor's degree (as opposed to 28% of whites and 17% of black) (see Business–Higher Education Forum, 2002, pp. 24, 25). As Crandall and Stein (2001) noted: one of every two teachers in American schools is likely to have an English-language learner in class; the majority of these ELLs are likely to be attending the schools with the least resources (highest free or reduced lunch numbers, oldest textbooks, etc.); they are likely to be educated by the largest number of uncertified teachers or teachers teaching out of field; and this is the group with the highest mobility rates for students, teachers, and administrators. The challenges are indeed daunting. Facts such as these and others that are rapidly emerging suggest that our school systems will need to become more and more effective in meeting the needs of English-language learners – a problem that we imagine will confront educators in many parts of the world as the movement of peoples across national borders increases and intensifies. Thus, although scholars may disagree on whether the English-language learner must develop CALP or second-language instructional competence (SLIC) in order to participate effectively in advanced instruction, there is no debate but that the numbers of such learners is increasing rapidly and that their education seems to present a special set of challenges to mainstream education (see, for example, August and Hakuta 1997).

References

August, D. and K. Hakuta (eds.). 1997. *Improving Schooling for Language-Minority Children: A Research Agenda*. Washington, DC: National Academy Press.

Baker, C. and N. H. Hornberger (eds.). 2001. *An Introductory Reader to the Writings of Jim Cummins*. Clevedon, UK: Multilingual Matters.

Business–Higher Education Forum. 2002. *Investing in People: Developing all of America's Talent on Campus and in the Workplace*. Washington, DC: American Council on Education.

Cloud, N., F. Genesee and E. Hamayan. 2000. *Dual Language Instruction: A Handbook for Enriched Education*. Boston, MA: Heinle & Heinle.

Crandall, J. and H. Stein. 2001. "There's no time for learning: All we do is test." Paper presented at the annual meeting of the National Council of Teachers of English. Baltimore, MD.

Dutcher, Nadine in collaboration with G. Richard Tucker. 1994. "The use of first and second languages in education: A review of educational experience." Washington, DC: World Bank, East Asia and the Pacific Region, Country Department III.

Extra, G. and T. Vallen. 1997. "Migration and multilingualism in Western Europe: A case study of the Netherlands." *Annual Review of Applied Linguistics*, 17, 151–69.

Hamayan, E. 1997. "Teaching exceptional second language learners." In G. R. Tucker and D. Corson (eds.), *Encyclopedia of Language and Education, Volume 4: Second Language Education*, pp. 85–93. Dordrecht: Kluwer Academic Publishers.

Lambert, W. E. 1991. "And then add your two cents' worth.' In A. Reynolds (ed.), *Bilingualism, Multiculturalism and Second Language Learning: The McGill Conference in Honour of Wallace E. Lambert*. Hillsdale, NJ: Lawrence Erlbaum.

Lambert, W. E. 1992. "Challenging established views on social issues: The power and the limitations of research." *American Psychologist*, 4, 533–42.

Lambert, W. E. and D. M. Taylor. 1990. *Coping with Ethnic and Racial Diversity in Urban America*. New York: Praeger.

Peyton, J. K., D. A. Ranard and S. McGinnis (eds.). 2001. *Heritage Languages in America: Preserving a National Resource*. Washington, DC/McHenry, IL: Center for Applied Linguistics/Delta Systems.

Taylor, D. M. and W. E. Lambert. 1996. "The meaning of multiculturalism in culturally diverse urban America." *Journal of Social Psychology*, 136, 727–40.

World Bank. 1995. "Priorities and strategies for education." Washington, DC: The International Bank for Reconstruction and Development.

Further Reading

Baker, C. 1993. *Foundations of Bilingual Education and Bilingualism*. Clevedon, UK: Multilingual Matters.

Baker, C. and S. Prys Jones. 1998. *Encyclopedia of Bilingualism and Bilingual Education*. Clevedon, UK: Multilingual Matters.

Belcher, D. and U. Connor (eds.). 2001. *Reflections on Multiliterate Lives*. Clevedon, UK: Multilingual Matters.

Grosjean, F. 1982. *Life with Two Languages: An Introduction to Bilingualism*. Cambridge, MA: Harvard University Press.

Hakuta, K. 1986. *Mirror of Language: The Debate on Bilingualism*. New York: Basic Books.

Hoffman, C. 1991. *An Introduction to Bilingualism*. London: Longman.

Romaine, S. 1995. *Bilingualism*. (2nd ed.), Oxford: Blackwell.

Zentella, A. C. 1997. *Growing Up Bilingual*. Oxford: Blackwell.

17

A Social Psychology of Bilingualism

Wallace E. Lambert

Other contributions in this series [in the *Journal of Social Issues*] have drawn attention to various aspects of bilingualism, each of great importance for behavioral scientists. For instance, we have been introduced to the psychologist's interest in the bilingual switching process with its attendant mental and neurological implications, and his interest in the development of bilingual skill; to the linguist's interest in the bilingual's competence with his two linguistic systems and the way the systems interact; and to the social-anthropologist's concern with the socio-cultural settings of bilingualism and the role expectations involved. The purpose of the present paper is to extend and integrate certain of these interests by approaching bilingualism from a social-psychological perspective, one characterized not only by its interest in the reactions of the bilingual as an individual but also by the attention given to the social influences that affect the bilingual's behavior and to the social repercussions that follow from his behavior. From this perspective, a process such as language switching takes on a broader significance when its likely social and psychological consequences are contemplated, as, for example, when a language switch brings into play contrasting sets of stereotyped images of people who habitually use each of the languages involved in the switch. Similarly, the development of bilingual skill very likely involves something more than a special set of aptitudes because one would expect that various social attitudes and motives are intimately involved in learning a foreign language. Furthermore, the whole process of becoming bilingual can be expected to involve major conflicts of values and allegiances, and bilinguals could make various types of adjustments to the bicultural demands made on them. It is to these matters that I would like to direct attention.

1 Linguistic Style and Intergroup Impressions

What are some of the social psychological consequences of language switching? Certain bilinguals have an amazing capacity to pass smoothly and automatically from one linguistic community to another as they change languages of discourse or as they turn from one conversational group to another at multilingual gatherings. The capacity is something more than Charles Boyer's ability to switch from Franco-American speech to Continental-style French when he turns from the eyes of a woman to those of a waiter who wants to know if the wine is of the expected vintage. In a sense, Boyer seems to be always almost speaking French. Nor is it the tourist guide's ability to use different languages to explain certain events in different languages. In most cases they are not fluent enough to pass and even when their command is good, their recitals seem to be memorized. Here is an example of what I do mean: a friend of mine, the American linguist, John Martin, is so talented in his command of various regional dialects of Spanish, I am told, that he can fool most Puerto Ricans into taking him for a Puerto Rican and most Columbians into taking him for a native of Bogota. His skill can be disturbing to the natives in these different settings because he is a potential linguistic *spy* in the sense that he can get along too well with the intimacies and subtleties of their dialects.

The social psychologist wants to know how this degree of bilingual skill is developed, what reactions a man like Martin has as he switches languages, and what social effects the switching initiates, not only the suspicion or respect generated by an unexpected switch but also the intricate role adjustments that usually accompany such changes. Research has not yet gone far enough to answer satisfactorily all the questions the social psychologist might ask, but a start has been made, and judging from the general confidence of psycholinguists and sociolinguists, comprehensive answers to such questions can be expected in a short time.

I will draw on work conducted by a rotating group of students and myself at McGill University in Montreal, a fascinating city where two major ethnic-linguistic groups are constantly struggling to maintain their separate identities and where bilinguals as skilled as John Martin are not at all uncommon. Two incidents will provide an appropriate introduction to our work. One involves a bus ride where I was seated behind two English-Canadian ladies and in front of two French-Canadian ladies as the bus moved through an English-Canadian region of the city. My attention was suddenly drawn to the conversation in front wherein one lady said something like: "If I couldn't speak English I certainly wouldn't shout about it", referring to the French conversation going on behind them. Her friend replied: "Oh, well, you can't expect much else from them". Then one of the ladies mentioned that she was bothered when French people laughed among themselves in her presence because she felt they might be making fun of her. This was followed by a nasty interchange of pejorative stereotypes about French Canadians, the whole discussion prompted, it seemed, by what struck me as a humorous conversation of the two attractive, middle class French Canadian women seated behind them. The English ladies couldn't understand the French conversation, nor did they look back to see what the people they seemed to know so much about even looked like.

The second incident involved my daughter when she was about 12 years old. She, too, has amazing skill with English and two dialects of French, the Canadian style and the European style. One day while driving her to school, a lycée run by teachers from France, I stopped to pick up one of her friends and they were immediately involved in conversation, *French-Canadian* French style. A block or two farther I slowed down to pick up a second girlfriend when my daughter excitedly told me, in English, to drive on. At school I asked what the trouble was and she explained that there actually was no trouble although there might have been if the second girl, who was from France, and who spoke another dialect of French, had got in the car because then my daughter would have been forced to show a linguistic preference for one girl or the other. Normally she could escape this conflict by interacting with each girl separately, and, inadvertently, I had almost put her on the spot. Incidents of this sort prompted us to commence a systematic analysis of the effects of language and dialect changes on impression formation and social interaction.

2 Dialect Variations Elicit Stereotyped Impressions

Over the past eight years, we have developed a research technique that makes use of language and dialect variations to elicit the stereotyped impressions or biased views which members of one social group hold of representative members of a contrasting group. Briefly, the procedure involves the reactions of listeners (referred to as judges) to the taped recordings of a number of perfectly bilingual speakers reading a two-minute passage at one time in one of their languages (e.g., French) and, later, a translation equivalent of the same passage in their second language (e.g., English). Groups of judges are asked to listen to this series of recordings and evaluate the personality characteristics of each speaker as well as possible, using voice cues only. They are reminded of the common tendency to attempt to gauge the personalities of unfamiliar speakers heard over the phone or radio. Thus they are kept unaware that they will actually hear two readings by each of several bilinguals. In our experience no subjects have become aware of this fact. The judges are given practice trials, making them well acquainted with both versions of the message, copies of which are supplied in advance. They usually find the enterprise interesting, especially if they are promised, and receive, some feedback on how well they have done, for example, if the profiles for one or two speakers, based on the ratings of friends who know them well, are presented at the end of the series.

This procedure, referred to as the *matched-guise* technique, appears to reveal judges' more private reactions to the contrasting group than direct attitude questionnaires do (see Lambert, Anisfeld and Yeni-Komshian, 1965), but much more research is needed to adequately assess its power in this regard. The technique is particularly valuable as a measure of *group* biases in evaluative reactions; it has very good reliability in the sense that essentially the same profile of traits for a particular group appear when different samples of judges, drawn from a particular subpopulation, are used. Differences between subpopulations are very marked, however, as will become apparent. On the other hand, the technique apparently has little reliability when measured by test–retest ratings produced by the same group of judges; we believe this type of unreliability is due in large part to the main statistic used, the difference between an individual's rating of a pair of guises on a single trait. Difference scores give notoriously low test–retest reliability coefficients although their use for comparing means is perfectly appropriate (Bereiter, 1963; and Ferguson, 1959, 285f).

Several of our studies have been conducted since 1958 in greater Montreal, a setting that has a long history of tensions between English- and French-speaking Canadians. The conflict is currently so sharp that some French-Canadian (*FC*) political leaders in the Province of Quebec talk seriously about separating the Province from the rest of Canada, comprising a majority of English Canadians (*ECs*). In 1958–59, (Lambert, Hodgson, Gardner and Fillenbaum, 1960) we asked a sizeable group of *EC* university students to evaluate the personalities of a series of speakers, actually the matched guises of male bilinguals speaking in Canadian-style French and English. When their judgements were analyzed it was found that their evaluations were strongly biased against the *FC* and in favor of the matched *EC* guises. They rated the speakers in their *EC* guises as being better looking, taller, more intelligent, more dependable, kinder, more ambitious and as having more character. This evaluational bias was just as apparent among judges who were bilingual as among monolinguals.

We presented the same set of taped voices to a group of *FC* students of equivalent age, social class and educational level. Here we were in for a surprise for they showed the same bias, evaluating the *EC* guises significantly *more* favorably than the *FC* guises on a whole series of traits, indicating, for example, that they viewed the *EC* guises as being more intelligent, dependable, likeable and as having more character! Only on two traits did they rate the *FC* guises more favorably, namely kindness and religiousness, and, considering the whole pattern of ratings, it could be that they interpreted too much religion as a questionable quality. Not only did the *FC* judges generally downgrade representatives of their own ethnic-linguistic group, they also rated the *FC* guises much more negatively than the *EC* judges had. We consider this pattern of results as a reflection of a community-wide stereotype of *FCs* as being relatively second-rate people, a view apparently fully shared by certain subgroups of *FCs*. Similar tendencies to downgrade one's own group have been reported in research with minority groups conducted in other parts of North America.

3   Extensions of the Basic Study

3.1   The follow-up study

Some of the questions left unanswered in the first study have been examined recently by Malcolm Preston (Preston, 1963). Using the same basic techniques, the following questions were asked: (*a*) Will female and male judges react similarly to language and accent variations of speakers? (*b*) Will judges react similarly to male and female speakers who change their pronunciation style or the language they speak? (*c*) Will there be systematic differences in reactions to *FC* and Continental French (*CF*) speakers?

For this study, 80 English-Canadian and 92 French-Canadian first year college age students from Montreal served as judges. The *EC* judges in this study were all Catholics since we wanted to determine if *EC* Catholics would be less biased in their views of *FCs* than the non-Catholic *EC* judges had been in the original study. Approximately the same number of males and females from both language groups were tested, making four groups of judges in all: an *EC* male group, an *EC* female, a *FC* male and a *FC* female group.

The 18 personality traits used by the judges for expressing their reactions were grouped, for the purposes of interpretation, into three logically distinct categories of personality: (a) *competence* which included intelligence, ambition, self-confidence, leadership and courage; (b) *personal integrity* which included dependability, sincerity, character, conscientiousness and kindness; (c) *social attractiveness* which included sociability, likeability, entertainingness, sense of humor and affectionateness. Religiousness, good looks and height were not included in the above categories since they did not logically fit.

3.2   Results: evaluative reactions of English-Canadian listeners

In general it was found that the *EC* listeners viewed the female speakers more favorably in their French guises while they viewed the male speakers more favorably in their English guises. In particular, the *EC* men saw the *FC* lady speakers as more intelligent, ambitious, self-confident, dependable, courageous and sincere than their English counterparts. The *EC* ladies were not quite so gracious although they, too, rated the *FC* ladies as more intelligent, ambitious, self-confident (but shorter) than the *EC* women guises. Thus, *ECs* generally view *FC* females as more competent and the *EC* men see them as possessing more integrity and competence.

Several notions came to mind at this point. It may be that the increased attractiveness of the *FC* woman in the eyes of the *EC* male is partly a result of her inaccessibility. Perhaps also the *EC* women are cognizant of the *EC* men's latent preference for *FC* women and accordingly are themselves prompted to upgrade the *FC* female, even to the point of adopting the *FC* woman as model of what a woman should be.

However, the thought that another group is better than their own should not be a comfortable one for members of any group, especially a group of young ladies! The realization, however latent, that men of their own cultural group prefer another type of women might well be a very tender issue for the *EC* woman, one that could be easily exacerbated.

To examine this idea, we carried out a separate experiment. The *Ss* for the experiment were two groups of *EC* young women, one group serving as controls, the other as an experimental group. Both groups were asked to give their impressions of the personalities of a group of speakers, some using English, some Canadian-style French. They were, of course, actually presented with female bilingual speakers using Canadian French and English guises. Just before they evaluated the speakers, the experimental group was given false information about *FC* women, information that was designed to upset them. They heard a tape recording of a man reading supposedly authentic statistical information about the increase in marriages between *FC* women and *EC* men. They were asked to listen to this loaded passage twice, for practice only, disregarding the content of the message and attending only to the personality of the speaker. We presumed, however, that they would not likely be able to disregard the content since it dealt with a matter that might well bother them – *FC* women, they were told, were competing for *EC* men, men who already had a tendency to prefer *FC* women, a preference that they possibly shared themselves. In contrast, the control group received quite neutral information which would not affect their ratings of *FCs* in any way. The results supported the prediction: The experimental *Ss* judged the *FC* women to be reliably more attractive but reliably less dependable and sincere than did the control *Ss*. That is, the favorable reactions toward *FC* women found previously were evident in the judgments of the control group, while the experimental *Ss*, who had been given false information designed to highlight the threat posed by the presumed greater competence and integrity of *FC* women, saw the *FC* women as men stealers – attractive but undependable and insincere. These findings support the general hypothesis we had developed and they serve as a first step in a series of experiments we are now planning to determine how judgments of personalities affect various types of social interaction.

Let us return again to the main investigation. It was found that *FC* men were not as favorably received as the women were by their *EC* judges. *EC* ladies liked *EC* men, rating them as taller, more likeable, affectionate, sincere, and conscientious, and as possessing more character and a greater sense of humor than the *FC* versions of the same speakers. Furthermore, the *EC* male judges also favored *EC* male speakers, rating them as taller, more kind, dependable and entertaining. Thus, *FC* male speakers are viewed as lacking integrity and as being less socially attractive by both *EC* female, and, to a less marked extent, *EC* male judges. This tendency to downgrade the *FC* male, already noted in the basic study, may well be the expression of an unfavorable stereotyped and prejudiced attitude toward *FCs*, but, apparently, this prejudice is selectively directed toward *FC* males, possibly because they are better known than females as power figures who control local and regional governments and who thereby can be viewed as sources of threat or frustration, (or as the guardians of *FC* women, keeping them all to themselves).

The reactions to Continental French (*CF*) speakers are generally more favorable although less marked. The *EC* male listeners viewed *CF* women as slightly more competent and *CF* men as equivalent to their *EC* controls except for height and religiousness. The *EC* female listeners upgraded *CF* women on sociability and self-confidence, but downgraded *CF* men on height, likeability and sincerity. Thus, *EC* judges appear to be less concerned about European French people in general than they are about the local French people; the European French are neither downgraded nor taken as potential social models to any great extent.

3.3   Evaluative reactions of French-Canadian listeners

Summarizing briefly, the *FC* listeners showed more significant guise differences than did their *EC* counterparts. *FCs* generally rated European French guises *more* favorably and Canadian French guises *less* favorably than they did their matched *EC* guises. One important exception was the *FC* women who viewed *FC* men as more competent and as more socially attractive than *EC* men.

The general pattern of evaluations presented by the *FC* judges, however, indicates that they view their own linguistic cultural group as *inferior* to both the English-Canadian and the European French groups, suggesting that *FCs* are prone to take either of these other groups as models for changes in their own manners of behaving (including speech) and possibly in basic values. This tendency is more marked among *FC* men who definitely preferred male and female representatives of the *EC* and *CF* groups to those of their own group. The *FC* women, in contrast, appear to be guardians of *FC* culture at least in the sense that they favored male representatives of their own cultural group. We presume this reaction reflects something more than a preference for *FC* marriage partners. *FC* women may be particularly anxious to preserve *FC* values and to pass these on in their own families through language, religion and tradition.

Nevertheless, *FC* women apparently face a conflict of their own in that they favor characteristics of both *CF* and *EC* women. Thus, the *FC* female may be safe-guarding the *FC* culture through a preference for *FC* values seen in *FC* men, at the same time as she is prone to change her own behavior and values in the direction of one of two foreign cultural models, those that the men in her group apparently favor. It is of interest that *EC* women are confronted with a similar conflict since they appear envious of *FC* women.

3.4   The developmental studies

Recently, we have been looking into the background of the inferiority reaction among *FC* youngsters, trying to determine at what age it starts and how it develops through the years. Elizabeth Anisfeld and I (1964) started by studying the reactions of ten year old *FC* children to the matched guises of bilingual youngsters of their own age reading French and English versions of *Little Red Riding Hood*, once in Canadian-style French and once in standard English. In this instance, half of the judges were bilingual in English and half were essentially monolingual in French. Stated briefly, it was found that *FC* guises were rated significantly *more* favorable on nearly all traits. (One exception was height; the *EC* speakers were judged as taller.) However, these favorable evaluations of the *FC* in contrast to the *EC* guises were due almost entirely to the reactions of the monolingual children. The bilingual children saw very little difference between the two sets of guises, that is, on nearly all traits their ratings of the *FC* guises were essentially the same as their ratings of *EC* guises. The results, therefore, made it clear that, unlike college-age judges, *FC* children at the ten year age level do not have a negative bias against their own group.

The question then arises as to where the bias starts after age ten. A recent study (Lambert, Frankel and Tucker, 1966) was addressed to solving this puzzle. The investigation was conducted with 375 *FC* girls ranging in age from 9 to 18, who gave their evaluations of three groups of matched guises, (a) of some girls about their own age, (b) of some adult women, and (c) of some adult men. Passages that were appropriate for each age level were read by the bilingual speakers once in English and once in Canadian-style French. In this study attention was given to the social class background of the judges (some were chosen from private schools, some from public schools) and to their knowledge of English (some were bilingual and some monolingual in French). It was found that definite preferences for *EC* guises appeared at about age twelve and were maintained through the late teen years. There was, however, a marked difference between the private and public school judges: the upper middle class girls were especially biased after age 12, whereas the pattern for the working class girls was less pronounced and less durable, suggesting that for them the bias is short-lived and fades out by the late teens. Note that we probably did not encounter girls from lower class homes in our earlier studies using girls at *FC* collèges or universités.

The major implication of these findings is that the tendency for certain subgroups of college-age *FCs* to downgrade representatives of their own ethnic-linguistic group, noted in our earlier studies, seems to have its origin, at least with girls, at about age 12, but the ultimate fate of this attitude depends to a great extent on social-class background. Girls who come from upper middle class *FC* homes, and especially those who have become bilingual in English, are particularly likely to maintain this view, at least into the young adult years.

The pattern of results of these developmental studies can also be examined from a more psychodynamic perspective. If we assume that the adult female and male speakers in their *FC* guises represent parents or people like their own parents to the *FC* adolescent judges, just as the same-age speakers represent someone like themselves, then the findings suggest several possibilities that could be studied in more detail. First, the results are consistent with the notion that teen-age girls have a closer psychological relation with their fathers than with their mothers in the sense that the girls in the study rated *FC* female guises markedly inferior to *EC* ones, but generally favored or at least showed much less disfavor for the *FC* guises of male speakers. Considered in this light, social-class differences and bilingual skill apparently influence the degree of same-sex rejection and cross-sex identification: by the mid-teens the public school girls, both monolinguals and bilinguals, show essentially no rejection of either the *FC* female or male guises, whereas the private school girls, especially the bilinguals, show a rejection of both female and male *FC* guises through the late teens. These bilinguals might, because of their skill in English and their possible encouragement from home, be able to come in contact with the mothers of their *EC* associates and therefore may have developed stronger reasons to be envious of *EC* mothers and fathers than the monolingual girls would have.

Similarly, the reactions to "same-age" speakers might reflect a tendency to accept or reject one's peer-group or one's self, at least for the monolinguals. From this point of view, the findings suggest that the public school monolinguals are generally satisfied with their *FC* image since they favor the *FC* guises of the same-age speakers at the 16 year level. In contrast, the private school monolinguals may be expressing a marked rejection of themselves in the sense that they favor the *EC* guises. The bilinguals, of course, can consider themselves as being potential or actual members of both ethnic-linguistic groups represented by the guises. It is of interest, therefore, to note that both the public and particularly the private school bilinguals apparently favor the *EC* versions of themselves.

4   Two Generalizations

This program of research, still far from complete, does permit us to make two important generalizations, both relevant to the main argument of this paper. First, a technique has been developed that rather effectively calls out the stereotyped impressions that members of one ethnic-linguistic group hold of another contrasting group. The type and strength of impression depends on characteristics of the speakers – their sex, age, the dialect they use, and, very likely, the social-class background as this is revealed in speech style. The impression also seems to depend on characteristics of the audience of *judges* – their age, sex, socio-economic background, their biliguality and their own speech style. The type of reactions and adjustments listeners must make to those who reveal, through their speech style, their likely ethnic group allegiance is suggested by the traits that listeners use to indicate their impressions. Thus, *EC* male and female college students tend to look down on the *FC* male speaker, seeing him as less intelligent, less dependable and less interesting than he would be seen if he had presented himself in an *EC* guise. Imagine the types of role adjustment that would follow if the same person were first seen in the *FC* guise and then suddenly switched to a perfect *EC* guise. A group of *EC* listeners would probably be forced to perk up their ears, reconsider their original classification of the person and then either view him as becoming too intimate in "their" language or decide otherwise and be pleasantly amazed that one of their own could manage the other group's language so well. Furthermore, since these comparative impressions are widespread throughout certain strata of each ethnic-linguistic community, they will probably have an enormous impact on young people who are either forced to learn the other group's language or who choose to do so.

The research findings outlined here have a second important message about the reactions of the bilingual who is able to convincingly switch languages or dialects. The bilingual can study the reactions of his audiences as he adopts one guise in certain settings and another in different settings, and receive a good deal of social feedback, permitting him to realize that he can be perceived in quite different ways, depending on how he presents himself. It could well be that his own self-concept takes two distinctive forms in the light of such feedback. He may also observe, with amusement or alarm, the role adjustments that follow when he suddenly switches guises with the same group of interlocutors. However, research is needed to document and examine these likely consequences of language or dialect switching from the perspective of the bilingual making the switches.

Although we have concentrated on a Canadian setting in these investigations, there is really nothing special about the Canadian scene with regard to the social effects of language or dialect switching. Equally instructive effects have been noted when the switch involves a change from standard American English to Jewish-accented English (Anisfeld, Bogo and Lambert, 1962); when the switch involves changing from Hebrew to Arabic for Israeli and Arab judges, or when the change is from Sephardic to Ashkenazic style Hebrew for Jewish listeners in Israel (Lambert, Anisfeld and Yeni-Komshian, 1965). Our most recent research, using a modified approach, has been conducted with American Negro speakers and listeners (Tucker and Lambert, 1967). The same type of social effects are inherent in this instance, too: Southern Negroes have more favorable impressions of people who use what the linguists call *Standard Network Style* English than they do of those who speak with their own style, but they are more impressed with their own style than they are with the speech of educated, Southern whites, or of Negroes who become too "white" in their speech by exaggerating the non-Negro features and over-correcting their verbal output.

5   Social-Psychological Aspects of Second-Language Learning

How might these intergroup impressions and feelings affect young people living in the Montreal area who are expected by educators to learn the other group's language? One would expect that both French-Canadian youngsters and their parents would be more willing, for purely social-psychological reasons, to learn English than *ECs* to learn French. Although we haven't investigated the French Canadians' attitudes toward the learning of English, still it is very apparent that bilingualism in Canada and in Quebec has long been a one-way affair, with *FCs* much more likely to learn English than the converse. Typically, this trend to English is explained on economic grounds and on the attraction of the United States, but I would like to suggest another possible reason for equally serious consideration. *FCs* may be drawn away from Canadian style French to

English, or to bilingualism, or to European style French, as a psychological reaction to the contrast in stereotyped images which English and French Canadians have of one another. On the other hand, we would expect *EC* students and their parents in Quebec, at least, to be drawn away from French for the same basic reasons. It is, of course, short-sighted to talk about groups in this way because there are certain to be wide individual differences of reaction, as was the case in the impression studies, and as will be apparent in the research to be discussed, but one fact turned up in an unpublished study Robert Gardner and I conducted that looks like a group-wide difference. Several samples of Montreal *EC*, high school students who had studied French for periods of up to seven years scored no better on standard tests of French achievement than did Connecticut high schoolers who had only two or three years of French training.

6   Instrumental and Integrative Motivation

When viewed from a social-psychological perspective, the process of learning a second language itself also takes on a special significance. From this viewpoint, one would expect that if the student is to be successful in his attempts to learn another social group's language he must be both able and willing to adopt various aspects of behavior, including verbal behavior, which characterize members of the other linguistic-cultural group. The learner's ethnocentric tendencies and his attitudes toward the other group are believed to determine his success in learning the new language. His motivation to learn is thought to be determined by both his attitudes and by the type of orientation he has toward learning a second language. The orientation is *instrumental* in form if, for example, the purposes of language study reflect the more utilitarian value of linguistic achievement, such as getting ahead in one's occupation, and is *integrative* if, for example, the student is oriented to learn more about the other cultural community, as if he desired to become a potential member of the other group. It is also argued that some may be anxious to learn another language as a means of being accepted in another cultural group because of dissatisfactions experienced in their own culture while other individuals may be as much interested in another culture as they are in their own. In either case, the more proficient one becomes in a second language the more he may find that his place in his original membership group is modified at the same time as the other linguistic-cultural group becomes something more than a reference group for him. It may, in fact, become a second membership group for him. Depending upon the compatibility of the two cultures, he may experience feelings of chagrin or regret as he loses ties in one group, mixed with the fearful anticipation of entering a relatively new group. The concept of *anomie* first proposed by Durkheim (1897) and more recently extended by Srole (1951) and Williams (1952), refers to such feelings of social uncertainty or dissatisfaction.

My studies with Gardner (1959) were carried out with English-speaking Montreal high school students studying French who were evaluated for their language learning aptitude and verbal intelligence, as well as their attitudes and stereotypes toward members of the French community, and the intensity of their motivation to learn French. Our measure of motivation is conceptually similar to Jones' (1949 and 1950) index of interest in learning a language which he found to be important for successful learning among Welsh students. A factor analysis of scores on these various measures indicated that aptitude and intelligence formed a common factor which was independent of a second one comprising indices of motivation, type of orientation toward language and social attitudes toward *FCs*. Furthermore, a measure of achievement in French taken at the end of a year's study was reflected equally prominently in both factors. This statistical pattern meant that French achievement was dependent upon both aptitude and verbal intelligence as well as a sympathetic orientation toward the other group. This orientation was much less common among these students than was the instrumental one, as would be expected from the results of the matched-guise experiments. However, when sympathetic orientation was present it apparently sustained a strong motivation to learn the other group's language. Furthermore, it was clear that students with an integrative orientation were more successful in learning French than were those with instrumental orientations.

A follow-up study (Gardner, 1960) confirmed and extended these findings. Using a larger sample of *EC* students and incorporating various measures of French achievement, the same two independent factors were revealed, and again both were related to French achievement. But whereas aptitude and achievement were especially important for those French skills stressed in school training, such as grammar, the development of such skills, skills that call for the active use of the language in communicational settings, such as pronunciation accuracy and auditory comprehension, was determined in major part by measures of an integrative motivation to learn French. The aptitude variables were insignificant in this case. Further evidence from the intercorrelations indicated that this integrative motive was the converse of an authoritarian ideological syndrome, opening the possibility that basic personality dispositions may be involved in language learning efficiency.

In this same study information had been gathered from the parents of the students about their own orientations toward the French community. These data suggested that integrative or instrumental orientations toward the other group are developed within the family. That is, the minority of students with an integrative disposition to learn French had parents who also were integrative and sympathetic to the French community. However, students' orientations were not related to parents' skill in French nor to the number of French acquaintances the parents had, indicating that the integrative motive is not due to having more experience with French at home. Instead the integrative outlook more likely stems from a family-wide attitudinal disposition.

7   Language Learning and Anomie

Another feature of the language learning process came to light in an investigation of college and postgraduate students undergoing an intensive course in advanced French at McGill's French Summer School. We were interested here, among other matters, in changes in attitudes and feelings that might take place during the six-week study period (Lambert, Gardner, Barik and Tunstall, 1961). The majority of the students were Americans who oriented themselves mainly to the European-French rather than the American-French community. We adjusted our attitude scales to make them appropriate for those learning European French. Certain results were of special interest. As the students progressed in French skill to the point that they said they "thought" in French, and even dreamed in French, their feelings of anomie also increased markedly. At the same time, they began to seek out occasions to use English even though they had solemnly pledged to use only French for the six-week period. This pattern of results suggests to us that these already advanced students experienced a strong dose of anomie when they commenced to *really* master a second language. That is, when advanced students became so skilled that they begin to think and feel like Frenchmen, they then became so annoyed with feelings of anomie that they were prompted to develop strategies to minimize or control the annoyance. Reverting to English could be such a strategy. It should be emphasized however, that the chain of events just listed needs to be much more carefully explored.

Elizabeth Anisfeld and I took another look at this problem, experimenting with 10-year old monolingual and bilingual students (Peal and Lambert, 1962). We found that the bilingual children (attending French schools in Montreal) were markedly more favorable towards the "other" language group (i.e., the *ECs*) than the monolingual children were. Furthermore, the bilingual children reported that their parents held the same strongly sympathetic attitudes toward *ECs*, in contrast to the pro-*FC* attitudes reported for the parents of the monolingual children. Apparently, then, the development of second language skill to the point of balanced bilingualism is conditioned by family-shared attitudes toward the other linguistic-cultural group.

These findings are consistent and reliable enough to be of general interest. For example methods of language training could possibly be modified and strengthened by giving consideration to the social-psychological implications of language learning. Because of the possible practical as well as theoretical significance of this approach, it seemed appropriate to test its applicability in a cultural setting other than the bicultural Quebec scene. With measures of attitude and motivation modified for American students learning French, a large scale study, very similar in nature to those conducted in Montreal, was carried out in various settings in the United States with very similar general outcomes (Lambert & Gardner, 1962).

One further investigation indicated that these suggested social-psychological principles are not restricted to English and French speakers in Canada. Moshe Anisfeld and I (1961) extended the same experimental procedure to samples of Jewish high school students studying Hebrew at various parochial schools in different sectors of Montreal. They were questioned about their orientations toward learning Hebrew and their attitudes toward the Jewish culture and community, and tested for their verbal intelligence, language aptitude and achievement in the Hebrew language at the end of the school year. The results support the generalization that both intellectual capacity and attitudinal orientation affect success in learning Hebrew. However, whereas intelligence and linguistic aptitude were relatively stable predictors of success, the attitudinal measures varied from one Jewish community to another. For instance, the measure of a Jewish student's desire to become more acculturated in the Jewish tradition and culture was a sensitive indicator of progress in Hebrew for children from a particular district of Montreal, one where members of the Jewish sub-community were actually concerned with problems of integrating into the Jewish culture. In another district, made up mainly of Jews who recently arrived from central Europe and who were clearly of a lower socio-economic level, the measure of desire for Jewish acculturation did not correlate with achievement in Hebrew, whereas measures of pro-Semitic attitudes or pride in being Jewish did.

8   Bilingual Adjustments to Conflicting Demands

The final issue I want to discuss concerns the socio-cultural tugs and pulls that the bilingual or potential bilingual encounters and how he adjusts to these often conflicting demands made on him. We have seen how particular social atmospheres can affect the bilingual. For example, the French-English bilingual in the Montreal setting may be pulled toward greater use of English, and yet be urged by certain others in the *FC* community not to move too far in that direction, just as *EC's* may be discouraged from moving toward the French community. (In a similar fashion, dialects would be expected to change because of the social consequences they engender, so that Jewish accented speech should drop away, especially with those of the younger generation in American settings, as should Sephardic forms of Hebrew in Israel or certain forms of Negro speech in America.) In other words, the bilingual encounters social pressure of various sorts: he can enjoy the fun of linguistic spying but must pay the price of suspicion from those who don't want him to enter too intimately into their cultural domains and from others who don't want him to leave his "own" domain. He also comes to realize that most people are suspicious of a person who is in any sense two-faced. If he is progressing toward bilingualism, he encounters similar pressures that may affect his self-concept, his sense of belonging and his relations to two cultural-linguistic groups, the one he is slowly *leaving*, and the one he is *entering*. The conflict exists because so many of us think in terms of in-groups and out-groups, or of the need of showing an allegiance to one group or another, so that terms such as own language, other's language, *leaving* and *entering* one cultural group for another seem to be appropriate, even natural, descriptive choices.

9   Bilinguals and Ethnocentrism

Although this type of thought may characterize most people in our world, it is nonetheless a subtle form of group cleavage and ethnocentrism, and in time it may be challenged by bilinguals who, I feel, are in an excellent position to develop a totally new outlook on the social world. My argument is that bilinguals, especially those with bicultural experiences, enjoy certain fundamental advantages which, if capitalized on, can easily offset the annoying social tugs and pulls they are normally prone to. Let me mention one of these advantages that I feel is a tremendous asset.[1] Recently, Otto Klineberg and I conducted a rather comprehensive international study of the development of stereotyped thinking in children (Lambert and Klineberg, 1967). We found that rigid and stereotyped thinking about in-groups and out-groups, or about own groups in contrast to foreigners, starts during the pre-school period when children are trying to form a conception of themselves and their place in the world. Parents and other socializers attempt to help the child at this stage by highlighting differences and contrasts among groups, thereby making his own group as distinctive as possible. This tendency, incidentally, was noted among parents from various parts of the world. Rather than helping, however, they may actually be setting the stage for ethnocentrism with permanent consequences. The more contrasts are stressed, the more deep-seated the stereotyping process and its impact on ethnocentric thought appear to be. Of relevance here is the notion that the child brought up bilingually and biculturally will be less likely to have good versus bad contrasts impressed on him when he starts wondering about himself, his own group and others. Instead he will probably be taught something more truthful, although more complex: that differences among national or cultural groups of peoples are actually not clear-cut and that basic similarities among peoples are more prominent than differences. The bilingual child in other words may well start life with the enormous advantage of having a more open, receptive mind about himself and other people. Furthermore, as he matures, the bilingual has many opportunities to learn, from observing changes in other people's reactions to him, how two-faced and ethno-centric *others* can be. That is, he is likely to become especially sensitive to and leery of ethnocentrism.

10   Bilinguals and Social Conflicts

This is not to say that bilinguals have an easy time of it. In fact, the final investigation I want to present demonstrates the social conflicts bilinguals typically face, but, and this is the major point, it also demonstrates one particular type of adjustment that is par-ticularly encouraging.

In 1943, Irving Child (1943) investigated a matter that disturbed many second-generation Italians living in New England: what were they, Italian or American? Through early experiences they had learned that their relations with certain other youngsters in their community were strained whenever they displayed signs of their Italian background, that is, whenever they behaved as their parents wanted them to. In contrast, if they rejected their Italian background, they realized they could be deprived of many satisfactions stemming from belonging to an Italian family and an Italian com-munity. Child uncovered three contrasting modes of adjusting to these pressures. One subgroup rebelled against their Italian background, making themselves as American as possible. Another subgroup rebelled the other way, rejecting things American as much as possible while proudly associating themselves with things Italian. The third form of adjustment was an apathetic withdrawal and a refusal to think of themselves in ethnic terms at all. This group tried, unsuccessfully, to escape the conflict by avoiding situa-tions where the matter of cultural background might come up. Stated in other terms, some tried to belong to one of their own groups or the other, and some, because of strong pulls from both sides, were unable to belong to either.

Child's study illustrates nicely the difficulties faced by people with dual allegiances, but there is no evidence presented of second-generation Italians who actually feel them-selves as belonging to both groups. When in 1962, Robert Gardner and I (1962) studied another ethnic minority group in New England, the French-Americans, we observed the same types of reactions as Child had noted among Italian-Americans. But in our study there was an important difference.

We used a series of attitude scales to assess the allegiances of French-American adolescents to both their French and American heritages. Their relative degree of skill in French and in English were used as an index of their mode of adjustment to the bicultural conflict they faced. In their homes, schools and community, they all had ample opportunities to learn both languages well, but subgroups turned up who had quite different patterns of linguistic skill, and each pattern was consonant with each subgroup's allegiances. Those who expressed a definite preference for the American over the French culture and who negated the value of knowing French were more proficient in English than French. They also expressed anxiety about how well they actually knew English. This subgroup, characterized by a general rejection of their French background, resembles in many respects the rebel reaction noted by Child. A second subgroup expressed a strong desire to be identified as French, and they showed a greater skill in French than English, especially in comprehension of spoken French. A third group apparently faced a conflict of cultural allegiances since they were ambivalent about their identity, favoring certain features of the French and other features of the American culture, Presumably because they had not resolved the conflict, they were retarded in their command of both languages when compared to the other groups. This relatively unsuccessful mode of adjustment is very similar to the apathetic reaction noted in one subgroup of Italian-Americans.

A fourth subgroup is of special interest. French-American youngsters who have an open-minded, nonethnocentric view of people in general, coupled with a strong aptitude for language learning are the ones who profited fully from their language learning opportunities and became skilled in *both* languages. These young people had apparently circumvented the conflicts and developed means of becoming members of both cultural groups. They had, in other terms, achieved a comfortable bicultural identity.

It is not clear why this type of adjustment did not appear in Child's study. There could, for example, be important differences in the social pressures encountered by second-generation Italians and French in New England. My guess, however, is that the difference in findings reflects a new social movement that has started in America in the interval between 1943 and 1962, a movement which the American linguist Charles Hockett humorously refers to as a "reduction of the heat under the American melting pot". I believe that bicultural bilinguals will be particularly helpful in perpetuating this movement. They and their children are also the ones most likely to work out a new, nonethnocentric mode of social intercourse which could be of universal significance.

Notes

1   For present purposes, discussion is limited to a more *social* advantage associated with bilingualism. In other writings there has been a stress on potential intellectual and *cognitive* advantages, see Peal and Lambert (1962) and Anisfeld (1964); see also Macnamara (1964) as well as Lambert and Anisfeld (1966). The bilingual's potential utility has also been discussed as a linguistic mediator between monolingual groups because of his comprehension of the subtle meaning differences characterizing each of the languages involved, see Lambert and Moore (1966).

References

Anisfeld, Elizabeth. A comparison of the cognitive functioning of monolinguals and bilinguals. Unpublished Ph.D. thesis, Redpath Library, McGill University, 1964,

Anisfeld, Elizabeth, and Lambert, W. E. Evaluational reactions of bilingual and monolingual children to spoken language. *Journal of Abnormal and Social Psychology*, 1964, 69, 89–97.

Anisfeld, M., Bogo, N., and Lambert, W. E. Evaluational reactions to accented English speech. *Journal of Abnormal and Social Psychology*, 1962, 65, 223–231.

Anisfeld, M., and Lambert, W. E. Social and psychological variables in learning Hebrew. *Journal of Abnormal and Social Psychology*, 1961, 63, 524–529.

Bereiter, C. Some persisting dilemmas in the measurement of change. In Harris, C. W. (Ed.), *Problems in measuring change*. Madison: The University of Wisconsin Press, 1963.

Child, I. L., *Italian or American? The second generation in conflict*. New Haven: Yale University Press, 1943.

Durkheim, E. *Le suicide*. Paris: F. Alcan, 1897.

Ferguson, G. A. *Statistical analysis in psychology and education*. New York: McGraw-Hill, 1959.

Gardner, R. C. and Lambert, W. E. Motivational variables in second-language acquisition. *Canadian Journal of Psychology*, 1959, 13, 266–272.

Gardner, R. C. Motivational variables in second-language acquisition. Unpublished Ph.D. thesis, McGill University, 1960.

Jones, W. R. Attitude towards Welsh as a second language. A preliminary investigation. *British Journal of Educational Psychology*, 1949, 19, 44–52.

Jones, W. R. Attitude towards Welsh as a second language, a further investigation. *British Journal of Educational Psychology*, 1950, 20, 117–132.

Labov, W. Hypercorrection by the lower middle class as a factor in linguistic change. Columbia University, 1964. (Mimeo)

Lambert, W. E., Hodgson, R. C., Gardner, R. C., and Fillenbaum, S. Evaluational reactions to spoken languages. *Journal of Abnormal and Social Psychology*, 1960, 60, 44–51.

Lambert, W. E., Gardner, R. C., Olton, R., and Tunstall, K. A study of the roles of attitudes and motivation in second-language learning. McGill University, 1962. (Mimeo)

Lambert, W. E., Gardner, R. C., Barik, H. C., and Tunstall, K. Attitudinal and cognitive aspects of intensive study of a second language. *Journal of Abnormal and Social Psychology*, 1963, 66, 358–368.

Lambert, W. E., Anisfeld, M., and Yeni-Komshian, Grace. Evaluational reactions of Jewish and Arab adolescents to dialect and language variations. *Journal of Personality and Social Psychology*, 1965, 2, 84–90

Lambert, W. E., Frankel, Hannah, and Tucker, G. R. Judging personality through speech: A French-Canadian example. *The Journal of Communication*, 1966, 16, 305–321.

Lambert, W. E., and Anisfeld, Elizabeth. A reply to John Macnamara. Mimeographed and submitted to *Studies*, 1966.

Lambert, W. E., and Moore, Nancy. Word-association responses: Comparison of American and French monolinguals with Canadian monolinguals and bilinguals. *Journal of Personality and Social Psychology*, 1966, 3, 313–320.

Lambert, W. E., and Klineberg, O. *Children's views of foreign peoples: A cross-national study*. New York: Appleton, 1967.

Macnamara, J. The Commission on Irish: Psychological aspects. *Studies*, 1964, 164–173.

McDavid, R. I. The dialects of American English. In Francis, W. N. (Ed.), *The structure of American English*, New York: Ronald, 1958.

Peal, Elizabeth, and Lambert, W. E. The relation of bilingualism to intelligence. *Psychological Monographs*, 1962, 76, Whole No. 546.

Preston, M. S. Evaluational reactions to English, Canadian French and European French voices. Unpublished M.A. thesis, McGill University, Redpath Library, 1963.

Srole, L. Social dysfunction, personality and social distance attitudes. Paper read before American Sociological Society, 1951, National Meeting, Chicago, Ill. (Mimeo)

Tucker, G. R., and Lambert, W. E., White and Negro listeners' reactions to various American-English dialects. McGill University, 1967. (Mimeo)

Williams, R. N. *American society*. New York: Knopf, 1952.

18

BICS and CALP: Origins and Rationale for the Distinction

Jim Cummins

The acronyms BICS and CALP refer to a distinction introduced by Cummins (1979) between basic interpersonal communicative skills and cognitive academic language proficiency. The distinction was intended to draw attention to the very different time periods typically required by immigrant children to acquire conversational fluency in their second language as compared to grade-appropriate academic proficiency in that language. Conversational fluency is often acquired to a functional or peer-appropriate level within about two years of initial exposure to the second language whereas at least five years is typically required to catch up to native speakers in academic aspects of the second language (Collier 1987; Hakuta, Butler and Witt 2000; Klesmer 1994; Cummins 1981a). Failure to take account of the BICS/CALP (conversational/academic) distinction has resulted in discriminatory psychological assessment of bilingual students and premature exit from language support programs (e.g. bilingual education) into mainstream classes (Cummins 1984).

1 Evolution of the Distinction

Skutnabb-Kangas and Toukomaa (1976) brought attention to the fact that Finnish immigrant children in Sweden often appeared to educators to be fluent in both Finnish and Swedish but still showed levels of verbal academic performance in both languages considerably below grade/age expectations. Similarly, analysis of psychological assessments administered to English language learners (ELL) showed that teachers and psychologists often assumed that children had overcome all difficulties with English when they could converse easily in the language (Cummins 1984). Yet these students frequently performed poorly on English academic tasks as well as in psychological assessment situations, with the result that they were often diagnosed as suffering from learning disabilities or communication disorders. Psychologists assumed that the verbal IQ tests were valid for these bilingual students because they could converse easily in English and appeared to understand instructions and questions.

The need to distinguish between conversational fluency and academic aspects of L2 performance was highlighted by the reanalysis of large-scale language acquisition data from the Toronto Board of Education (Cummins 1981a). These data showed clearly that there was a gap of several years, on average, between the attainment of peer-appropriate fluency in L2 and the attainment of grade norms in academic aspects of L2. Conversational aspects of proficiency reached peer-appropriate levels usually within about two years of exposure to L2 but a period of 5–7 years was required, on average, for immigrant students to approach grade norms in academic aspects of English.

The distinction between BICS and CALP was intended to draw educators' attention to these data and to warn against premature exit of ELL students (in the United States) from bilingual to mainstream English-only programs on the basis of attainment of surface-level fluency in English. In other words, the distinction highlighted the fact that educators' conflating of these aspects of proficiency was a major factor in the creation of academic difficulties for bilingual students.

At a more theoretical level, the BICS/CALP distinction also served to qualify John Oller's (1979) claim that all individual differences in language proficiency could be accounted for by just one underlying factor, which he termed *global language proficiency*. Oller synthesized a considerable amount of data showing strong correlations between performance on cloze tests of reading, standardized reading tests, and measures of oral verbal ability (e.g. vocabulary measures). However, it is problematic to incorporate all aspects of language use or performance into just one dimension of general or global language proficiency. For example, if we take two monolingual English-speaking siblings, a 12-year-old child and a six-year-old, there are enormous differences in these children's ability to read and write English and in the depth and breadth of their vocabulary knowledge, but minimal differences in their phonology or basic fluency. The six-year old can understand virtually everything that is likely to be said to her in everyday social contexts and she can use language very effectively in these contexts, just as the 12-year old can. In other words, some aspects of children's first language development (e.g. phonology) reach a plateau relatively early whereas other aspects (e.g. lexical knowledge) continue to develop throughout our lifetimes. Thus, these very different aspects of proficiency cannot be considered to reflect just one unitary proficiency dimension.

Another way of expressing this difference is to note that native speakers of any language come to school at age 5 or so virtually fully competent users of their language. They have acquired the core grammar of their language and many of the sociolinguistic rules for using the language appropriately in familiar social contexts. Yet, schools spend another 12 years (and considerable public funds) attempting to extend this basic linguistic repertoire into more specialized domains and functions of language. CALP or academic language proficiency is what schools focus on in this endeavor. It reflects the registers of language that children acquire in school and which they need to use effectively if they are to progress successfully through the grades. For example, knowing the conventions of different genres of writing (e.g. science reports, persuasive writing, etc.) and developing the ability to use these forms of expression or *registers* effectively are essential for academic success.

Conversational and academic language registers represent subsets of what James Paul Gee (1990) has termed *primary* and *secondary discourses*. Primary discourses are acquired through face-to-face interactions in the home and represent the language of initial socialization. Secondary discourses are acquired in social institutions beyond the family (e.g. school, business, religious and cultural contexts) and involve acquisition of specialized vocabulary and functions of language appropriate to those settings.

Secondary discourses can be oral or written and are central to the social life of non-literate cultures as much as they are in literate cultures. Examples of secondary discourse common in many non-literate cultures are the conventions of story-telling or the language of marriage or burial rituals which are passed down through oral tradition from one generation to the next. Oral forms of secondary discourse are in no way inferior to written forms, as illustrated in the fact that two of the greatest "literary" achievements of humanity, the Homeric epics of the *Odyssey* and the *Iliad*, existed for many centuries only in oral form before being written down.

The BICS/CALP distinction was elaborated into two intersecting continua (Cummins 1981a) that highlighted the range of cognitive demands and contextual support involved in particular language tasks or activities (context-embedded/context-reduced, cognitively undemanding/cognitively demanding). The BICS/CALP distinction was maintained within this elaboration and related to the theoretical distinctions of several other theorists (e.g. Bruner's (1975) *communicative* and *analytic competence*, Donaldson's (1978) *embedded* and *disembedded language*, and Olson's (1977) *utterance* and *text*). The terms used by different investigators have varied but the essential distinction refers to the extent to which the meaning being communicated is strongly supported by contextual or interpersonal cues (such as gestures, facial expressions, and intonation present in face-to-face interaction) or supported primarily by linguistic cues that are largely independent of the immediate communicative context.

2   Critiques of the BICS/CALP Distinction

Early critiques of the conversational/academic distinction were advanced by Carole Edelsky and her colleagues (Edelsky et al. 1983) and in a volume edited by Charlene Rivera (1984). Edelsky (1990) later reiterated and reformulated her critique and other critiques were advanced by Martin-Jones and Romaine (1986) and Wiley (1996). The major criticisms are as follows:

- the conversational/academic language distinction reflects an autonomous perspective on language that ignores its location in social practices and power relations (Edelsky et al. 1983; Wiley 1996).
- CALP or academic language proficiency represents little more than "test-wiseness" – it is an artifact of the inappropriate way in which it has been measured (Edelsky et al. 1983).
- The notion of CALP promotes a "deficit theory" insofar as it attributes the academic failure of bilingual/minority students to low cognitive/academic proficiency rather than to inappropriate schooling (Edelsky 1990; Edelsky et al. 1983; Martin-Jones and Romaine 1986).

In response to these critiques, Cummins and Swain (1983) pointed out that the construct of academic language proficiency does not in any way depend on test scores as support for either its construct validity or relevance to education. Furthermore, they argued that the BICS/CALP distinction has served to highlight how schools create academic difficulties for bilingual students. The notion of CALP was always presented as an intervening variable mediating between sociocultural and educational factors and student outcomes rather than as a direct causal variable of student outcomes.

In a more recent response, Cummins (2000) noted that the BICS/CALP distinction has been integrated since 1986 with a detailed sociopolitical analysis of how schools construct academic failure among subordinated groups. The framework analyzes how coercive relations of power in the wider society affect both educational structures and the ways in which educators define their roles. Educational structures (e.g. English-only instruction) and educator role definitions (e.g. low expectations for ELL students), in turn, have resulted in patterns of interactions between educators and subordinated group students that have constricted students' academic language development and identity formation. The framework documents educational approaches that challenge this pattern of coercive power relations and promote the generation of power in the interactions between educators and students (Cummins 1996).

Evidence that the BICS/CALP distinction is not just an artifact of test scores comes from several sources. For example, the following observations were made by Carolyn Vincent (1996) in an ethnographic study of a program serving second-generation Salvadorean students in Washington, DC:

> All of the children in this study began school in an English-speaking environment and within their first two or three years attained conversational ability in English that teachers would regard as native-like. This is largely deceptive. The children seem to have much greater English proficiency than they actually do because their spoken English has no accent and they are able to converse on a few everyday, frequently discussed subjects. Academic language is frequently lacking. Teachers actually spend very little time talking with individual children and tend to interpret a small sample of speech as evidence of full English proficiency. However, as the children themselves look back on their language development they see how the language used in the classroom was difficult for them, and how long it took them to acquire English. (p. 195)

The research of Biber (1986) and Corson (1995) also provides evidence of the linguistic reality of the distinction. Corson highlighted the enormous lexical differences between typical conversational interactions in English (BICS) as compared to academic or literacy-related uses of English (CALP). The high-frequency everyday lexicon of English conversation derives predominantly from Anglo-Saxon sources while academic language is primarily Graeco-Latin in origin (see also Coxhead 2000).

Similarly, Biber's (1986) factor analysis of more than one million words of English speech and written text from a wide variety of genres revealed underlying dimensions very consistent with the distinction between conversational and academic aspects of language proficiency. For example, when factor scores were calculated for the different text types on each factor, telephone and face-to-face conversation were at opposite extremes from official documents and academic prose on Textual Dimensions 1 and 2 (Interactive vs. Edited Text, and Abstract vs. Situated Content).

3   Conclusion

The BICS/CALP distinction was not proposed as an overall theory of language but as a very specific conceptual distinction that has important implications for policy and practice. To say that BICS and CALP are conceptually distinct is not the same as saying that they are separate or acquired in different ways. Developmentally they are not necessarily separate; all children acquire their initial conceptual foundation (knowledge of the world) through conversational interactions in the home. Similarly, discussion about conceptual issues is an important, and in many situations essential, way of deepening our understanding of concepts and developing critical literacy. By the same token, cognitive skills are involved, to a greater or lesser extent, in most forms of social interaction.

This intersection of the cognitive and social aspects of language proficiency, however, does not mean that they are identical or reducible one to the other. The implicit assumption that conversational fluency in English is a good indicator of "English proficiency" has resulted in countless bilingual children being "diagnosed" as learning-disabled or retarded. Despite their developmental intersections, BICS and CALP are conceptually distinct as reflected in their very different developmental patterns and contrasting lexical composition.

The criticisms of the BICS/CALP distinction derive, to some extent, from what critics have "read into" the distinction. None of the critics has disputed the basic realities from which the distinction derives. To reiterate:

- In monolingual contexts, the distinction reflects the difference between the language proficiency acquired through interpersonal interaction by the vast majority of six-year-old children and the proficiency developed through schooling and literacy that continues to expand throughout our lifetimes.
- Research studies since the early 1980s have shown that immigrant students can quickly acquire considerable fluency in the target language when they are exposed to it in the environment and at school but despite this rapid growth in conversational fluency, it generally takes a minimum of about five years (and frequently much longer) for them to catch up to native speakers in academic aspects of the language.

A final point concerns the "validity" of any theoretical construct. Theories must be consistent with the empirical data to have any claim to "validity." However, any theory represents only one of potentially many ways of organizing or viewing the data. Theories frame phenomena and provide interpretations of empirical data within particular contexts and for particular purposes. They generate predictions that are, in principle, falsifiable. If a theory is not consistent with the data, then it must be rejected, or refined to achieve that consistency. However, no theory is "valid" or "true" in any absolute sense. A theory represents a way of viewing phenomena that may be relevant and useful in varying degrees depending on its purpose, how well it communicates with its intended audience, and the consequences for practice of following through on its implications (its "consequential validity"). The generation of knowledge (theory) should be part of a collaborative dialogue (Cummins 2000).

In this respect, the response (both critical and supportive) to the BICS/CALP distinction has resulted in clarifications, elaborations, and refinements. The distinction represents *one way* of interpreting and communicating the research data to policy-makers and practitioners with the goal of improving educational experiences and outcomes for bilingual students. I believe it has served a useful purpose in this regard but at some point it may cease to serve this purpose or be subsumed into a more comprehensive framework that communicates to practitioners and policy-makers in a more effective way. Hopefully, the collaborative dialogue that is theory generation will usher in such a comprehensive framework sooner rather than later.

References

Biber, D. 1986. "Spoken and written textual dimensions in English: Resolving the contradictory findings." *Language*, 62, 384–414.

Bruner, J. S. 1975. "Language as an instrument of thought." In A. Davies (ed.), *Problems of Language and Learning*, pp. 61–88. London: Heinemann.

Collier, V. P. 1987. "Age and rate of acquisition of second language for academic purposes." *TESOL Quarterly*, 21, 617–41.

Corson, D. 1995. *Using English Words*. New York: Kluwer.

Coxhead, A. 2000. "A new academic word list." *TESOL Quarterly*, 34(2), 213–38.

Cummins, J. 1979. "Cognitive/academic language proficiency, linguistic interdependence, the optimum age question and some other matters." *Working Papers on Bilingualism*, No. 19, 121–9.

Cummins, J. 1981a. "Age on arrival and immigrant second language learning in Canada: A reassessment." *Applied Linguistics*, 1, 132–49.

Cummins, J. 1981b. "The role of primary language development in promoting educational success for language minority students." In California State Department of Education (ed.), *Schooling and Language Minority Students: A Theoretical Framework*. Los Angeles: Evaluation, Dissemination and Assessment Center, California State University.

Cummins, J. 1984. *Bilingualism and Special Education: Issues in Assessment and Pedagogy*. Clevedon, UK: Multilingual Matters.

Cummins, J. 1996. *Negotiating Identities: Education for Empowerment in a Diverse Society*. Los Angeles: California Association for Bilingual Education.

Cummins, J. 2000. *Language, Power and Pedgagogy: Bilingual Children in the Crossfire*. Clevedon, UK: Multilingual Matters.

Cummins, J. and M. Swain. 1983. "Analysis-by-rhetoric: Reading the text or the reader's own projections? A reply to Edelsky et al." *Applied Linguistics*, 4, 23–41.

Donaldson, M. 1978. *Children's Minds*. Glasgow: Collins.

Edelsky, C. 1990. *With Literacy and Justice for All: Rethinking the Social in Language and Education*. London: Falmer Press.

Edelsky, C., S. Hudelson, B. Flores, F. Barkin, B. Altweger, and K. Jilbert. 1983. "Semilingualism and language deficit." *Applied Linguistics*, 4, 1–22.

Gee, J. P. 1990. *Social Linguistics and Literacies: Ideologies in Discourses*. New York: Falmer Press.

Hakuta, K., Y. G. Butler, and D. Witt. 2000. *How Long Does it Take English Learners to Attain Proficiency?* Santa Barbara: University of California Linguistic Minority Research Institute.

Klesmer, H. 1994. "Assessment and teacher perceptions of ESL student achievement." *English Quarterly*, 26(3), 8–11.

Martin-Jones, M. and S. Romaine. 1986. "Semilingualism: A half-baked theory of communicative competence." *Applied Linguistics*, 7, 26–38.

Oller, J. 1979. *Language Tests at School: A Pragmatic Approach*. London: Longman.

Olson, D. R. 1977. From utterance to text: The bias of language in speech and writing. *Harvard Educational Review*, 47, 257–81.

Rivera, C. 1984. *Language Proficiency and Academic Achievement*. Clevedon, UK: Multilingual Matters.

Wiley, T. G. 1996. *Literacy and Language Diversity in the United States*. Washington, DC: Center for Applied Linguistics and Delta Systems.

Vincent, C. 1996. *Singing to a Star: The School Meanings of Second Generation Salvadorean students*. PhD dissertation, George Mason University, Fairfax, VA.

19

Linguistic Diversity, Schooling, and Social Class: Rethinking Our Conception of Language Proficiency in Language Minority Education

Jeff MacSwan and Kellie Rolstad

In the last half century, concern for the low educational achievement of linguistic minority children has led to a debate for and against bilingual education – that is, an education in which subject-matter, including literacy, is taught in both the child's native language and the majority language, English here. Attempting to enlighten the debate, Cummins (1980) introduced a distinction between basic interpersonal communicative skills (BICS) and cognitive-academic language proficiency (CALP). Cummins believed that teachers and other decision-makers might perceive language minority children who speak English on the playground or with classmates as ready for all-English classes, where he believed they might experience academic failure because they had not yet learned "cognitive-academic" aspects of English. Moreover, Cummins hypothesized that this aspect of language proficiency was specifically a property of the *first language*: "There exists a reliable dimension of proficiency in a first language which is strongly related to cognitive skills and which can be empirically distinguished from interpersonal communication skills such as oral fluency, accent, and sociolinguistic competence" (1980, p. 177).

While we join Cummins in supporting bilingual education programs,[1] we believe there are undesirable conceptual consequences of the BICS/CALP distinction as it is currently formulated. Specifically, we argue that the distinction confounds language ability and academic achievement, and does not take into account crucial differences between first and second language development; in this connection, we further argue that a consequence of the BICS/CALP distinction is the ascription of special status to the language of the educated classes, a view we find indistinguishable from classical prescriptivism, the idea that the variety of language spoken by more prestigious social groups is inherently "more correct" and thus regarded as superior to other varieties (Crystal 1986). We end by presenting an alternative conception of the relationship between school achievement and language development, which – for those who prefer acronyms – we call SLIC, or *second language instructional competence*, defined as the stage of second language (L2) development at which the learner is able to understand instruction and perform grade-level school activities using the L2 alone, in the local educational context.

1   The BICS/CALP Distinction

Although Cummins's BICS/CALP distinction persuaded many educators against prematurely mainstreaming English learners, a number of researchers responded with criticism (Edelsky et al. 1983; Genesee 1984; Spolsky 1984; Troike 1984; Martin-Jones and Romaine 1986; Wiley 1996). A frequent concern was that conflating *knowledge of language* and *academic knowledge* as "cognitive-academic language proficiency" produced a conception of language proficiency that granted special status to the language of school – and hence to the language of the educated classes.

We argue that Cummins's view that schooling has the effect of improving our language implies that the language of the educated classes is in certain respects intrinsically richer than – or an improved version of – the language of the unschooled or working class. Further, we argue that because the BICS/CALP distinction is applied in the context of *native language development* – not just *second language* – it is conceptually indistinguishable from prescriptivism and related deficit views of working-class language.

Cummins identifies "schooling and literacy" as the agency by which this more advanced stage of development, called CALP or "academic language," is reached:

> In monolingual contexts, the [BICS/CALP] distinction reflects the difference between the language proficiency acquired through interpersonal interaction by virtually all 6-year-old children and the proficiency developed through schooling and literacy which continues to expand throughout our lifetimes. For most children, the basic structure of their native language is in place by the age of 6 or so but their language continues to expand with respect to the range of vocabulary and grammatical constructions they can understand and use and the linguistic contexts within which they can function successfully. (Cummins 2000a, p. 63)

Consider other recent definitions:

> In short, the essential aspect of academic language proficiency is the ability to make complex meanings explicit in either oral or written modalities by means of language itself rather than by means of contextual or paralinguistic cues such as gestures and intonations. (Cummins 2000a, p. 59)

And

> Considerably less knowledge of language itself is usually required to function appropriately in interpersonal communicative situations than is required in academic situations. ... In comparison to interpersonal conversation, the language of text usually involves much more low frequency vocabulary, complex grammatical structures, and greater demands on memory, analysis, and other cognitive processes. (Cummins 2000b, pp. 35–6)

Let us consider for a moment a few of the specific properties Cummins associates with academic language – characteristics of the linguistic system which he believes distinguish BICS from CALP, or conversational language from academic language, in the first language context. CALP is said to involve the ability to make meanings explicit by means of language itself rather than by means of gestures and intonations. However, there is no reason to believe, and no evidence to support, the presumption that academics are better at explaining their craft than the less schooled are at explaining theirs, or that accompanying gestures are less useful to academics than to others. Imagine a typical professor, for instance, trying to talk in detail about farming, boat building, or auto repair. Academics would typically lack knowledge of relevant vocabulary in these contexts – words which would be "low frequency" for them, but not for many others. Moreover, we might wonder why one would consider academic language to involve "complex grammatical structures" in comparison to non-academic language. Are double negatives less complex than single negatives? Is *ain't*, a socially stigmatized contraction, less complex than *won't*, a socially acceptable one? Minimally, we would expect to see an explicit and theoretically defensible definition of linguistic complexity accompanying the claim that academic language is more complex than non-academic language, and then we would expect empirical evidence showing that, for some distinctive trait *t* of academic language which meets the definition of linguistic complexity, there is no trait *t'* of non-academic language which is as linguistically complex as *t*. Historically, a number of attempts have been made to distinguish languages or language varieties in such terms, but none have succeeded (Bernstein 1971; Crystal 1986; Milroy and Milroy 1999).

Although Cummins has frequently stressed that he did not intend to rank CALP above BICS (Cummins 1979, 2000a, 2000b), it is essentially *necessary* in his framework for BICS to precede CALP developmentally in order for his basic argument to succeed. Cummins's proposal was that, while BICS develops fairly rapidly in immigrant children, producing "surface fluency" early on, several more years are usually required before children develop sufficient levels of CALP to warrant placement in an all-English classroom. Cummins argued that this developmental dimension was essential to a theory of language proficiency, advocating that such a theory "must incorporate a developmental perspective so that those aspects of communicative proficiency mastered early by native speakers and L2 learners can be distinguished from those varying across individuals as development progresses" (1981 p. 11).

More recently, Cummins has asserted that BICS and CALP follow "different developmental patterns" (2000a p. 62), disapproving of August and Hakuta's (1997) interpretation of BICS as developmentally prior to CALP (p. 61). However, if the sequential order of BICS and CALP in immigrant children were dependent on individual experiences and situations, as Cummins (2000a p. 61) has asserted, then BICS would not normally precede CALP: Many (perhaps most) immigrant children have their first exposure to English in the classroom, where CALP is supposed to be found, and may seldom speak English on the playground, where BICS is presumably spoken. If BICS does not necessarily precede CALP in development, then the originally intended usefulness of the distinction is severely weakened, since educators might just as well expect CALP to develop first, and in no less time than BICS. On the other hand, if BICS and CALP *are* developmentally related, with BICS coming before CALP – as

Cummins (1981 p. 11) maintained in earlier work – then the two forms are explicitly ranked, with CALP being a developmentally more advanced form of language than BICS. Thus, if we preserve the developmental ranking of BICS and CALP, the implication of Cummins's framework is that the *language* of school itself – not just its social rewards or content – is an advanced or improved version of non-academic language. Put differently, in the context of first language development, the distinction implies that the language of the educated classes is inherently superior to the language of the working class.

In response to criticisms, Cummins (2000b) has written that "the greater relevance of academic language proficiency for success in school, as compared to conversational proficiency, does not mean that it is intrinsically superior in any way" (p. 75). If "academic language proficiency" were indeed understood in terms of *contextual relevance* or *situational/cultural appropriateness*, the notion would not be problematic. Indeed, when features of literary discourse (peculiar vocabulary, impersonal author, distant setting, special order of events, and so on) are present in the oral language of children, as may be seen even among very young middle-class children (Scollon and Scollon 1982), then achievement in school literacy becomes much easier, since much of the enterprise of learning to read and write has been accomplished before the child reaches school.

However, this "middle-class advantage" relates not to some presumed superior quality of the oral language of middle-class children, but to the special alignment of their particular home experiences and speech registers with those encountered at school. As Wiley (1996) has put it,

> . . . language proficiency is important in understanding academic success not because it is associated with universal cognitive thresholds, or common underlying language proficiencies, but because it is associated with the norms, practices, and expectations of those whose language, cultural, and class practices are embodied in the schools. Failing to appreciate this, we are left with the illusion that school practices involve universal, higher order cognitive functions and that all other uses of language are merely basic. (pp. 172–3)

Our disagreement with Cummins, then, is over the specific way in which CALP is defined: Rather than identifying cultural and linguistic *differences* which privilege some children, Cummins describes CALP as having specific context-independent properties from which advantages related to academic achievement are derived, and sees schooling as the agency by which basic conversational skills are transformed into the linguistically complex language of the educated classes – more specifically, Cummins distinguishes CALP from BICS by asserting that the former is characterized by an expanded range of vocabulary and complex grammatical structures (Cummins 2000a, p. 63; Cummins 2000b, pp. 35–6), an ability to make complex meanings explicit (Cummins 2000a, p. 59), and greater demand on memory, analysis, and other cognitive processes (Cummins 2000b, pp. 35–6). Considerable research has shown that there simply is no human language or language variety which does not have complex grammatical structures, or the mechanisms to create new words as new situations arise, or to make complex meanings explicit by means of language itself (Crystal 1986; Milroy and Milroy 1991). The common belief that academic language has specially enriched properties results from a long tradition of prescriptivist dogma, now propagated primarily in the academy – a tradition which has had the principal effect of justifying social inequalities in terms of "objectively assessed" deficiencies located in language, culture, and behavior.

Native language growth is inwardly driven, and all normal children achieve linguistically. During the most active acquisition period (ages 2–6), for instance, children learn approximately 10 to 12 new words a day, often on one exposure and under highly ambiguous circumstances (Gleitman and Landau 1994). Children know things about elementary aspects of sentence structure for which they have no evidence at all (Chomsky 1986; Pinker 1994). In a review of research on child language in the pre-school years, Tager-Flusberg (1997 p. 188) reported that, "by the time children begin school, they have acquired most of the morphological and syntactic rules of their language," and possess a grammar essentially indistinguishable from adults.

Our language continues to change in various ways as we encounter new experiences, and both schooling and school-based literacy are certainly among common life experiences in literate societies that can influence the structure and vocabulary of our language throughout our lives (MacSwan 2000). But schooling is not unique in this regard; any sustained experience can lead to new specialized vocabulary, new speech styles, and even structural changes. For instance, a skilled boatbuilder will know numerous vocabulary items completely foreign to non-specialists, will have expressions and a way of talking that academics find difficult to understand, and will use his language along with other cognitive resources to accomplish the goals and tasks of the trade.

Hence, in the context of children's native language, it is important to think critically about how we characterize linguistic changes that may take place as a result of schooling. "Proficiency" is presumed to be quantifiable, and *levels* of language proficiency are presumed to be ordered with respect to one another. If we claim that the usual effects of schooling on native language constitute *improvements* or *gains* in native language proficiency, in ways that other typical sustained experiences do not, then we have developed a conception of language proficiency that is not easily distinguished from classical prescriptivism.[2] In other words, if we say that schooling has a special effect on language proficiency which makes it better (higher, expanded), then we imply that the language proficiency of the unschooled or working class is inferior (lower, basic) in comparison to that of the educated classes.

Cummins explicitly endorses the view that schooling improves our language. For example, he asserts that instruction in school has the effect of *extending* "students' basic knowledge of syntax, semantics, and phonology . . . into new functional registers or genres of language" (2000b p. 75), and vigorously challenges the view, adopted here and elsewhere (MacSwan 2000), that schooling plays little role in developing language proficiency in the context of native language ability (2000b pp. 106–8). However, while the language used at school may differ in some respects from that used in other contexts, one cannot conclude that school has the effect of *improving* children's language, as Cummins claims. Schooling may change our language, but what results is *different*, not more complex. In the same way, taking up a new line of work, moving to a new region of the country, or undergoing an apprenticeship to work as a craftsman may very well make one's language *different* – but not more *complex*. Therefore, in the absence of relevant empirical evidence that shows academic language to be a "complex" or "expanded" version of non–academic language, we strongly reject the view that school improves our language, or that the language of the educated classes is in any sense richer or more complex than the language of the unschooled.

Numerous scholars have characterized the BICS/CALP distinction and related ideas as a kind of deficit theory (Edelsky et al. 1983; Martin-Jones and Romaine 1986; Wiley 1997; MacSwan 2000). Valencia (1997) defined a deficit theory as one which posits "that the student who fails in school does so because of internal deficits or deficiencies" manifested "in limited intellectual abilities, linguistic shortcomings, lack of motivation to learn and immoral behavior" (p. 2). The transmitters of these deficits, according to Valencia (1997), have typically been located in genetics, culture, class, and familial socialization. Because the acquisition of a native language is an inherent human ability, and because it reflects aspects of our biology and community lives, appealing to *levels* of native language proficiency appears to do precisely what Valencia warned against: It attempts to explain school failure in terms of a presumed "low ability level" of the child in his or her own native language.

Again, Cummins nowhere intended these consequences, and has vigorously defended the BICS/CALP distinction against claims that it represents a deficit theory (Cummins and Swain 1983; Cummins 2000b). We believe that it does, but wish to suggest here that the implications of deficiency inherent in the distinction may be largely avoided by carefully distinguishing between language ability and academic achievement, and between first and second language ability in school-age children.

2   Language Ability and Academic Achievement

Cummins sees literacy as "one aspect of communicative proficiency" (1981, p. 14) or "general language proficiency" (2000b, p. 131), and as a component of CALP more specifically (2000b, p. 70). In Cummins's framework, literacy is an aspect of language proficiency that develops later in life, layered atop the "basic fluency" or "species minimum" that is BICS. A more traditional view, however, which was part of the effort to repudiate traditional prescriptivism, took literacy to be a kind of technology used to represent language graphically. In this view, expertise in the use of print is no more an index of language proficiency than expertise in the use of photography is of visual acuity.

In fact, writing is a very recent human invention which became widespread and publicly accessible only about 500 years ago, with the advent of moveable type, and has been rejected by some societies as unimportant (Gaur 1992). By contrast, language existed long before the technology of writing, and exists in all human societies today. But given Cummins's conception of language proficiency, we are led inescapably to the conclusion that societies which do not use writing systems have relatively *low* "language proficiency," restricted only to BICS, in contrast to the "highly proficient" language abilities represented in the academy in literate societies. In our view, then, literacy is an aspect of academic achievement, not a stage of language development.

Unfortunately, confounding language ability and academic achievement can have real-life negative consequences for linguistic minorities. Indeed, it has become a common belief among teachers and policy-makers that some school-age children know

Table 1 Items on "Level C" of the ITP Spanish which require students to answer in complete sentences

Item	Required student response	Prompt
1. ¿Qué está haciendo el niño? [What is the body doing?]	El (niño) está leyendo/estudiando. [The body is reading/studying.]	Picture of boy looking at book.
2. ¿Cuántos manos tengo yo? [How many hands do I have?]	Usted tiene dos manos./Tú tienes . . . [You have two hands.]	None.
3. ¿Pueden correr los caballos? [Can horses run?]	Sí, pueden correr. [Yes, they can run.]	None.
4. ¿Vuelan los elefantes como los pájaros? [Do elephants fly like birds?]	No, los elefantes no vuelan. [No, elephants don't fly.]	None.

no language at all. In the Los Angeles Unified School District, for instance, the *Los Angeles Times* reported that 6,800 children were classified as "non-nons," and said to be "nonverbal in both English and their native language" (Pyle 1996). Children are so classified as a result of native language assessments, required for non–English speakers in five states and recommended in four others (Council of Chief State School Officers 1991) with large numbers of immigrant children. However, like the BICS/CALP distinction itself, these tests typically confound academic achievement with language ability, with the result that perfectly capable Spanish-speaking children are labeled as "non-speakers" of their own language.

Consider, for instance, the Idea Proficiency Test I Oral–Spanish (IPT-S) (Amori and Dalton 1996), a very widely used test of oral language (not literacy) which ranks students as "Non-speakers," "Limited Speakers," and "Fluent speakers" of Spanish. The authors of the IPT-S claim to be assessing in part a child's level of CALP, but further assert that test items also assess syntax, vocabulary, comprehension, and verbal expression – presumably BICS (Amori and Dalton 1996, pp. 14–15).

However, an examination of the contents of the IPT-S immediately reveals that the test is much more an assessment of academic knowledge than of language ability. For instance, the second part of the IPT-S asks four questions to which students are required to provide answers in complete sentences, as shown in Table 1. Students who miss these (or any other) four questions on this part are labeled "limited Spanish speaking."[3] After a first incorrect response, the test administrator directs the student to "answer the question in a complete sentence."

Putting aside the inconsistency in the implicit definition of a "complete sentence" and the fantastical and decontextualized nature of the items, we must ask whether the ability to recognize or produce a complete sentence on demand ought to factor into a native speaker's knowledge of language. Indeed, few of us would produce answers like those required above if asked these questions. The natural response to item 1, for instance, is simply *leyendo* or *estudiando* ("reading/studying").

Indeed, one's ability to answer in a fragment reveals detailed covert knowledge of linguistic structure. For instance, if asked a question such as item 4 in table 1, we rely on our knowledge of the internal structure of the phrase to determine possible shortened forms of the sentence (in English or Spanish), such as *No* and *No, they don't*; we can also reflect on our knowledge of language to determine which shortened versions are not structurally possible (e.g., *No, they / No, they do*). In fact, answering the question in the desired way requires that we suspend our knowledge of pragmatics, which tells us that we can delete recoverable information, in order to comply with an institutional requirement to respond in a so-called complete sentence.

We only learn about complete sentences in school, which is why the ability to produce or identify them should be regarded as part of the domain of academic achievement, not an aspect of knowledge of language. A language is a set of expressions generated by a grammar, which maps meaning to sound (Chomsky 1986; Pinker 1994). Very early on, children exhibit complex knowledge of word order, word structure, pronunciation, discourse structure, and appropriate use of language in distinct situations. All normal children exhibit this knowledge, regardless of their specific cultural background or life experiences. By contrast, knowledge of particular communities and cultural practices – including those internal to the school – depend upon one's interests, opportunities, and specific environment. If we define *language proficiency* in such a way as to include this sort of highly particular cultural knowledge, what should be regarded as a simple cultural difference suddenly becomes a linguistic dividing line which enormously privileges those with more socially valued cultural capital in hand. Only a small segment of the human race experiences formal schooling, and even fewer excel at it; but all of us know a language.

Confounding these constructs in our conception of native language proficiency is, in our view, an egregious error, with serious negative consequences for linguistic minorities. In the next section, we consider some relevant developmental differences between first and second language in typical school-age bilingual children before proposing some specific ways in which our conception of language proficiency in language minority education might be refined.

3   First and Second Language in School-age Early Sequential Bilinguals

We have argued that the association of the BICS/CALP distinction with a school-age child's native language makes it a species of prescriptivism because it represents *linguistic differences* – in this case, differences that are rooted primarily in social class membership – as *linguistic ability differences*. However, L2 learners[4] exhibit errors of a sort which school-age children do not exhibit in their native language. Unlike school-age L1 speakers, L2 learners have developed only partial knowledge of the structure of their target language, and exhibit substantial errors associated with tense, case, grammatical agreement, word order, phonology, and other aspects of structure. We refer to these forms as "errors" because they differ from the target language in terms of core aspects of the grammatical system, and in this respect are akin to the developmental errors observed in very young pre-school children acquiring their native language.[5]

In addition, while all normal human beings acquire the language of their speech community effortlessly and without instruction, L2 acquisition often meets with only partial success, and frequently depends upon considerable effort and purposely structured input (Bley-Vroman 1989; Coppieters 1987). Evidence suggests, too, that L2 development proceeds with considerable variation in rate and ultimate attainment (Snow and Hoefnagel-Höhle 1978), particularly as the age of onset of exposure to the L2 increases (Bialystok and Hakuta 1994). By contrast, native speakers exhibit remarkable uniformity in language growth (Chomsky 1986; Pinker 1994).

We argued that the BICS/CALP distinction leads to a deficit view of children in the context of native language because language is an inherent human ability which reflects aspects of our biology and community lives. L2 teaching, on the other hand, typically occurs at school, in a context that is outside of our communities, and corresponding L2 learning is subject to considerable variation in rate and ultimate attainment, and appears to be dependent upon extra-linguistic factors. Therefore, following Valencia's (1997) definition of a deficit model, describing a child as having limited ability in an L2 does not suggest "internal deficits or deficiencies" related to the child's genetic makeup, culture, class, or familial socialization. The L2 is specifically not a part of the child's home culture and environment. Thus, unlike attributed ability differences in a child's native language, which are intimately related to biological and cultural identity, ability differences in an L2 will very likely be perceived as a component of success in the academic environment quite generally. For these reasons, the critique of prescriptivism has historically been related only to the context of mature, normal native language ability, and does not apply in the L2 context.

In sum, we believe that the language proficiency construct, in the context of linguistic minority education, crucially must distinguish between language ability and academic achievement, and that blending these constructs in the context of native language ability, in particular, leads to unintended – and undesirable – conceptual consequences. Furthermore, distinguishing between first and second language allows us to clarify that the BICS/CALP distinction implies deficiencies inherent in the child's community only when applied to the first language context. In our final section, we offer an alternative line of thought which we think will avoid some of the pitfalls of the BICS/CALP framework.

4   Conclusion: An Alternative View, An Alternative Acronym

Separating achievement and language as distinct psychological constructs allows us to contrast the learning situation of majority language and minority language children in school. While majority language children have the single objective of mastering academic content (math, social studies, science, reading and writing) in school, language minority children have *two* objectives which they must meet in order to be academically successful: Like majority language children, they must master academic content; but unlike children in the majority, they must also learn the language of instruction at school. Bilingual instruction allows them to keep up academically while they take the time needed to master English. Also, in the course of developing children's knowledge of school subjects, bilingual education provides background knowledge which serves as a context for children to better understand the presentation of new academic subject-matter in the L2, and also helps them make inferences about the meaning of new words and grammatical structures they encounter in the new language (Krashen 1996).

Once children have learned English sufficiently well to understand content through all-English instruction, they have developed *second language instructional competence*, or SLIC. Unlike CALP, SLIC does not apply to native language development, and does not ascribe any special status to the language of school. Also, while CALP appears to equate cognitive and academic development, SLIC simply denotes the stage of L2 development in which the learner is able to understand instruction and perform grade-level school activities using the L2 alone, in the local educational setting. A child who has not yet developed SLIC is not considered cognitively less developed; she simply has not yet learned enough L2 to effectively learn through it. The SLIC concept thus avoids the implication that the child is deficient, and still allows us to stress the need for the child to continue to receive interesting, cognitively challenging instruction that she can understand during the time needed to achieve L2 instructional competence.

While we applaud the original intent of the BICS/CALP distinction, we believe that some refinements are needed in view of the unintended negative consequences of CALP outlined here. By distinguishing between academic achievement and language ability, and between first and second language development in school-age children, we may be better able to characterize the language situation of linguistic minorities and their achievement in school. We hope the notion of *second language instructional competence* contributes to this goal.

Notes

1   For a review of research on the effectiveness of bilingual education, see August and Hakuta (1997).
2   On the other hand, BICS/CALP proponents might argue that new experiences of any kind might have an enriching effect on language and "cognitive development," leading to gains in language proficiency and achievement, and that CALP describes gains in native language proficiency in the narrow context of schooling. On this view, we would no longer be able to compare or rank proficiency levels across domains (farmer language, banker language, school language, basketball language), so describing CALP (school language) as "expanded" in relation to BICS (language associated with other environments) would be impossible, undermining the usefulness of the distinction; and if school language is not necessarily associated with greater cognitive ability than other forms of language, then its relationship to achievement in school would also need to be recast.
3   According to the IPT-S scoring procedures, kindergarteners who take the test for initial identification must miss nine items on this part of the test to be regarded as "limited Spanish speaking"; kindergarteners who take the test for redesignation, like all others, are "limited" after just four "errors" (Amori and Dalton 1996, p. 39). Of course, no justification is presented for these arbitrary decisions.
4   For our purposes, an L2 learner is one who began learning a second (or other subsequent) language some time after the first was settled, around the age of 5 or so. For discussion, see Bhatia and Ritchie (1999, pp. 579–82) and Gass and Selinker (2001, pp. 100–4).
5   We wish to be precise in our definition of "error" in the second language context. We assume that a second language learner possesses a learning mechanism LM that generates values for a grammar G on inferences from a target T, where T is primary linguistic data from the second language; LM maps G from an initial state, G_0, to a steady state, G_S, where G_S is compatible with T. An

error is a linguistic expression compatible with $G_0 < G_n < G_S$. Some researchers prefer to think of such expressions as instances of "negative transfer" from the native language, while others think of them as analogous to developmental errors in child language acquisition. For our purposes, this issue is not relevant, and neither is the nature of the initial state G_0; but see Schwartz (1998) for some interesting discussion.

References

Amori, B. and E. F. Dalton. 1996. *Technical Manual: IDEA Oral Language Proficiency Test Spanish (IPT I Oral Grades K-6)*, 2nd edn. Brea, CA: Ballard & Tighe, Publishers.

August, D. and K. Hakuta (eds.). 1998. *Educating Language-Minority Children*. Washington, DC: National Academy Press.

Bhatia, T. K. and W. C. Ritchie. 1999. "The bilingual child: Some issues and perspectives." In W. C. Ritchie and T. K. Bhatia (eds.), *Handbook of Child Language Acquisition*, pp. 569–646. San Diego: Academic Press.

Bernstein, B. 1971. *Class, Codes and Control: Volume 1, Theoretical Studies Toward a Sociology of Education*. London: Routledge and Kegan Paul.

Bialystok, E. and K. Hakuta. 1994. *In Other Words: The Science and Psychology of Second-Language Acquisition*. New York: Basic Books.

Bley-Vroman, R. 1989. "What is the logical problem of foreign language learning?" In S. M. Gass and J. Schachter (eds.), *Linguistic Perspectives on Second Language Acquisition*. New York: Cambridge University Press.

Chomsky, N. 1986. *Knowledge of Language: Its Nature, Origin, and Use*. New York: Praeger.

Coppieters, R. 1987. "Competence differences between native and near-native speakers." *Language*, 63, 544–73.

Council of Chief State School Officers. 1991. *Summary of State Practices Concerning the Assessment of and the Data Collection about Limited English Proficient (LEP) Students*. Washington, DC: Council of Chief State School Officers, State Education Assessment Center/Resource Center on Educational Equity.

Crystal, D. 1986. "The prescriptive tradition." In D. Crystal (ed.), *The Cambridge Encyclopedia of Language*. Cambridge: Cambridge University Press.

Cummins, J. 1979. "Linguistic interdependence and the educational development of bilingual children." *Review of Educational Research*, 49, 221–51.

Cummins, J. 1980. "The cross-linguistic dimensions of language proficiency: Implications for bilingual education and the optimal age issue." *TESOL Quarterly*, 14(3), 175–87.

Cummins, J. 1981. "The role of primary language development in promoting educational success for language minority students." In *Schooling and Language Minority Students: A Theoretical Framework*. Sacramento: California State Department of Education.

Cummins, J. 1994. "Primary language instruction and the education of language minority students." In C. F. Leyba (ed.), *Schooling and Language Minority Students: A Theoretical Framework*, 2nd edn, pp. 3–46. Sacramento: California State Department of Education.

Cummins, J. 2000a. "Putting language proficiency in its place: Responding to critiques of conversational/academic language distinction." In J. Cenoz and U. Jessner (eds.), *English in Europe: The Acquisition of a Third Language*. Clevedon, UK: Multilingual Matters.

Cummins, J. 2000b. *Language, Power and Pedagogy: Bilingual Children in the Crossfire*. Clevedon, UK: Multilingual Matters.

Cummins, J. and M. Swain. 1983. "Analysis-by-rhetoric: Reading the text or the reader's own projections? A reply to Edelsky et al." *Applied Linguistics*, 4(1), 23–41.

Edelsky, C., S. Hudelson, B. Flores, F. Barkin, J. Altweger and K. Jilbert. 1983. "Semilingualism and language deficit." *Applied Linguistics*, 4, 1–22.

Gass, S. M. and L. Selinker. 2001. *Second Language Acquisition: An Introductory Course*, 2nd edn. Mahwah, NJ: Erlbaum.

Gaur, A. 1992. *A History of Writing*. London: The British Library.

Genesee, F. 1984. On Cummins' theoretical framework. In C. Rivera (ed.), *Language Proficiency and Academic Achievement*, pp. 20–7. Clevedon, UK: Multilingual Matters.

Gleitman, L. and B. Landau. 1994. *The Acquisition of the Lexicon*. Cambridge, MA: MIT Press.

Krashen, S. 1996. *Under Attack: The Case Against Bilingual Education*. Culver City, CA: Language Education Associates.

MacSwan, J. 2000. "The Threshold Hypothesis, semilingualism, and other contributions to a deficit view of linguistic minorities." *Hispanic Journal of Behavioral Sciences*, 20(1), 3–45.

Martin-Jones, M. and S. Romaine. 1986. "Semilingualism: A half-baked theory of communicative competence." *Applied Linguistics*, 7(1), 26–38.

Milroy, J. and L. Milroy. 1999. *Authority in Language: Investigating Standard English*. New York: Routledge.

Pinker, S. 1994. *The Language Instinct: How the Mind Creates Languages*. New York: William Morrow and Company.

Pyle, A. 1996. "Teaching the silent student." *Los Angeles Times*. June 11.

Schwartz, B. 1998. "The second language instinct." *Lingua*, 106, 133–60.

Scollon, R. and S. Scollon. 1982. *Narrative, Literacy, and Face in Interethnic Communications*. Norwood, NJ: Ablex.

Snow, C. E. and M. Hoefnagel-Höhle. 1978. "The critical period for language acquisition: Evidence from second language learning." *Child Development*, 49, 1114–28.

Spolsky, B. 1984. "A note on the dangers of terminology innovation." In C. Rivera (ed.), *Language Proficiency and Academic Achievement*, pp. 41–3. Clevedon, UK: Multilingual Matters.

Tager-Flusberg, H. 1997. "Putting words together: Morphology and syntax in the preschool years." In J. Berko-Gleason (ed.), *The Development of Language*, pp. 159–209. Boston, MA: Allyn and Bacon.

Troike, R. 1984. SCALP: Social and cultural aspects of language proficiency. In C. Rivera (ed.), *Language Proficiency and Academic Achievement*, pp. 44–54. Clevedon, UK: Multilingual Matters.

Valencia, R. 1997. "Introduction." In R. Valencia (ed.), *The Evolution of Deficit Thinking: Educational Thought and Practice*. London: Falmer Press.

Wiley, T. 1996. *Literacy and Language Diversity in the United States*. McHenry, IL: Center for Applied Linguistics and Delta Systems, Co.

Discussion Questions

1. Following Lambert's model, conduct a survey of a variety of people in your community (possibly from different language groups) about their opinions of people who speak different languages. Try to determine what stereotypes, if any, exist about the speakers of various *guises* (i.e., various languages or various regional or social dialects of a particular language). You may wish to use, or adapt, a frame such as the following

    German speakers are usually hard-working:
    Agree very much ____:____:____:____:____ Disagree very much
    French speakers are all very friendly:
    Agree very much ____:____:____:____:____ Disagree very much
    British English is more proper than American English:
    Agree very much ____:____:____:____:____ Disagree very much

2. Lambert observes that some bilinguals switch cultural identity when they switch languages. Interview someone who views himself or herself as bilingual and bicultural. What differences, if any, do they perceive in their interactions with members of the two different cultural groups? Are there behavioral norms that differ for the two groups? Does your informant report having any problems switching between the two cultures? Does he or she ever feel a conflict between this possible dual identity?

3. In his article, Cummins discusses situations in which bilingual children might acquire conversational skills (BICS), but lag behind their monolingual counterparts in the development of academic skills (CALP). Might the opposite situation also be possible (i.e., could a person – either adult or child – have good academic skills but poor conversational skills in a language)? If possible, what if anything would this observation imply about the claim that BICS must precede CALP?

4. Do you agree or disagree with MacSwan and Rolstad's claim that "Cummins's view that schooling has the effect of improving our language implies that the language of the educated classes is in certain respects intrinsically richer than – or an improved version of – the language of the unschooled or working class" (p. 330)? Why?

5. MacSwan and Rolstad present two different perspectives of literacy: that of Cummins which views literacy "as 'one aspect of communicative proficiency'" (p. 334) and one that MacSwan calls "a more traditional view," which "[takes] literacy to be a kind of technology used to represent language graphically. In this view, expertise in the use of print is no more an index of language proficiency than expertise in the use of photography is of visual acuity" (p. 334). Which view do you think is more accurate? Why?

6. Discuss how Cummins's construct of CALP and MacSwan's of second language instructional competence (SLIC) might fit well with Hymes's use of communicative competence and/or genre (see Part II).

Part VIII

Diglossia

Introduction

"Diglossia" is a neat example of the importance of concepts and conceptualization in the description of languages. Greek and Arabic have been especially problematic in their description. As Sotiropoulis points out, the term was first used by Karl Krumbacher in 1902 in his book *Das Problem der neugriechischen Schriftsprache*. A later reference to diglossia is in French, by the French linguist Marçais in 1930 about "La Diglossie arabe". The American linguist Charles Ferguson also attempted to deal with the problem of description of Arabic, but instead of describing the language in terms of its discrete features, he found a more adequate approach in describing a speech community of Arabic:

> I wanted to characterize a particular kind of language situation, taking a clear case that was relatively easy and uncontroversial to characterize. However, the idea of doing that was to make the clear case just one slot in a taxonomy of some sort . . . Ultimately the taxonomy would be replaced by some set of principles or frame of reference in terms of which this kind of thinking about language and this kind of research should be done. My goals, in ascending order were: clear case, taxonomy, principle, theory. (Ferguson 1991: 215).

Ferguson clearly had theory building in mind, and he expressed the hope that other people would write articles about other cases, and so they have, in the hundreds (Hudson 1992).

In Ferguson's "classic" definition of diglossia there are several features of the situation and of language use, which are part of or entailed in that description. There are no native speakers of the High (H) form, which must be learned by formal study, a situation which favors the elite classes. This in turn entails that, when there is language shift in a diglossic situation, the shift is to the Low (L) form as the lower classes just don't know the H. Clear cases of diglossia only involve one language, and so only one ethnic group and one culture; there is no ethnic strife, and when conflict occurs it is most often along lines of social class or religion. Joshua Fishman saw functional complementary distribution of the language varieties as the most salient feature of diglossia and extended it, as you will read in his article "Bilingualism with and without diglossia," to bilingual situations. This new conceptualization deleted the entailments just discussed. There are native speakers of both languages, there is often ethnic strife, and language shift is rarely to the L variety. Nor does the H form necessarily have the very high status which it does in clear cases of diglossia, to the point that its speakers deny the very existence of the L form.

One cannot copyright a theoretical concept like diglossia. Ferguson commented: "diglossia when it is used by a French linguist nowadays always implies the oppression of some lower classes by upper classes and I never even thought of that when I was writing about diglossia" (1997: 83). Oppression of an ethnic minority as well may be more accurate because most French writers have used Fishman's definition and have applied diglossia to bi/multilingualism, especially in decolonized countries.

There is today considerable disagreement and confusion about the meaning of diglossia. It is not helpful to look up "diglossia" in britannica.com and find, following a definition of classic diglossia, "Sociolinguists may also use the term to denote bilingualism, the speaking of two or more languages by members of the same community, as for example in New York City" with reference to the Puerto Rican community. That Spanish-speaking Puerto Ricans speak Spanish to Hispanics and English to Anglos is just plain bilingualism, not a case of functional complementary distribution. Basically, it is this confusion between diglossia and bilingualism which Alan Hudson is attempting to sort out with a theory-building rationale based on defining characteristics.

Next time you read an article about diglossia, make sure you know what definition the writer is using, or the explanations may confuse rather than enlighten you.

References

Ferguson, Charles. 1991. "Diglossia revisited," in Alan Hudson (ed.), *Studies in Diglossia*, special issue of *Southwest Journal of Linguistics*, 10: 1.

Ferguson, Charles. 1997. "History of sociolinguistics," in C. B. Paulston and G. R. Tucker (eds), *The Early Days of Sociolinguistics: Memories and Reflections*, pp. 77–86. Dallas: SIL.

Hudson, Alan. 1992. "Diglossia: a bibliographic review," *Language in Society*, 21: 611–74.

Krumbacher, Karl. 1902. *Das Problem der neugriechischen Schriftsprache*. Munich: Verlag der Akademie.

Marçais, W. 1930. "La Diglossie arabe." *L'Enseignement public*, 97.

Sotiropoulis, D. 1977. "Diglossia and the national language question in modern Greece," *Linguistics*, 19: 5–31.

Further Reading

Fasold, Ralph. 1984. *The Sociolinguistics of Society*. Oxford: Blackwell.

Hudson, Alan (guest editor). 2002. Diglossia, special issue of *International Journal of The Sociology of Language*, 157.

20

Diglossia

Charles Ferguson

In many speech communities two or more varieties of the same language are used by some speakers under different conditions. Perhaps the most familiar example is the standard language and regional dialect as used, say, in Italian or Persian, where many speakers speak their local dialect at home or among family or friends of the same dialect area but use the standard language in communicating with speakers of other dialects or on public occasions. There are, however, quite different examples of the use of two varieties of a language in the same speech community. In Baghdad the Christian Arabs speak a 'Christian Arabic' dialect when talking among themselves but speak the general Baghdad dialect, 'Muslim Arabic', when talking in a mixed group. In recent years there has been a renewed interest in studying the development and characteristics of standardized languages (see especially Kloss, 1952, with its valuable introduction on standardization in general), and it is in following this line of interest that the present study seeks to examine carefully one particular kind of standardization where two varieties of a language exist side by side throughout the community, with each having a definite role to play. The term 'diglossia' is introduced here, modeled on the French *diglossie*, which has been applied to this situation, since there seems to be no word in regular use for this in English; other languages of Europe generally use the word for 'bilingualism' in this special sense as well. (The terms 'language', 'dialect', and 'variety' are used here without precise definition. It is hoped that they occur sufficiently in accordance with established usage to be unambiguous for the present purpose. The term 'superposed variety' is also used here without definition; it means that the variety in question is not the primary, 'native' variety for the speakers in question but may be learned in addition to this. Finally, no attempt is made in this paper to examine the analogous situation where two distinct (related or unrelated) languages are used side by side throughout a speech community, each with a clearly defined role.)

It is likely that this particular situation in speech communities is very widespread, although it is rarely mentioned, let alone satisfactorily described. A full explanation of it can be of considerable help in dealing with problems in linguistic description, in historical linguistics, and in language typology. The present study should be regarded as preliminary in that much more assembling of descriptive and historical data is required; its purpose is to characterize diglossia by picking out four speech communities and their languages (hereafter called the defining languages) which clearly belong in this category, and describing features shared by them which seem relevant to the classification.

The defining languages selected are Arabic, Modern Greek, Swiss German, Haitian Creole. (See the references at the end of this Reading.)

Before proceeding to the description it must be pointed out that diglossia is not assumed to be a stage which occurs always and only at a certain point in some kind of evolution, e.g., in the standardization process. Diglossia may develop from various origins and eventuate in different language situations. Of the four defining languages, Arabic diglossia seems to reach as far back as our knowledge of Arabic goes, and the superposed 'Classical' language has remained relatively stable, while Greek diglossia has roots going back many centuries, but it became fully developed only at the beginning of the nineteenth century with the renaissance of Greek literature and the creation of a literary language based in large part on previous forms of literary Greek. Swiss German diglossia developed as a result of long religious and political isolation from the centers of German linguistic standardization, while Haitian Creole arose from a creolization of a pidgin French, with standard French later coming to play the role of the superposed variety. Some speculation on the possibilities of development will, however, be given at the end of the paper.

For convenience of reference the superposed variety in diglossia will be called the H ('high') variety or simply H, and the regional dialects will be called L ('low') varieties or, collectively, simply L. All the defining languages have names for H and L, and these are listed in the accompanying table.

Arabic

H is called		L is called
Classical (= H)	*'al-fuṣḥā*	*'al-ʿāmmiyyah,* *'ad-dārij*
Egyptian (= L)	*'il-faṣīḥ, 'in-nahawi*	*'il-ʿammiyya*

SW. German

Stand. German(= H)	*Schriftsprache*	*[Schweizer] Dialekt,* *Schweizerdeutsch*
Swiss (= L)	*Hoochtüütsch*	*Schwyzertüütsch*

H. Creole

French (= H)	*français*	*créole*

Greek

H and L	*katharévusa*	*dhimotikí*

It is instructive to note the problems involved in citing words of these languages in a consistent and accurate manner. First, should the words be listed in their H form or in their L form, or in both? Second, if words are cited in their L form, what kind of L should be chosen? In Greek and in Haitian Creole, it seems clear that the ordinary conversational language of the educated people of Athens and Port-au-Prince respectively should be selected. For Arabic and for Swiss German the choice must be arbitrary, and the ordinary conversational language of educated people of Cairo and of Zürich city will be used here. Third, what kind of spelling should be used to represent L? Since there is in no case a generally accepted orthography for L, some kind of phonemic or quasi-phonemic transcription would seem appropriate. The following choices were made. For Haitian Creole, the McConnell-Laubach spelling was selected, since it is approximately phonemic and is typographically simple. For Greek, the transcription was adopted from the manual *Spoken Greek* (Kahane et al., 1945), since this is intended to be phonemic; a transliteration of the Greek spelling seems less satisfactory not only because the spelling is variable but also because it is highly etymologizing in nature and quite unphonemic. For Swiss German, the spelling backed by Dieth (1938), which, though it fails to indicate all the phonemic contrasts and in some cases may indicate allophones, is fairly consistent and seems to be a sensible systematization, without serious modification, of the spelling conventions most generally used in writing Swiss German dialect material. Arabic, like Greek, uses a non-Roman alphabet, but transliteration is even less feasible than for Greek, partly again because of the variability of the spelling, but even more because in writing Egyptian colloquial Arabic many vowels are not indicated at all and others are often indicated ambiguously; the transcription chosen here sticks closely to the traditional systems of Semitists, being a modification for Egyptian of the scheme used by Al-Toma (1957).

The fourth problem is how to represent H. For Swiss German and Haitian Creole standard German and French orthography respectively can be used even though this hides certain resemblances between the sounds of H and L in both cases. For Greek either the usual spelling in Greek letters could be used or a transliteration, but since a knowledge of Modern Greek pronunciation is less widespread than a knowledge of German and French pronunciation, the masking effect of the orthography is more serious in the Greek case, and we use the phonemic transcription instead. Arabic is the most serious problem. The two most obvious choices are (1) a transliteration of Arabic spelling (with the unwritten vowels supplied by the transcriber) or (2) a phonemic transcription of the Arabic as it would be read by a speaker of Cairo Arabic. Solution (1) has been adopted, again in accordance with Al-Toma's procedure.

1 Function

One of the most important features of diglossia is the specialization of function for H and L. In one set of situations only H is appropriate and in another only L, with the two sets overlapping only very slightly. As an illustration, a sample listing of possible situations is given, with indication of the variety normally used:

	H	L
Sermon in church or mosque	x	
Instructions to servants, waiters, workmen, clerks		x
Personal letter	x	
Speech in parliament, political speech	x	
University lecture	x	
Conversation with family, friends, colleagues		x
News broadcast	x	
Radio 'soap opera'		x
Newspaper editorial, news story, caption on picture	x	
Caption on political cartoon		x
Poetry	x	
Folk literature		x

The importance of using the right variety in the right situation can hardly be over-estimated. An outsider who learns to speak fluent, accurate L and then uses it in a formal speech is an object of ridicule. A member of the speech community who uses H in a purely conversational situation or in an informal activity like shopping is equally an object of ridicule. In all the defining languages it is typical behavior to have someone read aloud from a newspaper written in H and then proceed to discuss the contents in L. In all the defining languages it is typical behavior to listen to a formal speech in H and then discuss it, often with the speaker himself, in L.

(The situation in formal education is often more complicated than is indicated here. In the Arab world, for example, formal university lectures are given in H, but drills, explanation, and section meetings may be in large part conducted in L, especially in the natural sciences as opposed to the humanities. Although the teachers' use of L in secondary schools is forbidden by law in some Arab countries, often a considerable part of the teachers' time is taken up with explaining in L the meaning of material in H which has been presented in books or lectures.)

The last two situations on the list call for comment. In all the defining languages some poetry is composed in L, and a small handful of poets compose in both, but the status of the two kinds of poetry is very different, and for the speech community as a whole it is only the poetry in H that is felt to be 'real' poetry. (Modern Greek does not quite fit this description. Poetry in L is the major production and H verse is generally felt to be artificial.) On the other hand, in every one of the defining languages certain proverbs, politeness formulas, and the like are in H even when cited in ordinary conversation by illiterates. It has been estimated that as much as one-fifth of the proverbs in the active repertory of Arab villagers are in H (*Journal of the American Oriental Society*, 1955, vol. 75, pp. 124 ff.).

2 Prestige

In all the defining languages the speakers regard H as superior to L in a number of respects. Sometimes the feeling is so strong that H alone is regarded as real and L is reported 'not to exist'. Speakers of Arabic, for example, may say (in L) that so-and-so doesn't know Arabic. This normally means he doesn't know H, although he may be a fluent, effective speaker of L. If a non-speaker of Arabic asks an educated Arab for help in learning to speak Arabic the Arab will normally try to teach him H forms, insisting that these are the only ones to use. Very often, educated Arabs will maintain that they never use L at all, in spite of the fact that direct observation shows that they use it constantly in all ordinary conversation. Similarly, educated speakers of Haitian Creole frequently deny its existence, insisting that they always speak French. This attitude cannot be called a deliberate attempt to deceive the questioner, but seems almost a self-deception. When the speaker in question is replying in good faith, it is often possible to break through these attitudes by asking such questions as what kind of language he uses in speaking to his children, to servants, or to his mother. The very revealing reply is usually something like: 'Oh, but they wouldn't understand [the H form, whatever it is called].'

Even where the feeling of the reality and superiority of H is not so strong, there is usually a belief that H is somehow more beautiful, more logical, better able to express important thoughts, and the like. And this belief is held also by speakers whose command of H is quite limited. To those Americans who would like to evaluate speech in terms of effectiveness of communication it comes as a shock to discover that many speakers of a language involved in diglossia characteristically prefer to hear a political speech or an expository lecture or a recitation of poetry in H even though it may be less intelligible to them than it would be in L.

In some cases the superiority of H is connected with religion. In Greek the language of the New Testament is felt to be essentially the same as the *katharévusa*, and the appearance of a translation of the New Testament in *dhimotikí* was the occasion for serious rioting in Greece in 1903. Speakers of Haitian Creole are generally accustomed to a French version of the Bible, and even when the Church uses Creole for catechisms and the like, it resorts to a highly Gallicized spelling. For Arabic, H is the language of the Qur'an and as such is widely believed to constitute the actual words of God and even to be outside the limits of space and time, i.e. to have existed 'before' time began with the creation of the world.

3 Literary Heritage

In every one of the defining languages there is a sizable body of written literature in H which is held in high esteem by the speech community, and contemporary literary production in H by members of the community is felt to be part of this otherwise existing literature. The body of literature may either have been produced long ago in the past history of the community or be in continuous production in another speech community in which H serves as the standard variety of the language. When the body of literature represents a long time span (as in Arabic or Greek) contemporary writers – and readers – tend to regard it as a legitimate practice to utilize words, phrases, or constructions which may have been current only at one period of the literary history and are not in widespread use at the present time. Thus it may be good journalistic usage in writing editorials, or good literary taste in composing poetry, to employ a complicated Classical Greek participial construction or a rare twelfth-century Arabic expression which it can be assumed the average educated reader will not understand without research on his part. One effect of such usage is appreciation on the part of some readers: 'So-and-so really knows his Greek [or Arabic]', or 'So-and-so's editorial today, or latest poem, is very good Greek [or Arabic].'

4 Acquisition

Among speakers of the four defining languages adults use L in speaking to children and children use L in speaking to one another. As a result, L is learned by children in what may be regarded as the 'normal' way of learning one's mother tongue. H may be heard by children from time to time, but the actual learning of H is chiefly accomplished by the means of formal education, whether this be traditional Qur'anic schools, modern government schools, or private tutors.

This difference in method of acquisition is very important. The speaker is at home in L to a degree he almost never achieves in H. The grammatical structure of L is learned without explicit discussion of grammatical concepts; the grammar of H is learned in terms of 'rules' and norms to be imitated.

It seems unlikely that any change toward full utilization of H could take place without a radical change in this pattern of acquisition. For example, those Arabs who ardently desire to have L replaced by H for all functions can hardly expect this to happen if they are unwilling to speak H to their children. (It has been very plausibly suggested that there are psychological implications following from this linguistic duality. This certainly deserves careful experimental investigation. On this point, see the highly controversial article which seems to me to contain some important kernels of truth along with much which cannot be supported – Shouby (1951).)

5 Standardization

In all the defining languages there is a strong tradition of grammatical study of the H form of the language. There are grammars, dictionaries, treatises on pronunciation, style, and so on. There is an established norm for pronunciation, grammar, and vocabulary which allows variation only within certain limits. The orthography is well established and has little variation. By contrast, descriptive and normative studies of the L form are either non-existent or relatively recent and slight in quantity. Often they have been carried out first or chiefly by scholars OUTSIDE the speech community and are written in other languages. There is no settled orthography and there is wide variation in pronunciation, grammar, and vocabulary.

In the case of relatively small speech communities with a single important center of communication (e.g., Greece, Haiti) a kind of standard L may arise which speakers of other dialects imitate and which tends to spread like any standard variety except that it remains limited to the functions for which L is appropriate.

In speech communities which have no single most important center of communication a number of regional L's may arise. In the Arabic speech community, for example, there is no standard L corresponding to educated Athenian *dhimotikí*, but regional standards exist in various areas. The Arabic of Cairo, for example, serves as a standard L for Egypt, and educated individuals from Upper Egypt must learn not only H but also, for conversational purposes, an approximation to Cairo L. In the Swiss German speech community there is no single standard, and even the term 'regional standard' seems inappropriate, but in several cases the L of a city or town has a strong effect on the surrounding rural L.

6 Stability

It might be supposed that diglossia is highly unstable, tending to change into a more stable language situation. This is not so. Diglossia typically persists at least several centuries, and evidence in some cases seems to show that it can last well over a thousand years. The communicative tensions which arise in the diglossia situation may be resolved by the use of relatively uncodified, unstable, intermediate forms of the language (Greek *mikti*, Arabic *al-lugah al-wustā*, Haitian *créole de salon*) and repeated borrowing of vocabulary items from H to L.

In Arabic, for example, a kind of spoken Arabic much used in certain semiformal or cross-dialectal situations has a highly classical vocabulary with few or no inflectional endings, with certain features of classical syntax, but with a fundamentally colloquial base in morphology and syntax, and a generous admixture of colloquial vocabulary. In Greek a kind of mixed language has become appropriate for a large part of the press.

The borrowing of lexical items from H to L is clearly analogous (or for the periods when actual diglossia was in effect in these languages, identical) with the learned borrowings from Latin to Romance languages or the Sanskrit *tatsamas* in Middle and New Indo-Aryan. (The exact nature of this borrowing process deserves careful investigation, especially for the important 'filter effect' of the pronunciation and grammar of H occurring in those forms of middle language which often serve as the connecting link by which the loans are introduced into the 'pure' L.)

7 Grammar

One of the most striking differences between H and L in the defining languages is in the grammatical structure: H has grammatical categories not present in L and has an inflectional system of nouns and verbs which is much reduced or totally absent in L. For example, Classical Arabic has three cases in the noun, marked by endings; colloquial dialects have none. Standard German has four cases in the noun and two non-periphrastic indicative tenses in the verb; Swiss German has three cases in the noun and only one simple indicative tense. *Katharévusa* has four cases, *dhimotikí* three. French has gender and number in the noun, Creole has neither. Also, in every one of the defining languages there seem to be several striking differences of word order as well as a thorough-going set of differences in the use of introductory and connective particles. It is certainly safe to say that in diglossia *there are always extensive differences between the grammatical structures of H and L*. This is true not only for the four defining languages, but also for every other case of diglossia examined by the author.

For the defining languages it may be possible to make a further statement about grammatical differences. It is always risky to hazard generalizations about grammatical complexity, but it may be worthwhile to attempt to formulate a statement applicable to the four defining languages even if it should turn out to be invalid for other instances of diglossia (cf. Greenberg, 1954).

There is probably fairly wide agreement among linguists that the grammatical structure of language A is 'simpler' than that of B if, other things being equal,

1. the morphophonemics of A is simpler, i.e. morphemes have fewer alternants, alternation is more regular, automatic (e.g., Turkish-*lar*~-*ler* is simpler than the English plural markers);

2. there are fewer obligatory categories marked by morphemes or concord (e.g., Persian with no gender distinctions in the pronoun is simpler than Egyptian Arabic with masculine–feminine distinction in the second and third persons singular);

3. paradigms are more symmetrical (e.g., a language with all declensions having the same number of case distinctions is simpler than one in which there is variation);

4. concord and rection are stricter (e.g., prepositions all take the same case rather than different cases).

If this understanding of grammatical simplicity is accepted, then we may note that in at least three of the defining languages the grammatical structure of any given L variety is simpler than that of its corresponding H. This seems incontrovertibly true for Arabic, Greek, and Haitian Creole; a full analysis of standard German and Swiss German might show this not to be true in that diglossic situation in view of the extensive morphophonemics of Swiss.

8   Lexicon

Generally speaking, the bulk of the vocabulary of H and L is shared, of course with variations in form and with differences of use and meaning. It is hardly surprising, however, that H should include in its total lexicon technical terms and learned expressions which have no regular L equivalents, since the subjects involved are rarely if ever discussed in pure L. Also, it is not surprising that the L varieties should include in their total lexicons popular expressions and the names of very homely objects or objects of very localized distribution which have no regular H equivalents, since the subjects involved are rarely if ever discussed in pure H. But *a striking feature of diglossia is the existence of many paired items, one H one L, referring to fairly common concepts frequently used in both H and L, where the range of meaning of the two items is roughly the same, and the use of one or the other immediately stamps the utterance or written sequence as H or L.* For example, in Arabic the H word for 'see' is *ra'ā*, the L word is *šāf*. The word *ra'ā* never occurs in ordinary conversation and *šāf* is not used in normal written Arabic. If for some reason a remark in which *šāf* was used is quoted in the press, it is replaced by *ra'ā* in the written quotation. In Greek the H word for 'wine' is *ínos*, the L word is *krasí*. The menu will have *ínos* written on it, but the diner will ask the waiter for *krasí*. The nearest American English parallels are such cases as *illumination ~ light, purchase ~ buy*, or *children ~ kids*, but in these cases both words may be written and both may be used in ordinary conversation: the gap is not so great as for the corresponding doublets in diglossia. Also, the formal–informal dimension in languages like English is a continuum in which the boundary between the two items in different pairs may not come at the same point, e.g., *illumination, purchase*, and *children* are not fully parallel in their formal–informal range of usage.

A dozen or so examples of lexical doublets from three of the sample languages are given below. For each language two nouns, a verb, and two particles are given.

Greek

H		L
íkos	house	*spíti*
ídhor	water	*neró*
éteke	gave birth	*eyénise*
alá	but	*má*

Arabic

ḥiδā'un	shoe	*gazma*
'anfun	nose	*manaxīr*
δahaba	went	*rāḥ*
mā	what	*'ēh*
'al'āna	now	*dilwa'ti*

Creole

homme, gens	person, people	*moun* (not connected with *monde*)
âne	donkey	*bourik*
donner	give	*bay*
beaucoup	much, a lot	*âpil*
maintenant	now	*kou–n–yé–a*

It would be possible to present such a list of doublets for Swiss German (e.g., *nachdem* ≅ *no* 'after', *jemand* ≅ *öpper* 'someone', etc.), but this would give a false picture. In Swiss German the phonological differences between H and L are very great and the normal form of lexical pairing is regular cognation (*klein* ≅ *chly* 'small', etc.).

9 Phonology

It may seem difficult to offer any generalization on the relationships between the phonology of H and L in diglossia in view of the diversity of data. H and L phonologies may be quite close, as in Greek; moderately different, as in Arabic or Haitian Creole; or strikingly divergent, as in Swiss German. Closer examination, however, shows two statements to be justified. (Perhaps these will turn out to be unnecessary when the preceding features are stated so precisely that the statements about phonology can be deduced directly from them.)

1. *The sound systems of H and L constitute a single phonological structure of which the L phonology is the basic system and the divergent features of H phonology are either a subsystem or a parasystem.* Given the mixed forms mentioned above and the corresponding difficulty of identifying a given word in a given utterance as being definitely H or definitely L, it seems necessary to assume that the speaker has a single inventory of distinctive oppositions for the whole H–L complex and that there is extensive interference in both directions in terms of the distribution of phonemes in specific lexical items. (For details on certain aspects of this phonological interference in Arabic, cf. Ferguson, 1957.)

2. *If 'pure' H items have phonemes not found in 'pure' L items, L phonemes frequently substitute for these in oral use of H and regularly replace them in tatsamas.* For example, French has a high front rounded vowel phoneme /ü/; 'pure' Haitian Creole has no such phoneme. Educated speakers of Creole use this vowel in *tatsamas* such as *Luk* (/lük/ for the Gospel of St Luke), while they, like uneducated speakers, may sometimes use /i/ for it when speaking French. On the other hand /i/ is the regular vowel in such *tatsamas* in Creole as *linèt* 'glasses'.

In cases where H represents in large part an earlier stage of L, it is possible that a three-way correspondence will appear. For example, Syrian and Egyptian Arabic frequently use /s/ for /q/ in oral use of Classical Arabic, and have /s/ in *tatsamas*, but have /t/ in words regularly descended from earlier Arabic not borrowed from the Classical. (See Ferguson, 1957.)

Now that the characteristic features of diglossia have been outlined it is feasible to attempt a fuller definition. DIGLOSSIA *is a relatively stable language situation in which, in addition to the primary dialects of the language (which may include a standard or regional standards), there is a very divergent, highly codified (often grammatically more complex) superposed variety, the vehicle of a large and respected body of written literature, either of an earlier period or in another speech community, which is learned largely by formal education and is used for most written and formal spoken purposes but is not used by any sector of the community for ordinary conversation.*

With the characterization of diglossia completed we may turn to a brief consideration of three additional questions: How does diglossia differ from the familiar situation of a standard language with regional dialects? How widespread is the phenomenon of diglossia in space, time, and linguistic families? Under what circumstances does diglossia come into being and into what language situations is it likely to develop?

The precise role of the standard variety (or varieties) of a language *vis-à-vis* regional or social dialects differs from one speech community to another, and some instances of this relation may be close to diglossia or perhaps even better considered as diglossia. As characterized here, diglossia differs from the more widespread standard-with-dialects in that no segment of the speech community in diglossia regularly uses H as a medium of ordinary conversation, and any attempt to do so is felt to be either pedantic and artificial (Arabic, Greek) or else in some sense disloyal to the community (Swiss German, Creole). In the more usual standard-with-dialects situation the standard is often similar to the variety of a certain region or social group (e.g., Tehran Persian, Calcutta Bengali) which is used in ordinary conversation more or less naturally by members of the group and as a superposed variety by others.

Diglossia is apparently not limited to any geographical region or language family. (All clearly documented instances known to me are in literate communities, but it seems at least possible that a somewhat similar situation could exist in a non-literate community where a body of oral literature could play the same role as the body of written literature in the examples cited.) Three examples of diglossia from other times and places may be cited as illustrations of the utility of the concept. First, consider Tamil. As used by the millions of members of the Tamil speech community in India today, it fits the definition exactly. There is a literary Tamil as H used for writing and certain kinds of formal speaking and a standard colloquial as L (as well as local L dialects) used in ordinary conversation. There is a body of literature in H going back many centuries which is highly regarded by Tamil speakers today. H has prestige, L does not. H is always superposed, L is learned naturally, whether as primary or as a superposed standard colloquial. There are striking grammatical differences and some phonological differences between the two varieties. (There is apparently no good description available of the precise relations of the two varieties of Tamil; an account of some of the structural differences is given by Pillai (1960). Incidentally, it may be noted that Tamil diglossia seems to go back many centuries, since the language of early literature contrasts sharply with the language of early inscriptions, which probably reflect the spoken language of the time.) The situation is only slightly complicated by the presence of Sanskrit and English for certain functions of H; the same kind of complication exists in parts of the Arab world where French, English, or a liturgical language such as Syriac or Coptic has certain H-like functions.

Second, we may mention Latin and the emergent Romance languages during a period of some centuries in various parts of Europe. The vernacular was used in ordinary conversation but Latin for writing or certain kinds of formal speech. Latin was the language of the Church and its literature, Latin had the prestige, there were striking grammatical differences between the two varieties in each area, etc.

Third, Chinese should be cited because it probably represents diglossia on the largest scale of any attested instance. (An excellent, brief description of the complex Chinese situation is available in the introduction to Chao (1947, pp. 1–17).) The *weu-li* corresponds to H, while Mandarin colloquial is a standard L; there are also regional L varieties so different as to deserve the label 'separate languages' even more than the Arabic dialects, and at least as much as the emergent Romance languages in the Latin example. Chinese, however, like modern Greek, seems to be developing away from diglossia toward a standard-with-dialects in that the standard L or a mixed variety is coming to be used in writing for more and more purposes, i.e. it is becoming a true standard.

Diglossia is likely to come into being when the following three conditions hold in a given speech community: (1) There is a sizable body of literature in a language closely related to (or even identical with) the natural language of the community, and this literature embodies, whether as source (e.g., divine revelation) or reinforcement, some of the fundamental values of the community. (2) Literacy in the community is limited to a small elite. (3) A suitable period of time, of the order of several centuries, passes from the establishment of (1) and (2). It can probably be shown that this combination of circumstances has occurred hundreds of times in the past and has generally resulted in diglossia. Dozens of examples exist today, and it is likely that examples will occur in the future.

Diglossia seems to be accepted and not regarded as a 'problem' by the community in which it is in force, until certain trends appear in the community. These include trends toward (1) more widespread literacy (whether for economic, ideological or other reasons), (2) broader communication among different regional and social segments of the community (e.g., for economic, administrative, military, or ideological reasons), (3) desire for a full-fledged standard 'national' language as an attribute of autonomy or of sovereignty.

When these trends appear, leaders in the community begin to call for unification of the language, and for that matter, actual trends toward unification begin to take place. These individuals tend to support either the adoption of H or of one form of L as the standard, less often the adoption of a modified H or L, a 'mixed' variety of some kind. The arguments explicitly advanced seem remarkably the same from one instance of diglossia to another.

The proponents of H argue that H must be adopted because it connects the community with its glorious past or with the world community and because it is a naturally unifying factor as opposed to the divisive nature of the L dialects. In addition to these two fundamentally sound arguments there are usually pleas based on the beliefs of the community in the superiority of H: that it is more beautiful, more expressive, more logical, that it has divine sanction, or whatever their specific beliefs may be. When these latter arguments are examined objectively their validity is often quite limited, but their importance is still very great because they reflect widely held attitudes within the community.

The proponents of L argue that some variety of L must be adopted because it is closer to the real thinking and feeling of the people; it eases the educational problem since people have already acquired a basic knowledge of it in early childhood; and it is a more effective instrument of communication at all levels. In addition to these fundamentally sound arguments there is often great emphasis given to points of lesser importance such as the vividness of metaphor in the colloquial, the fact that other 'modern nations' write very much as they speak, and so on.

The proponents of both sides or even of the mixed language seem to show the conviction – although this may not be explicitly stated – that a standard language can simply be legislated into place in a community. Often the trends which will be decisive in the development of a standard language are already at work and have little to do with the argumentation of the spokesmen for the various viewpoints.

A brief and superficial glance at the outcome of diglossia in the past and a consideration of present trends suggests that there are only a few general kinds of development likely to take place. First, we must remind ourselves that the situation may remain stable for long periods of time. But if the trends mentioned above do appear and become strong, change may take place. Second, H can succeed in establishing itself as a standard only if it is already serving as a standard language in some other community and the diglossia community, for reasons linguistic and non-linguistic, tends to merge with the other community. Otherwise H fades away and becomes a learned or liturgical language studied only by scholars or specialists and not used actively in the community. Some form of L or a mixed variety becomes standard.

Third, if there is a single communication center in the whole speech community, or if there are several such centers all in one dialect area, the L variety of the center(s) will be the basis of the new standard, whether relatively pure L or considerably mixed with H. If there are several such centers in different dialect areas with no one center paramount, then it is likely that several L varieties will become standard as separate languages.

A tentative prognosis for the four defining languages over the next two centuries (i.e. to about AD 2150) may be hazarded:

SWISS GERMAN:	Relative stability.
ARABIC:	Slow development toward several standard languages, each based on an L variety with heavy admixture of H vocabulary. Three seem likely: Maghrebi (based on Rabat or Tunis?), Egyptian (based on Cairo), Eastern (based on Baghdad?); unexpected politico-economic developments might add Syrian (based on Damascus?), Sudanese (based on Omdurman–Khartoum), or others.
HAITIAN CREOLE:	Slow development toward unified standard based on L of Port-au-Prince.
GREEK:	Full development to unified standard based on L of Athens plus heavy admixture of H vocabulary.

This paper concludes with an appeal for further study of this phenomenon and related ones. Descriptive linguists in their understandable zeal to describe the internal structure of the language they are studying often fail to provide even the most elementary data about the socio-cultural setting in which the language functions. Also, descriptivists usually prefer detailed descriptions of 'pure' dialects or standard languages rather than the careful study of the mixed, intermediate forms often in wider use. Study of such matters as diglossia is of clear value in understanding processes of linguistic change and presents interesting challenges to some of the assumptions of synchronic linguistics. Outside linguistics proper it promises material of great interest to social scientists in general, especially if a general frame of reference can be worked out for analysis of the use of one or more varieties of language within a speech community. Perhaps the collection of data and more profound study will drastically modify the impressionistic remarks of this paper, but if this is so the paper will have had the virtue of stimulating investigation and thought.

Note

A preliminary version of this study, with the title 'Classical or colloquial, one standard or two', was prepared for presentation at the symposium on Urbanization and Standard Languages: Facts and Attitudes, held at the meeting of the American Anthropological Association in November 1958, in Washington, D.C. The preliminary version was read by a number of people and various modifications were made on the basis of comments by H. Blanc, J. Gumperz, B. Halpern, M. Perlmann, R. L. Ward and U. Weinreich.

References on the Four Defining Languages

The judgements of this paper are based primarily on the author's personal experience, but documentation for the four defining languages is available, and the following references may be consulted for further details. Most of the studies listed here take a strong stand in favor of greater use of the more colloquial variety since it is generally writers of this opinion who want to describe the facts. This bias can, however, be ignored by the reader who simply wants to discover the basic facts of the situation.

Modern Greek

Hatzidakis, G. N. (1905), *Die Sprachfrage in Griechenland*, Chatzedaka, Athens.
Kahane, H., Kahane, R. and Ward, R. L. (1945), *Spoken Greek*, Washington.
Krumbacher, K. (1902), *Das Problem der neugriechischen Schriftsprache*, Munich.
Pernot, H. (1898), *Grammaire Grecque Moderne*, Paris, pp. vii–xxxi.
Psichari, J. (1928), 'Un Pays qui ne veut pas sa langue', *Mercure de France*, 1 October, pp. 63–121. Also in Psichari, *Quelque travaux. . . .*, Paris, 1930, vol. I, pp. 1283–1337.
Steinmetz, A. (1936), 'Schrift und Volksprache in Griechenland', Deutsche Akademie (Munich), *Mitteilungen*, pp. 370–379.

Swiss German

Dieth, E. (1938), *Schwyzertütsch Dialäkschrift*, Zurich.

Greyerz, O. von (1933), 'Vom Wert und Wesen unserer Mundart', *Sprache, Dichtung, Heimat*, Berne, pp. 226–247.

Kloss, H. (1952), *Die Entwicklung neuer germanischer Kultursprachen von 1800 bis 1950*, Pohl, Munich.

Schmid, K. (1936), 'Für unser Schweizerdeutsch', *Die Schweiz: ein nationales Jahrbuch 1936*, Basel, pp. 65–79.

Senn, A. (1935), 'Das Verhältnis von Mundart und Schriftsprache in der deutschen Schweiz', *Journal of English and Germanic Philology*, vol. 34, pp. 42–58.

Arabic

Al-Toma, S. J. (1957), 'The teaching of Classical Arabic to speakers of the colloquial in Iraq: a study of the problem of linguistic duality', Doctoral dissertation, Harvard University.

Chejne, A. (1958), 'The role of Arabic in present-day Arab society', *The Islamic Literature*, vol. 10, no. 4, pp. 15–54.

Lecerf, J. (1932), *Littérature Dialectale et renaissance arabe moderne* (Damascus, 1932–3), pp. 1–14; *Majallat al-majmaʿal-ʿilmī al-ʿarabī* (Dimashq), vol. 32, no 1 ʿAdad xāss bilmu'tamar al-'awwal lilmajāmiʿ al-lugawiyyah al-ʿilmiyyah al-ʿarabiyyah (Damascus, January 1957).

Marçais, W. (1930–31), Three articles, *L'Enseignement Public*, vol. 97, pp. 401–9; vol. 105, pp. 20–39, 120–33.

Haitian Creole

Comhaire-Sylvain, S. (1936), *Le Créole haitien*, Wetteren and Port-au-Prince.

Hall, R. A., Jr. (1953), *Haitian Creole*, Menasha, Wis.

McConnell, H. O., and Swan, E. (1945), *You Can Learn Creole*, Port-au-Prince.

Other references

Chao, Y. R. (1947), *Cantonese Primer*, Harvard University Press.

Ferguson, C. A. (1957), 'Two problems in Arabic phonology', *Word*, vol. 13, pp. 460–78.

Greenberg, J. H. (1954), 'A quantitative approach to the morphological typology of language', in R. Spencer (ed.), *Method and Perspective in Anthropology*, University of Minnesota Press, pp. 192–220.

Pillai, M. (1960), 'Tamil – literary and colloquial', in C. A. Ferguson and J. J. Gumperz (eds.), *Linguistic Diversity in South Asia*, Indiana University Research Center in Anthropology, Folklore and Linguistics: Publication 13, pp. 27–42.

Shouby, E. (1951), 'The influence of the Arabic language on the psychology of the Arabs', *Middle East Journal*, vol. 5, pp. 284–302.

21

Bilingualism With and Without Diglossia; Diglossia With and Without Bilingualism

Joshua A. Fishman

The psychological literature on bilingualism is so much more extensive than its socio-logical counterpart that workers in the former field have often failed to establish contact with those in the latter. In the past decade a very respectable sociological (or sociolog-ically oriented) literature has developed dealing with bilingual societies. It is the purpose of this paper to relate these two research traditions to each other by tracing the inter-action between their two major constructs: bilingualism (on the part of psychologists) and diglossia (on the part of sociologists).

1 Diglossia

In the few years that have elapsed since Ferguson (1959) first advanced it, the term diglossia has not only become widely accepted by sociolinguists and sociologists of lan-guage, but it has been further extended and refined. Initially it was used in connection with a society that used two (or more) languages for internal (intra-society) communi-cation. The use of several separate codes within a single society (and their stable main-tenance rather than the displacement of one by the other over time) was found to be dependent on each code's serving functions distinct from those considered appropriate for the other. Whereas one set of behaviors, attitudes and values supported, and was expressed in, one language, another set of behaviors, attitudes and values supported and was expressed in the other. Both sets of behaviors, attitudes and values were fully accepted as culturally legitimate and complementary (i.e., nonconflictual) and indeed, little if any conflict between them was possible in view of the functional separation between them. This separation was most often along the lines of an H(igh) language, on the one hand, utilized in conjunction with religion, education and other aspects of high culture, and an L(ow) language, on the other hand, utilized in conjunction with everyday pursuits of hearth, home and work. Ferguson spoke of H and L as superposed languages.

To this original edifice others have added several significant considerations. Gumperz (1961, 1962, 1964a, 1964b, 1966) is primarily responsible for our current awareness that diglossia exists not only in multilingual societies which officially recognize several "languages" but, also, in societies which are multilingual in the sense that they employ separate dialects, registers or functionally differentiated language varieties of whatever kind. He has also done the lion's share of the work in providing the conceptual ap-

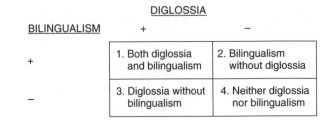

Figure 1   The relationships between bilingualism and diglossia

paratus by means of which investigators of multilingual speech communities seek to discern the societal patterns that govern the use of one variety rather than another, particularly at the level of small group interaction. On the other hand, I have attempted to trace the maintenance of diglossia as well as its disruption at the national level (1964, 1965a, 1965c, 1965d, 1965f, 1966a, 1966b), and in addition have attempted to relate diglossia to psychologically pertinent considerations such as compound and coordinate bilingualism (1965e). The present paper represents an extension and integration of these several previous attempts.

For purposes of simplicity it seems best to represent the possible relationships between bilingualism and diglossia by means of a fourfold table such as that shown in Figure I.

2   Speech Communities Characterized by Both Diglossia and Bilingualism

The first quadrant of Figure I refers to those speech communities in which both diglossia and bilingualism occur. At times such communities comprise an entire nation, but of course this requires very widespread (if not all-pervasive) bilingualism. An example of this type of nation is Paraguay, where almost the entire population speaks both Spanish and Guarani (Rubin, 1962; 1966). The formerly monolingual rural population has added Spanish to its linguistic repertoire in order to talk and write about education, religion, government, high culture and social distance or, more generally, the status stressing spheres; whereas the majority of city dwellers (being relatively new from the country) maintain Guarani for matters of intimacy and primary group solidarity even in the midst of Spanish urbanity.[1] A further example is the Swiss-German cantons in which the entire population of school age and older alternates between High German (H) and Swiss German (L), each with its own firmly established and highly valued functions (Ferguson, 1959; Weinreich, 1951; 1953).

Below the level of nationwide functioning there are many more examples of stable diglossia co-occurring with widespread bilingualism. Traditional (pre-World War I) Eastern European Jewish males communicated in Hebrew (H) and Yiddish (L). In more recent days their descendents have continued to do so adding to their repertoire a Western language (notably English) for *intragroup* communication as well as in domains of *intergroup* contact (Fishman, 1965c; Weinreich, 1951, 1953; 1962).[2] A similar example is that of upper and upper middle class males throughout the Arabic world who use classical (koranic) and vernacular (Egyptian, Syrian, Lebanese, Iraqui, etc.) Arabic and, not infrequently, also a Western language (French or English, most usually) for purposes of *intragroup* scientific or technological communication (Blanc, 1964; Ferguson, 1959; Nader, 1962).

All of the foregoing examples have in common the existence of a fairly large and complex speech community in which the members have available to them both a range of *compartmentalized* roles as well as ready *access* to these roles. If the *role repertoires* of these speech communities were of lesser range, then their *linguistic repertoires* would also be(come) more restricted in range, with the result that separate languages or varieties would be(come) superfluous. In addition, were the roles not compartmentalized, i.e., were they not *kept separate* by dint of association with quite separate (though complementary) values, domains of activity and everyday situations,[3] one language (or variety) would displace the other as role and value distinctions merged and became blurred. Finally, were widespread access not available to the variety of compartmentalized roles (and compartmentalized languages or varieties), then the bilingual population would be a small, privileged caste or class (as it is or was throughout most of traditional India or China) rather than a broadly based population segment.

These observations lead to the conclusion that many modern speech communities that are normally thought of as monolingual are, rather, marked by both diglossia and bilingualism if their several registers (speech varieties related to functional specificity; Halliday, 1964) are viewed as separate varieties or languages in the same sense as the examples listed above. Wherever speech communities exist whose speakers engage in a considerable range of roles (and this is coming to be the case for all but the extremely upper and lower levels of complex societies); wherever access to several roles is encouraged or facilitated by powerful social institutions and processes; and finally, wherever the roles are clearly differentiated (in terms of when, where and with whom they are felt to be appropriate), both diglossia and bilingualism may be said to exist. The benefit of this approach to the topic at hand is that it provides a single theoretical framework for viewing bilingual speech communities and speech communities whose linguistic diversity is realized through varieties not (yet) recognized as constituting separate "languages". Thus, it becomes possible for us to note that while nations characterized by diglossia and widespread bilingualism (the latter term being understood in its usual sense of referring to separate languages) have become fewer in modern times, those characterized by diglossia and diversified linguistic repertoires have increased greatly as a consequence of modernization and growing social complexity. The single theory outlined above enabling us to understand, predict and interrelate both of these phenomena is an instance of enviable parsimony in the behavioral sciences.[4]

3 Diglossia Without Bilingualism

There are situations in which diglossia obtains whereas bilingualism is generally absent (quadrant 3). Here, two or more speech communities are united religiously, politically or economically into a single functioning unit notwithstanding the socio-cultural cleavages that separate them. At the level of this larger (but not always voluntary) unity, two or more languages or varieties are recognized as obtaining. However, one (or both) of the speech communities involved is (are) marked by relatively impermeable group boundaries such that for "outsiders" (and this may well mean all those not born into the speech community, i.e., an emphasis on ascribed rather than on achieved status) role access and linguistic access are severely restricted. At the same time linguistic repertoires in one or both groups are limited due to role specialization.

Examples of such situations are not hard to find (see, e.g., the many instances listed by Kloss, 1966). Pre-World War I European elites often stood in this relationship with their countrymen, the elites speaking French or some other fashionable H tongue for their *intragroup* purposes (at various times and in various places: Danish, Salish, Provençal, Russian, etc.) and the masses speaking another, not necessarily linguistically related, language for their intragroup purposes. Since the majority of elites and the majority of the masses never interacted with one another *they did not form a single speech community* (i.e. their linguistic repertoires were discontinuous) and their intercommunications were via translators or interpreters (a certain sign of *intragroup* monolingualism). Since the majority of the elites and the majority of the masses led lives characterized by extremely narrow role repertoires their linguistic repertoires too were too narrow to permit widespread societal bilingualism to develop. Nevertheless, the body politic in all of its economic and national manifestations tied these two groups together into a "unity" that revealed an upper and a lower class, each with a language appropriate to its own restricted concerns.

Thus, the existence of national diglossia does *not* imply widespread bilingualism amongst rural or recently urbanized African groups (as distinguished from Westernized elites in those settings); nor amongst most lower caste Hindus, as distinguished from their more fortunate compatriots the Brahmins, nor amongst most lower class French-Canadians, as distinguished from their upper and upper middle class city cousins, etc. In general, this pattern is characteristic of polities that are economically underdeveloped and unmobilized, combining groups that are locked into opposite extremes of the social spectrum and, therefore, groups that operate within extremely restricted and discontinuous linguistic repertoires. Obviously, such polities are bound to experience language problems as their social patterns alter in the direction of industrialization, widespread literacy and education, democratization, and modernization more generally. Since such polities rarely developed out of initial socio-cultural consensus or unity, the educational, political and economic development of the lower classes is likely to lead to secessionism or to demands for equality for submerged language(s). The linguistic states of Eastern Europe and India, and the language problems of Wales, Canada and Belgium stem from origins such as these.[5] This is the pattern of development that may yet convulse modern African nations if their de-ethnicized Westernized elites and diglossic language policies continue to fail to create bilingual speech communities, incorporating the masses, within their ethnically arbitrary political boundaries.

4   Bilingualism Without Diglossia

We turn next to those situations in which bilingualism obtains whereas diglossia is generally absent (quadrant 2). Here we see even more clearly than before that bilingualism is essentially a characterization of individual linguistic behavior whereas diglossia is a characterization of linguistic organization at the socio-cultural level. Under what circumstances do bilinguals of similar cultural extraction nevertheless function without the benefit of a well understood and widely accepted social consensus as to which language is to be used between which interlocutors, for communication concerning what topics or for what purposes? Under what circumstances do the varieties or languages involved lack well defined or protected separate functions? Briefly put, these are circumstances of rapid social change, of great social unrest, of widespread abandonment of prior norms before the consolidation of new ones.

Many studies of bilingualism and intelligence or of bilingualism and school achievement have been conducted within the context of bilingualism without diglossia, often without sufficient understanding on the part of investigators that this was but one of several possible contexts for the study of bilingualism. As a result many of the purported "disadvantages" of bilingualism have been falsely generalized to the phenomenon at large rather than related to the absence or presence of social patterns which reach substantially beyond bilingualism (Fishman, 1965b, 1966c).

The history of industrialization in the Western world (as well as in those parts of Africa and Asia which have experienced industrialization under Western "auspices") is such that the means (capital, plant, organization) of production were often derived from one speech community while the productive manpower was drawn from another. Initially both speech communities may have maintained their separate diglossia-with-bilingualism patterns or, alternatively, that of an overarching diglossia without bilingualism. In either case, the needs as well as the consequences of rapid and massive industrialization and urbanization were frequently such that members of the speech community providing productive manpower rapidly abandoned their traditional sociocultural patterns and learned (or were taught) the language of the means of production much earlier than their absorption into the sociocultural patterns and privileges to which that language pertained. In response to this imbalance some react(ed) by further stressing the advantages of the newly gained language of education and industry while others react(ed) by seeking to replace the latter by an elaborated version of their own largely pre-industrial, pre-urban, pre-mobilization tongue.

Under circumstances such as these no well established, socially recognized and protected functional differentiation of languages obtains in many speech communities of the lower and lower middle classes. Dislocated immigrants and their children (for whom a separate "political solution" is seldom possible) are particularly inclined to use their mother tongue and other tongue for intragroup communication in seemingly random fashion (Nahirny and Fishman, 1965; Fishman, 1965f). Since the formerly separate roles of the home domain, the school domain and the work domain are all disturbed by the massive dislocation of values and norms that result from simultaneous immigration and industrialization, the language of work (and of the school) comes to be used at home (just as in cases of more radical and better organized social change the language of the home comes to be established in school and at work). As role compartmentalization and value complementarity decrease under the impact of foreign models and massive change the linguistic repertoire also becomes less compartmentalized. Languages and varieties formerly kept apart come to influence each other phonetically, lexically, semantically and even grammatically much more than before. Instead of two (or more) carefully separated languages each under the eye of caretaker groups of teachers, preachers and writers, several intervening varieties may obtain, differing in degree of interpenetration. Such fused varieties may, within time, become the mother tongue and only tongue of a new generation. Thus, bilingualism without diglossia tends to be transitional[6] both in terms of the linguistic repertoires of speech communities as well as in terms of the speech varieties involved per se. Without separate though complementary norms and values to establish and maintain functional separation of the speech varieties, that language or variety which is fortunate enough to be associated with the predominant drift of social forces tends to displace the other(s). Furthermore, pidginization is likely to set in when members of the "work force" are so dislocated as not to be able to maintain or develop significantly compartmentalized, limited access roles (in which they might be able to safeguard a stable mother tongue variety) and, furthermore, cannot interact sufficiently with those members of the "power class" who might serve as standard other-tongue models.

5   Neither Diglossia nor Bilingualism

Only very small, isolated and undifferentiated speech communities may be said to reveal neither diglossia nor bilingualism (Gumperz, 1962; Fishman, 1965d). Given little role differentiation or compartmentalization and frequent face to face interaction between all members of the speech community no fully differentiated registers or varieties may establish themselves. Given self-sufficiency no regular or significant contacts with other speech communities may be maintained. Nevertheless, such groups – be they bands or clans – are easier to hypothesize than to find. All communities seem to have certain ceremonies or pursuits to which access is limited, if only on an age basis. Thus, all linguistic repertoires contain certain terms that are unknown to certain members of the speech community, and certain terms that are used differently by different subsets of speakers. In addition, metaphorical switching (Blom and Gumperz, 1966) for purposes of emphasis, humor, satire or criticism must be available in some form even in relatively undifferentiated communities. Finally, such factors as exogamy, warfare, expansion of population, economic growth and contact with others all lead to internal diversification and, consequently, to repertoire diversification. Such diversification is the beginning of bilingualism. Its societal normification is the hallmark of diglossia. Quadrant four tends to be self liquidating.

Many efforts are now underway to bring to pass a rapprochement between psychological, linguistic and sociological work on bilingualism. The student of bilingualism, most particularly the student of bilingualism in the context of social issues and social change, may benefit from an awareness of the various possible relationships between individual bilingualism and societal diglossia illustrated in this paper. Since all bilingualism occurs in a social context, and since this context is likely to influence both the manifestations and the concomitants of bilingualism, it is incumbent on the student of bilingualism to differentiate accurately between the particular and the more general phenomena that pertain to his field of study.

Notes

1   Note that Guarani is not an official language (i.e., recognized and utilized for purposes of government, formal education, the courts, etc.) in Paraguay. It is not uncommon for the H variety alone to have such recognition in diglossic settings without this fact threatening the acceptance or the stability of the L variety within the speech community. However, the existence of a single "official" language should not divert the investigator from recognizing the fact of widespread and stable bilingualism at the levels of societal and interpersonal functioning.

2   This development differs significantly from the traditional Eastern European Jewish pattern in which males whose occupational activities brought them into regular contact with various strata of the non-Jewish coterritorial population utilized one or more coterritorial languages (usually involving H and L varieties of their own, such as Russian, German or Polish on the one hand, and Ukrainian, Byelorussian or "Baltic" varieties, on the other), but did so for *intergroup* purposes almost exclusively.

3   The compartmentalization of roles (and of domains and situations as well) requires the redefinition of roles, domains and situations in any encounter in which a seemingly inappropriate topic must be discussed between individuals who normally stand in a given role-relationship to each other. Under such circumstances one or other factor is altered (the roles are redefined, the topic is redefined) so as to preserve the cultural norms for appropriateness (grammaticality) of behavior between interlocutors.

4   A theory which tends to minimize the distinction between languages and varieties is desirable for several reasons. It implies that *social* consensus (rather than inherently linguistic desiderata) differentiates between the two and that separate varieties can become (and have become) separate languages given certain social encouragement to do so, just as purportedly separate languages have been fused into one, on the ground that they were merely different varieties of the same language.

5   Switzerland as a whole is not a case in point since it is *not* an example of discontinuous and hierarchically stratified speech communities under a common political regime. Switzerland consists of geographically stratified speech communities under a common regime. Except for the Swiss-German case there is hardly any societally patterned bilingualism in Switzerland. Only the Jura region, the Romansch area and a very few other small areas have (had) a recent history of diglossia without bilingualism.

6   At an individual level this need not be the case since translation bilingualism can be maintained for intragroup communication purposes and for individual vocational purposes without the formation of natural bilingual speech communities.

References

Blanc, Haim. *Communal dialects of Baghdad*. Cambridge: Harvard University Press, 1964.

Blom, Jan-Peter and Gumperz, John J. Some social determinants of verbal behavior. Unpublished paper presented at the annual meeting of The American Sociological Association, 1966a.

Ferguson, Charles A. Diglossia. *Word*, 1959, 15, 325–340.

Fishman, Joshua A. Language maintenance and language shift as fields of inquiry. *Linguistics*, 1964, (9), 32–70.

Fishman, Joshua A. *Yiddish in America*. Bloomington, Ind.: Indiana University Research Center in Anthropology, Folklore and Linguistics. Publication 36, 1965c. (Also: *International Journal of American Linguistics*, 1965a, 31, Part II, (2).)

Fishman, Joshua A. Bilingualism, intelligence and language learning. *Modern Language Journal*, 1965b, 49, 227–237.

Fishman, Joshua A. *Language Loyalty in the United States.* The Hague: Mouton, 1965c.

Fishman, Joshua A. Varieties of ethnicity and language consciousness. *Monograph Series on Languages and Linguistics* (Georgetown University), 1965d, 18, 69–79.

Fishman, Joshua A. Who speaks what language to whom and when? *Linguistique,* 1965e, (2), 67–88.

Fishman, Joshua A. Language maintenance and language shift; The American immigrant case within a general theoretical perspective. *Sociologus,* 1965f, 16, 19–38.

Fishman, Joshua A. Billingual sequences at the societal level. *On teaching English to speakers of other languages,* 1966a, 2, 139–144.

Fishman, Joshua A. Some contrasts between linguistically homogeneous and linguistically heterogeneous polities. *Sociological Inquiry,* 1966b, 36, 146–158.

Fishman, Joshua A. Sociolinguistic perspective on the study of bilingualism. Unpublished manuscript, 1966c.

Gumperz, John J. Speech variation and the study of Indian civilization. *American Anthropologist,* 1961, 63, 976–988.

Gumperz, John J. Types of linguistic communities, *Anthropological Linguistics,* 1962, 4, (1), 28–40.

Gumperz, John J. Linguistic and social interaction in two communities. *American Anthropologist,* 1964a, 66, part 2, 137–154.

Gumperz, John J. Hindi-Punjabi code-switching in Delhi. In Morris Halle (Ed.), *Proceedings of the International Congress of Linguists.* The Hague: Mouton, 1964b.

Gumperz, John J. On the ethnology of linguistic change. In William Bright (Ed.), *Sociolinguistics.* The Hague: Mouton, 1966, 27–38.

Halliday, Michael A. K. The users and uses of language. In M. A. K. Halliday, A. McIntosh, and P. Strevens, *The Linguistic Sciences and Language Teaching.* London: Longmans-Green, 1964, Chap. 4, 75–110.

Kloss, Heinz. Types of multilingual communities, a discussion of ten variables. *Sociological Inquiry,* 1966, 36.

Nader, Laura. A note on attitudes and the use of language. *Anthropological Linguistics,* 1962, 4, (6), 24–29.

Nahirny, Vladimir C. and Fishman, Joshua A. American immigrant groups: ethnic identification and the problem of generations. *Sociological Review,* 1965, 13, 311–326.

Rubin, Joan. Bilingualism in Paraguay. *Anthropological Linguistics,* 1962, 4, (1), 52–58.

Rubin, Joan. Language and education in Paraguay. In Joan Rubin, *National Bilingualism in Paraguay.* The Hague: Mouton, 1968.

Weinreich, Max. Inveynikste tsveyshprakikeyt in a skenaz biz der haskale; faktn un bagrifn. [Intra-group bilingualism in Ashkenaz until the enlightenment; facts and concepts]. *Goldenc Keyt,* 1959, No. 35, 3–11.

Weinreich, Uriel. Research problems in bilingualism, with special reference to Switzerland. Unpublished Dissertation, Columbia University, 1951.

Weinreich, Uriel. *Languages in contact.* New York: Linguistic Circle of New York, 1953.

Weinreich, Uriel. Multilingual dialectology and the new Yiddish atlas. *Anthropological Linguistics,* 1962, 4, (1), 6–22.

22

Toward the Systematic Study of Diglossia

Alan Hudson

1 Introduction

In its ideal form, the phenomenon of diglossia as originally described by Charles Ferguson (1959; chapter 20 in this volume: page references are to the original publication) may be understood as a highly specific type of sociolinguistic situation, characterizable in terms of particular synchronic and diachronic attributes. The identification of those attributes which are held in common by all instances of diglossia, and which differentiate them from other sociolinguistic situations, serves to locate diglossia within a broad typology of sociolinguistic situations and contributes to a general theory concerning the relationship between change in linguistic varieties and repertoires of varieties, on the one hand, and change in the social functions of language and the social organization of speech commnities, on the other.

Synchronically, diglossia may be distinguished from other types of sociolinguistic situations by reference to a number of general descriptive parameters. These include at least some of the following: (1) the social constitution of the diglossic speech community, (2) the type of code matrix, or repertoire of linguistic varieties, existing within the community, (3) the distribution of linguistic varieties, both in terms of knowledge and use, across the various social networks within the community, (4) the distribution of linguistic varieties across various contexts for social interaction, (5) the relative significance of situational, as opposed to social, stratification of linguistic varieties, and (6) the pattern of communal attitudes toward language which both derive from and support the particular social and functional allocation of codes within the community. To the extent that a diglossic characterization of a speech community on any one of these parameters consistently implies a diglossic characterization on one or more of the remaining parameters, then the classification, and the notion of diglossia itself, is demonstrated to be nonarbitrary.

Diglossia may also be distinguished from other sociolinguistic situations by reference to its diachronic attributes. These attributes have to do with (1) the social and linguistic circumstances which precede and give rise to the phenomenon of diglossia, (2) its course of development during its florescence, (3) the social and linguistic circumstances which attend its decline, and (4) the types of sociolinguistic situations which follow upon its extinction. The validity and utility of any particular definition of diglossia is confirmed to the extent that its synchronic representation, as discussed above, can be shown reliably to be associated with particular sociohistorical conditions, and can plausibly be interpreted as being linked causally to them. Thus the static description of diglossia is embedded within a dynamic, evolutionary perspective.

2   Ferguson's Description of Diglossia

Ferguson's characterization of a diglossic code matrix is stated from the beginning in terms that brook no ambiguity. The concept of diglossia is clearly intended to encompass only situations where "two or more varieties of the same language are used by some speakers under different conditions" (1959: 325), and not situations "where two distinct (related or unrelated) languages are used side by side throughout a speech community, each with a clearly defined role" (1959: 325, n. 2). The relationships between the varieties in a diglossic code matrix are such, however, that a "very divergent" superposed variety coexists in complementary functional distribution with the primary dialects of the language (Ferguson 1959: 336), and that there are always "extensive differences" between the grammatical structures of the two varieties (1959: 333). More recent extensions of the notion of diglossia to multilingual speech communities, or typologies of diglossia which subcategorize on the basis of the degree of genetic relatedness between codes, implicitly ignore the possibility that the particular code relationships identified by Ferguson are the direct outcome of social processes distinct from those involved in the emergence of societal multilingualism, on the one hand, or of finely graduated dialectal variation on the other.

According to Ferguson, the vernacular variety in diglossia is acquired naturally, and therefore, one may suppose, universally, while the elevated variety is acquired mainly by the means of formal education (1959: 331). Because formal education makes significant demands upon the resources of the community, access to the opportunities to acquire the high variety will typically be distributed asymmetrically, even in those cases where access to appropriate educational processes is not restricted to particular hereditary or other elites. Differential access to opportunities for acquisition of the prestige variety is inevitably reflected in differential ability to employ the code on a given occasion.

Both in Ferguson's original presentation of diglossia and in virtually all subsequent interpretations of his work, the issue of the differential functional allocation of codes has occupied center stage. This is scarcely surprising in view of the great importance attached by Ferguson himself to the strict complementarity of the functions of the high and low varieties: "In one set of situations only H is appropriate and in another only L, with the two sets overlapping only very slightly" (1959: 328). There is little room within such a characterization for a notion of fluid diglossia, "where several functions are less rigidly attached to a particular code", or for a continuum of diglossia types ranging between extremes of fluidity and rigidity in their association with their particular functions (Pauwels 1986: 15).

For those members of a diglossic community who control the high variety as well as the low, and who command access to those social occasions on which use of the high variety is appropriate, selection between the two varieties on a given occasion is a function of the social situation itself rather than a function of the social identities of the participants. Use of the high or low variety in a given situation is, moreover, reciprocal between interlocutors and thus determined by considerations other than the social distance between them. In this, diglossic speech communities contrast dramatically with other types of speech communities, such as those of traditional Javanese society, where highly divergent levels are used to signal status differences between speakers (Errington 1986: 338, 1991: 200).

Ferguson's account of the social context for the emergence of diglossia takes as its point of departure the assumption that diglossia is not a state "which occurs always and only at a certain point in some kind of evolution" (1959: 326–7), but rather one which "may develop from various origins and eventuate in different language situations" (1959: 327). While taking a polygenetic stance on the social origins of diglossia, however, it is clear that Ferguson views one recurring set of circumstances as contributing significantly to its emergence. Diglossia is likely to come into existence (1) when there exists a sizeable body of literature in a language closely related to the natural language of the community, and this literature embodies some of the fundamental values of the community, (2) when literacy in the community is restricted to a small elite, and (3) when a considerable period of time, on the order of several centuries, elapses following the establishment of the first two conditions (1959: 338).

The conditions specified by Ferguson as being conducive to the emergence of diglossia are likewise highly suggestive of those to be expected in what Gumperz describes as "more typical intermediate societies characterized by the existence of peasant, herder or even tribal strata or population[s] in various degrees of integration in the socially dominant groups" (1968: 467–8). In certain such societies, where government remains in the hands of a small ruling group, extreme structural differences between administrative and vernacular codes may develop and be maintained, even as relatively greater proportions of the population become mobilized and are drawn into national life (Gumperz 1968: 469). On the other hand, in a society where there exists a long-standing tradition of literacy in the mother tongue, and where the transition to industrial society is made at an early date, the emergence of discontinuous register ranges characteristic of diglossic speech communities may be permanently forestalled (Ure 1982: 17).

Certain developments in the speech community, which may be characterized broadly as tendencies toward mobilization and democratization, portend the decline, and ultimately the demise, of diglossia. These developments, in Ferguson's view, are (1) the spread of literacy, (2) the broadening and intensifying of communication between the various regional and social segments of the community, and (3) the rise of popular sentiment in favor of a standard national language as a symbol of autonomy (1959: 338). These same developments, the broadened participation of the middle classes in a general, vernacular-based education and the rise in language loyalty toward the vernacular variety, are among those identified by Kahane (1986: 499) as contributing to the decline of prestige varieties generally. They may be seen at work in the decline of Latin as a prestige language in Europe (Kahane 1986: 499; Parker 1983: 338–9), in the recent modernization of the code matrix in many formerly diglossic Arabic-speaking communities (Ibrahim and Jernudd 1986: 6; Walters 1996: 166), in the replacement of Ottoman Turkish by vernacular Turkish in the late nineteenth and early twentieth centuries (Gallagher 1971; Karpat 1984), the replacement of Ge'ez by Amharic in Ethiopia following the reforms of Menelik II in the early twentieth century (Fellman 1975b), the decline of Old Church Slavic following the reign of Peter the Great (Comrie 1991), the rise of a colloquial written style in Japanese during the Meiji era (Coulmas 1991; Neustupny 1974), and the abandonment of Classical Chinese in the decade following the May 4th 1919 literary revolution in China (Peyraube 1991).

The high variety in diglossia is likely to remain as the established standard "only if it is already serving as a standard language in some other community and the diglossia community, for reasons linguistic and non-linguistic, tends to merge with the other community" (Ferguson 1959: 339). However, any move toward the utilization of the high variety across all functions, to the exclusion of the vernacular variety, naturally presupposes a dramatic change in the diglossic pattern of language acquisition such that the vernacular is gradually discarded and the high variety, or some modified form of it, is now acquired as the primary variety (Ferguson 1959: 331). More typical by far is that "H fades away and becomes a learned or liturgical language studied only by scholars or specialists and not used actively in the community" (Ferguson 1959: 339). In these circumstances, "the creation of a third norm, which represents a merger of the original two norms[,] is a characteristic feature of diglossic situations" (Wexler 1971: 345–6, n. 22). The typical fate of the high variety in classical diglossia, namely its displacement by the vernacular variety and its vestigial survival in the lexicon of certain specialized registers of the vernacular (Coulmas 1991: 169; Kahane and Kahane 1979: 194; Sotiropoulos 1982: 19), contrasts dramatically with the gradual hegemonic advance of the high variety and the displacement of the low in the typical instance of heterogenous language contact.

3   Fishman's Treatment of Diglossia and its Impact

Of all of the attempts to differentiate or to generalize Ferguson's original definition of diglossia, none has been more influential than Fishman's essay on the relationship between bilingualism and diglossia (1967; chapter 21 in this volume: page references are to the original publication) and its various recensions over a period of more than thirty years (Fishman 1970, 1980, 1985, 1989). Although Fishman's and Ferguson's approaches to diglossia have often been characterized as antithetical, there are certain conceptual continuities between them which should be recorded here. Both Ferguson's and Fishman's studies are fundamentally typological in nature (Johnson 1975: 37), the former implicitly so, by reference to a number of criterial attributes held, in combination, to distinguish diglossia from other types of sociolinguistic situations, and the latter explicitly, by reference to a variety of possible intersections between the incidence of individual bilingualism, on the one hand, and the presence or absence of social compartmentalization of speech varieties, on the other. Both studies are concerned, moreover, with the complementary distribution of speech varieties across situational contexts, in accordance with patterns which are recognized by the speech community as culturally legitimate. Both studies portray diglossic repertoires as repertoires in which one variety, or range of varieties, is acquired in the natural manner of a vernacular mother tongue, whereas a second variety, or range of varieties, is acquired later in the process of socialization, under the influence of formal educational processes outside the environment of home and family. Finally, the two studies share a concern for the evolutionary framework for diglossia, exploring as they do the social conditions contributing to its emergence and decline, as well as the roles of functional complementarity and acquisitional process in the maintenance of a compatible long-term relationship between the constituent codes.

The most concise definition which Fishman offers of diglossia is that it is *"an enduring societal arrangement*, extending at least beyond a three generation period, such that two 'languages' each have their secure, phenomenologically legitimate and widely implemented functions" (1980: 3). The "languages" in question, it is clear, may in fact be distinct languages, or, alternatively, varieties of the same language which are sufficiently different from one another that, without schooling, the elevated variety cannot even be understood by speakers of the vernacular (1980: 4). Each language variety expresses, and is supported by, its own particular set of behaviors, attitudes, and values, which are "fully accepted as culturally legitimate and complementary" by the members of the speech community (1967: 29–30). Diglossia is the "stable, societal counterpart to individual bilingualism" (1980: 3) in that, while the latter is "a characterization of individual linguistic versatility" (1970: 83), the former represents "a well understood and widely accepted social consensus as to which language is to be used between which interlocutors, for communication concerning what topics or for what purposes" (1967: 34).

It is not at all obvious that the nature and degree of structural relatedness between the constituent codes in a code matrix is a sociologically revealing parameter in sociolinguistic typology generally, or in the typology of diglossia more particularly. It is clear that speech varieties which are closely related to each other may be in relatively stable functional complementation, as in the cases of Arabic, Greek, and Swiss German diglossia, or may be in some degree of competition with each other for the same functional niche, as in the cases of Frisian and Dutch, Occitan and French, Galician and Spanish, and Ukrainian and Russian. Conversely, genetically unrelated languages may be in serious rivalry with each other, as in the case of innumerable immigrant–host and colonial–indigenous contacts worldwide, or may be in stable, well-defined functional complementation, as in the case of Yiddish and Hebrew, and, arguably, Guaraní and Spanish. However, whereas codes which are structurally related to each other may be in stable functional complementation or not, codes which are not structurally related are overwhelmingly more likely, by virtue of the historical origins of the contact between them, to be in conflict when used by a single speech community for within-group communication. In the latter case, over the longer term, it is H that typically displaces L, often incorporating certain substrate influences from L as it does so, whereas, in the case of classical diglossia, it is L, in effect, that displaces H, incorporating certain superstrate influences from H in the process. Thus, a sociolinguistic typology based primarily upon structural relatedness between codes would group the Occitan–French situation in southern France together with, say, the Dhimotikí–Katharevousa situation in Greece, rather than with the Nahuatl–Spanish situation in Mexico. Yet the Occitan–French situation has a great deal more in common, sociologically, with the Nahuatl–Spanish situation (Eckert 1980; Hill 1983) than it does, for instance, with that of Schwyzertüütsch and Standard German in Switzerland, and should properly be classified as a case of heterogeneous language conflict, albeit one with specific additional characteristics arising from the potential for structural marginalization, or dialectalization, of Occitan inherent in its close affinity with French. The task facing students of diglossia, then, is to determine under what circumstances it is possible for two varieties, structurally related or not, to achieve cultural legitimacy within a single speech community and maintain a functionally compartmentalized coexistence which is transmitted intact from generation to generation indefinitely.

Fishman, no less than Ferguson, is concerned with the social origins of diglossia and with its course of development across time. While recognizing that traditional society is more compatible with diglossia, Fishman emphatically rejects the view that "diglossia obtains only under rather primitive, highly traditional and rigidly stratified sociocultural conditions" (1985: 51–2, 1989: 195) or that diglossia patterns *necessarily* coincide with high rates of illiteracy in H (1985: 51, 1989: 195). What all diglossic situations have in common, according to Fishman, is strict compartmentalization, whether of the functional or of the political variety. Diglossia is to be found, accompanied by widespread bilingualism, "wherever speech communities exist whose speakers engage in a considerable range of roles . . . wherever access to several roles is encouraged or facilitated by powerful social insitutions and processes; and finally, wherever the roles are clearly differentiated" (Fishman 1967: 32). On the other hand diglossia is to be found without bilingualism in situations where two or more distinct speech communities, marked by relatively impermeable group boundaries, are united, often involuntarily, within a single political or other social arrangement (Fishman 1967: 33). In contrast, diglossia is absent in speech communities characterized by limited role differentiation, whether as a result of the face-to-face nature of daily interaction in the community, the emphasis on open social networks and fluid role relationships characteristic of modernization, or the disestablishment of previous norms under the influence of radically disruptive social processes such as immigration and rapid industrialization.

Given its origins in culturally legitimate functional compartmentalization of roles, diglossia is necessarily a relatively stable phenomenon. Rigid functional compartmentalization contributes most directly to stability by eliminating any competition between the diglossic varieties for the same spheres of social interaction. Indirectly, functional compartmentalization contributes to stability by way of its implications for the language acquisition process: Since the elevated variety is never used for social interaction in the informal domains of the home and neighborhood, there is no opportunity for the youngest generation to acquire it as a native variety or to develop a degree of facility in it comparable to that acquired in their natural primary varieties. The functions of home and school in the acquisition of communicative competence in diglossic communities are reversed relative to their functions in nondiglossic societies. In the latter, "children typically become bilingual at a very early age, when they are still largely confined to home and neighborhood, since their elders . . . carry into the domains of intimacy a language learned outside its confines", while formal educational institutions, on the other hand, "tend to render individuals increasingly monolingual in a language other than that of hearth and home" (Fishman 1970: 83). In diglossic speech communities, by contrast, children "do not attain their full repertoires at home or in their neighborhood play groups" and, indeed, "those who most commonly remain at home or in the home neighborhod . . . are most likely to be functionally monolingual" (Fishman 1970:

79). Furthermore, whereas educational institutions in nondiglossic, bilingual societies tend to replace preexisting repertoires with others considered necessary for entry into mainstream society, those in diglossic communities augment preexisting repertoires with the additional varieties necessary for the complete expression of ethnocultural identity.

Since diglossia depends for its long-term survival upon compartmentalization of social roles, those societal processes which result in decompartmentalization of social behavior tend also to result in decompartmentalization of the linguistic repertoire and, therefore, in functional redundancy between codes. Functional redundancy, according to Fishman, leads in turn to structural interpenetration of linguistic varieties, and, inexorably, to language shift (1967: 35–6, 1980: 8, 9). Little wonder, then, that traditional societies offer more hospitable environments for the emergence and maintenance of diglossic arrangements, given that the transition from traditional to modern involves much that is inimical to the maintenance of compartmentalization in social behavior. Modernization brings with it industrialization and urbanization, democratization of education, literacy, and communication, the potential for greater mobility, and a shift in emphasis from ascribed to achieved social status. All of these processes "tend to diminish compartmentalization, whether in the language repertoire or in the social behaviour repertoire outside of language use *per se*" (Fishman 1980: 5). The resulting competition between linguistic varieties for the same ecological niche leads, in fairly short order, to the displacement of the socially and politically weaker variety by the stronger.

4 Toward a Working Definition of Diglossia

As noted above, between Ferguson's and Fishman's accounts of diglossia, there exist certain highly significant conceptual and theoretical continuities. The very essence of diglossia, in both cases, has to do with the existence in some speech communities of two or more significantly discrepant speech varieties, one of which is a universally available vernacular variety, and the other to some degree a superposed variety, used and acquired to a greater extent in more formal contexts. In addition, both the original and extended versions of diglossia are characterized by pervasive and rigid functional compartmentalization of the diglossic speech varieties. This, perhaps, is less a defining characteristic of diglossia than it is a necessary prerequisite for long-term maintenance of significantly discrepant codes within a single-speech economy, although the question persists as to how rigid functional compartmentalization of codes might be achieved and maintained in the first place.

As desirable as may be the conceptual parsimony achieved by extending Ferguson's notion of diglossia to instances of functionally compartmentalized societal bilingualism (Fishman 1967: 33), it is nonetheless the case that such parsimony is purchased at some considerable expense to evolutionary sociolinguistic theory (cf. Fellman 1975a: 38, 39), for the cases of diglossia described by Ferguson, in particular those of Arabic and Greek, are not comparable, in origin or in outcome, to the case of Spanish and Guaraní in Paraguay, or to similar cases of bilingualism elsewhere in the world which have commonly been cast as instances of diglossia. There is a significant correlate, in fact, to the distinction drawn here between diglossia in Ferguson's original sense and diglossia in the sense of functionally differentiated societal bilingualism, one which generally appears to have passed unnoticed in the debate over terminology. In instances of societal bilingualism, when language shift occurs, "the language with stronger rewards and sanctions associated with it wins out" (Fishman 1980: 8); the H variety, in other words, displaces the L. On the other hand, when shift occurs in the terminal stages of classical diglossia, it is, in effect, the prestige variety which is displaced by the vernacular (Ferguson 1959: 339; Kahane and Kahane 1979: 193). There are, to be sure, exceptions to both principles which remain to be accounted for in a more refined theory: The ongoing displacement of L-variety German by *Hochdeutsch* in urban German-speaking areas outside Switzerland (Schiffman 1991) might well be construed as a reversal of the usual pattern of shift for classical diglossia, while the displacement of Anglo-French by English in fourteenth-century England, although conforming to the general pattern for western prestige languages (Kahane and Kahane 1979), nonetheless may be viewed as a reversal of the pattern for societal bilingualism. In spite of these reversals, however, the contrast in the patterns of shift generally encountered in classical diglossia and in societal biligualism is persistent and striking.

Pending the adoption of a uniform definition of diglossia, hypotheses such as those adumbrated here cannot be put to the empirical test, and conflicting conclusions as to the origins, development, outcomes, and effects of diglossia are inevitable (Hudson-Edwards 1984: 6). While some will find diglossia, in the sense of the differential functional allocation of codes in general, to be a prerequisite for the maintenance of socially and politically weaker languages in multilingual settings, others will find it only incidental, at best, to the maintenance of weaker languages, and others still will see it as a form of linguistic capitulation to the more powerful languages in such situations; some will find diglossia to be intimately associated with the social stratification of literacy, while others may categorically reject such views as ideological interference (Fishman 1985: 51); some may see in traditional, stratified societies of a certain kind the most fertile conditions for the emergence of diglossia-like code repertoires (Gumperz 1968: 469), while others may find diglossia to be compatible not only with traditional societies but with "political, econotechnical or ideological/religious/philosophical arrangements of whatever kind" (Fishman 1985: 52). The source of this disagreement, at least in part, is the multiple ambiguity which has crept into the term diglossia as a result of its use with reference to quite disparate sociolinguistic situations. A return to a consistent definition of whatever kind is therefore essential if the study of diglossia is to contribute in a significant way to understanding "the organization and change of verbal repertoires in relation to the main processes of societal evolution" (Hymes 1984: 44), and the consistent definition advocated here, perhaps with some refinement, is that of Ferguson (1959).[1]

Note

This paper is an abbreviated and slightly revised version of Hudson (1991). For further details, consult the original version. For a more elaborate formulation of a possible theory of diglossia, see Hudson (2002).

References

Comrie, Bernard. 1991. "Diglossia in the Old Russian period." *Southwest Journal of Linguistics* 10(1): 160–72.

Coulmas, Florian. 1991. "Does the notion of diglossia apply to Japanese?: Some thoughts and some documentation." *Southwest Journal of Linguistics* 10(1): 125–42.

Eckert, Penelope. 1980. "Diglossia: Separate and unequal?" *Linguistics* 18: 1053–64.

Errington, J. Joseph. 1986. "Continuity and change in Indonesian language development." *Journal of Asian Studies* 45: 329–53.

Errington, J. Joseph. 1991. "A muddle for the model: Diglossia and the case of Javanese." *Southwest Journal of Linguistics* 10(1): 189–213.

Fellman, Jack. 1975a. "On 'diglossia'." *Language Sciences* 34: 38–9.

Fellman, Jack. 1975b. "The resolution of diglossia in an African setting: The Ethiopian case." *La Monda Lingvo-Problemo* 5: 178–83.

Ferguson, Charles A. 1959. "Diglossia." *Word* 15: 325–40. (Chapter 20 in this volume.)

Fishman, Joshua A. 1967. "Bilingualism with and without diglossia; diglossia with and without bilingualism." *Journal of Social Issues* 23(2): 29–38. (Chapter 21 in this volume.)

Fishman, Joshua A. 1970. *Sociolinguistics: A brief introduction*. Rowley, MA: Newbury House.

Fishman, Joshua A. 1980. "Bilingualism and biculturism as individual and as societal phenomena." *Journal of Multilingual and Multicultural Development* 1: 1–15.

Fishman, Joshua A. 1985. "Bilingualism and biculturism as individual and as societal phenomena." Joshua A. Fishman, Michael H. Gertner, Esther G. Lowy and William G. Milán (eds.), In *The Rise and Fall of the Ethnic Revival*, pp. 39–56. Berlin: Mouton.

Fishman, Joshua A. 1989. "Language and ethnicity in minority sociolinguistic perspective." Clevedon, UK: Multilingual Matters.

Gallagher, Charles F. 1971. "Language reform and social modernization in Turkey. Can language be planned?" In Joan Rubin and Björn H. Jernudd (eds.), *Sociolinguistic Theory and Practice for Developing Nations*, pp. 159–78. Honolulu: The University Press of Hawaii.

Gumperz, John J. 1968. "Types of linguistic communities." In Joshua A. Fishman (ed.), *Readings in the sociology of language*, pp. 460–72. The Hague: Mouton.

Hill, Jane H. 1983. "Language death in Uto-Aztecan." *International Journal of American Linguistics* 49: 258–76.

Hudson, Alan. 1991. "Toward the systematic study of diglossia." *Southwest Journal of Linguistics* 10(1): 1–22.

Hudson, Alan. 2002. "Outline of a theory of diglossia." *International Journal of the Sociology of Language*, 157.

Hudson-Edwards, Alan. 1984. "Rediscovering diglossia." *Southwest Journal of Linguistics* 7: 5–15.

Hymes, Dell. 1984. "Sociolinguistics: Stability and consolidation." *International Journal of the Sociology of Language* 45: 39–45.

Ibrahim, Muhammed H. and Björn H. Jernudd. 1986. Introduction [to "Aspects of Arabic socio-linguistics"]. *International Journal of the Sociology of Language* 61: 5–6.

Johnson, Bruce C. 1975. "More on diglossia." *Language Sciences* 37: 37–8.

Kahane, Henry. 1986. "A typology of the prestige language." *Language* 62: 495–508.

Kahane, Henry and Renée Kahane. 1979. "Decline and survival of western prestige languages." *Language* 55: 183–98.

Karpat, Kemal H. 1984. "A language in search of a nation: Turkish in the nation-state." In Aldo Scaglione (ed.), *The Emergence of National Languages*, pp. 175–208. Ravenna, Italy: Longo Editore.

Neustupny, J. V. 1974. "The modernization of the Japanese system of communication." *Language in Society* 3: 33–50.

Parker, Ian. 1983. "The rise of the vernaculars in early modern Europe: An essay in the political economy of language." In Bruce Bain (ed.), *The sociogenesis of language and human conduct*, pp. 323–51. New York: Plenum.

Pauwels, Anne. 1986. "Diglossia, immigrant dialects and language maintenance in Australia: The case of Limburgs and Swabian." *Journal of Multilingual and Multicultural Development* 7: 13–30.

Peyraube, Alain. 1991. "Some diachronic aspects of diglossia/triglossia in Chinese." *Southwest Journal of Linguistics* 10(1): 105–24.

Sotiropoulos, Dimitrios. 1982. "The social roots of Greek diglossia." *Language Problems and Language Planning* 6: 1–28.

Ure, Jean. 1982. "Introduction: Approaches to the study of register range." *International Journal of the Sociology of Language* 35: 5–23.

Walters, Keith. 1996. "Diglossia, linguistic variation, and language change in Arabic." In Mushira Eid (ed.), *Perspectives on Arabic Linguisics VIII*. Papers from the Eighth Annual Symposium on Arabic Linguistics, pp. 157–97. Amsterdam: John Benjamins.

Wexler, P. 1971. "Diglossia, language standardization and pluralism." *Lingua*, 27: 330–54.

Discussion Questions

1. In chapter 20, Ferguson gives some examples of formal vs. informal vocabulary items in English, e.g. *illumination ~ light, purchase ~ buy* (p. 352). List some other examples of formal (H) vs. informal (L) linguistic forms from your community's language use. Describe situations where each would be used.

2. If you have access to a speaker from a country where there is a diglossic situation, interview that speaker. Elicit his or her opinions about both the L and the H. Try to determine the range of uses that the L and H cover. Is there any overlap?

3. Ferguson and Fishman list many geographic areas and languages that they do not examine carefully (e.g, Italy, India and China). Choose one of these, or another area of interest to you, and investigate the language use situation. What is the pattern of use of each of the languages in this country or region? Is it more similar to bilingualism or to diglossia, or does it exhibit one of the other patterns described by Fishman?

4. Considering the language situation of the place you chose in question 3, examine the sociohistorical conditions that gave rise to the current linguistic situation. Does your information support the claims discussed by Hudson in chapter 22, for example that "diglossia patterns necessarily coincide with high rates of illiteracy in H" (p. 372)?

Part IX

Group Multilingualism

Introduction

Most countries in the world are multilingual, which is to say that they contain ethnic groups in contact and sometimes in competition. Multilingualism is at least as old as our earliest written records. The Sumerian-Akkadian empire in the third millennium BC governed a multitude of people in two languages, and in the Old Testament's Book of Esther the court official Mordecai sends out an official decree from Xerxes the Great (486–465 BC) in 127 translations to all the provinces of the Persian empire. The Roman empire was governed through Latin in the west and koine Greek in the east as lingua francas, languages of wider communication (LWC). Latin remained the lingua franca in the west until French took over much later under the powerful kings Louis. It was not until after World War II that English became the LWC of global usage.

The Romantic movement in Europe during the nineteenth century coincided with the rise of nationalism and with the idea of "one nation, one language," still a very powerful notion. Even so, it is mostly a fictitious one: there are very few countries where only one language is spoken. In Europe, only Iceland and Portugal are autochthonously monolingual. Nevertheless, nation and language paired into the ideal of one national language, which survives till this day. With this rather anachronistic ideal grew an ideology which held that the coexistence of many languages was likely to lead to strife and internal crises, and that one national language would solve such problems. The US English-Only Movement, roundly criticized by linguists and educators alike (Gonzalez 2001) can be seen as one such manifestation.

It is against the background of such beliefs that one should read and understand Joshua Fishman's article. He sets out to demonstrate – with very sophisticated methodology – that it is not multilingualism, linguistic heterogeneity in his words, which causes civil strife. This is not to deny that civil strife exists in multilingual states: Esman (2001: 356) cites "the recognition, thoroughly documented in [Viberg and Scherrer's *Ethnicity and Intra-state Conflict*], that more than two thirds of all armed conflicts since the end of the Cold War have been intra-state disputes with significant ethno-national components." Rather, it is a question of the factors which lead to such disputes. Paulston (1994) has discussed language as a social resource which is available to ethnic groups in their competition for access to the goods and services of a nation. When these ethnic groups, instead of seeing socioeconomic opportunities, perceive themselves as the target of stigmatization, economic exploitation and systematic unemployment, they are likely to use the original mother tongue as a strategy of mobilization, and so language strife becomes a corollary factor. If language and ethnicity had not been available, other strategies for mobilization would have been found, such as religion, labor unions and the like.

Another major concern for multilingual polities deals with language shift or maintenance of the various ethnic groups. The superordinate group frequently adopts a policy of assimilation and language shift for its linguistic minorities; if the subordinate ethnic group accepts these goals, strife is rare. The Occitan-speaking people of southern France have willingly shifted with little conflict. Likewise most immigrants shift to the language of the receiving country. But when an ethnic group wants to maintain its language and sees no motivation or rewards for assimilation and shift, the language policies of the mainstream may not be successful. Many of the indigenous populations of the Americas have seen themselves isolated from the mainstream reward system and have continued life in their traditional culture and in their original mother tongue. Paulston's article addresses some theoretical issues in understanding language maintenance and shift grounded in actual case studies in a comparative approach.

Yet other concerns in multilingual nations are choice of national language (Ricento 2000), of alphabet or writing system (Fierman 1991; Laitner, 1977), and of medium of education. South Africa after apartheid has opted for eleven official languages: English, Afrikaans, and nine indigenous African languages, a situation which demonstrates good will and aspirations of a "rainbow" nation but is not very practical. At present there is a marked use of English in government, in the army, and in multilingual local politics; people seem more concerned about building a new nation than worrying about what language they do it in or, in the words of Alan Davies in another context, "language is not the central driving force in human affairs: ideas are" (Davies 2001: 379). It is mostly when language becomes symbolic or symptomatic of other social driving forces that it becomes truly important.

Choice of medium of education is probably overtly the most troubling problem in multilingual countries. There is a vast literature on the role, function and (non)success of foreign and second languages in education. (See also parts X and XI.)

References

Davies, Alan. 2001. "Book review of Thomas Clayton, *Education and the Politics of Language.*" *Journal of Multilingual and Multicultural Development.* 22 (4): 376–9.

Esman, Milton J. 2001. "Book review of Hakan Wiberg and Christian Scherrer, *Ethnicity and Intra-state Conflict.*" *Journal of Multilingual and Multicultural Development.* 22 (4): 356.

Fierman, William. 1991. *Language Planning and National Development: The Uzbek Experience.* Berlin: Mouton de Gruyter.

González, Roseann Duenas. 2001. *Language Ideologies: Critical Perspectives on the Official English Movement.* Mahwah, NJ: Erlbaum.

Laitner, D. 1977. *Politics, Language and Thought: The Somali Experience.* Chicago: Chicago University Press.

Paulston, Christina Bratt. 1994. *Linguistic Minorities in Multilingual Settings.* Amsterdam: Benjamins.

Ricento, Thomas (ed.). 2000. *Ideology, Politics, and Language Policies: Focus on English.* Amsterdam: Benjamins.

Further Reading

Annamalai, E. 2001. *Managing Multilingualism in India: Political and Linguistic Manifestations*. Thousand Oaks, CA: Sage.

Coulmas, Florian (ed.). 1991. *A Language Policy for the European Community*. Berlin: Mouton de Gruyter.

Deprez, Kas and Theo de Plessis (eds.). 2000. *Multilingualism and Government*. Pretoria: Van Schaik.

Edwards, John. 1994. *Multilingualism*. London: Routledge.

Fase, Willem, Koen Jaspaert and Sjaak Kroon (eds.). 1992. *Maintenance and Loss of Minority Languages*. Amsterdam: Benjamins.

Fishman, Joshua A. (ed.). 1978. *Advances in the Study of Societal Multilingualism*. The Hague: Mouton.

Harlech-Jones, B. 1990. *You Taught Me Language: The Implementation of English as a Medium of Instruction in Namibia*. Capetown: Oxford University Press.

Lewis, E. Glyn. 1972. *Multilingualism in the Soviet Union*. The Hague: Mouton.

Mesthrie, Rajend (ed.). 1995. *Language and Social History: Studies in South African Sociolinguistics*. Capetown: Philip.

Turrell, M. Teresa. 2001. *Multilingualism in Spain*. Clevedon, UK: Multilingual Matters.

Wright, Sue and Helen Kelly-Holmes (eds.). 1998. *Managing Language Diversity* (Australia). Clevedon, UK: Multilingual Matters.

23

Empirical Explorations of Two Popular Assumptions: Inter-Polity Perspective on the Relationships between Linguistic Heterogeneity, Civil Strife, and Per Capita Gross National Product

Joshua A. Fishman

Among the major charges against linguistic heterogeneity that are encountered in the popular press in political discussions are the claims that it leads to or exacerbates civil strife, on the one hand, and that it lowers national productivity, on the other hand, in both cases because linguistic heterogeneity – and, by extension, bilingual education too, as an undertaking that fosters or promotes linguistic heterogeneity – presumably counteracts rationality, civility, optimal communication, and the smooth operations of society, government, and industry alike. These are charges to which some of my own recent research pertains,[1] and it may prove instructive to compare popular thinking and sociolinguistic scholarship in this connection.

Each of the foregoing charges can be translated into a formal inter-polity hypothesis, namely:

1. The greater the degree of linguistic heterogeneity in a country ("degree of linguistic heterogeneity" being operationalized as the proportion of the population claiming as its own the major mother tongue of any given country; the smaller that proportion, the greater the degree of linguistic heterogeneity, and, correspondingly, the larger that proportion, the smaller the degree of linguistic heterogeneity), the greater the frequency and severity of civil strife in that country.
2. Similarly, the greater the degree of linguistic heterogeneity in a country, the lower the per capita gross national product in that country.

1   How Can This Problem be Studied Empirically?

Until quite recently, it would have been virtually impossible to do conclusive, world-wide, empirical research on hypotheses such as the above because of the large number of countries (that is, polities) and the large number of additional variables that need to be examined in order to rigorously test these hypotheses. There are approximately 170 polities in the world today, and if these were simply to be compared two at a time, in order to determine whether the linguistically more homogeneous one differs significantly (with respect to severity or frequency of civil strife and/or with respect to per capita gross national product) from the linguistically less heterogeneous one, over twenty-five thousand individual comparisons would have to be made. Obviously, it would be both inordinately difficult to undertake and then to make sense out of so many comparisons.

Actually, however, the methodological problem indicated above for two variables and 170 countries is compounded many times over, if we realize that in order to test our hypotheses we also need to simultaneously consider many, many other variables that are descriptive of the countries of the world *in addition to* the two that we are focusing upon. What we really want to know is whether linguistically more heterogeneous and less heterogeneous polities differ in connection with civil strife and per capita gross national product *over and above* (independently of) the differences between such countries due to any and all other factors to which civil strife and per capita gross national product may be indirectly related.

Civil strife, for example, should be considered, too, when we are looking into the relationship between degree of linguistic heterogeneity and per capita gross national product. This is necessary so that we can tell whether any relationship encountered between the degree of linguistic heterogeneity and per capita gross national product, whatever that may be, is masked by or even due to the relationship between civil strife and per capita gross national product. And the same is also true, of course, with respect to the degree of religious heterogeneity, the degree of racial heterogeneity, the proportion of the annual budget allocated to military expenses, and so on, and so on. *Only if we can also consider all other possibly contributing variables can we tell whether linguistic heterogeneity per se really makes an independent (that is, a nonredundant) contribution to per capita gross national product.* However, there are an almost endless number of such "other possibly contributing variables" (indeed, political scientists have perfected about 230 different dimensions (238 to be exact), all in all, for describing countries), and all of these need to be utilized simultaneously, together with linguistic heterogeneity, when attempting to account for inter-polity differences in civil strife or in per capita gross national product.

Thus, our task is to compare all countries simultaneously on all variables simultaneously if we really want to find out whether the degree of linguistic heterogeneity is *a truly independent (necessary, nonredundant) correlate* of either civil strife or per capita gross national product. The price of bananas and the number of gloves sold on a particular day may correlate substantially. However, only if we include all other variables that might also possibly influence the cost of bananas on a particular day (for example, average daily temperature in the banana groves, daily transportation costs between the groves and the markets, labor costs in the groves and in the markets, et cetera, et cetera) can we safely avoid coming to the specious conclusion that the number of gloves sold is really genuinely (that is, independently) related to the cost of bananas. Does this sound like an impossibly tall order: to analyze hundreds of countries and hundreds of variables simultaneously? Do we have the necessary data to do that, and do we have the necessary methods to do that?

2 The Data and Methods Utilized in This Study

Fortunately, the variety and even the quality of the data we need has been provided by the cross-polity data banks that American political scientists, both in government and in academia, have prepared and repeatedly revised and expanded during the past quarter century. These data banks provide sifted, corrected, and continually updated data on all the countries of the world in conjunction with over 230 different economic, political, social, cultural, historical, geographic, and demographic variables. This data is not perfect, but it is the best available today anywhere in the world, and, since quite a bit of American economic, political, and military planning and policy is based on this data, it must at least be reasonably good on the whole, and it may even be quite a bit better than that.

The analytic methods to do what needs to be done have been provided by statisticians and computer specialists who have relatively recently perfected approaches (primarily cumulative multiple correlation and factor analysis) that make it relatively easy, on the one hand, to examine huge amounts of multivariate data and, on the other hand, to parsimoniously zero in on the relatively few variables in any large data set that are really the only independent (and, therefore, the only crucial) variables in explaining or in accounting for the variation in any given criterion variable. My co-workers and I are, I believe, the first to put both the exhaustive data sets and the new statistical analytic methods to joint use in relating inter-polity variation in linguistic heterogeneity to cross-polity variation in civil strife and in per capita gross national product.

Perhaps an apology is in order for this brief detour into methodological issues, which, no matter how brief it may be to the specialist, inevitably seems overly long and insufficiently understandable to the nonspecialist. My concern is basically related to the usual scholarly preoccupation that findings, interpretations, and conclusions rest upon foundations that are as firm as possible. It is also related to an attempt to get away from a contrasted approach, which may be referred to as "the favorite country approach." Journalists, politicians, and academics alike, we are all good at arguing from "preferred cases": cases that predictably provide *negative* answers to the questions we have initially posed about linguistic heterogeneity's possibly harmful consequences by examining them only in connection with Switzerland (where linguistic heterogeneity results in neither heightened civil strife nor in lowered per capita gross national product); or cases that answer these same questions in the *positive* by referring only to India, without even pausing to consider the many other dimensions (besides linguistic heterogeneity) on which Switzerland and India differ substantially and in ways that are directly related to civil strife and/or per capita gross national product. It is to escape from this more usual approach of arguing from "preferred (and biased) cases" that I have gone out of my way to study *all* available variables and *all* documentable countries simultaneously in order to clarify the true (that is, the independent) relationship between linguistic heterogeneity, civil strife, and per capita gross national product.[2]

3 Examining Civil Strife

Political scientists have kept records on four different indicators of civil strife in all of the countries of the world: (1) magnitude and frequency of conspiracy against the established government, (2) magnitude and frequency of internal warfare due to revolution, sedition, or secession, (3) magnitude and frequency of internal turmoil (riots, strikes, protests), and (4) a composite average of the above three.[3] The last is the only measure of civil strife that will be discussed in this paper, although essentially identical results obtain from analyses of the contribution of linguistic heterogeneity to civil strife as measured by each of the other measures of civil strife as well.[4]

A cumulative multiple correlation analysis that begins by aiming over 230 variables at the composite civil strife measure (our criterion or dependent variable at this point) reveals that the differences in composite-magnitude and frequency of civil strife across all of the countries of the world are both highly predictable and parsimoniously predictable. Out of about 230 possible predictors of this criterion, only a certain thirteen make truly independent contributions that, taken together, yield the optimal multiple correlation of .82 (see table 1 with respect to variable 1). Particularly noteworthy for our purposes is the fact that *linguistic heterogeneity is not a member of this optimal subset of predictors.* Of course, linguistic heterogeneity does have a certain correlation (.21) with civil strife and, therefore, if we were to disregard, for a moment, its redundancy with other variables it would, at most, explain only 4 percent (or $.21^2$) of the total variance in civil strife. However, when linguistic heterogeneity is confronted with all other possible predictors of civil strife, it is eclipsed entirely, and it becomes clear that it itself explains nothing at all in connection with civil strife that is not explained better (that is, less redundantly or more independently) by other variables. What are the variables that displace linguistic heterogeneity from any consideration as an independent predictor of civil strife? They are variables such as (1) short-term deprivation, (2) persistent deprivation, (3) the absence of coercive potential by the government, and (4) the presence of organized outlaw groups that exert pressure for their own particular benefit. Just a few variables such as these immediately come to the fore to form the relatively small optimal subset of thirteen indispensable predictors that, when taken together, account for 68 percent (or $.82^2$) of the worldwide inter-polity variance in composite civil strife.

A cumulative multiple correlation of .82 is quite an impressive accomplishment, but, of course, this still leaves about 32 percent of the variance in civil strife to be accounted for by variables not yet utilized (that is, by variables not yet in the total data set of about 230 variables) or by better measures of the variables that *have* been utilized in this data set. In either case, it is relatively certain that linguistic heterogeneity will not be among them, because we have already utilized it in two different measurement modes[5] and the results have been identical: linguistic heterogeneity simply does not appear in the optimal subset of independent variables needed for the maximal and most parsimonious prediction of civil strife. We may have the conviction that in one country or another linguistic heterogeneity *does* make an important contribution to the explanation of civil strife, and perhaps that is indeed so. Civil strife in each country is overdetermined by its own historical circumstances, but in the world as a whole, across all countries and across all historical circumstances, once deprivation, central coercive potential, and the presence of organized anomie groups are taken into consideration, it is entirely unwarranted to posit linguistic heterogeneity itself as a co-cause of civil strife. Whatever minor and redundant importance it may have is entirely attributable to its redundancy with the stronger independent predictors that do wind up in the optimal subset of predictors of civil strife.

Table 1 Linguistic heterogeneity, civil strife, and p.c. gross national product

Criterion	Maximum CR obtained	Most powerful predictors	r with LH	LH in opt. sub.?	Fact. struct. of opt. sub.
1. Civil strife	.82 ($CR^2 = 68\%$)	• Short- and long-term *deprivation* • Absence of central coercive power • Presence of organized lawless groups	.21 ($r^2 = 4\%$)	No	I, II, III
2. p.c. GNP	.90 ($CR^2 = 81\%$)	• Government *modernization* • p.c. newspaper circulation • Multiparty parliamentary government	−.32 ($r^2 = 10\%$)	No	I, II, III
3. LH	.88 ($CR^2 = 78\%$)	• Christianity or Islam dominant religion • Religious and racial homogeneity • Western or early westernized	–	–	I, IV, V

Note: The correlation between civil strife and p.c. GNP = −.28 ($r^2 = 82\%$).

4 Examining Per Capita Gross National Product

Turning now to our second criterion variable, we proceed to ask whether worldwide inter-polity variance in linguistic heterogeneity makes an independent contribution to the explanation or prediction of worldwide inter-polity variance in per capita gross national product.[6] Once again it becomes evident that the worldwide interpolity variance in our second criterion variable is highly predictable on the basis of a relatively small subset of optimal predictors. Out of our original pool of 238 available variables, only a certain ten are needed in order to yield a cumulative prediction of .90 and, once again, linguistic heterogeneity is not a member of this optimal subset (see table 1 with respect to variable 2). Linguistic heterogeneity naturally has its own correlation with per capita gross national product, a correlation of −.32, which, at best (that is, were it to be nonredundant) would indicate that linguistic heterogeneity could explain only 10 percent (or $.32^2$) of the worldwide inter-polity variation in per capita gross national product. However, linguistic heterogeneity is far from being a nonredundant predictor of per capita gross national product. When linguistic heterogeneity is confronted with all other possible predictors of per capita gross national product it is eclipsed entirely, indicating that in itself it really explains nothing at all about per capita gross national product.

The cross-polity variables that do wind up in the optimal subset of predictors of worldwide inter-polity variation in per capita gross national product are primarily (1) governmental modernization, (2) per capita newspaper circulation, (3) presence of a multiparty and parliamentary-republican government, and (4) industrial rather than agricultural concentration of the work force. All in all, these cumulatively account for 81 percent (or $.90^2$) of the total worldwide inter-polity variation in per capita gross national product, leaving 19 percent still to be accounted for either by additional variables, above and beyond the 238 already conceptualized, operationalized, and defined to date, or, alternatively, by the same variables measured more reliably and more validly. Even then it seems unlikely that linguistic heterogeneity would wind up in the optimal subset of predictors of per capita gross national product, because it is probably not sufficiently independent of the optimal subset of predictors, nor sufficiently powerful in comparison to them, to do so. There are simply much more immediate and much more independent predictors of cross-polity variation in per capita gross national product for us to be able to posit linguistic heterogeneity as a serious copredictor, over and above what is contributed by governmental modernization, parliamentary democracy, popular literacy, and large-scale industrialization.[7]

5   Examining Linguistic Heterogeneity as a Criterion Variable

We have twice looked at linguistic heterogeneity as an independent (or nonredundant) predictor variable and have found it to be a distinctly weak one.[8] We can now try to arrive at a clearer understanding of what inter-polity variation in linguistic heterogeneity *is* related to by viewing it itself as a criterion variable and then asking what other variables in our data set tend to predict inter-polity variation in linguistic heterogeneity. Once again, we obtain a relatively small and parsimonious optimal subset of predictors that, when taken together via cumulative multiple correlation procedures, yield a correlation of .88 (see table 1 with respect to variable 3). The most powerful variables in the optimal subset, a subset that accounts for 78 percent (or $.88^2$) of the worldwide cross-polity variance in linguistic heterogeneity, are (1) Christianity or Islam as the dominant religion of a polity, (2) degree of religious and racial homogeneity, (3) whether a polity is historically a former Spanish colony, and (4) whether a polity is Western or early-Westernized rather than late-Westernized under colonial auspices.

Several comments are in order about the above optimal subset of predictors. First of all, they are all *negatively* correlated to the criterion of linguistic heterogeneity; that is, they all tend to make for linguistic homogeneity rather than for heterogeneity. Second, we should note that neither civil strife nor per capita gross national product are in this subset, further confirming what we have reported in the two prior analyses, immediately above. Finally, it should be noted that if deprivation is the major underlying dimension of civil strife, and if modernization is the major underlying dimension of per capita gross national product, then homogenization, whether religious, demographic, or political-developmental, seems to be the major underlying (negative) predictor of linguistic heterogeneity. Obviously, at a deeper conceptual level, there *are* weak relationships between the three *criteria* that we have been predicting (civil strife, per capita gross national product, and linguistic homogeneity) as well as between their respective *optimal subsets of predictors*. This can be gleaned from the fact that civil strife and per capita gross national product correlate −.28 with each other, somewhere in between the correlation of linguistic heterogeneity with civil strife (.21) and the correlation of linguistic heterogeneity with per capita gross national product (−.32). Nevertheless, these links are weak, and no one criterion is among the best predictors of the other two. This means that each can be best predicted without the other, because each is influenced by the other not only weakly but indirectly, that is, via the influence of more primary and less redundant predictors.

The inescapable implication of these findings would be that lingua francas and bilingualism enable many polities to attain higher per capita gross national product and to avoid civil strife regardless of their degree of linguistic heterogeneity. It also implies that polities that are low in per capita gross national product and high in civil strife are, on the whole, characterizable as such regardless of their degree of linguistic heterogeneity, some of them being linguistically very homogeneous indeed. There may actually be very few, if any, countries that are communicationally penalized due to linguistic heterogeneity per se because folk bilingualism on a regional basis, elitist bilingualism on a nationwide basis, and the spread of national (and international) languages everywhere facilitate interactive processes. Furthermore, education, urbanization, commerce and industry, the mass media, and travel or migration all inevitably lead either to the erosion of minority languages (such erosion continuing to be particularly rapid and widespread in the United States)[9] or to the establishment of widespread and stable minority bilingualism along sociofunctional lines (referred to as *diglossia*), wherein each language is normatively accepted in minority society with minimally redundant functions of its own.[10]

6   Another Approach

That our three criteria are weakly (and redundantly) related but fundamentally separate is demonstrable by yet another approach known as "factor analysis." The optimal subset of variables for cumulatively predicting civil strife contains thirteen variables. The optimal subset of variables for cumulatively predicting per capita gross national product contains ten variables. The optimal subset of variables for cumulatively predicting linguistic heterogeneity (when the latter is measured as a continuous variable) also contains ten variables. These three subsets of optimal predictors are totally nonredundant; that is, there is no predictor that is optimal for more than one criterion. This itself is a powerful indicator of the major extent to which these three criteria are separate and distinct from each other.

However, thirty-three predictors are too many to keep in mind simultaneously and, therefore, difficult to understand or to discuss meaningfully. Factor analysis is a statistical method that enables us to derive from any large set of measures the smallest number of maximally different "dimensions" (that is, *factors*) to which the large set can be mathematically reduced. If we apply this technique to our original universe of 238 variables, we discover that it can be quite successfully reduced to about 20 factors, the first five of which alone account for more than half of the total variance in the original universe. Obviously, this means that there is quite a bit of redundancy in the original matrix, and that many of the original predictors correlate highly with each other and may even be different ways of measuring the same thing. If we now examine our three optimal subsets of predictors relative to this underlying factor structure in the data universe from which they were selected (via the cumulative multiple prediction method that we discussed quite early in this paper), the following picture emerges (see table 1): the optimal subset of predictors in connection with civil strife are primarily associated with factors I, II, and III. This is also the case in connection with the optimal subset of predictors in connection with per capita gross national product. However, when we turn to the optimal subset of predictors of our third criterion, linguistic heterogeneity, we find that these are primarily associated with factors I, IV, and V. It must be stressed that these factors are orthogonal, that is, unrelated to ("maximally different" from) each other. What the three optimal subsets of predictors have in common is factor I, the well-known "common factor" that "varimax orthogonal" factor analysis is expected to yield. Thereafter, the factor structure of the optimal predictors of linguistic hetero-geneity differs greatly from the factor structure of the optimal predictors of either civil strife or per capita gross national product, and the total variance accounted for by the differences in factor structure is much greater than the total variance accounted for by their similarities.[11]

7   Why is There Even a Weak Correlation Between Our Three Criteria?

Why do even weak relationships obtain between the three criteria we have been study-ing? Another type of statistical analysis, known as "path analysis," might possibly help clarify this question somewhat, but rather than burden this presentation by yet a third statistical technique,[12] let us permit ourself the instant gratification of a brief specula-tive interlude. All of the variables that political scientists have perfected for the study of inter-polity differences and similarities may be thought of as dealing with positive and negative "resources" vis-à-vis polity functioning. Most of these resources, by design, are *current resources*, and no historical dimension is supplied in connection with them. However, over centuries, those polities whose resources were relatively greater or more accessible generally attained modernization, unification, and democratization more quickly. In the past, the processes of modernization, unification, and democratization probably did undercut linguistic heterogeneity. However, by the end of the twentieth century, the period to which the bulk of our data pertains, we are dealing with the end results of the above, hypothetical, trends. Now, in an age of social, economic, demo-graphic, and even cultural planning by rich countries as well as by poor ones, by stable countries as well as by unstable ones, the relationships that may once have existed, par-ticularly along a long-term historical dimension, are now exceedingly attenuated and indirect at best.

Polities that value, accept, and cultivate linguistic heterogeneity have learned to do so while simultaneously fostering per capita gross national product and counteracting civil strife. There has been less politicized ethnolinguistic factionalism in the half century since the end of the Second World War, notwithstanding the large numbers of Third World polities that have come into existence since then, than in the half century preceding it. The underdeveloped, nondemocratic, multiethnic empires and colonies (where ethnolinguistic animosity was often stirred up by colonial masters seeking to divide the indigenous population) that may have given ethnolinguistic diversity a bad name ("Balkanization") in former times are hardly the proper model to use nowadays in order to understand the relationships between the criteria we have been studying. The weak relationships between these criteria are both resultants of past circumstances, and indications that those circumstances do not now commonly obtain in the world at large.

8   Might There be Some Positive Consequences of Linguistic Heterogeneity?

Thus far, we have done no more than discredit the necessarily negative consequences that are commonly attributed to linguistic heterogeneity. However, the absence of negative consequences is not at all the same thing as the presence of positive consequences. The verifiability of any positive consequences of linguistic heterogeneity, if, indeed, there are any, is a question for future research to pursue. It may be that the pursuit of such consequences will be an equally thankless one, since in that connection, too, linguistic heterogeneity may be an exceedingly weak independent (that is, nonredundant) inter-polity dimension. Perhaps what is involved, insofar as any possible positive consequences of linguistic heterogeneity are concerned, is not so much the *degree* of such heterogeneity as the type of policy adopted vis-à-vis linguistic heterogeneity. A serious problem in connection with the exploration of whatever positive correlates there may be of linguistic heterogeneity is the sad fact that political and other social scientists have not yet exhaustively studied the countries of the world with respect to those very dimensions that seem to me to present the best prospects of yielding such findings. Taking these two considerations together, (1) positive policies (or positive language-status planning) with respect to linguistic heterogeneity and (2) possibly positive consequences of linguistic heterogeneity, I would opt to investigate linguistic heterogeneity and such variables as (1) proportion of the minority-language population that has acquired the majority or dominant language (examining oralcy and literacy separately), (2) proportion of the minority-language population that has completed secondary education and received higher education, (3) proportions of the minority-language population that is employed and that is living above the poverty line, (4) some measure of positiveness of intergroup relations, and (5) some measure of degree of bilingualism and biliteracy in the dominant-language population.

These possibly positive consequences of a more positive (culturally pluralistic) policy toward linguistic heterogeneity are no more than hunches derived from the social science literature. Their exploration will require a combination of expanded inter-polity data, statistical sophistication, and sociolinguistic expertise. Their exploration will get us away from constant "damage control" with respect to linguistic heterogeneity, where we are always concerned with either containing or disproving the alleged negative consequences of linguistic heterogeneity, and into the domain of "positive bilingualism," that is, into the domain philosophically advanced by J. G. Herder, B. L. Whorf, and H. Kallen.[12]

Another lead that deserves to be investigated, which flows directly from the above discussion, is the possibility that, if the policy toward linguistic heterogeneity is nonaccepting, negative, or punitive, then the converse of the above tentative hypotheses might be confirmed, as might some of the other negative consequences of linguistic heterogeneity that have long been suspected. It would be more than I dare hope for to believe that such further research (of either kind) might overcome the emotional and nonrational climate in which issues of linguistic heterogeneity have long been discussed. Emotional issues do not respond easily to empirical evidence. Nevertheless, having devoted much of my life to the empirical study of emotional sociolinguistic issues, I continue to believe that the possibly positive and the possibly negative correlates of linguistic heterogeneity have been too little studied contextually, and that those who are not afraid of being "confused by the facts" and not too impatient to pursue the facts wherever they may lead, have a great deal of work ahead of them before light can begin to counterbalance heat in this sensitive area.[13]

Notes

1   This paper summarizes four previous studies, all of which I conducted together with Frank R. Solano, and one of which also benefited from the collaboration of Grant D. McConnell.

2   Prior to my own most recent research, almost all worldwide interpolity studies of linguistic heterogeneity concentrated on only a very few variables at a time (see, for example, Pool 1969; McRae 1983, 5–33 and particularly 24–25). My own early contribution to research on the interpolity correlates of linguistic heterogeneity *did* examine all variables available at that time, but it did so, by and large, one variable at a time rather than via statistical approaches that permitted all variables to be examined simultaneously and contrastively with each other (see Fishman 1966). The analytic approaches that I have adopted in the present round of studies (cumulative multiple correlation and factor analysis) seek to accomplish the same analyses, ceteris paribus, that would be undertaken if countries were matched on all variables and then compared only on two remaining variables: linguistic heterogeneity and the particular criterion variable under study (civil strife or per capita gross national product). The latter methodology, so commonly expected by the intelligent layman, usually cannot be followed in the social sciences because of sampling limitations, on the one hand (for example, in our studies the number of countries is finite and cannot be increased for research purposes) and, on the other hand, the very large number of other variables that need to be controlled. Even more directly tackled by our adopted methodologies is the problem of indirect causes, cumulative multiple correlation analysis actually being the method of choice if such concerns are to be set aside.

3   For full details as to the separate as well as the composite worldwide inter-polity measurement of civil strife, see Feierabend and Feierabend 1972.

4   This section briefly summarizes Fishman and Solano 1990. The correlation between linguistic heterogeneity and civil strife reported in the present paper is that which obtains when the former is measured as a continuous variable. A lower correlation obtains (.12) when linguistic heterogeneity is measured as a dichotomous variable. For $N = 200$, a correlation of .18 is significant at the .01 level and a correlation of .14 is significant at the .05 level.

5   Two measures of linguistic heterogeneity were employed, a dichotomous measure and a continuous measure. The dichotomous measure characterized each polity as either having or not having at least 15 percent of its population claiming a mother tongue other than the dominant mother tongue of the country. The continuous measure characterized each polity by the exact proportion of its population claiming a mother tongue other than the dominant mother tongue of that country. The identical nature of findings utilizing these two different measures of linguistic heterogeneity is reported in Fishman, Solano, and McConnell 1990.

6   This section briefly summarizes Fishman and Solano 1989a. The correlation between linguistic heterogeneity and per capita gross national product reported in the present paper is that which obtains when the former is measured as a continuous variable. A lower correlation obtains (.25) when linguistic heterogeneity is measured as a dichotomous variable. For $N = 200$, a correlation of .18 is significant at the .01 level and a correlation of .14 is significant at the .05 level.

7   Popular literacy may be as much a cause as a consequence of per capita gross national product, as far as cumulative multiple correlation analysis is concerned, but linguistic heterogeneity is apparently neither the one nor the other in a strong or nonredundant fashion.

8   This section briefly summarizes Fishman and Solano 1989b.

9   International perspective on language spread more generally and on recent language shift in particular may be gained from Dow 1987–88; Fishman et al. 1985, particularly chapter 6, "Mother-Tongue Claiming in the United States since 1960: Trends and Correlates"; and Veltman 1983.

10   A history of the diglossia concept and the huge literature devoted to it, as well as a review of its current status and suggestions for the modification of this concept, are all available in Britto 1986.

11   For the substantive specification and resultant naming of these factors, see the discussions in Fishman and Solano 1989a, 1989b, and 1989c.

12   For a discussion of "positive bilingualism" and a review of Herder's, Whorf's, and Kallen's theoretical contributions to that topic, see Fishman 1978.

13   I am greatly indebted to my colleagues and friends Ofelia Garcia, Ricardo Otheguy, and S. R. Sridhar for their comments and queries, which helped me revise an earlier draft of this paper.

References

Britto, Francis. 1986. *Diglossia: A Study of the Theory with Application to Tamil*. Washington, D.C.: Georgetown University Press.

Dow, James R., ed. 1987–88. "New Perspectives on Language Maintenance and Language Shift." *International Journal of the Sociology of Language*, nos. 68 and 69 (entire issues).

Feierabend, I. K., and R. L. Feierabend, eds. 1972. *Anger, Violence, and Politics: Theories and Research*. Englewood Cliffs, N.J.: Prentice-Hall.

Fishman, Joshua A. 1966. "Some Contrasts between Linguistically Homogeneous and Linguistically Heterogeneous Polities." *Sociological Inquiry* 6: 146–58. Reprinted, in *Language Problems of Developing Nations*, edited by Joshua A. Fishman, Charles A. Ferguson, and Jyotirindra Das Gupta, 53–68. New York: Wiley. 1968.

Fishman, Joshua A. 1978. "Positive Pluralism: Some Overlooked Rationales and Forefathers." In *International Dimensions in Bilingual Education*, edited by James E. Alatis, 42–52. (Same as *Georgetown University Round Table on Language and Linguistics*.) Washington, D.C.: Georgetown University Press. Reprinted in Fishman et al. 1985, 445–55.

Fishman, Joshua A., and Frank R. Solano. 1989a. "Cross-Polity Linguistic Homogeneity and Per Capita Gross National Product: An Empirical Explanation." *Language Problems and Language Planning*, 13 (2): 103–18.

Fishman, Joshua A., and Frank R. Solano. 1989b. "Societal Factors Predictive of Linguistic Homogeneity/Heterogeneity at the Inter-Polity Level." *Cultural Dynamics*, 1: 414–37.

Fishman, Joshua A., and Frank R. Solano. 1990. "Cross-Polity Perspective on the Importance of Linguistic Heterogeneity as a Contributory Factor in Civil Strife." *Canadian Review of Studies in Nationalism*, 17: 131–46.

Fishman, Joshua A., Frank R. Solano, and Grant D. McConnell. 1991. "A Methodological Check on Three Cross-Polity Studies of Linguistic Homogeneity/Heterogeneity." In *Languages in School and Society: Policy and Pedagogy*, edited by Mary McGroarty and Christian Faltis. Berlin: Mouton de Gruyter.

Fishman, Joshua A., M. Gertner, E. Lowy, and W. Milán. 1985. *The Rise and Fall of the Ethnic Revival*. Berlin: Mouton de Gruyter.

McRae, Kenneth D. 1983. *Conflict and Compromise in Multilingual Societies*. Waterloo, Ont.: Wilfred Laurier University Press.

Pool, Jonathan. 1969. "National Development and Language Diversity." *La Monda Lingvo-Problem* 1:140–56. Reprinted, slightly revised, in *Advances in the Sociology of Language*, edited by Joshua A. Fishman, 213–30. The Hague: Mouton. 1972.

Veltman, Calvin. 1983. *Language Shift in the United States*. Berlin: Mouton de Gruyter.

24

Linguistic Minorities and Language Policies

Christina Bratt Paulston

1 Introduction

Most nations in the world are multilingual, i.e. they contain ethnic groups in contact and not infrequently in competition. The major language problems which face the policy-makers of such nation-states are choice of national or official language(s), choice of alphabet, and choice of medium of instruction. People have rioted and faced death over unpopular choices, frequently in defense of their own language but not necessarily so. The 1976 Soweto riots in South Africa concerned a change of medium of instruction in the schools from English to Afrikaans, neither of which language was native to the students. At other times there have been peaceful implementation and acceptance of national languages which are not native to the various ethnic groups. Tanzania is one of the very few African ex-colonies which have an indigenous African language as a national language, and although Swahili is native to a very small group, it has peacefully and successfully become implemented and accepted as the national language in contradistinction to neighboring Kenya which still uses English. In Singapore, the clear preference of the Chinese for their children is instruction in English.

What generalizations can we make about language policies in multilingual states and how can we predict success and failure? We know that there are basically three possible linguistic outcomes of the prolonged contact of ethnic groups: language maintenance, bilingualism, or language shift. Bilingualism may also involve the spread of a lingua franca, a language of wider communication. An understanding of language maintenance and shift and of the social conditions under which they occur constitutes a major means for understanding language policies which seek to regulate the interactions of ethnic groups within a modern nation-state. A language policy which goes counter to existing sociocultural forces is not likely to be successful. The difficulty lies in understanding and identifying what are the relevant social determinants of maintenance and shift.

We have, at present, a very poor understanding of what social variables are germane to language in ethnic group relations and of the consequences. In this paper I explore some possibilities of understanding by means of a comparative approach of case studies.

The case studies I touch on concern Catalonia, Tanzania, and Peru. As will be seen, they represent a range of different illustrative situations, but I have also chosen them because I have first-hand experience of them. The basic point to be made is that ethnic groups use language when available as a social resource when it is to their advantage to do so, not otherwise. I examine some case studies to illustrate this point and others that follow from it. The comparison of case studies is probably the most fruitful approach to the study of language and ethnicity, of language maintenance and shift at any theoretical level. In addition to the search for causal factors, another major task is to identify and eventually typologize under what social conditions maintenance and shift take place.

2   Catalonia

It is well known that when a politically and socially strong language exists alongside a minority and, hence, weaker language in the same region, a language hierarchy known as diglossia is usually produced. In Catalonia, however, the social stratification of the two languages is unique. In relation to Spanish, Catalonia is a minority language, hence weaker, and in a subordinate position. But at the same time, it is the language of a large part of the economic and intellectual middle class, as well as the language of local political power. Spanish, on the other hand, is the language of immigrants and the lower strata of the population. That is, even if Spanish is, in principle, the stronger language from certain perspectives, it is also the less prestigious. (Siguan 1988: 4)

Catalonia represents a case of language maintenance beyond what one might have expected. Catalan, a Romance language, is spoken in Catalonia, situated in the north-eastern part of Spain. It is also spoken in Valencia and the Balearic Islands, parts of Sardinia, in the Roussillon area of France and in Andorra, where it is the official language. Dialect differences have never been much of a concern, maybe because "the Catalan of the 'great epoch' was remarkable for its uniformity and lack of dialectalization. Whether this came about only because of the imposition of a 'chancery standard' is difficult to say" (Posner 1966: 259). Certainly dialects did develop during the times when Castilian (Spanish) was the official administrative language but today Siguan can write about Catalan: "It is fully systematized with its own dictionary, grammar, and orthography, which are accepted without dispute" (1984: 108).

Estimates of the number of Catalan speakers vary according to the source and range from six to nine million.

Catalonia developed as the Spanish March, a buffer block between Muslim Spain and France. It became a major Mediterranean mercantile nation during the thirteenth and fourteenth centuries, and Middle Catalan flourished during the thirteenth to fifteenth centuries with serious work written in science and philosophy. Catalan was also used for administration and law.

During the late fifteenth century, with the marriage of Ferdinand of Aragon and Catalonia to Isabella of Castile in 1469, the center of political gravity shifted to Madrid and Castile, and changes took place "which transformed an important Mediterranean state into a dependent principality and finally into a cluster of Spanish provinces" (Pi-Sunyer 1974: 122).

Catalan speakers of the upper classes, who increasingly dealt with the Castilian elite in economic and political terms, became bilingual. Catalan remained the language of the Catalan people, and the substantial cultural and economic activity of the region made its continued use a matter of preference. (Taylor 1984: 3)

But in 1716, Philip V of the new Bourbon dynasty followed the French model of linguistic unity and issued a decree which forbad the use of Catalan: "Books in Catalan must be forbidden, nor must it be spoken or written in schools and instruction in Christian doctrine must be in Castilian" (Read 1978: 152). Catalan remained politically repressed (with a brief interlude during the Second Spanish Republic 1931–9) until the death of General Franco in 1975. Nevertheless, with the advent of industrialization in the eighteenth century, Catalonia eventually became the most prosperous region in Spain. Concomitant with the economic recovery, a cultural and linguistic renaissance, *La Renaixenca*, took place, which merged with *Catalanisme*, "a community awareness . . . spurred on by the new middle classes" (Siguan 1984: 105). In spite of the political repression of Catalan, which Vallverdú termed *persecuted bilingualism* during the early Franco regime (1973: 140), the Catalans refused to give up their language, and a study in 1979 (Shabad and Gunther) showed that 97% of native Catalans spoke the language and that 78% of all residents did so regardless of place of birth. Another survey found that 45–50% of schoolchildren in Catalonia are Catalan speakers. The latter figure reflects the massive migration into Catalonia from the rest of Spain (McNair 1980: 35).

Article 3 of the 1978 Spanish Constitution decrees Castilian and the regional languages to be both official within their community. Clearly, Catalan is doing very well. While there are problems, primarily with implementation in the educational sector and with the large number of Castilian-speaking immigrants from the rest of Spain, there is no indication of anything other than the continued maintenance of Catalan.

Why is Catalan flourishing when Galician within the same nation-state is not? Elsewhere (Paulston 1987a) I compare Catalan to Occitan (which is dying), and have argued that Catalan represents a case not of ethnicity but of geographic nationalism (more of this later), which in combination with a strong economy accounts for centuries of persecuted language maintenance with bilingualism. The Catalans avoid direction from Madrid and look to Paris and western Europe for cultural inspiration. They take great pleasure in emphasizing cultural values different from the rest of Spain, to the point of stereotyping:

> Catalans are often characterized by both insiders and outsiders as ambitious, intelligent, sensible, industrious people. Catalans themselves are very proud of what they see as one of their most traditional traits, *seny*. Literally "sense", it refers to level-headed, feet-on-the-ground common sense. (Woolard 1983: 17)

The work ethic, negotiation and compromise are all time-honored traditions. They are very stubborn and proud of it. Most important, the sense of shame Eckert discusses for Occitan is totally absent for the Catalans: "There are few Catalans who doubt that they are in some way 'better' than Castilians (the hereditary enemy?)" (Pi-Sunyer 1978: personal communication).

While Occitan is associated with peasants and poor workers, Catalan is solidly middle-class (as well as working-class): "Since the features of the Catalan character were most fully codified for the 19th century bourgeoisie, whose family-based mercantile and industrial enterprises marked them off from the wealthy land-owning class of the rest of Spain, it has been difficult to extricate Catalan identity from its bourgeois background" (Woolard 1983: 19).[1] The history of Catalonia is a history of landowning farmers, of artisans, shopkeepers, workshop owners (the *menestralia*), of merchants and industrialists, of a concern for the serious business of making money. Not only does Catalonia exhibit the basic defining characteristics of nationalism such as territory, intellectual leaders (exiled during the Franco regime), a middle class and property, stubborn loyalty, a common enemy (which Franco did his best to justify), a cultural "external distinction, internal cohesion," and a goal-orientation of political self-determination, she perceives herself as a nation. Woolard, in her work on language and ethnicity in Catalonia, writes in a footnote:

> It is difficult to eliminate confusion over terminology in discussing Catalonia, "Nation" and "nationalism" in this chapter always refer to Catalonia and to Catalanist political sentiment, not to Spain or Spanish-oriented loyalty. "Nationalism" has been used rather than 'regionalism' because Catalan political activists conceive of their homeland as a nation. While the term is rarely defined, it is often invoked in debate and is a tremendously powerful concept for both supporters and opponents of Catalan nationhood. (Woolard 1983: 34)

Since Catalonia's history and development include a variety of ethnic groups (Romans, Visigoths, Occitans, French, Castilians, Italians, Jews), this sense of nationalism is not ethnically but territorially based, similar to that of the United States, in fact. Writing about "open" nationalism, Kohn's comments about the Americans equally well apply to the Catalans: "[They] owe their nationhood to the affirmation of the modern trends of emancipation, assimilation, mobility, and individualism" (1968: 66). It is only that the Catalans were modern very early on; Giner (1980) makes the case that they were the first capitalists in Europe and one can argue the case that Catalan nationalism was well in effect before the industrial revolution. In geographic nationalism, speaking the national language (whether official or not) is an important marker of group membership and in the past immigrants to Catalonia have typically learned Catalan in addition to Castilian. At present, under the Statutes of Autonomy of Catalonia 1979, there is increased social and political pressure for the use of Catalan:

> Social class enters into these language policy consideration in another way as well: in both the public and private sector of the Catalan economy, access to white-collar jobs is being increasingly restricted to those reasonably fluent in Catalan. . . . a disproportionately large number of non-Catalan-speaking immigrants have low-status occupations. (Shabad and Gunther 1982: 468, 470)

The basic incentive for learning Catalan for the immigrants is economic, just as it was for learning French for the Occitan speakers. In Brudner's (1972) terms: Jobs select language-learning strategies. But it is far from clear that economic incentives are sufficient for language maintenance, and although it is rare that superordinate groups in a favored economic position do shift languages, it does happen, an example being the Normans in England. Rather, economic incentives are probably a necessary but not sufficient condition for language maintenance, and my argument is that the set of behaviors, attitudes and perceptions which we associate with nationalism provides that sufficient condition. In the words of Pi-Sunyer:

The lesson from Catalonia is not that economic and political forces should be disregarded – on the contrary, they should be studied with consummate care – but that these alone will not explain the phenomenon of nationalism. Not because nationalism does not respond to these forces, but because they will be interpreted and altered by specific cultures and societies – which are themselves undergoing change. (Pi-Sunyer 1985: 273)

3 Tanzania

In opting for Swahili as its sole official and national language, Tanzania has most departed from policies established under colonial rule. Although English is still the medium of post-primary education (and its role was re-affirmed in 1983), its overall position has been reduced. This also applies to the vernaculars. The uniform practice of using Swahili is a symbol of both socioeconomic egalitarianism and national integration, reflecting the nation's socialistic policies. (Scotton 1988: 219)

Tanzania represents a case of successful choice and implementation of a national and official indigenous language in Africa and, as such, is a rare case, since most sub-Saharan African states have an ex-colonial language as their national language. Some reasons for the ex-colonial language choice are: 1) the vested interests of elite groups, 2) the fact that textbooks and curricula are already in place, 3) the economic costs of standardizing languages(s), printing textbooks and training teachers, 4) the language attitudes of prestige of the colonial languages and their use as international languages, and finally, and in many cases most importantly, 5) their use as trans-ethnic languages.

Swahili is a Bantu language, used as a lingua franca by about 25 million ethnically diverse people living in East Africa (as well as in Tanzania, Swahili is a national language in Kenya and is also spoken in Uganda, Burundi, Ruanda, Zambia, Somalia, Mozambique, and Zaire [now the Democratic Republic of the Congo]). It is a native language for some two million people, on Zanzibar and on the East African coast from Somalia to Mozambique, and has many dialects, which was one of the problems of later standardization. Swahili as a lingua franca pre-dates the rise of modern education and independent national governments. It developed as a trade language in the monsoon trade, controlled by Arabs, with Arabia, India, Malaysia, China, and Indonesia. The ruling class was mixed Arab–African, and Swahili language and culture spread as trade and town spread and a new civilization evolved, ethnically diverse, maritime, Muslim, urban, mercantile, literate in Arabic with a writing tradition for Swahili in Arabic script. (Later, the European missionaries in control of education during early colonization changed that.) Zanzibar came to dominate trade and inland trade and sent large trading caravans (Swahili: *safari*) inland as far as Zaire and Zambia for ivory and slaves. They used the Zanzibar dialect of Swahili.

When the missionaries arrived in the 1860s, they needed a language for communication, and they settled on Swahili as the most practical choice. By the 1890s, the Germans had administrative control of what was then Tanganyika, and the German administrators and settlers along with the missionaries were learning Swahili. Swahili newspapers were founded, and village headmen made reports in Swahili. Schools used Swahili as the medium of instruction. The colonial administration (first German and consequently English) followed this practice and used Swahili to reach the people. (This was not so in Kenya and Uganda, where English was used.) Under the German administration, Swahili was sufficient for membership in the junior civil service, while beyond that level a knowledge of German was needed. The British required both Swahili and English for the junior civil service. Consequently an attitude developed that Swahili was second-best, but in Tanzania, where the Germans had used Swahili as the medium of instruction, there was a positive attitude toward the language as academically capable.

In 1961, Tanganyika became a republic with Julius Nyerere as president; in 1964 Tanganyika and Zanzibar became the United Republic of Tanzania, and in 1977 President Nyerere's socialist Chama Cha Mapinduzi Party (CCM) was granted political supremacy by the constitution. The official language planners in Dar es Salaam explained to me as socialist philosophy the rationale for the use of Swahili, "the need to consolidate the base, i.e. general literacy for the masses" (presumably a requirement for socialism and equity), but they also pragmatically saw the need "to maintain the elite infrastructure [i.e. in English] for the study of engineering, veterinary medicine, agriculture, and medicine" (Fieldnotes, Dar es Salaam, 1986). If anything, I saw a concern that they had been too successful with Swahili, and that efforts were now directed toward English.

The language-planning success with Swahili in Tanzania contrasts with the failure in neighboring Kenya, which failure probably has two main causes: 1) ethnic strife along tribal boundaries, i.e. vested interest groups, which use language as a resource for competition; and 2) language attitudes as a result of colonial policy which accord English the highest prestige and see Swahili as a way of keeping Blacks in their place.

One can, of course, interpret the success in Tanzania as a result of socialist philosophy, but that would be inaccurate since the success pre-dates the CCM. Rather, it was a historical accident of the coming together of a number of factors: 1) there was an indigenous language available with a centuries-long tradition as a lingua franca; 2) the language was already standardized and had been used as a medium of education by the missionaries and the Germans with concomitant positive attitudes; 3) Swahili is a Bantu language of the same language family as most of the 130-plus languages spoken in Tanzania and therefore easy to learn. The Kenyans make much of how hard it is to learn Swahili for non-Bantu speakers, but it should be mentioned as an aside that the Masai in Tanzania seem to have no difficulty; 4) although the British supplanted Swahili with English, or maybe because of this, it was relatively easy for Nyerere and his socialist movement for independence to embrace Swahili as a symbol of nationalism and freedom from oppression; 5) maybe most importantly, Swahili was not the native language of any one dominant group (it had only 12,000 speakers on the mainland), and among the 130 tribes there is really no clearly dominant group, so they escape the curse of special-interest groups; 6) finally, there is in the urban centers considerable intermarriage between tribal members, and this exogamy favors Swahili which then becomes the children's native tongue. In the urban centers, the situation now favors shift.

4   Peru

Neither a law nor an educational policy can change the social reality of a country, but they can undoubtedly open the way for fundamental changes in the structure of society, thereby making it more amenable to the idea of greater access to material goods and rights in the contemporary world. (Escobar 1988: 388)

Peru represents a case of unsuccessful choice and implementation of an indigenous language as official language (co-equal with Spanish) in Latin America. The military revolutionary government of General Velasco Alvarado designated Quechua as an official language in Decree Law 21156 of May 27, 1975, but it remained basically a law on paper only which, even so, lasted only four years before it was overturned (along with Velasco) in 1979 in the present constitution. The present constitution declares Spanish as the only official language of the nation but recognizes Quechua and Aymara as languages which may be used officially.

Peru is a country of three zones (and cultures): the *costa*, the *sierra*, and the *selva*; coast, mountains, and jungle, the latter two frequently instances of great geographic isolation. There is considerable contrast between the urban and the rural population where, as Escobar points out, the rural is linked with "Indianness," while the urban is associated with modernism. The population in 1981 was 17,515,000, of whom 65.1% were urban and 34.9% rural. These figures were almost reversed from the 1940 national census, which showed 64.5% of the 6,208,000 population to be rural. We see, then, a country which has experienced considerable population growth and also urbanization as a result of internal migration (primarily to Lima, the capital), but the point Escobar makes is that "it has not caused the sudden conversion of a basically rural country with few urban nuclei in the interior into an urbanized, modern, and homogeneous land that has shaken the symptoms of cultural plurality and provincial multilingualism" (1988: 380). There are many ethnic groups and subgroups in Peru but the basic stratification is between the superordinate Hispanic culture and the subordinate Indian culture, of which the most important and numerous are the Quechua (2–3 million) and Aymara (265,000). (Figures are from Kloss and McConnell 1979. Census taking in the sierra and the selva have notorious inherent difficulties, and the figures are best thought of as approximations.)

History may give us some insights into why Peru could not do what Tanzania succeeded in doing. The Quechua-speaking Inca empire was invaded, conquered, and colonized by Pizarro and the Spanish in the sixteenth century. The main goal held by the Spanish for the Indians was castellanization, which had two aspects: learning Spanish and becoming Christianized. But the priests in the early days found it more efficient to spread the word of God in the indigenous language (cf. Swahili) and, in fact, used Quechua which they helped spread across the empire (Heath and Laprade 1982). The then king Philip II actually supported the use of the indigenous language.

Opposition came later from priests from Spain who claimed creole (*'born in Peru'*) priests had an unfair advantage. Eventually the policy became to teach and preach in Spanish, and apart from interventionist groups like the Summer Institute of Linguistics (North American Protestant missionaries), any other policy has never really been generally implemented. There have been noble attempts, as in the Revolution of 1968 and its Education Reform, with its National Bilingual Education Policy of 1972. "The intention of the Reform was to create an educational system that would build up the Peruvian nation along humanistic, democratic and nationalistic lines" (Hornberger 1985: 52). The objectives (about which there were considerable disagreements among the intellectuals) of the Bilingual Education Policy as summarized by Hornberger were 1) consciousness-raising, 2) the creation of a national culture, and 3) the use of Spanish as the common language in Peru (1985: 61). Another interpretation is to see the policy as an attempt to mobilize the population in a feeling of nationalism along the lines of Haugen's internal cohesion – external distinction (Haugen 1966; chapter 25 in this volume).

Quechua has a number of different dialects, some mutually unintelligible, and six varieties were officially standardized after it was declared an official language in 1975. Certainly this variation carried problems of implementation, but it should be recalled that Swahili also has a number of dialects. Rather, the basic problem lay in what it meant to speak Quechua, and in fact the promulgation was never implemented.

Peru was colonized by men with far fewer women than was North America, and the result was widespread miscegenation, so that most Peruvians not of recent external migration are racially mixed or mestizo, which is to say that most are part (or all) Indian in origin. But race is not defined by caste as we tend to do, but rather by social class and culture, of which language is an integral part.

With a starched hat, braids, and long wide skirts, and a community-centered world view expressed in Quechua, you are an Indian. But go to the city, cut off your hair and wear European-style clothing, and accept in Spanish a Latin egocentric worldview, and you become mestizo. In fact, it is a very arduous but common process, usually taking one or two generations (Patch 1967). Typically, only the Indian and a few scholars of the upper class will admit to knowing Quechua; for the slowly growing middle class, where you find the public school teachers and the administrators, the Indian heritage is still too uncomfortably close.

In other words, to embrace Quechua is to announce to the world that you are Indian, a word so stigmatized in Peruvian Spanish that its official euphemism now is *campesino*, "peasant". Clearly, any nationalistic fervor, any "internal cohesion – external distinction" rallying around Quechua as it has rallied around Swahili in Tanzania, could not be supported if the precondition meant self-identification as an Indian.

5 Analysis and Discussion

The major point about multilingualism, which is not readily recognized in the literature, is that maintained group bilingualism is unusual. The norm for groups in prolonged contact with a nation-state is for the subordinate group to shift to the language of the dominant group, whether over three generations or over several hundred years. Where shift does not take place, there are identifiable reasons, of which the major two are lack of incentive (usually economic) and lack of access to the dominant language; another one is that the political unit may not be a nation-state, as was the case with the federated soviets.

The mechanism for language shift is bilingualism, often with exogamy. Groups will vary in their degree of ethnic maintenance and in their *rate* of shift of which one major influence is the origin of the contact situation. Voluntary migration results in much faster shift than does annexation or colonization. Other factors are continued access to a standardized, written L1 with cultural prestige and tradition in contradistinction to a non-standard, non-written language of no prestige. Sacred languages are also a factor. Ethnic groups also vary in their ethnic pride or ethnic stubbornness; Spicer (1980) refers to the more stubborn ones as persistent peoples. This is a topic that deserves work in the future as it will provide exceptions to some of my present generalizations.

I have discussed elsewhere at length a theoretical framework for explaining and predicting the language behavior of ethnic groups in contact within a contemporary nation-state (Paulston 1987b, 1994) and will merely touch on it very briefly here. The proposition is that linguistic groups form four distinct types of social mobilization, ethnicity, ethnic movements, ethnic nationalism, and geographic nationalism, which under certain specified social conditions result in differential linguistic outcomes of language maintenance and shift.

5.1   Ethnicity

Royce defines ethnic identity as "the sum total of feelings on the part of group members about those values, symbols, and common histories that identify them as a distinct group. 'Ethnicity' is simply ethnic-based action" (Royce 1982: 18). There is, in fact, little power struggle and not much purpose with ethnicity and so the common course is assimilation and concomitant language shift. Ethnicity will not maintain a language in a multilingual setting if the dominant group allows assimilation, and incentive and opportunity of access to the national language are present. The immigrant groups to Sweden (with the exception of the Finns) are a very good example of this point. Voluntary migration, access to public schools and thus to the national language, and economic incentives in the form of available jobs all contribute to assimilation and language shift. The very liberal Swedish educational language policies of mother tongue instruction will not succeed in bringing about L1 maintenance and will at most contribute to a few generations of bilingualism before complete shift to Swedish.

The Indian groups of Peru are another example of ethnicity and language shift within a nation-state. The shift is infinitely slower than in Sweden and we can identify such factors as colonization, far less economic incentive and more difficulty in access to Spanish because of geographic isolation, which contribute to that slower shift. We also need to consider the stigmatized status of things Indian and the cultural definition of race. The rewards clearly lie within Hispanic culture, and under these conditions General Velasco's language policies of bilingual education and Quechua as an official language clearly failed to stir up national consciousness, to bring about a sense of nationalism.

5.2   Ethnic movements

Ethnicity becomes an ethnic movements when ethnicity as an unconscious source of identity turns into a conscious strategy, usually in competition for scarce resources. An ethnic movement is ethnicity turned militant, its protagonists ethnic discontents who perceive other groups as being opposed to them, an opposition drawn along ethnic boundaries.

While ethnicity stresses the content of the culture, ethnic movements will be concerned with boundary maintenance, in Barth's terms, with *us* against *them*. It is very much a conscious, cognitive ethnicity in a power struggle with the dominant group for social and economic advantage, a struggle which frequently leads to violence and social upheaval. Many ethnic movements have charismatic leaders, probably always members of the ethnic group, but they need not have an intellectual elite or a significant middle class.

Ethnic movements by themselves probably cannot maintain a language but will affect rate of shift so that the shift is much slower and spans many more generations. None of these case studies exemplifies an ethnic movement and we need much more data. Peru does have *Sendero Luminoso*, the terrorist Maoist Shining Path movement (now almost eliminated), but its leadership is university-educated and functions mainly in Spanish. More importantly, their claims are drawn not along ethnic boundaries but rather along those of social class.

5.3 Nationalism

Shafer concludes that it is impossible to fit nationalism into a short definition (1972: 5), but I will attempt to identify some salient features. Cottam insists that nationalism is best interpreted as the manifestation of nationalistic behavior and that a nationalist is seen as "an individual who sees himself as a member of political community, a nation, that is entitled to independent statehood, and is willing to grant that community a primary and terminal loyalty" (Cottam 1967: 3). Group cohesion to the end, the goal of self-determination, a perceived threat of opposing forces, and access to or hope of territory are characteristics of all national movements.

The improvement of one's own lot in life, or at least of one's children's, is probably a common goal of all national movements; the motivation is one of perceived self-interest, a self-chosen state. Very often, nationalism takes place as a protest against oppression, against the common enemy, whether it be against a (dominant) group within the same nation or against another state.

Goals in national movements, besides general independence, tend to be quite definite and specific. These goals are often legitimized by or based on historical past events or conditions.

A national movement must have a well-developed middle class, in which condition it differs from ethnic movements. Alba's (1975) anecdote of the Catalan workers who considered issues of language immaterial is representative. "We don't care if we are exploited in Castilian or Catalan," was their rejoinder, and they aligned themselves with the workers' unions and the socialist party rather than mobilizing themselves along national lines. Without a stake in property, nationalism is not perceived as furthering one's self-interest.

Ethnic nationalism and geographic nationalism share many features, and the major difference is probably the same as the one Hans Kohn outlines for "open" and "closed" nationalism. In ethnic or closed nationalism the ethnic group is isomorphic with the nation-state. The emphasis is on the nation's autochthonous character, on the common origin and ancestral roots.

Kohn calls "open" nationalism a more modern form; it is territorially based (hence geographic nationalism) and features a political society, constituting a nation of fellow citizens regardless of ethnic descent.

In ethnic nationalism, language is a prime symbol of the nation, but that is not necessarily the case with geographic nationalism. In fact, the United States does not even legally have a national language. At the same time, although one cannot change one's genes, one can learn a new language, and in a nation which does not care about genes but uses language to define membership, as does Catalonia, learning the new language obviously held both practical and symbolic significance: knowing the national language became the hallmark of membership and in-group status.

Catalonia exemplifies a nation which has sustained language maintenance in spite of prohibition and prosecution. The monolingual Spanish-medium schools were not successful in bringing about a shift from Catalan to Spanish although they were successful in establishing widespread bilingualism. The educational language policies were not successful because they went counter to the prevailing social forces of strong economic incentives, geographic nationalism, and stubborn pride, all of which favored the maintenance of Catalan.

Tanzania, on the other hand, is a case of highly successful language policies, both in choice of national language and in choice of medium of instruction. I have earlier listed a number of reasons for this success, but ultimately the most explanatory factor lies in the situation, unusual in Africa, that most educated Tanzanians identify themselves first as Tanzanian and only second as members of a tribe (I have heard them speak very derogatorily about the exceptions), that is, the success of the language policies is a function of geographic nationalism. The major social institution for the spread of Swahili has been the public schools, and probably also the armed forces. Along the coast, urbanization also contributes to the successful implementation of Swahili.

6   Conclusions

In this paper I have argued that the main linguistic outcomes of the prolonged contact of ethnic groups within a modern nation-state are language maintenance, bilingualism, or language shift. An understanding of language maintenance and shift and the social conditions under which they occur constitutes a major means of understanding language policies, which seek to regulate the interactions of ethnic groups within a nation-state. A language policy which goes counter to existing sociocultural forces is not likely to be successful.

The paper has explored the social variables germane to language in ethnic group relations in a comparative approach of case studies. The case studies concerned are Catalonia, Tanzania, and Peru. I propose that linguistic groups form four distinct types of social mobilization, ethnicity, ethnic movements, ethnic nationalism and geographic nationalism, which under certain specified social conditions result in differential linguistic outcomes of language maintenance and shift.

Notes

1   The *Bandera Roja* party (the Catalan communist branch) at one time engaged "in the exclusive use of the Spanish language explaining to all and sundry that Catalan was 'the language of the bourgeoisie,' and therefore to be avoided" (Giner 1980: 47).

References

Alba, Victor. 1975. *Catalonia: A Profile.* New York: Praeger.

Barth, F. 1969. *Ethnic Groups and Boundaries.* Boston, MA: Little Brown & Co.

Bennett, J. W. 1975. *The New Ethnicity: Perspectives from Ethnology.* St. Paul, MN: West Publishing.

Brudner, Lilyan. 1972. "The Maintenance of Bilingualism in Southern Austria." *Ethnology* 11 (1): 39–54.

Castile, G. P. and G. Kushner. 1981. *Persistent Peoples.* Tucson: University of Arizona Press.

Cooper, R. L. 1982a. "A framework for the study of language spread." In Cooper 1982b.

Cooper, R. L. (ed.). 1982b. *Language Spread: Studies in Diffusion and Social Change.* Arlington, VA: Center for Applied Linguistics, and Bloomington, IN: Indiana University Press.

Cottam, R. W. 1964. *Nationalism in Iran.* Pittsburgh, PA: University of Pittsburgh Press.

Crewe, W. (ed.). 1977. *The English Language in Singapore.* Singapore: Eastern Universities Press.

Deutsch, K. W. 1968. "The trend of European nationalism – the Language Aspect." In Fishman 1968.

Eckert, P. 1983. "The paradox of national language movements," *Journal of Multilingual and Multicultural Development* 4 (4): 289–300.

Elazar, D. and M. Friedman. 1976. *Moving Up: Ethnic Succession in America.* New York: Institute on Pluralism and Group Identity of the American Jewish Committee.

Escobar, A. (ed.). 1972a. *El reto del multilinguismo en el Peru* (= Peru-Problema, 9.) Lima: Instituto de Estudios Peruanos.

Escobar, A. 1972b. *Lenguaje y discriminacion social en America Latina.* Lima: Milla Batres.

Escobar, A. 1988. "Bilingualism in Peru." In Paulston 1988.

Fishman, J. A. (ed.). 1968. *Readings in the Sociology of Language.* The Hague: Mouton.

Fishman, J. A. 1972. *Language and Nationalism: Two Integrative Essays.* Rowley, MA: Newbury House.

Fishman, J. A. 1977. "Language maintenance." *Harvard Encyclopedia of American Ethnic Groups.* Cambridge: Cambridge University Press.

Fishman, J. A. 1978. *Advances in the Study of Societal Multilingualism.* The Hague: Mouton.

Gal, S. 1979. *Language Shift: Social Determinants of Linguistic Change in Bilingual Austria.* New York: Academic Press.

Giner, S. 1980. *The Social Structure of Catalonia.* Sheffield: University of Sheffield, The Anglo-Catalan Society.

Haugen, E. 1966. "Dialect, language, nation." *American Anthropologist* 68 (4): 922–35.

Heath, S. B. and R. Laprade. 1982. "Castilian colonization and indigenous languages: the cases of Quechua and Aymara." In Cooper 1982b.

Hornberger, N. 1985. "Bilingual education and Quechua language maintenance in Highland Puno, Peru." Unpublished PhD dissertation. Madison, WI: University of Wisconsin.

Jakobson, R. 1968. "The beginning of national self-determination in Europe." In Fishman 1968.

Kabir, M. 1985. "Nationalistic movements in Bangladesh." Unpublished PhD dissertation. Pittsburg, PA: University of Pittsburgh.

Kloss, H. and G. D. McConnell. 1985. *Linguistic Composition of the Nations of the World: Europe and the USSR.* Quebec: University of Laval Press.

Kohn, H. 1944. *The Idea of Nationalism: A Study of its Origins and Background.* New York: Macmillan.

Kohn, H. 1968. "Nationalism." *1968 International Encyclopedia of the Social Sciences* 11: 63–70.

Lieberson. S., G. Dalton and M. E. Johnston. 1975. "The course of mother tongue diversity in nations." *American Journal of Sociology* 81 (1): 34–61.

Lieberson, S. and T. J. Curry. 1971. "Language shift in the United States: some demographic clues." *International Migration Review* 5: 125–37.

MacDougall, J. A. and C. S. Foon. 1976. "English language competence and occupational mobility in Singapore." *Pacific Affairs* 49: (2): 294–312.

Mannheim, B. 1984. "Una Nacion acorrolada: Southern Peruvian Quechua language planning and politics in historical perspective." *Language in Society* 13: 291–309.

McNair, J. 1980. "The contribution of the schools to the restoration of regional autonomy in Spain." *Comparative Education* 16 (1): 33–44.

Molde, B. and D. Sharpe. 1984. "Second International Conference on Minority Languages (special issue)." *Journal of Multilingual and Multicultural Development* 5: 3–4.

Myrdal, G. 1974. "The case against romantic ethnicity." *Center Magazine*. 26–30.

Nahir, M. 1984. "Language planning goals: a classification." *Language Problems and Language Planning* 294–327.

Painter, M. 1983. "Aymara and Spanish in Southern Peru: the relationship of language to economic class and social identity." In A. Miracle (ed.), *Bilingualism* Athens, GA: University of Georgia Press.

Patch, R. W. 1967. "La Parade, Lima's market. Serrano and Criollo, the confusion of race with class." *AVFSR, West Coast South America Series* XIV 2: 3–9.

Paulston, C. B. 1982. *Swedish Research and Debate about Bilingualism.* Stockholm: National Swedish Board of Education.

Paulston, C. B. 1987a. "Catalan and Occitan: comparative test cases for a theory of language maintenance and shift." *International Journal of the Sociology of Language*, 63: 31–62.

Paulston, C. B. 1987b. "Linguistic consequences of ethnicity and nationalism in multilingual Settings." In *Multicultural Education.* Paris: Organization for Economic Cooperation and Development.

Paulston, C. B. (ed.). 1988. *International Handbook of Bilingualism and Bilingual Education.* New York: Greenwood Press.

Paulston, C. B. 1994. *Linguistic Minorities in Multilingual Settings.* Amsterdam: John Benjamins.

Pi-Sunyer, O. 1974. "Elites and non-corporate groups in the European Mediterranean: a reconsideration of the Catalan case." *Comparative Studies in Society and History* 16: 117–31.

Pi-Sunyer, O. 1985. "Catalan nationalism." In E. A. Tiryakian and R. Rogowski (eds.). *New Nationalisms of the Developed West.* Boston: Allen and Unwin.

Posner, R. 1966. *The Romance Languages.* Garden City, NY: Anchor.

Read, Jan. 1978. *The Catalans.* London: Faber & Faber.

Royce, A. P. 1982. *Ethnic Identity: Strategies of Diversity.* Bloomington, IN: Indiana University Press.

Scotton, C. M. 1988. "Patterns of bilingualism in East Africa." In Paulston 1988.

Shabad, G. and R. Gunther. 1982. "Language, nationalism, and political conflict in Spain." *Comparative Politics* 14 (4): 443–77.

Shafer, Boyd C. 1976. *Nationalism: Its Nature and Interpreters.* Washington, DC: American Historical Association.

Shafer, Boyd C. 1972. *Faces of Nationalism.* New York: Harcourt Brace Jovanovich.

Siguan, M. 1988. "Bilingual education in Spain." In Paulston 1988.

Siguan, M. 1984. "Language and education in Catalonia." *Prospects: Quarterly Review of Education (UNESCO)* XIV (1): 107–19.

Siguan, M. (ed.). 1983. *Lenguas y Educacion en el Ambito del Estado Espanol.* Barcelona: Ediciones de la Universidad de Barcelona.

Snyder, L. L. 1976. *Varieties of Nationalism: A Comparative Study.* Hinsdale, IL: Dryden Press.

Spicer, E. H. 1980. *The Yaquis: A Cultural History.* Tucson: University of Arizona Press.

Stein, W. 1972. *Mestizo Cultural Patterns: Culture and Social Structure in the Peruvian Andes.* Buffalo, NY: New York State University Press.

Veltman, C. 1983. *Language Shift in the United States.* The Hague: Mouton.

Whiteley, W. 1969. *Swahili – the Rise of a National Language.* London: Methuen.

Woolard, K. A. 1983. The politics of language and ethnicity in Barcelona, Spain." Unpublished PhD dissertation. Berkeley, CA: University of California, Department of Anthropology.

Woolard, K. A. 1984. "A formal measure of language attitudes in Barcelona: a note from work in progress." *International Journal of the Sociology of Language* 47: 63–71.

Discussion Questions

1. Describe the positive and negative consequences that multilingualism might have for a society.
2. Choose one multilingual society and collect information related to some of the following indicators of the impact of multilingualism on a society:
   - official language policies (e.g. regulations on language use in education, government agencies)
   - the proportion of bilinguals in the population
   - literacy rates and the level of formal education for the various language groups in the languages of the society
   - economic indicators (e.g. poverty rate, income level) for the various language groups.

   Are there other factors, not mentioned by Fishman in chapter 23, that you would include? What conclusions do you draw based upon the data that you have collected?
3. If you know someone who has experienced "ethnic violence," interview him or her to find out what his or her perceptions are as to the causes of the violence. Does the person believe that language was a factor?
4. Interview three to five people in your community to solicit their opinions concerning the pros and cons of actively promoting bilinguality in modern societies. Do your informants believe that multilingualism could lead to social unrest?
5. Fishman claims that the historical dimension is lacking from the list of variables used by political scientists. Paulston, on the other hand, looks deeply into the historical factors which create linguistically heterogeneous societies. Is there any evidence in Paulston's historical accounts to support or disprove Fishman's conclusion that linguistic heterogeneity does not contribute to civil strife or lower gross national product?
6. Apply Paulston's concept of "social mobilization" to the society you researched for question 2. Which of her types (ethnicity, ethnic movements, ethnic nationalism, or geographic nationalism) best represents the situation? Discuss whether your research provides evidence for maintenance of bi-/multilingualism or for language shift.
7. Interview one or two immigrants to your country and ask whether they have maintained their mother tongue. If they have, ask whether they have maintained literacy skills as well as oral proficiency. What reasons do the informants give for maintaining or not maintaining their language?

Part X

Language Policy and Planning

Introduction

The past four decades have been particularly rich ones for scholars concerned with language policy and language planning issues. The first article in this section, originally written by Einar Haugen for discussion at a seminar held at Indiana University during the summer of 1964, juxtaposed a brief diachronic summary of work by linguists concerned with the *structure* of language and those who had been more recently concerned with the description of the social uses or *functions* of language in communication. His broad-ranging paper foreshadowed an emerging interest by scholars in a subfield of sociolinguistics to be known as Language Policy and Planning that would blossom during the 1970s thanks, in large part, to sponsorship by the Ford Foundation of a series of international conferences on language problems in developing countries, including those at Airlie House, Virginia in 1966 (see Fishman, Ferguson and Das Gupta 1968), Laval University in Moncton, New Brunswick in 1967 (see Kelly 1969), the University of Dar es Salaam in 1968 (see Whiteley 1971), the East–West Center in Honolulu in 1969 (see Rubin and Jernudd 1971), and Glen Cove, NY in 1973 (see Ohannessian, Ferguson and Polomé 1975). Scholars working during the 1960s and 1970s were united by the common belief that it was possible (and in some cases desirable) to plan, affect, modify or systematically change the status of a language or languages within a polity. Toward this end, a number of so-called sociolinguistic surveys were carried out in various settings (see, for example, Whiteley 1974; Harrison, Prator and Tucker 1975) to collect information that might later be used by policy-makers to codify, expand or restrict the use(s) of language(s) in specific settings to perform certain functions.

In the second chapter of this part, Nahir summarizes the then (early 1980s) extant literature and extracts the common elements that characterize the *functions* and the *goals* common to the field of language planning. His treatment draws upon the earlier work of Haugen, Ferguson and others and extends the discussion to focus on the activities of language-planning agencies in numerous settings around the world (for example in China, Israel, and Québec). In 1994, the *Annual Review of Applied Linguistics* was devoted to the topic of language policy and planning; and by that time much of the work foreshadowed by Haugen and Nahir had blossomed and come to fruition. Tucker (1994, p. 277), writing in a summary to that volume, noted that five somewhat interrelated themes characterized the then current state of work in the area, namely "the role(s) of language policy or planning activities in foreshadowing or marking major world (political) events;

concern with ethnic revitalization; the correlates and consequences of continuing migration and mobility; the differential perceptions of the role of the mother tongue in primary education; and the potential contributions of language planning to educational and national development." Indeed these issues remain current today.

The final contribution in this part, by Hornberger, exemplifies two aspects of the work referred to above in the *Annual Review*, namely those dealing with the role of literacy in the mother tongue in primary education and the potential contributions of language planning to educational and national development. This work continues to be extremely relevant today, as evidenced by the publication of the results of a survey conducted by staff from the Center for Applied Linguistics (2001) to describe successful innovative programs that have been implemented to expand educational opportunities for underrepresented groups in multilingual countries.

References

Center for Applied Linguistics. 2001. *Expanding Educational Opportunity in Linguistically Diverse Societies*. Washington, DC: Center for Applied Linguistics.

Fishman, J. A., C. A. Ferguson and J. Das Gupta. (eds.). 1968. *Language Problems of Developing Nations*. New York: John Wiley & Sons.

Harrison, W. W., C. H. Prator and G. R. Tucker. 1975. *An English-Language Policy Survey of Jordan*. Arlington, VA: Center for Applied Linguistics.

Kelly, L. G. (ed.). 1969. *Description and Measurement of Bilingualism: An International Seminar, University of Moncton, June 6–14, 1967*. Toronto: University of Toronto Press.

Ohannessian, S., C. A. Ferguson and E. Polomé. (eds.). 1975. *Language Surveys in Developing Nations: Papers and Reports on Sociolinguistic Surveys*. Arlington, VA: Center for Applied Linguistics.

Rubin, J. and B. H. Jernudd. (eds.). 1971. *Can Language be Planned?: Sociolinguistic Theory and Practice for Developing Nations*. Honolulu: University Press of Hawaii.

Tucker, G. R. 1994. "Language planning issues for the coming decade." In W. Grabe (ed.), *Annual Review of Applied Linguistics* pp. 277–83. *14*, New York: Cambridge University Press.

Whiteley, W. H. (ed.). 1971. *Language Use and Social Change*. London: Oxford University Press.

Whiteley, W. H. (ed.). 1974. *Language in Kenya*. Nairobi: Oxford University Press.

Further Reading

Bender, M. L., J. D. Bowen, R. L. Cooper and C. A. Ferguson. (eds.). 1976. *Language in Ethiopia*. London: Oxford University Press.

Bongaerts, T. and K. de Bot. (eds.). 1997. *Perspectives on Foreign-Language Policy: Studies in Honor of Theo van Els*. Philadelphia: John Benjamins.

Cooper, R. L. 1989. *Language Planning and Social Change*. Cambridge: Cambridge University Press.

Kaplan, R. B. and R. B. Baldauf, Jr. (eds.). 1997. *Language Planning: From Practice to Theory*. Clevedon, UK: Multilingual Matters.

Ohannessian, S. and M. E. Kashoki. (eds.). 1978. *Language in Zambia*. London: International African Institute.

Polomé, E., P. C. Hill and N. H. Kuhanga (eds.). 1980. *The Languages of Tanzania*. London: Oxford University Press.

Ricento, T. (ed.). 2000. *Ideology, Politics and Language Policies: Focus on English*. Amsterdam: John Benjamins.

Whiteley, W. H. (ed.). 1971. *Language Use and Social Change*. London: Oxford University Press.

25

Dialect, Language, Nation

Einar Haugen

The taxonomy of linguistic description – that is, the identification and enumeration of languages – is greatly hampered by the ambiguities and obscurities attaching to the terms 'language' and 'dialect'. Laymen naturally assume that these terms, which are both popular and scientific in their use, refer to actual entities that are clearly distinguishable and therefore enumerable. A typical question asked of the linguist is: 'How many languages are there in the world?' Or: 'How many dialects are there in this country?'

The simple truth is that there is no answer to these questions, or at least none that will stand up to closer scrutiny. Aside from the fact that a great many, perhaps most, languages and dialects have not yet been adequately studied and described, it is inherent in the very terms themselves that no answer can be given. They represent a simple dichotomy in a situation that is almost infinitely complex. Hence they have come to be used to distinguish phenomena in several different dimensions, with resultant confusion and overlapping. The use of these terms has imposed a division in what is often a continuum, giving what appears to be a neat opposition when in fact the edges are extremely ragged and uncertain. Do Americans and Englishmen speak dialects of English, or do only Americans speak dialect, or is American perhaps a separate language? Linguists do not hesitate to refer to the French language as a dialect of Romance. This kind of overlapping is uncomfortable, but most linguists have accepted it as a practical device, while recognizing, with Bloomfield, 'the purely relative nature of the distinction' (1933, p. 54).

The two terms are best understood against the perspective of their history. In English both words are borrowed from French. *Language* is the older, having partially displaced such native words as 'tongue' and 'speech' already in Middle English. The oldest attestation in the OED is from 1290: 'With men þat onder-stoden hire langage.' The French word is itself late, being a popular derivative of Latin *lingua* with the probable form **linguāticum*, first attested in the twelfth century. *Dialect*, on the other hand, first appears in the Renaissance, as a learned loan from Greek. The oldest OED citation is from 1579 in reference to 'certain Hebrue dialectes', while the earliest French I have found (in Hatzfeld and Darmesteter's dictionary) is only sixteen years earlier and speaks of Greek as being 'abondante en dialectes'. A 1614 citation from Sir Walter Raleigh's *The History of the World* refers to the 'Aeolic Dialect' and confirms the impression that the linguistic situation in ancient Greece was both the model and the stimulus for the use of the term in modern writing.

There was need for some such term in Greece, since there was in the classical period no unified Greek norm, only a group of closely related norms. While these 'dialects' bore the names of various Greek regions, they were not spoken but written varieties of Greek, each one specialized for certain literary uses, e.g., Ionic for history, Doric for the choral lyric, and Attic for tragedy. In this period the language called 'Greek' was therefore a group of distinct, but related written norms known as 'dialects'. It is usually assumed that the written dialects were ultimately based on spoken dialects of the regions whose names they bore. These spoken dialects were in turn descended by normal linguistic divergence from a Common Greek language of an older period, which can be reconstructed by comparison of the dialects with each other and with their Indo-European kinsmen. In the post-classical period, however, the Greek dialects disappeared and were replaced by a rather well-unified Greek norm, the *koiné*, essentially the dialect of Athens. So, in the Hellenistic period 'Greek' became the name of a norm that resulted from a linguistic convergence. The differences among the dialects were eliminated in favor of a single, triumphant language, based on the dialect of the cultural and administrative center of the Greeks.

The Greek situation has provided the model for all later usage of the two terms 'language' and 'dialect'. Much of the unclarity in their application stems from the ambiguities present in that situation. This has become evident with their extension to other countries and with their adoption into the technical terminology of linguistics. In a descriptive, synchronic sense 'language' can refer either to a *single* linguistic norm, or to a *group* of related norms. In a historical, diachronic sense 'language' can either be a common language on its way to dissolution, or a common language resulting from unification. A 'dialect' is then any one of the related norms comprised under the general name 'language', historically the result of either divergence or convergence.

Since this historical process can be indefinitely repeated, the two terms are cyclically applicable, with 'language' always the superordinate and 'dialect' the subordinate term. This is also clear from the kind of formal structures into which they can be placed: 'X is a dialect of language Y,' or 'Y has the dialects X and Z' (never, for example, 'Y is a language of dialect X'). 'Language' as the superordinate term can be used without reference to dialects, but 'dialect' is meaningless unless it is implied that there are other dialects and a language to which they can be said to 'belong'. Hence every dialect is a language, but not every language is a dialect.

In addition to the ambiguities provided by the synchronic and diachronic points of view distinguished above, increasing knowledge concerning linguistic behavior has made the simple application of these two contrasting terms ever more difficult.

In French usage a third term developed, *patois*, which applied primarily to the spoken language. The term *dialecte* is defined in the dictionary of the Académie Française and other French dictionaries as *variété régionale d'une langue*. Littré (1956) explicitly requires that a dialect 'include a complete literary culture' (*comportant une complète culture littéraire*). As pointed out by André Martinet (1964), this usage reflects the special French situation, in which there were a number of regional written standards, which were then superseded by the written standard of Paris. The French dialects were regional, like the Greek, and literary, but not functionally distinguished like the Greek. When the dialects ceased to be written, they became *patois*: 'Après le XIVe siècle, il se forma une langue littéraire et écrite, et les dialectes devinrent des patois' (Littré). Even more succinctly, Brun (1946) writes: 'Un patois est un dialecte qui s'est degradé.' A patois, then, is a language norm not used for literary (and hence official) purposes, chiefly limited to informal situations. Thus Provençal might be considered a French dialect, but its local, spoken varieties are all *patois*. This distinction introduces a new dimension in our discussion: the social functions of a language. In terms of the language–dialect distinction, we may say that a patois is a dialect that serves a population in its least prestigious functions. The distinction of patois–dialect is therefore not one between two kinds of language, but between two functions of language. The definition in Littré (and others like it) clearly suggests a pejorative attitude toward the patois, since it no longer carries with it 'a complete literary culture'.

In English the term 'patois' has never been seriously adopted in the description of language, and 'dialect' has carried the full burden of both scientific and popular usage. Older writers, cited in the OED, often used it for any specialized variety of the language, e.g., 'the lawyer's dialect'. Samuel Butler (*Hudibras*, 1663) railed against 'a Babylonish dialect, which learned pedants much affect'. General usage has limited the word largely to the regional or locally based varieties, such as 'Lancashire dialect' or 'Irish dialect' in reference to varieties of English. It is less customary to speak of 'London dialect' or 'Boston dialect', except in reference to the lower-class speech of those cities. Nor is it common to speak of 'British dialect' in reference to cultivated English speech, and Americans are generally resentful of being told they speak 'American dialect' when reference is had to the speech of educated people. Martinet is therefore beside the mark when he writes that in America 'the term denotes every local form of English but without any suggestion that a more acceptable form of the language exists distinct from the dialects' (1964). It is quite different with the word 'accent': an American may inoffensively be described as having a 'New England accent' or a 'Southern accent,' and, of course, all Americans speak of the English as having an 'English accent'. 'Dialect' is here as elsewhere a term that suggests informal or lower-class or rural speech. In general usage it therefore remains quite undefined whether such dialects are part of the 'language' or not. In fact, the dialect is often thought of as standing outside the language: 'That isn't English.' This results from the *de facto* development of a standard language, with all the segregation of an elite and the pyramidal power structure that it has usually implied.

As a social norm, then, a dialect is a language that is excluded from polite society. It is, as Auguste Brun (1946) has pointed out, a language that 'did not succeed'. In Italy, Piedmontese is from every linguistic point of view a language, distinct from Italian on the one hand and French on the other, with a long tradition of writing and grammatical study. But because it is not Tuscan, and Tuscan became the standard language of all Italy, Piedmontese is only a 'dialect', yielding ground to Italian with every generation and kept alive only by local pride and linguistic inertia (Clivio, 1964). Only if a 'dialect' is watered down to an 'accent' – that is, an intonation and a set of articulations, with an occasional lexical item thrown in for color – does it (say in Germany or Italy or England) become *salonfähig*. As a complete structure it is out in the cold limbo of modern society. In America the stigma is placed not so much on local dialects, since these are few and rarely heard, as on 'bad' English, which is quite simply lower-class dialect. The language of the upper classes is automatically established as the correct form of expression. They cannot say only, 'L'état, c'est moi,' but also 'Le langage, c'est le mien'.

In trying to clarify these relationships, linguistic science has been only moderately successful. Even in the Renaissance it was perfectly clear to serious students of the subject that the term 'language' was associated with the rise of a nation to conscious unity and identity. George Puttenham wrote in his book *The Arte of English Poesie* (1589): 'After a speech is fully fashioned to the common understanding, and accepted by consent of a whole country and nation, it is called a language.' This kind of historical development, by which convergence was achieved at the expense of deviating varieties, was familiar to the men of that age. But the arbitrary tower-of-Babel approach to linguistic divergence was dispelled by the discovery, in the early nineteenth century, of historical regularity. The realization that languages have resulted from dialect-splitting gave a new content to the terms and made it possible to begin calling languages like English and German 'dialects' of a Germanic 'language'.

But in the mid-nineteenth century, when scientific study of the rural and socially disadvantaged dialects began, a generation of research was sufficient to revolutionize the whole idea of how a dialect arises. The very notion of an area divided into a given number of dialects, one neatly distinct from the next, had to be abandoned. The idea that languages split like branches on a tree gave way to an entirely different and even incompatible idea, namely, that individual linguistic traits diffused through social space and formed isoglosses that rarely coincided. Instead of a dialect, one had a *Kernlandschaft* with ragged edges, where bundles of isoglosses testified that some slight barrier had been interposed to free communication. Linguistics is still saddled with these irreconcilable 'particle' and 'wave' theories; this in effect involves the differing points of view from which any linguistic structure can be seen: as a unitary structure (a 'language'), or as one of several partially overlapping structures (the 'dialects').

Without going into the problems raised by this conflict, we may simply state that the 'particle' theory of language as a unified structure is a fruitful hypothesis, making it possible to produce an exhaustive and self-consistent description. But it excludes as 'free variation' a great many inconsistencies within the speech of any informant, and it fails to account for the fact that communication is possible between users of identifiably different codes. Comparative grammar succeeded in reconstructing the common structure from which 'dialects' could be derived. Contrastive grammar has tried to program the differences between languages in order to ease the learner's task or, on a higher theoretical plane, to arrive at a linguistic typology. But there is still no calculus that permits us to describe the differences between languages in a coherent and theoretically valid way.

Our discussion has shown that there are two clearly distinct dimensions involved in the various usages of 'language' and 'dialect'. One of these is *structural*, that is, descriptive of the language itself; the other is *functional*, that is, descriptive of its social uses in communication. Since the study of linguistic structure is regarded by linguists as their central task, it remains for sociologists, or more specifically, sociolinguists, to devote themselves to the study of the functional problem.

In the *structural* use of 'language' and 'dialect', the overriding consideration is genetic relationship. If a linguist says that Ntongo has five dialects, he means that there are five identifiably different speech-forms that have enough demonstrable cognates to make it certain that they have all developed from one earlier speech-form. He may also be referring to the fact that these are mutually understandable, or at least that each dialect is understandable to its immediate neighbors. If not, he may call them different languages, and say that there is a language Ntongo with three dialects and another, Mbongo, with two. Ntongo and Mbongo may then be dialects of Ngkongo, a common ancestor. This introduces the synchronic dimension of comprehension, which is at best an extremely uncertain criterion. The linguist may attempt to predict, on the basis of his study of their grammars, that they should or should not be comprehensible. But only by testing the reactions of the speakers themselves and their interactions can he confirm his prediction (Voegelin and Harris, 1951; Hickerson, Turner and Hickerson, 1952). Between total incomprehension and total comprehension there is a large twilight zone of partial comprehension in which something occurs that we may call 'semicommunication'.

In the *functional* use of 'language' and 'dialect,' the overriding consideration is the uses the speakers make of the codes they master. If a sociolinguist says that there is no Ntongo language, only dialects, he may mean that there is no present-day form of these dialects that has validity beyond its local speech community, either as a trade language or as a common denominator in interaction among the various dialect speakers. A 'language' is thus functionally defined as a superposed norm used by speakers whose first and ordinary language may be different. A 'language' is the medium of communication between speakers of different dialects. This holds only within the limits established by their linguistic cognacy: one could not speak of Ntongo as a dialect of English just because its speakers use English as a medium of intercommunication. The sociolinguist may also be referring to the fact that the 'language' is more prestigious than the 'dialect'. Because of its wider functions it is likely to be embraced with a reverence, a language loyalty, that the dialects do not enjoy. Hence the possibility of saying that 'Mbongo is only a dialect, while Ngkongo is a language'. This means that Ngkongo is being spoken by people whose social prestige is notoriously higher than that of people who speak Mbongo. When used in this sense, a dialect may be defined as an undeveloped (or underdeveloped) language. It is a language that no one has taken the trouble to develop into what is often referred to as a 'standard language'. This dimension of functional superiority and inferiority is usually disregarded by linguists, but it is an essential part of the sociolinguist's concern. It becomes his special and complex task to define the social functions of each language or dialect and the prestige that attaches to each of these.

What is meant by an 'undeveloped' language? Only that it has not been employed in all the functions that a language can perform in a society larger than that of the local tribe or peasant village. The history of languages demonstrates convincingly that there is no such thing as an inherently handicapped language. All the great languages of today were once undeveloped. Rather than speak of undeveloped languages as 'dialects', after the popular fashion, it would be better to call them 'vernaculars', or some such term, and limit 'dialect' to the linguist's meaning of a 'cognate variety'. We are then ready to ask how a vernacular, an 'undeveloped language', develops into a standard, a 'developed language'. To understand this we will have to consider the relation of language to the nation.

The ancient Greeks and Romans spread their languages as far as their domains extended, and modern imperialists have sought to do the same. But within the modern world, technological and political revolutions have brought Everyman the opportunity to participate in political decisions to his own advantage. The invention of printing, the rise of industry, and the spread of popular education have brought into being the modern nation-state, which extends some of the loyalties of the family and the neigborhood or the clan to the whole state. Nation and language have become inextricably intertwined. Every self-respecting nation has to have a language. Not just a medium of communication, a 'vernacular' or a 'dialect', but a fully developed language. Anything less marks it as underdeveloped.

The definition of a nation is a problem for historians and other social scientists; we may accept the idea that it is the effective unit of international political action, as reflected in the organization of the United Nations General Assembly. As a political unit it will presumably be more effective if it is also a social unit. Like any unit, it minimizes internal differences and maximizes external ones. On the individual's personal and local identity it superimposes a national one by identifying his ego with that of all others within the nation and separating it from that of all others outside the nation. In a society that is essentially familial or tribal or regional it stimulates a loyalty beyond the primary groups, but discourages any conflicting loyalty to other nations. The ideal is: internal cohesion – external distinction.

Since the encouragement of such loyalty requires free and rather intense communication within the nation, the national ideal demands that there be a single linguistic code by means of which this communication can take place. It is characteristic that the French revolutionaries passed a resolution condemning the dialects as a remnant of feudal society. The dialects, at least if they threaten to become languages, are potentially disruptive forces in a unified nation: they appeal to local loyalties, which could conceivably come into conflict with national loyalty. This is presumably the reason that France even now refuses to count the number of Breton speakers in her census, let alone face the much greater problem of counting the speakers of Provençal. On the other hand, a nation feels handicapped if it is required to make use of more than one language for official purposes, as is the case in Switzerland, Belgium, Yugoslavia, Canada and many other countries. Internal conflict is inevitable unless the country is loosely federated and the language borders are stable, as is the case in Switzerland.

Nationalism has also tended to encourage external distinction, as noted above. In language this has meant the urge not only to have one language, but to have one's own language. This automatically secludes the population from other populations, who might otherwise undermine its loyalty. Here the urge for separatism has come into sharp conflict with the urge for international contact and for the advantages accruing both to individual and nation from such contact. Switzerland is extreme in having three languages, no one of which is its own; Belgium has two, both of which belong to its neighbors. The Irish movement has faltered largely under the impact of the overwhelming strength of English as a language of international contact. The weakness of the New Norwegian language movement is due to the thorough embedding of Danish in the national life during four centuries of union; what strength the movement has had is derived from the fact that Danish was not one of the great international languages.

Whenever any important segment of the population, an elite, is familiar with the language of another nation, it is tempting to make use of this as the medium of government, simply as a matter of convenience. If this is also the language of most of the people, as was the case when the United States broke away from England, the problem is easily solved; at most it involves the question of whether provincialisms are to be recognized as acceptable. But where it is not, there is the necessity of linguistically re-educating a population, with all the effort and disruption of cultural unity that this entails. This is the problem faced by many of the emerging African and Asian nations today (Le Page, 1964). French and English have overwhelming advantages, but they symbolize past oppression and convey an alien culture. The cost of re-education is not just the expense in terms of dollars and cents, but the malaise of training one's children in a medium that is not their own, and of alienation from one's own past.

The alternative is to develop one's own language, as Finland did in the nineteenth century, or Israel did in the twentieth. Different languages start at different points: Finland's was an unwritten vernacular, Israel's an unspoken standard. Today both are standards capable of conveying every concept of modern learning and every subtlety of modern literature. Whatever they may lack is being supplied by deliberate planning, which in modern states is often an important part of the development process.

It is a significant and probably crucial requirement for a standard language that it be written. This is not to say that languages need to be written in order to spread widely or be the medium of great empires. Indo-European is an example of the first, Quechua of the Inca Empire an example of the second (Buck, 1916). But they could not, like written languages, establish models across time and space, and they were subject to regular and inexorable linguistic change. It is often held that written language impedes the 'natural' development of spoken language, but this is still a matter of discussion (Zengel, 1962; Bright and Ramanujan, 1964). In any case the two varieties must not be confused.

Speech is basic in learning language. The spoken language is acquired by nearly all its users before they can possibly read or write. Its form is to a great extent transmitted from one generation of children to the next. While basic habits can be modified, they are not easily overturned after childhood and are virtually immovable after puberty. The spoken language is conveyed by mouth and ear and mobilizes the entire personality in immediate interaction with one's environment. Writing is conveyed by hand and eye, mobilizes the personality less completely, and provides for only a delayed response. Oral confrontation is of basic importance in all societies, but in a complex, literate society it is overlaid and supplemented by the role of writing.

The permanence and power of writing is such that in some societies the written standard has been influential in shaping new standards of speech. This is not to say that writing has always brought them into being, but rather to say that new norms have arisen that are an amalgamation of speech and writing. This can of course take place only when the writing is read aloud, so that it acquires an oral component (Wessén, 1937). There is some analogy between the rise of such spoken standards and that of pidgin or creole languages (Meillet, 1925, p. 76; Sommerfelt, 1938, p. 44). The latter comprise elements of the structure and vocabulary of two or more languages, all oral. They have usually a low social value, compared to the oral standards, but the process of origin is comparable. The reawakening of Hebrew from its century-long dormant state is comprehensible only in terms of the existence of rabbinical traditions of reading scripture aloud (Morag, 1959). Modern Hebrew has shown a rapid adaptation to the underlying norms of its new native speakers, so that it has become something different from traditional Hebrew. Similarly with the standard forms of European languages: one is often hard put to say whether a given form has been handed down from its ancestor by word of mouth or via the printed page. 'Spelling pronunciations' are a well-known part of most oral standards, even though purists tend to decry them.

While we have so far spoken of standard languages as if they were a clear and unambiguous category, there are differences of degree even among the well-established languages. French is probably the most highly standardized of European languages, more so than, for example, English or German. French, as the most immediate heir of Latin, took over many of its concepts of correctness and its intellectual elaboration. French in turn became a model for other standard languages, and its users were for centuries nothing loth to have it so considered. When English writers of the eighteenth century debated whether an English academy should be established to regulate the language, the idea of such an institution came from France. The proposal was rejected largely because the English did not wish to duplicate what they regarded as French 'tyranny'.

In France, as in other countries, the process of standardization was intimately tied to the history of the nation itself. As the people developed a sense of cohesion around a common government, their language became a vehicle and a symbol of their unity. The process is reasonably well documented in the histories written for the older European languages. But the period since the French Revolution has seen a veritable language explosion, which has been far less adequately studied. In many countries a process that elsewhere took centuries of effort on the part of a people and its writers has been compressed into a few short years or decades. In a study of the new standards developed since 1800 for Germanic languages, Heinz Kloss has suggested that there may be a typical profile for what he has called the *Ausbau* of a new language (Kloss 1952, p. 28). First comes its use for purely humorous or folkloristic purposes. Then lyric writers may adopt it, followed by prose narrators. But it has not reached a crucial stage of development until success is achieved in writing serious expository prose, or what he calls *Zweckschrifttum*. Beyond this comes the elaboration of the language for purposes of technical and scientific writing and government use. Each of these 'domains' (as Fishman (1964) has called them) constitutes a challenge for the language in its attempt to achieve full development.

While making a survey of the world's standard languages, Ferguson proposed (1962) to classify them along two dimensions: their degree of standardization (St. 0, 1, 2) and their utilization in writing (W 0, 1, 2, 3). Zero meant in each case no appreciable standardization or writing. St. 1 meant that a language was standardized in more than one mode, as in the case, for example, with Armenian, Greek, Serbo-Croatian, and Hindi-Urdu. He also included Norwegian, but it is at least arguable that we are here dealing with two languages. St. 2 he defined as a language having a 'single, widely accepted norm which is felt to be appropriate with only minor modifications or variations for all purposes for which the language is used'. W 1 he applied to a language used for 'normal written purposes', W 2 to one used for 'original research in physical science', and W 3 to one used for 'translations and résumés of scientific work in other languages'.

These categories suggest the path that 'underdeveloped' languages must take to become adequate instruments for a modern nation. The 'standardization' to which Ferguson refers applies primarily to developing the form of a language, i.e., its linguistic structure, including phonology, grammar and lexicon. We shall call this the problem of *codification*. Ferguson's scale of 'utilization in writing' applies rather to the *functions* of a language. We shall call this the problem of *elaboration*, a term suggested by a similar usage of Bernstein's (1962) and corresponding to Kloss's *Ausbau*. As the ideal goals of a standard language, codification may be defined as *minimal variation in form*, elaboration as *maximal variation in function*.

The ideal case of minimal variation in form would be a hypothetical, 'pure' variety of a language having only one spelling and one pronunciation for every word, one word for every meaning, and one grammatical framework for all utterances. For purposes of efficient communication this is obviously the ideal code. If speakers and listeners have identical codes, no problems of misunderstanding can arise due to differences in language. There can be none of what communication engineers call 'code noise' in the channel (Hockett, 1958, pp. 331–2). This condition is best attained if the language has a high degree of stability, a quality emphasized by many writers on the subject (e.g., Havránek, 1938). Stability means the slowing down or complete stoppage of linguistic change. It means the fixation forever (or for as long as possible) of a uniform norm. In practice such fixation has proved to be chimerical, since even the most stable of norms inevitably changes as generations come and go. At all times the standard is threatened by the existence of rival norms, the so-called 'dialects', among its users. It is liable to interference from them and eventually to complete fragmentation by them.

Apparently opposed to the strict codification of form stands the maximal variation or elaboration of function one expects from a fully developed language. Since it is by definition the common language of a social group more complex and inclusive than those using vernaculars, its functional domains must also be complex. It must answer to the needs of a variety of communities, classes, occupations, and interest groups. It must meet the basic test of *adequacy*. Any vernacular is presumably adequate at a given moment for the needs of the group that uses it. But for the needs of the much larger society of the nation it is not adequate, and it becomes necessary to supplement its resources to make it into a language. Every vernacular can at the very least add words borrowed from other languages, but usually possesses devices for making new words from its own resources as well. Writing, which provides for the virtually unlimited storage and distribution of vocabulary, is the technological means enabling a modern standard language to meet the needs of every specialty devised by its users. There are no limits to the elaboration of language except those set by the ingenuity of man.

While form and function may generally be distinguished as we have just done, there is one area in which they overlap. Elaboration of function may lead to complexity of form, and, contrariwise, unity of form may lead to rigidity of function. This area of interaction between form and function is the domain of *style*. A codification may be so rigid as to prevent the use of a language for other than formal purposes. Sanskrit had to yield to Prakrit, and Latin to the Romance languages, when the gap between written and spoken language became so large that only a very few people were willing to make the effort of learning them. Instead of being appropriate for 'all purposes for which the language is used', the standard tends to become only one of several styles within a speech community. This can lead to what Ferguson (1959) has described as 'diglossia', a sharp cleavage between 'high' and 'low' style. Or it may be a continuum, with only a mild degree of what I have called 'schizoglossia', as in the case of English (Haugen, 1962). In English there is a marked difference between the written and spoken standards of most people. In addition, there are styles within each, according to the situation. These styles, which could be called 'functional dialects', provide wealth and diversity within a language and ensure that the stability or rigidity of the norm will have an element of elasticity as well. A complete language has its formal and informal styles, its regional accents, and its class or occupational jargons, which do not destroy its unity so long as they are clearly diversified in function and show a reasonable degree of solidarity with one another.

Neither codification nor elaboration is likely to proceed very far unless the community can agree on the *selection* of some kind of a model from which the norm can be derived. Where a new norm is to be established, the problem will be as complex as the sociolinguistic structure of the people involved. There will be little difficulty where everyone speaks virtually alike, a situation rarely found. Elsewhere it may be necessary to make some embarrassing decisions. To choose any one vernacular as a norm means to favor the group of people speaking that variety. It gives them prestige as norm-bearers and a headstart in the race for power and position. If a recognized elite already exists with a characteristic vernacular, its norm will almost inevitably prevail. But where there are socially coordinate groups of people within the community, usually distributed regionally or tribally, the choice of any one will meet with resistance from the rest. This resistance is likely to be the stronger the greater the language distance within the group. It may often be a question of solidarity versus alienation: a group that feels intense solidarity is willing to overcome great linguistic differences, while one that does not is alienated by relatively small differences. Where transitions are gradual, it may be possible to find a central dialect that mediates between extremes, one that will be the easiest to learn and most conducive to group coherence.

Where this is impossible, it may be necessary to resort to the construction of a new standard. To some extent this has happened naturally in the rise of the traditional norms; it has been the aim of many language reformers to duplicate the effect in new ones. For related dialects one can apply principles of linguistic reconstruction to make a hypothetical mother tongue for them all. Or one can be guided by some actual or supposed mother tongue, which exists in older, traditional writings. Or one can combine those forms that have the widest usage, in the hope that they will most easily win general acceptance. These three procedures – the comparative, the archaizing, and the statistical – may easily clash, to make decisions difficult. In countries where there are actually different languages, amounting in some African nations to more than a hundred, it will be necessary either to recognize multiple norms or to introduce an alien norm, which will usually be an international language like English or French.

Finally, a standard language, if it is not to be dismissed as dead, must have a body of users. *Acceptance* of the norm, even by a small but influential group, is part of the life of the language. Any learning requires the expenditure of time and effort, and it must somehow contribute to the well-being of the learners if they are not to shirk their lessons. A standard language that is the instrument of an authority, such as a government, can offer its users material rewards in the form of power and position. One that is the instrument of a religious fellowship, such as a church, can also offer its users rewards in the hereafter. National languages have offered membership in the nation, an identity that gives one entrée into a new kind of group, which is not just kinship, or government, or religion, but a novel and peculiarly modern brew of all three. The kind of significance attributed to language in this context has little to do with its value as an instrument of thought or persuasion. It is primarily symbolic, a matter of the prestige (or lack of it) that attaches to specific forms or varieties of language by virtue of identifying the social status of their users (Labov, 1964). Mastery of the standard language will naturally have a higher value if it admits one to the councils of the mighty. If it does not, the inducement to learn it, except perhaps passively, may be very low; if social status is fixed by other criteria, it is conceivable that centuries could pass without a population's adopting it (Gumperz, 1962, 1964). But in our industralized and democratic age there are obvious reasons for the rapid spread of standard languages and for their importance in the school systems of every nation.

The four aspects of language development that we have now isolated as crucial features in taking the step from 'dialect' to 'language', from vernacular to standard, are as follows: (*a*) selection of norm, (*b*) codification of form, (*c*) elaboration of function, and (*d*) acceptance by the community. The first two refer primarily to the form, the last two to the function of language. The first and the last are concerned with society, the second and third with language. They form a matrix within which it should be possible to discuss all the major problems of language and dialect in the life of a nation:

	Form	*Function*
Society	Selection	Acceptance
Language	Codification	Elaboration

Note

This paper was written as a contribution to the work of the Seminar on Sociolinguistics, held at the Indiana University Linguistic Institute in the summer of 1964, under the direction of Charles A. Ferguson. It has profited from extensive discussion with the members of the Seminar.

References

Bernstein, B. (1962), 'Linguistic codes, hesitation phenomena and intelligence', *Language and Speech*, vol. 5, pp. 31–46.

Bloomfield, L. (1933), *Language*, Holt, Rinehart & Winston.

Bright, W., and Ramanujan, A. K. (1964), 'Sociolinguistic variation and language change', in *Proceedings of the Ninth International Congress of Linguists*, Mouton.

Brun, A. (1946), *Parlers Régionaux: France Dialectale et Unité Française*, Didier.

Buck, C. D. (1916), 'Language and the sentiment of nationality', *Amer. Polit. Sc. Rev.*, vol. 10, pp. 44–69.

Clivio, G. (1964), *Piedmontese: a Short Basic Course*, mimeographed, Center for Applied Linguistics, Washington, D.C.

Dictionnaire de l'Académie Française (1932), Paris, 8th edn.

Ferguson, C. A. (1959), 'Diglossia', *Word*, vol. 15, pp. 325–40.

Ferguson, C. A. (1962), 'The language factor in national development', *AL*, vol. 4, no. 1, pp. 23–7.

Fishman, J. A. (1964), 'Language maintenance and language shift as a field of inquiry', *Linguistics*, vol. 9, pp. 32–70.

Gumperz, J. J. (1962), 'Types of linguistic communities', *AL*, vol. 4, no. 1, pp. 28–40.

Gumperz, J. J. (1964), 'Hindi-Punjabi code switching in Delhi', in *Proceedings of the Ninth International Congress of Linguists*, Mouton.

Hatzfeld, A. and Darmesteter, A. (1920), *Dictionnaire Général de la Langue Française*, Paris, 6th edn.

Haugen, E. (1962), 'Schizoglossia and the linguistic norm', *Monograph Series on Languages and Linguistics*, Georgetown University, Washington, no. 15, pp. 63–9.

Havránek, B. (1938), 'Zum Problem der Norm in der heutigen Sprachwissenschaft und Sprachkultur', in J. Vachek (ed.), *A Prague Reader in Linguistics*, Bloomington, Ind.

Hickerson, H., Turner, G. D., and Hickerson, N. P. (1952), 'Testing procedures for estimating transfer of information among Iroquois dialects and languages', *IJAL*, vol. 18, pp. 1–8.

Hockett, C. F. (1958), *A Course in Modern Linguistics*, Macmillan.

Kloss, H. (1952), *Die Entwicklung Neuer Germanischen Kultursprachen von 1800 bis 1950*, Pohl, Munich.

Labov, W. (1964), 'Phonological correlates of social stratification', in J. J. Gumperz and D. Hymes (eds). *The Ethnography of Communication, AmA*, vol. 66, no. 6, part 2, pp. 164–76.

Le Page, R. B. (1964), *The National Language Question: Linguistic Problems of Newly Independent States*, Oxford University Press.

Littré, E. (1956), *Dictionnaire de la Langue Française*, Paris.

Martinet, A. (1964), *Elements of General Linguistics*, University of Chicago Press.

Meillet, A. (1925), *La Méthode Comparative en Linguistique Historique*, Institute for Sammenlignende Kulturforskning, Oslo.

Morag, S. (1959), 'Planned and unplanned development in modern Hebrew', *Lingua* vol. 8, pp. 241–63.

Murray, J. A. H. *et al.* (ed.), *Oxford English Dictionary* (1888 ff.), Oxford University Press.

Sommerfelt, A. (1938), 'Conditions de la formation d'une langue commune', *Actes du IV Congrès International de Linguistes*, Copenhagen.

Voegelin, C. F., and Harris, Z. S. (1951), 'Methods for determining intelligibility among dialects of natural languages', *Proceedings of the American Philosophical Society*, vol. 95, pp. 322–9.

Wessén, E. (1937), 'Vårt riksspråk: Nagra huvudpunkter av dess historiska utveckling', *Modersmalslärarnas Förenings årsskrift*, pp. 289–305.

Zengel, M. S. (1962), 'Literacy as a factor in language change', *AmA*, vol. 64, 132–9.

26

Language Planning Goals: A Classification

Moshe Nahir

1 Introduction

Language planning may be defined as deliberate, institutionally organized attempts at affecting the linguistic or sociolinguistic status or development of language. Much of the theoretical work in the field has been devoted to developing various typologies and dichotomies. This study proposes a classification of language planning functions, or goals, that the respective agencies – academies, committees, commissions, and so forth – have been engaged in or seeking since language planning began several centuries ago. The classification includes goals that such agencies *can* adopt if and when activities are recognized as indicators of language-related needs that these agencies can then meet. An attempt is also made to show how these LP goals relate to LP *processes* as described in Haugen's model (1966a, 1966c, 1983).

2 Language Planning Processes

Neustupný, a language planning theorist, recently observed that "a need for an explanatory theory in language planning has been perceived" (1983: 1) and proposed a "language planning paradigm" in which he lists several concepts (e.g., Language Correction, Language Treatment, and Communication Planning) relevant to language planning. His paradigm is certainly useful as a contribution to a future theoretical framework for language planning, yet virtually all theorists to date have been largely engaged in *language planning processes*, as reflected in the various typologies and dichotomies introduced in the last two decades. Haugen's model ("the major dimensions of language planning," Fishman 1973), for example, attempts to describe the processes or steps (Selection, Codification, Implementation, and Elaboration) that language planners have taken (Haugen 1966c, 1983). This model, however, still "does not tell us why they have done it, nor what goals they have hoped to attain" (1983: 274). Haugen's four steps are only theoretical "starting points, since they say nothing about the end points, the goals to be reached, or the ideals and motivations that guide planners" (1983: 269f).

With few partial exceptions (e.g., Rabin 1971a; Haugen 1966a), then, language planning goals have been neither established nor delineated. In order to meet such a need, I suggested some time ago a classification of Language Planning Functions that

Table 1 Language planning goals and language planning processes

GOAL	PROCESSES			
	Selection	*Codification*	*Implementation*	*Elaboration*
Purification	X	X	X	X
Revival	X	X	X	X
Reform	X	X	X	X
Standardization	X	X	X	X
Spread	X	X	X	X
Lexical modernization (and so forth)	X	X	X	X

language planning agencies have been engaged in (Nahir 1977). The distinction between language planning *processes* and language planning functions, or *goals*, may be illustrated by an example cited by Haugen. Following a brief discussion of language as a source or reflector of discrimination against women, he concludes that the attempt to correct the situation is a case of language planning: "Women have identified a language problem: the very language itself conflicts with their desired role in society, and they wish to make a new *Selection* and *Codification*, which some of them are trying to *implement* and *elaborate*" (Haugen 1983: 283). Now the "identification" of the problem, on the one hand, and the respective steps of "selection" and "codification" that follow the identification are not identical. Haugen's and others' models and typologies (e.g., Corpus Planning vs. Status Planning, Kloss 1969; Policy Approach vs. Cultivation Approach, Neustupný 1970; and Language Choice and Policy Formulation, Codification, Elaboration, Implementation, and Evaluation, Eastman 1983) begin to deal with the issue or the problem only after the issue or the problem has been identified and established and the relevant goals have been set.

The proposed typology has attempted, then, to identify goals and problem areas, labeled Language Planning Aspects or Functions, that have been or may be set and then practiced by language planning agencies. The activity that takes place while seeking the goals or fulfilling the functions follows some processes of the kind proposed by Haugen. Thus, the sequence is first establishing a *function* or a *goal*, consciously or unconsciously, then proceeding with the four *steps* that, in turn, involve various language planning *activities*. Language planning goals, as established in the classification, could thus be cross-tabulated with Haugen's model (table 1), not unlike Fishman's cross-tabulation of Ferguson's three "socio-functional indicators of development" – Graphization, Standardization, and Modernization – with the "Haugen-Neustupný processes" (Fishman 1973: 81).

3 Language Planning Goals (Functions)

The classification mentioned above (Nahir 1977) suggests, then, that language planning as practiced by the agencies involved – academies, commissions, committees, and so on

– has consisted of one or more of five functions or goals as "major" or "minor." This classification, however, tends to be diachronic, identifying and focusing on goals adopted and sought by past or present agencies, such as the French Academy, the Hebrew Language Academy, the Irish Language Commission, the Norwegian Language Council, and the Quebec French Language Bureau.

Further observation now reveals six more goals that either have been or can be adopted by various agencies. Numerous activities carried out throughout the world indicate the existence of language-related problems, needs, and aspirations that can be solved or met by existing or new agencies. These activities and indicators can then be categorized into one of a total of eleven language planning functions or goals. While some of the new goals may have been recently adopted by LP agencies, others have yet to be recognized and adopted. Furthermore, some of the activities discussed here in relation to the given goals may not be labeled as pertaining to language planning by current definitions of the field. Their role in this study is strictly that of *indicators* of social, linguistic, or communicative needs, problems, or aspirations. These activities/ indicators are cited in the search for and identification of the respective possible new goals to be adopted by existing or future agencies.

While earlier models attempt to analyze what steps agencies take in the process of planning language, this expanded classification attempts to establish *what they have been or may be seeking*, that is, to cover the totality of the functions that they have engaged in or goals they have sought to date or that they may adopt under current sociolinguistic conditions. Incidentally, a case in which almost all the goals presented here have been sought is that of modern Norwegian, which was one of the first to be investigated comprehensively (Haugen 1966a), thus greatly enhancing interest in the field and the development of tools for its study.

Finally, some general observations on the proposed classification ought to be noted.

1.   A clear distinction must be made between *Language Planning Activities* involved in carrying out specific functions or in seeking specific goals, and the *Language Planning Goals* themselves; identical activities may lead to different goals and vice versa. For example, when the Canadian Public Service Commission provides French or English language training to public servants, it is seeking the goal of Language Spread. The same type of activity, however, could be related to other goals, such as Language Revival or Language Maintenance. Conversely, different activities may have to be implemented in seeking the same goal. For example, in the growing search for Stylistic Simplification in the United States, as elsewhere, relevant activities include legislation, courses offered to writers and others, and textbook preparation. Perhaps the LP goal/LP activity distinction may be further clarified by noting that a goal represents an LP agency's *intention*, declared or otherwise, while an activity represents, in relation to the goal, the *implementation* aspect of the agency – what is actually being done, by whom, how, and so forth.

2.   As indicated earlier, LP goals as presented in this classification are not mutually exclusive. LP agencies may pursue one or more goals simultaneously. Further, where several goals are pursued, some may be viewed as "major goals" and others as "minor goals" (cf. Nahir 1977). For example, Quebec's LP agencies have pursued Language Maintenance as a "major goal" in recent decades. At the same time, however, they have

also been engaged in Purification and in Language Spread (the spread of French among the Province's English monolinguals) as "minor goals."

3.   LP goals pursued by one or more agencies in a given speech community may be contradictory. The Hebrew Language Academy's major goal in recent decades has been Lexical Modernization. Some of the Academy's achievements, however, have been contradictory to, or even canceled by, activities related to its minor goal, External Purification. Similar conflicts may conceivably exist between other goals – for example, between (External) Purification and Interlingual Communication or between the latter goal and Stylistic Simplification.

4.   LP goals are not static. As soon as they have been achieved, LP agencies adopt new goals or even disband. When the revival of Hebrew was completed at the turn of this century, for example, the Hebrew Language Committee (later Academy) replaced Language Revival as a major goal with both Language Spread and Language Standardization (see also Nahir 1978a). An LP agency may, of course, replace, modify, or abandon goals when a change takes place in the community's respective needs or aspirations.

5.   Some overlap may at times appear to exist between certain goals as presented. This may result, as indicated, from the occasional similarity between a goal and a particular activity. An example is the goal of Stylistic Simplification, certain manifestations of which may be seen as overlapping with Terminological Unification. A careful observation reveals, however, that the respective needs, motivations, and intentions, as well as the ultimate goals they create, are on the whole clearly distinct.

6.   Finally, it ought to be noted that this classification seeks to *describe* what LP agencies have been engaged in – that is, what they have attempted to achieve – as observed in various case studies and in other literature and to discuss what LP agencies are *capable* of doing, given the right conditions, or, conversely, what observed activities indicate the existence of *sociolinguistic needs and aspirations* that can be met by existing or newly formed LP agencies. In other words, the objective is to describe either what LP agencies have done or what they could do. This classification does not attempt to state what LP agencies ought to do, although the boundary between this and a description of what they could do may not always be distinctly observable.

4   Language Purification

Two types of Language Purification may be observed.[1]

1.   *External Purification* is prescription of usage in order to preserve the "purity" of language and protect it from foreign influences. Various agencies, notably language academies, have engaged in language purification for centuries, ever since the Italian Academy and the French Academy were formed in 1582 and 1635, respectively. Some of the better-known academies that followed and were influenced by these were those in Spain (1713), Sweden (1786), and Hungary (1830). Some current examples may be found in Israel, Jordan, Canada, Quebec, Iceland, and elsewhere. Selection, codification, and implementation activities by the respective academies and similar bodies have largely consisted of the creation of prescriptive grammars and dictionaries. The latter included, among others, forms expected to replace borrowings.

The objection to borrowings has somewhat diminished in recent decades. In the specialized dictionaries recently published by Israel's Hebrew Language Academy, for example, a much higher percentage of foreign terms may be found than in those published earlier (Nahir 1974).[2] Barring unforeseen political, religious, or other pressures, one may safely expect this trend to continue universally. As Rau found, "the natural tendency to borrow could not be completely checked by official command" (1954: 4).

At the same time a renewed growth in purism may be observed in various parts of the world, as, for example, in France, Spain, and Hispanic America. The increasing rate of one-way concept-borrowing and subsequent lexical borrowing that has been taking place almost universally from the technologically advanced countries, notably the United States, has initiated fears in a growing number of speech communities that the borrowing languages may be swamped by the foreign language (usually English) and eventually lose their linguistic identity. Language purism has also been popular recently in some countries in Asia and Africa, where language planning agencies engaged in language spread or standardization and others have rejected "international" terms, even technical ones, in order to fight "Western cultural colonialism."

On the whole, however, it seems that, following the development of modern scientific linguistics since the turn of the century, preoccupation with puristic issues has lost ground except, as above, where excessive borrowing, mostly lexical, is seen as threatening the independent existence or unique identity of the borrowing language. Still, with the more recent advent of sociolinguistics generally and language planning in particular, the beginnings of a scholarly interest in the area may be observed in a small but growing number of studies describing puristic attitudes and external purification, for example, in Iceland (Halldórsson 1979) and Israel (Nahir 1974).

2.   *Internal Purification* involves "protecting" the accepted standard code as it exists at a given time against deviation that occurs from *within* in the form of non-normative, "incorrect" usage in a language. It is distinct from External Language Purification in that the latter involves "protecting" a language against foreign languages and the "impurity" resulting from their influence. Usually both types of purification have been practiced by the same language planning agencies.

As has been the case with External Purification, the pressure to defend language from internal undesirable development began with the language academies mentioned above. Influential personalities, however, were also active in this movement. As early as 1712, Jonathan Swift in "A Proposal for Correcting, Improving, and Ascertaining the English Tongue" suggested following the French example and changing "many gross improprieties, which, however authorized by practice, and grown familiar, ought to be discarded. . . . Many words . . . deserve to be utterly thrown out of our language, many more to be corrected" (Swift 1712, published 1883: vol. 9, 147; quoted from Kachru 1975: 58).

Numerous, varied considerations have motivated language normativists attempting to curb "incorrect" usage. For some, universal use of "correct" standard would democratize language. For others, "incorrect" usage would result in the loss of the identity of the language and whatever that implies. For still others, the motivation is the desire to improve the socioeconomic status of individuals or groups. Opponents, however, interpret these as mere disguise for elitism: "The old concepts of 'good style' and correctness reflect only *one* norm-conception, namely that of the social elite" (Skyum-Nielsen 1978: 3).

Whatever the motivation, normative policies and their implementation are still quite widespread. One of the tasks of Quebec's language planning agencies, for example, is fostering correct spoken and written use of language.[3] Examples of implementation through education include, among many others, Japan, where the communities strictly control the selection of "model textbooks" (Neustupný 1976), and Israel, where school texts need approval by the Ministry of Education, which by law must follow the Hebrew Language Academy's decisions, as do all government-affiliated agencies. Also, all Israeli high schools have been using "improve your language" texts, albeit with uncertain results.[4]

Implementation by the media is also commonly practiced. It includes "language correction" columns in the press (e.g., in Japan, Israel, Sweden, Poland) and on radio (e.g., Israel's "A Moment of Hebrew"). In fact, Israel's broadcasting authority employs a representative of the Hebrew Language Academy as a language watchdog. In Sweden, among other relevant activities, a telephone service gives advice on correct language, and "correct language" texts are published for popular use (Jernudd 1977). Activities in Poland include, in addition to corrections suggested in the press and on radio, establishing language advising centers in some of the largest cities and, for the past twenty years, organizing a festival on language problems and language treatment (Niedzielski 1979).

Few, if any, modern linguists believe in the intrinsic merit of "correct" language. Still, just as few would probably deny its socioeconomic usefulness. It seems therefore that, whatever its rationale, it is here to stay for quite some time.

5   Language Revival

Language Revival is the attempt to turn a language with few or no surviving native speakers back into a normal means of communication in a community.

The modern trend that began about the middle of the nineteenth century in favor of national identity and independence has been accompanied by or resulted in numerous language problems and aspirations, mostly related to the adoption and standardization of national languages (see below). Some of these cases involved old nations, newly aware of their national identity and heritage, which formed movements with the aim of restoring their old, little-used languages to their previous status (e.g., Irish, Welsh), or even completely "reviving" "dead" or historical languages or their vernaculars (e.g., Hebrew, Cornish). This objective was clearly defined by a commission set up in Ireland in 1964 to examine the progress of the revival and advise on future steps: "What we understand by the Revival is that the [Irish] language should once again be a normal means of conversation and communication among Irish people. This has been the objective of the Irish language movement from its inception and of the political movement which stemmed from it, and this has been the linguistic objective of every government since the foundation of the state."[5] The Hebrew Language Committee's objective, declared in 1911, was, similarly, for Hebrew to become a language spoken in "all matters of life, at home, in the schools, in public life, in commerce and business, in industry, art and science."[6]

The number of language revival attempts has been small. Certain conditions must be met before the desire to revive a language exists: there must be an old language to be revived and a direct historical or cultural affinity with the historical nation whose language is to be revived. These conditions involve a rare combination, which severely limits the number of revival attempts, and even more so the number of successes, which would require certain additional conditions, involving an almost unprecedented combination. And, in fact, all such attempts have practically failed, with the exception of Hebrew at the turn of this century (the only "near-success" according to Haugen 1966b: 26). These attempts have involved the Irish, the Welsh, the Provençals, the Frisians, the Bretons, and others. As to the success of the Hebrew revival, it was probably due largely to the prevalence of the required conditions – a *need* for a means of communication resulting from the "right" (if unfortunate) historical circumstances, and an *old revivable language*. Yet several other sociocultural factors – national, political, religious, and educational – have also been crucial to the favorable outcome of the sociolinguistic experiment that, as Fishman observes, "has encouraged other smaller language communities . . . to strive to save *their* ethnic mother tongue (or their traditional cultural tongues) from oblivion" (Fishman 1972: 2).[7]

6 Language Reform

Language Reform is deliberate change in specific aspects of language, intended to facilitate its use. Usually this involves changes in, or simplification of, orthography, spelling, lexicon, or grammar.

Obviously, *reform* is used here in its narrow sense. Viewing it broadly might render it a partial synonym of *language planning*. At least some LP goals in this classification – for example, Language Purification and Language Standardization – would then have to be eliminated, as they would have to be viewed merely as types of language reform. While this may seem economical, it would result in failure to identify distinct, specific goals LP agencies may have.

Language Reform, unlike the above two goals or functions, has usually been motivated by a desire to facilitate language use, although the particular direction of the reform has often been affected by ideological, political, religious, or other considerations. Reform is normally a relatively brief undertaking. Attempts at reforming languages have been known and justified for centuries. One of the leaders of the French Revolution, Barère, stated: "We have revolutionized the government, the laws, the habits, the customs, commerce, and thought; let us also revolutionize the language which is their daily instrument."[8] The Estonian Johannes Aavik, a more modern reformer, in his *The Extreme Possibilities of Language Reform* (1924), claims that language is like an instrument or a machine, which can and should be improved. Since all natural languages are imperfect, they, too, should be improved – that is, reformed – at every level: grammar, orthography, spelling, and lexicon. According to Tauli, another language planning theoretician, "there is no element of a language that cannot be altered deliberately" (1968: 151).

Language reform involving one or more language levels is known to have taken place since the beginning of the nineteenth century in numerous countries, for example, Hungary, Norway, Estonia, Spain, Germany, Greece, Iceland, Albania, China, Israel, Indonesia, Poland, Czechoslovakia, Russia (in Russian, Yiddish, and other languages), and India. A most celebrated case, of course, investigated extensively by Heyd (1954), was that of Turkey early in this century, when Kemal Atatürk led a massive and largely successful reform in Turkish orthography and lexicon. Language reforms recently investigated include, among others, those involving Hebrew (Rabin 1971b), Polish (Niedzielski 1979), Norwegian (Haugen 1966a; Gundersen 1977), Irish (Ó Murchú 1977), Dutch (Geerts et al. 1977), Chinese (DeFrancis 1977; Cheng 1979), and several languages in East and Southeast Asia (DeFrancis 1967). In fact, some of the latter appeared in a recent anthology devoted to developments in the creation and reform of writing systems (Fishman 1977).

7   Language Standardization

Language Standardization is the attempt to turn a language or dialect spoken in a region, usually a single political unit, into one that is accepted as the major language of the region and, as a result, is often considered its best form. This may be a local dialect or language or even a foreign language (a "language of wider communication"). Standardization may take place in more than one dialect or language concurrently and result in two or even more major languages used in a region for either the same or different functions – official, educational, commercial, and so forth.

Probably more language planning agencies are currently engaged in Language Standardization as a major function than in any other, notably in Africa and Asia, due to changes in political conditions – the unification of small political units, the division of others, and the newly achieved independence of previously colonized territories coupled with a widespread rise in nationalism. The potential of language has been rapidly and universally recognized: "Language is a uniquely powerful instrument in unifying a diverse population and in involving individuals and subgroups in the national system" (Kelman 1971: 21). Indeed, in the late nineteenth and the early twentieth centuries Europe witnessed linguistic instability rather similar to that of modern Africa and Asia. For example, the number of national languages grew from sixteen in 1800 to thirty in 1900 and to fifty-three in 1937, paralleled by a growth in the number of states from fifteen in 1871 to twenty-one in 1914 and to twenty-nine in 1937 (Deutsch 1942: 606).

Language Standardization has been give considerable attention by theoreticians such as Ferguson (1968), Fishman (1971a), and others. Two pioneers who studied the issue in depth are Ray (1963), who defined Language Standardization in terms of three "necessary components" – Efficiency, Rationality, and Commonalty – and Le Page (1964). Le Page (1964: 77f.) suggested seven possible factors a language planning agency must consider in selecting a language or a dialect to be standardized:

a. The demography and sociology of the language(s) in question;
b. The past history of the linguistic situation (including educational and literary);
c. The structural nature of the language(s) involved – as described scientifically by
    linguists;
d. The political, social, economic and cultural situation of the country;
e. The organization and structure of the educational system;
f. The cost of any change in the language situation;
g. The extent of ruthlessness the government or its agency is prepared to apply in
    implementing the decisions.

Garvin succinctly summarized the rationale for language standardization: "Both official and national languages have to have a high level of standardization as a matter of cultural necessity. This means primarily that these language should have the structural properties of a standard language to the highest possible extent, both that of flexible stability and that of intellectualization" (1974: 75). To the list of functions that a standard language is to fulfill, Garvin adds one he calls "the participatory function, that is, the function of the language to facilitate participation in world–wide cultural developments" (ibid.: 76). This seems to be true at least where the language to be standardized is one of "wider communication."

Interest in the practical aspect of language standardization was evident even while relevant theories were developed. Early case studies by theoreticians (e.g., Ray 1963; Le Page 1964; Haugen 1966b) have generated descriptions of the processes involved, particularly codification and implementation, in a growing number of communities in both developing and developed countries – for example, China (Barnes 1973), Latvia (Rūķe-Draviņa 1977), Albania and Albanian-speaking Yugoslavia (Byron 1979), Czechoslovakia (Salzmann 1980), and The Gambia (Richmond 1982).

8 Language Spread

Language Spread (or Spreading) is the attempt to increase the number of speakers of a language at the expense of another language (or languages). This is, in fact, what from the perspective of the language or its speakers has been labeled *language shift* (Fishman et al. 1966; Fishman 1977), with the difference that, unlike the latter, it is an attempt to *cause* speakers of a given language to shift to another. However, since the concern here is with the goals of the LP agency, *language spread* is more accurately descriptive.

This function has been motivated either by pragmatic or, more often, by political considerations, especially in bilingual or multilingual countries where it has been felt that adopting one of the languages or dialects spoken in the country, or even a "language of wider communication," as an official and/or national language, would facilitate the functioning of the government and other institutions or contribute to the political unification of the country. These motivations are often similar to those behind the decision to standardize a given language. Furthermore, where the rationale behind the decision to spread a language is political, typically in newly independent states or emerging nations (see Language Standardization, above), the adoption of this goal necessarily requires the concurrent or at least subsequent standardization of the language.

It makes little political sense to spread the use of a language in order to "nationalize" it unless it is also codified and implemented as a standard language. The converse, on the other hand, is not necessarily applicable. A nonstandard language spoken by a large section of the population in a country may be selected as its national language, which then calls for its standardization. In this case there is no need to spread it, although the LP agency may still wish to increase the number of its speakers. This, however, is not a condition for its selection or for its effective functioning in its new role.

There often exists, then, a relationship between the considerations that prompt LP agencies to engage in Language Standardization and Language Spread. One of the many cases where both goals are concurrently sought is that of Yugoslav-Albanian, where, as Byron notes, "without adoption of the preferred dialect by speakers outside the geographical or social boundaries of this dialect, the favored code would, despite its status, remain a merely *local* speech variety. It could not then qualify as a standard language, which, by definition, is a supra-local linguistic variety" (1979: 43). Another example of Language Standardization and Language Spread interdependence is that of Modern Hebrew early in this century; by the time it was successfully revived as a vernacular (approximately 1916), it was still spoken by only 40 percent of Palestine's Jewish community (1916 census – see Bachi 1956). Its spread and concurrent standardization were concluded three decades later when, spoken by 71 percent of the population (Bachi 1956; Hofman and Fisherman 1971), it was declared the national and – with the minority's Arabic – the official language of the newly established Israel (Nahir 1978a). These and other dual-goal cases certainly warrant Byron's call for further research on the relationship between language (or dialect) shift and language standardization (1979: 43). It seems to be safe to expect that the investigation of different cases will reveal greatly varying degrees and types of such relationships. It may also draw attention to other relationships, such as that between Language Spread and Language Maintenance.

Other cases where Language Spread has been adopted as a planning goal, mostly combined with at least some measure of Language Standardization, include Tanzania (Whitely 1971; Polomé 1979), the USSR (Lewis 1971), and Quebec (Bourhis 1984). The most outstanding case of language spread, however, is probably that of Malay-Indonesian, which, spoken by 15 million native speakers only a few decades ago, is now spoken by over 125 million, and is the sixth largest language in the world (Le Page 1964; Alisjahbana 1971).

9   Lexical Modernization

Lexical Modernization is word creation or adaptation as a way to assist developed, standard languages (at times referred to as "mature") that have borrowed concepts too fast for their natural development to accommodate.

Terminological work may be dichotomized as belonging in either of two categories. 1. It may constitute an activity that is *part* of either the process of codification or implementation (perhaps also elaboration) while seeking either one of the language planning goals, such as revival and reform in Hebrew and Turkish, respectively, at the turn of the century (Nahir 1978a; Heyd 1954). This often involves developing, growing, or previously unwritten languages (at times referred to as "immature"), where the attempt is made, among other activities, to enrich their lexicon so as to close the gap between them and modern technology, thought, and knowledge. This, then, is an *activity*, not a goal or function. 2. Term creation and adaptation may serve as a means to adjust developed, standard languages in which newly borrowed ideas and concepts or technological and scientific innovations find the lexicon "unprepared," that is, the natural development of the language has not supplied the necessary terminology. What is required for such a language is the collection of concepts imported into the community, or even formed within it, and the creation or designation of new terms for them. This is not an activity in the process of achieving some goals – say, revival, reform, or standardization – but *the goal or the function itself*, that of aiding a language in keeping up with modern life as represented in the language of an outside speech community, especially when it is the source of "word immigration" or even an "invasion of words, expressions and phrases" (Selander 1980). It presupposes a developed, standard status for the given language. Therefore, a language undergoing revival or standardization, for example, can only be lexically modernized in this sense if it has first achieved a "standard" status.

Lexical Modernization is practiced in numerous countries – Norway, Denmark, Sweden, Finland, Iceland, Israel, Hungary, Egypt, West and East Germany, France, Vietnam, India, and the Soviet Union, among others (Guxman 1968; Tauli 1968; Fishman 1971b). The major activity of LP agencies seeking this goal is systematically collecting new ideas and concepts imported into the community and creating (or adopting) new terms for them. Again, lexical work as an *activity* in pursuit of a goal and lexical modernization as a *goal* must not be confused. They may belong to altogether different levels.

The beginnings of scholarly interest in this LP goal are becoming evident. A recent study, for example, discusses in some detail the procedures and operation of a subcommittee of the Hebrew Language Academy engaged in the lexical modernization of Modern Hebrew (Fellman and Fishman 1977; see also Nahir 1974, 1979). De Bessé similarly describes terminology committees established by the French government in the 1970s: coordinated by the Haut Comité de la Langue Française, their task was "to make an inventory of lexical gaps in a given field and to propose the terms necessary to designate a new concept or to replace a loan word" (1980: 43).

With the rapid growth in international relations, communication, and mobility, and the resulting increase in concept borrowing, we may expect the number and workload of language planning agencies seeking this goal to rise steadily.

10 Terminology Unification

Terminology Unification is establishing unified terminologies, mostly technical, by clarifying and defining them, in order to reduce communicative ambiguity, especially in the technological and scientific domains.

This goal, like that of Lexical Modernization, is more typical of developed, standard languages. It has been recognized that in many such languages the same concepts or phenomena often have different names, or, conversely, the same names are often used to describe different concepts or phenomena. The possible resulting confusions are self-evident. One such notorious case concerns a British military unit in World War II that received, among other supplies, a certain liquid labeled *inflammable*. Not surprisingly, the prefix was read as a negative marker, with disastrous consequences. Perhaps this is what has led to the growing use of *flammable* as standard,[9] although most dictionaries still define the two identically.

Similar ambiguities probably occur in most if not all languages. In Hebrew, for example, certain words have opposing meanings – for example, *hig'il* 'to cause to be dirty' and its opposite 'to clean'; *kiles* 'to scorn' and 'to praise'; *nifkad* 'to be counted in a census or roll call' and 'to be absent or missing'; *na'ana* 'to receive a reply' and 'to reply.'

The greatest concern with this function has been evident, however, in the technological and scientific fields. The Swedish government, for example, set up a committee on the "cultivation of medical language" in 1977. It was felt that "the same medical phenomenon could have several names which would hinder flow and search of literature and which could lead to loss of time and money as well as delay research procedures."[10]

Other examples illustrate the same trend. According to the first president of the Hebrew Language Academy, H. H. Tur-Sinai, its objective was, among other things, "to establish a unified norm for the use of terminology so that [the terms] will be understood by all" (*Zemanim*, December 18, 1953). Similarly, one of the three objectives of the Arab Language Academy, specified in a 1976 law, was "to unify terminology in the various fields and to compile terminological glossaries and dictionaries."[11]

A major activity involved in the goal of Terminology Unification is terminology definition, which delineates the functions and semantic boundaries of terms, thus attaining a "systematicity of terminology" (Jernudd 1973: 20). One of the aims of the Swedish Center of Technical Terminology (Tekniska Nomenklaturcentralen, or TNC) is, according to its director, "to create and maintain semantic order in already available terminology" (Selander, in Jernudd 1973: 20). Similarly, one of the activities of the Israel Institute of Standards is defining terminologies it receives from the Hebrew Language Academy, both for its own use in performing its major task and for general use. In the process it unifies these terminologies and discards duplicates. Thus the IIS serves also as an LP agency with Terminology Unification as its goal.[12] Still another example is that of Norway, where the Norwegian Language Council in 1977 published the results of nine years' work on the planned development of a unitary terminology in linguistics.[13]

Finally, the significance of this function is reflected in the growing volume of related activity, as, for example, in the number of professional meetings held recently in many parts of the world (e.g., Quebec, Germany, France, Austria, the Soviet Union), and in relevant courses and even entire programs newly offered by universities and language planning agencies (e.g., in Denmark and Sweden). In fact, some leading scholars have even called for the recognition of the subject as an independent branch of applied linguistics "for the purposes of research and teaching at universities" (e.g., Eugen Wüster, in Felber 1980; Rondeau 1979). A step in this direction was the publication in 1980 of an issue of the *International Journal of the Sociology of Language* (ed. J. C. Sager) devoted in its entirety to the *Standardization of Nomenclature*, with case studies on Sweden (Einar Selander), Czechoslovakia (L. Drozd and M. Roudný), France (Bruno De Bessé), and South Africa (A. D. De V. Cluver) and several studies on the theory of terminology standardization as it relates to effective communication (Helmut Felber, R. L. Johnson and J. C. Sager).

11   Stylistic Simplification

Stylistic Simplification is simplifying language *usage* in lexicon, grammar, and style, in order to reduce communicative ambiguity between professionals and bureaucrats on the one hand and the public on the other, and among professionals and bureaucrats themselves.

Both language planning agencies and the professional literature have recently come to focus on deficiencies resulting from the use of ambiguous, often archaic style and lexicon and overly complex grammar and on possible remedies for such deficiencies and their undesirable effects. These deficiencies may involve two types of relationships: 1. Professional (scientist, bureaucrat, etc.) vs. consumer (patient, client, etc.), where the latter may be a professional (scientist, etc.) in another field. 2. Professional (scientist, etc.) vs. professional (scientist, etc.) – both in the same field. Of most immediate concern has been the professional–consumer relationship. Skyum-Nielsen finds that as a result of developments in science and technology, "the layman and the expert have difficulties in understanding each other. . . . This communication barrier forms an obstacle to the realization of the . . . idea of democracy" (1978: 3). Rubin is also interested in the communicative aspect of the problem: "The language used by professionals may inhibit the accomplishment of the purpose of the professional interaction" (1978: 3). Some lawyers, she finds, are beginning to "question whether justice can be achieved by [legal] language when the lay public cannot adequately participate in the legal process" (ibid.). Alfred Kahn, a chief advisor to former President Carter, touches upon a possible motivation: "legalese" and "bureaucratese" are used "to put people down, to conceal, to substitute for clarity."[14]

Finally, a recent court case, Carlson vs. N. Y. Life Insurance, has shown how "legalese" can stand in the way of justice. Andrew Schiller, a linguist, was appointed by the court to testify as to whether a reading of the policy would convey to the average insured the actual meaning of the policy and to establish the semantic values of some of its key elements as they might be understood by "ordinary men" (Schiller 1980).

Despite the realization that a problem exists, this has not yet been reflected in many language planning agencies adopting the goal or function of Stylistic Simplification. One pioneer is the Swedish Language Council, for which, according to Bertil Molde, its director, "the internationally known problem of difficult and complicated 'officialese' is a main field of interest" (Molde 1975: 4).

Increasing scholarly interest in the precise measure of the problem is evident. In a comprehensive study, for example, Veda and Robert Charrow (1979) investigated the comprehensibility of standard jury instructions. They attempted to find to what extent the average person understands jury instructions and what vocabulary, grammatical, and semantic constructions and contextual features cause people to misunderstand standard jury instructions. They found that 50 percent of the legal concepts were misunderstood and that the difficulty of legal concepts had little to do with misinter-pretation (20 percent). The cause, then, was linguistic and stylistic.

Other researchers have investigated similar problems in medical language (e.g., Shuy 1974, 1979; Ford 1976; Van Naerssen 1978; Barber 1979) and in the language of other professions. Some of the findings of such investigations have recently been published by Alatis and Tucker (1979).

Whether or not this research has a practical impact in the field, awareness of the problem is rising and is reflected in a growing volume of relevant institutional activity, including legislation. Examples include former President Carter's "simple and clear" language regulations (1978), and laws passed in several states (e.g., the New York Sullivan Act 1978) requiring that consumer contracts and other documents be written in "plain, simple" or "understandable non-technical" English. The number of such states has been rapidly growing.[15] Similar legislation has also been passed recently in Denmark, where a government agency was established to ensure that laws of general interest be "transformed into readable pamphlets and brochures" (Skyum–Nielsen 1978).

Other relevant activities include simplification of loan forms by some U.S. banks; projects such as the preparation of kits, teacher's guides, and so forth, undertaken at several university law schools (e.g., at the University of Manitoba in Winnipeg, Canada) and aimed at "making law comprehensible to the layman"; various publications and other activities of the Document Design Center in Washington, D.C., established by the American Institute for Research (Battison 1980); offering courses to improve the comprehensibility of writers in technology and the professions; and the publication of books dealing with "plain language" in legal and other documents. Such activities may well be viewed as indicators of the existence of a problem that is bound to grow with the development of science, technology, and government.

12   Interlingual Communication

Interlingual Communication is facilitating linguistic communication between members of *different* speech communities by enhancing the use of either an artificial (or "auxili-ary") language or a "language of wider communication" as an additional language used as a *lingua franca* either throughout the world or in parts thereof for verbal or written communication. Interlingual communication may also involve attempts at modifying certain linguistic features in one or more cognate languages in order to facilitate com-munication among their speakers. A major relevant activity is that of language spread-ing (which ought not to be confused with Language Spread as an LP *goal*).

12.1   Worldwide interlingual communication

12.1.1   *Auxiliary languages*
A recent upsurge in the scholarly preoccupation with auxiliary (or "international," "artificial") languages is clearly evident. The structure of such languages and their role in interlingual communication (the popular designation *international communication*

seems inadequate here since it fails to distinguish between political and linguistic boundaries) have been studied for over a century. In recent decades these languages have been investigated by linguists, sociolinguists, and other social scientists, particularly those interested in the emergence, development, and function of Esperanto, the language spoken in "a voluntary, non-ethnic, non-territorial speech community formed by conscious linguistic choice rather than by birthright membership" (Wood 1979a: 433). Both the cultural and linguistic aspects of auxiliary languages have been studied (e.g., Jacob 1947; McQuown 1950; Sapir 1957; Tonkin 1968; Forster 1971, 1982; Wood 1979a; Braga 1979).

Concurrently, the number of institutions offering courses or programs in auxiliary languages, particularly Esperanto, has increased considerably. At the same time, the number of Esperanto speakers has grown to over a million (Wood 1979a). Many LP agencies are active in either corpus or status planning in auxiliary languages. In fact, some agencies are international, with branches in various countries. One such agency is the Universala Esperanto Asocio, located in Rotterdam. Its goal, as quoted in Joan Rubin's *Directory of Language Planning Organizations* (1979), is to "promote and spread the use of the international auxiliary language Esperanto worldwide, and thereby advance friendly relations among all the peoples of the world" (1979: 45).

12.1.2   English as a lingua franca

The widespread study, acquisition, and use of English as a second language, a *lingua franca*, is so apparent that it hardly needs elaboration. In recent decades English has become a language, as Ferguson puts it, that "you 'can get around in' . . . which people actually use to communicate across language boundaries . . . most used as a second language (or third or fourth)" (1978: 26). English is also the language of instruction in parts of Asia and Africa and is most commonly utilized for scientific publication and at international meetings including many in Eastern Bloc countries, where Russian as a second language is a required school subject. Although political, social, and linguistic factors may play a considerable role in the acceptance or rejection of a language, either as a national language or as a *lingua franca*, acceptance can ultimately occur only when, as in all behavior, using the language reinforces its user – that is, when the expected reward is attractive enough, or when speaking it promises to meet a strong enough need.[16] Thus, in a snowball fashion (or the "rich become richer" process) the very popularity of a language results in the feasibility of its study by new potential users, which, in turn, further motivates its acquisition and use. Such a process, involving the mechanism of "self-fulfilling prophecy," has been globally occurring in the case of English.

Several surveys and studies by organizations and scholars have recently formalized and analyzed the status of English as a *lingua franca*. These include, inter alia, a number of case studies by Fishman and his collaborators (1977); reports and surveys by the International Communications Agency and the British Council;[17] and some of the findings in a study of "The Foreign Language Needs of U.S. Corporations Doing Business Abroad" (Inman 1980) and in another on international short-wave radio stations using English and other "languages of wider communication" (Wood 1979b).

According to some scholars the status of English interlingual communication has its risks and problems. Ferguson, for example, calls for a national language policy in the

United States that would "acknowledge the special place of English in the language situation of the world and in . . . our own country, [aiming at] further spreading of English as a world language, without, however, tying it directly to our own political and cultural values" (Ferguson 1978: 31). The East–West Culture Learning Institute in Honolulu, Hawaii, has also recognized the existence of actual or potential related problems. Accordingly, it has recently embarked on a project, Language for International Communication, to "explain how individuals and organizations may deal more effectively with language problems related to use of an international language in an international setting,"[18] such as international business, research and development projects, professional organizations, and educational programs.

12.2   Regional interlingual communication

In addition to the spread of *lingua francas* for universal use, Interlingual Communication may also involve attempts at advancing either the use of regional *lingua francas* or mutual intelligibility within a group of cognate languages in a given region.

12.2.1   Regional lingua franca

Users of a regional *lingua franca* may be speakers of either related or unrelated languages. Examples of this include, among others, Russian, which, it is claimed, serves the role of a "cross-national" language in the USSR (Isayev 1977; Lewis 1971) and Spanish in the Andrés Bello speech communities, where its use as a regional *lingua franca* is promoted in order to remove severe language barriers among the numerous communities. An international conference on this issue held recently in Peru reflected a substantial interest on the part of scholars and educators in the removal of language barriers in the region.[19]

12.2.2   Mutual intelligibility between cognate languages

Improving mutual intelligibility between speakers of a group of cognate languages in a given region involves partially standardizing the respective linguistic codes within the group, in order to minimize the differences between these languages and thus facilitate communication between their speakers. All Nordic national language committees, for example, are committed by their statutes to cooperate with all others "to avoid new and unnecessary differences between the languages and . . . to try to close the gaps between [them]" (Molde 1975; cf. also Haugen 1966b). The goals of the Nordic Language Committee, formed in 1978 and representing language committees in Denmark, Finland, the Faroes, Greenland, Iceland, and Norway, are "to strengthen the Nordic language community, to further cooperation on language cultivation and planning . . . and to handle language problems of concern to more than one Nordic language."[20] Relevant scholarly activity on these and similar issues is increasingly evident in the Nordic countries.[21]

Another case in which the improvement of interlingual communication between cognate languages in a given region has been the goal is that of Malay–Indonesia, in which the standardization of the spelling systems of its two varieties, spoken in Malaysia and Indonesia, respectively (Bahasa Malaysia and Bahasa Indonesia), was begun in 1959 and successfully concluded by 1972 (Omar 1975). The spelling reform in Dutch in the Netherlands and Belgium represents the same goal. The search for a unified spelling in the Dutch-speaking area (the Netherlands and northern Belgium), already begun in the mid-nineteenth century, in 1944 resulted in the formation of a joint Belgian-Dutch commission that was to form "a uniform orthography for the Dutch language . . . to be valid in the Netherlands and in Belgium" (*Belgisch Staatsblad* 3208, April 5, 1946, quoted in translation in Geerts et al. 1977). The commission's proposals became law in both countries in 1947 and were to be applied in both official and educational use. This law, initiating what has become known as the 1947–1954 spelling reform, was followed by the "1967–1969 proposals" (Geerts et al. 1977). To date, the respective LP agencies as well as other interested groups in both the Netherlands and Belgium continue in their search for a unified spelling acceptable to all.

13 Language Maintenance

Language Maintenance is the preservation of the use of a group's native language, as a first or even as a second language, where political, social, economic, educational, or other pressures threaten or cause (or are perceived to threaten or cause) a decline in the status of the language as a means of communication, a cultural medium, or a symbol of group or national identity.

Language Maintenance may be categorized as either Dominant Language or Ethnic Language Maintenance.

13.1 Dominant language maintenance

This is typical of a society being or feeling threatened by an outside "invading" language(s) even though its own language is still dominant and spoken by the majority as a native language. Such threat may be *external* – from technologically, politically, or economically influential communities – usually resulting in linguistic borrowing rather than in actual language shift. In such cases (e.g., Hebrew in Israel), language planning agencies have often resorted to (External) Language Purification. In most cases, however, the threat of an "invading" language is perceived or posed from *within* the community's boundaries, by a prestigious minority language that is dominant elsewhere. Such a threat may result in an agency adopting Language Maintenance as its goal. Canada's province of Quebec may serve as an illustration. Although the majority (80 percent according to the 1976 census) have been native speakers of French, English – a minority language within and dominant without – has long been considered a threat to the French language and the culture it represents. Successful Language Maintenance activities have considerably removed this threat since a new government in 1977 made French the Province's official language. Its aim was "to reduce functional bilingualism . . . by replacing the presence of . . . English . . . by French" (McConnell 1977: 4). Specifically, this legislation attempted to affect the status of French as an official language, as the language of instruction at schools, and as the language of work. As a result, Quebec is currently undergoing a significant cultural and linguistic adjustment, with

French becoming dominant in all areas. Incidentally, adopting this function necessitated the subsequent adoption in Quebec of the function of Language Spread (of French) with activities directed at Quebec's many English monolinguals, who were now forced to use French more extensively.[22]

Another case of Dominant Language Maintenance is that of Greenland, where Greenlandic, clearly the dominant language, has long been threatened by Danish, the language of the island's parent country, both from within and without. However, probably because no language planning agency enjoys political or legal authority in Greenland (Kleivan 1979), the maintenance of Greenlandic has been less successful than that of French in Quebec.

13.2   Ethnic language maintenance

This involves the preservation of a *minority* ethnic language by raising its status and facilitating and encouraging its study, acquisition, and use by members of the community. Ethnic language maintenance has been practiced in numerous communities throughout the world where ethnic language loyalties have weakened. Scholarly interest in the issue is also evident in recent decades. An early, exhaustive investigation has been carried out by Fishman and several collaborators, who studied language loyalty and maintenance in the numerous ethnic languages of the United States (Fishman et al. 1966). This study is of interest to language planners, since, as Fishman states, "most of the circumstances influencing minority group language maintenance efforts throughout the modern world are available for study within the continental limits of the United States, drawing on experience over the past two centuries" (ibid.: 25).

Recent interest in minority ethnic languages and their legitimization stems from several factors. One is the recognition in the United States since the early 1960s of the usefulness of non-English languages as a valuable national resource or "a huge and valuable treasure which should be recognized as such" (Lemaire 1966: 275).[23] Another factor, albeit still rather fragile, is "the general movement towards cultural pluralism, egalitarianism, and recognition of differences" (Rubin 1978: 3). Finally, it has also been observed that ethnolinguistic groups in the United States will not be able to be fully American unless "they are given every possibility of being fully French, Portuguese, Spanish, or whatever as well" (Lambert 1977: 45); and if that is done, "the United States will be a greater nation and a more interesting one" (ibid.). Due to America's leadership role in recent decades, the prevalence of similar views and feelings in other parts of the world may easily be observed.

Current implementation activities related to this goal include, among others, bilingual education in various parts of the world. A popular program in the United States (recently reduced by the present administration) was one aimed at students with "limited English," which was initiated in 1975 following the Lau vs. Nichols Supreme Court decision and which became known as "the *Lau* Remedies." Bilingual education programs have reportedly received almost universal ethnic community approval. Some scholars believe that these programs have met an urgent need and that language planning agencies could assist them by providing to groups wishing to preserve their ethnic languages "foreign linguistic aid" – planning, strategy, administration, problem solving, and so forth (Mackey 1978).

While language maintenance in the United States is still drawing scholars' attention (e.g., Thompson 1974; Spolsky and Kari 1974), similar cases from other areas are increasingly brought to light in the professional literature, as, for example, in Spolsky (1978) and in collections by Alatis (1978), Mackey and Ornstein (1979), Wood (1979c), and Cobarrubias and Fishman (1983). Some of the programs involved seem to be quite effective. Schweda (1980) reports on an interesting, large-scale project carried out since 1970 in a French-speaking area in northern Maine by the St. John Valley Bilingual Education Program (SJVBEP). This community, situated between English-speaking Maine and a French-speaking part of New Brunswick in Canada, has witnessed a growing shift to the dominant English. The objective of the program, evaluated by HEW criteria as one of the best in the U.S. bilingual education system, is to change the "negative attitudes Franco-Americans have toward themselves" (Schweda 1980: 12). Activities include preparation of French textbooks suitable for students living in St. John Valley, thus eliminating the need for texts that have imported from France both its culture and language variety, which are of little interest or use to local students.

Finally, it should be noted that cases of Language Maintenance may at times be confused with Language Revival. Some recent attempts to restore North America's native Indian languages can indeed be designated as cases of "Revival" (St. Clair 1980), since they have ceased to be spoken as native languages by significant numbers (see the definition of Revival). Other such attempts, however, actually belong in the Language Maintenance category, since they involve languages *still spoken*, albeit under pressure and in danger of being replaced by others.

14   Auxiliary-Code Standardization

Auxiliary-Code Standardization is standardizing or modifying the marginal, auxiliary aspects of language such as signs for the deaf, place names, and rules of transliteration and transcription, either to reduce ambiguity and thus improve communication or to meet changing social, political, or other needs or aspirations. Although place names, transliteration and transcription rules, and so forth, could conceivably be viewed as mere aspects of some other goals – for example, Terminology Unification or Stylistic Simplification – they seem to be sufficiently marginal and unique in the problems and solutions involved to justify viewing them as constituting a separate, independent goal.

Place-name change or standardization is probably the most common aspect of this function – it has been practiced by the U.S. Board of Geographic Names since 1890 – although standardizing signs for the deaf and rules of transliteration can also be observed in many parts of the world. A familiar problem involves street names. A recently reported fire at "Pine" in Santa Cruz, California, resulted in dispatching firefighters to Pine Street, Place, and Avenue. It is easy to guess the same firefighters' reluctant response at receiving a call to "Redwood," of which their county has twenty-nine Drives, Lanes, and Avenues. A commission established to propose changes will have to rename about 20 percent of the county's streets.

In multilingual Singapore, a committee established by the government to make decisions on language corpus planning has published since 1976 lists of standard translated terms in Chinese for geographical names, names of national and international organizations, titles of civil servants, and so on (Kuo 1980).

Due to the political, social, or emotional significance of names, signs, and the like, place naming is frequently motivated by such considerations rather than by genuine communicative need. The Dutch authorities in Friesland, for example, have recently been persuaded, following a lengthy campaign, to allow Frisian place names on Frisian postal addresses; the target now is the approval of the Frisian equivalents of *Mr.*, *Mrs.*, and *Miss*.[24] The U.S. Board of Geographical Names is another example: it is currently considering changing Mt. McKinley to its Tanana Indian name, Denali. Certain hurricanes have been given men's names to equalize evil between the sexes (Rubin 1978). Cape Canaveral in Florida, renamed Cape Kennedy following the president's assassination in the early sixties, was recently given back its original name. Such changes often take place when the "right" political party is in power. In Israel, an airport, a university, and major streets in most cities were renamed after Ben-Gurion, the country's first prime minister. Since the opposition party won the elections in 1977, the number of major roads and streets renamed after its own late leaders has grown considerably. Political considerations have also motivated the renaming of the capital of Canada's Province of Saskatchewan, when established, from Pile of Bones to its present Regina, after the queen of England.[25]

15   Conclusion

As indicated briefly in the introduction, an attempt has been made in this classification to identify, define, and delineate not only goals or functions that language planning agencies have adopted and engaged in but also those that they can adopt and engage in if and when the need to do so is recognized. This is why much of the discussion, particularly in the second part of the classification, has focused on examples of various field or scholarly activities, by agencies or individuals, which either led to the adoption of certain goals or indicate a need to define and adopt other goals. These activities/indicators have been categorized by their common denominators, the specific goals that, if achieved, will meet the indicated needs.

These goals, or *seeking* them, must be seen, of course, as clearly distinct from language planning *processes* as established in Haugen's model, which should lead to *achieving* the goals. The activities discussed, among others, constitute the steps in his processes. In other words, this classification deals with *what* language planners attempt to achieve, while Haugen's model deals with the question of *how* they go about achieving it.

The eleven goals, or functions, in the proposed classification may also be viewed as a means to summarize the up-to-date totality of language-related communicative, political, social, economic, religious, or other needs and aspirations and the resulting language planning activities, or what language planning is actually about. Needs and aspirations in the future are of course likely to change, leading to different goals for language planning agencies.

Notes

A revision of a paper presented at the Annual Meeting of the European Linguistic Society, Budapest, 1980. I am grateful to Professors Paul Garvin, Richard E. Wood, and Janet Byron, and my wife, Tsippora H. Nahir, for their invaluable comments.

1 Since the order in which the functions, or goals, are presented is of little significance, those included in the earlier classification of Language Planning Functions (Nahir 1977) are presented first. For the readers' convenience they are briefly discussed, too, with certain changes, the result of hindsight.

2 For more on this, see Tauli (1968: 70).

3 See Bills 22 and 101.

4 For the effectiveness of the use of this textbook and a comparison between educated speech and "correct language" in Modern Hebrew, see Nahir (1978b).

5 Commission on the Restoration of the Irish Language, *The Restoration of the Irish Language* (1965), p. 13.

6 *Records of the Hebrew Language Committee* (Jerusalem, 1912), p. 11; reprinted by the Hebrew Language Academy on the 80th anniversary of the founding of the Committee (1970); my translation from Hebrew.

7 For discussions of various aspects of the Hebrew revival, see Bachi (1956), Fellman (1973), and Nahir (1974, 1978a). See also a discussion of the sociocultural factors involved in the revival in Nahir (1983).

8 Quoted in C. J. Hayes, *The Historical Evaluation of Modern Nationalism* (New York: Macmillan, 1941), p. 64.

9 I am grateful to Richard E. Wood for drawing this to my attention.

10 From P. A. Pettersson, *Språkvård*, February 12, 1978, reported by B. H. Jernudd, *Language Planning Newsletter* 4/4 (1978).

11 M. H. Ibrahim, "The Arabic Language Academy of Jordan," *Language Planning Newsletter* 5/4 (1979): 2.

12 For a description of the lexical work of this and other non-Academy agencies in Israel, see Nahir (1979).

13 Reported by Richard E. Wood, *Language Planning Newsletter* 4/1 (1978).

14 Claude Adams, *Winnipeg Free Press*, November 6, 1978.

15 This process has been regularly followed in recent issues of *Simply Stated*, newsletter of the Document Design Center of the American Institute for Research.

16 "Need" as a condition for language use and as a factor in the revival of Hebrew has been discussed in Nahir (1977, 1983).

17 *Linguistic Reporter* 22/3 (1979).

18 East–West Culture Learning Institute Information Sheet, Honolulu, Hawaii (1980).

19 Ernesto Zierer summarizes the contents of the conference in *Linguistic Reporter* 22/5 (1980): 8. Its objectives are discussed in *Language Planning Newsletter* 5/4 (1979).

20 Abstracted from Catherina Grünbaum's article in *Språkvård*, February 19, 1978, reported by Björn H. Jernudd, *Language Planning Newsletter* 4/4 (1978): 8.

21 Richard E. Wood, *Language Planning Newsletter* 6/1 (1980).

22 In fact, the Office de la Language Française, one of Quebec's language planning agencies, has been active in other functions as well, such as (Internal) Language Purification, Lexical Modernization, and Terminology Unification, as charged by a series of laws (Bills 63, 22, 101; McConnell 1977).

23 For a recent analysis of the foreign-language resources in the United States, see Berryman et al. (1979).

24 *Frisian News Items* 36/5 (1980).

25 I am grateful to Richard E. Wood for drawing this example to my attention.

References

Aavik, Johannes. 1924. *Keeleuuenduse äärmised võimalused* (The Extreme Possibilities of Language Reform). Tartu: n.p.

Alatis, James E. (ed.). 1978. *International Dimensions of Bilingual Education.* Washington, D.C.: Georgetown University Press.

Alatis, James E. and G. Richard Tucker (eds.). 1979. *Language in Public Life.* Washington, D.C.: Georgetown University Press.

Alisjahbana, S. Takdir. 1971. "Language Policy, Language Engineering, and Literacy in Indonesia and Malaysia." In Thomas A Sebeok (ed.), *Current Trends in Linguistics.* The Hague: Mouton, vol. 8, 1087–1109.

Bachi, Roberto. 1956. "A Statistical Analysis of the Revival of Hebrew in Israel." *Scripta Hierosolymitana* 3: 179–247.

Barber, Bernard. 1979. "Communication between Doctor and Patient: What Compliance Research Shows." In James E. Alatis and G. Richard Tucker (eds.), 119–125.

Barnes, Dayle. 1973. "Language in Mainland China: Standardization." In Joan Rubin and Roger Shuy (eds.), 34–54.

Battison, Robbin. 1980. "Document Design: Language Planning for Paperwork." *Language Planning Newsletter* 6/4: 1–5.

Berryman, Sue E. et al. 1979. *Foreign Language and International Studies Specialists: The Marketplace and National Policy.* Santa Monica, Cal.: Rand Corporation.

Bourhis, Richard Y. (ed.). 1984. *Conflict and Language Planning in Quebec.* Clevedon, UK: Multilingual Matters.

Braga, Giorgio. 1979. "International Languages: Concept and Problems." *International Journal of the Sociology of Language* 22: 27–49.

Byron, Janet. 1979. "Language Planning in Albania and in Albanian-Speaking Yugoslavia." In Richard E. Wood (ed.), 15–44.

Charrow, Veda R. and Robert P. Charrow. 1979. "Characteristics of the Language of Jury Instructions." In James E. Alatis and G. Richard Tucker (eds.), 163–185.

Cheng, Chin-Chuan. 1979. "Language Reform in China in the Seventies." In Richard E. Wood (ed.), 45–57.

Cobarrubias, Juan and Joshua A. Fishman (eds.). 1983. *Progress in Language Planning.* Berlin: Mouton.

Commission on the Restoration of the Irish Language. 1965. *The Restoration of the Irish Language.* Dublin: Stationery Office.

De Bessé, Bruno. 1980. "Terminology Committees in France: Balance and Perspectives." *International Journal of the Sociology of Language* 23: 43–49.

DeFrancis, John. 1967. "Language and Script Reform." In Thomas A. Sebeok (ed.), *Linguistics in East Asia and South East Asia. Current Trends in Linguistics.* The Hague: Mouton, vol. 2, 130–150.

DeFrancis, John. 1977. "Language and Script Reform in China." In Joshua A. Fishman (ed.), 121–148.

Deutsch, Karl W. 1942. "The Trend of European Nationalism – the Language Aspect." Reprinted in Joshua A. Fishman (ed.), *Readings in the Sociology of Language.* The Hague: Mouton, 1968, 598–606.

Eastman, Carole M. 1983. *Language Planning: An Introduction.* San Francisco: Chandler and Sharp.

Felber, Helmut. 1980. "In Memory of Eugen Wüster, Founder of the General Theory of Terminology." *International Journal of the Sociology of Language* 23: 7–14.

Fellman, Jack. 1973. *The Revival of a Classical Tongue: Eliezer Ben-Yehuda and the Modern Hebrew Language.* The Hague: Mouton.

Fellman, Jack and Joshua A. Fishman. 1977. "Language Planning in Israel: Solving Terminological Problems." In Joan Rubin et al. (eds.), 79–95.

Ferguson, Charles A. 1968. "Language Development." In Joshua A. Fishman et al. (eds.), *Language Problems of Developing Nations*. New York: Wiley, 27–36.

Ferguson, Charles A. 1978. "Language and Global Interdependence." In E. M. Gerli et al. (eds.), *Language in American Life*. Washington, D.C.: Georgetown University Press, 23–31.

Fishman, Joshua A. 1971a. "The Impact of Nationalism on Language Planning." In Joan Rubin and Björn H. Jernudd (eds.), 3–20.

Fishman, Joshua A. 1971b. "The Sociology of Language: An Interdisciplinary Social Science Approach to Language in Society." In Joshua A. Fishman (ed.), *Advances in the Sociology of Language*. Reprinted, The Hague: Mouton, 1976, vol. 1, 217–404.

Fishman, Joshua A. 1972. *The Sociology of Language*. Rowley, Mass.: Newbury House.

Fishman, Joshua A. 1973. "Language Modernization and Planning in Comparison with Other Types of National Modernization and Planning." *Language in Society* 2: 23–43. Reprinted in Joshua A. Fishman (ed.), *Advances in Language Planning*. The Hague: Mouton, 1974, 79–102.

Fishman, Joshua A. (ed.). 1977. *Advances in the Creation and Revision of Writing Systems*. The Hague: Mouton.

Fishman, Joshua A. et al. 1966. *Language Loyalty in the United States*. The Hague: Mouton.

Fishman, Joshua A., Robert L. Cooper, and Andrew W. Conrad. 1977. *The Spread of English: The Sociology of English as an Additional Language*. Rowley, Mass.: Newbury House.

Ford, J. C. 1976. "A Linguistic Analysis of Doctor Patient Communication Problems." Dissertation, Georgetown University, Washington, D.C.

Forster, Peter G. 1971. "Esperanto as a Social and Linguistic Movement." In *Pensiero e Linguaggio in Operazioni* (Thought and Language in Operation), II, 201–215.

Forster, Peter G. 1982. *The Esperanto Movement*. The Hague: Mouton.

Garvin, Paul L. 1973. "Some Comments on Language Planning." In Joan Rubin and Roger Shuy (eds.), 24–33. Reprinted in Joshua A. Fishman (ed.), *Advances in Language Planning*. The Hague: Mouton, 1974, 69–78.

Geerts, Guido et al. 1977. "Successes and Failures in Dutch Spelling Reform." In Joshua A. Fishman (ed.), 179–245.

Gundersen, Dag. 1977. "Successes and Failures in the Reformation of Norwegian Orthography." In Joshua A. Fishman (ed.), 247–265.

Guxman, M. M. 1968. "Some General Regularities in the Formation and Development of National Languages." In Joshua A. Fishman (ed.), *Readings in the Sociology of Language*. The Hague: Mouton, 766–784.

Halldórsson, Halldór. 1979. "Icelandic Purism and Its History." In Richard E. Wood (ed.), 76–86.

Haugen, Einar. 1966a. "Dialect, Language, Nation." *American Anthropologist* 68: 922–935.

Haugen, Einar. 1966b. *Language Conflict and Language Planning: The Case of Modern Norwegian*. Cambridge: Harvard University Press.

Haugen, Einar. 1966c. "Linguistics and Language Planning." In William Bright (ed.), *Sociolinguistics*. The Hague: Mouton, 50–71. Reprinted in Anwar S. Dil (ed.), *The Ecology of Language: Essays by Einar Haugen*. Stanford, Cal.: Stanford University Press, 1972, 159–190.

Haugen, Einar. 1983. "The Implementation of Corpus Planning: Theory and Practice." In Juan Cobarrubias and Joshua A. Fishman (eds.), *Progress in Language Planning*. The Hague: Mouton, 269–289.

Heyd, Uriel. 1954. *Language Reform in Modern Turkey*. Jerusalem: Israel Oriental Society.

Hofman, John E. and Haya Fisherman. 1971. "Language Shift and Maintenance in Israel." *International Migration* Review 5/2: 204–226. Reprinted in Joshua A. Fishman (ed.), *Advances in the Sociology of Language*. The Hague: Mouton, 1972, vol. 2, 342–364.

Ibrahim, M. H. "The Arabic Language Academy of Jordan." *Language Planning Newsletter* 5/4 (1979): 1–3.

Inman, Marianne. 1980. "Foreign Languages and the U.S. International Corporation." *Modern Language Journal* 64/1: 64–74.

Isayev, M. I. 1977. *National Language in the U.S.S.R.: Problems and Solutions*. Moscow: Progress Publishers.

Jacob, H. 1947. *A Planned Auxiliary Language*. London: Dobson.

Jernudd, Björn H. 1973. "Language Planning as a Type of Language Treatment." In Joan Rubin and Roger Shuy (eds.), 11–23.

Jernudd, Björn H. 1977. "Three Language Planning Agencies and Three Swedish Newspapers." In Joan Rubin et al. (eds.), 143–149.

Kachru, Braj B. 1975. "Lexical Innovations in South Asian English." *International Journal of the Sociology of Language* 4: 55–74.

Kelman, Herbert C. 1971. "Language as an Aid and Barrier to Involvement in the National System." In Joan Rubin and Björn H. Jernudd (eds.), 21–52.

Kleivan, Inge. 1979. "Language and Ethnic Identity: Language Policy and Debate in Greenland." In William F. Mackey and Jacob Ornstein (eds.), 117–156.

Kloss, Heinz. 1969. *Research Possibilities on Group Bilingualism: A Report*. Quebec: International Center for Research on Bilingualism.

Kuo, Eddie C. Y. 1980. "Language Planning in Singapore." *Language Planning Newsletter* 6/2: 1–5.

Lambert, Wallace E. 1977. "Culture and Language as Factors in Learning and Education." In Fred R. Eckman (ed.), *Current Themes in Linguistics: Bilingualism, Experimental Linguistics, and Language Typologies*. Washington, D.C.: Hemisphere Publishing, 15–48.

Lemaire, Hervé B. 1966. "Franco-American Efforts on Behalf of the French Language in New England." In Joshua A. Fishman et al., 253–279.

Le Page, R. B. 1964. *The National Language Question*. London: Oxford University Press.

Lewis, E. Glyn. 1971. "Migration and Language in the U.S.S.R." *International Migration Review* 5: 147–179. Reprinted in Joshua A. Fishman (ed.), *Advances in the Sociology of Languages*. The Hague: Mouton, vol. 2, 310–341.

McConnell, Grant D. 1977. "Language Treatment and Language Planning in Canada." *Language Planning Newsletter* 3/4: 1–6.

Mackey, William F. 1978. "The Importation of Bilingual Education Models." In James E. Alatis (ed.), 1–18.

Mackey, William, F. and Jacob Ornstein (eds.). 1979. *Sociolinguistic Studies in Language Contact: Methods and Cases*. The Hague: Mouton.

McQuown, Norman A. 1950. Review of *A Planned Auxiliary Language* by H. Jacob, *Language* 26: 175–185. Reprinted in Dell Hymes (ed.), *Language in Culture and Society*. New York: Harper and Row, 1964, 555–563.

Molde, Bertil. 1975. "Language Planning in Sweden." *Language Planning Newsletter* 1/3: 1–4.

Nahir, Moshe. 1974. "Language Academies, Language Planning, and the Case of the Hebrew Revival." Dissertation, University of Pittsburgh.

Nahir, Moshe. 1977. "The Five Aspects of Language Planning: A Classification." *LPLP* 1/2: 107–123.

Nahir, Moshe. 1978a. "Language Planning Functions in Modern Hebrew." *LPLP* 2/2: 89–102.

Nahir, Moshe. 1978b. "Normativism and Educated Speech in Modern Hebrew." *International Journal of the Sociology of Language* 18: 49–67. Reprinted in Moshe Nahir (ed.), *Hebrew Teaching and Applied Linguistics*. Washington, D.C.: University Press of America, 1981, 355–382.

Nahir, Moshe. 1979. "Lexical Modernization in Hebrew and the Extra-Academy Contribution." In Richard E. Wood (ed.), 105–116.

Nahir, Moshe. 1983. "Sociocultural Factors in the Revival of Hebrew." *LPLP* 7/3: 263–284.

Neustupný, J. V. 1970. "Basic Types of Treatment of Language Problems." *Linguistic Communications* 1: 77–98. Reprinted in Joshua A. Fishman (ed.), *Advances in Language Planning*. The Hague: Mouton, 1974, 37–47.

Neustupný, J. V. 1976. "Language Correction in Contemporary Japan." *Language Planning Newsletter* 2/3: 1–5.

Neustupný, J. V. 1983. "Towards a Paradigm for Language Planning." *Language Planning Newsletter* 9/4: 1–4.

Niedzielski, Henry. 1979. "Language Consciousness and Language Policy in Poland." In Richard E. Wood (ed.), 134–159.

Omar, Ashmah Haji. 1975. "Supranational Standardization of Spelling System: The Case of Malaysia and Indonesia." *International Journal of the Sociology of Language* 5: 77–92.

Ó Murchú, Máirtín. 1977. "Successes and Failures in the Modernization of Irish Spelling." In Joshua A. Fishman (ed.), 267–289.

Polomé, Edgar C. 1979. "Tanzanian Language Policy and Swahili." In Richard E. Wood (ed.), 160–170.

Rabin, Chaim. 1971a. "A Tentative Classification of Language Planning Aims." In Joan Rubin and Björn H. Jernudd (eds.), 177–180.

Rabin, Chaim. 1971b. "Spelling Reform – Israel 1968." In Joan Rubin and Björn H. Jernudd (eds.), 95–121.

Rau, G. Subba. 1954. *Indian Words in English: A Study in Indo-British Cultural and Linguistic Relations.* London: n.p.

Ray, P. S. 1963. *Language Standardization.* The Hague: Mouton.

Richmond, Edmun B. 1982. "The Development of a National Literacy Program: The Gambia Project." *LPLP* 6/2: 154–164.

Rondeau, G. 1979. "Une nouvelle branche de la linguistique appliquée: La terminologie." *AILA Bulletin* 26/2: 1–13.

Rubin, Joan. 1978. "The Approach to Language Planning within the United States." *Language Planning Newsletter* 4/4: 1–6; 5/1: 1–6.

Rubin, Joan. 1979. *Directory of Language Planning Organizations.* Honolulu, Hawaii: East-West Center.

Rubin, Joan and Björn H. Jernudd (eds.). 1971. *Can Language Be Planned?* Honolulu, The University Press of Hawaii.

Rubin, Joan and Roger Shuy (eds.). 1973. *Language Planning: Current Issues and Research.* Washington, D.C.: Georgetown University Press.

Rubin, Joan et al. (eds.). 1977. *Language Planning Processes.* The Hague: Mouton.

Rūķe-Draviņa, Velta. 1977. *The Standardization Process in Latvian.* Stockholm: Almqvist and Wiksell.

Sager, J. C. (ed.). 1975. *Standardization of Nomenclature. International Journal of the Sociology of Language* 23.

St. Clair, Robert N. 1980. "What Is Language Renewal?" In Robert St. Clair and W. Leap (eds.), *Language Renewal among Native American Indians.* Rosslyn, Va.: National Clearinghouse for Bilingual Education.

Salzmann, Zdeněk. 1980. "Language Standardization in a Bilingual State: The Case of Czech and Slovak, Two Closely Cognate Languages." *LPLP* 4/1: 38–54.

Sapir, Edward. 1957. "The Function of an International Auxiliary Language." In David E. Mandelbaum (ed.), *Culture, Language and Personality.* Berkeley: University of California Press.

Schiller, Andrew. 1980. "The Language of Accidental Death and Dismemberment: A Case of Forensic Linguistics." Unpublished mimeograph.

Schweda, Nancy L. 1980. "Bilingual Education and Code-Switching in Maine." *Linguistic Reporter* 23/1: 12–13.

Selander, Einar. 1980. "Language for Professional Use from the Swedish Point of View." *International Journal of the Sociology of Language* 23: 17–28.

Shuy, Roger. 1974. "Problems of Communication in the Cross-Cultural Medical Interview." *Working Papers in Sociolinguistics* 19. Austin, Texas: Southwest Educational Development Laboratory.

Shuy, Roger. 1979. "Language Policy in Medicine: Some Emerging Issues." In James E. Alatis and G. Richard Tucker (eds.), 126–136.

Skyum-Nielsen, Peder. 1978. "Language Problems and Language Treatment in the Danish Speech Community." *Language Planning Newsletter* 4/1: 1–5.

Spolsky, Bernard. 1978. *Educational Linguistics: An Introduction*. Rowley, Mass.: Newbury House.

Spolsky, Bernard and James Kari. 1974. "Apachean Language Maintenance." *International Journal of the Sociology of Language* 2: 91–100.

Swift, Jonathan. 1712. "A Proposal for Correcting, Improving, and Ascertaining the English Tongue." In Walter Scott (ed.), *The Works of Jonathan Swift* (with notes), vol. 9. London: n.p., 1883.

Tauli, Valter. 1968. *Introduction to a Theory of Language Planning*. Acta Universitatis Upsaliensis, Studia Philologiae Scandinavicae. Uppsala: University of Uppsala.

Thompson, Roger M. 1974. "Mexican American Language Loyalty and the Validity of the 1970 Census." *International Journal of the Sociology of Language* 2: 7–18.

Tonkin, Humphrey. 1968. "Code or Culture? The Case of Esperanto." *Era* 4.

Van Naerssen, Margaret M. 1978. "ESI, in Medicine: A Matter of Life and Death." *TESOL Quarterly* 12/2: 193–203.

Whiteley, Wilfred H. 1971. "Some Factors Influencing Language Policies in Eastern Africa." In Joan Rubin and Björn H. Jernudd (eds.), 141–158.

Wood, Richard E. 1979a. "A Voluntary Non-Ethnic, Non-Territorial Speech Community." In William F. Mackey and Jacob Ornstein (eds.), 433–450.

Wood, Richard E. 1979b. "The Politics of Language: Language Choice in Transnational Radio Broadcasting." *Journal of Communication* 29/2: 112–123.

Wood, Richard E. 1979c. *National Language Planning and Treatment*. Special Issue, *Word* 30: 1–2.

27

Literacy and Language Planning

Nancy H. Hornberger

In a world which is simultaneously coming together as a global society while it splinters apart into ever smaller ethnically-defined pieces, the two-faced potential of literacy to both open and bar doors of opportunity becomes increasingly evident. (See Barton 1994 on the globalisation and diversification of literacy itself.) As the new literacy studies of the past decade turn our attention to the variety of literacy practices and their inextricable links to cultural and power structures in society (Street, 1993a:7), and bring to light 'the often ignored language and literacy skills of non-mainstream people and . . . the ways in which mainstream, school-based literacy often serves to perpetuate social inequality while claiming, via the literacy myth, to mitigate it' (Gee, 1991:268), long-dominant assumptions that literacy is a technical skill, neutral, universal, and key to both individual and societal development, and that there is a 'great divide' of difference between oral and literate cultures (cf. Street, 1988), give way to the realisation that not only are there continuities across oral and literate traditions, but that there are also contradictions inherent within literacy itself (Graff, 1986:72–74; Hornberger 1994–6).

Nowhere are these tensions more evident than in multilingual nations, where literacy development faces the challenge of attending to a multilingual population, many of whom do not speak the country's official language. The variety among these multilingual nations is great. A recent UNESCO document suggests that multilingual nations can be characterised in terms of four main contextual possibilities, depending on whether there exists within the nation: no one linguistic majority (e.g. Nigeria, with three major languages and 400 others), a locally developed lingua franca (e.g. Swahili in the East African countries), a predominant indigenous language (e.g. Quechua in Peru, Ecuador, and Bolivia), or multiple language with literary and religious traditions (e.g. India with over 1000 languages and twelve scripts) (UNESCO, 1992:15–18 as cited by Fordham, 1994).

In a memorable piece entitled 'The Curse of Babel,' Einar Haugen argued eloquently that 'language (diversity) is not a problem unless it is used as a basis for discrimination' (1973:40). More recently, Dell Hymes has reminded us of the difference between actual and potential equality among languages – that while all languages are potentially equal, they are, for social reasons, not actually so (1992:2–10). The same is true for literacies: all literacies are potentially equal, but, for social reasons, not actually so. Literacy is, simultaneously, potential liberator and weapon of oppression (Gee, 1991:272). For literacy developers in multilingual contexts, then, the question is not so much: how to develop literacy? but, which literacies to develop for what purposes?

A persistent model of literacy development has been that of national literacy; competing models include mother tongue literacy, multiple literacies, local literacies, and biliteracies. National literacy implies the existence of a national literacy, one national literacy, such as those promoted in much of Europe, in the US and other Western developed nations. Joshua Fishman (1968; 1971) suggests that the choice of one or another national language reflects either an underlying *nationalism* which seeks sociocultural integration based on authenticity or an underlying *nationism* which seeks politico-geographic integration based on efficiency. Yet, Fishman also suggests that the choice for one national language is not the only possibility; rather, given that not all language differences that exist are noted let alone ideologised by their speakers, that conscious and even ideologised language differences need not be divisive, and that most new nations are not ethnic nations, another possible national language policy choice is diglossia, wherein a language of wider communication (LWC) is the language of government, education, and industrialisation, while local languages are used for home, family, and neighbourhood purposes. I suggest that the same can be said for national literacy and local literacies.

Mother tongue literacy offers an alternative to the national literacy model. The axiomatic principle that people acquire literacy best in their own mother tongue, as formulated in UNESCO's 1953 statement, has been widely implemented in mother tongue literacy education throughout the world for the past four decades especially (Limage, 1994). Mother tongue literacy as an alternative or complement to national literacy is not without controversy however; the objections and limitations reviewed and refuted in that early UNESCO document are still very much with us. Objections include that the language lacks a grammar and an alphabet, that the child already knows his/her mother tongue, that the use of the mother tongue will prevent acquisition of the second language, and that the use of vernacular languages impedes national unity; while practical limitations cited are those of inadequate vocabulary, shortage of educational materials, multiplicity of languages in a locality or country, need for reading material, shortage of suitably trained teachers, popular opposition to use of the mother tongue, and special problems surrounding the choice of a lingua franca or pidgin for mother tongue literacy instruction. Nearly all of these objections and limitations have met with creative and effective solutions in one case or another over the past forty years, yet the desirability of mother tongue literacy remains a debated point.

Other alternative models are those of multiple literacies, and more recently, local literacies, as introduced by Street. By multiple literacies, he intends to underline the fact that literacy is not one uniform technical skill, but rather it is something different in each different context and society in which it is embedded (Street, 1984). By local literacies, he refers to those literacy practices that are closely connected with local and regional identities and indeed often overlooked by international or national literacy campaigns. In Street (1994a), he suggests three possible local literacies: local literacies that consist of the different languages and writing systems within a national context; local literacies that are invented, 'often by indigenous peoples in the face of the dominant literacies of colonial powers' (1994); and vernacular literacies, which involve *not* a different language nor a different writing system, but a different literacy practice (here, vernacular is used in the sense of everyday, but not to refer to vernacular language; cf. Street, 1993a:221).

Finally, in my own work (Hornberger, 1989, 1990b, 1992, 1994), I suggest the model of biliteracies, and by extension, multiliteracies, as another alternative. In this model, any instance – whether it be an individual, a situation, or a society – in which communication occurs in two or more languages in or around writing, is an instance of biliteracy. The model situates biliteracies (or instances of biliteracy) within nine nested and intersecting continua which define biliterate development, biliterate media and contexts of biliteracy. Thus, biliteracies are seen as developing along intersecting first language–second language, receptive–productive, and oral–written language skills continua; through the medium of two (or more) languages/literacies whose linguistic structures vary from similar to dissimilar, whose scripts range from convergent to divergent, and to which the developing biliterate individual's exposure varies from simultaneous to successive; and in contexts which range from micro to macro levels and are characterised by varying mixes along the monolingual–bilingual and oral–literate continua.

What all of these latter models of literacy – mother tongue literacy, multiple literacies, local literacies, biliteracies – have in common are notions of a variety and diversity of literacies, reflective and constitutive of specific contexts and identities (cf. Street, 1992). Given such a model of literacy, how can we approach our earlier question, which literacies to develop for what purpose? We need a framework which outlines our options, which identifies different literacies and their different goals and uses, in order to begin to address the question.

Language planning, referring to 'deliberate efforts to influence the behaviour of others with respect to the acquisition, structure, or functional allocations of their language codes' (Cooper, 1989:45), offers one such possible framework for thinking about literacy planning. Table 1 represents my attempt to integrate some two decades of language planning scholarship into one coherent framework for this purpose. The paragraphs below provide a skeletal explanation of the table.[1]

The first use of the term language planning in the literature dates back to 1959, when Haugen used it in his study of language standardisation in Norway (1959:8). The first use of the widely accepted status planning/corpus planning distinction was by Heinz Kloss (1969); while acquisition planning as a third type of language planning was introduced twenty years later (Cooper, 1989). With respect to language/literacy planning, we may think of status planning as those efforts directed toward the allocation of functions of languages/literacies in a given speech community; corpus planning as those efforts related to the adequacy of the form or structure of languages/literacies; and acquisition planning as efforts to influence the allocation of users or the distribution of languages/literacies, by means of creating or improving opportunity or incentive to learn them, or both. These three types comprise the vertical axis of the table.

The horizontal axis presents another distinction made early in the language planning literature, between policy and cultivation approaches to language planning (Neustupný, 1974). The policy approach, seen as attending to matters of society and nation, at the macroscopic level, emphasising the distribution of languages/literacies, and mainly concerned with standard language, is often interpreted to be the same as the status language planning type; while the cultivation approach, seen as attending to matters of language/literacy, at the microscopic level, emphasising ways of speaking/writing and their distribution, and mainly concerned with literary language, is often

Table 1 Language planning goals: An integrative framework

Approaches	Policy planning (on form)	Cultivation planning (on function)
Types	Goals	Goals
Status planning (about uses of language)	Standardisation status Officialisation Nationalisation Proscription	Revival Maintenance Interlingual communication → International → Intranational Spread
Acquisition planning (about users of language)	Group Education/school Literature Religion Mass media Work	Reacquisition Maintenance Foreign language/second language Shift

Corpus planning (about language)	Standardisation
	  Corpus
	  Auxiliary code
	  Graphisation
		Modernisation
		  Lexical
		  Stylistic
		Renovation
		  Purification
		  Reform
		  Stylistic simplification
		  Terminology unification

Based on Ferguson, 1968; Kloss, 1968; Stewart, 1968; Neustupný, 1974; Haugen, 1983; Nahir, 1984; Cooper, 1989.

interpreted to be synonymous with corpus planning. Yet the match is not perfect, and Haugen offers a more finely-tuned interpretation which maps these two binary distinctions (status/corpus and policy/cultivation) onto a fourfold matrix defined by society/language and form/function axes and comprising selection of norm, codification of norm, implementation of function, and elaboration of function as the four dimensions (1972; 1983). His is the interpretation I use here, with the addition of acquisition planning as a third type, thus yielding six, rather than four dimensions of language/literacy planning.

Language/literacy planning types and approaches do not in and of themselves carry a political direction, however, and thus cannot begin to answer our question about which literacies to develop for which purposes. Rather, it is the goals that are assigned to the language literacy planning activities that determine the direction of change envisioned (cf. Hornberger, 1990a:21), and it is to these that we now turn. In my interpretation, and as represented in the table, goals are at the heart of language/literacy planning. The matrix of types and approaches defines the parameters, but the goals identify the range of choices available within those parameters. In what follows, I present some 30 goals upon which there seems to be some consensus in the literature; however, I make no claim that these are the only possible goals.

An early formulation of language planning goals was Ferguson's (1968) discussion of standardisation, graphisation, and modernisation, which I have placed in the figure under corpus policy and corpus cultivation planning, respectively (Ferguson's cover term, language development, seems to correspond to corpus planning). The definitions Ferguson provided then for language planning can be applied to literacy planning today: standardisation, referring to the development of a literacy norm which overrides regional and social literacies, and graphisation, referring to the provision of a writing system for a hitherto unwritten language, both attend to the formal aspects of languages/literacies (cf. Haugen's codification, 1983:271–2); while modernisation, referring to the lexical and stylistic development of a language literacy for its expansion into hitherto unused domains, attends to the cultivation of languages/literacies for particular functions.

In a pair of articles, Moshe Nahir (1977; 1984) identified eleven goals of language planning, nine of which I interpret as representing cultivation planning, of the status and corpus types, respectively. Revival, maintenance, spread, and interlingual communication all exemplify status cultivation, or the cultivation of a language/literacy's status by increasing its functional uses (cf. Haugen's implementation, 1983:272[2]); while lexical modernisation, purification, reform, stylistic simplification, and terminology unification belong to corpus cultivation, that is, the cultivation of a language/literacy's form for additional functions (cf. Haugen's elaboration, 1983:273–6). Nahir's remaining two goals, standardisation and auxiliary code standardisation will be taken up below.

Beginning then with status cultivation planning, we have revival, maintenance, interlingual communication, and spread. I provide brief paraphrases of Nahir's (1984) original definitions and examples, with my own *italicised* additions emphasising the applicability of these goals to literacy. Revival as a language/literacy planning goal refers to the effort to restore a language with few or no speakers *or a literacy with few or no users* to use as a normal means of communication in a community; Hebrew is the oft-cited example of success. Maintenance, says Nahir, is the effort to preserve the use of the native language, *or native literacy*, in situations where the status of the language/*literacy* as a means of communication, a cultural medium, or a symbol of group or national identity is (or is perceived to be) under threat due to political, social, economic, educational or other pressures; here Nahir gives the maintenance of French in Quebec and of minority languages in the US as examples of dominant and ethnic language maintenance, respectively. Interlingual communication refers to efforts toward facilitating communication between members of different speech communities, whether by use of an artificial or auxiliary language/*literacy* (e.g. Esperanto for international communication), or a language/*literacy* of wider communication (e.g. Spanish as a regional language in Latin America, or English as an intranational language in India), or by adapting cognate languages for greater mutual intelligibility (e.g. the Scandinavian languages). Finally, spread, such as the remarkable spread of Bahasa Indonesia/Malay from about 15 million to 125 million speakers in a few decades, refers to the attempt to increase the number of speakers of a language *or users of a literacy* at the expense of another language/*literacy*.

Turning now from the cultivation of a language/literacy's status by increasing its functional uses to the cultivation of a language/literacy's form for additional functions, Nahir's five goals, for each of which he provides abundant examples, are: lexical mod-

ernisation – assisting in the development of terms for new borrowed concepts: purification – prescribing correct usage and protecting against internal change: reform –
deliberate change in specific aspects of the language or literacy, with the intention of
improving it; stylistic simplification – reducing ambiguity in lexicon, grammar, and
style, particularly as it occurs in professional jargon and terminology unification –
reducing ambiguity in terminology, particularly technical and scientific terminology.

Note that while lexical modernisation corresponds to Ferguson's (1968) original
modernisation (which included both lexical and stylistic modernisation), the remaining four corpus cultivation goals (purification, reform, stylistic simplification and terminological unification) do not. Cooper's (1989) addition of renovation, as a fourth
corpus planning goal, to Ferguson's original standardisation, graphisation and modernisation, provides the appropriate rubric for these latter four subgoals. Indeed, as
Cooper (1989:154) points out, the distinction between modernisation and renovation
(both of which belong to corpus cultivation planning in my framework) is that while
modernisation finds ways for existing language/literacy forms to serve new functions,
renovation does the opposite, finding new forms to serve new functions. It is to this
latter goal, renovation, that the subgoals purification, reform, stylistic simplification and
terminological unification all belong.

Nahir's remaining two goals, standardisation and auxiliary code standardisation,
bring us to a closer look at the term standardisation. In the language planning literature, the term covers a broad spectrum of meanings, as the following sample of definitions will serve to illustrate:

> Language standardisation is the attempt to turn a language or dialect spoken in a region
> . . . into one that is accepted as the major language of the region . . . (Nahir, 1984:303–4)

> Standardisation . . . consists basically of creating a model for imitation and of promoting
> this model over rival models. (Ray, 1963:70, cited by Karam, 1974:114)

> Language standardisation . . . (means) prescription of linguistic norms . . . (Tauli,
> 1974:62)

> Language standardisation is the process of one variety of a language becoming widely
> accepted throughout the speech community as . . . the 'best' form of the language . . . The
> concept of standardisation also includes the notions of increasing uniformity of the norm
> itself and explicit codification of the norm. It is sometimes extended also to include . . .
> the choice of one language instead of another as an official or national language . . .
> (Ferguson, 1968:31)

The notion of standardisation which emerges from these definitions is one of a language planning goal that embraces both process and product (Nahir vs. Tauli); both
language status and language corpus (Nahir vs. Ray and Tauli; cf. Ferguson); and means
ranging from recognising or accepting an existing standard (Ferguson), to creating,
selecting, or imposing one (Nahir, Ray, Tauli). Given the breadth of its application, I
have located it under both status and corpus planning in the figure, such that status
standardisation refers to language planning activities that accept or impose a language
as the standard; while corpus standardisation refers to language planning activities that
codify the linguistic forms of that standard as a uniform norm. Related to the latter is

auxiliary code standardisation which seeks to establish uniform norms for auxiliary aspects of language/literacy such as 'signs for the deaf, place names and rules of transliteration and transcription, either to reduce ambiguity and thus improve communication or to meet changing social, political, or other needs or aspirations' (Nahir, 1984:318).

Turning from corpus standardisation back to status standardisation, we enter the status policy dimension of planning (cf. Haugen's selection, 1983:270–1); here the figure includes, along with status standardisation, three goals, none of which appear in Ferguson's, Nahir's, or Cooper's typology, but which are nevertheless widely recognised language planning activities: officialisation, nationalisation, and proscription.

Officialisation refers to planning activity making a given language/literacy official (following Stewart, 1968). Cooper suggests that there are three types of official languages/literacies and uses the case of Israel to exemplify the distinction: statutory official, that is, declared official (e.g. Hebrew and Arabic); working official, that is, used by the government in day-to-day business (e.g. Hebrew, Arabic and English); or symbolic official, that is, used by the government for symbolic purposes (e.g. Hebrew); further, Cooper notes that languages/literacies may be official at the national or the provincial/regional level (1989:100–4).

Another distinction within officialisation is that between vernacularisation and internationalism (Cobarrubias, 1983:66) where vernacularisation refers to the choice and development of an indigenous language/literacy as official language/literacy (e.g. Quechua in Peru in 1975), while internationalism reflects the choice of an international language/literacy of wider communication as official language/literacy (e.g. English in India).

Nationalisation refers to planning activity establishing a national language/literacy (cf. Heath, 1985). While the national language/literacy may also be the national official language/literacy (e.g. Spanish in Mexico), it is not necessarily so. There may be one distinctive indigenous, non-official national language/literacy alongside another, official one (e.g. Guarani and Spanish in Paraguay as national and official, respectively); there may also be multiple, indigenous, regional, non-official languages/literacies alongside another, official one (e.g. in Senegal, French is the official and Jola, Manding, Pulaar, Sereer, Soninke, and Wolof are national languages/literacies (Diop, 1986)).

Proscription refers to planning activity that proscribes the use of a given language/literacy (cf. Kloss, 1968). History provides ample examples of such activity: the Basque language was banned during the first years of Franco's regime in Spain (Cobarrubias, 1983:45); Quechua was banned in Peru from the time of the Tupac Amaru revolt in the late 18th century up to the time of its officialisation in 1975 (Cerrón-Palomino, 1989:21).

As noted above, Cooper introduces acquisition planning as a third planning type (1989:157–63), distinguished from status planning by being about the users rather than the uses of a language/literacy; but by the same token having more in common with status than with corpus planning. Acquisition planning can be classified, he suggests, according to its overt goal, for which he identifies the possibilities of: reacquisition, maintenance, foreign language/second language acquisition, and to which I add shift as a fourth possible goal, thus producing an exact correspondence with the four status cultivation goals (revival, maintenance, interlingual communication and spread). As for acquisition policy planning, the latter five of Stewart's functions, as discussed and amended by Cooper in his discussion of status planning, make up the six goals here, identified in terms of the domains in which users are targeted to receive opportunity and/or incentive to learn the given language/literacy group: education/school, literature, religion, mass media, and work.

What does this figure tell us, in terms of our question: which literacies for which purposes? Beyond identifying possible goals for development of a particular literacy, the figure can also provide a reminder that, no matter what the goal, language/literacy development proceeds best if goals are pursued along several dimensions at once. Fishman has argued that status planning and corpus planning 'are usually (and most effectively) engaged in jointly' (1979:12). The same is true for the more elaborate schematic of planning types/approaches represented by the figure above: language/literacy planning will be most effectively carried out if all six dimensions are attended to. To take a simple example: to declare a language/literacy the national official language/literacy, while not providing incentive or opportunity for it to be a school language nor a writing system and standardised grammar for it, will not go far toward achieving the stated goal.

Similarly, to endow a national official language/literacy with a new writing system that makes it more compatible with certain regional first languages/literacies (reform), while not providing incentive or opportunity for it to be learned nor a cross-regional communicative purpose for its use, will also not go far toward achieving its goal. On the other hand, to undertake a planning activity that not only selects a national official language/literacy, but also seeks to extend its use into interlingual communication, and therefore makes provision to offer opportunity and incentive for people to learn it as a second language through the domains of religion, work, and education; as well as ensuring that its writing system is standardised and its lexicon modernised, offers far greater promise of success.

What the figure does not show, however, is that planning for a given language/literacy never occurs in a vacuum with regard to other languages/literacies. It is a figure that suggests focus on one language/literacy in isolation from others, and it is therefore incomplete with respect to our question about multiple/local/biliteracies and how we plan for them. For this last dimension, we turn to yet another language planning concept – orientations. Ruiz (1984:16) defines orientation as 'a complex of dispositions [largely unconscious and pre-rational] toward language and its role, and toward languages and their role in society.' He goes on to outline three orientations (which are neither the only possible ones, nor are they mutually exclusive of each other):

(1)   a language as problem orientation which would tend to see local languages as problems standing in the way of the incorporation of cultural and linguistic minority groups in society, and to link language issues with the social problems characteristic of such groups – poverty, handicap, low educational achievement, and little or no social mobility;

(2)   a language as right orientation which would tend to see local languages as a basic human and civil right for their speakers, and to seek the affirmation of those rights, often leading to confrontation, since a claim to something is also a claim against something else;

(3)   a language as resource orientation which would tend to see local languages as resources not only for their speakers, but for society as a whole, and to seek their cultivation and development as resources, in recognition of the fact that they are exhaustible not by use, but by lack of use.

'We can leave the oil in the ground, and it will still be there to use in a hundred years; the more we use it, and the more we use it unwisely, the less we have of it later. Just the opposite is true of language and culture. The more we use these, the more we have of them; but the longer we neglect their use, the closer we are to extinguishing them. That has already happened for some languages, and we may be starting to see the consequences. The world will one day end, but the overriding cause is more likely to be a shortage of human resources like language and culture than a shortage of physical resources like coal and oil' (1981:28). The resource orientation applied to local literacies suggests that local literacies will thrive where multiple literacies are seen as a resource, and not a problem.

Consider the example of Quechua literacy in Peru. There, as in other multilingual nations, popular and political voices, as well as educators themselves, commonly assert that there is no point in fostering indigenous local, mother tongue literacy since very little (or no) writing exists in the indigenous mother tongue (in this case, Quechua).[3] In another paper (Hornberger, 1994), I refute that assumption using case studies of three biliterate adults to explore functions and uses of Quechua literacy already existent in Peru: Faustino Espinoza, an 82 year old self-taught scholar of rural origins who uses Quechua literacy for the promotion of the Quechua language; Maria Centeno, a 62 year old city-reared housewife and mother who uses Quechua literacy to teach the Word of God; and Rufino Chuquimamani, a 41 year old rural-born schoolteacher and bilingual education consultant who uses Quechua literacy to investigate and promulgate Quechua knowledge. I go on to argue that, not only does it follow logically that increasing numbers of indigenous mother tongue readers and writers would inevitably lead to more indigenous mother tongue writing, but perhaps more importantly, the promotion of indigenous mother tongue literacy increases the potential for full literate development and fuller social participation of hitherto marginalised sectors of the national society. To return to our opening metaphor of literacy as both a door and a bar to opportunity; if it is true that literacy practices position us, it is also true that they may be sites of negotiation and transformation (cf. Street 1994b). Though literacy may not in actuality be a causal factor in individual and societal development, planning for the development of local literacies opens up the possibility that it can be an enabling one.

Notes

1   Throughout the following discussion, in order to underline my emphasis here on the usefulness of these concepts for literacy planning, I will often use the paired term language/literacy (or languages/literacies) where the original scholar referred only to language (implicitly including literacy).

2   Note that Nuessel (1988:185–7) also groups these four together, under the function which he designates as restorative-augmentative (as opposed to the normative function, which encompasses the other seven goals); he further suggests that the four goals bear a hierarchical relation to each other,

such that revival would be primary, to be followed by maintenance, which in turn could be followed by spread and/or interlingual communication.

3   Quechua, often known as the language of the Incas, is spoken today in Ecuador, Bolivia and several other Andean republics, in addition to Peru, with the total number of speakers exceeding 10 million. For a brief period in the 1970s in Peru, Quechua enjoyed the status of official language co-equal with Spanish (cf. Hornberger, 1988a, b); the current Constitution, however, recognises only that Quechua and Aymara are in official use in zones established by law.

References

Barton, David (1994) Globalisation and diversification: Two opposing influences on local literacies. *Language and Education* 8 (1–2), 3–8.

Cerrón-Palomino, Rodolfo (1989) Language policy in Peru: A historical overview. *International Journal of the Sociology of Language* 77, 11–33.

Cobarrubias, Juan (1983) Ethical issues in status planning. In J. Cobarrubias and J. Fishman (eds) *Progress in Language Planning: International Perspectives* (pp. 41–86). Berlin: Mouton.

Cooper, Robert L. (1989) *Language Planning and Social Change*. Cambridge: CUP.

Diop, Amadou (1986) Language planning problems in Senegal. Unpublished manuscript, University of Pennsylvania.

Ferguson, Charles A. (1968) Language development. In J. Fishman, C. A. Ferguson and J. Das Gupta (eds) *Language Problems of Developing Nations* (pp. 27–35). New York: John Wiley and Sons.

Fishman, Joshua A. (1968) Nationality–nationalism and nation–nationism. In J. A. Fishman, C. A. Ferguson and J. Das Gupta (eds) *Language Problems of Developing Nations* (pp. 39–51). New York: John Wiley and Sons.

Fishman, Joshua A. (1971) The impact of nationalism on language planning. In J. Rubin and B. Jernudd (eds) *Can Language Be Planned? Sociolinguistic Theory and Practice for Developing Nations* (pp. 3–20). University Press of Hawaii.

Fishman, Joshua A. (1979) Bilingual education, language planning, and English. *English World-Wide* 1 (1), 11–24.

Fordham, Paul (1994) Language choice. *Language and Education* 8 (1–2), 65–8.

Gee, James P. (1991) The legacies of literacy: From Plato to Freire through Harvey Graff. In M. Minami and B. Kennedy (eds) *Language Issues in Literacy and Bilingual/Multicultural Education*. Cambridge, Massachusetts: Harvard Educational Review (pp. 266–85) (reprinted from *Harvard Educational Review* (1988) 58, 195–212).

Graff, Harvey J. (1986) The legacies of literacy: Continuities and contradictions in Western society and culture. In S. de Castell, A. Luke and K. Egan (eds) *Literacy, Society and Schooling: A Reader* (pp. 61–86). Cambridge: Cambridge University Press.

Haugen, Einar (1959) Planning for a standard language in Norway. *Anthropological Linguistics* 1 (3), 8–21.

Haugen, Einar (1966) Linguistics and language planning. In William Bright (ed.) *Sociolinguistics* (pp. 50–71). Harmondsworth: Penguin.

Haugen, Einar (1972) Dialect, language, nation. In J. B. Pride and J. Holmes (eds) *Sociolinguistics* (pp. 97–111). Harmondsworth: Penguin.

Haugen, Einar (1983) The implementation of corpus planning: Theory and practice. In J. Cobarrubias and J. Fishman (eds) *Progress in Language Planning: International Perspectives* (pp. 269–90). Berlin: Mouton.

Heath, Shirley Brice (1985) Bilingual education and a national language policy. In J. Alatis and J. Staczek (eds) *Perspectives on Bilingualism and Bilingual Education* (pp. 75–88). Washington DC: Georgetown University Press.

Hornberger, Nancy H. (1988a) *Bilingual Education and Language Maintenance: A Southern Peruvian Quechua Case*. Dordrecht/Providence: Foris. (Reissued by Mouton).

Hornberger, Nancy H. (1988b) Language planning orientations and bilingual education in Peru. *Language Problems and Language Planning* 12 (1), 14–29.

Hornberger, Nancy H. (1989) Continua of biliteracy. *Review of Educational Research* 59 (3), 271–96.

Hornberger, Nancy H. (1990a) Bilingual education and English-only: A language planning framework. *The Annals of the American Academy of Political and Social Science* 508, 12–26.

Hornberger, Nancy H. (1990b) Creating successful learning contexts for bilingual literacy. *Teachers College Record* 92 (2), 212–29.

Hornberger, Nancy H. (1992) Biliteracy contexts, continua, and contrasts: Policy and curriculum for Cambodian and Puerto Rican students in Philadelphia. *Education and Urban Society* 24 (2), 196–211.

Hornberger, Nancy H. (1994) Continua of biliteracy: Functional Quechua literacy and empowerment in Peru. In L. Verhoeven (ed.) *Attaining Functional Literacy: Theoretical Issues and Educational Implications.* Philadelphia: John Benjamins.

Hornberger, Nancy H. (1994–6) Oral and literate cultures. In H. Günther, O. Ludwig, and H. Wenzel (eds) *Writing and Its Use: An Interdisciplinary Handbook of International Research.* Berlin: Walter de Gruyter.

Hymes, Dell H. (1992) Inequality in language: Taking for granted. *Working Papers in Educational Linguistics* 8, 1–30.

Karam, Francis (1974) Toward a definition of language planning. In J. Fishman (ed.) *Advances in Language Planning* (pp. 103–24). The Hague: Mouton.

Kloss, Heinz (1968) Notes concerning a language-nation typology. In J. Fishman, C. Ferguson and J. das Gupta (eds) *Language Problems of Developing Nations.* New York: Wiley and Sons.

Kloss, Heinz (1969) *Research Possibilities on Group Bilingualism: A Report.* Quebec: International Center for Research on Bilingualism.

Limage, Leslie (1994) Lessons from UNESCO on language issues and literacy and the issues so far. *Language and Education* 8 (1–2), 95–100.

Nahir, Moshe (1977) The five aspects of language planning – A classification. *Language Problems and Language Planning* 1 (2), 107–22.

Nahir, Moshe (1984) Language planning goals: A classification. *Language Problems and Language Planning* 8 (3), 294–327.

Neustupný, J. V. (1974) Basic types of treatment of language problems. In J. Fishman (ed.) *Advances in Language Planning* (pp. 37–48). The Hague: Mouton.

Nuessel, Frank (1988) National language academics: The hierarchical aspect of goals in language planning. In J. Lihani (ed.) *Global Demands on Language and the Mission of the Language Academies* (pp. 183–9). University of Kentucky.

Ruiz, Richard (1981) Ethnic group interest and the social good: Law and language in education. Unpublished manuscript, University of Wisconsin, Madison.

Ruiz, Richard (1984) Orientations in language planning. *NABE Journal* 8 (2), 15–34.

Stewart, William (1968) A sociolinguistic typology for describing national multilingualism. In J. Fishman (ed.) *Readings in the Sociology of Language* (pp. 531–45). The Hague: Mouton.

Street, Brian (1984) *Literacy in Theory and Practice.* Cambridge: Cambridge University Press.

Street, Brian (1988) A critical look at Walter Ong and the 'Great Divide'. *Literacy Research Center* 4 (1), 1, 3, 5.

Street, Brian (1992) Literacy practices and the construction of personhood: Cross-cultural perspectives. Unpublished manuscript, University of Sussex.

Street, Brian (1993a) *Cross-cultural Approaches to Literacy.* Cambridge: Cambridge University Press.

Street, Brian (1994a) What do we mean by 'local literacies'? *Language and Education* 8 (1–2), 9–17.

Street, Brian (1994b) Cross-cultural perspectives on literacy. In L. Verhoeven (ed.) *Attaining Functional Literacy: Theoretical Issues and Educational Implications.* Philadelphia: John Benjamins.

Tauli, Valter (1974) The theory of language planning. In Joshua Fishman (ed.) *Advances in Language Planning* (pp. 49–67). The Hague: Mouton.

UNESCO (1953) *The Use of Vernacular Languages in Education.* Paris: UNESCO.

Discussion Questions

1. Imagine that an internal revolution has occurred in a country and what was previously one nation has now been divided into two countries. Linguists would likely argue that the residents of the two newly formed states speak dialects of the same language – perhaps the former national language. However, the residents of the two independent republics might claim that they really speak different languages. Should these varieties be classified as separate languages or as dialects? Why?

2. Consider the following hypothetical situations. Propose a course of action for each problem and indicate the goals and processes involved (as described by Nahir, pp. 423–6) and whether your proposal involves corpus, status or acquisition planning (as described by Hornberger, p. 452).

   a) Imagine that you are a member of the legislative body of a newly formed republic. Your citizens speak three mutually intelligible varieties of the same language, but use two different scripts (A and B). Script A is your own script and is more common among the elite of the country. However, the other two language varieties (spoken by the numerical majority) use script B. You must decide whether or not to teach both scripts in the schools, only one of the two, or to have regional differences. Cost is a consideration since you are not a wealthy country.

   b) You are a member of the Royal Academy of language Z. You must decide whether or not to officially reform the writing system of your language: it no longer reflects pronunciation and different countries that speak Z have already begun their own reforms. There are however many people who worry that if the spelling system is reformed future generations will be prevented from understanding the highly esteemed literature of the past, as it is written in Old Z.

   c) New legislation has been proposed in your country which will make the nation's most common language the official language of the schools and public or legal institutions. You are an immigrant who fears that many people in the immigrant community would be denied access to services if this legislation were put into effect.

   d) You are a member of an indigenous group which has been bilingual in your native language and the dominant (national) language for many generations. Recently more and more of the tribal members have attended university in the dominant language and have begun to work in mainstream professions. As a result use of the native language has begun to decline. You are interested in preserving the indigenous language and advocate its use in the public schools.

3. Investigate the language policies of your own country or community. How are minority groups or immigrants who are not proficient in the national language dealt with? Who decides what language will be used in legislation or education? Are there any controversies about language use?

Part XI

Multilingualism, Policies, and Education

Introduction

Bilingual education "can be defined generically as education involving two languages as media of education" (Christian and Genesee 2001: 1). It has been around, if at times with other names, for a very long time, wherever the children of ethnic groups in contact needed schooling. The purpose of bilingual education (BE) has been highly varied, depending on the context, as can be seen from this typology of implicit goals:

1. to assimilate individuals or groups into the mainstream of society. The aim is to socialize people for full participation in the community;
2. to unify a multilingual community. The aim is to bring unity to a multi-ethnic, multi-tribal, or multi-national linguistically diverse polity;
3. to enable people to communicate with the outside world. The aim is to introduce a language of wider communication in addition to the unifying national language so as to make it possible for nationals to interact with foreigners;
4. to gain an economic advantage for individuals or groups. The aim is to provide language skills which are saleable in the job market and can put a person ahead on job and status;
5. to preserve ethnic or religious ties. The preservation of ethnic or religious identity in an individual or group may or may not go against general national goals;
6. to reconcile different political, or socially separate, communities. Language can mediate between social or political groups. The implication may be that the more fortunate have a responsibility to the less fortunate which can be fulfilled partially be learning their language to communicate with them;
7. to spread and maintain a colonial language. This goal, which is similar to the mainstream goal, is to socialize an entire population to a colonial existence and a colonial language;
8. to embellish and strengthen the education of elites. Much of bilingual education in the world is primarily for elites, and much of that which is now generally available to all began as education for elites;
9. to give equal status to languages of unequal prominence in the society. As a democratic or egalitarian policy, two languages of unequal status in a nation may be treated as exactly equal under the law;

10.   to deepen understanding of language and culture. Languages can be used in education to introduce cultures of other times and places, to open new views of reality, or to give insights into human nature (Ferguson et al. 1977: 163–72).

One fact is obvious. Bilingual education frequently serves the interests of the elites or the dominant groups in the education of their children. Gaarder's (1977) crucial distinction between elite bilingualism and folk bilingualism bears repeating. Elitist bilingualism is the hallmark of intellectuals and the learned in most societies, and, one might add, of upper-class membership in many societies, such as those of continental Europe. It is a matter of choice. This is not so with folk bilingualism, which is the result of contact between ethnic groups and competition within a single state, where one of the peoples becomes bilingual involuntarily in order to survive.

Much of the research on BE is contradictory or confusing. One reason for this is the emotional nature of issues in folk bilingualism, whether for language maintenance or shift. Language touches deep roots in nationalism and ethnic membership, and neither researchers nor readers remain immune. It makes for selective use of data. Another reason is a tendency to confuse linguistic factors with sociopolitical concerns. It is the focus on the language rather than on the social conditions which skews the data and distorts the issues. One cannot expect the language medium of education to overcome the social facts of poorly funded schools, a demoralized and poorly trained teacher corps, discrimination and un(der)employment. Nor can research findings persuade against ideologically based political agendas like mother-tongue education for so-called Blacks during the days of apartheid in South Africa or the Unz initiative of 1998, which in effect outlawed BE in California. It is against the background of this scene that Tucker's article on global perspectives on bilingual education should be read and understood. In a non-polemical fashion, he attempts to sort out facts we do know about two languages in education around the world.

A newly developing field is that of language rights. Language rights of a limited nature have been approved by UNESCO and are now awaiting introduction to the United Nations for a vote of approval. Much of the emotional approach to the topic stems from the attempt to create social justice for linguistic minorities, with one of the top demands the right to mother tongue education. Paulston's chapter attempts to sort out this highly contentious set of claims: language rights are an important new topic because their existence usually reveals past and present injustice towards or exploitation of the weak in the world.

References

Christian, Donna and Fred Genesee (eds.). 2001. *Bilingual Education*. Alexandria, VA: TESOL.
Ferguson, Charles, Catherine Houghton and Marie H. Wells. 1977. "Bilingual education: An international perspective," in Bernard Spolsky and Robert Cooper (eds.), *Frontiers of Bilingual Education*. Rowley, MA: Newbury House.
Gaarder, Bruce. 1977. *Bilingual Schooling and the Survival of Spanish in the United States*. Rowley, MA: Newbury House.

Further Reading

August, Diane and Kenji Hakuta. 1998. *Educating Language-Minority Children*. Washington, DC: National Academy Press.

Baetens-Beardsmore, Hugo (ed.). 1993. *European Models of Bilingual Education*. Clevedon, UK: Multilingual Matters.

Baker, Colin. 1996. *Foundations of Bilingual Education and Bilingualism*. Clevedon, UK: Multilingual Matters.

Baker, Colin and Sylvia Prys Jones (eds.). 1998. *Encyclopedia of Bilingualism and Bilingual Education*. Clevedon, UK: Multilingual Matters.

Broeder, Peter and Gus Extra. 1998. *Language, Ethnicity and Education*. Clevedon, UK: Multilingual Matters.

Crawford, James. 2000. *At War with Diversity; US Language Policy in an Age of Anxiety*. Clevedon, UK: Multilingual Matters.

Cummins, Jim. 2000. *Language, Power, and Pedagogy: Bilingual Children in the Crossfire*. Clevedon, UK: Multilingual Matters.

Cummins, Jim and Merrill Swain. 1986. *Bilingualism in Education: A Canadian Case Study*. Clevedon, UK: Multilingual Matters.

Garcia, Ofelia. 1991. *Bilingual Education; Focusschrift in Honor of Joshua A. Fishman*. Amsterdam: Benjamins.

Lambert, Wallace and G. Richard Tucker. 1972. *The Bilingual Education of Children: The St. Lambert Experiment*. Rowley, MA: Newbury House.

Lindholm-Leary, Kathryn. 2001. *Dual Language Education*. Clevedon, UK: Multilingual Matters.

Paulston, Christina Bratt. 1988. *International Handbook of Bilingualism and Bilingual Education*. New York: Greenwood.

Tollefson, James W. (ed.). 2002. *Language Policies in Education*. Mahwah, NJ: Erlbaum.

Tosi, Arturo. 1984. *Immigration and Bilingual Education: A Case Study of Movement of Population, Language Change and Education Within the EEC*. Oxford: Pergamon Press.

28

A Global Perspective on Bilingualism and Bilingual Education

G. Richard Tucker

1 Introduction

The number of languages spoken throughout the world is estimated to be approximately 6,000 (Grimes 1992). Although people frequently observe that a small number of languages such as Arabic, Bengali, English, French, Hindi, Malay, Mandarin, Portuguese, Russian and Spanish serve as important link languages or languages of wider communication around the world, these are very often spoken as second, third, fourth or later-acquired languages by their speakers (see, for example, Cheshire 1991; Comrie 1987; Edwards 1994). The available evidence seems to indicate that governments in many countries deliberately present a somewhat skewed picture of monolingualism as normative by the explicit or implicit language policies that they adopt and promulgate (Crystal 1987). Thus, fewer than 25% of the world's approximately 200 countries recognize two or more official languages – with a mere handful recognizing *more than two* (e.g., India, Luxembourg, Nigeria). However, despite these conservative government policies, available data indicate that there are many more bilingual or multilingual individuals in the world than there are monolingual. In addition, many more children throughout the world have been, and continue to be, educated via a second or a later-acquired language – at least for some portion of their formal education – than the number of children educated exclusively via first language. In many parts of the world, bilingualism or multilingualism and innovative approaches to education which involve the use of two or more languages constitute the normal everyday experience (see, for example, Dutcher 1994; World Bank 1995).

2 Multiple Languages in Education

The use of multiple languages in education may be attributed to, or be a reflection of, numerous factors such as the linguistic heterogeneity of a country or region (e.g., Luxembourg or Singapore); specific social or religious attitudes (e.g., the addition of Sanskrit to mark Hinduism or Pali to mark Buddhism); or the desire to promote national identity (e.g., in India, Nigeria, the Philippines). In addition, innovative language education programs are often implemented to promote proficiency in international language(s) of wider communication together with proficiency in national and regional languages. The composite portrait of language education policies and practices throughout the world is exceedingly complex – and simultaneously fascinating. In Eritrea, for instance, an educated person will likely have attended some portion of schooling taught via Tigrigna *and* Arabic *and* English – and developed proficiency in reading these languages which are written using three different scripts (Ge'ez, Arabic, and Roman)! In Oceania, to take a different example, linguists estimate that a mere 4% of the world's population speaks approximately 20% of the world's 6,000 languages. In Papua New Guinea, a country which has a population of approximately 3 million linguists have described more than 870 languages (Summer Institute of Linguistics 1995). Here it is common for a child to grow up speaking one local indigenous language at home, another in the market place, adding Tok Pisin to her repertoire as a lingua franca, and English if she continues her schooling. Analogous situations recur in many parts of the world such as India which has declared 15 of its approximately 1,650 indigenous languages to be "official"; or Guatemala, or Nigeria, or South Africa – to name but a few countries in which multilingualism predominates, and in which children are frequently exposed to numerous languages as they move from their homes into their communities and eventually through the formal educational system.

3 Prevalent Educational Myths

Despite the prevalence of innovative language education programs around the world, the number of sound, critical, longitudinal and published evaluations remains relatively small, and there are a plethora of *prevalent educational myths* which continually circulate:

- Creoles are not real languages; therefore they cannot be used as media of instruction;
- If the major goal is to develop the highest degree of proficiency and subject–matter mastery via English (or French or XYZ), the more time spent educating the child via English (or French or XYZ), the better;
- Anyone who can speak a language can teach successfully via that language;
- In multilingual countries, it is too "expensive" to develop materials and to train teachers in a number of different languages;
- There is one, and only one, "correct solution" to the choice and sequencing of language(s) for purposes of initial literacy training and content instruction for all multilingual countries.

Against this backdrop, Nadine Dutcher (1994) and I carried out for the World Bank a comprehensive review of the use of first and second languages in education, in which we examined, in some detail, the literature from research conducted in three different types of countries: (1) those with no (or few) mother tongue speakers of the language of wider communication (e.g., Haiti, Nigeria, the Philippines); (2) those with some mother tongue speakers of the language of wider communication (e.g., Guatemala); and (3) those with many mother tongue speakers of the language of wider communication (e.g., Canada, New Zealand, the United States).

Next I describe what I hope will be a few of the familiar highlights of this review – findings which are also consonant with those contained in "Section 3: Case Studies in

Multilingual Education" in the splendid recent volume edited by Cenoz and Genesee (1998) as well as with the papers in the special issue of the *Journal of Multilingual and Multicultural Education* (1996, vol. 17) and selected papers in two of the volumes of the *Encyclopedia of Language and Education* (Cummins and Corson 1997; Tucker and Corson 1997). Interested readers may also wish to review the excellent case study by Gonzalez and Sibayan (1988) as well as the recent volume by Baker and Jones (1998).

4   Conclusions from Extant Research

My reading of the available literature, together with the personal research that I have conducted over the past three decades in varied language education settings through-out the world, leads me to a number of relatively straightforward conclusions.

- The language of school is *very* different from the language of home;
- The development of cognitive/academic language requires *time* (four to seven years of formal instruction);
- Individuals most easily develop literacy skills in a familiar language;
- Individuals most easily develop cognitive skills and master content material that is taught in a familiar language;
- Cognitive/academic language skills, once developed, and content-subject material, once acquired, *transfer* readily;
- The *best* predictor of cognitive/academic language development in a second language is the level of development of cognitive/academic language proficiency in the first language;
- Children learn a second language in different ways depending upon their culture, their group, and their individual personality.

Therefore: If the goal is to help the student ultimately develop the highest possible degree of content mastery and second-language proficiency, time spent instructing the child in a familiar language is a wise investment (cf. Lambert's notion (1980) of "additive" bilingualism).

5   Common Programmatic Threads

Furthermore, Dutcher and I noted that the following common threads run through *all* of the successful programs that we reviewed whose goal was to provide students with multiple language proficiency and with access to academic content material (even though, we noted, a wide range of models is available for implementation):

- Development of the mother tongue is encouraged for cognitive development, and as a basis for learning the second language;
- Parental and community support and involvement are present;
- Teachers are able to understand, speak, and use with a high level of proficiency the language of instruction whether it is their first or second language;

- Teachers are well trained, they have cultural competence and subject-matter knowledge and they continually upgrade their training;
- Recurrent costs for innovative programs are about the same as they are for "traditional" programs (although there may be additional one-time start-up costs);
- Cost–benefit calculations can typically be estimated in terms of the cost savings to the education system, improvements in years of schooling, and enhanced earning potential for students with multiple language proficiency.

The results from published, longitudinal, and critical research undertaken in varied settings throughout the world indicate clearly that the development of multiple language proficiency is possible, and indeed that it is viewed as desirable by educators, policymakers, and parents in many countries. Ironically, that which is viewed as desirable in Eritrea or Luxembourg or the Netherlands or Nigeria or the Philippines or South Africa, to name but a few countries, is not similarly viewed in the United States. Although the focus of this paper is specifically on bilingual education internationally, the findings summarized above are clearly consistent with those reported by researchers in the United States and Canada (see, for example, Brisk 1998; Christian 1996; Thomas and Collier 1996).

6   Cross-cutting Themes

I next comment briefly on two cross-cutting themes which seem to me to be critical linchpins for moving forward policy or planning discussions within the domain of language education reform: (1) the critical role of the child's mother tongue in initial literacy attainment and content-subject mastery and the subsequent transfer of skills across languages; and (2) the natural tension between importing a model versus importing a "cycle of discovery."

6.1   Nurturing the first language

Despite decades of sound educational research, there still remains a belief in many quarters that somehow when an additional language is introduced into a curriculum, the child must go back and relearn all over again concepts already mastered. Although there remains much to be learned about the contexts and strategies that facilitate transfer across languages, the fact that such transfer occurs should not be a topic for debate. The work of Hakuta (1986) and his colleagues provides clear evidence that a child who acquires basic literacy or numeracy concepts in one language can transfer these concepts and knowledge easily to a second or third or other later-acquired languages. The literature, and our practical experience, is replete with examples which confirm the importance of nurturing the child's mother tongue. Gonzalez (1998), in particular, writes and speaks especially compellingly about the need to develop basic functions of literacy, numeracy, and scientific discourse in the L_1 to the fullest extent possible while facilitating transfer to the L_2. Our imperfect understanding of the constructs of so-called Basic Interpersonal Communication Skills (or contextualized language abilities) and Cognitive Academic Language Proficiency (or decontextualized language abilities), and of the cognitive processes that facilitate or impede cross-language transfer of skills, underscores the need for additional basic research on this important topic, but this should not detract from the utility and the practical importance of the underlying concept.

6.2   Importation of models versus importation of "cycles of discovery"

At this stage one is obviously tempted to call for the widespread implementation of new programs based on the results of documented experiences from settings such as Canada, the Philippines, or some of the other countries mentioned previously. However, it may be instructive to underscore the observations made by Swain (1996) at an international conference on bilingualism held in Brunei Darussalam. There, she described some of the critical attributes of Canadian immersion programs and shared with participants the ways in which she and colleagues have continued to reflect upon the products of their earlier research in order to better understand and clarify some of the basic processes underlying successful and unsuccessful language education. She described the need to "transfer" the stages and processes of evaluation, theory building, genera-tion of hypotheses, experimentation, and further evaluation that will help to ensure the implementation of programs appropriate for the unique sociocultural contexts in which they will operate. That is, she cautioned that it is not a particular model of innovative language education (and, in particular, a Western model) that should be transferred, for example to Brunei Darussalam or Namibia or Peru, but rather a "cycle of discovery."

Swain reminded us that the so-called threshold levels of L_2 skills required for suc-cessful participation in formal education may differ quite dramatically across content areas, and that a majority of children face a language "gap" which must be bridged when they move from learning the target language to using the target language as a medium of instruction. Many policy-makers have characterized bilingual education as a "high risk" undertaking by which they mean that it is necessary to attend to a complex set of interacting educational, sociolinguistic, economic, and political factors.

7   Key Issues Warranting Further Attention

Based upon a review of available literature, it is possible to identify four areas which deserve additional attention.

- Sociolinguistic research throughout the world;
- A more thorough examination of the concept and parameters of transfer;
- The development, reproduction and distribution of materials in the so-called truly less commonly spoken languages (e.g., the majority of the African languages spoken in Namibia, the majority of the languages in Papua New Guinea);
- The development of a cadre of trained teachers who are proficient speakers of these languages.

Despite several decades of rather extensive sociolinguistic fieldwork in many areas, there remains much to be done to describe the language situation in many parts of the world.

For example, personnel from the World Bank were recently engaged in a preliminary educational mission to Guinea-Bissau but discovered that they knew relatively little about the distribution and status of languages and their speakers throughout the country, which makes sound educational planning problematic. Many of the world's languages have yet to be written, codified or elaborated. Furthermore, there are no materials available for initial literacy training or for advanced education; nor are there teachers who have been trained to teach via many of the world's languages. These are all issues that have been identified as crucial by the World Bank in a recent report of priorities and strategies for enhancing educational development in the twenty-first century (World Bank 1995) – and they are issues which must be dealt with effectively before systemic reform which will encourage multilingual proficiency can be widely implemented.

8   Conclusions

By way of summary, let me identify a number of important questions that must be addressed whenever parents, educators and administrators discuss the prospects of multilingual education for their communities:

- What are the explicit or implicit goals for formal education in the region?
- Is there general satisfaction throughout the region with the level of educational attainment by all participants (both those who terminate their education relatively early and those who wish to go on to tertiary studies)?
- Is the region relatively homogeneous or is it heterogeneous linguistically and culturally and how would bilingual education complement the linguistic and cultural characteristics of the community?
- Does the region have an explicit or implicit policy with respect to the role of language in education, and how would bilingual education fit or not fit with this existing policy? Is this policy based upon tradition or the result of language (education) planning?
- What priorities are accorded to goals such as the development of broadly based permanent functional literacy, the value of education for those who may terminate their schooling at an early age, and the power of language to foster national identity and cohesiveness?
- Are the language(s) selected for instruction written, codified, standardized, and elaborated?
- Is there a well-developed curriculum for the various levels/stages of formal education (i.e., a framework which specifies fairly explicitly a set of language, content, cognitive, and affective objectives that are then tied to or illustrated by exemplary techniques and activities, and supported by written materials)?
- Are sufficient core *and* reference materials available for teachers and for students in the language(s) of instruction? If not, are there trained individuals available who can prepare such materials?
- Is there a sufficient number of trained and experienced teachers who are fluent speakers of the language(s) of instruction *and* who are trained to teach via that language(s)?

Questions such as these (see Tucker 1991, 1998) must be considered by community leaders as they consider the implementation of any innovative language education program.

As Courtney Cazden (1990) noted in her report for UNICEF, "despite the centrality of language achievements in the developmental agenda of the [child], language issues are rarely in the forefront of thinking about how to plan environments for young children"; "The prevalence of multilingualism in the world adds a particular urgency to the recommendation to attend [to the quality of language instruction available to the child]."

The cumulative evidence from research conducted over the last three decades at sites around the world demonstrates conclusively that cognitive, social, personal, and economic benefits accrue to the individual who has an opportunity to develop a high degree of bilingual proficiency when compared with a monolingual counterpart. The message for educators is clear (see also Tucker 1990): draw upon community resources and involve diverse stakeholders in all phases of program planning and implementation, implement carefully planned and well-articulated sequences of study, utilize trained committed teachers, and begin innovative language education programs that will lead to bilingual or multilingual proficiency for participants as early as possible. The graduates of such programs should be culturally rich, linguistically competent and socially sensitive individuals prepared to participate actively in our increasingly global economy.

References

August, Diane and Kenji Hakuta (eds.). 1997. *Improving Schooling for Language-minority Children: A Research Agenda*. Washington, DC: National Academy Press.

Baker, Colin and Sylvia Prys Jones. 1998. *Encyclopedia of Bilingualism and Bilingual Education*. Clevedon, UK: Multilingual Matters.

Brisk, María Estela. 1998. *Bilingual Education: From Compensatory to Quality Schooling*. Mahwah, NJ: Lawrence Erlbaum.

Cazden, Courtney, Catherine E. Snow and C. Heise-Baigorria. 1990. "Language planning in preschool education with annotated bibliography." Report prepared for the Consultative Group on Early Childhood Care and Development, UNICEF.

Cenoz, Jasone and Fred Genesee (eds.). 1998. *Beyond Bilingualism: Multilingualism and Multilingual Education*. Clevedon, UK: Multilingual Matters.

Cheshire, Jenny (ed.). 1991. *English Around the World: Sociolinguistic Perspectives*. Cambridge: Cambridge University Press.

Christian, Donna. 1996. "Language development in two-way immersion: Trends and prospects." In James. E. Alatis (ed.), *Georgetown University Round Table on Languages and Linguistics 1996*, pp. 30–42. Washington, DC: Georgetown University Press.

Comrie, Bernard (ed.). 1987. *The World's Major Languages*. New York: Oxford University Press.

Crystal, David. 1987. *The Cambridge Encyclopedia of Language*. Cambridge: Cambridge University Press.

Cummins, Jim and David Corson (eds.). 1997. *Second Language Education. Encyclopedia of Language and Education: Volume 5*. Dordrecht, Netherlands: Kluwer Academic Publishers.

Dutcher, Nadine in collaboration with G. Richard Tucker. 1994. "The use of first and second languages in education: A review of educational experience." Washington, DC: World Bank, East Asia and the Pacific Region, Country Department III.

Edwards, John. 1994. *Multilingualism*. London: Routledge.

Gonzalez, Andrew. 1998. "Teaching in two or more languages in the Philippine context." In Jasone Cenoz and Fred Genesee (eds.), *Beyond Bilingualism: Multilingualism and Multilingual Education*, pp. 192–205. Clevedon, UK: Multilingual Matters.

Gonzalez, Andrew and Bonifacio P. Sibayan. 1988. *Evaluating Bilingual Education in the Philippines (1974–1985)*. Manila: Linguistic Society of the Philippines.

Grimes, Barbara. F. 1992. *Ethnologue: Languages of the World*. Dallas, TX: Summer Institute of Linguistics.

Hakuta, Kenji. 1986. *Mirror of Language: The Debate on Bilingualism*. New York: Basic Books.

Lambert, Wallace E. 1980. "The two faces of bilingual education." *NCBE Forum*, 3.

Summer Institute of Linguistics. 1995. *A Survey of Vernacular Education Programming at the Provincial Level Within Papua New Guinea*. Ukarumpa, Papua New Guinea: Summer Institute of Linguistics.

Swain, Merrill. 1996. "Discovering successful second language teaching strategies and practices: From program evaluation to classroom experimentation." *Journal of Multilingual and Multicultural Development*, 17 (1–2): 89–104.

Thomas, Wayne P. and Virginia Collier. 1996. "Language-minority student achievement and program effectiveness." *NABE News*, 19 (6): 33–5.

Tucker, G. Richard. 1990. "Cognitive and social correlates of additive bilinguality." In James E. Alatis (ed.), *Georgetown University Round Table on Languages and Linguistics: 1990*, pp. 90–101. Washington, DC: Georgetown University Press.

Tucker, G. Richard. 1991. "Developing a language-competent American society: The role of language planning." In Allan. G. Reynolds (ed.), *Bilingualism, Multiculturalism, and Second Language Learning*, pp. 65–79. Hillsdale, NJ: Lawrence Erlbaum.

Tucker, G. Richard. 1996. "Some thoughts concerning innovative language education programs." *Journal of Multilingual and Multicultural Development*, 17 (1–2).

Tucker, G. Richard. 1998. "A global perspective on multilingualism and multilingual education." In Jasone Cenoz and Fred Genesee (eds.), *Beyond Bilingualism: Multilingualism and Multilingual Education*, pp. 3–15. Clevedon, UK: Multilingual Matters.

Tucker, G. Richard and David Corson (eds.). 1997. *Second Language Education. Encyclopedia of Language and Education: Volume 4*. Dordrecht, Netherlands: Kluwer Academic Publishers.

Tucker, G. Richard and Richard Donato. 1995. "Developing a second language research component within a teacher education program." In James. E. Alatis (ed.), *Georgetown University Round Table on Languages and Linguistics: 1995*, pp. 453–70. Washington, DC: Georgetown University Press.

World Bank. 1995. Priorities and strategies for education. Washington, DC: The International Bank for Reconstruction and Development.

29

Language Policies and Language Rights
Christina Bratt Paulston

1   Introduction

"Major language legislation in the area of language policy is evidence, within certain political contexts, of contracts, conflicts and inequalities among languages used within the same territory" (Turi 1994, p. 111). So does Turi begin his essay "Typology of Language Legislation." He further states that the fundamental goal of all legislation about language is to resolve the linguistic problems which stem from these language conflicts and inequalities by legally establishing and determining the status and use of the concerned languages. It is a good capsule description of the study of language rights, a new field that has developed recently within language planning and sociolinguistics, because language rights is basically about the legislation – or absence of legislation – for the rights and privileges of languages and their speakers.

A quick glance at any on-line library catalog will verify the newness of this topic. In a library search at the University of Pittsburgh, of the 81 book titles found using the keyword phrase "language rights," 48 were written in the past decade. For the phrase "linguistic rights," all 18 were written since 1979 (with 15 in the 1990s), and for "linguistic human rights," all were written in the 1990s (one is an update of a United Nations report from 1979). Most of these writings concern conditions in Europe and North America; in Europe, these are mostly directly traceable to the European Union and a concern for its minority languages (e.g. Coulmas 1991, Rouland et al. 1996) and to the collapse of the Soviet empire. In Canada, they focus on the long-impending and now acute crisis in Quebec. In the United States, the interest can be traced to the Civil Rights Act of 1964 and the Voting Rights Act of 1965 (Leibowitz 1982, Teitelbaum & Hiller 1977), not only because of the zeitgeist that led to their enactment but primarily because these acts form the legal precedent to most subsequent language legislation in the United States. Also an important impetus for this new interest has been increased immigration from the third world, the Bilingual Education Act of 1968, and the backlash English-Only movement. Formerly colonized areas and nations continue to show a concern for language rights, but this concern typically surfaces under other headings, such as official languages, medium of instruction, or language standardization.

The literature on language policies as language rights and linguistic human rights falls into two major camps. First are the historical and present-day descriptive accounts of official or nonofficial language policies in practice. Some of the best of these have been written by lawyers – not necessarily easy to read (e.g. De Witte 1993) – historians

(Giordan (1992) and Vilfan (1993) are my personal favorites), and political scientists. Typically these accounts are descriptive and atheoretical, and language rights are mostly treated as a dependent or resultant variable. There is no attempt – or perhaps even interest – to predict the consequences of language rights. Language rights are often considered as individual rights, according to the legal situation.

The other camp is exhortatory – at times quite wildly so – and often ideologically biased and can range from ethnic nationalism – e.g. in the Baltic States – to federalist extremism – e.g. in Quebec. These writings are basically concerned with social change or future developments in which language rights is clearly the independent or causal variable. Linguists, anthropologists, politicians, and educators all figure prominently here – some, of course, also belong to the first camp. In the majority, the rights advocated here are based on the notion of group or collective rights.

There is also a middle camp between the two – and a useful literature it is – formed by special-interest groups and organizations such as the Mexican American Legal Defense Fund (MALDEF), the Puerto Rican Legal Defense and Education Fund (PRLDEF), the National Association of Bilingual Education (NABE), and the Center for Applied Linguistics, all of which have distinguished publication lists (see also Domínguez & López 1995). In addition, there is a nonideological and rather nostalgic concern for endangered and disappearing languages, mostly on the part of linguists (Hale et al. 1992, Robins & Uhlenberg 1991). The Endangered Language Fund, Inc, newly founded, is dedicated to the scientific study of endangered languages. The following message, part of its formal statement, on Linguist List (Vol. 7-1595, Nov. 11, 1996), strikes me, though surely it is not intended to, as consumer rights cast as language rights: "Languages have died off throughout history, but never have we faced the massive extinction that is threatening the world right now. As language professionals, we are faced with a stark reality: Much of what we study will not be available to future generations."

2 Definitions

Three terms commonly used in the literature to denote the field are "language rights," "linguistic rights," and "linguistic human rights." There is a remarkable lack of definitions in the literature; the three terms are commonly used synonymously. In addition, they may differ in the law from country to country, resulting in no generally accepted standard legal definition, as Joseph Lo Bianco, Chief Executive of the National Languages and Literacy Institute of Australia, pointed out at the Comparative Education Societies' World Congress in 1996. Language rights and linguistic rights usually do mean the same thing. The latter form is presumably influenced by *derechos lingüisticos* and *droits linguistiques*, as they are known in Spanish and French, respectively. Language rights, in the sense of the German *Sprachenrecht*, may be interpreted, according to Vilfan (1993; for an interesting review, see Ager 1994), as the legal regulation of the use of languages in public life as part of the arrangements dealing with interethnic regulations in a country with a mixed ethnic structure. Other areas of regulation deal with language use in schooling and religious life, the political representation of ethnic groups, and the international protection of minority groups, as well as the rights of members of nondominant ethnic groups in using their particular language in administrative and judicial legal procedures. One objective of language rights for a nondominant ethnic group is the recognition of that group's existence. This implies "the degree of status sought by the group as part of its efforts to overcome a feeling of inferiority acting to hamper members of such a nondominant group in their endeavours both to maintain their ethnic identity and advance in terms of social mobility" (Vilfan 1993).

In his US *Federal Recognition of the Rights of Minority Language Groups*, Leibowitz (1982) does not define language rights outright but does so indirectly in terms of access – political, legal, economic (especially employment (Piatt 1993)), and educational – in a narrative summary of the legislative, administrative, and judicial efforts made to recognize the needs and secure the civil rights (sic) of minority-language citizens. In addition, one may add the concern over access to social policies and health care (Hamel 1997a).

Turi (1994) commented that language legislation is typically aimed at the speakers of a language rather than at the language itself unless that legislation is clearly a public policy law. As an exception, he cited the France Quick Case in which Cour d'appel de Paris in 1984 acquitted a firm of using terms such as "bigcheese" and "hamburger" on the grounds that the French consumers understood them. This ruling was overturned by France's Cour de cassation, which argued that "French language legislation protected the French language rather than francophones," Turi (1994) adds cryptically "without entering into much detail." Some cases cannot help but strike an anglophone as quite amusing.

Linguistic human rights (LHRs), however, is a different concept. Its awkward stylistic tautology – if it is linguistic it must, of course, already be human – derives from the attempt to link language with human rights, i.e. to reframe the issues of language rights in terms of human rights, now a generally accepted notion. "The challenge to lawyers, politicians and language professionals is to see how a human rights perspective can support efforts to promote linguistic justice," wrote Phillipson et al. (1994) in a recent and first major publication on *Linguistic Human Rights: Overcoming Linguistic Discrimination*.

The expression "human rights" is relatively new. It takes the place of "natural rights" and has come into general parlance only since World War II and the atrocities of Nazi Germany. Forerunners to the United Nations' *Universal Declaration of Human Rights* (1948) "as a common standard of achievements for all peoples and all nations" (*Encyclopedia Britannica* 1993) were the US Declaration of Independence, in which it is written that "We hold these truths to be self-evident, that all men are created equal, that they are endowed by their creator with certain inalienable rights, that among these are Life, Liberty and the Pursuit of Happiness" (1776), and the French Declaration of the Rights of Man and the Citizen, which states that "men are born and remain free and equal in rights" these being "Liberty, Property, Safety and Resistance to Oppression" (1789).

The moot point whether language rights are individual or collective (see discussion below) has its roots in the conjunction of Roman law (individual) with Germanic tribal law (collective) at the collapse of the Roman empire. Today LHRs proponents tend to take for granted that both individual and collective rights apply. Human rights are often discussed in terms of "three generations of human rights" proposed by the French jurist Karel Vasak, based on the themes of the French revolution: liberté, égalité, and fraternité. Liberty represents "freedom from"; equality represents individual and collective "rights to" (language rights, had he thought of them, would fit here); and fraternity represents collective "solidarity rights" such as self-determination, economic and social development, and benefit from the common heritage of mankind (e.g. earth-space resources). The latter emerged from the claims of the so-called third-world nations in the postcolonial period, the legitimacy of these being a function of context.

The human rights of the first two "generations" are typically conceived as "quintessentially general or universal in character, in some sense equally possessed by all human beings everywhere, including in some instances even the unborn. In stark contrast to the 'Divine Rights of Kings' and other such conceptions of privilege, human rights extend, in theory, to every person on Earth without discrimination irrelevant to merit" (*Encyclopedia Britannica* 1993). It is precisely this notion of *droits universels* of LHRs which becomes the basic problem with this putative concept (see also Capotorti 1991).

The question of language rights concerns ethnic minorities in most cases, and a word of caution is due here. "Minority" implies quantitative differences only, but as a number of writers (Giordan 1992, Paulston 1994, Vilfan 1993) have pointed out, the most salient difference is that of a superordinate/subordinate status relationship. As Vilfan discusses, it is more correct to speak about privileged or dominant and nonprivileged or nondominant ethnic groups. Dominance, or its lack, depends "upon numerous circumstances, for instance social structure, the dispersion of social groups, the electoral system, historical traditions and the respective prestige of the 'historical nations' involved" (Vilfan 1993).

3   Language Rights and Language Policies as Language Planning

Language policies are probably best considered as a subset of language planning, an important field of sociolinguistics that emerged in the 1960s, triggered by real-world problems (Fishman et al. 1968, Whiteley 1971). This new field of language planning found itself consistently dealing with language policies for linguistic minorities. Even the absence of explicit policy, as Heath (1976) pointed out, is in itself an act of language policy.

This is not to say that historians and political science people do not also write about language policies. They do so, and very well, but they typically deal with them as events (i.e. case studies) or as contextual or dependent variables. For a theoretical understanding of the consequences of language rights, of the causal effect of language rights as language policy, the field of language planning is probably the most rewarding approach to pursue (see e.g. Grabe 1994).

The term "language planning" is usually limited to "the organized pursuit of solutions to language problems, typically at the national level" (Fishman 1973). A recent framework that integrates earlier scholarship is Hornberger's (1994) work on theoretical approaches to language planning and language policy, discussed again in Ricento &

Hornberger (1996). Nancy Hornberger considers policy (concerning matters of society and nation) and cultivation (relating to language and literacy at the microscopic level) planning (Neustupný's (1974) terms originally). She also uses Cooper's (1989) distinction of three types of planning, which Cooper adapted from Kloss (1969): status planning (about uses of language), acquisition planning (about users of language), and corpus planning (about language). Most language policy relating to language rights falls under status planning, e.g. recent choice of national languages as in South Africa, or under acquisition planning, e.g. choice of medium of instruction.

Ricento & Hornberger point out that planning often results in unintended outcomes. (Fishman (1973) had earlier termed such failure "unexpected system linkages.") Implementation may be poor and evaluation nonexistent or dependent on the values of who does the evaluating. They list some issues in the ongoing development of language planning of which the following are of interest here (see e.g. Tollefson 1991, 1995): (*a*) the investigation of specific language policies in specific contexts to provide "richer" explanation (the importance of the context is stressed throughout the article and from my viewpoint rightly so); (*b*) the shift of interest from the nation building and modernization in third-world countries to language rights globally and the perpetuation of structural socioeconomic inequalities and language revitalization; and (*c*) the discovery by English-language teaching (ELT) professionals of critical theory and the historical-structural approach:[1] (*i*) Language policies represent the interests of those in power. (*ii*). Such interests serve to maintain the socioeconomic interests of the elites. (*iii*). These ideologies permeate society at all levels and all its institutions. (*iv*). Individuals do not have freedom of language choice, neither in education nor in social life. They go on to point out that none of the theoretical approaches of language planning policies they discuss can "predict the consequences of a particular policy or show a clear cause/effect relationship between particular policy types . . . and observed outcomes" (Ricento & Hornberger 1996). To which I would add, as they also do later: "Language policy must be evaluated not only by official policy statements or laws on the books but by language behavior and attitudes in *situated*, especially institutional *contexts*" (italics mine; Ricento & Hornberger 1996).

It is indeed the major argument of this review that any real insight into the nature of language rights can only be reached if we consider such rights emic rather than universal. Linguistic human rights is a tempting and facile conceptualization for advocacy purposes, but it holds little explanatory power and may ultimately backfire in that its claims are too strong and therefore more easily dismissed.

4   Principal Concerns

4.1   The territoriality versus the personality principles

Officially bilingual or multilingual nations often resort to either the territoriality or the personality principle in their language legislation. McRae (1983), who has written about many multilingual countries, discussed these principles in an early, excellent article. According to McRae (1975), "[t]he principle of territoriality means that the rules of language to be applied in a given situation will depend solely on the territory in question." Belgium or Switzerland would be examples. "[T]he principle of personality means that the rules will depend on the linguistic status of the person or persons concerned" (McRae 1975). Federal, if not provincial, Canadian legislation affirms the right to services in French or English regardless of territory (see Nelde et al. 1992). After a lengthy discussion of the historical development, McRae adds three further dimensions of language policy, namely the distinction between linguistic equality and minority status, the degree of domain comprehensiveness, and the degree of centralization in decision making. He goes on to demonstrate how these dimensions, combined with the territoriality–personality axis, afford a basis for the analysis and evaluation of language policies in a number of selected countries. "The criteria for the choice of a particular combination of options can be seen as resting on two groups of factors: (1) a set of given environmental factors, including in particular the relative numbers of the language groups, their geographical distribution, economic and social status, levels of political development, and so on and (2) a combination of goals based on the value structure of the society concerned or of one of its constituent groups" (McRae 1975). He concludes that the number of relevant variables seems large enough that no two linguistic situations will be alike in all significant aspects; therefore, one cannot generalize about the relative merits of territoriality or personality per se as alternative principles of language planning. McRae's arguments are worth keeping in mind when one considers universal language rights.

In a more recent discussion, based on the situations in Belgium, Canada, and Quebec, Nelde et al. (1992) argue basically the same point: "Because of the inappropriateness of adopting either a model based upon the territoriality or the personality principles and given the essential need for compromise in most concrete situations, the measures we formulate are located somewhere in between both principles." (For a similar discussion of Catalonia, see Woolard (1985).) They acknowledge state intervention in language planning in legislative functions (promulgation of laws), executive functions (writing and implementation of laws), administrative functions (introduction and assurance of respect for laws), and judiciary functions (arbitration on the constitutionality and on the respecting of laws) – a distinction of functions I find quite helpful. They go on to point out, however, that "the motor of linguistic planning" is made up of collectivities, i.e. special-interest groups, not necessarily based on territorial linguistic communities. For example, francophones in Quebec were both for and against the latest referendum vote on sovereignty for Quebec. This leads the authors to consider the personality principle in terms of individual and collective rights. They cite Woehrling (1989, my translation): "Language is a collective possession which can only be used and maintained in a group. . . . The collective nature of these rights does not disappear simply because they are legally attributed to individuals and they can individually claim the benefit." The resultant three concepts – territorial, individual, and collective rights – prevail in linguistic rights, by which I presume the authors mean they are the primary legal bases or foundations for language rights. There is a sizable literature on these concepts – territoriality, personality, individual, collective – but I have found the Nelde–Labrie–Williams model to be the most helpful. They conclude inter alia that language planning should "genuinely take into account the situational and contextual characteristics of the linguistic groups" (Nelde et al. 1992), a common argument in the language rights literature.

It is interesting in this context to consider the Bord na Gaeilge (1988) report *The Irish Language in a Changing Society*. The report mentions that legislation inevitably interprets rights as attaching to individuals rather than to groups or collectivities and that non-Irish speakers are allowed to build houses in Gaeltacht areas and so become a threat to the survival of the minority language: "Individual rights become a threat to the common good" (Bord na Gaeilge 1988, p. 95). Compare the Irish situation to that of Åland, a set of islands in the Baltic which is an autonomous region of Finland but is Swedish speaking. The European Union recently approved the so-called Ålandprotocol, which grants as exception the right that only Ålanders can buy land and farm the soil (Berglund 1995). No reason is given in the report for this legislation, but if anything is based on territorial rights, this certainly is – especially in contrast with the Irish legislation. Whatever the intention of the law, it will certainly serve to maintain Swedish on the islands (the rest of Finland shows shift from Swedish to Finnish).

4.2   Universal versus emic language rights

The leading proponents of LHRs are Tove Skutnabb-Kangas and Robert Phillipson (1994 – see especially the bibliography; see also Gomes de Matos 1993). A fairly succinct introduction to this topic is the article "Linguistic Rights and Wrongs" (Phillipson & Skutnabb-Kangas 1995), in which they recapitulate their basic arguments: Linguistic rights are one type of human rights, part of a set of inalienable, universal norms for just enjoyment of one's civil, political, economic, social, and cultural rights (p. 483). After a review of human rights and LHRs, they make the generalization that lack of linguistic rights is one of the causal factors in certain conflicts, and that linguistic affiliation is a rightful mobilizing factor in conflicts with multiple causes where power and resources are unevenly distributed along linguistic and ethnic lines (1995). They end their article with what a Universal Declaration of Linguistic Human Rights "should guarantee, in our view":

> A.   everybody can: 1. identify with their mother tongue(s) and have this identification accepted and respected by others; 2. learn the mother tongue(s) fully, orally (when physiologically possible) and in writing (which presupposes that minorities are educated through the medium of their mother tongue(s)); 3. use the mother tongue in most official situations (including schools).
> B.   everybody whose mother tongue is not an official language in the country where s/he is resident, can become bilingual (or trilingual, if s/he has 2 mother tongues) in the mother tongue(s) and (one of) the official language(s) (according to his or her own choice).
> C.   any change of mother tongue is voluntary, not imposed.

It is interesting to compare Phillipson & Skutnabb-Kangas (1995) with the Declaration of Linguistic Rights, which was actually signed in June 1996 in Barcelona and co-chaired by UNESCO and CIEMEN (a Barcelona-based organization specializing in linguistic rights issues), and which is ultimately headed for the United Nations. The following (from Argemi 1996) is an extract from the Declaration, Article 3 (note the "may" in point 2):

1.   This Declaration considers the following to be inalienable personal rights which may be exercised in any situation: the right to be recognized as a member of a language community; the right to use one's own language in private and in public; the right to the use of one's own name; the right to interrelate and associate with other members of one's language community of origin; the right to maintain and develop one's own culture and all the other rights related to language which are recognized in the International Covenant on Civil and Political Rights of 16 December 1966 and the International Covenant on Economic, Social and Cultural Rights of the same date.

2.   This Declaration considers that the collective rights of language groups may include the following, in addition to the rights attributed to the members of language groups in the foregoing paragraph, and in accordance with the conditions laid down in paragraph 2.2: the right for their own language and culture to be taught; the right of access to cultural services; the rights to an equitable presence of their language and culture in the communications media; the right to receive attention in their own language from government bodies and in socio-economic relations.

3.   The aforementioned rights of persons and language groups must in no way hinder the interrelation of such persons or groups with the host language community or their integration into that community. Nor must they restrict the rights of the host community or its members to the full public use of the community's own language throughout its territorial space.

By emic (but see Harris 1976 for a range of meanings possible but not intended here) rights I intend nothing more than culture-, language-, and context-specific rights. It is not a term used in the literature on language rights, if close at hand for a linguist; nor is it discussed at all as a contrast to universal rights. The thought first occurred to me as discussant at a session on Minority and International Perspectives on Linguistic Human Rights at the AAA meeting in 1994. Ana Celia Zentella (1997) had argued the rights for the minority language (Spanish in Puerto Rico), followed later by a presentation by Ina Druviete proclaiming the rights of the national language (Latvian in Latvia with undeniable – and understandable – overtones against the now barely minority Russian). On the notion that rights *to* are at the same time rights *against* something (Hamel 1997b), I merely pointed out that their claims were contradictory and that we needed to resolve them, as it seemed to me that both were right. They later conferred and informed me that I was wrong in saying they disagreed, because they did not. Hence stems my fledgling thought that language rights are not universal, and my concern that such universal claims merely serve to weaken potential rights since many claimed rights patently cannot be enforced in some situations, echoing Lo Bianco: "rights are always modified by the pragmatic capacity of their enforcement" (personal communication, 1996). In addition, as Nelde et al. (1992) point out, it is an accepted fact in the legal domain in Canada that linguistic rights are based on political compromise and therefore must be interpreted by the courts with more discretion than is usually the case for other fundamental rights (1992).

Courtney Cazden somewhere has discussed the event of a child erasing a blackboard: It may be in punishment, it may be as reward, or it may be the routine of that particular classroom, but until you have an emic understanding, you will not understand what is happening. On the whole, the notion of emic understanding, where the same event may have different significance in different cultures, or where different events/phenomena may have the same significance, is ignored in the discussions of language rights. The more important is Hamel's "Language conflict and linguistic human rights in indigenous Mexico: a sociolinguistic framework" (1997a), where he argues for the necessity to relate LHRs to a sociolinguistic analysis, which takes into account not only the surface structures of language but also the cultural schemes and patterns, similar to Dell Hymes's communicative competence construct. He argues convincingly that to deal with an Indian minority in matters of the Mexican judicial system, using concepts and notions of the Western world will still be bewildering even if it is done in the Indian language. Surface structure of language is not enough. I do not expect that Hamel intended his work as an argument against universal language rights, but nevertheless that is its effect.

5   Conclusion

What should follow here is a discussion in terms of language rights of the English-Only/English Plus movement (Adams & Brink 1990, Cazden & Snow 1990, Crawford 1992, Gomez de Garcia 1996, Lang 1995, Wiley & Lukes 1996, Wong 1988); of the Canadian situation and the Quebec secession movement (Corson & Lemay 1996, Coulombe 1995, Edwards 1995); Australian language policies (Baldauf & Luke 1990, Herriman 1996, Lo Bianco 1987); the Arctic and Saami movements (Blom et al. 1992, Collis 1990, Corson 1995, Nordisk Kontakt 1993); and so on, i.c. language rights issues in specific localities around the world; but space does not permit a mapping of this diversity.

According to Giordan (1992), "the optimal development of the linguistic and cultural riches constituted by this diversity is a major condition for the realization of a democratic society capable of guaranteeing peace in this geopolitical space" (my translation). Giordan is writing about Europe, but he could just as well have meant the world. Language rights is an important new topic for us, because their existence usually reveals past and present injustice or exploitation against the weak in the world. Our responsibility as academics is the careful exploration of the nature of language rights and their consequences.

Note

1   There is in the United States a marked lack of academic intercourse between ELT and bilingual education (BE) professionals. The issues Ricento & Hornberger discuss were all written about in the 1970s by scholars working in the field of (bilingual) education. See my chapter "The Conflict Paradigm," in Paulston (1980).

References

Adams K, Brink D, eds. 1990. *Perspectives on Official English: The Campaign for English as the Official Language of the USA.* Berlin: Mouton de Gruyter

Ager D. 1994. Review of *Ethnic Groups and Language Rights*, ed. S Vilfan with G Sandvik, L Wils. Aldershot: Dartmouth

Argemi A. 1996. Universal Declaration of Linguistic Rights: responding to a need. *Contact Bull. Eur. Bur. Lesser Used Lang.* 13:3–4

Baldauf RB, Luke A, eds. 1990. *Language Planning and Education in Australasia and the South Pacific.* Clevedon, Engl: Multilingual Matters

Berglund J-E. 1995. Ålandsprotokollet ändras ej av EUs regeringskonferens (The Åland protocol not changed by EU's government conference). *Nord. Kontakt tema* 2:12–13

Blair P. 1994. *The Protection of Regional or Minority Languages in Europe.* Fribourg: Inst. Féd. Fribg. Suisse

Blom G, Graves P, Kruse A, Thomsen BT, eds. 1992. *Minority Languages: The Scandinavian Experience.* Oslo: Nord. Lang. Secr.

Bord na Gaeilge. 1988. *The Irish Language in a Changing Society: Shaping the Future.* Dublin: Bord na Gaeilge

Capotorti F. 1991. *Study of the Rights of Persons Belonging to Ethnic, Religious, and Linguistic Minorities.* New York: United Nations

Cazden CB, Snow CE, eds. 1990. English plus: issues in bilingual education. *Ann. Am. Acad. Polit. Soc. Sci.* 508. Newbury Park, CA: Sage

Collis DRF, ed. 1990. *Arctic Languages: An Awakening.* Paris: UNESCO

Cooper R. 1989. *Language Planning and Social Change.* Cambridge: Cambridge Univ. Press

Corson D. 1995. Norway's 'Sámi language act: emancipatory implications for the world's aboriginal peoples. *Lang. Soc.* 24:493–514

Corson D, Lemay S. 1996. *Social Justice and Language Policy in Education: The Canadian Research.* Toronto: OISE Press

Coulmas F, ed. 1991. *A Language Policy for the European Community.* Berlin: Mouton de Gruyter

Coulombe PA. 1995. *Language Rights in French Canada.* New York: Lang

Crawford J. 1992. *Hold Your Tongue: Bilingualism and the Politics of "English-only".* Reading, MA: Addison-Wesley

De Witte B. 1993. Conclusion: a legal perspective. In *Ethnic Groups and Language Rights,* ed. S Vilfan, pp. 303–14. Aldershot: Dartmouth

Domínguez F, López N. 1995. *Sociolinguistic and Language Planning Organizatioins.* Lang. Int. World Dir. Amsterdam: Benjamins

Druviete I. 1997. Linguistic human rights in the Baltic States. In *Linguistic Human Rights from a Sociolinguistic Perspective,* ed. RE Hamel. *Int. J. Sociol. Lang.* 127

Edwards J. 1995. Monolingualism, bilingualism, biculturalism and identity. *Curr. Issues Lang. Soc.* 2:5–57

Encyclopedia Britannica. 1993. Human rights. 20:656–64

Fishman JA. 1973. Language modernization and planning in comparison with other types of national modernization and planning. *Lang. Soc.* 2:23–42

Fishman JA, Ferguson CA, das Gupta J, eds. 1968. *Language Problems of Developing Nations.* New York: Wiley

Giordan H. 1992. *Les minorités en Europe: droits linguistiques et Droits de l'Homme.* Paris: Kimé

Gomes de Matos F. 1993. Ten years' work in linguistic rights: a selected bibliography. *Sociolinguist. Newsl.* 7:52–53

Gomez de Garcia J. 1996. Official English and the Native American: another tribe heard from. *Appl. Linguist. Forum* 16:5–7

Grabe W, ed. 1994. Language policy and planning. *Annu. Rev. Appl. Linguist.,* Vol. 14. Cambridge: Cambridge Univ. Press

Hale K, Krauss M, Watahomigie L, Yamamoto A, Craig C, et al. 1992. Endangered languages. *Language* 68:1–42

Hamel RE. 1997a. Language conflict and language shift: a sociolinguistic framework for linguistic human rights. *Int. J. Sociol. Lang.* 127

Hamel RE, ed. 1997b. Linguistic human rights from a sociolinguistic perspective. *Int. J. Sociol. Lang.* 127

Harris M. 1976. History and significance of the emic/etic distinction. *Annu. Rev. Anthropol.* 5:329–50

Heath SB. 1976. A National Language Academy? *Int. J. Sociol. Lang.* 11:9–43

Herriman M. 1996. Language policy in Australia. In *Language Policies in English Dominant Countries*, ed. M Herriman, B Burnaby, pp. 35–61. Clevedon: Multilingual Matters

Hornberger NH. 1994. Literacy and language planning. *Lang. Educ.* 8:75–86

Kloss H. 1969. *Research Possibilities on Group Bilingualism: A Report.* Quebec: Int. Cent. Res. Bilingual.

Lang P. 1995. *The English Language Debate: One Nation, One Language?* Springfield, NJ: Enslow

Leibowitz AH. 1982. *Federal Recognition of the Rights of Minority Language Groups.* Rosslyn, VA: Natl. Clgh. Biling. Educ.

Lo Bianco J. 1987. *National Policies on Languages.* Canberra: Aust. Gov. Publ. Serv.

McRae KD. 1975. The principle of territoriality and the principle of personality in multilingual states. *Int. J. Sociol. Lang.* 4:33–54

McRae KD. 1983. *Conflict and Compromise in Multilingual Societies.* Waterloo, Ont: Laurier

Nelde PH, Labrie N, Williams CH. 1992. The principles of territoriality and personality in the solution of linguistic conflicts. *J. Multiling. Multicult. Dev.* 13:387–406

Neustupny J. 1974. Basic types of treatment of language problems. In *Adv. Lang. Plan.*, ed. JA Fishman, pp. 37–48. The Hague: Mouton

Nordisk Kontakt. 1993. *Arktis. Engl. summ.*, Vol. 2

Paulston CB. 1980. *Bilingual Education: Theories and Issues.* Rowley, MA: Newbury House

Paulston CB. 1994. *Linguistic Minorities in Multilingual Settings.* Amsterdam: Benjamins

Phillipson R, Rannut M, Skutnabb-Kangas T. 1994. Introduction. In *Linguistic Human Rights.* Berlin: Mouton de Gruyter

Phillipson R, Skutnabb-Kangas T. 1995. Linguistic rights and wrongs. *Appl. Linguist.* 16:483–504

Piatt B. 1993. *Language on the Job: Balancing Business Needs and Employee Rights.* Albuquerque: Univ. N. M. Press

Ricento TK, Hornberger NH. 1996. Unpeeling the onion: language planning and policy and the ELT professional. *TESOL Q.* 30:401–27

Robins HR, Uhlenberg EM, eds. 1991. *Endangered Languages.* Oxford: Berg

Rouland N, Pierre-Caps S, Poumarede J. 1996. *Droits des Minorités et des Peuples Autochtones.* Paris: Presses Univ. Fr.

Skutnabb-Kangas T, Phillipson R, eds. 1994. *Linguistic Human Rights.* Berlin: Mouton de Gruyter

Teitelbaum H, Hiller RJ. 1977. *The Legal Perspective: Bilingual Education*, Vol. 3. Arlington, VA: Cent. Appl. Linguist.

Tollefson J. 1991. *Planning Language, Planning Inequality: Language Policy in the Community.* London: Longman

Tollefson J, ed. 1995. *Power and Inequality in Language Education.* Cambridge: Cambridge Univ. Press

Turi J-G. 1994. Typology of language legislation. See Skutnabb-Kangas & Phillipson 1994, pp. 111–19

Vilfan S, ed. 1993. *Ethnic Groups and Language Rights.* Aldershot: Dartmouth

Whiteley WH, ed. 1971. *Language Use and Social Change: Problems with Multilingualsim with Special Reference to Eastern Africa.* Oxford: Oxford Univ. Press

Wiley TG, Lukes M. 1996. English-only and standard English ideologies in the US. *TESOL Q.* 30:511–35

Woehrling J. 1989. Les droits linguistiques des minorités et le projet de modification de la Constitution du Canada. In *Langue et Droit*, ed. P Pupier, J Woehrling. Montreal: Wilson & Lafleur

Wong S-LC. 1988. Educational rights of language minorities. In *Language Diversity Problems or Resource?*, ed. SL McKay, S-LC Wong, pp. 367–86. New York: Newbury House

Woolard KA. 1985. Catalonia: the dilemma of language rights. In *Language of Inequality*, ed. N Wolfson, J Manes, pp. 91–109. Berlin: Mouton de Gruyter

Zentella AC. 1997. The Hispanophobia of the official English movement in the USA. In *Linguistic Human Rights from a Sociolinguistic Perspective*, ed. RE Hamel. *Int. J. Sociol. Lang.* 127

Discussion Questions

1. Using Tucker's conclusions (p. 466) as a guide, discuss what language should be used to educate children in the following language situations. You may need to collect some background information for each situation before making your recommendations.

    a) A former Soviet Republic where the local language is widely spoken and highly esteemed, but educational materials are more available in Russian.

    b) Monolingual Spanish speakers who migrate to the United States and live in a bilingual (Spanish–English) community.

    c) The Basque area of Spain, where local people are either bilingual in Basque and Spanish or monolingual Spanish speakers.

    d) Monolingual Chinese speakers who live in a monolingual English-speaking community in Australia.

2. How do the situations in question 1 show support for Paulston's call for an emic view of linguistic human rights?

3. In recent years the English-Only movement seems to have gained momentum in the United States – one of its main goals has been to eliminate bilingual instruction in the schools. The thinking behind this movement is that immigrants should be assimilated into the society and to do this they must learn English. Delaying instruction in English is seen as an impediment to integration. According to Tucker, is there any support for this logic? What arguments can be made against this thinking? What potential benefits (individual or societal) can be gained from bilingual instruction?

4. Considering the English-Only movement mentioned in question 3, answer the following questions:

    a) Is access to instruction in the native tongue a right?

    b) Would denying access to the majority/dominant language violate the rights of the minority speakers?

5. Consult a speaker of another (minority) language in your community. What has been his or her experience in terms of language use in school and language use in public or legal situations? What are his or her opinions about linguistic human rights, as listed in the Declaration of Linguistic Rights (chapter 29, p. 479)?

Index

Aavik, J. 429
Abipon of Argentina 34, 42
accent 240, 413
address forms *see* pronouns of address
Africa
　diglossia 362
　language planning 427, 430, 437
　marginal languages 293, 294
　nation and language 417, 420
　Swahili as lingua franca 398, 449
African-American vernacular English,
　construction of dialect norms 232, 251,
　253, 254–60, 266–8
Afrikaans 167, 298n, 380, 394
age, and linguistic strategies 208, 212
age-grading 4
Al-Toma, S. J. 347
Åland 478
Alaska, trade jargons 292
Alatis, J. E. 436, 441
Alba, V. 403
Albania, Albanian 430, 431, 432
alphabets 380, 394
Alsatian 22
Anzaldua, G. 50
American Anthropological Association meeting
　(1994), session on Minority and
　International Perspectives on Linguistic
　Human Rights 479
American Anthropologist 110n
American Council of Learned Societies 10
American Dialect Society 9
American English 146, 149, 150, 152, 154,
　234–5, 313, 411, 413
　see also African-American vernacular English;
　Negro English
American Indian studies 6
American Indians 50, 380

languages 441
　pan-Indian vernacular 268n
American Institute for Research 436
American Linguistic Institutes *see* Linguistic
　Society of America Institutes
Anang of Nigeria 33
Andorra 395
Anisfeld, E. 311, 313, 316
Anisfeld, M. 316
Année sociologique, L' 17
Annual Review of Applied Linguistics 409, 410
anomie 314, 315–17
anthropological linguistics, as term 5, 6
anthropology
　and development of sociolinguistics 2, 5–6,
　8–9, 13, 14, 15, 201
　and ethnography of speaking 27–8
Appalachian English 251
Arabic 11, 31
　diglossia 343, 345, 346–58, 361, 369, 371,
　373
　language planning 434, 455
　language switching 313
　as LWC 464, 465
Arabs, communication 44–5, 361
Aranta 18
Araucanians of Chile 34
archaic language 22
ARCI (Italian Recreational and Cultural
　Association) 54
Arctic movement 480
Ardener, S. 201
Argentina, Abipon 34, 42
Armenian 418
artificial languages 436–7
Ashanti 31
Asia
　language planning 427, 430, 437

nation and language   417
    style shifting and social stratification   237–8
Athabaskan Indian narratives   136nn
Atlas Linguistique de la France (Gilliéron and
    Edmont)   9, 17–18, 21
August, D.   331
Australia
    aboriginal languages   18
    language policy   480
    speech   37
Austria, speech   37
authenticity, of oral narratives   107–8
Auxiliary-Code Standardization   441–2, 453,
    454, 455
auxiliary languages   436–7, 453
Aymara   400

Baker, C.   466
Bali, individuals   281
Balkanisation   390
Baltic States   473
Barber, B.   436
Barère, Bertrand   429
Barik, H. C.   315
Barnes, D.   431
Barth, F.   36, 49, 403
Bartlett, F. C.   139
basic interpersonal communicative skills (BICS)
    302, 322–8, 467
    critical discussion of concept   329–40
Basque   22, 455
Basso, K. H.   50, 63
Bateson, G.   219, 226n
Bauman, R.   48, 52, 63
Bean, J. M.   273
Beauvoir, S. de   199
Becker, A. L.   214, 283
Bederman, G.   199
Beeman, W. O.   212
Belgium
    diglossia   362
    language legislation   477
    language planning   439
    official languages   416
belief systems   45
    see also religion
Bell, A.   118
Bell, S. E.   127
Bellinger, D.   216
Bengali   11, 464
Bernstein, B.   9, 19, 249, 331, 419
Besnier, N.   127

Biber, D.   325
Bible   231, 238, 379
Bickerton, D.   287
BICS   302, 322–8, 467
    critical discussion of concept   329–40
Bilibili islanders   37
bilingual education   382, 440–1, 480n
    common programmatic threads   466–7
    conception of language proficiency   329–40
    conversational/academic language   302–3,
        322–8
    cross-cutting themes   467–8
    definition   461
    ethnography of communication   35
    global perspectives   462, 464–71
    important questions for consideration
        469–70
    key issues for further research   468–70
    prevalent myths   465–6
    purpose   461–2
    research conclusions   466
bilingualism   20, 290, 301–4, 388, 394, 404
    global perspective   464–71
    language and social life   30, 31
    and language/style shift   236, 240, 402
    relationship to diglossia   344, 359–66, 371,
        373–4
    social psychology   301–2, 305–21
biliteracies   450–1, 456–7
Birdwhistell, R. L.   146
Black English   146, 148, 150–1, 152–3, 154
blasons   52
Bleier, R.   199
Bloch, B.   5
Bloomfield, L.   4, 5, 9, 36, 411
Blu, K. I.   52, 58
Bly, R.   223
body language   *see* non-verbal communication
Bolivia   449
Bord na Gaeilge   478
Bordewich, F. M.   260
Bourdieu, P.   48
Brazil, marginal languages   292, 294, 295, 298n
Brenneis, D.   209
Brenner, M.   273
Breton   22, 416, 429
Briggs, C. L.   273
Bright, W.   7, 10, 11, 110n
Britain, D.   189
British Council   437
British Guiana   295
broken speech   297

Brown, P.   177, 179, 209, 281
Brown, R.   72, 209, 210, 211, 212, 213
Brudner, L.   397
Brun, A.   413
Bruner, J. S.   324
Burke, Kenneth   43
Burton, P.   201
Burundi   398
Bush Negroes   298nn
Butler, Samuel   413
Byrne, Sister St G.   157
Byrnes, H.   223
Byron, J.   431, 432

CALP   302, 303, 322–8
    critical discussion of concept   329–40
Calvet, L.-J.   1, 2, 21, 22, 231
Cameron, D.   201
campanilismo   51–2
Campbell, Joseph   223
Canada
    bilingual education   467, 468
    bilingualism   306–19, 322–3
    diglossia   362
    language planning   425, 426, 442
    language rights   472, 477, 479, 480
    linguistic norms   244
    official languages   416
    see also Quebec
Carlson vs. N. Y. Life Insurance   435
Casey, E. S.   63
caste   11
Catalonia, Catalan   22
    language rights   477
    linguistic minorities and language policies
        394, 395–8, 403, 404
Cazden, C.   470, 479
Cenoz, J.   466
Center for Applied Linguistics   410, 473
Central African Republic   33
Chambers, J. K.   252, 253, 266
Chandler, M.   226n
chanting   45
Charrow, R. P.   435–6
Charrow, V. R.   435–6
Chicago school   291
Chicano American identity   50
Chikobava, A.   23n
Child, I.   318, 319
Chile, oratory   34
China, Chinese
    diglossia/bilingualism   355, 361, 370

language planning   409, 430, 431, 441
    as LWC   464
    marginal languages   292, 293
Chinook jargon   292, 293
Chomsky, N.   10, 27, 231, 232
Christian, D.   251, 461
Cicourel, A.   110n, 273
CIEMEN   478
Cino Da Pistoia   67n
civil strife   see conflict
Clarke, S.   217
Coates, J.   116, 118, 127, 131, 218
Cobarrubias, J.   441
Cochiti of New Mexico   36–7
code switching   30–1, 140, 141, 146, 148, 287
    Tuscan Contrasto   53
codes   44
cognitive academic language proficiency
        (CALP)   302, 303, 322–8, 467
    critical discussion of concept   329–40
Cohen, M.   20, 21, 22, 23n
Cohen, P.   251
Cohen, R.   49
Coke, Sir Edward   173, 174
Colby, B.   75
collective rights   473, 474, 479
colonialism   21, 22, 287, 294–5, 297
communication
    effects on language   369, 373, 388
    ethnography of   12, 15, 148
communicative competence (Hymes)   12, 27,
        480
Comparative Education Societies' World
        Congress (1996)   473
complementary schismogenesis (Bateson)
        226n
compliments   72, 177–95
    content   187–90
    definition   177–8
    functions   178–81, 182, 188, 190, 192–3
    gender in paying   72, 181–93
    as power play   190–3
conflict   2
    bilingualism and social conflict   318–19
    diglossia   343, 371–2
    and language rights   478
    and linguistic strategies   221–4
    multilingualism and civil strife   379–80,
        382–93
    nation and language   416
Conley, J. M.   216
contextualization cues   72, 140–6

perceptual bases   146–53
Contrasto, identity and place in Tuscan   48–68
conversation analysis   7, 72, 106–9
    contextualization conventions   72, 139–55
    see also linguistic strategies
conversational/academic language   322–8
    critical discussion of concepts   329–40
    critiques of BICS/CALP distinction   324–5
    evolution of BICS/CALP distinction
        322–4
Cooper, R. L.   451, 454, 455–6, 476
coordinate clauses   84–5, 86
Corneille, Pierre   158
Cornish   428
Corsaro, W.   222
Corson, D.   325, 466
Corston, S.   127
Cortellazzo, M.   52
Cottam, R. W.   403
Coulmas, F.   472
Craig, B.   268n
Crandall, J.   302
creoles   1, 15, 22, 287–9, 417, 465
    dialects   290, 291, 293–7
    diglossia   346–57
    Dutch creole   296
    French creole   288–9, 295, 296–7, 298n,
        346–58
    Portuguese creole   294
    predecessor of AAVE   254, 268n
critical theory   2, 476
Crystal, D.   15, 71, 331, 332
Cuba   295
cultural colonialism   427
cultural identity   260, 265, 267, 302
cultural relativity   5, 72, 115, 135
culture
    and compliments   180, 193
    and contextualization conventions   72, 146,
        147, 151, 154
    cross-cultural research   8
    and gender   200, 204
    and individuation   281–2
    and linguistic strategies   208, 212–13,
        216–17, 219, 223–4
    and listener feedback   129
    Maori/Pakeha   114–15, 126, 127, 129–30,
        133–4, 135
    role of language   32
Cummins, J.   302, 322, 324–5, 466
    critical discussion of his BICS/CALP
        distinction   329–40

Curaçao   296
Currie, H. C.   1, 11
Czechoslovakia
    language planning   430, 431, 435
    linguistic norms   243
    speech   37

D'Amico-Reisner, L.   185
Danish   416, 440
Davies, Alan   380
Davis, Alva L.   11
De Bessé, B.   433
De Simonis, P.   52
De Witte, B.   472
Declaration of Linguistic Rights   478–9
deficit theory of language   199, 334, 337
Del Giudice, L.   52–3
Democratic Republic of the Congo   398
democratization   373
Denmark
    language planning   433, 436, 438
    see also Danish
deprivation   386, 387
    see also poverty
descriptive linguistics   6, 9, 27, 32–46, 357
developing countries, international conferences
        on language problems   409
Dialect Notes   9
dialect switching   140, 313
dialectology, and development of
        sociolinguistics   9–12,14, 20, 21–2, 231
dialects   293, 317, 368
    change   317
    communicative functions   148–9
    diglossia   368
    distinguished from language   411–14,
        419–21
    linguistic minorities and language policies
        395, 401
    matched-guise research technique   307–8
    and speech forms   44
    structural/functional dimensions   411–21
    style shifting   234–6
    Tuscan   53
    see also creoles
Dieth, E.   347
diglossia   11, 22, 343–58, 388, 419, 450
    acquisition   349–50
    definitions   343–4, 371, 373–4
    diachronic attributes   367–8
    function   347–8, 368–9, 371–2
    grammar   351–2

diglossia *cont.*
  lexicon 352–3
  literary heritage 349
  phonology 353–7
  prestige of languages 348–9
  relationship to bilingualism 344, 359–66,
    371, 372–4
  stability 350–1, 371, 372–3
  standardization 350
  synchronic attributes 367
  systematic study of 367–76
disappearing languages 473
discourse analysis 10, 15, 71, 208, 282
Dittmar, N. 21
Diver, W. 103nn
dominant language maintenance 439–40
Donaldson, M. 324
Dorval, B. 220
drum languages 297n
Druviete, I. 479
dumb barter 290
Duranti, A. 50, 127, 209
Durkheim, E. 17, 18, 314
Dutch
  language planning 430, 439
  see also Netherlands
Dutcher, N. 465, 466
Dyson, K. K. 201

East–West Culture Learning Institute, Hawaii
  438
Eastern Bloc, language planning 437
Eastern Europe, diglossia 362
Eastman, C. M. 424
Eckert, P. 201, 223, 396
Ecuador 449
Edelsky, C. 324, 330, 334
Edmont, E. 9, 17, 21
education
  classroom communication 148–9, 151, 153
  development 410
  and development of sociolinguistics 2, 8
  and diglossia 370, 373
  and language regulation 473
  linguistic minorities 1, 329–40, 394
  mother tongue literacy 369, 370, 410, 450,
    457
  and multilingualism 380
  and narrative structure 135
  social psychology of second-language
    learning 313–14
  and social stratification 240–1

  standard languages 421
  see also bilingual education
education of linguistic minorities studies 1
Egypt, language planning 433
Ekman, P. 147
elicitation sessions 109–10
elite bilingualism 462
Ellwood, Thomas 166
Emerson, Ralph Waldo 281
Encyclopedia of Language and Education 466
Endangered Language Fund, Inc 473
endangered languages 473
England *see* United Kingdom
English
  Canadian English 244, 306–17, 439–40
  development and standardization of 411,
    413–14, 418, 419–20
  educational medium 394
  forms of speech 44
  language variation 231–2, 234–50
  learning 302–3, 322–3, 325, 326, 329, 330,
    331, 337–8
  as LWC 379, 399, 420, 437–8, 453, 455,
    464, 465
  as official language 380, 417, 455
  pronouns of address 156, 158, 159, 166,
    169, 170, 173–5, 209
  teaching 476
  vernacular dialect norms 251–71
  see also American English; Indian English;
    Pidgin English
Enlightenment 33
Erickson, F. 142, 147, 208, 209
Eritrea
  multiple languages in education 465, 467
Ervin-Tripp, S. 27, 39
Escobar, A. 400
Eskimo trade jargons 292
Esman, M. J. 379
Esperanto 19, 437, 453
Estonia, Estonian 297
  language reform 430
Ethiopia, diglossia 369
ethnic identity
  and construction of vernacular dialect norms
    260, 261, 265, 267
  in Tuscan *Contrasto* 48–68
ethnic minorities
  language maintenance 440–1
  language rights 473–4, 475
  United States 302
ethnic movements, and language shift 402–3

ethnic nationalism 403–4, 473
ethnicity 462
  and conversation interpretation 143, 145,
    146, 147, 148, 150, 151, 153
  and group multilingualism 379–80
  and language shift 380, 402
  language variation 239–40, 248
  linguistic strategies 208
  and Maori/Pakeha narrative 131
ethnocentrism, and bilingualism 317–18
ethnography 11, 14
  of communication 12, 15, 148
  of compliments 181–93
  of speaking 27–47, 71
ethnolinguistics, as term 6
ethnological philology, as term 6
ethnomethodology 15
Europe
  development of sociolinguistics 2, 9, 17–24
  diglossia 362
  pronouns of address 156–76, 209
European Union 472, 478
evaluative narrative function 75, 102
external language purification 426–7, 439
Extra, G. 301

face-threatening acts
  compliments as 179, 180, 182, 183, 184,
    188, 189, 192, 193
  public-opinion surveys 281
Farnsworth, R. 166
Faroes, language planning 438
Fasold, R. W. 251, 252
Fay, P. B. 157
federalist extremism 473
Feld, S. 57–8
Fellman, J. 433
Ferguson, C. A. 7, 8, 9, 11, 12, 20, 343, 344,
    359, 367, 368–70, 373, 374, 409, 418, 419,
    424, 430, 437–8, 453, 454, 455
Fernando Po 294
Ferrara, K. 273
Fillenbaum, S. 307
Fillmore, C. 141
Finland, Finnish
  bilingualism of emigrants to Sweden 322
  language planning 433, 438
  language shift 478
  listener narrative feedback 129
  national language 417
Firth, J. R. 9, 32
Fischer, J. L. 11, 245

Fishman, J. A. 7, 8, 12, 343, 344, 360, 370–3,
    374, 379, 391n, 392nn, 418, 423, 424, 429,
    430, 433, 437, 440, 441, 450, 456, 475, 476
Flathead Indians 31
folk bilingualism 462
folklore 35, 223
Ford, J. C. 436
Ford Foundation 409
Fordham. S. 260
form, formalism 9, 21, 22, 71
  narrative analysis 74–104, 110
formulaic expressions 142, 146, 148, 149–51,
    153, 154
  see also compliments
Fox, George 166
Fox, J. R. 36
Frake, C. O. 42, 50
France 395
  development of sociolinguistics 17–18, 21, 22
  dialectology 9
  language planning 425, 426, 427, 433, 435
  language rights 474–5
  language shift 380
  see also French
Frank. J. 223
free narrative clauses 83–4, 85, 86, 102
Freed, A. 199
Freeman, R. 199
French
  development and standardization of 411,
    412–13, 416, 418
  and diglossia 371, 372
  and Haiti creole 289, 295, 296–7, 346–58
  linguistic strategies 209, 216
  as LWC 464
  as official language 417, 420
  pronouns of address 156, 157, 158, 159, 161,
    162, 163–5, 167, 169, 170, 173, 174–5, 209
  see also France
French Africa, pronouns of address 166
French-Americans 240, 318–19
French-Canadians, Canadian French 244,
    306–17, 439, 453
  diglossia 362
Freudian theory 158, 175, 225
Friedrich, P. 11, 20, 209, 283
Frisian 371, 429, 442
Froissart, Jean 158
Fromm-Reichmann, F. 112n
function, functionalism 6, 9, 22, 31, 110, 201
  development and standardization of
    dialect/language 409, 411–21

functional narrative analysis   74–104
   evaluative   75
   referential   75, 93, 102

Gaarder, B.   462
Gal, S.   201
Galician   22, 371, 396
Gambia, The   431
Gardner, P. M.   31
Gardner, R. C.   307, 314, 315, 316, 318–19
Garfinkel, H.   7, 8, 45, 110n
Garvin, P. L.   431
Gauchat, L.   20
Gbeya of Central African Republic   33
Gedike, F.   156
Gee, J. P.   323, 449
Geerts, G.   439
gender   4, 199–202
   and compliments   72, 181–93
   and conflict and verbal aggression   221–4
   and conversation interpretation   143
   and language planning   424
   linguistic strategies and gender domination
      208–28
   and linguistic variation   245–6
   and listener's narrative role   136n
   and public-opinion surveys   273
   sexism   199–200, 203–7
   social psychology of bilingualism   308–11
gender studies   28
generative grammar   10, 27
Genesee, F.   330, 461, 466
genres, speech components   45
Georges, R. A.   56
Georgetown University   8
Germany, German
   code switching   30
   dialectology   9
   diglossia   360, 374
   language planning   430, 433
   linguistic strategies   223
   pronouns of address   156, 157, 159, 162,
      163–5, 167, 169, 175
   sociolinguistics   21
   speech   37, 42
   standardization   418
   see also Swiss German
gesture codes   297n
ghost stories   102
Gilgamesh   223
Gilliéron, J.   9, 17–18, 21
Gilman, A.   72, 209, 210, 211, 212, 213

Giner, S.   397
Giordan, H.   473, 475, 480
Gleason, J. B.   216
glossolalia   31
GNP   see gross national product
Goffman, E.   7, 8, 28, 110n, 141
Gonzalez, A.   466, 467
Goodwin, C.   111n, 127
Goodwin, M.   118
Gorer, G.   219
grammar
   conversation analysis   148, 154
   creation by talking   282–3
   speech communities   36–7
   Tuscan Contrasto   53
Grand, C.   156, 161, 173
graphization   452, 453, 454
   see also writing, writing systems
Greece, Greek
   development and standardization   411–12,
      415, 418
   diglossia   343, 346–57, 371, 373
   language planning   430
   as lingua franca in Roman empire   379
   linguistic strategies   216–17, 223–4
Green, E. W.   255
Greenland, language planning   438, 440
greeting rituals   135
Grégoire, Antoine   18
Gregory I, Pope   158
gross national product (GNP), and
      multilingualism   382–93
group ideology, and pronouns of address   156,
      165–9
group multilingualism   see multilingualism
group rights   473, 474, 479
Guarani   30, 360, 371, 373, 455
Guatamala   465
Guerin de la Grasserie, R.   17–18, 22
Guiana   294
Guinea-Bissau   469
Gujerati   167
Gumperz, J. J.   7, 8, 9, 11, 12, 27, 28, 36, 37,
      72, 110n, 139, 148, 150, 154, 200, 208,
      225n, 359, 369
Gunter, R.   397
Guttman, L.   170

Haiti   288–9, 295, 296–7, 298n
   diglossia   346–58
Hakuta, K.   331, 467
Hale, K.   473

Hall, E. T.   146
Halliday, M.   9
Hamel, R. E.   480
Harrison, W. W.   409
Harvard University   6
Haugen, E.   11, 12, 20, 401, 409, 423, 424,
   429, 431, 442, 449, 451, 452, 453
Hausa   293
Hawaii   127, 297
Hearn, Lafcadio   296
Heath, S. B.   475
Hebrew
   development and standardization   411, 417,
      434
   diglossia/bilingualism   360, 371
   social psychology of learning   316–17
   see also Israel; Jews
Herbert, R. K.   179, 181, 182, 183, 186
Herder, J. G.   391
Heritage, J.   55
Heritage-language Learner   302
Hermann, E.   20
Hertzler, J. O.   7
Herzog, M.   268n
Heyd, U.   430
Hill, P. C.   22
Hindi   167, 464
Hindi-Urdu   418
historical linguistics   11, 20, 232
historical-structural approach   476
Hockett, C.   5, 319
Hodgson, R. C.   307
Hodson, T. C.   1
Hoenigswald, H. M.   11
Hogan, R. F.   11
Holland, G.   226n
Holmes, J.   4, 71, 72, 183
Homer   324
homogenization, and linguistic heterogeneity
   386, 387–8
Hopper, P.   282
Horn, L. R.   71
Hornberger, N. H.   401, 410, 451, 457,
   475–6
Houis, M.   22
Hudson, A.   344
Hughes, L. A.   221
Hungary
   language planning   426, 430, 433
   speech   37
Hymes, D.   6, 7, 8, 9, 11, 12, 14, 27, 28–9, 71,
   110n, 181, 282, 287, 374, 449, 480

Iceland   379
   language planning   426, 427, 430, 433,
      438
Idea Proficiency Test I Oral-Spanish (IPT-S)
   335
identity
   and dialect variation   260, 261, 265, 267
   in Tuscan Contrasto   48–68
   see also ethnic identity
IJAL   11
immigrants
   broken speech   297
   diglossia/bilingualism   363
   language shift   380, 402
India
   communication   31, 45
   diglossia/bilingualism   361, 362
   language and social status   11
   language planning   430, 433, 453, 455
   multilingualism   384, 449
   official languages   464, 465
   pronouns of address   167
   rhetorical strategy   152–3, 154
Indian English   146, 150–1, 152–3, 154
Indiana University, Linguistic Institute (1964)
   10
individual   232, 272–85
Indo-European languages   169, 412, 417
Indonesia, language planning   430
industrialization   363, 369, 373, 396
Inman, M.   437
insults   193
interactional sociolinguistics   71–2
   see also interpretive sociolinguistics
interlingual communication   436–9, 453, 456
internal language purification   427–8, 443n
International Communications Agency   437
International Journal of the Sociology of
   Language   434–5
international languages   436–7
interpretive sociolinguistics   28, 72
   and contextualization conventions   139–55
   Maori/Pakeha stories   126–7
   norms of interpretation   44–5
interviewing   see public-opinion surveys
Iran, linguistic strategies   212
Iraq, diglossia   345
Irish   416
   language planning   425, 428, 429, 430
   language rights   478
Iroquois   34
isoglosses   414

Israel
    bilingualism 313, 317
    language planning 409, 425, 426, 427,
        428–9, 430, 432, 433, 434, 439, 442, 443n,
        455
    see also Hebrew; Jews
Italian Americans 50, 318, 319
Italian Spanish 297
Italy, Italian
    bilingualism 318–19
    class stratification and language variation
        239–40
    development of sociolinguistics 19, 22
    dialects/language 413
    identity and place in Tuscan *Contrasto*
        48–68
    language planning 426
    pronouns of address 156, 157, 158, 159,
        161, 162, 163–5, 167, 169, 173, 175

Jaberg, K. 20
Jakobson, R. 32
Jamaica 289
James, D. 217
Japan, Japanese 370
    language planning 428
    linguistic strategies 212, 216
    listener's narrative role 129
    speech style 39
Java 369
Javanese, Suriname 212–13
Jefferson, G. 108
Jespersen, O. 173, 297n
Jews
    argument 223
    class stratification and language variation
        239–40
    diglossia/bilingualism 313, 316–17, 360,
        371
    see also Hebrew; Israel
Johnson, D. M. 179, 181–2, 183, 186
Johnston, O. M. 156
Johnstone, B. 118, 232, 273
jokes 52, 102
Jones, S. P. 466
Jones, W. R. 314
Jong, Erica 218–19
Jonson, Ben 170, 173–4
Joos, M. 39
Jordan, language planning 426
*Journal of Multilingual and Multicultural
    Education* 466

Journal of Pidgin and Creole Studies 287
Journal of the American Oriental Society
    348
Jung, Carl Gustav 4

Kahane, H. 369
Kahn, A. 435
Kakava, C. 223–4
Kallen, H. 391
Kaluli songs 57–8
Keenan, E. 217
Kelman, H. C. 430
Kennedy, A. G. 157
Kenya, national language 394, 398, 399
Kenyon, J. 236
key, speech component 28, 43
Kinloch, P. 115, 129
Kiparsky, P. 4
Kitchen Kafir, Natal 292
Kittredge, G. 9
Klagsbrun, F. 225n
Klineberg, O. 317–18
Kloss, H. 418, 419, 424, 451, 476
Knapp, M. L. 190
Kochman, T. 148
Koerner, K. 4, 20
Kohn, H. 397, 403
Komarovsky, M. 218
Kroeber, A. L. 33
Kroskrity, P. V. 49
Krumbacher, K. 343
Kuiper, K. 193
Kurath, H. 9, 10

Labov, W. 4–5, 7, 8, 9, 11, 12, 13, 20, 22, 36,
    71, 200
    application of analytical framework to Maori
        and Pakeha stories 116–35
    critique 105–8, 110
    variationism 14, 231–2, 251, 268n
Lacoste, Robert 166
Lakoff, R. 199–200, 203, 215
Lambert, W. E. 201, 244, 301–2, 307, 311,
    313, 315–16, 317–19, 440
language
    change 15, 17, 232, 287, 357; *see also below*
        standardization
    distinguished from dialect 411–14
    diversity 139
    functions *see* function, functionalism
    law 472, 474, 476–8, 479
    modernization 453, 454

norms   *see* linguistic norms
purification   424, 426–8, 429, 439, 443n,
   453, 454
reform   424, 429–30, 453, 454
revival   424, 425, 428–9, 441, 453
rules   241–3
as social fact   17, 18
social stratification   236–41
speech forms   44
spread (planning goal)   424, 425, 426,
   431–2, 440, 453
spreading (planning process)   436
stability   419
standardization   424, 426, 429, 430–2,
   438–9, 451, 453, 454; *see also* standard
   languages
structure   *see* structure, structuralism
switching   305, 313
transfer   468
use   20, 22, 201, 409, 411–21; *see also*
   function, functionalism
variation   *see* variation, variationism
see also language maintenance; language
   planning; language policies; language
   rights; language shift; linguistic . . .
language and culture courses   6, 14, 15
language and gender studies   1, 199, 200, 201
language behavior   8, 14
language contact approach   11, 12, 22
language field   37
Language for International Communication
   project   438
language maintenance   380, 394, 401, 402–14,
   425, 432, 439–41, 453
   Catalan as case of   395, 396, 397
language planning   11, 15, 287, 409–10
   acquisition planning   452, 455–6, 476
   corpus planning   452, 453, 454, 456, 476
   goals   409, 423–48, 452–4
   and language rights   475–6
   and literacy   449–59
   nationalization   455
   officialization   455
   orientations   456–7
   processes   418–21, 423–4, 425, 432–3, 436,
      440–1, 442
   proscription   455
   status planning   451, 452, 453, 454, 455,
      456, 476
language policies   287, 409–10, 461–3, 464–71
   as language planning   475–6
   and language rights   472–82

and linguistic minorities   380, 394–406
   and multilingualism   390–1
language policy and planning   1, 409, 475
language rights   462, 472–82
   definitions   473–5
   as language planning   475–6
   territoriality versus personality principles
      476–8
   universal versus emic rights   478–80
language shift   380, 394, 395, 401–4, 431–2
   and diglossia   344, 374
languages of wider communication (LWC)
      288, 290, 293, 294, 379, 388, 394, 464,
      465
   and language planning   436–9, 450, 453
   see also English; French; Latin; Spanish;
      Swahili
Latin   31, 169, 379, 418, 419
   diglossia   355, 369
   pronouns of address   157–8, 169
Latin America
   diglossia/bilingualism   371, 373
   language planning   427, 453, 455
   marginal languages   295
   regional languages   453
   sociolinguistics   2
Latvia   431, 479
laughter   129
law
   language of   435–6
   language rights   472, 474, 476–8, 479
Le Page, R. B.   430, 431
Leap, W.   268n
Lehtonen, J.   129
Leibowitz, A. H.   474
Lemaire, H. B.   440
Lettish   297
Levelers   167
Lévi-Strauss, C.   18, 107
Levinson, S. C.   177, 179, 209, 281
Lévy-Bruhl, L.   18
Lewandowska-Tomaszczyk, B.   180, 181
Lewis, J.   251
Lewis, M. M.   19
lexicon
   development of knowledge   323
   and diglossia   352–3
   modernization   424, 426, 432–3, 443n,
      453–4
   patterns in compliments   184–7
Lind, E. A.   216
Linde, C.   117, 118

lingua francas *see* languages of wider
  communication
linguistic anthropology, as term 6
linguistic atlases 9–10, 21
linguistic community 37
linguistic competence (Chomsky) 27
linguistic ethnology, as term 6
linguistic geography 9–12, 231
linguistic heterogeneity 379–80, 382–93, 464
  empirical study of relationship with civil
    strife and GNP 382–9
  positive consequences 390–1
  reasons for correlation between civil strife,
    GNP and 389–90
  see also multilingualism
linguistic human rights 472, 473, 474–5,
  478–80
linguistic minorities 1, 380
  and language policies 394–406, 462
  language shift 401–4
  see also minority languages
linguistic norms 243–4
  construction of vernacular dialect norms
    251–71
linguistic rights *see* language rights
Linguistic Society of America Institutes 8, 15
  (1964) 10, 11–12
  (1966) 7, 110n
linguistic strategies 208–28
  conflict and verbal aggression 221–4
  indirectness 215–17
  interruption 217–18
  relativity 215–24
  silence versus volubility 218–20
  theory 209–15
  topic raising 220
linguistics 1–2, 8–9, 12–13, 14, 17
  see also descriptive linguistics; form,
    formalism; function, functionalism;
    historical linguistics; structure,
    structuralism
literacy 287, 334, 369, 374
  development 449–59
literature
  in creole dialect 296
  diglossia 349
  linguistic strategies 214–15, 218–19, 223
  pronouns of address 157, 158, 159, 170,
    173–5
Littré, É. 161, 412, 413
Lo Bianco, J. 473, 479
local literacies 450–1, 456–7

Logli, Altamante 54–64
Lowell, J. R. 9
LSA *see* Linguistic Society of America
  Institutes
Lumbee vernacular English 232, 260–5, 266
Luxembourg 464, 467

McConnell, G. D. 439
McDavid, R. I., Jr. 10, 11, 20
McDermott, R. P. 209
McElhinney, B. 199
McGill University, Montreal 306, 315
Mackey, W. F. 441
McRae, K. D. 476
MacSwan, J. 302, 334
McWhorter, J. 287
Madagascar, linguistic strategies 217
makeshift languages 290
Malay 464
Malay-Indonesian, language planning 432,
  438–9, 453
Malbec 165
Malinowski, B. 18, 31, 45
Maori 31
  story-telling, compared to Pakeha 114–38
Marçais, W. 343
Marcellesi, J. B. 22
marginal languages 22, 290–8
Mariani 66n
Marlowe, Christopher 174
Marr, N. 19–21
Martin, J. 306
Martin-Jones, M. 324, 330, 334
Martinet, A. 4, 20, 412, 413
Marxism 2, 19–21, 22
Mascarenes 294
mass media 388
Mauss, M. 18
Mead, M. 219
medical language 436
Meillet, A. 4, 5, 9, 17, 18, 20, 21
Merritt, M. 277
Messenger, J. C., Jr 33
metalinguistics, as term 6
Metge, J. 115, 129
Mexican American identity 50
Mexican American Legal Defense Fund
  (MALDEF) 473
Mexico, Mexicans
  diglossia/bilingualism 371
  language planning 455
  language rights 480

language variation   240
Migliorini, B.   19
Milroy, J.   232, 331, 332
Milroy, L.   232, 265, 331, 332
minimum languages   290
minority languages   22
  erosion   388
  and language rights   472, 479
  maintenance   440–1
  see also linguistic minorities
miscommunication   28, 72, 135, 140–55
Mitchell-Kernan, C.   148
Modern Greek   *see* Greece, Greek
modernization   373, 386, 387, 388, 453
Moerman, M.   110n, 127
Molde, Bertil   435
Molière   170, 174
monolingualism   379, 464
Moreau de Saint-Méry, L. E.   298n
morphology   32
mother tongue
  and diglossia   369, 370
  education   462, 466–8
  and language maintenance   380, 394–406
  language rights   478
  literacy   410, 450, 457
Motu pidgin   292
Moussirou-Mouyama, A.   22
Mozambique   398
multilingual nations, and literacy   449
multilingualism   11, 20, 22, 287, 301, 302,
    379–81
  and diglossia   344, 368
  and education   464–5, 470
  and social conflict and GNP   379–80,
    382–93
multiple literacies   450–1, 456–7

Nahir, M.   409, 424, 453–5
Nahuatal   371
Namibia   468
narrative   71
  abstract   117, 119, 121, 125
  closure   122, 127
  codas   100–2, 117, 119, 127, 134
  (complicating) action   93–4, 102, 117–19,
    121, 122–5, 127, 134
  coordinate clauses   84–5, 86
  definition   88–9, 116–17
  displacement sets   83, 85–7, 88
  evaluation   94–9, 102, 117–19, 120, 121,
    122, 125–6, 127, 131, 134

free clauses   83–4, 85, 86, 88, 93, 102
  implicitness   122, 126–7, 134, 135
  listener's role   127–33, 134, 135
  orientation   93, 102, 117, 119, 125, 131
  primary sequences   92, 102
  resolution   100–2, 117, 119, 120, 121, 122,
    125, 127, 134
  restricted clauses   85–7, 88, 102
  role of narrator   119–28, 134
  surface structure   90–2
  temporal juncture   87–8
  temporal sequence   81–2
narrative analysis   71–2, 74–104
  basic framework   81–92
  importance of context   126, 127, 128, 130,
    134
  later developments   105–13
  Maori and Pakeha story-telling   71–2,
    114–38
  overall structure of narratives   93–102
narrative clauses   83–90, 102
  definition   88
narrative heads   89–90
narrative sequences   90–2
Natal, marginal languages   292
nation, and language planning   410, 411–22
National Association of Bilingual Education
    (NABE)   473
National Council of Teachers of English   232
national identity   428, 464
national languages   369, 379, 380, 388, 394,
    416, 428, 431, 450, 455, 456, 464, 479
  Swahili in Tanzania   398–9
national literacy model   450
nationalism   379, 416, 430, 450, 462
  geographic   396, 397–8, 403–4
  and language shift   403–4
Native Americans   *see* American Indians
Negro English   235, 239, 240, 244, 248, 294–5,
    313, 317
  AAVE and construction of dialect norms
    232, 251, 253, 254–60, 266–8
Nelde, P. H.   477, 479
Netherlands
  bilingual education   467
  colonies and marginal languages   296
  language planning   430, 439, 442
  sociolinguistics   22
Neustupný, J.   37, 423, 424, 476
New Guinea   31, 37
  see also Papua New Guinea
New Norwegian   416

New Zealand
  gender and compliments 181–2, 183, 184,
    186, 187–8, 189, 190–1, 192, 193
  Maori and Pakeha story-telling 114–38
  song/speech 31
Newmeyer, F. J. 12
Nida, E. 1
Nigeria 31, 33, 449, 464, 465, 467
non-verbal communication 119, 133, 146–7,
  169
Nordic languages 438, 453
Norman, M. 221
North Carolina Language and Life Project
  254, 262
Norway, Norwegian
  code switching 31
  language and social status 11
  language planning 425, 430, 433, 434, 438,
    451
  marginal languages 293
  nation and language 416, 418
Ntongo 415
Nuessel, F. 457n
Nukulaclac gossip 127

O'Barr, W. M. 216
Occitan 22, 371, 372, 380, 396, 397
Oceania 465
Ochs, E. 50
official languages 394, 396, 431, 432, 455, 456,
  464, 465
  Peru 400–1
  Tanzania 398–9
Ogbu, J. 260
Ohio Valley Sociological Society 7
oho-chant 42
Oka, I. G. N. 214
Old Church Slavic 370
Old Testament 231, 379
Oller, J. 323
Olson, D. R. 324
Ong, W. J. 221
oral cultures 324, 449
Ornstein, J. 441
Outer Banks dialect 254–9, 267
overlapping 130, 150, 217–18

Pagliai, V. 29, 50
Pali 464
Paliyans of south India 31
Pāṇini 4
Papiamento Spanish 296

Papua New Guinea 465, 468
  pidgins 288, 292
Paraguay
  code switching 30
  diglossia/bilingualism 360, 373
  language planning 455
paralinguistic signals 118, 147, 150, 151
Parépou, Alfred 298n
patois 412–13
Paules, G. F. 211
Paulston, C. B. 379–80, 396, 402, 462, 475
Pecori, G. 52
peer group influence 246
peer reviews 179, 181–2, 186–7
Persian empire 379
Peru 449
  language planning 455, 457
  linguistic minorities and language policies
    394, 400–1, 402, 403
phatic communication 31
Philippines
  bilingual education 464, 467, 468
  Yakan speech events 42
Philips, S. U. 208
Phillipson, R. 22, 474, 478
phonetic signs, conversation analysis 146, 148
phonology 32
  construction of vernacular dialect norms
    264
  and diglossia 353–7
  and language development 323
  and language variation 234
Pi-Sunyer, O. 395, 396, 397–8
pidgin and creole studies 1
Pidgin English 292–3, 297
pidgins 15, 287–9, 290, 364, 417
Piedmontese 413
Piestrup, A. M. 148–9
Pike, K. L. 5, 10, 39
Pillai, M. 355
Pinter, Harold 214–15, 218
Pitcairn Island 294
place, in Tuscan Contrasto 48–68
place names 48, 50, 53–6, 441–2, 455
plantation creole dialects 291, 294–7
Poeti Bernescanti 53
poetry, identity, and place in Tuscan Contrasto
  48–68
Poland
  compliments 180, 181
  language planning 428, 430
Polanyi, L. 118, 129

politeness
  linguistic strategies   212
  listening to narrative   132–3, 134
  Maori   115, 133
  pronouns of address   168
  public-opinion surveys   281–2
  see also compliments
political science   2
Polomé, E.   7, 8, 18, 22
Poplack, S.   254
Portugal, Portuguese   379
  creoles   294
  as LWC   464
  pronouns of address   158
  sociolinguistics   22
Posner, R.   395
post-colonial states
  language rights   472
  language standardization   430
post-colonialism, and development of
    sociolinguistics   2
postmodernism   199, 201
poverty, and development of sociolinguistics
    2, 8
power   2, 22
  and compliments   184, 190–3
  and gender   200, 208–28
  and identity and ethnicity   49
  language rights and policies   476, 478
  pronouns of address   72, 158–60, 161–2,
    165–9, 173–5
pragmatics   1, 10, 15, 28, 71–2
Prakrit   419
Pravda   19, 21
prescriptivism   329, 330, 333, 334, 336, 337
Preston, M.   308
Pride, J.   4
pronouns of address   30, 72, 156–76, 209
  contemporary differences among French,
    Italian and German   163–5
  as expressions of transient attitudes   172–5
  gender and language variation   245
  group style   169–72
  semantic evolution of t and v   157–63
  semantics, social structure and ideology
    165–9
Propp, V.   75
prosodic signs
  contextualization conventions   140, 146,
    148, 149, 150, 151, 152, 153, 154
  narrative structure   118, 124, 125
Provençal   413, 416, 429

psycholinguistics   40
public-opinion surveys   272–85
  individual variation among interviewers
    273–80
  issues for linguistic practice and theory
    282–3
  nature of   272–3
  reasons for individual variation   280–2
Publications of the American Dialect Society
    15n
Puerto Rican Legal Defense and Education
    Fund (PRLDEF)   473
Puerto Ricans, NY   50
Puerto Rico   295, 479
Puttenham, George   414
Pyle, A.   335

Quakers   166–7
quantitative sociolinguistics   231
  see also variation, variationism
Quebec
  language planning   409, 425–6, 428, 432,
    439–40, 453
  language rights   472, 473, 477, 480
  language variation   244
  social psychology of bilingualism   306–19
Quechua   400–1, 402, 417, 449, 455, 457

Rabin, C.   423
race
  and development of sociolinguistics   2, 8
  narrative analysis   118
  and official language in Peru   401
  and vernacular dialect norms   265, 267–8
  see also ethnicity
Racine, Jean   158, 173
Radcliffe-Brown, A. R.   18
Raleigh, Sir Walter   411
Rampton, B.   65n
Rau, G. S.   427
Ray, P. S.   430, 431, 454
Read, J.   396
Redfield, J.   283
referential narrative function   75, 93, 102
reflection   55
reflexivity   55, 63
region, linguistic strategies   208
regional dialectology   231
regional dialects   9–12, 306
  diglossia   345
regional interlingual communication   438–9,
    453

regional languages 21, 22, 464
regional lingua francas 438
registers 15, 44
Reinecke, J. E. 289
religion
    and bilingual education 464
    and diglossia 343, 349
    and language regulation 473
    and speech 30–1, 42
Religious Society of Friends 166–7
restricted narrative clauses 85–7, 102
Revill, P. M. 43
rhythmic signs 146, 148, 149
Ricento, T. K. 475–6
Richmond, E. B. 431
Rickford, J. R. 287
Riessman, C. K. 127
Riley, W. K. 13
Rivera, C. 324
Rizzo, T. 222
Robespierre, Maximilien de 165
Robins, C. 251
Robins, H. R. 473
Roen, D. H. 179, 181–2, 183, 186
Rolstad, K. 302
Romaine, S. 324, 330, 334
Roman Empire 157–8, 159, 379, 415
    see also Latin
Romance languages 355, 419
Romantic movement 379
Rondeau, G. 434
Rossi-Landi, F. 22
Rouland, N. 472
Royce, A. P. 49, 402
Ruanda 398
Rubin, J. 435, 437, 440
Ruiz, R. 456–7
Rūķe-Draviņa, V. 431
rural dialects 260
rural languages 21–2
Russenorsk jargon 293
Russia, Russian
    diglossia 371
    language planning 430, 438
    as LWC 464
Rymes, B. 118, 127

Saami movement 480
Sabir 288
Sacks, H. 7, 8, 110n, 112n
St. John Valley Bilingual Education Program
    (SJVBEP) 441

Sajavaara, K. 129
Salzmann, Z. 431
Samarin, W. 11, 33
Samoa, compliments 180
Samoan Americans 50
Sankoff, D. 254
Sanskrit 419, 464
Santo Domingo 295
Sapir, E. 5, 32, 252
Sattel, J. W. 218, 219
Saussure, F. de 4, 5, 9, 17, 19, 21
Saville-Troike, M. 28
Savitz, L. 7
Scalogram Analysis 170–3
Scandinavian languages 438, 453
Schatzman, L. 75
Scheflen, A. E. 147
Schegloff, E. A. 7, 71, 108, 110n, 111n,
    209
Schiffrin, D. 223
Schiller, A. 435
Schilling-Estes, N. 252, 267
schizoglossia 419
Schliebitz, V. 156, 173
Schlobinski, P. 21
Schuchardt, H. 287, 291, 297
Schultz, J. J. 142
Schultze, E. 292, 297n
Schweda, N. L. 441
Scollon, R. 28, 136nn, 208, 219, 220, 225n
Scollon, S. 28, 136nn, 208, 219
Scotton, C. M. 398
Searle, J. 28
second-language instructional competence
    (SLIC) 303, 329–30, 337–8
second-language learning 456
    social psychology 313–17
    see also bilingual education
Segerstedt, T. 19
semantics 32
    conversation analysis 147, 149, 154
    of pronouns of address 156–76
    Tuscan Contrasto 53
Senegal 455
Serbo-Croatian 418
sermons 45, 238
settlers' creole dialects 291, 293–4
Sévigné, Mme de 159
sexism, linguistic 199–200, 203–7
Shabad, G. 397
Shafer, B. C. 403
Shakespeare, William 158, 173, 174

Shaw, G. B.   28
Shouby, E.   350
Shultz, J.   208
Shuy, R. W.   1, 11, 13, 220, 231, 245, 436
Sibayan, B. P.   466
Sierra Leone   294, 298n
Sifianou, M.   226n
signs for the deaf   441, 455
Siguan, M.   395, 396
silence   31, 115, 128, 129, 134, 135
   versus volubility   218–20
Silverberg, W. V.   175
Singapore
   education   394
   language planning   442
   multilingualism   464
Skutnabb-Kangas, T.   478
Skyum-Nielsen, P.   428, 435, 436
slang   22, 240
SLIC   303, 329–30, 337–8
Snyder, G.   44
social class
   and acquisition of Standard English   247
   and development of sociolinguistics   10, 11,
      19–21, 22
   diglossia   343
   and language variation   247, 248–9
   and linguistic strategies   208
   narrative analysis   75, 118
   and pronouns of address   156, 170, 172
   and verbal skills   248–9
   see also social stratification
social conflict
   and bilingualism   318–19
   see also conflict
social constructionism   136n1
social dialects   4, 15
Social Dialects and Language Learning
      conference (1964)   11–12
social justice/injustice   2, 287, 462
social psychology   2
   of bilingualism   301–2, 305–21, 359
social relationships   30–47
social relativism   72
Social Science Research Council   9
social status   see social class
social stratification   236–41
   see also social class
social structures
   and development of sociolinguistics   2, 8
   pronouns of address   165–9
socialization   200, 370

sociolinguistics
   definitions   1, 15
   Europe   2, 9, 17–24
   as field of study   1–2
   methodology   13–14
   origins of term   1, 10–11, 32
   principles   234–50
   terminology   14–15
   US   2, 4–16, 22, 110n1
sociology
   and bilingualism   359
   and development of sociolinguistics   2, 6–9,
      13, 14
sociology of language, term   1, 7, 14, 15, 18,
      19
sociopolitical context
   bilingual education   462
   and conversation   150
   diglossia/bilingualism   317, 360–4, 369, 371,
      372, 373, 374
   and gender   200
   language policies in multilingual states
      394–404
   Maori/Pakeha story-telling   118, 126,
      128
   pidgins and creoles   287
   vernacular norms   266–7
   see also culture
Solano, F. R.   391n, 392nn
solidarity
   compliments as   178, 182, 191, 193
   and gender   208–22
   insults and   193
   pronouns of address   156, 159–63, 164–9,
      171–5
Somalia   398
Sommerfelt, A.   18, 20, 22
song
   identity and place in Tuscan *Contrasto*
      48–68
   and speech   31
Sotiropoulis, D.   343
South Africa
   Afrikaans pronouns   167
   compliments   182
   language planning   435
   language policy and education   394, 462,
      465, 467
   official languages   380
Southeast Asian languages, style shifting and
      social stratification   237–8
Southern Speech Journal   11

Spain, Spanish
  BICS/CALP distinction   335
  code switching   30
  diglossia/bilingualism   360, 371
  language planning   426, 427, 430, 438, 453,
    455
  as LWC   400–1, 453, 464
  pronouns of address   156, 157, 158, 159,
    165, 167, 169
  regional languages   22, 395–8, 404
  sociolinguistics   21
  style   236, 306
Spanish America   see Latin America
special-interest groups/organizations, and
    language rights   473, 477
speech, speaking
  components   40–6
  contextualization conventions   139–55
  diversity   30
  ethnography   27–47, 71
  language standardization   417–18
  pacing and pausing   220
  social differences in verbal skills   248–9
  styles   39
  ways of speaking   40
speech acts   15, 28, 32, 38–9, 45, 72
  see also compliments
speech communities   4, 36–7, 244
  and diglossia/bilingualism   360–4, 369
  and vernacular norms   267
speech events   28, 38, 45
  see also public-opinion surveys
speech field   37
speech network   37
speech situations   28, 38
Spicer, E. H.   402
Spolsky, B.   330
spontaneity, of oral narratives   107–8
Sprechbund (Neustupný)   37
Srole, L.   314
Stalin, Joseph   19–21
Standard English   289
  dialect and   148–9
  stages in acquisition   246–8
Standard French   289
standard languages
  creoles and   287, 288–9, 295
  development   413, 415–21
  and diglossia   343, 345–58, 369
  see also language, standardization
Stein, H.   302
stereotypical thinking   307–8, 317–18

Stewart, W.   456
Stidston, R. O.   157
story-telling, Maori and Pakeha   114–38
Strauss, A.   75
Street, B.   450
structure, structuralism   5, 9, 10, 11, 17, 19,
    20, 107
  language policy and planning   409, 411–21
  variationism and   232, 234–50
Stubbe, M.   130
style   419–20
  gender and complimenting   184–7
  pronouns of address   156, 169–72
  shifting/switching   140, 234–41, 245, 247
  simplification   425, 426, 435–6, 441, 453,
    454
  social psychology   305–7
  see also diglossia
substitute languages   290
Sumerian-Akkadian empire   379
Summer Institute of Linguistics   400
Suriname   294, 296
  Javanese and respect/deference   212–13
Swahili   293, 394, 398–9, 401, 404, 449
Swain, M.   324–5, 468
Swann, J.   71, 200, 201
Sweden, Swedish
  bilingualism and language proficiency   322
  development of sociolinguistics   19
  language planning   426, 428, 433, 434,
    435
  language rights   478
  language shift   402
Sweet, Henry   28
Swift, Jonathan   427
Swiss German   346–57, 360, 371
Switzerland
  diglossia/bilingualism   365n
  language rights   477
  linguistic heterogeneity   384
  official languages   416
syntax   32, 149, 234
  compliments   184–6

Ta'ase, E. K.   50
Tabouret-Keller, A.   20
Tager-Flusberg, H.   333
Tagliamonte, S.   254
Taki-taki English   296
talk-in-interaction   106–10
Tamanoi, M. A.   52
Tamil, diglossia   354–5

Tannen, D.   28, 179, 191, 200, 208, 209, 210, 213, 216, 217, 219, 220, 221, 223–4, 225nn, 226n, 283
Tanzania, language policy and planning   394, 398–9, 404, 432
Tauli, V.   430, 454
Tax, Sol   6
Taylor, D. M.   302
Taylor, P. B.   395
telephone public-opinion surveys   *see* public-opinion surveys
terminology unification   426, 433–5, 441, 443n, 453, 454
Tewa of Arizona   49
Texas A&M University, Public Policy Resources Laboratory   274
text linguistics   71
    see also narrative analysis
Thai conversation   127
Thiam, N.   22
Thomas, E. R.   255, 258
Thoreau, Henry David   281
Tigrigna   465
Times, The   206
Tocqueville, Alexis de   281
Tok Pisin   288, 465
Tonti, Realdo   51–2, 54–64
Toolan, M. J.   117
trade jargons   290–3, 294, 297
transcription rules   441, 455
transformational generative grammar (TGG)   10, 27
transliteration rules   441, 455
Trobriand Islands   45
Troike, R.   330
Trudgill, P.   200
Tucker, G. R.   1–2, 313, 409, 436, 462, 466
Tunstall, K.   315
Tupi Lingua Geral   292, 298n
Tur-Sinai, H. H.   434
Turi, J.-G.   472, 474
Turkey, Turkish   369
    language reform   430, 432
Tuvalu   127
Tylbor, H.   209

Uchida, A.   200
Uganda   398, 399
Uhlenberg, E. M.   473
Ukrainian   371
UNESCO   449, 450, 462, 478
UNICEF   470

United Kingdom
    bilingualism   374
    code switching   31
    compliments   180
    development of sociolinguistics   9, 19, 22
    language and class   239
    linguistic strategies   219
    silence versus volubility   219
    vernacular norms   266
United Nations   462, 478
    Universal Declaration of Human Rights   474
United States
    address forms   168–9
    argument   223
    bilingual education   462, 467, 480n
    bilingualism   302, 316, 318–19, 322–3, 325
    compliments   179, 181, 182, 184–5, 186, 189, 190
    contextualization conventions   152–3, 154
    development of sociolinguistics   2, 4–16, 22, 110n
    dialects   232, 234–5, 251–71
    English-only/English plus movement   379, 472, 480
    ethnic identity   49–50
    ethnography of speech   31, 34, 36–7, 42
    individualism   281
    language planning   425, 427, 440–1, 442, 453
    language policy   462
    language rights   472, 474, 480n
    linguistic atlases   9–10
    linguistic norms   232, 244, 251–71
    linguistic strategies   212–13, 216–17, 219, 223
    listener's narrative role   129
    marginal languages   294, 295
    national/official language   404, 416
    public-opinion surveys   272–85
    social stratification of language   239
Universal Declaration of Linguistic Human Rights   478
Universala Esperanto Asocio   437
universals   14
University of California, Berkeley   6
University of California, Los Angeles   7
    Lake Arrowhead conference (1964)   10–11, 12
    Linguistic Institute (1966)   7, 110n
University of Pennsylvania   6, 7, 14
University of Texas   8
urban language   11, 260

urban sociolinguistics   21, 22
urbanization   373, 388, 404
USSR
  language planning   432, 433
  language rights   472
  linguistic norms   243
  sociolinguistics   19–21

Valencia, R.   334, 337
Vallen, T.   301
Vallverdú, F.   396
Van Naerssen, M. M.   436
variation, variationism   11, 12, 14, 15, 17, 72,
    200, 201, 231–50, 287
  see also dialectology; linguistic geography
varieties, form of speech   44
Vasak, Karel   475
Vendryes, J.   20, 298n
Venezuela, Waiwai speech events   42
vernacular dialect norms   232, 251–71
  AAVE   254–60
  factors to be considered   266–8
  fundamental issues   251–3
  Lumbee vernacular English   260–5
  neglect of   251
vernacular language   244
  see also vernacular dialect forms
Vietnam, language planning   433
Vilfan, S.   473, 474, 475
Villena Ponsoda, J. A.   21
Vincent, C.   325
Virgin Islands   296
Visweswaran, K.   65n
Vizenor, G. R.   50
Volochinov, V.   19, 20

Waiwai of Venezuela   42
Wales, Welsh
  diglossia   362
  language planning   428, 429
  motivation in learning   314–15
Waletzky, J.   71, 117
  critique   105–8, 110
Watanabe, S.   212
Watson, K. A.   127
Weinreich, M.   4, 20
Weinreich, U.   4, 11, 12, 20, 268n

Wellington Caucus of Spoken New Zealand
    English (WCSNZE)   115–16
Welsh   see Wales, Welsh
Wenker, Georg   9
West, C.   217
West Africa, marginal languages   293, 294
West Indies   294
Wexler, P.   370
White, S.   129
Whiteley, W.   22
Whitney, W. D.   4
Whorf, B. L.   32, 39, 391
Wiley, T. G.   324, 330, 332, 334
Williams, R. N.   314
Wishram Chinook   31, 42
Woehrling, J.   477
Wolfowitz, C.   212
Wolfram, W. A.   13, 232, 251, 252, 255, 267
Wolfson, N.   127, 181, 183, 184, 189, 190
women's movement   199
Wood, R. E.   437, 441
Woolard, K. A.   396, 397
World Bank   465–6, 469
Wrede   20
writing, writing systems   334, 380
  and language planning   452, 453, 454,
    456
  and language standardization   417–18
Wüster, E.   434

Yakan of Philippines   42
Yamada, H.   212
Yana myths   42
Yiddish   297, 360, 371
Yoruba   298n
Yugoslav-Albanian   431, 432
Yugoslavia
  official languages   416
  pronouns of address   167, 169

Zambia   398
Zanzibar   398
Zen philosophy   44
Zentella, A. C.   50, 479
Zierer, E.   443n
Zimmerman, D. H.   217
Zuni   31